ecial indexes

D0983582

Studies in Church History

12

CHURCH SOCIETY AND POLITICS

CHURCH SOCIETY AND POLITICS

PAPERS READ AT
THE THIRTEENTH SUMMER MEETING AND
THE FOURTEENTH WINTER MEETING
OF THE
ECCLESIASTICAL HISTORY SOCIETY

EDITED BY
DEREK BAKER

PUBLISHED FOR
THE ECCLESIASTICAL HISTORY SOCIETY
BY
BASIL BLACKWELL · OXFORD
1975

ISBN 0 631 16970 9
Library of Congress Catalog
Card No.: 73–82131

Printed in Great Britain
by Crampton & Sons Ltd, Sawston, Cambridge

PREFACE

The present volume of *Studies in Church History* is the twelfth to be produced by the Ecclesiastical History Society and the third to be published by the Society itself in collaboration with Basil Blackwell. 'Church, Society and Politics' was the theme of the thirteenth summer meeting of the Society, held at the University of York, and of the fourteenth winter meeting. The twenty-three papers included in this volume are a selection from those read at these two meetings. To them has been added a short memoir on David Knowles, the first president of the Society.

The Society is grateful to the British Academy for generous financial assistance in the production of this volume.

Derek Baker

CONTENTS

CONTENTS

DAVID KNOWLES

The Ecclesiastical History Society was founded in 1961 by the initiative and inspiration of Clifford Dugmore; and it was Professor Dugmore who invited David Knowles to lecture to the opening meeting, and proposed his name for election as first President. To their friendship the Society owes much. Already in 1950 they were associated in the *Journal of Ecclesiastical History*, and David Knowles remained a member of the Advisory Committee (from 1966 the Advisory Editorial Board) until his death. His first lecture to the Society was on 'The Medieval Archbishops of York';[1] and his Presidential (1962) was a very characteristic critical survey in his best manner on 'Some recent work on early Benedictine history'.[2] In our early conferences he was a familiar figure, an image of spiritual friendship and scholarly aspiration to inspire his colleagues; we saw in him one of the great ecclesiastical historians of his day, and our friend.

The outline of his life is familiar to readers of W. A. Pantin's appreciation in *The Historian and Character and other Essays* (Cambridge 1963); and he himself described his formation as a historian in his lecture on 'Academic History'.[3] 'At school I was never, either in fact or in desire, an historian. I was a classic, and in my school days the only spell that bound me was that of great literature.' He went on to describe how he passed on from the classics and English poetry to the great works of literary history: Macaulay, Gibbon, Grote, Clarendon and many others. He joined the Downside community in 1914, but it was only in the late 1920s that he became a monastic historian. His first book, *The American Civil War*, was published in 1926. 'My inspiration came, at an infinite distance, from Thucydides. I did not approach the subject primarily in order to discover the truth, but to share with others what the story had meant for me'.[4] He went on to describe how reviews of the book brought home the serious professional nature of the historian's task, and how, not long after, he began work for *The Monastic Order* by going through *Domesday Book* 'copying out every entry relating to a monastic house'.

---

[1] A bye-product of the related paper 'The English Bishops 1070–1532' in *Medieval Studies presented to Aubrey Gwynn, S.J.*, ed J. A. Watt, J. B. Morrall and F. X. Martin (Dublin 1961) pp 283–96.

[2] *SCH* 1, pp 35–46.

[3] 'Academic History', *History*, 47 (1962) pp 223–32.

[4] *Ibid* p 229–30.

The Monastic Order in England was published in 1940. 'There was something very heartening in getting such a book in the summer of Dunkirk and the Battle of Britain'.[5] Hitherto he had been known to a few historians; from now on his reputation grew rapidly wider. In 1944 he became a Fellow of Peterhouse; in 1947 he succeeded my father, Z. N. Brooke, as Professor of Medieval History at Cambridge, and he was elected a Fellow of the British Academy; in 1954 he was translated to the Regius Chair, from which he retired in 1963. He was much else besides: President of the Royal Historical Society (1956–60); honorary fellow of two colleges, honorary doctor of many universities, including his own.

He did not see the Church's history as divorced from the general study of man's past. 'The life of Napoleon, the influence of Neoplatonism in the twelfth century, and the origins and business methods of a great brewery or soap-factory are all equally the materials of history', he wrote.[6] But he went on: '. . . Nevertheless it is surely true that human understanding and sympathy and love have always been elements in the make-up of the greatest historians.' In his own mind and approach an intense involvement somehow combined with an objectivity almost Olympian. His judgements could be sharp; yet he was justly famed for his kindness and fairness. In 'Cardinal Gasquet as an Historian',[7] he reconciled Coulton and Gasquet, a feat even he could hardly have accomplished in their lifetime, in a feast of wit which was wholly fair to both, yet hid the faults of neither. 'Towards the end of his life, indeed, Gasquet's capacity for carelessness amounted almost to genius . . . He lacked that passion for absolute intellectual chastity, which . . . in an historian is as much an occupational requirement as is absolute integrity in a judge'. 'In Gasquet's case the triumphal car had a good start, but Vengeance came limping after in the person of George Gordon Coulton'. Gasquet had his virtues as a man, and even as an historian; and they are enumerated without fear or favour.

If he lives on in his friends and pupils as well as in his writings, then David Knowles will be seen to have made a major contribution to several branches of medieval history. But in this context, as a reminder of what he has meant to the history of the Church, let us dwell for a

---

[5] Pantin in *The Historian and Character*, p xxiii.
[6] 'Academic History', p 231.
[7] The Creighton Lecture for 1956, reprinted in *The Historian and Character*, chapter 11: the quotations are from pp 254, 261, 257–8.

moment on his greatest work, *The Monastic Order* and *The Religious Orders in England* (3 vols, Cambridge 1948–59). In the spoken word he could convey, all the more because of his still, small voice and figure, the power of his intellectual and spiritual stature. So in his best books these are revealed in some of the finest prose dedicated to historical writing in this century. Much of his happiest writing is in the last volume of the series, and its combination of spiritual insight with wit, shrewdness of judgement and detachment helps us to understand the way in which he won homage and fealty from secular historians – and so helped secure the recognition of his historical interests as a valid and important part of history. But my own favourite will always be the first volume, for it changed my life. I well recall *The Monastic Order* sitting on my father's desk, and he – always inclined to severity in his first judgement on books – astonishing me by the warmth of enthusiasm which he showed only when really roused. Soon after, to my father's entertainment, I began to read it and to note misprints and minor errors – and there were such in all David Knowles' works, fine scholar though he was; but when I began to try my novice scalpel on one of my father's own works, he felt the time had come for more constructive tasks. So began the work of collaboration out of which (other things apart) eventually came *The Heads of Religious Houses*,[8] and, long before (1942) my first meeting with David Knowles. When he began to work, literary and narrative history were going out of fashion among professional historians, and especially among medievalists, but he came to history from English literature, and first read and wrote history as literature. He had also been trained as a scholar, and had sat at the feet both of Abbot Cuthbert Butler and of Abbot Ramsay, whose work on the text of Cyprian he aided; he had met Edmund Bishop. Thus he came to *The Monastic Order* with a strong sense of the nature of critical scholarship and a love of narrative history; and he had chosen one of the few medieval fields in which the evidence supports and invites both ample narrative and analysis. He also brought a devotion to the subject which illuminates many of its pages. His final judgement was severe, for he quotes on the last page Christ's terrifying call to perfection, which he, following John Cassian and many others, expected a monk to answer. Yet the book is also infused with the warm charity and human understanding which fills so many of his writings, and which we knew in him. *The*

---

[8] Ed Knowles, C. N. L. Brooke and Vera C. M. London (Cambridge 1972); see p vii for the roles of M.D.K. and Z.N.B. in the origin of the project.

Monastic Order wrought a change in monastic history and in much more; just as all of us who knew and loved him were touched and chastened by his presence.

University of London
Westfield College   Christopher Brooke

Additional note: the lecture on 'The Medieval Archbishops of York' referred to previously was published as the Oliver Sheldon Memorial Lecture (York Civic Trust 1961).

INTRODUCTION

'That men, that *all* men, should be allowed to worship their Maker in their *own way*, is, I think, not to be doubted; but if the government once begins to meddle it must establish somewhat of a *uniform creed*, and that this creed will not suit all men is very certain. Whether the government *ought ever to meddle* with religion is a question that I will not now attempt to discuss; but this I am not afraid to assert: that without *a state religion*, a kingly government and an aristocracy will never long exist, in any country upon earth . . . and as all history will clearly prove, *without a state religion a kingly government cannot exist*. If this be the case, it must be allowed that the government is bound to protect its own religion, which is to be done only by *keeping down others* as much as is necessary to secure a predominance to that of the state. . . . Indeed, *if we allow that a state religion is necessary*, this is no question at all. . . . But, in another view of the matter, in a *moral* view, I mean, it may still be a question with some persons . . . I say in a *moral* view; for, as to *religion* without morality, none but fools or knaves do, or ever did, profess it.'[1]

When William Cobbett wrote in May 1811 his purpose was to castigate the dissenters of his day – 'as much like the Dissenters of old times as *horse-dung* is like an *apple*' – but his remarks have a wider significance, and both here and elsewhere in his *Political Works* relate to the theme of this volume, and to the particular papers which compose it. Few would entirely agree with Cobbett that 'the short but true history of the causes of the Reformation' was '*the taking of the tithes from Catholic Priests and giving them to Protestant Priests, keeping back a part to be given to favourite Lords and Ladies*', or that 'the history of this grand event . . . was merely a shifting of the *Church Property* from one set of hands to another', but the acquisition, possession and protection of property is prominent in discussion of the changing attitudes of the post-conquest community at Durham and the fourteenth-century sequestration of the English alien priories; in the characterisation of the genevan reformation as a revolution, and above all in the meticulously critical examination of early christian attitudes to property and slavery with which this volume commences.

If, however, in Mr de Ste. Croix's words, it was the 'complete indifference' of early christians as christians 'to the institutions of the

---

[1] Quoted from *Cobbett's England*, ed J. Derry (London 1968) p 105.

world in which they lived' which inhibited christian influence upon the institutions and human relations of antiquity, imperial endorsement and adoption of christianity was soon to give rise to those complex liaisons to which Cobbett referred, and which enabled Tindall to declare that the church of England was 'a perfect creature of the civil power; I mean the polity and discipline of it'. The conditioning and limiting effects of such relationships are evident in professor Hill's remark that the seventh-century king 'who was holy without also being stern . . . was apt to prove a disaster' for his kingdom; they emerge in the portrayal of Fulk of Toulouse's enforced reinvolvement in the world from which he had fled, in the fifteenth-century preacher's reliance on an 'apocalyptic warrior-king' in the person of Henry V to reform society, in the politics of religious pacification and settlement in late sixteenth-century France and seventeenth-century Scotland, and in an eighteenth-century English debate about the nature of the church and its relationship to the state. In the nineteenth and twentieth centuries examination of developments in Sierra Leone and Borneo, and consideration of parliamentary debates and policies, disclose the same pressures and interrelationships, while two contributions to the wide-ranging contemporary debate on the church struggle in Germany in the 1930s conclude the volume.

When professor Robbins quotes an anonymous English woman writing in 1939 to the effect 'that if one defined Christianity as an acceptance of the spiritual meaning of the Church's teaching, with a sincere effort to apply it to everyday life, "one may discern Christianity as the *Leitmotiv* of the National Socialist philosophy in Germany" ' it is easy to see why he should conclude that 'interference in politics is, after all, a choice of evils', but it is as well to recall Cobbett's dictum that religion without morality was professed only by fools and knaves. In his evocative study of Gavazzi Dr Hall has laid stress on the role of religious idealism in great political movements, recalling that even Cavour was aware that 'only moral forces overcome moral obstacles'. In an earlier age, as both professor Morris and Dr Smalley have emphasised such influences stemmed from a medieval failure, or reluctance, to distinguish between the religious, the social and the political, but later and better categorised societies display similar influences, and make it plain that they stem as much from aggressive social concern as from primitive social confusion. Dr Cargill Thompson's magisterial consideration of Luther's views on the right of resistance to the emperor makes it clear that 'no issue of practical politics presented the first generation of German reformers with such acute moral problems', while professor McManners' elegant discussion of the so-called political jansenism of the eighteenth century does much to qualify the despair of a jansenist letter of 1695: if 'the earth is becoming empty of saints, while Heaven is filling up' it remained true that 'high principles were at stake and good men willing to suffer for them, even though their spirituality lacked the illumination of intellectual and literary genius' – and his assessment is as valid for men like Gavazzi in the Italy of the risorgimento as for the latter-day jansenists of pre-revolutionary France.

With Gavazzi and men like him, however, as Dr Hall has indicated, there is another dimension to consider. Professor Kingdon picked out the transformation of 'the predominant myth of the community' as one of the significant changes which made the reformation in Geneva a revolution. For Gavazzi too there was a predominant myth which inspired his political purposes and endowed him with a sustaining spiritual strength. Jowett, as Dr Hall recalls, might declare that 'words are not always ideas, nor are ideas always realities', but for Gavazzi – as for those who worshipped at the shrine of Waldef of Melrose some seven centuries earlier – words and ideas could be as substantial and influential as reality itself. There is an intangible numinous aspect and influence which demands attention and accords a significant place and role to fable and predominant myth, and which is vividly portrayed in Dr Hall's quotation from Leopardi: 'the years of childhood are in the memory of every man, the fabulous years of his life, as in a nation's memories the fabulous years are those of this nation's youth'. Material interests, secular purposes, bureaucratic structures, persecution, or even high moral earnestness and individual crises of conscience, do not entirely comprise the interaction of church, society and politics.

EARLY CHRISTIAN ATTITUDES TO PROPERTY AND SLAVERY[1]

by G. E. M. DE STE. CROIX

I BEGIN with the central fact about christian origins: that although the earliest surviving christian documents are in greek and although christianity spread from city to city in the graeco-roman world, its Founder lived and preached almost entirely outside the area of graeco-roman civilisation proper; the world in which he was active was not at all that of the *polis* (the city) but the very different world of the *chōra* (the countryside). This may require some explanation.

In the classical period, in Greece itself and in some of the early greek colonies in Italy and Sicily and on the west coast of Asia Minor, the word *chōra* was often used as a synonym for the *agroi* (the fields), the rural area of the *polis*;[2] and sometimes the word *polis* itself, in the special limited sense of its urban area, was contrasted with its *chōra*.[3] This usage continued in the hellenistic period (roughly the last three centuries BC) and under roman rule: every *polis* had its own *chōra* in the sense of its own rural area. However, except where a native population had been reduced to a subject condition[4] there was gener-

[1] This paper is a re-presentation of parts of my book, *The Class Struggle in the Ancient Greek World* (to be published by Duckworth about the autumn of 1976), which incorporates the substance of the J. H. Gray Lectures delivered at Cambridge university in February 1973, greatly expanded. Full documentation for those statements for which I have not provided proper references here will be found in that book, referred to below as *CSAGW*.

The best collection of early christian views concerning property (from the OT down to the early fifth century) is by [Paul] Christophe, [*L'usage chrétien du droit de propriété dans l'écriture et la tradition patristique*]=Collection *Théologie, Pastorale et Spiritualité*, no 14 (Paris 1964). I have made much use of this book (although at times it is uncritical), as of [C. J.] Cadoux, [*The Early Church and the World*] (Edinburgh 1925 & repr). Ernst Troeltsch, *The Social Teaching of the Christian Churches* I, trans Olive Wyon (London 1931) pp 1–200, has some useful material, but for my purposes does not lie sufficiently close to the historical background, and I have not cited it here.

[2] For example in Thuc. II.5.7, ἐκ τῆς χώρας is equivalent to ἐκ τῶν ἀγρῶν in 14.1; cf. ἐν τοῖς ἀγροῖς in 14.2, and the same expression and κατὰ τὴν χώραν in 16.1.

[3] As in Thuc. VI.4.2; Lyc., *C. Leocr.* 1; etc.

[4] I shall mention the main examples in *CSAGW*: they include Heracleia Pontica, Zeleia, Priene, Syracuse.

ally in the areas just mentioned no fundamental difference between those who lived in or near the urban centre of the *polis* and the peasants who lived in the countryside, even if the latter tended to be noticeably less 'urbane' (less cityfied) than the former; all were greek and participated in a common culture to a greater or less degree. But in those parts of Asia and Egypt into which greek civilisation penetrated in the time of Alexander the Great and in the hellenistic period the situation was very different. In Asia, from at least the time of Alexander (and probably, as I have argued elsewhere,[5] as early as the fifth century BC), the terms *chōra* and *polis* had come to be used on occasion with a recognised technical sense, which continued through-out the hellenistic period and beyond in Asia and Egypt: in this sense the *chōra* was the whole vast area not included in the territory administered by any greek *polis*; it was under the direct, autocratic rule of the kings, the successors of Alexander, and it was bureaucratic-ally administered, while the *poleis* had republican governments and enjoyed forms of precarious autonomy which differed according to circumstances. Under roman rule the same basic division between *polis* and *chōra* continued: but the great bulk of the *chōra* came by degrees under the administration of particular *poleis*, each of which had its own *chōra* (*territorium* in the latin west). The cities in the strict sense (the *poleis*) were greek in very varying degrees in language and culture; native languages and cultures prevailed in the *chōra*, where the population lived mainly in villages, the most common Greek term for which was *kōmai*. Graeco-roman civilisation was essentially urban, a civilisation of cities; and in the areas in which it was not native, in which it had not grown up from roots in the very soil, it remained largely an upper-class culture, parasitic on the countryside which supported it and to which it gave little in return.[6]

[5] In *The Origins of the Peloponnesian War* (London 1972) pp 154–5, 313–14.
[6] Perhaps the best account of this fundamental opposition between town and country in the greek east is in part V ('The Achievement of the Cities', pp 259–304) of A. H. M. Jones' great work, *The Greek City from Alexander to Justinian* (Oxford 1940) esp 285 *et seq.* Another major work by Jones, *Cities [of the Eastern Roman Provinces]* (frequently cited in *The Greek City*), has been reissued in a second edn (Oxford 1971), with the sections on Palestine in chap 10 (on 'Syria', pp 226–94) revised by M. Avi-Yonah. A recent work, limited to the late republic and principate, is [Ramsay] MacMullen, [*Roman Social Relations 50 B.C. to A.D. 284*] (London 1974): the first two chapters of this (I 'Rural', and II 'Rural-Urban', pp 1–56) have much well-chosen illustrative material. For the opinions of a scholar who knew the archaeological as well as the literary evidence particularly well, see [M.] Rostovtzeff, [*Social and Economic History of the Roman Empire*] (Oxford 1957) I, pp 261–73 (with II, pp 660 *et seq.*, esp pp 664–6), 344–52, 378–92. For an able account of the social and economic background of the great jewish

Early christian attitudes to property & slavery

The essential point I want to make is that – apart from Jerusalem, a special case as I shall explain presently – the mission of Jesus took place entirely in the *chōra*, in its *kōmai*, in the *agroi* of Palestine. Partly it was conducted altogether outside *polis* territory, in areas of Galilee and Judaea administered not by cities but directly by Herod Antipas the 'tetrarch' or by the roman governor of Judaea; but it is highly significant that on the rather rare occasions when we do find Jesus active inside *polis* territory, it is never in the *polis* itself, in the sense of its urban area, but always in its country district. As we shall see, whenever we have any specific information (as distinct from vague general statements) the terms used are such as to point unmistakably to the countryside – the *kōmai, kōmopoleis, agroi, chōra*, also the *merē, horia, paralios, perichōros*. There is of course a great dispute about how much reliable historical information can legitimately be extracted from the narratives of the gospels, even the synoptics. But I would emphasise that in so far as we can trust the specific information given us by the gospels there is no evidence that Jesus ever even entered the urban area of any greek city. That should not surprise us: Jesus, as I indicated at the beginning, belonged wholly to the *chōra*, the jewish countryside of Galilee and Judaea.

Palestine, which had been ruled by the Ptolemies for over a hundred years after the death of Alexander, became around 200 BC part of the seleucid kingdom. Just before the middle of the second century Judaea achieved a considerable degree of independence for nearly a century; but from 63 BC onwards the whole of Palestine and Syria was always effectively under roman control, although Judaea (and Samaria) did not actually become a roman province until AD 6, and Galilee and Peraea until 44.[7] In Palestine the native language at the beginning of the christian era was aramaic, which was spoken throughout the countryside and also by a good proportion of the inhabitants of many of the cities. By the time of Jesus, Palestine contained a number of genuine *poleis*, some of which were much more

---

revolt in Palestine of AD 66–70, see Heinz Kreissig, *Die sozialen Zusammenhänge des judäischen Krieges. Klassen und Klassenkampf im Palästina des 1. Jahrh. v.u.Z.=Schriften zur Geschichte und Kultur der Antike* no 1 (Berlin 1970).

[7] For the history of Palestine in the late hellenistic and early roman period, see the admirable new english version, by [Geza Vermes and Fergus Millar, *The History of the Jewish People in the Age of Jesus Christ (175 B.C.–A.D. 135)*, of Emil] Schürer's [*Geschichte des jüdischen Volkes im Zeitalter Jesu Christi*] (3/4 ed 1901–9), of which only vol 1 (Edinburgh 1973) has already appeared. The events of 63 BC to AD 44 are dealt with on pp 237–454.

hellenic in character than others.[8] With the exception of Tyre and Sidon, which I shall mention presently, the cities on the coast (Caesarea, Ascalon, Gaza and others) were too far from the main scene of Jesus's activity to be mentioned in the gospels, and we can ignore them here. The cities we need to notice are, first, Sepphoris and Tiberias, the only two in Galilee; next Samaria, between Galilee and Judaea, recently re-founded by Herod the Great as Sebaste (but never mentioned under that name in the new testament); thirdly the well-marked cluster of ten genuine cities administering a large area known as Decapolis, to the east and south-east of Galilee and the north-east of Judaea; and finally one or two cities at the periphery of the area within which Jesus moved: Caesarea Paneas, founded in 2 BC by Herod's son, Philip the tetrarch,[9] some 25 miles to the north of the lake of Galilee (and referred to in Mark and Matthew as Caesarea Philippi), and the ancient phoenician towns of Tyre and Sidon, of which Tyre lay on the coast, due west of Caesarea Paneas, with Sidon to the north of it.

Now the word *polis* is often used by greek authors (and in the septuagint) in a loose sense, of places which were not true cities but simply large villages or market-towns which were described more correctly by other expressions such as *mētrokōmiai, kōmopoleis*. In the gospels, Luke especially, the term *polis* is used on dozens of occasions for individual named places which were not technically cities at all: Nazareth, Capernaum, Nain, Chorazin, Bethsaida, Sychar of Samaria, Ephraim, Arimathea, Bethlehem – and Jerusalem.[10] The last

---

[8] See [Victor] Tcherikover, [*Hellenistic Civilization and the Jews*] (Philadelphia/Jerusalem 1959) pp 90–116; Jones, *Cities*, chap 10, esp pp 248–9, 255–9, 269–76; 'The Urbanization of Palestine', in *JRS* 21 (1931) pp 78–85; Rostovtzeff I², pp 269–73, II², 663–6 nn 32–6; M. Avi-Yonah, *The Holy Land from the Persian to the Arab Conquest (536 B.C. to A.D. 640). A Historical Geography* (Grand Rapids, Mich., 1966) esp pp 127–80.

[9] See Jones, *Cities* pp 282.

[10] Jerusalem appears as a *polis* in all four gospels. Otherwise, Mark has only Capernaum (which also appears as a *polis* in Luke and by implication in Matthew); Ephraim and Sychar appear only in John; Arimathea, Bethlehem and Nain only in Luke: Bethsaida (a *kōmē* in Mk. 8.22–3), Chorazin and Nazareth are found as *poleis* in Matthew and Luke. Perhaps I should emphasise here that Jerusalem was never at any time a *polis* in the technical sense, except when hellenising jews attempted to turn it into the *polis* of 'Antioch-by-Jerusalem' during a short period beginning in 175 BC: see Tcherikover pp 153 *et seq.*, esp pp 161–74, 188. If Jerusalem really had a theatre, amphitheatre and hippodrome (alien to the jewish way of life), it was only because these were provided by that ardent helleniser, Herod the Great – who is also said to have built the same three structures at Jericho, which no one would dream of calling a *polis*: see Schürer pp 304–5 n 56.

4

is a special case. From the early hellenistic period onwards, greek authors such as Hecataeus of Abdera and Agatharchides of Cnidos (*ap.* Jos., *C. Apion.* I. 197–8, 209) could call Jerusalem a *polis*, and in some respects it did qualify for that title, although I think it would be preferable to regard it essentially as the administrative capital of Judaea, of the *ethnos* (the 'nation') of the jews. In any event, it was very far from being a proper greek *polis*. Of the other places called *poleis* in the gospels, we might wish to call Bethsaida a 'town';[11] none of the others was really more than a village. And although much of the activity of Jesus is said in the gospels to have taken place in desert places or by the shore of the lake of Galilee or elsewhere in the country districts, we are sometimes told in very general terms that Jesus went through *poleis* (Mt. 11.1; compare Lk. 4.43), or *poleis* and *kōmai* (Mt. 9.35; Lk. 13.22), or *kōmai, poleis* and *agroi* (Mk. 6.56). But in such contexts the word *poleis* must be understood in the very loose and untechnical sense in which the evangelists (like some other greek authors) habitually use it. As I said earlier, wherever we have a specific reference to a visit by Jesus to one of the genuine *poleis*, it is in every single case made clear that it was the country district of the *polis* concerned to which Jesus went.[12]

Let us begin with Samaria. We can forget the bogus *polis* of Sychar (Jn. 4.5), a mere village of course, and the passage in Matthew (10.5) in which Jesus tells his disciples *not* to go into a *polis* of the Samaritans. That leaves us with only two passages in Luke: in 17.11 Jesus merely goes 'through the midst of Samaria and Galilee', and in 9.52 he sends messengers 'to a *kōmē* of the Samaritans' to prepare for his coming, which in fact never took place – Jesus went to another *kōmē* (9.55). There is never a mention of Sebaste, the city founded by Herod, which was a pagan town, with no large proportion of jewish settlers, and the only genuine *polis* in the Samareitis.

The Decapolis crops up in two passages in Mark and one in Matthew, and the manner of its appearance is significant. In Mt. 4.25 crowds *from* Decapolis (which had a large *chōra*) and elsewhere follow Jesus. In Mk. 7.31 Jesus comes from the borders of Tyre, through

---

[11] It was the capital of the (originally ptolemaic) toparchy of Gaulanitis, and it had been re-named Julias by Philip the tetrarch: see Jones, n 9 above.

[12] Whether 'he could no longer enter εἰς πόλιν', in Mk. 1.45, means 'into a city' or 'into the city concerned' (perhaps Capernaum, as in 1.21, but compare 39), it obviously refers to no more than the immediate situation: see 2.1 and much of the following narrative, esp for example 6.56.

Sidon,[13] to the lake of Galilee, via (as the text has it) 'the midst of the boundaries (or 'territory') of Decapolis'.[14] But it is Mk. 5.20 which brings out most clearly what I am trying to emphasise: that in these cases Jesus is clearly in the country district attached to a *polis* and not in the actual *polis* itself. It needs to be taken with its whole context: the story of the demoniac out of whom was cast the legion of devils (Mk. 5.1–20; Mt. 8.28–34; Lk. 8.26–39), whether this is to be located at Gadara or Gerasa,[15] both of which were cities of the Decapolis. In all three synoptics Jesus is in the *chōra* of the city, and the incident is pictured as taking place beside the lake of Galilee; the demoniac comes out of the city (Lk. 8.27) and indeed was always 'in the tombs and in the mountains' (Mk. 5.2–5); afterwards the swineherds go into the city (Mt. 8.33), and they tell the story in 'the *polis* and the *agroi*' (Mk. 5.14; Lk. 8.34), whereupon people ('the whole *polis*': Mt.8. 34) come out to Jesus (Lk. 8.35) and beg him to go away – in Lk. 8.37 it is 'the whole multitude of the *perichōros* of the Gerasenes' who do this. When Jesus tells the former demoniac to go home and publish the news of the divine work, he proclaims it, in Luke (8.39), 'throughout the whole *polis*', and in Mark (5.20) 'in the Decapolis'.

The situation is exactly the same on the two occasions on which

---

[13] I accept ἐκ τῶν ὁρίων Τύρου ἦλθεν διὰ Σιδῶνος as a preferable textual reading to καὶ Σιδῶνος ἦλθεν, though I doubt whether the territory of Sidon was in fact involved; compare [D. E.] Nineham, [*Saint Mark*] (Pelican Gospel Comm., 1963) p 203.

[14] A curiously roundabout route: see Nineham.

[15] Variant readings exist in each case for the name of the city into the *chōra* of which Jesus goes at the beginning of the story: the best reading in Mark and Luke is 'Gerasa' (εἰς τὴν χώραν τῶν Γερασηνῶν), in Matthew, 'Gadara' (... τῶν Γαδαρηνῶν). In some MSS of all three gospels there also occurs the reading 'Gergesa' (... τῶν Γεργεσηνῶν): this goes back to Origen, *Comm. in Johan.* VI.41, p 150, ed E. Preuschen, in the *GCS* Origen 4, (1903), who realised that the distance from the lake of Galilee of both Gerasa (nearly 40 miles) and Gadara (5 or 6 miles) is considerable, and in order to allow the swine to 'run violently down a steep place into the sea' proposed to substitute a place he called Gergesa, πόλις ἀρχαία περὶ τὴν νῦν καλουμένην Τιβεριάδα λίμνην, περὶ ἣν κρημνὸς παρακείμενος τῇ λίμνῃ. It has been suggested, however, that Origen was simply exercising his ingenuity on the basis of *Gen.* 10.16. A place with some such name as Gergesa may have existed: in the 6th century Cyril of Scythopolis (a city of Decapolis) refers to a locality in this area which he calls Chorsia (*Vita Sabae* 24, p 108.14 ed E. Schwartz, *Kyrillos von Scythopolis* = *TU* 49, ii (1939), and this may correspond with the modern Kursi – which however is said to have no precipice. But there is no trace elsewhere of any 'Gergesa', and even if such a place existed it cannot have been more than a *kōmē*, whereas the whole story demands that it be a *polis*, and indeed (see Mk. 5.19) a member of the Decapolis, as were Gerasa and Gadara. There was, by the way, another city of the Decapolis, namely Hippos (the old Susitha), lying to the east of the lake of Galilee and possessing a territory which included villages that adjoined the territory of Gadara (Jos., *Vita* [ix] 42), but it is never mentioned in the new testament.

Jesus is said to have visited the territory of cities outside his main area of action. It is not in Caesarea Philippi itself that he is found, but in its *kōmai* (Mk. 8.27) or *merē* (Mt. 16.13);[16] and when he visits Phoenicia it is to the *merē* or *horia* of Tyre and Sidon that he goes (Mt. 15.21–2; Mk. 7.24, 31), and he is there approached by a woman 'from those *horia*'. When multitudes come to him on another occasion from Tyre and Sidon, it is from their *paralios* (coastal district, Lk. 6.17). There is one reference in Matthew (11.21) and Luke (10.13) to the doing of 'mighty works' in Tyre and Sidon; but (and this nicely confirms what I have been saying) this is simply part of the reproach to the 'cities' (in reality, *kōmai*) Chorazin and Bethsaida (and Capernaum) that *if* the mighty works which had actually been done in them had been performed instead in Tyre and Sidon, they would have repented!

It will have been noticed that I have said nothing so far about the first two palestinian cities which I put at the head of my list above: Sepphoris and Tiberias, the only two real *poleis* of Galilee, which had been founded by Herod Antipas.[17] There is the best of reasons for this: just as we hear nothing in the gospels of Sebaste (the *polis* of the Samareitis), so we hear not a word of Sepphoris, and Tiberias is mentioned only in the fourth gospel (Jn. 6.1, 23; 21.1) in connection with the lake that bore its name, better known to us as the lake of Galilee. Yet Sepphoris was only about four miles from Jesus's home village of Nazareth, and Tiberias is on the shore of the lake of Galilee at almost the nearest point to Nazareth. One can understand that Jesus would not wish to enter Sebaste, a predominantly pagan city; but both Sepphoris and Tiberias were thoroughly jewish in population and religion, even if their civic institutions (those of Tiberias at any rate)[18] were of the standard greek pattern, and even if Sepphoris was to be exceptionally pro-roman during the great jewish revolt of 66–70.[19] Yet it need not surprise us to find no record of Jesus's presence in either of these cities: they were both regarded with hatred by the galilaeans in Josephus's

---

[16] Nineham pp 219, 228n, is unnecessarily puzzled by the use of the perfectly correct expression *kōmē* in Mk. 8.23, 26, 27.

[17] Sepphoris (re-founded): Jos. *AJ* 18. 27. Tiberias: Jos., *BJ* 2. 168; *AJ* 18. 36–8; *Vita* 37; and see M. Avi-Yonah, 'The Foundation of Tiberias', in *Israel Exploration Journal* 1 (1950–51) pp 160–9. For both these cities, see Jones, *Cities* pp 274–8.

[18] See Jones, *Cities* p 462 n 67. Compare also Tessa Rajak, 'Justus of Tiberias', *Classical Quarterly* 67, ns 23 (1973) pp 345–68, esp 346–50.

[19] See Jos., *BJ* 3. 30–4; *Vita* 30, 38–9, 103–4, 124, 232, 346–8, 373, 394–7, 411. (Tiberias had quite an influential pro-roman element: see Jos., *Vita* 32–42, 155 *et seq.*, 381, 391; compare 82 etc.)

army in 66,[20] and Jesus would no doubt have seen them as belonging to an alien world. In Mk. 1.38 it is the nearby *kōmopoleis* (the substantial villages) of Galilee in which he contemplates preaching: that represents the reality.

I dare say that some new testament scholars may object that I have made far too much of topographical evidence in the gospels which they themselves are in general reluctant to press.[21] To this I would reply that I am not using any of the gospel narratives for any topographical purpose: it is a matter of indifference to me whether, for example, the pericope containing the 'confession of Peter' (Mk. 8.27ff.; Mt. 16.13ff.) is rightly located near Caesarea Philippi rather than anywhere else. Nor have I drawn any conclusions from uses of the word *polis*. My one purpose has been to demonstrate that the synoptic gospels are unanimous and consistent in locating the mission of Jesus entirely in the countryside, not within the *poleis* proper, and therefore outside the real limits of hellenistic civilisation. It seems to me inconceivable that this can be due to the evangelists themselves, who (as we have seen) were very likely to dignify an obscure village like Nazareth or Capernaum[22] with the title of *polis* but would certainly not 'down-grade' a locality by making it a country district if in their source it appeared as a *polis*. I conclude, therefore, that in this respect the evangelists accurately reflect the situation they found in their sources; and it seems to me that these sources are very likely indeed to have presented a true picture of the general locus of the activity of Jesus.

Within a generation the message of Jesus had been transformed into what is sometimes described (perhaps not unfairly) as pauline christianity. This process cannot be understood by the historian (as distinct from the theologian) unless it is seen as the transfer of a whole system of ideas from the world of the *chōra* to that of the *polis*[23] – a

---

[20] For Tiberias, see Jos., *Vita* 98–100, 381–9 (esp 384), 392; for Sepphoris, 374, 384; compare 30, 375–80.

[21] Opinions differ greatly here, and none of the new testament scholars I have read has an approach at all similar to mine. There is some good material in G. Schille, 'Die Topographie des Markus-Evangeliums, ihre Hintergründe u. ihre Einordnung', in *Zeitschrift des Deutschen Palästina-Vereins* 73 (1957) pp 133–66, but his interests too are quite different from mine.

[22] The well-known synagogue that has been excavated at Capernaum was built more than a hundred years after the time of Jesus. Josephus, in the whole of his works, makes no reference to Nazareth and at most two to Capernaum: *BJ* 3. 519 (a mere spring), and perhaps *Vita* 403 (the village of Kepharnokos).

[23] See esp n 6 above. Here I should like to mention an excellent article which is relevant to

process necessarily involving the most profound changes in that system of ideas. And in my opinion it is in this process of transformation that the most serious problems of 'Christian origins' arise.

★   ★   ★   ★   ★

Jesus, then, lived and taught within an area which was neither greek nor roman but wholly jewish.[24] As I mentioned earlier, Galilee, within which by far the greater part of the activity of Jesus apparently took place, was not even a roman province during his lifetime: it was still a roman 'client kingdom', until 39 part of the tetrarchy of Herod Antipas, the son of Herod the Great. Of course Jesus was well aware of the roman imperial power that had already engulfed Judaea as a tributary province and could easily swallow up the remaining petty client kingdoms of Palestine whenever it wanted to. But he may well have had virtually no direct contact with the roman imperial administration before his final arrest and trial, on the pretence that he was a political agitator, indeed a 'resistance leader'. Even the 'publicans' (*publicani* in latin, *telōnai* in greek) who crop up in the gospels, such as Matthew (or Levi the son of Alpheus),[25] will have been employed by Herod Antipas, the tetrarch, and not by the roman governor of Judaea – who by the way at this date, as we know from a recently discovered inscription, had the title not of procurator but of praefectus.[26] How much contact Jesus had with greek culture it is not possible to say, but I think it is likely to have been minimal.

Now the graeco-roman world was obsessively concerned with wealth and status. In regard to the vast majority of the members of the upper classes whom we happen to know about from literary evidence or from honorific or funerary inscriptions or otherwise, it is of course their official careers which are best known to us; we seldom have any details of their wealth.[27] But wealth was by far the most important determinant of status. Ovid put it beautifully in three

---

the one aspect of this vast subject named in its title: Heinz Kreissig, 'Zur sozialen Zusammenstellung der frühchristlichen Gemeinde in ersten Jahrh. u.Z.', in *Eirene* 6 (1967) pp 91–100.

[24] This is best brought out, in my opinion, in the admirable recent book by [Geza] Vermes, [*Jesus the Jew. A Historian's Reading of the Gospels*] (London 1973): see esp pp 48–9.

[25] In Mk. 2.14 it is Levi the son of Alpheus, and Levi also in Lk. 5.27, 29; in Mt. 9.9 it is Matthew.

[26] See Schürer p 358 and n 22.

[27] [Richard] Duncan-Jones, [*The Economy of the Roman Empire. Quantitative Studies*] (Cambridge 1974) gives a useful list of 29 of the largest fortunes known to us under the principate, ranging from HS 400 million to about 2 million (App 7, pp 343–4), and a

9

words: *dat census honores*, 'it is property that confers rank' (*Amores* III. viii. 55). In the time of Jesus virtually all the great fortunes belonged to romans rather than greeks; but in the greek world there had always been wide variations of wealth and poverty, and these had become much more pronounced now that the democracy which had flourished in the fifth and fourth centuries was gradually being extinguished by the joint efforts of the greek propertied classes and the romans.[28]

The greeks, from archaic times through the classical and hellenistic periods and on into the roman age, habitually expressed political complexion and social status in a fascinating vocabulary which is an inextricable mixture of socio-economic and moral terminology, with two sets of terms applied more or less indiscriminately to the propertied and the non-propertied classes respectively. On the one hand we have not only words which mean property-owning, rich, fortunate, distinguished, well-born, influential,[29] but also, as alternatives for virtually the same set of people, words having a basically moral connotation and meaning literally the good, the best, the upright, the fair-minded and so forth.[30] And on the other hand we find applied to the lower classes, the poor, who are also the many, the mob, the populace, words with an inescapably moral quality, meaning essentially bad.[31] Even Solon, often regarded as the founder of the athenian democracy, could say in one of his poems that he had made laws equally for the *kakos* and the *agathos*[32] – for the 'lower class' and the 'upper class', of course, rather than 'the bad' and 'the good'; but nothing could alter the social fact that the upper class *were* 'the good',

---

detailed analysis of the wealth of one particular roman of distinction whom we know much better than most: Pliny the Younger (cap 1, pp 17–32).

[28] I shall explain how this happened in *CSAGW*.

[29] For example οἱ τὰς οὐσίας ἔχοντες, πλούσιοι, παχεῖς, εὐδαίμονες, γνώριμοι, εὐγενεῖς, γενναῖοι, δυνατοί, δυνατώτατοι.

[30] For example οἱ ἀγαθοί, καλοὶ κἀγαθοί, χρηστοί, ἐσθλοί, ἄριστοι, βέλτιστοι, δεξιώτατοι, χαρίεντες, ἐπιεικεῖς. I know of no detailed examination of the use of these greek terms comparable to that of J. Hellegouarc'h, *Le vocabulaire latine des relations et des partis politiques sous la République*[2] (Paris 1972), who studies the use of the corresponding latin terms *boni, optimi, optimates* etc on pp 484–505, and the equivalent of those given in n 31 below (for example *plebs, populus, populares, mali, improbi* etc) on pp 506–41. But see R. A. Neil, *The Knights of Aristophanes* (London 1909) pp 202–9, app II, 'Political use of moral terms'.

[31] For example (a) οἱ πένητες (sometimes used almost in the sense of 'the deserving poor'), ἄποροι (the propertyless), πτωχοί; (b) οἱ πολλοί, τὸ πλῆθος, ὁ ὄχλος, ὁ δῆμος, οἱ δημοτικοί; (c) οἱ κακοί, μοχθηροί, πονηροί, δειλοί, τὸ κάκιστον. Compare MacMullen app B: 'The Lexicon of Snobbery', and the works there cited on p 138.

[32] Solon, fr. 24.18–20 (ed E. Diehl, *Anthologia Lyrica Graeca* I[3]. 45); compare fr. 23.19–21; fr. 1.33.

the lower class 'the bad'. The roman governing class was as thoroughly devoted to property as the most wealth-conscious of the greeks. No surviving greek writer is quite as explicit about the over-riding importance of property rights as Cicero, the earliest known to me in a long line of thinkers, extending into modern times, who have seen the protection of private property rights as the prime function of the state. In the *De Officiis*, for example, after asking what greater mischief there could be than an equal distribution of property *(aequatio bonorum . . . qua peste quae potest esse maior?)*, Cicero goes on to declare that states were established above all with the aim of preserving property rights (II.73, compare 78, 83–5; I.21).

Let us now turn back to the jewish world inhabited by Jesus. The contrast between jewish and graeco-roman attitudes to questions of wealth and poverty comes out vividly in the account given in chapter 4 of Luke's gospel of the public preaching of Jesus at Nazareth. (The part I am interested in does not occur in parallel accounts in the other synoptics.) Jesus reads from the 61st chapter of Isaiah, opening with the words, 'the spirit of the Lord is upon me, because he has anointed me to preach the gospel to the poor' (Lk. 4.18). Now the word for 'poor' used here by Luke, as in the septuagint version of Isaiah, is *ptōchoi*, a very strong word indeed, which very often in greek means not just the poor but the down-and-out, the destitute, the beggar – Lazarus in the parable is a *ptōchos* (Lk. 16.20, 22). Classical scholars will remember the appearance of Poverty *(Penia)* as a charac-ter in the *Plutus* of Aristophanes (lines 415–612), and how angry she becomes when Chremylus refers to Penia and Ptocheia as sisters: no, says Penia, the *ptōchos* has nothing, whereas her man, the *penēs*, may toil and scrape, but he has enough to live on (lines 548–54).

I must just mention here that although the word *ptōchoi* does also appear in the septuagint version of Isaiah 61.1, it there translates a hebrew word which is sometimes better rendered – as indeed it is in the authorised version – by 'the meek'. But this takes us into irrelevant questions, which I am anyway not competent to deal with, of the various shades of meaning of the hebrew words expressing poverty, lowliness and the like. Some of these are as ambiguous as the english word 'humble', which can be purely social or purely moral or a mix-ture of the two. The only point I need make here is that in the hebrew terminology, unlike the greek, poverty and a lowly station in life are often associated with the moral virtues.[33]

[33] Perhaps it will be sufficient if I merely give a few references to the massive work of S.W

But let us return to Jesus. In Matthew's version of the beatitudes, in the so-called 'sermon on the Mount' (Mt. v–vii), Jesus is made to say 'Blessed are *hoi ptōchoi tōi pneumati*, the poor *in spirit*' (we might say, 'humble at heart'), 'for theirs is the kingdom of heaven'; and 'Blessed are those who hunger and thirst *after righteousness*, for they shall be filled' (5.3, 6); but Luke's corresponding version, in the 'Sermon on the Plain' (6.17–49), has simply 'Blessed are ye poor' (*ptōchoi*, without qualification), 'for yours is the kingdom of God', and 'Blessed are ye that hunger now' (not 'hunger *after righteousness*'), 'for ye shall be filled' (6.20–1). In both cases, of course, the fulfilment of the blessings is intended eschatologically: they will be realised not in this world but only in the Age to Come. And even the lucan version is echoing the large number of passages in the old testament (especially in the Psalms, Isaiah, Proverbs and Job) in which the poor and lowly as such are treated with special reverence – several different hebrew expressions are involved. In the thought-world of palestinian judaism, out of which Jesus came, it was not so much the rich and influential from whom the moral virtues were to be expected, as in the graeco-roman world, but the poor. An illuminating recent treatment of the beatitudes by David Flusser[33a] shows interesting connections with some of the literature of the Dead Sea sect. Although Flusser is sure that it is Mt. 5.3–5 which 'faithfully preserves the saying of Jesus and that Luke 6.20 is an abbreviation of the original text', he nevertheless insists that 'Matthew's "poor in spirit" also has a social content'.[34]

The main element in the preaching of Jesus was the message, 'repent, for the Kingdom of Heaven is at hand'. The meaning of this is that the end of the whole present dispensation is near: God will intervene and bring to a speedy end all the powers of this world. In preparation for these earth-shaking events men must repent of their sins and obey the law of God. In another sense of the expression 'Kingdom of Heaven' (or 'Kingdom of God'), that kingdom is within man's power to grasp *now*:[34a] if he repents and follows the right way of life, he can to that

---

Baron, *A Social and Religious History of the Jews*, which cites much modern literature: I² (1952 & repr) pp 152 (with 364 n 25), 262–7, 278 (with 414 n 36); II² (1952 & repr) pp 46, 241–2, 256, 269–74. See below n 33a.

[33a] D. Flusser, 'Blessed Are the Poor in Spirit', in *Israel Exploration Jnl* 10 (1960) pp 1–13. I agree with Vermes p 241 n 53 that Adolph Büchler, *Types of Jewish -Palestinian Piety from 70 B.C.E. to 70 C.E.* (1922), is 'a rich mine of information rather than a valid historico-critical assessment of the data'.

[34] p 11, compare pp 6–8.

[34a] Particularly interesting is the article by C. H. Roberts, 'The Kingdom of Heaven

extent enter into the kingdom even before the final cataclysm. Various consequences follow from this. One of the most important is that the possession of wealth is a positive hindrance to entering into the kingdom. 'It is easier for a camel to go through the eye of a needle than for a rich man to enter the Kingdom of God', said Jesus, after the man seeking eternal life who 'had great possessions' had gone away disconsolate on being told to sell all that he had and give it to the poor.[35] (Incidentally, this story is commonly referred to nowadays as that of 'The Rich *Young* Man', and that is certainly what Matthew calls him; but Mark and Luke make it clear that in their minds young is what he is not!)[36] There is one respect in which Matthew's account differs radically from that of the other two synoptics: Matthew (19.21) inserts into the command of Jesus the qualification, 'If you would be perfect' (*ei theleis teleios einai*), which is not in Mark (10.21) or Luke (18.22); and, as we shall see presently, it is in Matthew's formulation that the passage is invariably quoted by the early Fathers.[37]

Luke (16.19–31) is the only evangelist to give us the parable of Lazarus – who, as I said earlier, is specifically a *ptōchos*, here quite rightly translated 'beggar'. Expositors seldom bring out the fact that the terrible fate of the rich man (Dives, as we usually call him) is clearly seen as a direct result of his great wealth, for he feels (verses 27–8) that Lazarus alone will be able to teach his five surviving brothers how to avoid a similar fate. I need not cite any of the other evidence[38] showing that the possession of any substantial amount of property was regarded

---

(Lk. XVII.21)', in *Harvard Theological Review* 41 (1948) pp 1–8, showing that the much-disputed expression ἐντὸς ὑμῶν in Lk. 17.21 is most likely to mean that the kingdom is 'within your power' ('It is a present reality if you wish it to be so', p 8), rather than 'within you' or 'among you'.

[35] Mk. 10.17–31; Mt. 19.16–30; Lk. 18.18–30. For an interesting variant, see the extract from the so-called *Gospel according to the Hebrews*, quoted for example by Albert Huck, *Synopsis of the First Three Gospels* (9 ed, rev by H. Lietzmann, English ed by F. L. Cross, Oxford 1957) p 145n., from E. Klostermann and E. Benz, *Zur Überlieferung der Matthäuserklärung des Origenes* = TU 47, 2 (1931) pp 91–2; there is an English trans in [M. R.] James, [*The Apocryphal New Testament*] (Oxford 1924 & repr) p 6.

[36] In Mark and Luke he says he has observed the commandments ἐκ νεότητος: it is Matthew who calls him ὁ νεανίσκος. Incidentally, it is only Mark (10.21) who says that Jesus 'loved him' (or is it 'caressed him'?).

[37] For a desperate attempt by a modern christian scholar to retain, here and in the beatitudes, the matthaean version in preference, although realising that the other is much more likely to be the historically true one, see Christophe pp 37–8. Would it be unfair to paraphrase his exegesis by saying that Mark and Luke have what Jesus more probably *said*, Matthew what a modern christian feels he must surely have *meant*?

[38] Cadoux pp 61–6 quotes as usual all the texts, even if his interpretations cannot always be accepted.

by Jesus as a positive evil, because it was only too likely to ensnare its possessor and divert him from the primary task of seeking the kingdom of God.

There is just one other new testament passage, again in Luke alone, which I wish to mention: the Magnificat.[39] Here we find an interesting variant on the eschatological conception we have noticed already, according to which in the Age to Come the poor and hungry will be satisfied. We are still within the realm of eschatology, but the desired result is now conceived – in one form of the tradition of jewish apocalyptic – as having been in some mysterious way achieved already. 'He *hath* put down the mighty from their seats and *hath* exalted them of low degree. He *hath* filled the hungry with good things and the rich he *hath* sent empty away'. In the greek the 'mighty' are the *dynastai*, and Thomas Hardy took his title, 'The Dynasts', explicitly from this passage.[40] In fact nothing of the sort had actually happened: the dynasts were now more firmly in control than ever, as the roman principate began its long era of power. The picture in the Magnificat, in which the events are represented as having in a mystical sense occurred already, was a pleasantly harmless one from the point of view of the dynasts, who certainly cashed the blank cheque saint Paul later wrote them when he said, 'The powers that be are ordained of God', and enjoined strict obedience to the civil authorities.[41]

---

[39] Lk. 1.46–55 (esp 52–3). See [Joseph Vogt, 'Ecce ancilla domini', in *Vigiliae Christianae* 23 (1969) pp 241–63, repr in] Vogt [*Sklaverei u. Humanität*] (2 ed = *Historia*, Einzelschr. 8, 1972) pp 147–64, 168.

[40] See Thomas Hardy, *The Dynasts*, After Scene (p 522 of the 'Papermac' edition 1965), where the Semi-chorus I of the Pities has the line, 'Who hurlest Dynasts from their thrones', and Hardy quotes the greek of the Magnificat in a footnote. The term *dynastēs*, in the sense of a chief or prince, occurs from the 5th century BC onwards (see for example Thuc. VII. 33.4), and in the hellenistic period becomes almost a technical term for the ruler who is not actually a king. Thus in official formulae referring to ruling authorities, dynasts are linked with kings, cities and peoples (*ethnē*), in various combinations: see for example *OGIS* 229.11; 383.172–3, 228–9; 441.129–30, 131–2; *SIG*[3] 581.64; Diod. XIX.57.3.

[41] *Rom.* 13.1–7; *Titus* 3.1; compare *I Pet.* 2.13–17; *I Tim.* 2.1–2. There has been a long controversy over the nature of the 'powers' (*exousiai*) to whom every soul is commanded to be subject, in *Rom.* 13.1. It should be sufficient to refer to Clinton D. Morrison, *The Powers That Be* (= *Studies in Biblical Theology* no 29 (1960)), who has exhaustive bibliographies. The reader should be warned, however, that the author is a theologian and not a historian, and that some of his statements are such as no ancient historian could accept – for example p 125: 'Since the State was part of the cosmic order established by the Ruler of All . . ., the ancients considered subjection to the State a religious duty, and anarchy was synonymous with atheism. Wise and godly men had no alternative but submission to this order, and no doubt the Christian conscience was largely tempered by this common understanding'. Apologists for Paul must try to do better than this.

Early christian attitudes to property & slavery

I shall waste little time on the so-called 'communism' of the earliest apostolic community, which appears only momentarily in the opening chapters of Acts, while the christian church was a single small body,[42] and then ceases altogether, to reappear only within single monastic communities from the early fourth century onwards. This situation, which was already characteristic of certain essene and other communities among the jews,[43] is entirely absent from the remainder of the new testament, and even in the early chapters of Acts it is clear that communal ownership was not complete, and in any event had nothing to do with communal production. Later references which have sometimes been taken wrongly as evidence of a continuance of community of property are no more than idealisations of a situation in which charity is conceived as complete, as when Tertullian says, '*omnia indiscreta sunt apud nos, praeter uxores*' (*Apol.* 39.11), or when Justin boasts that christians share all their property with one another (I *Apol.* xiv.2).

*   *   *   *   *

At this point, before I go on to consider the attitude of the fathers to the question of property-ownership, I want to turn aside and deal with early christian attitudes to the specific problem of slavery, which of course is partly one aspect of the larger question of property in general, for slaves ranked very high indeed among the forms of property considered essential for the good life in classical antiquity. The main organisational difference between the economy of the ancient world and our own is that in antiquity the propertied classes derived their

---

[42] *Acts* 2.44–5; 4.32–7; 5.1–11; cf. Jn. 12.6; 13.29. I need refer only to [Rudolf] Bultmann, [*Theology of the New Testament*] (1952 & repr) I p 62: 'It is self-evident that in an eschatological congregation awaiting the near end of the world no special economic system was set up. What is often called the community of property in the earliest Church on the basis of Acts 2:45; 4:34ff. is in reality a practical sharing of property on the basis of love. To call this actual communism is out of the question, for it lacks both a social programme and organized production'.

[43] For the ancient greek and latin texts relating to the essenes, see *Antike Berichte über die Essener*, ed Alfred Adam=*Kleine Texte für Vorlesung und Übungen*, no 182 (1961). There is of course a large literature on the essenes: see the select bibliography in vol 9 of the Loeb edition of Josephus, by L. H. Feldman (1965), App D, pp 561–3. This has been growing since the appearance of the 'Dead Sea Scrolls', emanating (in my view) either from the essenes themselves or from a closely related sect. For a useful recent bibliography dealing with all the recent discoveries in the Judaean desert, see Schürer I, pp 118–22. G. Vermes, *The Dead Sea Scrolls* (Penguin, 1962 & repr) is the best English version: see esp pp 29–30. And compare R. de Vaux, *Archaeology and the Dead Sea Scrolls* (London 1973) esp 129–30. Doubtless jewish influences also lie behind such passages in the 'Apostolic Fathers' as *Didache* 4.8 (contrast 1.5–6; 4.9, 11); Hermes, *Shepherd*, Vision III.vi.6 (contrast for example Mandate II.4–6; Similitude II.5–10); *Barnabas* 19.8.

surplus, which enabled them to live as they pleased, not from the exploitation of free wage labour (which was relatively rare and was never of any great importance in the economy) but from unfree labour[44] – that of chattel slaves above all, but also to some extent that of serfs (such as the spartan helots or the majority of the *coloni* of the later roman empire) or of debt-bondsmen. Of course, a very large part of both agricultural production and manufacture was carried on by small independent peasants and artisans; but anyone who wanted to live as a gentleman and have time to spend on such things as politics or philosophy[45] or just a life of pleasure would have to rely mainly on exploiting slave labour. (There was hardly any alternative, except the letting of land or houses to tenants.)

Now of course in a class society, especially one resting largely on servile labour, the governing class will have to keep the threat of force up its sleeve, to ensure the subservience of those at whose expense it lives; and the greeks, and even more the romans, could treat refractory slaves with extreme harshness. During the debate in the roman senate in 61, on whether there should be the traditional mass execution of all the four hundred urban slaves of Pedanius Secundus, the *Praefectus Urbi*, who had been murdered by one of his slaves, the conservative lawyer Gaius Cassius told the nervous senators, 'You will not restrain that scum except by terror'; and the execution was duly carried out, in spite of a vigorous protest by the common people of Rome, who demonstrated violently for the relaxation of the savage ancient rule – which, incidentally, was still the law in the legislation of the christian emperor Justinian five centuries later.[46] But a ruling class seldom tries to rule by force alone; some kind of ideology is usually devised which both justifies the privileged position of the rulers and also seeks to persuade the ruled that the existing state of affairs is only right and proper and is even in their 'own best interests'.

[44] I shall have a great deal to say about this in *CSAGW* and can omit the evidence here.
[45] According to Arist., *Pol.* I.7, 1255^b35–7, such a man would not even trouble himself with the supervision of his slaves but would entrust it to an overseer.
[46] The story is given by Tac., *Ann.* XIV.42–3. It is strange that some standard works, such as W. W. Buckland, *The Roman Law of Slavery* (Cambridge 1908) pp 95 etc., and W. L. Westermann, *The Slave Systems of Greek and Roman Antiquity=Mem. Amer. Philos. Soc.* 40 (1955) p 82, speak of the *S.C. Silanianum* as ordering only the torture of the murdered master's slave household. It is quite clear that if they failed to give aid to their murdered master (whether killed by a fellow-slave or anyone else), all those slaves *sub eodem tecto* were held to be guilty and were not merely tortured but executed: see *CJ* VI.xxxv.12 (Justinian, AD 532); and many passages in *Dig.* XXIX.v, for example 1.§§ 18, 21, 22, 26, 27, 28, 31, 33; 3.§§ 16, 17; 14; and esp 19. Many heirs must have been very angry at being thus robbed of valuable property!

Early christian attitudes to property & slavery

Two main types of philosophical justification of slavery were constructed by the greeks and romans.[47] The first, the famous theory of 'natural slavery', which is implicit in Plato's thought and fully developed by Aristotle, grew naturally out of the historical fact that most greek slaves in the classical period were *barbaroi* – strictly, non-greeks, but 'barbarians' is normally used as the translation of the corresponding greek and latin words, as it is so convenient in practice, if often technically incorrect. Aristotle's theory was based upon the proposition, which he regarded as self-evident, that certain people (including virtually all barbarians) are slaves by nature, in the sense that they are actually better off when subjected to a master: for such a person, slavery is both beneficial and just. The essential view of Plato and Aristotle was nicely expressed, more vividly than by either of them, by the Virginian slaveowner, George Fitzhugh, in 1854: 'Some men are born with saddles on their backs, and others booted and spurred to ride them; *and the riding does them good*'![48] (Fitzhugh, of course, was quoting, and contradicting, some famous words spoken on the scaffold in 1685 by the English radical, Richard Rumbold.)[49] One passage in Aristotle's *Politics* that is particularly interesting is the one containing the advice that all slaves should be offered the reward of ultimate emancipation (VII.10, 1330ᵃ 32–3): Aristotle promises to give his reasons later, but unfortunately never does so. If we read this advice with earlier passages explaining how the slave can benefit from his association with his master, we may see a fairly precise parallel, at the individual level, with the theory of the 'tutelage of backward nations', one of the main planks in the ideology of modern western imperialism.

The other type of philosophical justification of slavery, which is particularly associated with the stoics, has its antecedent in a statement in the *Politics* of Aristotle (I.6, 1255ᵃ 25–6) which denies the very name of slave to the man who does not deserve to be in a condition of slavery – or, as we might say, denies that the man who does not deserve to be in slavery is 'really' a slave at all. This, and not the theory of 'natural slavery', became the standard view of thinking slaveowners in hellenistic and roman times. Even before Aristotle wrote there had been

---

[47] My treatment of this subject here is somewhat over-simplified, and I have cited little ancient evidence; but there is a much fuller analysis in my *CSAGW*.

[48] George Fitzhugh, *Sociology for the South, or the Failure of Free Society* (Richmond, Va., 1854) p 179.

[49] See *The Good Old Cause. The English Revolution of 1640–1660, Its Causes, Course and Consequences*². Extracts from contemporary sources, ed Christopher Hill and Edmund Dell (2 ed, rev, 1969) p 474.

protests against the hypothesis of 'natural' slavery[50] and even against the assumption that barbarians are naturally inferior to greeks. Indeed, the theory of 'natural slavery' is not at all prominent in antiquity after Aristotle's time, and when it does reappear it is mainly applied to peoples rather than individuals.[51] This may be in a merely rhetorical context, as when Cicero stigmatises jews and syrians as 'peoples born for slavery' (De Prov. Cons. 10), but we also find it seriously stated by a speaker in Cicero's dialogue De Republica (III.25/37) that a nation can benefit from being in a state of complete political subjection (servitus) to another.[52] There were, however, some distant but powerful echoes of the 'natural slavery' theory in much later times, when it played a highly significant role in christian Spain in the controversy concerning the rightfulness of enslaving negroes, and the indians of the Caribbean and of central and south America, in the fifteenth century onwards. At the great debate ordered by Charles V at Valladolid in 1550, to decide whether christian spaniards might lawfully wage war upon indians and enslave them, before even preaching the faith to them, Aristotle's doctrine was accepted in principle by both the leading disputants: the great scholar Juan Gines de Sepúlveda and the franciscan friar Bartolomé de las Casas. (The main book in English on this topic, upon which I am relying here, bears the delightful title, Aristotle and the American Indians.)[53] The main point of disagreement, it seems, was simply the factual question whether or not the indians were 'natural slaves'; it was hardly questioned that negroes were.

In the hellenistic period onwards, greek and roman thought on the subject of slavery, with hardly an exception, provides a set of uninspired variations on a single theme: that the state of slavery – like poverty and war, or liberty, riches and peace – is the result of accident, of Fortune rather than of Nature, and that it is a matter of indifference, affecting externals only; that the good and wise man is never 'really' a slave, even if that happens to be his actual condition, but is 'really' free; that it is the bad man who is 'really' a slave, because he is in bondage to his own lusts – a wonderfully comforting set of doctrines for

[50] See my The Origins of the Peloponnesian War, p 45.
[51] As it had sometimes been earlier, for example in Arist., Pol. VII.14, 1333^{b}38ff., esp 1334^{a}2.
[52] The source of Cic., De Rep. III.24/36 to 25/37, ed K. Ziegler (6 ed 1964) is often said to be Panaetius, but I agree with H. Strasburger, 'Poseidonios on Problems of the Roman Empire', in JRS 55 (1965) pp 40–53 (esp pp 44–5 & n 50) that this is unjustified.
[53] It is by Lewis Hanke (London 1959).

slaveowners. (I fancy that such austere philosophical notions are of greater assistance in the endurance of liberty, riches and peace than of slavery, poverty and war.) Ingenious developments can be found of this or that aspect of the standard view I have just described, and of course some authors emphasise one aspect of it, others another; but there is a general dreary similarity of sentiment. I think the fourteenth oration of Dio Chrysostom is probably the most entertaining example I know of this kind of perverse ingenuity.

It is often said that christianity introduced an entirely new and better attitude towards slavery. Nothing could be more false: Jesus accepted slavery as a fact of his environment,[54] just as it is accepted in the old testament; and his followers accepted and adapted the prevailing graeco-roman view which I have just described. The significance of the oft-quoted text in *Colossians* (3.11), 'There is neither Greek nor Jew, circumcision nor uncircumcision, barbarian, Scythian, bond nor free' is better understood in the light of the parallel text in *Galatians* (3.28): 'There is neither Jew nor Greek, there is neither bond nor free, *there is neither male nor female*; for ye are all one in Christ Jesus'. There is 'neither bond nor free' in exactly the same sense as there is 'neither male nor female': these statements are true *in a strictly spiritual sense*; the equality exists 'in the sight of God' and has no relation whatever to temporal affairs. The distinction between slave and master in this world is no more seen as needing to be *changed* than that between male and female. For saint Paul, Jesus has set all his followers free – from the flesh and all its works.[55] The exhortation to the christian slave to regard himself as 'Christ's freedman' (in the same sense that the Christian who is a free man is 'Christ's slave', *I Cor.* vii.22) may well have afforded him greater spiritual comfort than the pagan slave could obtain from the familiar philosophic view that if he was a good man he was 'really' free already; but it was basically the same view. And if, as by philosophic pagans, christian masters are briefly enjoined to treat their slaves fairly,[56] the yoke of slavery is fastened even more firmly

[54] See esp Lk. 17.7–9 (addressing potential slaveowners); also Mk. 12.2–5 (=Lk. 20.10–12; compare Mt. 21.34–6); 13.34; Mt. 10.24–5; 13.27–8; 18.23ff.; 22.3–10 (compare Lk. 14.17–23); 24.45–51; 25.14–30 (compare Lk. 19.13–22); Lk. 12.37–8; 43–8; 15.22, 26; and other texts.

[55] See for example Bultmann 1, pp 243–5, 246, 249, 331–3, 340–3; 2, pp 205, 214, compare 230–1.

[56] In the new testament, the only relevant passages I can find are *Coloss.* 4.1; *Ephes.* 6.9; also *Philem.* 10ff. (esp 16–18), a special case, Onesimus having been converted by Paul (10).

[57] See *Ephes.* 6.5–8; *Coloss.* 3.22–4; *I Tim.* 6.1–2; *Titus* 2.9–10; *I Pet.* 2.18–20. Compare

upon christian slaves as the emphasis on obedience to their masters becomes even more absolute. Certain phrases in the pauline epistles,[57] such as that in *Ephesians* (6.5), exhorting slaves to obey their masters 'with fear and trembling, in singleness of heart, *as unto Christ*', had sinister implications which were made explicit in two post-apostolic works, the *Epistle of Barnabas* (19.7) and the *Didache* (4.11): they expressly tell the slave that he must serve his master 'as a counterpart of God' (*hōs typōi theou*), 'in reverence and fear'. I know of nothing that goes as far as that in pagan literature. Whatever the theologian may think of christianity's claim to set free the soul of the slave, therefore, the historian cannot deny that it helped to rivet the shackles rather more firmly on his feet.[58] It performed the same social function as the fashionable philosophies of the graeco-roman world, and perhaps with deeper effect: it made the slave both more content to endure his earthly lot, and more tractable and obedient. Saint Ignatius, in his *Epistle to Polycarp* (4.3), is anxious that christian slaves should be neither despised nor 'puffed up' (*mē physiousthōsan*); that they should 'serve the more, to the glory of God'; and that they should 'not wish to be set free at the public cost, lest they become slaves of lust'. (I confess that I find the last phrase somewhat inconsequential, nor can I see exactly how an even more intense degree of labour on the part of the slave can enhance the glory of God.) The fifth Canon of the council of Elvira (in the late third century or the early fourth) punished with no more than seven years' excommunication even the intentional flogging to death by a woman of her slave-girl – perhaps one who had received the sexual attentions of the woman's husband. And baptism seems to have been refused to a slave by at least some churches without the consent of his master –

---

[57] *I Cor.* 7.20–4: here there has been much dispute about the meaning of vv. 20–1, which must certainly be taken as an injunction against seeking manumission, both because of the *ei kai* ('even if': the force of this is missed in the authorised version and by many commentators) and because of the *gar* at the beginning of v. 22. The sense is, 'Let each man remain in the calling [occupation] wherein he was called [converted to Christianity]. Were you a slave when you were called [converted]? Don't let it concern you; but even if you are able to become free, be content with your present condition, for he who was called in the Lord [converted], being a slave, is the Lord's freedman; similarly, he who was called being a free man is a slave of Christ'. Paul's point is that the believer's earthly condition, as slave or free, is of no importance.
[58] In his article, 'Slavery, Christian', in Hastings' *Encyclopaedia of Religion and Ethics* 11 (London 1920 & repr) p. 604a, L. D. Agate felt obliged to admit that the church tended, 'owing to its excessive care for the rights of the masters, even to perpetuate what would otherwise have passed away'. I doubt, however, if slavery would have 'passed away' any earlier in the absence of christianity.

perhaps only at first if a christian one,[59] but later even if a pagan.[60] Such a sacrifice of the immortal soul of a would-be christian slave to the property-rights of a master seems to me indefensible on christian premises.

The situation changed not at all when christianity succeeded to the seats of power in the fourth century, and the church[61] assumed a position even in the public life of the roman empire of the fourth and following centuries which I can only compare, functionally, with the role of what president Eisenhower called 'the military-industrial complex' in the United States today. Saint Augustine at least admitted that slavery was an evil in principle; but with that extraordinary perverse ingenuity which never ceases to astonish one, he saw it as God's punishment upon mankind for the sin of Adam.[62] (It did not occur to him that it might be thought blasphemous to attribute to an all-just Deity such a singularly indiscriminate method of collective punishment.) In thus suggesting that 'justly was the burden of servitude laid upon the back of transgression' Augustine represented slavery as something divinely ordained, and gave the institution an even weightier justification than it had ever received from pre-christian thinkers since the days when theories of 'natural slavery' were abroad. Indeed, Augustine and Ambrose went so far as to think that slavery could actually be good for the slave, an instructive form of correction and a blessing even[63] – for, as Ambrose put it, 'the lower the station in life, the more exalted the virtue'.[64] I have not been able to find in any early christian writer anything like a demand for the abandonment of slavery or even for a general freeing of existing slaves. The nearest

---

[59] See Hippol., *Apost. Trad.* 15 (ed Bernard Botte, *Hippolyte de Rome. La tradition apostolique d'après les anciennes versions*[2] = SC 11[b], 2 ed 1968)=xvi.4 in the English trans by Gregory Dix, *The Treatise on the Apostolic Tradition of St. Hippolytus of Rome*[2] (1968, 2 ed, rev by H. Chadwick). The date of the *Apost. Trad.* is very close to 215.

[60] *Can. Hippol.* X.63 (pp 76–7, ed H. Achelis, *TU* 6, 4, 1891); compare the arabic version, with a french trans, in R. G. Coquin, *Les canons d'Hippolyte*=PO 31, 2 (1966) can. 10, p 95=363.

[61] Strictly, the expression 'the church' is a theological rather than a historical concept, for the christians were never anything like a united body, and each sect (including of course the catholics) had a habit of denying the very name of christian to all 'heretics' and 'schismatics' – that is to say, those who were not within its communion. But the expression is too convenient to be abandoned entirely.

[62] Aug., esp *CD* XIX.xv–xvi.

[63] Aug., *CD* XIX.xv; Ambr., *Ep.* 77.6 ('is qui regere se non potest et gubernare, servire debet . . . pro benedictione igitur huiusmodi confertur servitus').

[64] Ambr., *Ep.* 2.19 ('quo status inferior, eo virtus eminentior'). Among other passages in Ambrose dealing with slavery, see *Ep.* 37 *passim*; 63.112; 75.4–5.

thing I know to this is in one of the *Hymns on the Nativity* (surviving only in syriac) of Ephraim, of Nisibis and Edessa in Mesopotamia: here Ephraim makes Mary say, 'Let the man who owns a slave give him his freedom'.[65] But immediately there follow the words, 'so that he may come and serve his Lord'; and in one of his *Hymns on the Epiphany* Ephraim makes it clear that in his eyes it is through baptism that the slave and the free man are equated[66] – the standard christian view. I have not even been able to discover any attack on slavery in heretical works, comparable to the pelagian onslaught on riches which I shall mention presently. At least two Christian scholars of modern times, C. J. Cadoux and R. M. Grant,[67] have declared that the gnostic *Acts of Thomas*[68] attack the very institution of slavery on the ground that all men are equal before God. In the text I see nothing of the sort, but only an expression of sympathy for slaves whose masters lay burdens on them as brute beasts and refuse to treat them as men like themselves.

In the roman lawyers (apparently pagans to a man), from the second or third century of the christian era to the sixth, we sometimes find the admission that slavery was *contra naturam, iuri naturali contraria*.[69] (Slavery indeed seems to have been regarded by at least some of the lawyers as the only feature of the *ius gentium* that did not form part of *ius naturale*.)[70] This is a line of thought that can be traced right back to the unnamed thinkers of the fifth or fourth century BC who are said by Aristotle to have declared that slavery, because it was based on force, was contrary to nature and wrong – not merely 'not according to nature' (*ou kata physin*) but '*contrary* to nature' (*para physin*), a significant difference.[71] This line of thought may or may not have descended to the roman lawyers through the stoics. Certainly some stoics – the ex-slave Epictetus, for example[72] – may occasionally have spoken as if they actually disapproved in principle of possessing slaves. But this is all

---

[65] Ephraem Syrus, *Hymn. de Nativ.* XVII.8, p 80, in the German trans of E. Beck, *CSCO* 187 (=Syr. 83) 1959. For this and the passage cited in the next note, see Vogt pp 161–2.

[66] Ephraem Syrus, *Hymn, de Epiph.* IV.6–8 (p 143).

[67] Cadoux p 454 (with the greek text in n 5); R. M. Grant, *Augustus to Constantine. The Thrust of the Christian Movement into the Roman World* (London 1971) p 301.

[68] *Act. Thom.* 83, in *Acta Apostolorum Apocrypha* II.ii.198–9, ed M. Bonnet (Leipzig 1903). There is a good English trans in James at p 402.

[69] *Dig.* I.v.4.1 (Florentinus); XII.vi.64 (Tryphoninus); I.i.4 (Ulpian); *Inst. J.* I.ii.2.

[70] See H. F. Jolowicz and Barry Nicholas, *Historical Introduction to the Study of Roman Law*[3] (Cambridge 1972) pp 106–7.

[71] See my *The Origins of the Peloponnesian War* p 45.

[72] See *Gnomologium Epicteteum* 36–7 (pp 486–7 in H. Schenkl's Teubner text of Epictetus, 1916)=fr. 42–3 Schweighäuser.

ultimately unreal, part of the smokescreen of plausible ideas by which the more fastidious thinkers of antiquity concealed from themselves the unpalatable truth about a ruthless world of which they were trying to make the best they could, according to their lights. The unreality of all this talk emerges most clearly from Epictetus's description of the ex-slave who ends up by becoming a senator: he is then subject, says Epictetus, to 'the fairest and sleekest slavery of all'![73] If being a senator was slavery, it was slavery in a pickwickian sense, a kind of slavery which the vast majority of the population of the graeco-roman world would have embraced eagerly enough.

In early christian thought, then, I have been able to find little or nothing that goes even as far in rejecting slavery as the purely theoretical statements of the roman lawyers to the effect that it is 'contrary to nature'. And at this point I must mention one thing that has long puzzled me. I realise that on christian principles a good case can perhaps be made for accepting the condition of slavery *for the slave*, in the way that stoics and epicureans accepted it, as well as saint Paul and so many of the other early christians, as something external and unimportant. This is so, even for those who might not go all the way with cardinal Newman when he declared that according to the teaching of his church 'it were better for sun and moon to drop from heaven, for the earth to fail, and for all the many millions who are upon it to die of starvation in extremest agony, as far as temporal affliction goes, than that one soul, I will not say, should be lost, but should commit one single venial sin, should tell one wilful untruth, though it harmed no one, or steal one poor farthing without excuse'.[74] But what of slavery as it affects the master? Surely the christian who prays not to be 'led into temptation' should proceed to renounce the total irresponsible domination over fellow human beings which belongs to the master of slaves and is only too likely to lead him (as we know it did) into the gravest temptation, to commit acts of cruelty and lust? I do not know when this was first realised; but it was evident to the genius of Tolstoy, who in a remarkable passage in *War and Peace* makes prince Andrey tell Pierre that what is most evil about serfdom is its effect upon those masters who have the power to punish their serfs as they please, and who, in doing so, 'stifle their remorse and become hardened'.[75] I can

---

[73] Epict., *Diss.* IV.i.40, p 360, ed H. Schenkl (1916).
[74] J. H. Newman, *Lectures on certain Differences felt by Anglicans in submitting to the Catholic Church* (London 1850) p 199; (new and rev ed Dublin 1857) p. 190.
[75] The conversation occurs in book V, during Pierre's visit to Andrey at Bogucharovo.

only conclude that what prevented the christian church from admitting the dangerous, brutalising effect of slavery (and serfdom) upon masters was the irresistible force of social reality – what I would call, with Marx, the class struggle: the absolute necessity for the dominant classes of the graeco-roman world to maintain those social institutions upon which their whole privileged position depended, and which they were not willing, or even able, to forgo.

I cannot speak from personal knowledge of christian literature much after the sixth century; but I would say that I know of no absolute condemnation of slavery as an institution by any christian writer during the middle ages: statements I have seen quoted from Theodore the Studite, Smaragdus Abbas and others always have some particular limited application.[76] I dare say it is only my own ignorance, but I know of no general, outright condemnation of slavery inspired by a christian outlook, before the petition of the mennonites of Germantown in Pennsylvania in 1688[77] – a sect very like the quakers, outside the main stream of christianity. Christian writers have often emphasised attempts by christians to prevent or at least discourage enslavement; but these efforts were rarely if ever extended for the benefit of those outside the christian fold, and writers who have drawn attention to them have often failed to mention that condemnation of the sin of enslaving christians is commonly accompanied by the tacit admission that enslaving non-believers is permissible, and even praiseworthy if enslavement is followed by conversion to the faith – a conversion which perhaps in some cases could hardly be attained by other means.

*　　*　　*　　*　　*

So much for slavery. I turn now to the more general problem of the attitude of the early fathers to the question of property-ownership.[78]

---

[76] For Smaragdus, see R. W. and A. J. Carlyle, *A History of Medieval Political Theory in the West* I² (London 1927) pp 208–9; [David Brion] Davis, [*The Problem of Slavery in Western Culture*] (New York 1966) pp 92–3. There is a great deal of interesting material in the latter work (the best general account of its subject) on christian attitudes to slavery; compare also C. R. Boxer, *The Portuguese Seaborne Empire 1415–1825* (London 1969, Pelican 1973) for example pp 20–5, 66 *et seq.*, and esp pp 265–8.

[77] A text often reprinted: see for example *Documents of American Hist.*,⁵ ed H. S. Commager (New York 1949) pp 37–8, no 26. And see Davis pp 308–9.

[78] The bibliography is vast, and I will only refer to Christophe, pp 55–214; and [Jean] Gaudemet, [*L'Église dans l'empire roman IVᵉ–Vᵉ siècles*] (Paris 1958) pp 569–73 (compare pp 694–8 on almsgiving), who give sufficient references to other modern work. A. R. Hands, *Charities and Social Aid in Greece and Rome* (London 1968), deals mainly with the pre-christian world, as does H. Bolkestein, *Wohltätigkeit und Armenpflege in vorchristlichen Altertum* (Utrecht 1939).

Early christian attitudes to property & slavery

There are of course considerable differences of emphasis, but I think it would be true to say that with hardly an exception all the orthodox writers seem to have no serious qualms in accepting that a christian may own property, under certain conditions, the most important of which are that he must neither seek it avidly nor acquire it unjustly; that he ought not to possess a superfluity but only a sufficiency; and that what he does have he may use but must not abuse: he must hold it as a kind of trustee[79] (if I may be permitted to use that peculiar technical term of English law) for the poor, to whom he must give charity. This last condition, the necessity for almsgiving, is the one upon which there is most insistence: the whole conception of course descended direct to christianity from judaism;[80] and here the christian churches do seem to have gone far beyond the ordinary pagan standard. (There are some interesting remarks about the absence of similar organised activities among the pagans, in the works of the emperor Julian.)[81] Occasional anticipations of the christian ideas I have just outlined can be found in earlier greek authors, as when Euripides makes Jocasta say that mortals do not hold their property as their own private possession: it belongs to the gods, and mortals merely have the care of it; the gods, whenever they want it, take it back again (*Phoen.* 555–7).

I shall return in a moment to the question of almsgiving, which is worth special attention, and I shall also have something to say on the question of sufficiency or superfluity of property. But I must first add a rider to what I have said about the general early christian view of property-ownership. The words of Jesus to the rich man seeking eternal life, which I discussed earlier, were not entirely disregarded; but it seems that the unqualified version of Mark and Luke was conveniently forgotten and the words of Jesus were always quoted in Matthew's formulation (19.21), in which the direction to sell all and give to the poor was prefaced by the qualification, 'If you would be perfect'. Out of scores of passages I have come across in the fathers I have not found one that even notices the discrepancy between the matthaean text and that of Mark and Luke. So complete was the refusal to recognise the

---

[79] Of many possible examples I will cite only Jerome, *Ep.* 130.14 (to the very wealthy Demetrias).

[80] See below, and some of the passages cited in n 33 above.

[81] For Julian, see esp. (1) *Ep.* 84a (ed J. Bidez and F. Cumont, *Iuliani Imp. Epist., Leges etc.* [1922]=84a Bidez [Budé]=49 Hertlein=22 W. C. Wright [Loeb III]). 429c–30a, 430bcd (compare 430d: no Jew is a beggar); (2) *Ep.* 89b (Bidez-Cumont and Bidez= Wright II.296–339). 305bcd; compare (3) *Misopog.* 363a; (4) *Orat.* VII (*ad Heracl.*). 224bc. I have not been able to make use of Jürgen Kabiersch, *Untersuchungen zum Begriff der Philanthropie bei dem Kaiser Julian* (Wiesbaden 1960).

existence of any other version than that of Matthew that when Clement of Alexandria, in his *Quis dives salvetur?*, sets out Mark's narrative of the whole story *in extenso* in his own text, explicitly as his source, he inserts Matthew's *ei theleis teleios einai*, at the point that corresponds to Mt. 19.21, without any indication that these words are not in Mark.[82] Saint John Chrysostom is even at pains to put the conditional clause in the forefront and to make out that Jesus did *not* merely say to the rich man, 'Sell what you have': he actually rubs it in, expanding the words of Jesus into 'I lay it down for your determination. I give you full power to choose. I do not lay upon you any necessity'.[83] Thus, by quoting the statement of Jesus in its qualified, matthaean form, the fathers were able to make use of the standard distinction between 'precept' and 'counsel': the command to sell all became literally a 'counsel of perfection'.[84] And I think it would be true to say that after the rise of monasticism in the fourth century there was a tendency to take 'If you would be perfect' to refer essentially to the adoption of the monastic life: thus when Jerome presses on his rich friend Julian the desirability of ridding himself of all his possessions (again of course on the basis of the matthaean text we have been considering), he is clearly advising him to become a monk.[85]

We can now return to almsgiving. There is an enormous amount of evidence of the high value attached to almsgiving by early christian thinkers which it would be superfluous to quote, and I shall concentrate on two passages, one from a latin and one from a greek father, both of which emphasise the expiatory character of almsgiving and thus demonstrate the jewish roots of christian thinking in this field. Optatus, in his work against the donatists, had occasion to allude to almsgiving when speaking of the visit of certain imperial emissaries (Macarius and others) to Africa in 347, in order to make charitable distributions provided by the emperor Constans.[86] He first claimed, on the strength

---

[82] Clem. Alex., *Quis dives salvetur?* iv.6; cf. x.1. The standard edition of this work is by O. Stählin, 2 ed by L. Früchtel, *GCS* 17²=Clemens Alex. III² (1970) pp 158–91. English readers will find useful the Loeb ed by G. W. Butterworth (London 1919 & repr), in which *The Rich Man's Salvation* is printed mainly in Stählin's text, with a good facing english trans and some notes, on pp 270–367.

[83] John Chrys., *Hom. II De Stat.* 5 (PG 49 (1859) col 40).

[84] Among very many examples see Aug. *Ep.* 157.23–39.

[85] Jerome, *Ep.* 118, esp §§ 4, 5, 6 (*init.*), 7 (*init.*). Compare *Ep.* 60, to Heliodorus, where the priest Nepotian is said to have lived in practice the life of a monk (§ 10) and thus fulfilled Mt. 19.21.

[86] Optatus III.3, pp 74.19 to 75.3, ed C. Ziwsa, *CSEL* 26 (1893). This work was published about 365–6, and a revised edition was issued some twenty years later.

of *Proverbs* 22.2, that it was God who had made both the poor and the
rich, and he then proceeded to explain that God had a very good reason
for establishing this distinction: it would of course have been perfectly
possible for him to give to both classes at once, but if he had done so,
the sinner would have had no means of atoning for his faults (*si
ambobus daret, peccator quae sibi succurreret invenire non posset*). To drive
his point home, Optatus now quotes what was for him another
inspired and canonical work, *Ecclesiasticus* (3.30): just as water quenches
fire, so do alms atone for sin (*sic eleemosyna extinguit peccatum*).[87] Later,
the theology of almsgiving – if I may call it that – may have become
more subtle (that is beyond the scope of this paper), but whenever
almsgiving is being discussed, the notion that it can be an atonement
for sin is seldom absent. This is certainly true of the second example I
said I would give of the christian concept of almsgiving, from a greek
father. This comes from the work by Clement of Alexandria, usually
referred to by its latin title, *Quis dives salvetur?*, which is actually the
earliest treatise to provide a detailed justification of property-ownership by christians, and is perhaps the most important work of its kind.
Clement puts most eloquently the argument that almsgiving can
actually purchase salvation, and he exclaims, 'What a splendid commerce! what divine trading!'[88] Needless to say, almsgiving often played
an important part in penance.[89] Too often, however, it seems to have
been resorted to as a means of self-advertisement,[90] contrary to the
admirable prescription of Jesus in Mt. 6.1–4.

The early christian attitude to property-ownership, as I have
described it, is open to criticism from more than one direction. I shall
concentrate on two respects in which it can now be seen to be unsatisfactory: first, the exceedingly important role it allotted to almsgiving; and secondly, its notion that a sufficiency of wealth was harmless enough, even if a superfluity was dangerous.

Until quite recently, of course, charity was accepted by the great
majority as an entirely admirable thing; and it is only in our own
generation that a large number of people have begun to criticise

[87] Compare another apocryphal passage, *Tobit* 12.9; and, from the old testament itself,
Prov. 13.8; *Dan.* 4.27 (LXX).
[88] Clem. Alex., *Quis dives salvetur?* (n 82 above) xxxii.1 (p 181); compare xix.4–6 etc.
The Greek of the words I have quoted in the text is ὦ καλῆς ἐμπορίας, ὦ θείας ἀγορᾶς;
and the passage continues, ὠνεῖται χρημάτων τις ἀφθαρσίαν ... πλεῦσον ἐπὶ ταύτην,
ἂν σωφρονῇς, τὴν πανήγυριν, ὦ πλούσιε κτλ.
[89] A good brief account of the whole difficult subject of penance is given by Gaudemet
pp 78–87, 667–81.
[90] See for example Paulinus of Nola, *Ep.* 34. 2, 7, 10 (*CSEL* 29 pp 303–12).

powerfully the whole principle of organised charity within the community as a remedy for social evils, not only because it provides the giver with a moral justification of his privileged position but also because it is increasingly felt by the recipient as something degrading, as a derogation from human dignity – a feeling with which, I must say, I myself entirely sympathise. (In the conception of the 'welfare state', such as it is, everyone contributes if he can; and he receives what he does receive not as charity, but as a social right – a fundamentally different principle.) The almsgiving upon which the early christians so prided themselves, therefore, appears to many of us nowadays in a very much less attractive light than it did in its own time and for centuries afterwards. My other criticism of the early christian position concerning property-ownership is that the concept of a 'sufficiency' of property, whenever it was introduced, was always left vague and was no better defined than by some such imprecise formula as *non plus quam necesse est*,[91] with the result that anyone except the ancient equivalent of a multi-millionaire could feel that he had no superfluity. Pliny the Younger could claim that he had no more than a 'modest fortune' (*Sunt quidem omnino nobis modicae facultates, Ep.* II.iv.3), yet he cannot have been worth much less than twenty million sesterces[92] and counts among the two or three dozen richest Romans we happen to know about during the principate,[93] even if his assets were hardly more than a fifteenth or a twentieth part of those attributed to the richest men of all, who may have owned three hundred or even four hundred million – and who themselves did not approach the great imperial families in wealth. The great fortunes became greater still in the fourth and fifth centuries,[94] and in those days it was even easier for the well-to-do to feel that they were possessed of only 'modest fortunes'.[95]

The orthodox christian position that I have outlined was held with only minor variations by virtually all the great names:[96] in the west, Irenaeus (who of course thought and wrote in greek), Tertullian, Cyprian, Lactantius, Hilary of Poitiers, Jerome, Augustine, and John Cassian; in the east, Clement of Alexandria, Gregory of Nyssa,

[91] Pelagius (?), *De Divit.* ii (p 32, ed Haslehurst: see n 124 below). Yet this is a work which is far more hostile to riches than most: see below.
[92] See Duncan-Jones pp 17–32, esp pp 18 n 4, 32 n 6.   [93] *Ibid* p 343 (no 21 in App 7).
[94] See A. H. M. Jones, *The Later Roman Empire* (Oxford 1964) 2, pp 554–5.
[95] See Gaudemet p 573, who alludes to 'le difficile problème de la mesure' in this regard. After asking what proportion of his wealth the rich man was expected to spend in charity, he replies, 'Son superflu doit assurer le nécessaire à ceux qui sont dans le besoin. Notions imprécises dont il serait vain de chercher la détermination'!
[96] Christophe gives much of the material.

Early christian attitudes to property & slavery

Gregory of Nazianzus,[97] John Chrysostom,[98] and Theodoret. So far I have found only three partial exceptions among the non-heretical writers. The first, Origen, I do not yet feel that I know well enough to be able to give a fair summary of his attitude. But I have noticed that Origen refused, for example, to countenance prayers for temporal benefits of any sort,[99] and that, unlike Clement, he did not try to allegorise away those biblical texts which attack wealth, while interpreting literally those usually quoted as permitting it – very much the reverse, in fact.[100] I would say that the very idea of wealth tended to make Origen feel uneasy. And he is insistent that priests must give up all property.[101] Much the same is true of my second exception: Basil, in whose writings contradictions are found which cannot be resolved except by admitting that Basil, whose whole thought was of a thoroughly monastic cast, sometimes applied to the outside world precepts which were really applicable only to a monastic community, in which the renunciation of all individual property was possible in a way that was simply impracticable in the graeco-roman world at large.[102] My third exception, perhaps a rather surprising name in this connection, is no less than Ambrose, certainly in the social sense one of

---

[97] Four lines in a poem by Greg. Naz. (*Carmina Theologica* II.xxxiii.113–16) are worth quoting: 'Cast away all and possess God alone, for you are the dispenser of riches that do not belong to you. But if you do not wish to give all, give the greater part; and if not even that, then make a pious use of your superfluity' (τοῖς περιττοῖς εὐσέβει).

[98] I have quoted above Chrysostom's exegesis of Mt. 19.21. As he is often justly remembered as a specially vehement and eloquent denouncer of the very rich, it is worth also recalling his curious defence of the wealth of Dives (in the parable of Lazarus) as God-given: see his *Homilies on Lazarus* III.4 (*PG* 48 (1859) cols 996–7); VI.9 (cols 1040–3), summarised by Christophe pp 138–9. See also Otto Plassmann, *Das Almosen bei Joh. Chrys.* (Diss., Bonn, 1960), a collection of material not utilised to much effect.

[99] He even took 'Give us this day' (Mt. 29.11) or 'day by day' (Lk. 11.3) 'our daily bread' to refer to incorporeal bread, food of the spirit: see his *De Orat.* (Περὶ εὐχῆς) 27, pp 363–75 ed P. Koetschau, in *GCS* Origenes II (1899).

[100] See for example Orig., *Comm. in Matth.* XV.14–20, esp 15, pp 391–5, ed E. Klostermann, *GCS* 40=Origenes X (1935). Compare XV.20 (pp 405–9), where Origen points out that it is only difficult, and not impossible, for a rich man to be saved – though it is clear that in his mind a divine miracle is needed, comparable to getting a camel through the eye of a needle! And see also Orig., *C. Cels.* VII.18, pp 169–71 ed Koetschau; see n 99 above.

[101] See Christophe p 93 for a french translation of the main passage: *Hom. in Genes.* XVI.5.

[102] The treatment of Basil's thought is perhaps the best part of Christophe: see his pp 107–29, esp 108–12, 119–21, 123–5,128–9. Decisive in favour of the view that Basil did not regard the mere ownership of property as an evil is Basil's so-called 'Shorter Rules' no 92 (*PG* 31, col 1145; Christophe, p 108); compare the 'Longer Rules' no 18 (*PG* 31, col 965; Christophe, pp 128–9).

the most exalted of all the early christian fathers – he was a member of the senatorial aristocracy, the son of a praetorian prefect of the Gauls and, at the time of his appointment to the bishopric of Milan in 374, the governor of the province of Aemilia and Liguria, of which Milan was the capital. (I know of no other early father who could be considered his social equal, except Paulinus of Nola.) Now Ambrose is far from consistent in his attitude to property rights; and some recent continental commentators, in their anxiety to rescue him from any such heinous offence as a belief in 'communism' (one monograph is entitled, *Il preteso comunismo di San Ambrogio*),[103] have given rather perverse interpretations of some of his writings, in particular a famous passage in the *De Officiis Ministrorum* (I.132) containing the words *usurpatio ius fecit privatum*.[104] The fact is that in such passages Ambrose shows great uneasiness on the whole question of property rights.[105] Yet he can allegorise away the statement of Jesus contained in all three synoptics (Mk. 10.25; Mt. 19.24; Lk. 18.25) that it is easier for a camel to pass through the eye of a needle than for a rich man to enter the kingdom of God; he can say that not all *paupertas* is *sancta* nor all *divitiae* necessarily *criminosae*, and that in good men riches can be *adiumenta virtutis*;[106] and of course he accepts almsgiving as the great

---

[103] By J. Squitieri (Sarno 1946). It will hardly repay the effort of reading it.

[104] It is absurd to pretend, as for example Squitieri and Christophe have done (see Christophe pp 168–74), that in *De Offic.* I.130–2 Ambrose is simply agreeing with Cicero, and that his '*usurpatio*' is equivalent to Cicero's '*vetus occupatio*' (Cic., *De Offic.* I.20–22). In § 131 Ambrose makes a *first objection* to Cicero's '*iustitiae primum munus*'; and in § 132, whereas Cicero had *accepted* the rule that while common possessions should be used for the common good, a man could use private possessions for his own good, Ambrose now, with the words 'next *they thought it* a form of justice that one should treat common [public] property as public, but private as private', raises a *second objection* to the ciceronian position: after the passage beginning '*sic enim deus*', for which there is no parallel in Cicero, he says, '*natura igitur ius commune generavit, usurpatio ius fecit privatum*', and he then carefully omits the sentence ('*ex quo ... societatis*') at the end of Cicero's § 21 which is the climax of Cicero's argument, asserting that it is right for a man to retain what he has acquired and that anyone who else who seeks to annex it will be violating a law of human society – a quintessentially ciceronian statement. Ambrose's use of the word *usurpatio* too is decisive, and Christophe's arguments (pp 172–4) against Calafato are obviously worthless. His conclusion that Ambrose is here 'maintaining the legitimacy of private property' has no justification. Of course in several other passages, listed by [F.] Homes Dudden, [*The Life and Times of St. Ambrose*] (1935) 2, pp 548–50, Ambrose takes private property for granted, although in others again (see pp 545–7) he regards it with aversion.

[105] On the whole I accept the account given by Homes Dudden, 2, pp 545–50. However, when he summarises Ambrose's attitude (p 547) as 'But wealth is not only unprofitable: it is positively demoralizing', most of the passages he proceeds to quote (though by no means all) require the substitution for 'wealth' of 'avarice' or 'seeking after wealth'. [106] Ambr., *Expos. Ev. Luc.* VIII.70–2, 13, 85 (in *CSEL* 22.iv).

panacea through which the taint of riches can be removed:[107] thus alone can riches become 'the ransom of a man's life' and 'the redemption of the soul',[108] for almsgiving 'purges from sin'.[109] And so, when Ambrose says that God intended the whole earth and its produce to be the common possession of all men,[110] and continues, *sed avaritia possessionum iura distribuit,* he nevertheless goes on to accept the existing situation, provided the property owner gives to the poor. His attitude is very nicely brought out in a passage in the *De Helia et ieiunio* (76), where he tells the sinner to redeem himself from his sins with his own money, thus using one poison to subdue another: *Et venenum frequenter antidoto temperatur, hoc est veneno venenum excluditur, veneno mors repellitur, vita servatur* – wealth itself is a poison, but almsgiving, which redeems from sin, turns wealth into sin's antidote!

Augustine seems not to have been troubled about property rights. With characteristic ingenuity he extracts an argument in his favour even from the parable of Lazarus: Lazarus, we are told, went to Abraham's bosom; well, Abraham was rich![111] (As this and many other such passages show, the level of argument in this field is not always high, and some may feel some sympathy for the pelagian who turned one of Augustine's own favourite weapons against him by advocating a figurative interpretation of Abraham in the parable!)[112] Sometimes in the fourth century the poor are warned that they must not think they can take the initiative and *demand* even the necessary minimum of subsistence from those christians who had vast possessions. Two centuries earlier Irenaeus, citing the scriptural parallel of the israelites 'spoiling the egyptians at the time of the exodus,[113] had expressed some sympathy for the man who, after being compelled to give years of forced labour to another, makes off with some small portion of his property.[114] But now Gregory of Nyssa is careful to show that no such initiative can be justified by an appeal to the 'spoiling of the egyptians' in Exodus as a precedent.[115]

---

[107] See Homes Dudden, 2, p 548 nn 5–8.

[108] Ambr., *Ep.* 63.92, quoting *Prov.* 13.8 and perhaps also *Dan.* 4.27 (LXX).

[109] *De Helia et ieiunio* 76, quoting *Tobit* 12.9.

[110] Ambr., *Expos. in Ps. CXVIII*, Sermo 8.22; compare *De Viduis* 4–5; *De Nabuth.* 2, 11; *Expos. Ev. Luc.* VII.124, 247.

[111] See for example Aug., *Ep.* 157.23–4; compare *Serm.* XIV.4 etc.

[112] See the pelagian *De Divit.* (cited in n 124 below) ix.1–3 (pp 50–2, ed Haslehurst).

[113] *Exod.* III.21–2; XI.2; XII.35–6.

[114] Iren., *Elench.* IV.xxx.1–3, ed W. W. Harvey (1857).

[115] Greg. Nyss., *Vita Moys.* II, pp 67–8, ed H. Musurillo, in Greg. Nyss. VII.i (Leiden 1964).

At this point I should like to mention one minor passage which is not very well known generally and indeed may come as a surprise to those who remember the condemnation by saint Cyprian and the other western bishops of the *libellatici* of the decian persecution, who had purchased certificates falsely stating that they had complied with the imperial order to sacrifice, and were treated as *lapsi*, though of a less serious kind than those who had actually sacrificed or offered incense. The text I have in mind is the twelfth 'canon' in the *Canonical Letter* issued at Easter 306, during the 'Great Persecution', by saint Peter, bishop of Alexandria,[116] acquitting of any religious offence those who had purchased immunity from sacrificing, on the ground that they had sustained a loss of property in order to save their souls. It is interesting to find here a very different (and surely much more sensible) attitude from that which had prevailed in the west during the decian persecution just over half a century earlier. As it happens, our evidence from the west in this respect is for the decian persecution only and from the east for the 'Great Persecution' only; but I have argued elsewhere that we can put all this evidence together and conclude that in the east the purchase of immunity from sacrificing was not regarded as sinful in either persecution.[117]

If we may ignore some passages in early judaeo-christian writings, it is only in the mouths of heretics that we find an unqualified denunciation of private property ownership. Usually, of course, we know nothing of their arguments, all our information being derived from orthodox condemnations of their views. In this category are at least four or five strains of heretical thought. First, there is the second-century work *On Justice* ascribed by Clement of Alexandria to Epiphanes and attacked by Clement as a carpocratian gnostic product which advocated not only equality and community of property but also community of women[118] – although I must say, I accept the view recently advanced that Clement's biographical and historical information about the author of this work, *Peri dikaiosunēs*, is worthless, although his actual quotations from it are genuine;[119] I believe it may have nothing to do with gnosticism or christian heresy. I need only

[116] See my 'Aspects of the "Great" Persecution', in *Harvard Theological Review* 47 (1954) pp 75–113, at p 84 n 44.
[117] See *Ibid* esp pp 87–8.
[118] Clem. Alex., *Strom.* III (ii) 5.1 to 9.3, pp 197–200 in *GCS* 52=Clemens Alex. II³, ed O. Stählin and L. Früchtel (1960) esp 6.1 to 8.1.
[119] See Heinz Kraft, 'Gab es einen Gnostiker Karpokrates?', in *Theologisches Zeitschrift* 8 (1952) pp 434–43.

give the briefest mention of the unimportant, if much discussed, *Pseudo-Clementine Homilies*, the fifteenth of which especially has some material denying to those who have chosen the heavenly kingdom the right to property in anything except bread and water and a single garment, and insisting that in them the possession of other property would be a sin, which could only be taken away by the abandonment of that property.[120] Among genuine christian heretics there are the followers of Eustathius of Sebaste condemned in the *Synodal Letter* of the mid-fourth-century council of Gangra for denying the possibility of salvation to rich people who do not give up all their possessions;[121] there are also the fourth-century dualists denounced by Cyril of Jerusalem, who rejected the ownership of property, with all other physical things, as belonging to the province of the devil;[122] and finally there are the various ascetic sects described as encratites and flourishing especially in Asia Minor, such as the apostolics or apotactites who are attacked in the 370s in the *Panarion* of Epiphanius for preaching that complete abstention from property (as well as marriage) was a necessity for all christians.[123] Unfortunately, we have no details of the arguments by which any of these sects sought to justify its interpretation of scripture against the orthodox position. I have been able to discover only one single surviving work which argues at length that the mere possession of wealth creates a tendency to sin and that it really is best to divest oneself of all one's possessions. This is a work probably written in the first decade of the fifth century, the *De Divitiis*, one of a group of pelagian works published by Caspari in 1890.[124] This has been attributed by

---

120 Ps.-Clem., *Homil.* XV.vii–x, esp vii.4–6, ix.2–3, pp 215–17, ed B. Rehm, in GCS 42 (1953). The *Homilies* in their present form date from the fourth century but seem to derive from an original of the third or even second century, which may have emanated from a jewish-christian sect with gnostic tendencies. See also Christophe pp 96–8, using a french translation.

121 Mansi 2 (1759) col 1102; HL, I.ii (1907) p 1032: the eustathians are said to believe that the rich who do not give up all their property have no hope of salvation. (Compare also the Epilogue to the Canons.) It is interesting to find, both from the *Synodal Letter* and from Canon 3 of this council (Mansi, col 1101; HL 1034), that the eustathians had also been inciting slaves to leave their masters, apparently to become monks: Can. 3 anathematises anyone who 'on a pretext of piety, teaches a slave to despise his master and to leave his service, and not to serve him with goodwill and all honour'.

122 Cyril Hierosol., *Catech.* VIII.6–7 (Migne, PG 33 cols 632–3).

123 Epiphan., *Panar.*, Haer. LXI, esp i.1; iii.1 (pp 380, 382, ed K. Holl. in GCS 31= Epiphan. II, 1922); compare Aug., *De Haeres.*, Haer. 40; and see also Basil, *Ep.* 188, can. 1; 189, can. 47; *C.Th.* XVI.v.7, 11, compare 9; *C.J.* I.v.5.

124 Pelagius (?), *Tractatus de Divitiis*, ed C. P. Caspari, *Briefe, Abhandlungen und Predigten*

de Plinval to Pelagius himself, and by others to one of the followers of Pelagius: Fastidius, Coelestius or Agricola. It has been much discussed in recent years.[125] I will only remark that although this remarkable treatise does recommend divesting oneself of all property (thus 'transferring it from earth to heaven', xix.4), it does not actually condemn *sufficientia*, and it regards even wealth not as an actual sin (vii.5) but as a *peccandi occasio* (xix.3), something that is very likely indeed to result in sin; if we keep the commandments of the new testament, then *per divitiarum contemptum, peccatorum aufertur occasio* (x.1). The most radical passage goes so far as to treat the existence of the few rich as the reason why there are so many poor: *pauci divites pauperum causa sunt multorum*; and so *tolle divitem et pauperem non invenies*, 'get rid of the rich and you won't find any poor' (xii.2). There is, however, not a word to suggest that this desirable end can be achieved by anything but religious persuasion; and – rather strangely, perhaps – there is no appeal to the 'primitive communism' (if I may call it that) of the earliest apostolic community at Jerusalem,[126] and indeed no advocacy at all of community of property, even as a theoretical ideal. I know of no evidence that any pelagian ever advocated the reform of secular institutions. I will only add that this work, the *De Divitiis*, in spite of some over-ingenious arguments and the usual inflated rhetoric, seems to me a far better approximation to the thought of Jesus, as expressed in the synoptic gospels (Luke especially), than at any rate the principal work on the orthodox side, Clement's *Quis dives salvetur?*, from which I quoted

---

aus den zwei letzten Jahrhunderten des kirchlichen Altertums und dem Anfang des Mittelalters (Christiania 1890) pp 25–67, repr in PL Suppl 1 (1958) cols 1380 et seq. and by [R. S. T.] Haslehurst, [*The Works of Fastidius*] (London 1927) pp 30–107: the last has a good facing English trans. There are other pelagian works touching on the same theme, for example the *Epist. II ad Geruntii filias (De contemnenda haereditate)*, in PL 30 cols 45–50.

[125] By Haslehurst; Georges de Plinval. *Pélage: ses écrits, sa vie et sa réforme. Etude d'hist. littér. et relig.* (Lausanne etc., 1943) esp pp 160–2, 189–91, 221–3; J. N. L. Myres, 'Pelagius and the End of Roman Rule in Britain', in *JRS* 50 (1960) pp 21–36; W. Liebeschuetz, 'Did the Pelagian Movement have Social Aims?', in *Historia* 12 (1963) pp 227–41; John Morris, 'Pelagian Literature', in *JTS* ns 16 (1965) pp 26–60; Liebeschuetz, 'Pelagian Evidence on the Last Period of Roman Britain?', in *Latomus* 26 (1967) pp 436–47; Peter Brown, *Religion and Society in the Age of St. Augustine* (London 1972) pp 183–207, 208–26 (the last particularly informative on Pelagius's circle). None of these works deals exclusively with the *De Divit.*, but they all bear upon it in one way or another.

[126] The only allusions I notice in the *De Divit.* (those in x.5, 6) to the earliest apostolic community make no reference to its 'communism'.

earlier.[127] Clement, of course, makes adroit use, here as elsewhere, of the allegorical method of interpretation which had been invented by pagan greek scholars in the classical period and perfected by hellenistic judaism in regard to the old testament (Philo provides some extraordinary examples); this type of exegesis flourished extravagantly at Alexandria in particular.[128] Clement does not scruple to make use of the argument (cap. 13) that only if a man possesses some property can he do the things the Lord requires: feed the hungry and give drink to the thirsty, clothe the naked and entertain the homeless – as Zacchaeus and others entertained the Lord himself (Lk. 19.1-10). 'What sharing (*koinōnia*) would be left among men,' he asks, 'if nobody had anything?' This at least is not quite as feeble as the passage in which Aristotle (*Pol.* II.5, 1263^{b}5-14) pretends that the very great delight of doing a kindness to friends or guests or comrades is possible only when there is private ownership of property – as if generosity or liberality could be expressed only in the form of material benefits.

*   *   *   *   *

It is time to sum up. Why did early christianity so signally fail to produce any important change for the better in graeco-roman society? Why did slavery and kindred forms of unfree labour such as the colonate persist, without christians even realising that they were evil in themselves and that they tended to brutalise both slaves and masters? Why after the empire became officially christian, did the extremes of wealth and poverty throughout the roman world (and especially in the west) become even greater, with enormous wealth concentrating in the hands of the senatorial class, and taxation becoming decidedly more oppressive? Why did punishments become even harsher and torture even more prevalent?[129]

The standard answer to all these questions is familiar to all of us:

---

[127] See pp 26–7 above and nn 82, 88.

[128] For the use of allegory by Clement, in *Quis dives salvetur?*, see esp v.2–4; xi.2–3; xiv.1–6; xv–xvii; xviii–xx; xxvi.2–7; xxvi.8 to xxvii.2. The most complete account I have found of allegory, from the beginnings to the time of Augustine and Gregory Nazianzen, is Jean Pépin, *Mythe et allégorie. Les origines grecques et les contestations judéo-chrétiennes* (Paris 1958). R. P. C. Hanson, *Allegory and Event. A Study of the Sources and Significance of Origen's Interpretation of Scripture* (London 1959) hardly goes back behind jewish and hellenistic allegory (pp 11–64). For the earlier stages, see J. Tate, in *Oxford Class. Dict.*[2] (1970) pp 45b–6b ('Allegory, Greek', and 'Latin'), and his articles there cited in *Class Rev.* 1927 and *Class. Quart.* 1929, 1930 and 1934.

[129] I discuss all these questions in *CSAGW*.

Jesus himself and the early christians were concerned exclusively with the relations between man and man, or man and God, and not at all with social, economic or political institutions – with the relations between men and men, if I may use that expression. That does not seem to me a very good answer, even as far as it goes, for although the new testament writers (like the early fathers) concentrate on questions of individual morality and make no attempt to prescribe a general code of economic or political behaviour, they do make a series of statements on political and economic questions which the church duly accepted as canonical and inspired: Saint Paul's disastrous 'The powers that be are ordained of God', which I quoted earlier, is only one among many such pronouncements.

But can the traditional christian position, which I have outlined, provide a satisfactory answer to my questions, even if it is adjusted in such a way as to shed those unpleasant features of early christian thought such as the acceptance of slavery and of political autocracy which so many christians today are unwilling to endorse? This of course is a matter of opinion. I will only say that in my opinion it was precisely the exclusive concentration of the early christians upon the personal relations between man and man, or man and God, and their complete indifference, as christians, to the institutions of the world in which they lived, that prevented christianity from even having much effect for good upon the relations between man and man. I suggest that the relations between man and man in any organised human society are severely conditioned by the relations between men and men – between different states, and between different classes and groups within states, relations governed as a rule by criteria very different from those which can be applied between man and man. It has often been realised that christianity has been conspicuously unsuccessful in preventing wars between nations. It took the church a long time to evolve a doctrine of the 'just war'[130] – although incidentally even the early roman republic had had a doctrine of the *bellum iustum*, derived from the principle of fetial law: that no war

---

[130] The evidence for early christian views on military service and war is most fully set out by Cadoux, pp 51–7, 116–22, 183–90, 269–81, 402–42, 564–96. See also Gaudemet, pp 706–9, who gives a brief summary of the main 4th/5th century views (esp those of Augustine, who went further than many early christians in defending war), with bibliography. Recent work, including the article by R. H. Bainton, 'The Early Church and War', in *Harvard Theological Review* 39 (1946) pp 189–212, is briefly reviewed by Jacques Fontaine, 'Christians and Military Service in the Early Church', in *Concilium* 7.1 (1965) pp 58–64.

was acceptable to the roman gods unless it was a defensive war, waged to protect Rome or her allies.[131] And the doctrine of the just war has never come to very much, because any country that goes to war can always justify itself easily enough in its own eyes. As for what I would call the class struggle, I cannot see that the christian churches have done much more than either deplore it in principle or ignore its very existence; and all too often they have explicitly underwritten the existing social and economic order in its crudest form. 'The rich man in his castle' – but I need not go on. Pope Pius XI's encyclical, *Quadragesimo anno*, of 1931, admits that the class struggle had been a serious danger forty years before, but then proceeds to speak of this danger as having been largely dispelled by Leo XIII's *Rerum novarum* – an opinion which has hardly been confirmed by the events of the years since 1931. There have, needless to say, been a few striking exceptions within the churches who have broken right away from their official policy, from John Ball in 1381[132] to Camilo Torres in our own time.[133]

When the early hebrew prophets, or Plato and Aristotle, tried to formulate a vision of the good society, they thought first in terms of the israelite nation or of the greek city: for Plato and Aristotle, the society as such had first to be good, to have good institutions, before men could lead the good life within it. Their successors, in both cases, tended to despair of creating a good society: for them, either the individual man (the stoic, in particular) had to discover how best to live his personal life in an indifferent if not hostile world, or else there was a Good Time Coming, but it would be achieved by some supernatural agency. In the latter case one could comfort oneself by imagining (as in jewish apocalyptic) that in some mysterious way the desired result had been achieved already: the passage in the Magnificat which I quoted earlier provides a good example. At the present time there is a debate going on among christians whether (to use the language I have employed) it may not be absolutely necessary to reform

---

[131] Itself nicely criticised in Cic., *De Rep.* III.12/20, ed K. Ziegler (6 ed, 1964) preserved in Lact., *Div. Inst.* VI.ix.4: it was the means by which the romans gave their aggression the appearance of legitimacy ('per fetiales bella indicendo, et legitime iniurias faciendo').

[132] The most convenient English version of the relevant part of Froissart is *Froissart's Chronicles*, ed and trans by John Jolliffe (London 1967), caps 73–4, pp 236–52 (esp 237–8). The traditional english version is *Froissart's Cronycles*, trans by Sir John Bouchier Lord Berners, I, 4 (Oxford 1928) pp 1095–1121 (esp 1096–7).

[133] *Revolutionary Priest. The Complete Writings and Messages of Camilo Torres*, ed John Gerassi (1971, paperback in *Pelican Latin American Library*, 1973).

the relations between men and men – in particular the relations between states and between classes within states – in order that the relations between man and man may not be for ever distorted and damaged. Among these relations between men and men, I would suggest that a central role is played by property-relations, including in particular the ownership of property and the way in which production is organised. Those of us who watch the debate within the churches, even from the outside, may feel that careful study of what actually happened in the early christian centuries, both in the field of ideas and in actual social life, might well shed some useful light on current problems and controversies, and as a result might have a powerful effect upon the future of man.

University of Oxford
New College

HOLY KINGS – THE BANE
OF SEVENTH-CENTURY SOCIETY

by ROSALIND M. T. HILL

IN his recent and excellent book *The Coming of Christianity* Henry
Mayr-Harting has some interesting things to say about lay society
and the monastic ideal. Taking as his sources those two fundamental guides to seventh-century history, Bede's *Historia Ecclesiastica*
and the *Penitential* of Theodore of Tarsus, he shows how the christian
pattern of holiness, as demonstrated especially in the monastic life,
could be observed also in the lives of Bede's heroic kings. 'The King'
he says, 'was a kind of Christ, and his life should show forth the
virtues of his prototype as they were cultivated in monastic circles.
Oswald demonstrated his generosity and charity, . . . Sigbert of the
East Saxons demonstrated his meekness, . . . Oswin of Deira demonstrated his humility . . . The Ecclesiastical History presents a gallery of
exemplary kings, each of whom had many virtues, but each of whom
is brought forward in a narrative of great care and skill to illustrate the
particular virtue in which Bede regarded him as pre-eminent.'[1]

That Bede considered it to be the duty of a historian to teach people
how to live the good life is beyond question. He says as much himself:
'If a history tells the good deeds of good men, the careful hearer is
stirred up to imitate that which is good'.[2] It is also true that he had a
very high regard for kingship. Unlike Gregory of Tours, he never
denounces the wickedness of a lawfully-acclaimed king of his own
people (although he blames Ecgfrith for acting 'rashly' against good
advice),[3] and even when he is describing the brutalities perpetrated by
an invading British king in his own country of Northumbria (and
Bede hated the Britons, with good reason) he says of Cadwallon that
he acted 'not like a conquering king but like a raging tyrant'.[4] His

The references to early histories and chronicles are by book (where appropriate) and
chapter. The references to laws are by code and numbering. They should be found valid
for all modern editions.

[1] H. Mayr-Harting, *The Coming of Christianity* (London 1972) p 255.
[2] Bede, *HE*, preface.
[3] *Ibid* IV 24.
[4] *Ibid* III 1.

information about Osred of Northumbria (whom we know from other sources to have been anything but 'a kind of Christ') is brief almost to vanishing point. Bede was, in fact, enough of a typical Anglo-Saxon of his age to believe that a lawful king could command the highest possible degree of earthly loyalty, and to believe also that loyalty was the highest possible expression of a layman's virtue. (Treachery is the only crime which he specifically condemns as *detestanda*.[5]) It was moreover, in Bede's view, the duty of a layman to protect and maintain the state and, if he were a king, to uphold that degree of public order without which the christian virtues could not flourish. At the end of the *Historia Ecclesiastica* he says that in the existing time of peace and quiet, many Northumbrians have preferred to enter monasteries rather than to train themselves and their sons in the use of arms. He adds, darkly, 'A later age will see the result of this'[6] – as, of course, it did, at the time of the viking invasions. Bede was a monk, who believed that the monastic life was a form of 'the perfect following of Christ', but it was not a form which he thought fit to recommend to everybody. After all, had not Christ himself commanded people to render unto Caesar the things that are Caesar's? And although Bede had been dedicated to the cloister in childhood, he was a Northumbrian of fighting ancestry, and I think that historians have been too ready to overlook this strand in his character. It is true that he tells us how Oswald demonstrated his generosity and charity by giving up his easter feast to the poor, and by adding to it the broken fragments of the great silver dish in which it was served,[7] – in itself a typical act of royal largesse, such as the scattering of gold and silver among the people of Tours by Clovis,[8] – but this is by no means the only thing which he tells us about Oswald. He was a king who, with a small army, drove his enemies from a place 'near the Roman Wall' to the Rowley Burn in what must have been a running fight across difficult country,[9] who kept his head in the face of certain death at the hands of a hostile army,[10] and who incidentally was feared by his young aunt by marriage as the potential murderer of his cousins, at that time small children.[11] In addition to this, Bede tells us that Oswald extended his authority over

[5] *Ibid* III 14.
[6] *Ibid* V 23.
[7] *Ibid* III 6.
[8] Gregory of Tours, *History of the Franks*, II 28.
[9] Bede, *HE*, III 1–2.
[10] *Ibid* III 12.
[11] *Ibid* II 20.

'all the people and provinces of Britain which are divided into four tongues, that is, of the Britons, Picts, Scots and English'.[12] He may well be exaggerating, since there is no evidence that Oswald's overlordship was accepted in Dalriada, south Wales or the land of the northern Picts, though it was probably he who brought under English rule the notable stronghold later called Edinburgh. Still, it is clear that Bede felt that a really good king should be distinguished by notable achievements in battle.

In Bede's account of Oswald's predecessor Edwin we see that he believed also that a good king should enforce with a strong hand the peace of his kingdom. He does not give us the story, preserved by the monk of Whitby,[13] of the marvellous discovery of Edwin's relics and their translation to York, although relics were of great interest to him and he had contact both with York and with Whitby. Instead he tells us how Edwin enforced good law throughout his kingdom, slaughtered his enemies,[14] and maintained his royal dignity, and how 'because of the greatness of fear as well as of love' in the hearts of his subjects, nobody ventured to steal the drinking-cups which he had caused to be set up for the use of travellers.[15] As for the three kings depicted as outstanding in meekness and humility, Sigbert of East Anglia, Sigbert of Essex and Oswin of Deira, Bede does indeed praise them for their virtues as good men, but there seems to be little evidence that he regarded them as good kings, although he says that men were attracted to Oswin's service by his physical beauty, courtesy of manner and open-handed largesse.[16] Sigbert of East Anglia, brought forcibly out of the monastery to which he had retired of his own choice, insisted on leading his army against Penda of Mercia with no better weapon than a staff. He was presumably trying to obey Christ's injunction to turn the other cheek, but he was killed, and succeeded by Anna, apparently a more warlike king, whom Bede calls 'a very good man'.[17] Sigbert of Essex was killed by his brothers, who declared that 'they were angry with the king, and were opposed to him, because he was too much given to sparing his enemies, and used serenely to forgive injuries done to himself as soon as he was asked to do so'.[18] Bede could not but

---

[12] *Ibid* III 6.
[13] *Anonymous Life of St Gregory* 18–9.
[14] Bede *HE* II 9.
[15] *Ibid* II 16.
[16] *Ibid* III 14.
[17] *Ibid* III 18.
[18] *Ibid* III 22.

approve of serene forgiveness, but it was no admirable quality in a king who was pledged to uphold the system of blood-price as the only acceptable alternative to blood-feud. In seventh-century England every man had, quite literally, his price, which would go to the maintenance of his widow and children and the strengthening of his kinship group if he were killed, and upon the proper payment of the recognised price for killing or injuring your neighbour the stability of society depended. Once let a king, pledged to enforce the good laws of his people, start being too freely influenced by the gospel precept about forgiving your enemies, and who knew where the thing might stop? Generosity was a good thing, but justice was a better. As for Oswin of Deira, a delightful young man whom Bede describes as 'fair to look upon, tall, cheerful and courteous, generous to all' and the leader of a large and mostly devoted band of followers, his humility and courtesy to Aidan (himself probably of royal descent) were such as to make the saint exclaim in sorrow 'I know that this king will not live long, for never before have I seen a humble king. Wherefore I think that he will soon be snatched out of this life, for this people is not worthy to have such a ruler'.[19] Aidan's prophecy was quickly fulfilled, and we need hardly call upon his celebrated second-sight to account for it. Really powerful kings in the seventh century did not apologise, even to saints.

In fact the essential quality which made a man a good ruler in seventh-century England, or indeed anywhere else in Europe at that time, was not the quality of an ideal monk but that of an ideal fighter, of a man who could keep his own warband in order, hold his frontiers secure (and if possible extend them) against his enemies, and preserve among his subjects such good peace as would permit them to go unharmed about their lawful business, and cultivate, under God's authority, those virtues which were most pleasing in his service. With the simple and surprising exception of Edward the confessor, this continued to be the ideal of successful kings right down to the sixteenth century. A king who failed to live up to it might, like Stephen, die in his bed; like Henry VI he might die with the reputation of a saint, but he died comparatively unlamented, and historians did not accord him a very good reputation as a king.

In order to maintain and extend his frontiers a king must be a good leader in war, and in order to preserve his people at home he must not only know the law which has been handed down to him by his wise

[19] *Ibid* III 14.

counsellors, he must be able to proclaim it, and have power to enforce
it. Bede never describes a scene in which the king appears as dispenser
of justice, for such was not his purpose in writing an ecclesiastical
history, but there can be no doubt that the authority which he described
as sufficient to enable a woman with her baby to walk in safety
'through the whole island from sea to sea'[20] would have had to be
enforced with a very firm hand. What else would suffice to protect the
roads at a time when young noblemen thought it a reasonable part of
their training for war to burn monastic barns[21] or to go out with their
followers on plundering expeditions?[22] Penalties would have to be
severe, and in fact we know from some seventh-century law-codes that
this is exactly what they were. Æthelbert of Kent exacts a double
penalty for any offence committed in the king's presence, or at meetings
called in his name, and imposes the heavy extra fine of fifty shillings
for infraction of his rights of lordship, after wergild has been duly paid
for the killing of any of his freeborn subjects.[23] Ine's law lays it down
that if you fight in the king's house you incur the death-penalty, which
can be remitted only at the king's pleasure, as well as losing all your
property,[24] and that mutilation is the appropriate punishment for
persistent law-breakers.[25]

The first great civilising force in seventh-century England was
christianity, but the second was undoubtedly law. Theodore of Tarsus,
who, in spite of his late start as an English archbishop, understood his
adopted people better than did many of their born rulers, recognised
this fact when he settled the blood-feud arising from the death of
Ælfwin at the battle of the Trent by having recourse to the English
system of wergild.[26] It was only when the ruler was strong enough to
enforce the rule of law that society could live in such peace that it was
possible for the gentler virtues to flourish. A king who was holy without
also being stern (and possibly rather ruthless) might be an admirable
man, but Bede realised that from the point of view of his kingdom he
was apt to prove a disaster.

University of London
Westfield College

20 *Ibid* II 16.
21 Eddi, *Life of St Wilfrid* 67.
22 Felix of Crowland, *Life of St Guthlac* 16–17.
23 Æthelbert, 2, 3, 5, 7.
24 Ine, 6.
25 Ine, 18, 37.
26 *HE* IV 19.

OUTSIDERS, INSIDERS, AND PROPERTY IN DURHAM AROUND 1100

by BERNARD MEEHAN

THE monastic community at Durham was founded by bishop William of St Calais in 1083. Its arrival from Jarrow and Wearmouth was accompanied by an act of aggression, when the secular clerks previously in residence were presented with the ultimatum of either becoming monks or leaving. All but one chose to leave. This action can be seen as setting the tone for the community's attitude to the world outside the see. In their historical writings, particularly Symeon's *Historia Dunelmensis Ecclesiae*, written between 1104 and 1109,[1] the Durham monks were self-assertive and defensive.

---

[1] The *Historia Dunelmensis Ecclesia* was last edited by [Thomas] Arnold, [*Symeonis Monachi Opera Omnia*] 2 vols RS 75 (1882) 1, pp 3–135. For the date of composition, see Arnold 1 p xix. The attribution to Symeon is not conclusive. He was named as author only in the Sawley copy, third in date, now MS Ff. 1. 27 in Cambridge University Library, described in *A Catalogue of the Manuscripts preserved in the library of the University of Cambridge* 5 vols (Cambridge 1856–67) 2 pp 318–29. The Durham MSS, Bishop Cosin's MS V. ii. 6, described in R.A B. Mynors, *Durham Cathedral Manuscripts* (Durham 1939) pp 60–1, and its early copy, British Museum Cotton MS Faustina A. v, described in *A Catalogue of the Manuscripts in the Cottonian Library*, ed J. Planta (London 1801) p 603, are both anonymous, as is the fourth copy, an early thirteenth century MS from Durham, described in J. Conway Davies, 'A Recovered Manuscript of Symeon of Durham', *Durham University Journal* 44 (1951) pp 22–8. See also [H. S.] Offler, *Medieval Historians [of Durham]* (Durham 1958) p 20 n 8. The work had been *maiorum auctoritate jussus* (Arnold 1 p 4), and it was only when it left Durham and became of more academic historical interest that it was felt necessary to know the author. Before the end of the twelfth century, Symeon had also been credited with writing the so-called *Historia Regum*, printed in Arnold 2 (1885) pp 3–283. On the problem of the MS which contains this work, see [P. Hunter] Blair, ['Some Observations on the *Historia Regum* attributed to Symeon of Durham'], in *Celt and Saxon*, ed Nora K. Chadwick (Cambridge 1963) pp 63–118 and Derek Baker, 'Scissors and Paste: Corpus Christi Cambridge MS 139 again', *SCH* 11 (1974) pp 83–123. Like MS Ff. 1. 27, MS 139 was also at Sawley, at least for a time, and the rubric ascribing authorship to Symeon is very similar to those in Ff. 1. 27, though whether they are all in the same hand, as Blair suggests (see Blair pp 74–6 and plate facing p 117) can not be regarded as certain. Baker has pointed out that MS 139 was put together in sections of different date; it is interesting that the rubric to the *Historia Regum* occurs at the bottom of the last folio of one section, and the text itself occurs in the next. The ascription to Symeon should perhaps thus be viewed with some suspicion. In his edition of the *Historia Regum*, [J. Hodgson] Hinde indicated some internal objections to seeing Symeon as author of both the *Historia Dunelmensis Ecclesiae* and the *Historia Regum*; see [*Symeonis Dunelmensis Opera et Collectanea*] 1, SS 51 (1867) pp xxvii–xxx.

The kings, bishops and earls discussed in this work were judged not according to the dictates of some preordained social order, but according to their treatment of the church, especially in a material sense. Concern with property, the need to show the historical roots of present holdings, was a thread which ran through the *Historia Dunelmensis Ecclesiae*. The monks' approach was perhaps slightly paranoic, in that all outsiders were seen as a potential threat. The contradiction was that the twelfth century monks were themselves usurpers of the tradition they so vigorously defended. For the community which eventually came to Durham via Jarrow and Wearmouth had been founded by men from Evesham in the south, though it is not possible to say with certainty how many of the twenty-three who came to Durham in 1083 were from the south, or how many survived to be numbered among those in the house after 1104.[2] The monks successfully appropriated the existing corpus of cuthbertine hagiography, and soon augmented it.[3] Their biggest coup, the event which sealed the community's sense of identification with the northumbrian past, was the fresh translation of Cuthbert's incorrupt body to the new cathedral in 1104.[4] The church itself, which the clerks had been content to dedicate both to Cuthbert and to the Holy Mother of God, became unequivocally *ecclesia sancti Cuthberti*.[5] Looking back from 1104, it was necessary to prove that the secular clerks had been unworthy guardians of the relics of Cuthbert, that they had represented a corruption of the tradition. Symeon described the fall from a regular monastic state among the descendants of those who had saved the relics from danish desecration:

> Ecclesiastical discipline they viewed with hatred, and preferred to follow the attractions of a looser life. For there was no one to hold them under ecclesiastical censure, since the worship of God had almost died out when the churches and monasteries were destroyed. Thus they lived a secular life, enslaved to the ways of the flesh, producing sons and daughters. Their successors in the

---

[2] For some discussion of this problem see Appendix.

[3] See the *Historia de Sancti Cuthberti* (Arnold 1 pp 196–214), the *De Miraculis et Translationibus Sancti Cuthberti* (Arnold 1 pp 229–61, 2 pp 333–62), and B. Colgrave, 'The Post-Bedan Miracles and Translations of St Cuthbert', in *The Early Cultures of North West Europe (H. M. Chadwick Memorial Studies)* ed C. Fox and B. Dickins (Cambridge 1950) pp 305–32.

[4] See Arnold 1 pp 247–61, and *Reginald[i Monachi Dunelmensis Libellus de admirandis Beati Cuthberti virtutibus]*, SS 1 (1835) pp 84–90.

[5] [H. H. E.] Craster, ['The Red Book of Durham',] *EHR* 40 (1925) pp 504–32, at p 529.

church of Durham knew nothing but a life ruled by the flesh, nor did they wish to know anything different. They were called clerks, but could not claim that rank in either dress or conversation.[6]

When bishop Walcher arrived in 1072, he was naturally grieved at this, and taught them to observe *clericorum morem in diurnis et nocturnis officiis*.[7] But by 1083, Symeon had to report that the clerks were *in nullo canonicorum regulam sequentes*.[8] Bishop William thus bound the new community of monks *inseparabiliter* to the relics of Cuthbert.[9] They were still seeking official entitlement to this position as late as 1123, when they obtained from pope Calixtus II a confirmation of their occupation of the cathedral, which was justified by 'the depraved and incorrigible behaviour of the secular clerics' formerly in residence.[10] By the early 1170s, however, when Reginald of Durham was writing, the monks were secure. The clerks could now be seen as part of the same tradition,[11] as men fit to witness the appearance of Cuthbert in a vision which cured a leper. The monks had often heard of this miracle from their brother Thurold, who had himself been told it *a veteranis Canonicis*.[12] It would be wrong to see the monks' objection to the clerks as part of the wider ideological animosity between the secular and the regular clergy in this period.[13] Symeon could, in fact, note that it was its body of canons which made Waltham in Essex, a Durham possession from 1072, such a celebrated church,[14] and bishop Walcher, who was so distressed by what he saw when he came to Durham, was himself not a monk.

On the evidence of the clerk's historical output, the monks would probably have found the outlook of their predecessors more sympathetic than they could at first have admitted. The pre-monastic chronicle

[6] Arnold 1 p 8.
[7] *Ibid* p 106.
[8] *Ibid* p 122.
[9] *Ibid* p 11.
[10] [Donald] Nicholl, [*Thurstan Archbishop of York*] (York 1964) p 91.
[11] See Reginald pp 28–9.
[12] *Ibid* p 41. It is not certain, however, that Thurold can be added to the names of those who were at Jarrow (see note 2 above), or whether he can be identified with the monk who comes eighty-ninth in the list in the *Historia Dunelmensis Ecclesiae* and had thus not professed up to 1104 x 9. Reginald speaks of Thurold in the past tense, and he was thus not alive in the 1170s, but it is not clear how someone not in the community between 1083 and 1104 could have spoken to the clerks.
[13] See R. Foreville and J. Leclercq, 'Un debat sur le sacerdoce des moines au XIIᵉ siècle', *Studia Anselmiana* 41 (1957) pp 8–118. See also Nicholl pp 171–2, and, for later examples, Knowles *Monastic Order* pp 662–78.
[14] Arnold 1 p 113.

pieced together by Craster and probably used by Symeon,[15] had the same preoccupation with recording the gifts of property made to the church in honour of Cuthbert. But the clerks adopted a noticeably less strident tone than the monks towards their property. Another Durham work, the De obsessione Dunelmi, may have been written by a clerk in the mid 1070s.[16] It contained an imperfect, heavily favourable account of the career of earl Uhtred of Northumbria, who died in 1016, and recorded the fate of the six estates which bishop Aldun gave to his daughter on her marriage to Uhtred. The marriage broke up and the estates suffered various vicissitudes. At least two and possibly three of the six estates were not said to return to the church, and, strangely, it was not suggested that they should.[17] Those who seized the lands were not threatened with divine vengeance and the so-called hereditary right to them of the earl's family was not questioned. By contrast, the pre-monastic chronicle and the Historia Dunelmensis Ecclesiae both reported the threats of excommunication which king Cnut uttered against those who dared to interfere with the lands he gave to the church. To the monks, however, the property of the church could be protected better by the addition of an exemplary miraculous element. The chronicle of the clerks contained no story like that of the fate which befell the man who stole Cuthbert's offerings.[18] The difference between the attitude of the clerks and the monks is seen most clearly in the two accounts of the visit of William the Conqueror to Durham in 1072. The clerks said that he entered the church with great devotion, and asked to be told about the life and miracles of Cuthbert, and about the origins of the see. The oldest and wisest in the house let him know that while Cuthbert lived, king Egfrid had treated him with veneration, and that after his death, succeeding Christian kings had shown their esteem by augmenting the liberty of his church. William responded to these and other hints by offering the shrine a mark of gold and a precious cloak, by affirming the privileges of the see, and by gifting the estate of Waltham.[19] As the clerks told it, this was a civilised encounter, with William's behaviour exemplary. The monks, however,

---

[15] Craster pp 523–9.

[16] Printed in Arnold 1 pp 215–20. For a more complete discussion of this tract, see Bernard Meehan, 'The siege of Durham, the battle of Carham, and the cession of Lothian', ScHR forthcoming.

[17] Two of the estates, however, seem to have been back with the church by 1141. See Acts of Malcolm IV, ed G. W. S. Barrow (Edinburgh 1960) pp 146–7.

[18] Arnold 1 pp 96–7.

[19] Craster p 528, and see p 530.

told a different story. They added to the clerks' chronicle precise details of what William gave the church,[20] and in their own account gave a more severe version of the meeting. They told an unlikely story of William's scepticism about the existence in Durham of Cuthbert's body, and of his determination to investigate for himself; if he had not found the body there as described, he had decided to put to death every person of consequence attending the feast of all saints, which was being celebrated at the time. But Cuthbert had matters well in hand, and when William was in church the next day he was afflicted with such a heat as caused him to rush from the church, forego the banquet prepared for him, and not draw rein till he reached the river Tees.[21] Some time later, he sent the tax collector Ranulf, possibly the later bishop, to collect tribute. Cuthbert had to take further action. He appeared to Ranulf as he slept and attacked him with his pastoral staff. Ranulf recovered only when carried beyond the boundaries of the diocese. King William had to be impressed by all this and confirmed the privileges of the see.[22] In both cases the result was the same – the demesne of the church was increased – but Symeon made it clearer that the church of Durham was protected from outside interference by the power of the patron saint. The clerks had simply a different outlook from the monks. They referred to the Conqueror as *gloriosus ac potentissimus*,[23] and though both Symeon and the clerks knew his predecessor Edward the Confessor as *piissimus*,[24] there is a general lack of such conventional pieties in Symeon's chronicle, which tended to see kings, if danes or scots, as warriors, pillagers and disturbers of the peace and wealth of Cuthbert; if english, as men who learned to respect Cuthbert and offer gifts to his church. It was not a matter of wonder that king Cnut came five miles barefoot to the shrine.[24a] Symeon treated kings neither with reverence nor with disrespect. He even avoided the temptation to embark on unfavourable comparisons with the saintly king Oswald, the contemporary of bishop Aidan, who did rate the predictable praise, and about whom there was a strong hagiographic tradition, enhanced by the discovery in 1104 of his head in Cuthbert's coffin.[25] In their coolness towards monarchy, the monks

[20] *Ibid* p 529.
[21] Arnold 1 p 106.
[22] *Ibid* pp 107–8.
[23] Craster p 528.
[24] *Ibid*, and Arnold 1 p 98.
[24a] Arnold 1 p 90.
[25] Arnold 1 p 255, and see pp 18–21.

were, however, firmly in the tradition of english twelfth and thirteenth century historians, who regarded kings with much less affection than did their french counterparts.[26] But to the monastic author of the *De Miraculis et Translationibus Sancti Cuthberti*, William became *rex gloriosus* when he sent an army to avenge the slaughter of bishop Walcher,[27] for it was above all their bishops who gained the respect of the monks. In economic terms alone this may have been justified, for until 1176 it was the bishop, not the king, who collected such revenues as taxes, fines, farm profits and the possessions of felons in Durham.[28]

The monks emphasised that the holders of the bishopric had to be conscious that they were treading in famous footsteps. 'Unless of honest and religious conversation,' Symeon warned, 'a man should not lightly venture to ascend the seat of St Aidan and St Cuthbert and those other holy bishops.'[29] The main requirement was that the bishops protect the cult of Cuthbert, and especially that they ensure its economic survival. Personal piety was largely an optional extra, but ideally it was required that the bishop come from inside the community. Symeon suggested that this was *secundum instituta canonum*.[30] But in recent years the church had not been served by ideal bishops. Essentially, the history of the church was a history of the bishops, and in earlier times the community could identify with the bishops, since only Sexhelm, the simoniac who was bishop for six months in the mid tenth century, had not been a monk. Symeon realised that even the secular clerks had had a grasp of the proprieties. Bishop Edmund, who suggested himself for the post in what may have been intended as a faint echo of Aidan's speech in Iona,[31] would not allow himself to be consecrated until he had taken monastic vows.[32] This had happened in 1023, and since then no member of the Durham community had been elected bishop. The monks were thus bitter and frustrated observers of the central aspect of the tradition they professed to be continuing. After the death of Edmund, Edred had bought the bishopric from king

---

[26] See R. W. Southern, 'England's First Entry into Europe', in *Medieval Humanism* (Oxford 1970) pp 135–57, at pp 150–1.

[27] Arnold 2 p 334.

[28] W. L. Warren, *Henry II* (London 1973) p 372.

[29] Arnold 1 p 85.

[30] *Ibid* p 85. Adherence to monasticism meant that the church of Durham retained the original character of the church at Lindisfarne (*ibid* p 18).

[31] See *Bede's Ecclesiastical History of the English People*, ed B. Colgrave and R. A. B. Mynors (Oxford 1969) pp 228–9.

[32] Arnold 1 pp 85–6. The final judgement on Edmund was that *nullius violentia res ecclesiasticas pessundari patiebatur* (*ibid* p 87).

Harthacnut, with money plundered from the church.[33] His immediate successors, Egelric and Egelwin, the brothers from Peterborough who held the see for thirty years between them, were the bishops most heavily criticised by Symeon. Egelric, who, ironically, came to Durham as a result of bishop Edmund's entreaties for a monk to teach him the monastic life,[34] was bishop for three years before being expelled by the clerks. They did this, Symeon felt, because, significantly, he was a stranger – *extraneus*[35] – though by now he had been in Durham for twenty-two years. Egelric, however, bribed earl Siward, and the earl forced the clerks to have him back. The bishop, Symeon said, was plotting along with his brother Egelwin and other monks from Peterborough to plunder the church. Their opportunity came when they decided to replace the wooden church at Chester-le-Street with one of stone, and discovered there some treasure hidden for safe-keeping during the tyranny of bishop Sexhelm. Egelric sent the treasure home to Peterborough, and soon followed it himself, leaving the bishopric in the hands of his brother.[36] Such a stern view of Egelric's behaviour was not supported by the *Historia Regum*, produced at Durham sometime after 1129.[37] This included a passage from Florence of Worcester which lacked all mention of treasure or

---

[33] *Ibid* p 91, and see Arnold 2 p 162.

[34] *Ibid* p 86.

[35] *Ibid* p 91. Strictly speaking, the first four bishops – Aidan, Finan, Colman and Tuda – had also been strangers, having come from Iona. Their successors, Eata and Cuthbert, came via Melrose, as did Ethelwold, the ninth bishop. Of the bishops up to Aldun, Edmund's immediate predecessor, it is not always indicated that they were elected, rather than someone's appointee; for example, Kynewulf seems to have appointed Higbald, his successor. But it may be assumed, from lack of evidence to the contrary, that they were members of the community; of Aldun, it is said that he was *habitu, sicut omnes predecessores ejus, et actu probabilis monachus* (*ibid* p 78). Sexhelm was a puzzling exception. He was a secular cleric, and a simoniac (*ibid* pp 20, 106), but it is not said where he came from, and it is not clear whom he bribed. It is inferred in two places that he became bishop after committing simony (*ibid*); elsewhere, it seems that his expulsion resulted from offences after his appointment: *Defuncto autem Uhtredo episcopo, Sexhelm loco ejus est ordinatus, sed vix aliquot mensibus in ecclesia residens, sancto Cuthberto illum expellente, aufugit. Cum enim, a via praedecessorum suorum aberrans, populum ipsius sancti et eos qui in ecclesia ejus serviebant avaritia succensus affligeret, exterritus a sancto per somnium jussus est quantocius abscedere* (*ibid* p 77).

[36] *Ibid* p 92.

[37] Blair (p 112) suggests that the section of the *Historia Regum* indisputably the work of Durham is the chronicle contained in Arnold 2 pp 98–283. The chronicle finishes in 1129, but it is not yet certain at what date in the twelfth century it was written. See H. S. Offler, 'The Tractate *De Iniusta Vexacione Willelmi Episcopi Primi*', *EHR* 66 (1951) pp 321–41, at p 322 n 3, and H. S. Offler, 'Hexham and the *Historia Regum*', *Transactions of the Architectural and Archaeological Society of Durham and Northumberland* 2 (1970) pp 51–62.

bribery, and said only that Egelric voluntarily relinquished his see and retired to Peterborough.[38] Strangely, the chronicle of the clerks, the successors of those whom Symeon reported as ejecting Egelric, was positively favourable. It portrayed Egelric as a man who could not resist the violence of those who were attacking the liberty of the church. Rather than allow his own weakness to ruin the church, he preferred to return to his own monastery and die without the bishopric. The chronicle added with satisfaction that those enemies of St Cuthbert who drove him away all came to a bad end.[39] Other sources agreed that it was Egelric's life which ended badly. The *Anglo-Saxon Chronicle* recorded that in 1070 he was accused of treason and imprisoned at Westminster.[40] Symeon, predictably, claimed that he was imprisoned because the king knew that Egelric had taken money from the church of Durham.[41] The explanation for the discrepancies is probably that Symeon simply expected the worst from someone he considered an outsider. Like his brother, Egelwin also ended his days in the Conqueror's custody, the english bishop imprisoned by the normans at Abingdon. Symeon claimed that this was also a punishment for theft from Durham.[42] For Egelwin *nihilominus ecclesiae nihil inferre, immo multo magis quam frater ejus ante illum ornamenta resque alias satagebat auferre.*[43] But Durham tradition was divided about Egelwin, because in other senses he had protected the see. The *Historia Regum* took from Florence of Worcester a passage which spoke of the translation of the relics of Oswin by the *reverendus vir Agelwinus.*[44] More importantly, when the Conqueror's army came north in 1069, Egelwin fled to Lindisfarne with the relics of Cuthbert and reached safety with the aid of a miraculous parting of the tide. This was the only aspect of his episcopacy known to the monk who wrote the *De Miraculis et Translationibus Sancti Cuthberti,*[45] and was discussed also by Symeon and by the *Historia Regum.*[46] This expedition of the Conqueror's was undertaken in revenge for the death of Robert Cumin, who had been appointed earl of Northumbria and then been burnt alive in the bishop's house in Durham. Symeon recorded this slaughter,[47] but not

---

[38] Arnold 2 p 173.
[39] Craster p 528, and see p 530.
[40] 'D' version. See *EHD* 2 p 151.
[41] Arnold 1 p 91.
[42] *Ibid* p 105. For the confusion of the two brothers in other sources, see E. A. Freeman, *The History of the Norman Conquest of England* 4 (Oxford 1871) pp 812–13.
[43] Arnold 1 p 94.   [44] Arnold 2 p 177.   [45] Arnold 1 pp 246–7.
[46] *Ibid* pp 100–1, and Arnold 2 p 189.   [47] Arnold 1 pp 98–9.

the role the bishop played. The *Historia Regum*, on the other hand, said that Egelwin warned Robert Cumin not to enter Durham, but that his advice was disregarded.[48] Egelwin seems to have had ambivalent feelings towards the normans. Where Symeon said that he left Durham because he was carrying off church property literally up his sleeve,[49] the *Historia Regum* presented the man who tried to prevent norman deaths as leaving his see because he saw the old english order in turmoil on all sides, and was disturbed at living among a foreign nation whose tongue and customs he did not know.[50]

The conquest produced similarly ambivalent feelings among the monks of Durham. They did not disguise the devastation of the north caused by William's men, or their plunder of the church.[51] But the strength of local feeling, shown in the murder of Robert Cumin and later of bishop Walcher, was not transmitted to the monks, even though Turgot, prior when Symeon was writing, had been imprisoned by the new regime in Lincoln.[52] Symeon hesitated to criticise the norman appointees after Egelwin who held the bishopric in apparent violation of the canons of which he had spoken earlier. Southern has recently shown that from the late eleventh century there was an english historical revival, a specifically benedictine phenomenon which saw the conquest as 'an event in the past to which every evil could be traced.' Along with Evesham, Canterbury, Worcester and Malmesbury, Southern names Durham as one of the great centres of this movement.[53] Certainly, those who wrote history at Durham after 1083 were benedictines, but they did not attack the conquest in personal terms. The difference between Durham and the other houses just named was that at Durham the benedictines were established by normans. The Conqueror and his son William Rufus were both benefactors of the church,[54] and it was known that Rufus was not so benevolent to other monasteries.[55] The monks therefore could not criticise their patrons. It was pointed out that Walcher was *de gente Hlothariorum*,[56]

---

[48] Arnold 2 pp 186–7.   [49] Arnold 1 p 105.   [50] Arnold 2 p 190.
[51] See Arnold 1 pp 101, 118; 2 p 188.
[52] Arnold 2 p 202. In discussing Walcher's death, William of Malmesbury noted that *Fusus ibi non paucus numerus Lotharingorum, quod praesul ipse nationis ejus erat*. See *Willelmi Malmesbiriensis Monachi, De Gestis Regum Anglorum*, ed W. Stubbs, 2 vols RS 90 (1889) 2 p 330.
[53] R. W. Southern, 'Aspects of the European Tradition of Historical Writing: 4. The Sense of the Past', *TRHS*, fifth series 23 (1973) pp 243–63, at pp 248–9.
[54] Arnold 1 pp 101, 108, 113, 128.
[55] *Ibid* p 128: *licet enim in alia monasteria et ecclesias ferocius ageret*.
[56] *Ibid* p 105.

and thus a stranger. He was a secular cleric, but was not to be identified with Sexhelm, and *vitae laudabilis conversatione religiosum praeferebat monachum.*[57] Great emphasis was placed on his efforts to reform the clerks, his welcome to Aldwin and his companions, and his preparations, cut short by death, to become a monk and build a cathedral.[58] But though Walcher could be summed up as *vir venerandae canitiei, sobrietate morum et honestate vitae tali dignus honore,*[59] he did have failings as a bishop. His position as earl after the imprisonment of earl Waltheof in 1075 seems to have involved him in an effort to balance the administration between norman and local factions. The scheme collapsed when one of his kinsmen, Gilbert, killed Ligulf, a member of the house of earl Waltheof. Walcher was involved in the resulting feud, and was killed in the church at Gateshead. Symeon was reluctant to take sides, but was forced to admit that Walcher had offended the natives – *indigenarum animos offendebat* – by giving his followers free rein to do whatever they liked, and by not restraining them when they did wrong.[60] He was buried, not surprisingly, by the monks of Jarrow.[61] Walcher's successor, William of St Calais, was another norman appointee to whom the monks owed a great debt. Because he had read that in earlier times the bishopric had been served by monks,[62] he settled the monks in Durham, and started to build the new cathedral.[63] He was, Symeon enthused, 'a man of great prudence and wisdom.'[64] He protected the monks and, importantly, he separated the monastic from the episcopal lands.[65] He ruled the monks, Symeon said, 'with the greatest discretion,'[66] and the operative word was surely *regebat.* The monks who attained office were expressly the bishop's appointments,[67] though this was not a violation of the *Rule.*[68] Symeon glossed over St Calais's rebellion against the king, his trial and exile.[69]

[57] *Ibid* pp 20, 106.
[58] *Ibid* pp 9, 106, 109–13.
[59] *Ibid* p 106.
[60] *Ibid* pp 114–17, and see David Douglas, *William the Conqueror* (London 1964) pp 240–1.
[61] Arnold I pp 117–18.
[62] *Ibid* p 10.
[63] *Ibid* pp 128–9.
[64] *Ibid* p 10.
[65] *Ibid* p 123.
[66] *Ibid* p 125: *summa discretione regebat.*
[67] *Ibid* p 123.
[68] *The Rule of St Benedict*, ed and trans J. McCann (London 1952) pp 148–9.
[69] Arnold I p 128: *per aliorum machinamenta orta inter ipsos dissensione, episcopus ab episcopatu pulsus ultra mare secessit, quem comes Normannorum non ut exulem, sed ut patrem suscipiens, in magno honore per tres annos, quibus ibi moratus est, habuit.*

Self-interest dictated that he could not blame either bishop or king for the quarrel, for while St Calais was away, William Rufus had defended the community, and when he returned, it was with quantities of gold and silver altar vessels and books.[70] Symeon thus argued that the dissension had arisen through the schemes of others. The vindication of St Calais was completed by a pamphlet which, Offler argues, was produced around 1114. It portrayed him as a wronged defender of ecclesiastical privilege appealing to the pope, but admitted the charge of treason.[71] The praise Symeon gave to St Calais may have been intended as an oblique criticism of a man who fell foul of the next king, Henry I – Ranulf Flambard, who was bishop when Symeon was writing. St Calais, Symeon said, *nihil unquam de ecclesia auferebat; quin potius semper inferre, et multis eam ac pretiosis ornamentorum speciebus studebat exornare.*[72] It is true, as Southern pointed out, that Flambard's wrongful exactions, of which he repented on his deathbed, were to a large extent directed towards building the cathedral.[73] But while Flambard may have, in the words of Symeon's continuator, defended the rights and liberties of his see *contra extraneos*,[74] the situation could not have been so clear while the bishop lived, and Symeon may have preferred to maintain a meaningful silence.[75]

All this is perhaps a slightly selective approach to Symeon's work. He shared the moralistic and miraculous background common to medieval historiography. He told some admonitory tales of the fate of women who defied custom and entered the church where Cuthbert's relics lay.[76] His attitude to clerical celibacy was what might loosely be termed 'gregorian.'[77] There was also in Durham some interest in affairs outside the see. This is typified by the *Historia Regum*, and by Symeon's tract on the archbishops of York.[78] But having said this, it must still be claimed that in the few crucial decades after their foundation, the monks' attitude to the outside world was governed by two primary considerations. They sought, firstly, to establish their continuity with the past, and the tradition they usurped and embellished

---

[70] *Ibid* p 128.
[71] See Offler, *'De Iniusta Vexacione'*.
[72] Arnold 1 p 125.
[73] R. W. Southern, 'Ranulf Flambard', in *Medieval Humanism* pp 183–205, at p 202.
[74] Arnold 1 p 139.
[75] See Offler, *Medieval Historians* p 7. For later relations between bishop and monks see [G. V.] Scammell, [*Hugh du Puiset*] (Cambridge 1956) pp 135–41.
[76] Arnold 1 pp 60–1, 95.
[77] *Ibid* pp 93, 131, and see Scammell pp 100–1.
[78] Arnold 1, pp 222–8.

was strong enough to envelop those who came north. Lawrence of Durham, the prior who came from Waltham, is acknowledged as a 'humanist,'[79] and was therefore, arguably, influenced by ideas not native to the north. But while in Durham, he wrote verse on Cuthbert, and on the troubles which William Cumin inflicted on the see in the 1140s.[80] For the monks, loyalty to the see was stronger than loyalty to their order. Symeon's continuator was able to castigate the cistercian who helped William Cumin as a *gyrovagus*,[81] one of the types of monk condemned by Benedict.[82] But Symeon himself could not hide that those who plundered the bishopric in the 1040s were fellow benedictines from Peterborough. The monks had to balance a protective attitude towards the bishops, the personification of continuity, with aggression towards outsiders, and when the two aims clashed, a certain tension became apparent. Secondly, the see had to survive territorially. The *Historia de Sancto Cuthberto* demonstrated that the influence of property questions was not unique to the twelfth century, and a recurrent controversy with St Albans, another bene-dictine community, that it was not unique to Durham. The problem was the church of Tynemouth, claimed by Durham, but in the possession of St Albans, probably from *c* 1090.[83] The row flared again in the 1170s, shortly before the St Albans' chronicler, Roger of Wendover (died 1236), was writing. Though he made no direct reference to Tynemouth, it seems likely that this is what stopped him from finding a good word for any bishop of Durham.[84] Where property was concerned, objective criteria could not apply. In ninth century Lindisfarne, the *Liber Vitae*, a book which came to lie on the

[79] See Colin Morris, *The Discovery of the Individual 1050–1200* (London 1972) pp 68–9, 100. Lawrence was prior 1149–54.

[80] See *Dialogi Laurentii Dunelmensis Monachi ac Prioris*, SS 70 (1878) 2, pp 12–38, 69–70.

[81] Arnold I p 147.

[82] *The Rule* p 14.

[83] See H. S. Offler, *Durham Episcopal Charters 1071–1152*, SS 179 (1968) pp 4–6, 30–2, 41–7; Arnold I pp 124–5; Nicholl pp 76–7.

[84] Wendover was the only chronicler to blame Walcher for his own death. He accused Walcher of buying the earldom and of reducing the population to poverty. See [Roger of Wendover, *Flores Historiarum*] 4 vols, ed [H. O.] Coxe, English Historical Society (London 1841–2) 2, pp 17–18. Wendover indulged in the usual monastic rhetoric against Ranulf Flambard (*ibid* p 165). Up to 1201, he seems to have used an earlier St Albans' chronicle which he may have embellished; see [Roger of Wendover, *Flores Historiarum*] 3 vols, ed [H. G.] Hewlett, RS 84 (1889) 3, pp xi–xxii. He accused Hugh du Puiset of bribing his king and pope; see Coxe 3, p 9. In fact, Hugh did buy the earldom; see Scammell pp 49–50. Wendover was violently opposed to Richard Marsh (bishop 1215–26) in his struggle with the monks of Durham; see Coxe 4, pp 68–71, Hewlett 3, p xxii, and Offler *Medieval Historians* p 15.

high altar at Durham, had been inscribed with the names of benefactors arranged according to rank: kings and earls came first, followed by queens and abbesses, then by hermits, abbots and so on. In twelfth century Durham, no such rigid stratification is apparent.[85]

University of Edinburgh

---

[85] See *Liber Vitae Ecclesiae Dunelmensis*, SS 136 (1923) p xvi, and see, for example, fols 14ᵛ and 16ᵛ, where, admittedly in part for reasons of space, the ninth century groupings are ignored.

APPENDIX

Symeon said that few of the recruits to Jarrow were northumbrians, more were *de australibus Anglorum partibus*.[1] He said that in 1083 twenty-three monks came from Jarrow and Wearmouth. The figure survives in the cottonian MS, but was erased from the Cosin's MS and did not appear in subsequent copies.[2] The names of those who had taken monastic vows in Durham between 1083 and the time of writing (1104 x 9) are contained in the Cosin's MS.[3] There are seventy-three names in the original hand, and here I agree with Arnold rather than J. Conway Davies, on where the original hand ends.[4] But Arnold was certainly mistaken in thinking that the other names in the list were all written in the same hand. Ælfredus (seventy-fourth) to Absalon (ninety-eighth) at the end of fol 7ᵛ are written in at least four different hands, and the names on fol 8, from Willelmus (ninety-ninth) to the last-named monk, Girardus, are in another.[5] Arnold was probably correct in identifying the original monks with the first twenty-three in the list.[6] Wulmorus (fifth), Turkillus (eighth) and Edmundus (twenty-second) were said by the *Historia Regum* to have been at Jarrow.[7] Aldwin (first), the first prior of Durham, had refounded Jarrow along with Elfwius, second in the list.[8] Turgot (sixth), who joined Jarrow later, was second prior,[9] and the capital letters in the MS for his name but not for that of Algarus, the next prior, indicate that he was probably prior when the bulk of the Cosin's MS was written. Leofwinus, fourth in the list, was made sacrist in 1083,[10] and Swartebrandus (fourteenth) and Gamelo (fifteenth) were reported as dying in Durham.[11]

That Symeon himself was at Jarrow was accepted by Arnold[12] and by Knowles.[13] The idea originated with Thomas Rud, who concluded that *Fuit ergo Symeon inter Monachos*

---

[1] Arnold 1 pp 109–10.
[2] *Ibid* p 122.
[3] *Ibid* pp 4–5.
[4] See Arnold 1 p 6 and J. Conway Davies in *The Durham Philobiblon* 1 (1949–55) p 11.
[5] I am grateful to Dr A. I. Doyle for permission to see the MS, and for discussion of this point. There is a similar but not identical list in the *Liber Vitae*, fols 42ʳ/ᵛ.
[6] Arnold 1 p xii.
[7] Arnold 2 pp 260–1.
[8] Arnold 1 p 109.
[9] *Ibid* pp 111, 127.
[10] *Ibid* p 123.
[11] *Ibid* pp 20–1, 88.
[12] *Ibid* pp x–xi.
[13] *The Monastic Order in England* (2 ed 1963) p 167.

Gyrwenses, priusquam Dunelmum traducti sunt.[14] This conclusion was based on the assumption, which should be regarded as no more than a possibility, that Symeon wrote both the *Historia Dunelmensis Ecclesiae* and the *Historia Regum*.[15] Rud quoted from the *Historia Regum* the passage in which the Durham monks stated their claim to the church of Tynemouth: *Wlmarum quoque, nostrae congregationis monachum, aliosque per vices fratres, qui ibidem officia divina peragerent, illuc de Gyrva transmissos meminimus . . . postremo, cum Albrius honorem comitatus suscepisset, ipse quoque nobis in Dunelmum translatis eundem locum donavit.*[16] It seems clear, however, that, even conceding that Symeon did write the *Historia Regum*, it is probably a mistake to think that whenever he used the first person plural he was speaking personally. It is at least as likely that in this case the memories were those of a community stressing links with its immediate past. The same explanation might apply to the following, from which Hinde and Arnold both deduced that Symeon had heard the choir at Durham in bishop Walcher's time: *Unde tota nepotum suorum successio magis secundum instituta monachorum quam clericorum consuetudinem candendi horas, usque ad tempus Walcheri episcopi, paterna traditione observavit, sicut eos canentes saepe audivimus, et usque hodie nonnullos de illa progenie narrantes audire solemus.*[17] Hinde suggested that Symeon was resident in Durham before the community moved from Jarrow,[18] Arnold that since Jarrow was only fifteen or sixteen miles away, Symeon could often have travelled to Durham to hear the music.[19] Again, it cannot be taken as certain that Symeon, even if the author of the *Historia Dunelmensis Ecclesiae*, was speaking personally. It may, however, be valid to see a connection between an interest in the choir and Symeon's later conjectural position as precentor, though 'precentor' may almost be a synonym for 'scholar'.[20] The conviction that Symeon was at Jarrow led Arnold to seek confirmation of this elsewhere in the *Historia Dunelmensis Ecclesiae*; since he dwelt on the motives of those who resettled Jarrow, 'Symeon may probably be regarded as one of these fervent neophytes from the south',[21] and the following eulogy on Aldwin provoked the unlikely observation that 'It is surely the natural inference from these words that Symeon himself was one of the monks whom Aldwin brought up with him from the south':[22] *Cujus memoriam ut in suis orationibus monachi Dunhelmenses indesinter agant, ipse meritis suis omnino exigit, quem praevium in ipsam provinciam ducem habuerunt, ubi exemplo illius et magisterio habitantes Christo servire coeperunt.*[23] This conclusion of Arnold's really does seem something of a *non sequitur*, but he was not deterred by this, nor by the knowledge that Symeon's name, standing thirty-eighth in the *Historia Dunelmensis Ecclesiae* list, was not among those first twenty-three monks who came to Durham. The explanation that occurred to him was that 'during his stay at Jarrow, Symeon was . . . a *clericus inter monachos degens*, as Turgot (p 111) had been before him, and that he was not regularly professed till two or three years after the establishment of the monastery at Durham, that is till 1085 or 1086'.[24] It is not possible to prove that Symeon was not at Jarrow, but the evidence that he was seems, in short, extremely flimsy.

---

[14] Thomas Rud, *Disquisitio de vero auctore hujus Historiae Dunelmensis Ecclesiae*, in Thomas Bedford, *Symeonis Monachi Dunhelmensis Libellus* (London 1732) pp i–xxxv, at pp xxx–ii n a.

[15] See note 1 above.

[16] Arnold 2 pp 260–1, and see note 83.

[17] Arnold 1 pp 57–8.

[18] Hinde p vii.

[19] Arnold 1 p x.

[20] See Knowles p 428; that Symeon was known as precentor is confirmed not only by the rubrics of MSS 139 and Ff. 1. 27, as Blair (p 75) thought, but also by the early twelfth century *Vision of Orm*, ed H. Farmer in *Analecta Bollandiana* 75 (1957) pp 72–82, at p 76.

[21] Arnold 1 p xi.

[22] *Ibid* p 127 n.   [23] *Ibid* p 127.   [24] *Ibid* p xii.

LEGEND AND REALITY:
THE CASE OF WALDEF OF MELROSE

by DEREK BAKER

THE *Life of Saint Waldef* by Jocelin of Furness[1] is the only
surviving account[2] of a man who would seem to have played a
prominent part in the political and ecclesiastical affairs of the
north in the middle years of the twelfth century, and who acquired a

---

[1] Jocelin [of Furness, *Vita Sancti Waldeni*], in *AS*, August I, (Paris/Rome 1867) pp 242–78.
The saint's name should be rendered *Waldevi*. The best resumé of the evidence relating
to Jocelin himself is given by McFadden (see n 3 below); [Derek] Baker, 'San Bernardo
[e l'elezione di York'], *Studi su San Bernardo* (Florence 1975) pp 85–146; [Derek] Baker,
'Patronage [in the early twelfth-century church: Walter-Espec, Kirkham and
Rievaulx'] *Festschrift Winfried Zeller* (Marburg 1975). Jocelin's life is delineated by
the works ascribed to him: the *Lives* of Kentigern, Patrick and Helena, besides that of
Waldef. The *Life of Kentigern* was commissioned by bishop Joscelin of Glasgow (1174–99)
and former abbot of Melrose (below n 49). In McFadden's view the *Life of Patrick*
comes next, preceding the *Life of Helena,* which is assigned to the period 1198–1207.
The *Life of Waldef* comes last in the series. Jocelin had a literary reputation and an
association with the community of Melrose, at least at one remove, through its ex-abbot
Jocelin. Little else is certain. There is no confirmation of Colgan's statement that
Jocelin was Welsh, and a monk of Chester, though some support for his claim that he
then became a monk at Down may be found in the composition of the *Life of Patrick,*
whose remains were discovered at Down in 1186. Contacts, however, were close
between Scotland and Ireland in general: Melrose itself sent its eighth abbot, Ralph to
be bishop of Down in 1202, and in 1211 he was to be found back at Melrose
consecrating the abbots of Fountains, Furness and Calder (*Chronicle of Melrose*). More
particularly, the founder of Inis Courcy, near Down, as a daughter house of Furness,
John de Courcy, was one of those to whom Jocelin dedicated his *Life of Patrick.* On
only one occasion does Jocelin refer to himself as a monk of Furness – in the preface to
his *Life of Waldef* – but the manuscripts of his works all agree in calling him a monk of
Furness, and it is probably best, for the present, to settle simply on that. Whether
further study of his works will allow greater precision it is difficult to say. Certainly, the
order of composition of his *Lives* is important here and McFadden's brief comments
are not altogether convincing (pp 9–10), but I have not seen his unpublished thesis which
might deal with this at greater length. As far as the *Life of Waldef* is concerned it is clear
that Jocelin was a writer of established reputation within the cistercian houses of the
north before he was invited to undertake a *Life* of the second abbot of Melrose. For an
extreme view of the merits of the *Life* see McFadden: for him Jocelin is 'a literary
artist of almost the first rank' (p 5 n 1), and his *Life* 'one of the most perfect – even
"classic" – specimens of hagiography' (p 13). I find myself in greater agreement with the
more superficial comment of Bulloch (p 127) – 'it would seem that he used his sources
honestly but uncritically, faithfully reproducing whatever he found there'.

[2] A *Vita Sancti Waltheni,* now lost, is ascribed to Waldef's fellow canon and monk
Everard, later first abbot of Holmcultram. See *AS* August I p 246[b], and below. John of

reputation for conventional sanctity. Apart from Jocelin's account, written almost fifty years after his subject's death, there are only a handful of contemporary references to Waldef. If the historian was limited to these Waldef would be a shadowy figure indeed, and the annals of the twelfth-century church would lose a man who appears, both in Jocelin's narrative and the pages of modern historians, almost as a second-rank Ailred.[3]

The story that Jocelin has to tell is simple in outline and treatment, and clear in purpose. Waldef (Waltheof) was the second son of Simon I of Senlis, earl of Northampton,[4] and Maud, the daughter of the Conqueror's niece Judith, and was probably named after his grand-father Waldef, earl of Northumbria, executed in 1076 for his alleged complicity in a plot against the Conqueror. He was, so Jocelin asserts, his mother's favourite. While his elder brother was a father's boy, building toy castles and fighting battles, Waldef built toy churches and mimed services.[5] Soon after the death of Simon I of Senlis his

---

Tynemouth's *De S. Wallevo* is an abbreviated version of Jocelin's *Life*, see C. Horstmann, *Nova Legenda Angliae* (Oxford 1901).

[3] Contemporary references to Waldef occur in [A. C.] Lawrie, [*Early Scottish Charters prior to 1153*] (Glasgow 1905); [G. W. S.] Barrow, *Regesta* [*Regum Scottorum*] I (Edinburgh 1960, repr 1971); [*Chronica de*] *Mailros*, ed J. Stevenson (Edinburgh 1835); Bernard's *Vita Sancti Malachiae* (below n 46); in connection with the York election dispute (below n 53), and in the pseudo-Ingulph (below n 60). For more recent comment see [Walter Daniel, *Life of Ailred*, ed F. M.] Powicke (Edinburgh 1950); [R. L. G.] Ritchie, [*The Normans in Scotland*] (Edinburgh 1954); [J. C.] Dickinson, [*The Origins of the Austin Canons and their Introduction into England*] (London 1950); [Donald] Nicholl, [*Thurstan, Archbishop of York (1114–140)*] (York 1964); [R. H. C.] Davis, [*King Stephen*] (London 1967); [Ailred of Rievaulx, *De Anima*, ed C. H.] Talbot, *MRS* suppl 1 (London 1952); [David Knowles, The] *M[onastic] O[rder in England]* (2 ed Cambridge 1963); [David] Knowles, ['The Case of] Saint William [of York'], *CHJ* 5 no 2 (1936) pp 162–77, 212–14; [J.] Wilson, ['The Passages of St Malachy through Scotland'], *ScHR* 18 (1921) pp 69–82; [Derek] Baker, '*Viri Religiosi* [and the York Election Dispute'], *SCH* 7 (1971) pp 87–100; [J. P. B.] Bulloch, ['St Waltheof'], *Records of the Scottish Church History Society*, 11 (Glasgow 1955) pp 105–32; [G.] McFadden, ['*The Life of Waldef* and its author Jocelin of Furness'], *Innes Review* (Glasgow 1955) pp 5–13; [A. O.] Anderson, [*Early Sources of Scottish History 500–1286*], 2 (Edinburgh 1922) pp 32–3, 40, 145–50, 207, 240, 274–5.

[4] Died at La Charité-sur-Loire in *c* 1111. See Anderson, p 146.

[5] Jocelin II. 11 (*AS* p 252ª): Comes Simon, praenominatus pater puerorum, primogenitum, tamquam Isaac Esau suum, arctius amabat; mater vero, mulier bona, Walthenum, velut Rebecca suum Iacobum, affectu propensiori diligebat. Cum fratres illi in puerili aetate constituti essent, sapiebant, agebant, ludebant ut parvuli: prior natu Simon collectis arbusculis seu ramusculis, secundum modulum suum, castellum construere consueverat; et ascendens canabum, velut sonipedem suum, et virgulam quasi lanceam accipiens et vibrans, cum coaetaneis suis circa fictitii et imaginarii castelli custodiam et defensionem solicitus, militiam simulabat. Walthenus vero puerulus ex virgulis vel lapillis quasi ecclesias, seque presbyterum tamquam Missam celebrantem expansis

Waldef of Melrose: legend and reality

widow married again, in the winter of 1113–14. Her second husband was earl David, the brother of Henry I's queen and of Alexander I of Scotland (1107–24), and future king of Scotland (1124–53). He now appears to have assumed responsibility for his step-children, and to have brought them up in his household.[6] At this early stage in the *Life* Jocelin has already been at pains to stress Waldef's exemplary character, and he now conducts him quickly and safely through the temptations and distractions of David's court to his renunciation of the world and entry into the augustinian house of Nostell, near Pontefract.[7] The king, apparently, had Waldef earmarked for the episcopate, and he feared that if he entered a religious house within Scotland, or on the lands of the earl his brother,[8] *violenter extractus* he would be promoted to a bishopric willy-nilly: hence his choice of Nostell, remote and reasonably secure.

Promotion followed quickly for Waldef. The next section of Jocelin's *Life* (II:20) records his unwilling acceptance of election as prior of Kirkham, referring to him as sacrist of Nostell. There follow in rapid

---

manibus praesentabat: et quia verba proferre non noverat, sonos cantum similantes edere solebat. A similar story, however, is told by Gerald of Wales of himself. See Ritchie p 247 n 4.

[6] Jocelin I: 14 (*AS* p 252b): In curia regis [sic] nutriebatur, educabatur, crescebat et confortabatur, et gratia Dei in eo evidentibus indiciis monstrabatur. In palatium namque claustrum, et in turba monachum, inter aulicos seipsum exhibuit solitarium. Both McFadden and Bulloch retail the story recorded in the *De Comitissa* that Maud's children by her first marriage were sent to Normandy – 'So David had possession of the countess and the earldom, and custody of the children. . . . The children who had been born to Simon and Matilda, and who were in David's custody, were taken to Normandy and committed to the keeping of Stephen, the count of Aumale, their mother's uncle. And they were so much educated under his tutelage that Simon, the eldest, received insignia of knighthood with count William, count Stephen's son. For this reason Henry, the king of the English, was indignant.' Anderson p 145, quoting from the *Life of Earl Waldef* (*De Comitissa* section) ed Francisque Michel, *Chroniques Anglo-Normandes*, 3 vols (Rouen 1836) 2, pp 126–31. Bulloch concludes (p 108) that 'it can only have applied to the daughters', but there is no reason why it should not be accepted. Waldef could have returned to David's household at a later date – perhaps after he became king, as Jocelin implies (I: 14). Though no certainty is possible here there can be no doubt as to the importance of the documents associated with the cult of earl Waldef to this discussion. Denholm-Young saw the *De Comitissa*, together with the *Vita et passio venerabilis viri Gualdevi*, as being the essential core of the documents printed by Michel, deriving from 'a common nucleus and narrative of the life and death of Siward, Waltheof and the countess Judith', while Anderson saw the *De Comitissa* as underlying the account of the pseudo-Ingulph. See Anderson p 33; n 46; and below pp 73–4, nn 60–4.

[7] *Ibid* I: 15 – II: 19.

[8] Comitis fratris sui. Simon II of Senlis seems to have received the earldom of Northampton sometime after 1136, see Davis pp 134–5, and below pp 73–4, nn 60–4. The chronology of Waldef's early life is uncertain, and is discussed further below.

succession references to Waldef's encounter with Malachy at York (II: 27-8); his involvement in the York election dispute (II: 29-30); his conversion from the augustinian to the cistercian life (III: 31-3) and his election as abbot of Melrose (III: 36). Apart from incidental references to Waldef's part in the foundation of Holmcultram, Kinlos and Cupar (IV: 49-50), and the attempt to install him as bishop of St Andrews in the last months of his life (VI: 79), the remaining two-thirds of Jocelin's *Life* is a mosaic of miraculous occurrences and visions, both before and after Waldef's death in 1159. His edifying death is followed by miracles, the institution of a popular cult, and a demonstration of incorruption at the opening of his tomb in 1170 in the presence of the bishop of Glasgow and other witnesses (IX: 121). More miracles follow, and at the burial of the ninth abbot of Melrose, William, in 1206[9] there was a second inspection of Waldef's tomb, and a further demonstration of incorruption. Jocelin tells us that he had heard of this inspection many times from one of the monks present, Robert the *caementarius*, and he concludes his *Life* with a panegyric of Waldef, comparing him, amongst other saints, to Cuthbert, also a monk of Melrose.

Jocelin's account was written at the request of the tenth abbot of Melrose, Patrick, who ruled for only one year, 1206-7, and, as Jocelin records, was dead before its completion. It is dedicated to William the Lion and his son Alexander, who succeeded to the throne in 1214. The outside limits of the period of composition are, therefore, 1206-1214, but there can be little doubt that it was the second exhumation of Waldef which provided the incentive to commission the *Life*, and it is likely that it was completed very soon after the death of abbot Patrick in 1207.[10] Jocelin was writing, in fact, almost fifty years after the death of Waldef, but, as he stressed, he had taken pains to establish the facts and present a true history.[11] This history, in all

---

[9] The *Chronicle of Melrose* records abbot William's death on 8 June 1206. Jocelin, however, is quite explicit about the date he gives – Anno ab Incarnatione Domini millesimo ducentesimo septimo, qui est annus quadragesimus octavus a decessu sancti Waltheni – and it is difficult to see how he could have been mistaken about an event so close to the date at which he must have been writing, though it should be noted that he dates Waltheof's death to 1160 not 1159 (VI: 91). Since abbot Patrick, who commissioned the *Life*, ruled only from 1206-7, according to the *Chronicle of Melrose*, 1206 may be preferred as the date of exhumation.

[10] There is, for example, no mention of the next abbot of Melrose, Adam, who had been the prior of the house. Some reference to him might be expected if the completion of the *Life* was delayed much beyond Patrick's death.

[11] Jocelin, Prologue (*AS* p 250ᵃ): nullaque in eis veritati opposita, sed quod a viris veridicis

Waldef of Melrose: legend and reality

essentials, has found a ready acceptance in all recent accounts of the events and developments in which Waldef was concerned. In one particular respect – William of Aumâle's offer to procure the archbishopric of York for Waldef, at a price (II: 29–30) – Jocelin adds significantly to what is otherwise known about these years: more generally he ensures Waldef a prominent place in the company of greater men like abbot William of Rievaulx, about whom much less is known.

Amongst recent historians the most coherent account is given by Powicke in the introduction to his edition of Walter Daniel's *Life of Ailred*.[12] It is essentially a paraphrase of Jocelin's *Life*, though it does suggest in addition that Waldef was already prior of Kirkham when Ailred entered Rievaulx, that the curious agreement contained in the Rievaulx cartulary, between the communities of Rievaulx and Kirkham for the transfer of the site of the priory to the cistercians, is to be associated with Waldef's desire to become a cistercian,[13] and that Ailred's short treatise on the monastic rule and profession, addressed to an augustinian, should be connected with the same crisis in Waldef's life.[14] Elsewhere he accepts the addition made to Walter Daniel's *Life of Ailred* in the fourteenth century which asserts that Ailred was brought up at David's court with prince Henry and Waldef,[15] and he repeatedly emphasises the friendship and intimacy

---

senioribus domus Melrosensis, omni exceptione maioribus accepi, me scripsisse fideliter agnoscant. In dictando ita stylum temperavi meum, ut nec humi repat, nec tumeat in altum, modum eligendo propter simplices planum et perlucidum et circumspectum, et vitando iuxta Tullium pompaticum, suffultum, et involutum. On Jocelin's reliability see the comments of Knowles, 'Saint William', p 165 n 10, and *MO* p 240.

[12] Powicke pp lxxi–iv, and at pp xiii, xxxii, xxxiii, xxxvi n 3, xxxix, xli, xlii n 1, xliv, xci, xcii, 3 n*, 10 n 3, 56 n 1. McFadden is primarily concerned with Jocelin and his *Life of Waldef*. His summary account of Waldef (pp 5–7) is almost entirely based upon Powicke, and while Bulloch deals at great length with Waldef his account is a recapitulation of Jocelin's *Life* with large excursions into related events and developments.

[13] In spite of the fact that he accepts a date of *c* 1139 for it. This agreement needs further consideration. It need only be said here that there seems to be no necessity to associate it with the career of Waldef at all. See Powicke p lxxiii; *Chartulary of Rievaulx*, ed J. C. Atkinson, SS 83, for 1887 (1889) pp xviii–xxxvi, 108–9; *Memorials of the Abbey of St. Mary of Fountains*, ed. J. R. Walbran, 2, 1, SS 67, for 1876 (1878) pp 177–93; below n 18; Baker, 'Patronage'.

[14] See Powicke p lxxiv for the references.

[15] The addition is made in a Bury St Edmund's manuscript, now Oxford Bodleian MS Bodley 240 (SC 2469), written in 1377 and the years following. The manuscript contains a number of saints' lives, including one of Ailred. This is essentially a summary of

between Ailred and Waldef. Ritchie, at various points in *The Normans in Scotland*[16] refers to Waldef, and if his treatment of the evidence is not always beyond question[17] his account in general accords with the accepted view, adding only that Waldef was the tutor of the young Malcolm IV, David I's grandson and successor. In Dickinson's book on the augustinians Waldef naturally appears, but only in incidental references.[18] These, in spite of some rather startling errors, are all derived from Jocelin's *Life*, and such differences as exist are only ones of emphasis, and derive from the author's viewpoint. In Nicholl's biography of Thurstan of York Waldef makes three brief appearances.[19] The first, largely, and in part inaccurately, derived from Ritchie, deals with Waldef's period at the Scottish court and his departure to Nostell. The second refers to the visit of saint Malachy to York, probably in November 1139, and his meeting with Waldef, as recorded by Jocelin (II: 27-8). The third is a passing reference in connection with the York election dispute. It is the same dispute which occasions Waldef's only appearance in Davis's *King Stephen*.[20] Talbot makes passing reference to Waldef in the introduc-

---

the *Life* by Walter Daniel. The manuscript also seems to contain some of the materials collected by John of Tynemouth at St Albans in the second quarter of the fourteenth century for his collection known as the *Sanctilogium Angliae* (now BM Cottonian MS Tiberius E.i.). The addition reads 'in curia David regis Scocie, cum Henrico filio regis et Walthevo postmodum abbate de Melros, nutritus et educatus.' Powicke notes that the addition may be derived from Jocelin, who refers (III. 32) to Ailred as 'coalumnum et amicissimum suum, a iuventute in curia regis David cum Henrico filio regis et eodem Waltheno nutritus et educatus'. See Powicke pp xxviii–xxxii, xxxiii, xxxix, xli, 3 n*, and *AS* August I, p 258° (not p 257 d.e. as given by Powicke p xxxiii n 1).

[16] Ritchie pp 247–53, and at pp 139, 171 n 4, 348 n 1, 355, 357, 410, 417.

[17] His references to Ailred, for example, need to be treated with considerable caution.

[18] Dickinson pp 123 n 4, pp 171–2, 177, 201, 213, 252, 253. It may be noted that he dates the agreement between Rievaulx and Kirkham (above n 13) 'before March 1154' (p 123 n 4), and makes the interesting suggestion that the canons of Kirkham may have withdrawn their objection to Waldef's departure to the cistercians (p 213). At p 171 he gives dates of c 1140–47 for Waldef's priorate. The latter date is certainly wrong, and perhaps arises from the attempt to reconcile Jocelin's reference to *Ailredum abbatum* (III: 32) with the crisis in Waldef's life. Though there is a reference to a *Life* of Waldef by Ailred at p 201 this is in fact Jocelin's *Life*, and Waldef was not abbot of Melrose at the time of his nomination to the see of York, but prior of Kirkham (p. 252).

[19] Nicholl pp 137, 235, 241. It was Simon II of Senlis who was the benefactor of Nostell, not his father, see Ritchie p 171 n 4. The date of c 1128 given for Waldef's entry into Nostell is presumably derived from Lawrie. The date given by Nicholl for Malachy's visit to York (November 1139) is not undisputed, but seems preferable to 1140, see Nicholl p 235. Wilson (p 73) argues unconvincingly for 1140 as the date of Malachy's visit, relating it to the death of Thurstan (5 February 1140).

[20] Davis p 99.

tion to his edition of Ailred's *De Anima*,[21] stating a connection between Ailred and Waldef on the basis of Ailred's *Genealogy of the Kings of England* which the text will not sustain.[22] Knowles touched on Waldef's career on two occasions. His treatment in the *Monastic Order*[23] is based on Jocelin and indebted, as he acknowledges, to Powicke. Apart from ascribing Ailred's conversion to the regular life to the example of Waldef[24] it differs little in tone or substance from Powicke's account. In his earlier examination of the York election dispute Knowles's brief references to Waldef,[25] though less enthusiastic,[26] are in agreement with his later account. Finally, Waldef's position and influence is given some consideration by Barrow in the first volume of his *Regesta*,[27] though he seems to find some difficulty in reconciling what is claimed for Waldef by Jocelin (IV: 50; VI: 79) with the evidence of the documents he is presenting.[28]

The general view of Waldef's life and importance, then, though seldom coherently given, and varying in detail, is consistent amongst modern historians, and is in agreement with the thirteenth-century

[21] Talbot pp 3, 4.
[22] Ailred's reference is to David's son Henry only, not to Henry and Waldef as Talbot asserts, though he quotes the relevant passage, p 4 n 4.
[23] *MO* pp 240–3, and at 219, 220, 245, 254, 635. At p 645 is a brief assessment of Jocelin's *Life*.
[24] Ailred 'must have been stirred by the action of his friend Waldef, the king's stepson and brother of Simon, earl of Northumberland [*sic*], who about 1130 became an Augustinian canon at Nostell, then under the rule of Aldulf. Within a few years the distinguished young canon became prior of Kirkham . . . and there Ailred was soon to find his friend again . . .', *MO* p 242.
Waldef's brother, Simon II of Senlis, became earl of Northampton possibly *c* 1136. His step-brother Henry became earl of Northumberland in 1139, see Davis pp 134–7, and above n 8.
[25] Knowles, 'Saint William' pp 164, 165.
[26] 'his high connections and his own ability made him . . . a candidate for the vacant archbishopric, but, though widely known and trusted, he was still a young man and, as events were to show, had not yet found his true vocation', p 164.
[27] Barrow, *Regesta* I. p 7, and at pp 11, 20, 21.
[28] Malcolmus rex, nepos Abbatis sancti in pueritia et iuventute ante regnum et in regno constitutus, monitis ipsius obsecundans et imperio, vitam suam ad eius arbitrium ac mores composuit, domum et regnum disposuit (Jocelin IV:50). 'More influential, doubtless, was the king's uncle and sometime tutor, Waltheof, abbot of Melrose since 1148, who refused the king's offer of the St Andrew's see in 1159 because he believed he had not long to live, and who, in fact, died on 3 August in that year. One would hardly expect a Cistercian abbot, especially one of Waltheof's humility and devotion, to be much at court; and, indeed, he is named as a witness very seldom' (Barrow, *Regesta I* p 7). See, too, the following paragraph.
Waldef witnesses once in fact, see Barrow *Regesta* I no 128, pp 190–1. His absence as a witness to the great charter of confirmation to Kelso, given at Roxburgh in the second quarter of 1159 should be noted. See Barrow, *Regesta* I no 131, pp 192–5.

Life of the saint by Jocelin of Furness, on which it is based. Waldef appears as a good example of the type of which Ailred is the nonpareil. Nobly born, and intended for a conventional ecclesiastical career, he had higher aspirations which enabled him to set a fine example, both in the world and in the regular life he chose to enter. He passed through the crises of his own life and of his times demonstrating an edifying sanctity, humility and wisdom. He exemplifies that essential christian example that did so much to cement the 'gregorian' reform of spiritual manners, attitudes and behaviour into the fabric of twelfth-century society, and he demonstrates how family influence and connection could facilitate the spiritualising of the secular world of court, feudatory and retainer. Knowles's 'distinguished young canon' and 'nobly-born prior' became a saint, and Jocelin's *Life* ends, literally, with odours of sanctity.

Yet if Jocelin is so emphatic about Waldef's sanctity no other contemporary, or near contemporary, is. The *Chronicle of Melrose*, recording Waldef's election in 1148 and death in 1159, is more concerned with his family relationships than anything else, and, in its laconic annals for these years, makes no other mention of Waldef during the period of his abbatiate.[29] There is no reference to the inspection of Waldef's relics, and demonstration of their incorruption in 1206,[30] and in 1240, when the bones of the abbots of Melrose were moved to a different part of the chapter house, far from being incorrupt Waldef's remains were impossible to move having been reduced to dust, except for a few small bones and teeth, which were taken away as relics.[31] Only with the translation of Waldef's relics, described in a few lines under 1171 *(sic)*, does the *Chronicle of Melrose* in any way resemble Jocelin's *Life*, the chronicler referring to 'the most holy body' of Waldef, and concluding *vere hic homo Dei est.*[32] So

29 *Mailros* p 73 (1148): Ricardus primus abbas de Melros discessit, et Walthevus frater Henrici comitis Northimbrorum, et Simonis comitis Norhamtune, factus est abbas de Malros (the first seven words are a later interlinear addition). *Ibid* p 76 (1159): Obiit pie memorie Waldevus abbas ii de Malros iii nonarum Augusti [3 August] qui fuit awnculus regis M[alcolm IV].

30 *Ibid* p 106.

31 *Ibid* p 151 (1240): Eodem anno levata sunt ossa abbatum de Melros que iacebant in introitu capituli, et in orientali parte eiusdem capituli decencius sunt tumulata; praeter ossa venerabilis patris nostri Wallevi, cuius sepulcrum apertum fuit et corpus eius incineratum inventum, ex quo qui assuerunt ex minutis ossibus secum asportaverunt, et reliqua in pace dimiserunt. Aderat ibi praesens miles bone oppinionis, dictus Gilellmus filius comitis, nepos domini regis; hic dentem precibus obtinuit, per quem, ut ipse postea retulit, infirmi multa secuti sunt beneficia.

32 *Ibid* p 84 (1171): Sepulcrum pii patris nostri dompni Wallevi abbatis secundi de Melros,

Waldef of Melrose: legend and reality

he may have been considered locally, but there is no evidence of wider, or more formal, recognition. The bollandist editors of Jocelin's *Life* conclude their survey of the evidence cautiously. They accept miracles and a cult, but cannot accept canonisation by the pope in the absence of reliable evidence.[33] Jocelin himself confirms this view when at the end of his account of the exhumation of 1170 he rounds on his namesake Joscelin, fourth abbot of Melrose (22 April 1170–1174), who had arranged the inspection of the relics, for not promoting the cause of Waldef.[34] His own *Life* was certainly commissioned and designed to promote Waldef's claims,[35] and from odd hints that he drops,[36] and from the structure of his account, it is likely that there

---

a bone memorie Ingeramo Glasguensi episcopo et iiii[or] abbatibus ad hoc vocatis' reseratum est, et corpus eius integrum inventum et vestimenta intacta, anno xii° obitus sui, xi kalendas Iunii [June 22]. Et post sacra missarum solempnia idem antistes et abbates, quos praenumeravimus, cum ipsius monasterii universo conventu, super ipsam sanctissimi corporis glebam posuerunt lapidem novum, id est, marmor politum; et facta est leticia magna, conclamantibus qui aderant et dicentibus, vere hic homo Dei est. Compare the much longer account given by Jocelin, (IX: 121–3, *AS* p 275[b]), and in particular his substitution of 'incorrupt and entire' for the 'entire' of the *Chronicle of Melrose*.

[33] Facile admittimus, hunc Walthenum ab immemorabili tempore in Scotia et Anglia solitos Sanctorum honores obtinuisse; sed non asseremus, illum ab Apostolica sede solenniter inter Sanctos relatum fuisse, donec fide digniora huius rei testimonia asserantur. (*AS* p 243[b]).

[34] Abbas vero Jocelinus per aliquanti temporis spatium episcopus de Glasgu effectus est, vir in multis laudandus; sed in hoc, quod sanctum Walthenum, qui specialiter illum dilexit, erexit, provexit, canonizare non sategit, ut pluribus videtur, vituperandus. (IX: 23, *AS* p 275[b]). The debate about Waldef's resting place, which immediately precedes the remarks about abbot Jocelin, postpones a decision 'donec auctoritate summi Pontificis, vel consensu et concessu, capituli Cisterciensis aliud sanciretur'. There is no reference to this in the surviving statutes of the general chapter. See too the words put into the pope's mouth in the account of the vision of Nicholas, chancellor of Malcolm IV, at Rome (VII: 95).

[35] See his prologue, addressed to William the Lion and the future Alexander II: Ipse est decus et decor prosapiae vestrae, regni tutor, tutela patriae, titulus pudicitiae, gemma vitae canonicae, speculum monasticae disciplinae. Hic, inquam, degens in mundo fuit cleri solatium, pauperum aerarium, egenorum sustentaculum, infirmorum remedium, virtutum praeclarum domicilium. Huius corpus sanctissimum, totius adhuc corruptionis expers, futurae resurrectionis praeclarum praefert indicium, et fidei ac spei nostrae probabile ac palpabile praebet experimentum. Huius itaque dilecti Deo et hominibus, cuius memoria in benedictione est, utpote quem Dominus similem illi fecit in gloria Sanctorum, vitam virtutibus vernantem, miraculis gloriosam, theoriis praedaris sublimatam, petente ac praecipiente domino Patricio, abbate de Melros, sed heu! morte praematura praerepto, tandem suscepi (*AS* p 250[a]). Slightly further on in his prologue he exhorts his readers 'diligite, visitate, veneramini locum requietionis eius'.

[36] For example his reference to the deposition of the third abbot of Melrose, William (22 April 1170) against a background of opposition to friends and protegés of Waldef – like the future abbot Joscelin – and active discouragement of Waldef's cult. It may well

DEREK BAKER

was an earlier campaign which lapsed when abbot Joscelin was promoted to the see of Glasgow in 1174. When Jocelin's *Life* is examined more closely it is possible to distinguish a number of component parts. In his prologue Jocelin emphasises that he has based his account on the most reliable evidence available, the testimony of the senior members of the community at Melrose,[37] and at a number of other places in the Life he mentions particular witnesses – Robert the *caementarius* at the exhumation of 1206 (IX: 133) Suenus, monk and sub-cellarer of Melrose (II: 23);[38] Walter, *conversus hospitarius* of Melrose, who recounts, after Waldef's death, miracles about which he had been sworn to secrecy in the saint's lifetime (IV: 57–9);[39] Lambert the conversus describing the transfiguration of Waldef which he had witnessed (V: 71–2); Bernulf the citizen of Roxburgh, 'whose son I have seen as a monk of Melrose', who told almost everyone at Melrose of his healing at the saint's tomb (IX: 124).[40] Before all others, however, stands Everard, of whom Jocelin gives a brief sketch in recording the foundation of Holmcultram in 1150. Everard, at first a canon of Kirkham, followed Waldef into the cistercian order, and accompanied him to Melrose, where he became his chaplain, and was party to his secrets. On the foundation of Holmcultram in Cumberland in 1150 Everard was sent as first abbot of the community which left Melrose. He ruled the new abbey successfully until his death in 1192.[41] Jocelin refers explicitly to

---

be that this reflects a conflict in the house between those who supported Waldef's claim to sanctity and those who opposed it. See IX: 120–1, and compare in Powicke the criticisms levelled at Ailred after his death. See too the reference 'In superiori libello de beato Waltheno' at VII: 92, which introduces the posthumous account of Waldef and reads better as a composition of *c* 1170 than of 1207: 'In superiori libello de beato Waltheno, quae memoratu digna sensebantur, diligenter ab his, qui noverunt investigavimus, investigata qualicumque stylo digesta notitiae praesentium ac posteriorum tradimus; omisimus tamen auribus accepta plura, quia, ut nobis visum est, probabilis testimonii defecit sufficientia (*AS* p 270a). [37] Above n 11.
[38] Apparently relating events at Kirkham.
[39] See the further references to Walter at VII: 96–8, which conclude 'Haec frater Waltherus multoties etiam cum lachrymis pluribus retulit, ex quorum relatu didici, quae scripsi.'
[40] Hoc miraculum fere cunctis in Melros degentibus innotuit.
[41] Erat isdem Everardus a pueritia divinis obsequiis mancipatus in Canonicatu, virum Dei prae ceteris Canonicis arctius amans in Christo ad monachatum secutus, in Melrosensi coenobio eiusdem capellanus, conscius secretorum Sancti est effectus. Hic multis annorum curriculis vivens domum, cui praefuit interius ad magnae religionis culmen erexit, et exterius praediis et possessionibus ditatum in altum pervexit: sicque plenus dierum et virtutum in senectute bona ibidem in Domino requiescit. (IV: 49, *AS* 262a).
   He seems to have been close to Waldef while still at Kirkham, see Jocelin's account of the eucharistic miracle at II: 22–3.

Waldef of Melrose: legend and reality

Everard on three occasions: in connection with the eucharistic miracle at Kirkham, recounted to him by Everard (II: 22–3),[42] in telling the story of Waldef's slaughter of a horse-fly, while accompanied by Everard (III: 40),[43] and in recording the exhumation of Waldef's remains in 1170 (IX: 122).[44] Apart from these references at least one other contribution by Everard may be assumed. Writing almost forty years ago Knowles[45] said of Jocelin's brief account of the York election dispute that there was 'no reason to question his statement', though it contained information found nowhere else: 'he clearly had Cistercian records before him'. It may be suggested that the source of Jocelin's account of events which occurred while Waldef was prior of Kirkham was his confidant Everard. It would be possible, too, to ascribe Jocelin's description of the encounter between Waldef and Malachy at York in 1139 to the same source, were it not for the close, if unacknowledged, relationship between Jocelin's text and that of Bernard's *Life of Malachy*.[46]

If the material which was derived from Everard, Robert the *caementarius* and Bernard, or which can be connected with the *Chronicle of Melrose*, is removed from Jocelin's *Life* little of any substance, though much of interest, is left. The vague, brief, conventional description of Waldef's early life, and time at Nostell, Kirkham and Rievaulx, is swamped by the unexceptional miraculous. Yet even

---

[42] Haec a viro venerabili Everardo, primo abbate de Helculii, narrante didici, et ex ore confessoris eius accepi. (*AS* p 256ᵃ). See Bulloch p 115 for reference to the occurrence of an identical miracle at Whithorn in the first half of the ninth century.

[43] Retulit etiam Domnus Everardus, primus abbas de Holcultran, quod quadam vice dum itineraret cum praefato Viro Dei. . . . (*AS* p 259ᵇ).

[44] Jocelin's words here indicate the extent to which he was indebted to Everard: Haec et alia in hanc formam abbas de Helcon plura replicando subiunxit (*AS* p 275ᵇ).

[45] Knowles, 'Saint William' p 165 n 10. See Jocelin II: 29–30, *AS* p 257ᵃ.

[46] Compare Jocelin II: 27–8, AS pp 256ᵇ–7ᵃ and [*Vita Sancti*] *Malachiae*, ed J. Leclercq and H. M. Rochais, *Sancti Bernardi Opera*, III, *Tractatus et Opuscula* (Rome 1963) pp 295–378, at pp 341–2 (XV: 35–6). The composition of the *Life of Malachy* can be dated between 1150 and March 1152, see *Malachiae* p 297. There are no differences of substance between the two, though Jocelin extends the account by remarking that the Irish ascribed the transformation of the horse given by Waldef to Malachy to the merits of Malachy, while the canons of Kirkham ascribed it to the merits of Waldef. McFadden (p 11) referred to Jocelin's hostile account of the Conqueror's dealings with Waldef of Northumbria, and it is possible that for this part of his *Life* (I: 6–9, AS p 251) Jocelin made use of some of the writings associated with the cult of Waldef which were in circulation in the twelfth century: he remarks at one point (I: 9): 'Extat libellus in eodem coenobio conscriptus de miraculis eius, ex quibus probatur, quod merito nomen martyris ei adscribitur, attribuiter et decus.' See the comments of N. Denholm-Young, *Bodleian Quarterly Record* 6, 69 (Oxford 1931) pp 225–30, the references there given; and n 6 above.

with this material it is likely that Jocelin is entering into other men's labours. The portents, visions and miracles which precede the exhumation of 1170, comprise by far the largest part of the *Life*—only seven out of the one hundred and thirty-six sections which constitute Jocelin's account are concerned with the years between the two exhumations of 1170 and 1206 – and they are carefully and circumstantially presented. Wherever possible the name and status of the witness is given, the circumstances described. This is surely the substance of a body of evidence collected to prove Waldef's sanctity, and to assist in a process of canonisation of which the demonstration of incorruption at the opening of Waldef's tomb in 1170 should have been the culmination. In the event there was no canonisation, and it is not altogether clear why the process lapsed. Perhaps Jocelin of Furness was right in blaming it on the neglect of the fourth abbot of Melrose.[47] More probably there had always been antagonism to the cult at Melrose itself. Jocelin records the opposition of the third abbot William,[48] and it is noticeable that those who attest Waldef's sanctity are, for the most part, humble members of the house.[49] It is unlikely

---

[47] See above nn 34, 36.

[48] Above n 36.

[49] Almost the only exception is the fourth abbot Joscelin, the prior of Melrose before he succeeded the deposed abbot William in 1170. He is said to have succeeded *ipso die* of William's deposition – 22 April 1170 – and the *Chronicle of Melrose* dates the investigation of Waldef's remains to 22 June, exactly two months later. It is possible to see this as a decisive rejection of abbot William's opposition; it is also possible that the new abbot had little option but to go along with the supporters of Waldef's cause at this early stage of his abbatiate. Joscelin's appointment to the see of Glasgow in 1174 makes it difficult to establish his attitude. He was certainly a good friend and benefactor to Melrose (*Mailros* p 100, s.a. 1198). He was well regarded there, died at the abbey on 17 March 1199, and was buried in the monks choir (*ibid* p 103 and n hh), but though he is described as a disciple and friend of Waldef he occurs in none of the stories about him (see Jocelin IX: 121, *AS* p 275b). For monks who witness to Waldef's sanctity see Jocelin III: 41; VI: 76; VIII: 117. For conversi V: 71; VI: 74; VI: 85; VII: 96; VII: 99; VII: 100; VIII: 109 (probably); VIII: 112. Thomas Good, the cellarer, occurs in IV: 52, in connection with miracles associated with the relief of famine. In similar fashion Walter, *conversus hospitarius*, occurs in IV: 57 in connection with miraculous guests. Some insight into Waldef's relations with his conversi is given at V: 73 – sedebat Sanctus iste inter laïcos fratres dispertiens eis spirituales escas. . . . In contrast to these miracles those added by Jocelin for the period after 1170 are much more varied. Besides two monks of Melrose (IX: 128, 129) and two conversi (IX: 130, 131), the witnesses include a citizen of Roxburgh (IX: 124), two Englishmen (IX: 125), a *breviregulus* (IX: 127) and a clerk of Westmoreland (IX: 132). Compare R. B. Brooke's account of the canonisation of Francis in *Latin Biography*, ed T. A. Dorey (London 1967) pp 177–96, and see McFadden, p 7, 'the collective imagination of the monks (and especially of the *conversi*) together with the hagiographical lore and writer's vision of Jocelin have given flesh and blood to these noble precepts'.

in the extreme that Jocelin, for all his protestation, could have gained much first-hand information from the monks of Melrose about the events of half a century before, but it may well be that a dossier on Waldef still existed, and that Jocelin used it and supplemented it with the few miracles which he records from the period after 1170.

One final source may have been available to him. In the preface to the bollandist edition of Jocelin's *Life* the editors refer to the claim that, like Waldef, Everard was a man of recognised sanctity, and, unlike him, a man of learning: he is said to have written lives of Adamnan, Cumin the white and Waldef.[50] There is no proof of these assertions, and Everard's claim for inclusion in the calendar of the saints is rejected, but his composition of a life of Waldef is less questionable, and gains some support from Jocelin's own comment about the evidence made available to him by Everard in connection with the events of 1170.[51] Elsewhere in the *Life of Waldef* there are indications that Jocelin was using a written source, or sources, which he had imperfectly assimilated. If Everard did write such a life then it is more likely to have been available to Jocelin at Holmcultram than Melrose, for Everard had been abbot of the daughter house for nine years before Waldef's death,[52] and it is probable that, in outline, it would have resembled Jocelin's account – slight, vague and inaccurate for the Waldef's childhood, youth and period at Nostell: broadening out from his arrival at Kirkham. On balance, then, it may be suggested that Jocelin's *Life of Waldef* contains little that is Jocelin's. Its essential elements would seem to be the testimony, and perhaps a pre-existing *Life*, of Everard and a dossier of miracles associated with

---

[50] *AS* pp 246b–247.
[51] See above n 44.
[52] Holmcultram was founded in 1150. Everard died in 1192. On the basis of these dates it would have been possible for Jocelin to have met Everard as he appears to claim that he did (see above nn 42, 43) – though at least fifteen years before he was asked to write the *Life of Waldef*. I am inclined to think, however, that these two references to Everard occurred in the postulated dossier of 1170, and do not, therefore, relate to Jocelin. It is quite likely, however, that the brief account of Everard given after the notice of the foundation of Holmcultram (see above n 41), which records Everard's death, was added by Jocelin. Holmcultram was not far from Calder or its mother-house Furness, and Everard seems to have been active in the diocese of Carlisle during his long abbatiate. In this connection the presence of Hardred, abbot of Calder, at the exhumation of 1170 is interesting (see *HRH* p 129, where this reference is not noted). Everard must surely have been one of the other unnamed abbots present.

Some account of Holmcultram is given in G. E. Gilbanks, *Some Records of a Cistercian Abbey* (London n.d.). For the records of the house see *MA* V pp 593–619 and [G. R. C.] Davis, *Medieval Cartularies [of Great Britain]* (London 1958) pp 55–6 , with references there given.

an early, but unsuccessful, attempt to achieve canonisation. In addition it borrows from Bernard's *Life of Malachy*, and perhaps from the *Chronicle of Melrose*. For the period after 1170, with which Jocelin himself was particularly concerned, it has little to say and nothing important to add. For the period before Waldef became prior of Kirkham neither at first nor second hand is it a reliable source. Where then does this leave Waldef?

Contemporary references to Waldef are few, and, in general, uninformative. He is referred to twice by John of Hexham in connection with the York election dispute, and in various letters concerned with that dispute: none of these do more than refer to him as prior of Kirkham.[53] He appears as a witness in only two scottish royal charters. In the earlier, issued before the death of the queen in 1131, he is described as *filius Reginae*.[54] In the later, a charter of Malcolm IV, he witnesses as abbot of Melrose.[55] Bernard's *Life of Malachy* is marginally more informative, referring to Waldef as former prior of Kirkham, 'but now a monk and father of monks at Melrose, a monastery of our order'.[56] By far the most informative source is the *Chronicle of Melrose*, but its brief references are confined to his election and death, and the exhumations of 1170 and 1240.[57] What the *Chronicle of Melrose* does supply, however, are some firm dates, and there are very few of these in Waldef's history.[58] It is clear that he became abbot of Melrose in 1148 and that he died on 3 August 1159. As prior of Kirkham he was in Rome in connection with the York election dispute in early March 1143,[59] and he is referred to by John of

[53] John of Hexham s.a. 1142 and 1144. See the references in Knowles, 'Saint William', and in C. H. Talbot, 'New Documents in the Case of Saint William of York', *CHJ* 11, 1 (1950) pp 1–15.

[54] Lawrie p 69, no LXXXIII: in favour of the church of St John in the castle of Roxburgh. Lawrie gives a date of *c* 1128, but the outside limits seem to be early 1126–1131. Ascelin the archdeacon, who witnesses the charter, is known to have been archdeacon before 31 December 1126 (Lawrie pp 54–5, no LXV) and bishop John of Glasgow was in Rome in the winter of 1125/6. The movements of David I are not certainly known for this period, though he seems to have been in the south between September 1126 and March 1127 (Barrow, *Regesta* I p 113). Queen Maud died in 1131.

[55] Barrow, *Regesta* I, pp 190–1, no 128, dated 1157–9: in favour of the cistercian abbey of Warden.

[56] *Malachiae* p 342: vir nobilis secundum saeculum, Wallenus nomine, tunc Prior in Kyrkeham regularium fratrum nunc vero monachus et monachorum pater in Mailros, monasterio Ordinis nostri.

[57] See above nn 29, 31, 32.

[58] Even Jocelin can only date Waldef's election as abbot of Melrose *circa idem tempus* (III: 36, *AS* p 258b).

[59] 7 March 1143, see Talbot p 6; Baker, 'San Bernardo'.

Waldef of Melrose: legend and reality

Hexham as prior of Kirkham in 1141. At the time of Malachy's visit to York in late 1139 he held the same position. At some point between 1126 and 1131 he was at the court of David I. It is possible to be precise about nothing else and, in particular, his date of birth is not certainly known. In this connection there is, however, one interesting, if dubious, piece of evidence. The author of the *History* of the pseudo-Ingulph, which ends in 1091, in dealing with the execution of earl Waldef of Northumbria under the year 1075, referred to the subsequent history of his widow Judith, and the first marriage of his eldest daughter, Maud, to Simon I of Senlis. Of this marriage, he said, there were three children, Simon, Waldef and Matilda, 'all of whom are still children and below the age of marriage'.[60] Of the historical Ingulph, who seems to have died on 16 November 1109, Orderic Vitalis has something to say,[61] but of his so-called *History* Stevenson remarked over a century ago that it was 'interesting as a work of fiction, but on the whole valueless as a historical document'.[62] It may be as well, however, to reserve judgement on the comment about the children of Simon I of Senlis and Maud. Some historical sources underlie the fantasies of the pseudo-Ingulph, and what he has to say of this family is not in conflict with the little other evidence available. Earl Waldef of Northumbria married the Conqueror's niece Judith in 1072. He was imprisoned in late 1075 and executed on 31 May 1076. In due course the Conqueror pressed Judith to marry Simon I of Senlis, but on her continued refusal Simon was given the hand of her daughter Maud, then about twelve, and the earldom of Northampton. Simon I does not appear in Domesday Book, but does witness Rufus's grant of Bath to John of Tours in 1091 as 'Symon *comes*',[63] suggesting a date for his bethrothal and marriage to Maud of *c* 1087. Maud must have been about thirty-six when her first husband died at La *Charité-*sur-Loire in about 1111, and given her age at marriage it is more likely that the three children of the marriage were born in the last years of the eleventh century than in the first decade of the twelfth – though in the absence of precise information it is impossible to be certain.[64]

---

[60] Adhuc impuberes et infantiles. [*The Church Historians of England*, ed J.] Stevenson, II. 2 (London 1854) pp 565–725, at p 670. See nn 6, 64.

[61] See the references in *HRH* p 42.

[62] Stevenson p xxi, see nn 6, 64.

[63] See E. A. Freeman, *History of the Norman Conquest*, IV (2 ed, rev, Oxford 1876) pp 393 n 2, 601–3; H[*andbook of*] B[*ritish*] C[*hronology*], ed F. M. Powicke and E. B. Fryde (2 ed London 1961) p 432 n 2, referring to *RRAN* I, no 315.

[64] She died in 1131 at about the age of fifty-six, and must have been about forty when the

If, however, the possibility of Waldef's birth by *c* 1100 is accepted then a fresh approach to his early life becomes necessary, and the silence of the sources about him is more intelligible. At first sight it is remarkable that Ailred should make no mention whatsoever of Waldef, but if there was a difference of some ten years or more in their ages it becomes entirely understandable, and also helps to explain why Ailred, but not Waldef, should have been brought up with David's son Henry.[65] When his mother married again Waldef would have been an adolescent with little interest in, or perhaps aptitude for, the business and pastimes of the court of his step-father, whether as earl or king. His absence as a witness in the royal charters which survive stands in sharp contrast to the appearance of prince Henry as early as *c* 1120, when he could not have been more than six years old, and regularly thereafter.[66] Perhaps unfairly one has the impression that Jocelin of Furness made the best of a bad job with Waldef's time in

---

only child of her second marriage to earl David was born (see Ritchie p 252 and n). Ritchie (p 247 n 3) says of Waldef's elder brother Simon, that he 'must have been seven or eight years older than Ailred'. No evidence is given, and I have been unable to find any, either for this statement or that in *HBC* that he was 'born probably after 1103,' see pp 432, 440. See Ritchie pp 408–10, 435, for further discussion, partly hypothetical, of the chronology of Maud's life and the evidence for it. Both McFadden and Bulloch refer to the *four* children of the marriage of Maud and Simon I of Senlis. No authority is given, but the source is presumably Jocelin I: 9 – 'Matildis vero . . . cum pervenisset ad mundum, opportuno tempore illustrissimo comite de Huntedunia, scilicet seniori Simoni de Samhet nupsit; de quo votivo germine duos filios et filias edidit'. The existence of a second daughter is not otherwise known, and may be discounted. The *De Comitissa* simply remarks 'And in process of time earl Simon begot children by countess Matilda: – Simon, Waltheof, Matilda. Waltheof was afterwards the abbot of Melrose', quoted Anderson p 145.

McFadden (p 5) is of the opinon that Waldef was born 'shortly after the year 1100', while Bulloch, relying on Jocelin's statement that Waldef was still 'in puerili toga constituto' (I: 14) when his father died abroad and his mother married again, asserts that Waldef was still under sixteen *c* 1110–13.

[65] See Ailred, *Genealogia Regum Anglorum*, in R. Twysden, *Historiae Anglicanae Scriptores Decem* (London 1652) cols 347–70. To David he declares 'ab ineunte aetate mea impendisti' (col 350), and of Henry – Cum quo ab ipsis cunabulis vixi et puer cum puero crevi, cuius etiam adolescentiam adolescens agnovi, quem iuventutis flores pulsantem sicut patrem suum quem prae cunctis mortalibus dilexi, iam senile flore fulgentem ut Christo servirem corpore quidem set nunquam mente vel affectu reliqui (col 368). For Ailred's date of birth see Powicke, p xxxiv. It is not, perhaps, without significance that Jocelin's reference to Ailred's time at David's court reads simply 'a iuventute in curia regis David cum Henrico filio et eodem Waltheno nutritus et educatus'. (III: 32, *AS* p 258a).

[66] See Lawrie p 28 no XXXV, p 55 no LXV, p 59 no LXXII, pp 68–9 nos LXXXII–LXXXIII. It is in the last of these that Waldef makes his sole appearance in the reign of David I. See above nn 6, 27–8.

David's household.[67] Certainly, as late as 1126-31 he was still simply *filius Reginae*, and he never plays a comparable part to that of his elder brother Simon, or of Ailred and Henry in the developments of the second third of the twelfth century. Nor is there any evidence, other than Jocelin's *Life*, that David I intended him for the episcopate or that he had the capabilities to adminster a diocese at such a time of change and reorganisation in the Scottish church.[68] It is, moreover, quite likely that David had a hand in his move to Nostell, rather than being opposed to it,[69] though it is impossible to date either his entry into Nostell, or his promotion, to Kirkham with any accuracy. All that can be said, on the basis of the scanty evidence available, is that his rise within the ranks of the augustinians was remarkably quick. If, as is generally assumed, he was the close friend who arranged Ailred's visit to Rievaulx in *c* 1134, he may have been prior of Kirkham by that date. But this, too, is all assumption. Walter Daniel does not say it was the prior of Kirkham who guided Ailred, nor does he name the friend[70] – a remarkable omission if it was Waldef, whom he might have been expected to know as abbot of the daughter-house of Melrose, and a regular visitor to Rievaulx.[71]

Certainly Waldef was established as prior by the end of 1139 when Malachy visited York,[72] but in contrast to the heads of other

---

[67] See Jocelin I: 13-17, *AS* p 252.

[68] It is not easy to disentangle the chronology of the episcopate for these years, but David I may have had the opportunity to nominate to the sees of Aberdeen, Dunkeld, Moray and Ross. Certainly neither St Andrews nor Glasgow were open to him, see *HBC* pp 281-301. For recent studies of aspects of the policy of David I with regard to the Scottish church see [G. W. S.] Barrow, *The Kingdom [of the Scots]* (London 1973) pp 165-211.　　　[69] See below.

[70] See Powicke pp xi-xii, 10, 13-14. There are other candidates: See Nicholl's comments about Aethelwold (Aldulf) of Nostell, in York for his consecration as bishop of Carlisle on 6 August 1133 (pp 147-51), and Ritchie pp 230-3 for David's appeal to the northern English barons in 1134, and Espec's leading part in their response. Either of these could have occasioned Ailred's trip *in partes Eboraci civitatis*. There are, in any case, difficulties in Walter Daniel's account of this embassy. David had been an early benefactor of Rievaulx, as a letter of Bernard requesting assistance for the struggling community at Fountains records, and was to establish a daughter house at Melrose in 1136. It is difficult to believe that Ailred knew nothing of Rievaulx before he went to Thurstan, or that he needed permission from Thurstan to visit it when, as Daniel later indicates, his business with the archbishop must have been concluded. If, as is likely, Ailred had business with both Thurstan and Espec in 1134, then it would have been surprising if he had not visited Rievaulx en route. See Powicke pp 10-16, and compare Jocelin III: 34-5 (below n 78) for Waldef's apparent reaction to the cistercian life when he entered the order.

[71] For references to Waldef's visits to Rievaulx see Jocelin V: 67-70, *AS* p 265[b].

[72] See Jocelin's reference to his reorganisation of life at Kirkham–(II: 21, *AS* p 255[b]) Omnes

75

augustinian priories, or cistercian abbeys, established under archbishop Thurstan of York he seems to have played little part in affairs.[73]
After Thurstan's death he was early involved in the subsequent election
dispute, first as a candidate, then as one of the opponents of William
Fitzherbert.[74] There is no sign, however, that he played a leading role,
and it is noticeable that the so-called 'party of reform' never put him
forward as an alternative to Fitzherbert, and they included men who
knew him well.[75] At some point after his return from Rome in
mid-1143 he abandoned his charge, and entered the cistercian order,
apparently on the advice of Ailred, first at Warden and then at
Rievaulx. Once again, it is impossible to be sure when this occurred,[76]
but the references to abbot William of Rievaulx, who died on 2 August
1145, in Jocelin's *Life* make it likely that he spent some time at
Rievaulx under him.[77] At the most, however, only four years can
have elapsed before his election as abbot of Melrose in 1148, and these
were years disturbed by doubts, second thoughts, and distaste for the
cistercian life.[78] Not, it might seem, the most obvious and natural
recommendation for the abbacy of Melrose to which he succeeded in
1148.

There was, in fact, little to distinguish Waldef from the mass of his
contemporaries. He does not stand out as a leader, nor did he hit con-

---

bonas consuetudines et sacra instituta, quae in diversis ecclesiis Canonicorum tener
cognovit, velut in fasciculam collecta, in domo, cui praefuit, observari diligenter
instituit – and Dickinson pp 171-2. This activity may be connected with the foundation,
by William of Aumale, of the priory of Thornton from Kirkham at this time.

[73] See Nicholl *passim.*

[74] For some comment on this see Baker, '*Viri Religiosi*'.

[75] The most significant figure, perhaps, is Aethelwold, prior of Nostell and, from 1133,
bishop of Carlisle in plurality. His support of Henry Murdac's candidacy in the election
of 1147 may be contrasted with his failure to support, or to suggest, Waldef. See Baker,
'San Bernardo'; Nicholl pp 244-5 and, for the close relationship of the major
augustinian houses to the York chapter, *ibid* pp 128-30.

[76] Jocelin gives no indication of date, and there are none in other sources.

[77] Jocelin V: 67-70, AS pp 265b-6a . . . Nonne me agnoscis specialem amicum tuum
Wilhelmum, huius loci abbatem primum. . . . ante sepulcrum amantissimi sui
Wilhelmi abbatis. Waldef had been closely associated with William in the early stages
of the York election dispute, travelling with him to Rome in 1143.

[78] Jocelin III: 34-5, AS pp 258b-9a: cum venerabilis Walthenus in probatorio peregisset
aliquanti temporis spatium, antiquo serpente sibilante, Ordinis arrepti observantia
vertebatur illi in fastidium: videbatur ei cibus et potus insipidus, asper et vilis vestitus,
labor manualis durus, vigiliarum et psalmodiae gravis, ac totius Ordinis tenor nimis
austerus. Recogitans pristinos annos in Canonicatu vel Prioratu suo, persuasum in mente
habuit, institutiones illorum, licet leviores, discretioni tamen viciniores ac per hoc
salvandis animabus aptiores . . . ita ut Ordinem Cisterciensem deserere ac ad
Canonicatum reverti deliberasset.

temporary headlines.[79] What he did have, however, to assist him in a remarkable succession of preferment was family influence. The *Chronicle of Melrose* remarked, at his election in 1148, 'Waldef, brother of earl Henry of Northumbria and earl Simon of Northampton was made abbot', and in the brief notice of his death in 1159 commented that he was 'the uncle of king Malcolm [IV]'. The same emphasis is to be found in Bernard's *Life of Malachy* – Waldef is *vir nobilis secundum saeculum* – and, of course, in Jocelin's *Life*. William the Lion and the future Alexander II are left in no doubt that Jocelin's saintly subject is their kinsman, though it might have occurred to them that the relationship was both fortuitous and artificial.

It is possible to see the influence of his royal patron from the very beginning of Waldef's ecclesiastical career. Jocelin's account of Waldef's choice of Nostell as a place of refuge from David and his brother Simon, and of escape from the king's ambitious plans for him, is scarcely convincing even taken by itself,[80] and when Scottish connections with northern English churchmen, and with the priory of Nostell in particular, are examined it falls completely.[81] It was David's brother and predecessor, Alexander I, who was responsible for bringing the augustinians to Scotland, and the first community, which was established at Scone probably *c* 1120, was drawn from Nostell. Robert, the first prior of Scone, was appointed bishop of St Andrews by Alexander I in 1124, and it is almost certain that the grants made at this time to the church of St Andrews by the king in association with earl David were intended to establish a community of canons to serve the cathedral church.[82] In the event it was not until 1144 that this project was achieved by bishop Robert, at the instigation of king David and with the assistance of Athelwold, bishop of Carlisle as well

---

[79] See nn 53–6 above. John of Hexham, for example, paid considerable attention to scottish affairs, and to developments in the scottish church, but has nothing to say of Waldef – see his account of the designation of Malcolm the Maiden as heir to the scottish throne, and to his subsequent accession (s.a. 1153, 1154), and compare Jocelin's claim on Waldef's behalf.

[80] . . . deliberat attentius super qualitate religionis et loco. Timebat enim, ne forte, si infra regnum regis Scotiae vel infra terram comitis fratris sui in aliqua domo Religionis susciperetur, diutius ibi demorari non permitteretur, aut inde violenter extractus ad aliquod culmen honoris ecclesiastici etiam invitus promoveretur.

Haec ille mente pertractans, inspirante Spiritu sancto, salubre consilium invenit, exiensque de terra illa et cognatione sua, veniensque ad locum Nostiel vocabulo extra ditionem regis et comitis, in ecclesia S. Oswaldi regis et martyris, habitum Canonici suscepit (II: 18–19, *AS* p 255b).

[81] See Nicholl pp 128–50; Barrow, *The Kingdom* pp 170–87.

[82] See Barrow, *The Kingdom* pp 170–3.

77

as prior of Nostell, who sent a canon from Nostell to be first prior of St Andrews. David's establishment of other augustinian communities, and his relations with the regular canons, and other orders, have been well described by Barrow, and there is no need to repeat this account here. One further illustration of David's close connection with Athelwold may, however, be seen in the establishment of an arrouaisian community at Stirling (Cambuskenneth) c 1147, most probably as a result of the adoption of the arrouaisian observance for the cathedral priory of Carlisle c 1139.[83] It is clear, then, that there was a close association between David and the augustinians in general, and between David and Athelwold in particular. As in the archdiocese of York under the leadership of Thurstan, and in partnership with the local magnates, so in Scotland augustinian communities were founded to assist in the establishment of a regular observance and an organised ecclesiastical structure.[84] How close this partnership was can be most clearly seen in the north of England, where the inter-relation of benefactors and witnesses in the charters not only of regular canons but of monks is striking.[85] There, the dominant figure is Thurstan, though at least with the canons the process had begun before his time. In Scotland there can be no doubt that the key figure is David I.

There was, however, no clear divide between the two realms. As Powicke and others have made clear, basing their views on Ailred's comments,[86] the magnates of the north, whichever side of the border they were, shared a common culture, attitudes and interests. There were issues, both secular and ecclesiastical, which could be divisive, but for the most part these could be resolved by compromise, and in the end usually were.[87] In general, contacts were close and relations cordial, and there were few better examples of this than the career of Waldef. His entry into Nostell under prior Athelwold is likely to have been made at David's suggestion.[88] Trained there, he might, like the first priors of Scone and St Andrews, expect preferment in line with the influence and policies of his royal patron. His promotion seems to have been rapid. Sacrist at Nostell, he was elected prior of Walter

[83] *Ibid* pp 181–4; Dickinson pp 250–1; Nicholl pp 146–7.
[84] See Nicholl pp 111–50.
[85] *Ibid* pp 144–6.
[86] For example, Powicke pp xlv–xlvii; Nicholl pp 137–40; Ritchie pp 142–270.
[87] As, for example, with the battle of the Standard, where the compromise proposed before the battle by Balliol and Bruce was adopted after it, see Nicholl pp 224–31.
[88] See above p 75.

Espec's foundation at Kirkham, where Espec had retained the right of presentation.[89] It was probably from the same quarter that his candidacy for the see of York arose after Thurstan's death in 1140. So far, as Bernard implied,[90] there was nothing distinguished about him except his birth, and the stresses of the York election dispute showed up the inadequacy of his vocation. As a cistercian at Warden, his brother Simon's hostility towards him is probably best explained as antagonism to the protegé of the Scottish royal house, whose former earldom of Huntingdon he now held. Back at Rievaulx he was rescued by David, and elected abbot of Melrose after the rather dubious resignation, or deposition, of his predecessor, the first abbot, Richard.[91] If, towards the end of his life, he was proposed for the vacant see of St Andrews – and there is only Jocelin's statement that he was – it can only have been on the ground of status, not of ability.[92]

If Waldef's ecclesiastical career is to be related to the patronage and policies of David I, and was shaped by them, it is necessary to qualify the connection generally assumed between them. In the *Monastic Order in England* Knowles, referring to the family of saint Margaret of Scotland, said that Waldef came from 'a nursery of saints',[93] and associated him with the piety and spiritual qualities of the Scottish house. This, however, is not Waldef's line. He looks back to earl

[89] *York Minster Fasti II*, ed Sir Charles Clay, *YAS, RecS* 124 for 1958 (1959) pp 70–1.

[90] See above n 56.

[91] *The Chronicle of Melrose* says simply 'Ricardus primus abbas de Melros discessit', and later records 'obiit Ricardus quondam abbas de Malros apud Clara Vallem in conventu' (pp 73, 1148; 74, 1149). Jocelin (III: 36) is more circumstantial – Circa idem tempus Richardus primus abbas de Melros, quamquam in pluribus laudabilis, cum se ob impetum irae indomabilem, conventui exhiberet intolerabilem, iuste exabbas effectus, officio ac loco cessit (*AS* p 259a). It was suggested by Morton that Richard was removed by abbot William of Rievaulx (died 1145). If the abbot of Rievaulx did play a direct part in Richard's resignation or deposition in 1148 the abbot in question must have been Ailred. There is, however, no clear evidence that the abbot of Rievaulx was so directly involved. See J. Morton, *The Monastic Annals of Teviotdale* (Edinburgh 1832) p 202; *Mailros* p 74 n h. It is not clear what part king David played in these events. Jocelin refers briefly to the anger of the king at the deposition of abbot Richard, but Jocelin's purpose is to emphasise the immediate reconciliation consequent upon the succession of Waldef – 'prae ceteris illum [rex] dilexit, protexit, nihilque mali de viro suspicari voluit'. It is difficult to believe that the community acted, or were able to act, without consulting the king, or that Ailred, if he was involved, did not proceed with David's approval. Certainly, Jocelin's own account makes it clear that there were charges to rebut – 'haec breviter tetigi, ne quis sanctum Conventum de Melros super depositione illius abbatis vel aliorum tale quid promerentium accusare audeat'.

[92] See Jocelin VI: 79, *AS* p 267a.

[93] *MO* p 242.

Waldef of Northumbria, who may have achieved a spurious sanctity after his execution in 1076, but who is better, and more characteristically, known for the slaughter he planned in the course of an inherited family feud.[94] His grandmother, Judith, the Conqueror's niece, was accused in some quarters of conspiring to achieve her husband's death.[95] His father and elder brother, the two Simons of Senlis, were capable feudal magnates, well able to look after themselves in the turbulent politics of the time. There remains the shadowy figure of his mother, but whatever her influence the family as a whole shows few signs of sanctity.

This is not to deny that Waldef did possess spiritual qualities, but rather to suggest that he should be seen in more conventional style than the mirror of saint Margaret, in which he is usually viewed, seems to disclose. The hyperbole of Jocelin of Furness, the concern to associate him with the tradition of Margaret, and to compare him with Ailred, distort both the picture and the significance of Waldef. In the glimpses we catch of him dispensing spiritual sustenance to his conversi in familiar conversation; in the impression he made on Everard; in the affectionate stories remembered and told of him by the humbler members of his house; in his inability, perhaps disinclination, to take a leading part in affairs, we get close to the average temper of the time. There is a confused and struggling spirituality here which never achieved great things, but which demonstrated, nonetheless, a real and compassionate christian example in the local context of Melrose. The comparison that springs naturally to mind is not with Ailred, but with the later twelfth-century abbot of Fountains Ralph Haget, like Waldef a man of influential local connection, whose spiritual qualities were affectionately remembered by his community.[96]

Where Waldef differs from Haget is in the attempt made to canonise him, and in this the monks of Melrose were not exceptional. Two of those who feature most prominently in Waldef's career were canonised – Ailred in 1190, and William Fitzherbert in 1226 – while for others the claim was made but never, apparently, recognised: William, first abbot of Rievaulx, and Everard, first abbot of Holmcultram, spring to mind, and John of Hexham (s.a. 1141) asserts that

[94] For the most recent account, with full references, see B. Meehan, 'The siege of Durham, the battle of Carham and the cession of Lothian', *Scottish Historical Review* (forthcoming).

[95] See Ritchie pp 137–9.

[96] See Derek Baker, 'Heresy and learning in early cistercianism', *SCH* 9 (1972) pp 103–5, and the references there given.

Thurstan's body was found incorrupt when his tomb was opened some years after his death. Local cults were no new phenomenon in the twelfth century, and Waldef was certainly more acceptable than some candidates for sanctity discussed by Guibert of Nogent a century before.[97] Indeed, if the monks of Melrose wanted to establish their own domestic cult, whether in 1170 or 1206, they had singularly little choice: both the first and third abbots resigned, or were dismissed, under a cloud, and the seventh abbot also resigned. Of the remainder up to the tenth abbot, Patrick, who commissioned Jocelin's *Life*, and who himself only ruled for one year, two departed to bishoprics, one to the abbacy of the mother house of Rievaulx, and the other two ruled for only three and four years respectively.[98] Against this background it is easy to see why the customs of Furness declared that only those abbots who ruled for a decade and died as abbots would be commemorated as abbots of the house.[99]

By these standards Waldef has a right to be commemorated, but not as a calendared saint of the universal church. His interest, and his significance are local. His career illustrates, at every turn, how the structure of the medieval church was established in the marches of

[97] See Nicholl pp 237-8; Colin Morris, 'A critique of popular religion: Guibert of Nogent on *The Relics of the Saints*', *SCH* 8 (1972) pp 55-60.

[98] For the first abbot, Richard, see n 91 above. For the third abbot, William, see pp 67-8, 70 above: the *Chronicle of Melrose* says that *humiliter dimisit*, and that he was succeeded by the prior of Melrose, Joscelin, *ipso die* (22 April 1170). Joscelin himself became bishop of Glasgow in 1174, a charge he kept until his death on 17 March 1199: he died, and was buried, at Melrose. The seventh abbot, Reiner, former abbot of Kinlos, and 'our monk', resigned after five years as abbot (23 March 1189 – 17 September 1194). His successor, Radulphus, also an ex-abbot of Kinlos, also left the house, for the bishopric of Down, having ruled for eight years (18 September 1194-1202). The sixth abbot, Arnold, became abbot of the mother house of Rievaulx having ruled Melrose for ten years (6 January 1179 – 2 March 1189). Laurence, the fifth abbot, a former abbot in Orkney, and 'our monk', was, in the opinion of the *Chronicle of Melrose* 'vir mire humilitatis et mansuetudinis et in divinis litteris plurimum eruditus'. He ruled for only three years (21 May 1175-1178). William, the ninth abbot, was a former abbot of Cupar, and master of the conversi at Melrose: he ruled the house for four years (1202 – 8 June 1206). His successor, Patrick, the sub-prior of Melrose, who commissioned Jocelin's *Life*, survived only one year as abbot (1206-7). The next four abbots rule for only six, one, one and three years respectively. Not until the fifteenth abbot Adam, who ruled for twenty-six years (6 August 1219-1245) is there any continuity of rule.

[99] See *MA* 5, p 250, *De successione abbatum*: Est hic sciendum quod contra usum aliorum monasteriorum huiusmodi ordinis, observatur consuetudo in monasterio Furnesii solum illos nominare et pronunciare abbates in mortuario suo qui per decennium integrum rexerunt ante decessum eorum, et postmodum obierunt abbates, et sic ibidem non nominantur abbates qui etiam post decennium abbaciatus sui cesserunt vel depositi fuerunt, seu qui ante completum decennium sui regiminis obierunt. (fol 1ʳ). See Davis, *Medieval Cartularies* pp 48-9 for references to the records of the house.

western christendom in the twelfth century, and underlines the interaction of policy, interest, patronage, personal contact and, sometimes, ideal in this achievement. In this process, for all that Jocelin claims for him, Waldef does not rank high. Both at Kirkham and at Melrose his was a subordinate command – but a significant one. Without men like Waldef the 'ecclesiastical strategy' of a David or a Thurstan could not have been realised, and without the spiritual qualities and witness of men of his type, unexceptional though they may have been, the oppressive, demanding ideals of a Hildebrand or Bernard could not have been diffused into western society. Perhaps, after all, I should concur with Jocelin of Furness and the chronicler of Melrose, and agree, in local terms, that in making known the ways of God to man *vere hic homo Dei est*.

University of Edinburgh

FULK OF TOULOUSE:
THE ESCAPE THAT FAILED

by BRENDA BOLTON

E lo dozes sera Folquetz de   And the twelfth one will be Fulk of
Marseilla, us mercadairetz Marseille, a merchant of importance
que a fait un fol sagramen   Who made an oath so mad
quan juret que chansos no fetz And swore his songs no more to write
et anz dizon que fo per vetz   This seemed to all to be in true sincerity
qe·s perjuret son escien   When he so consciously forswore.[1]

This short piece of a contemporary troubadour's song makes a
suitable introduction to Fulk of Toulouse who was first a jongleur and
troubadour, a citizen and merchant and later in life a monk and bishop.
Underlying most of this varied career was a desire on Fulk's part to
retreat from the world in order to achieve the *vita apostolica*.

The father of Fulk Anfos was a genoese merchant who had settled
in Marseille and who had left his fortune to his son. When we first
hear of Fulk in 1178 he was established as a rich and highly respected
citizen, a married man and father of two sons.[2] In addition to this he
enjoyed a reputation as a successful troubadour throughout all the
courts of the midi especially so in the court of Marseille.[3] This
combination of merchant and troubadour was not unusual and indeed
reflected the relatively open society of southern France at this time.

Some understanding of what this society was like can be gained by
examining the songs and poetry of Fulk and other contemporary
troubadours.[4] It is now generally accepted that these poems did not

---

[1] The song was written by the monk of Montaudon. [S.] Stronski, [*Le troubadour*]
Folquet de Marseille (Cracow 1910) p 48*. This critical edition of Fulk's poetry contains
a short but valuable biographical study. Pages from this section are asterisked thus *
while the page references to his poetry have no asterisk.

[2] *Ibid* p 8*.

[3] This court was presided over by Raymond Geoffrey Barral one of the most powerful
lords of the midi. He was favourable to the troubadours and supported not only Fulk
but Peire Vidal. Bertran de Born thought sufficiently highly of Barral to address one
of his *sirventés* to him. *Ibid* pp 15*–18*.

[4] From the very considerable volume of literature on the troubadours I have drawn upon
H. Moller, 'The social causation of the courtly love complex', *Comparative Studies in
Society and History* 1 (The Hague 1958–9) pp 137–63; W. Powell Jones, 'The Jongleur

portray any personal love experiences. This concentration upon courtly love was a highly stylised method of expression which allowed them to show both a considerable depth of meaning and an emotional involvement in order to emphasise educational and moral uplift. Such poetry was presented at social gatherings and became an intrinsic part of the value system of a significant number of the secular upper classes. This relatively open society allowed a degree of upward mobility and led to an apparent masculinisation of the upper social layers. The consequent imbalance in the sex ratio was further aggravated by the desire to avoid hypogamy. Marriage was regarded as another means of social ascent. Thus the symbolic contents of this courtly love poetry expressed not only hopes of marrying upwards but also reflected the totally competitive way of life of the knightly class. The troubadours conceived of courtly love poetry as a method of indicating ethical and moral behaviour which they often linked with an idealistic participation in a crusade as a possible equivalent to a lady's service. The symbolism had different layers of meaning but there was a common element which may be seen as an anxiety regarding acceptance, assuaged by self-improvement and devoted service. Such attitudes are not uncommon in any society which allows upward mobility.

Fulk was familiar with all these pressures and his life as a troubadour revealed his attempts to come to terms with them. He composed many songs dealing with love and the crusades. Crusading indeed became the major preoccupation in his later poetry. He himself was already beginning to move away from the competitive world. One song written at the court of Marseille between 1188 and 1192 indicated his new train of thought for it showed that he was aware of the inability of money to provide happiness.

Que rix diz hom qu'ieu sui e que be·m vai	They claim that I am rich and in good health
mas cel quo diz no sap ges ben lo ver	But those who say this are hardly aware of the truth
que benanansa non pot hom aver	For happiness only results from what is pleasing to the heart

---

Troubadours of Provence' *PMLA* 46 (1931) pp 307–11; H. Davenson, *Les Troubadours* (Paris 1961) and [C.] Morris, *The Discovery of the Individual [1050–1200]* (1972) especially pp 107–20.

Fulk of Toulouse: the escape that failed

de nulla re mas d'aisso qu'al cor plai	So that a poor man who is contented has more
per que n'a mais us paubres s'es joyos	Than a rich man deprived of joy and constantly
q'us rix ses joi qu'es tot l'an cossiros	burdened by sad thoughts.[5]

The last song he wrote dealt with the crusade in Spain and appeared to be so much a call to arms that Fulk's provençal biographer refers to it as the preaching song (the *prezicansa*).[6] In this Fulk exhorted the poor no less than the rich to take the cross and maintained that their salvation would come through death for the christian faith. It was becoming evident that Fulk was ready to move away from this troubadour life. The activities and moralising of that life were not enough to overcome his growing distaste for a life based on material wealth. Neither was it enough to overcome his disillusionment with the life of the courts. He, like other merchants such as Valdes or Francis, had witnessed at first hand the inequalities between rich and poor. As a troubadour his close contact with the courts had enabled him to assess the real worth of the life in which he had played such an intimate part. He found himself expressing his personal *renovatio* through a commitment to asceticism with a growing emphasis on poverty. He came to hold the augustinian view that poverty meant happiness and realised that the surest way to achieve this was by entry into an order. He chose to enter the austere cistercian order which was the one most compatible with his views. In 1195 or 1196 he retired from the world, entering with his wife and two sons the abbey of Le Thoronet in Provence.[7]

By the time that Fulk had entered the order the cistercians had become the leading crusading agents of the papacy. Their specific function was to mount a missionary campaign 'to evangelise a restive populace and a dechristianised world'.[8] Although the order had been somewhat shaken by its early call to the apostolate, many cistercians played a prominent role in the second and third crusades. In spite

---

[5] Stronski, *Folquet de Marseille* p 7*, song 7 lines 5–10 p 36.

[6] *Ibid* p 88*, song 19 pp 83–6. This poem, preaching crusade against the infidel, was written after the battle of Alarcos in 1195 and the defeat of the cistercian military order of Calatrava. The provençal biographer writes 'en Folquetz de Marceilla qu'era molt amies del rei de castela si fes una prezicansa per conortar los baros e la bona gen que deguessan secorre al bon rei'. *Ibid* p 8. [7] *Ibid* p 89*.

[8] [M-D.] Chenu, *Nature, Man and Society [in the Twelfth Century]* (Chicago 1968) p 213. On the earlier attempt see R. I. Moore, 'St Bernard's Mission to the Languedoc in 1145', *BIHR* 48 (1974) pp 1–10.

of the bitterness engendered by these failures they were ready to embark on an attack upon heresy wherever it appeared. This attack was two-fold, an academic onslaught and a practical operation on both the geographical and spiritual frontiers of orthodoxy. In Languedoc, their recent mobilisation by the papacy against the cathars had presented them with their most severe challenge yet.[9] To preach and engage in debate with these erudite heretics was one reason why the order needed men of talent who could manipulate words. Another reason was that the laity at all levels were generally illiterate and so were incapable of reading the bible or any other text for themselves. They were listeners and not readers and communication came to them through preachers, poets, jongleurs and learned heretics.[10] The troubadours provided men with such talent in communicating and Fulk's conversion was only one example of successful cistercian proselytising amongst them.[11] Perhaps such proselytising was not too difficult. Morris has discussed some of the similarities of troubadours and cistercians and sees in them a common desire to make personal experience and personal relations the focus of life. 'While the poet looked for love to inspire all the virtues of "courtesy", the monk hoped to find in friendship a common mind in Christ. Finally the expression of longing common to both groups must be linked with the assiduous attempts at self-understanding'.[12]

The cistercian order had acquired a political character and it was not appropriate that Fulk should be allowed to remain long in his monastery. Thus on the eve of the albigensian crusade, he found himself thrust into the politics of crusade-preaching. In 1205 he was elected to the bishopric of Toulouse. He took possession of his see on 5 February 1206 [13] and so simultaneously became involved in the

[9] *PL* 215 (1855) cols 355–60; *Potthast* 1 no 2229. The bull *Et si nostri navicula* of 1204 confirmed the legation of Renier da Ponza, Guy, Peter de Castelnau, Raoul de Fontefroide and Arnald Amaury abbot of Cîteaux.

[10] H. Grundmann, 'Hérésies savantes et hérésies populaires au moyen âge', in [J.] Le Goff, *Hérésies et Sociétés [dans l'Europe pré-industrielle 11–18 siècles]*, École pratique des hautes études. *Civilisations et Sociétés*, 10 (Paris 1968) pp 209–14. Also C. Morris, *Medieval Media* (university of Southampton 1972) in which he discusses the use of the song as a way of expressing values and ideas, in particular the cultural media brought to bear upon Valdes who was himself converted after hearing a *jongleur* recount the story of saint Alexis.

[11] Hélinand of Fontefroide a former *trouvère* became an eminent cistercian preacher while Bernard of Ventadour and Bertran de Born both became monks in the same order. [12] Morris, *The Discovery of the Individual*, pp 117.

[13] [C.] Devic and [J.] Vaissète, *Histoire générale [de Languedoc]*, 6 (Toulouse 1879) p 244. Fulk took as his sermon for that day the parable of the sower.

business affairs of the diocese. For Fulk to be entrusted with such an important see as Toulouse with all its political, social and religious problems indicated the high opinion which the cistercian order had of his abilities. Fulk himself was not lacking in confidence. Through preaching he hoped to appeal to the intellect of the heretics and through an insistence on episcopal rights accompanied by an attack on usury he hoped to induce an acceptance of the orthodox view of wealth. The new diocese presented him with many problems. Contemporary chroniclers such as William de Puylaurens and Peter de Vaux Cernay stressed the major role which a large city such as Toulouse played in the diffusion of heresy.[14] More recent consideration has modified this view and Violante has demonstrated the importance of the *contado* as a vital factor in the growth of italian heresy.[15] It was not by chance that Toulouse at the beginning of the thirteenth century, when heresy there was making enough stir to attract outside intervention, was also attempting to conquer an italian-style *contado*.[16] Nevertheless the mobility and dynamism of urban life, the break with traditional groupings and religious structures which were either oppressive or inadequate, all created stresses and tensions for the urban dweller. In this situation heresy could flourish whether the need was religious or not. Wherever an heretical preacher appeared he became the mouthpiece for all those frustrations and discontents with which neither the priests nor the court of Toulouse could deal.[17]

As a cistercian bishop Fulk was well-placed to collaborate with the legates and missionaries of his order against the heretics. In 1207 an influx of preachers brought to Toulouse by the abbot of Cîteaux led to a transformation of evangelical strategy.[18] Languedoc was divided into districts which were then distributed among the principal preachers and supervised by a *magister*. Whilst the cistercians continued

[14] [William of] Puylaurens, *Cronica* ed Beyssier in 'Guillaume de Puylaurens et sa chronique' in *Troisièmes mélanges d'histoire du moyen âge*, ed A. Luchaire, Bibliothèque de la Faculté des Lettres de Paris, 18 (Paris 1904) pp 119–75. Peter de Vaux Cernay, *Petri Vallium Sarnau monachi Hystoria albigensis*, ed P. Guérin and E. Lyon, 3 vols (Paris 1926–39).

[15] C. Violante, 'Hérésies urbaines et hérésies rurales en Italie du 11e au 13e siècle' in Le Goff, *Hérésies et Sociétés*, pp 171–97.

[16] [J. H.] Mundy, *Liberty and Political Power [in Toulouse 1050–1200]* (New York 1954) p 68.

[17] For an interesting discussion of this question see the review article by R. I. Moore, 'The Test of Religious Truth', *Times Higher Educational Supplement* 141 (28 June 1974) p 13.

[18] [C.] Thouzellier, *Catharisme et valdéisme [en Languedoc à la fin du xiie et au début du xiiie siècle]* (2 ed Paris 1969) pp 199, 205.

their preaching and attempts at conversion, pope Innocent III had harnessed what he felt might be an effective new method of evangelism. He diverted Diego of Osma and Dominic to aid the preachers in Languedoc by the example of their austerity and by their skill in words.[19] In 1207 Fulk and Dominic preached together at Pamiers in a great debate between heretics and catholics. Fulk was so confident of the success of the debate that he asked a local knight why people in the area did not expel heretics from their lands. The knight replied that this would be impossible since the heretics lived among them, were numbered among their relations and were seen to be living lives of perfection.[20] The eloquence and example of poverty which Dominic and the cistercians displayed were successful in attracting to orthodoxy a group of vaudois led by Durand de Huesca but no cathars appeared to have been converted.[21] In 1208 Fulk and the legate Navarre, bishop of Couserans, were sent to Rome by the southern bishops to ask for help. After hearing their report and learning of the murder of Peter de Castelnau, Innocent proclaimed the crusade against the heretics. He also renewed the special powers granted to the cistercians in 1204 adding the absolute right to exterminate heresy.[22] Peaceful preaching for conversion alone seemed to have failed.

Fulk who had entered a cistercian monastery to escape from the world thus found himself increasingly involved in preaching the politics of the albigensian crusade.[23] Not only did Fulk preach the crusade in Languedoc with Arnald-Amaury, abbot of Cîteaux, but he also travelled three times through France. He reached Flanders on these preaching campaigns and secured valuable help by attracting men and by raising large sums of money.[24] Fulk's role as a crusade-preacher was obviously very important. He preached continually wherever he was and even accompanied the crusaders in battle. By now convinced

---

[19] *Ibid* pp 194–5; *PL* 215 (1855) cols 1024–5; C. Thouzellier, 'La pauvreté, arme contre l'Albigéisme, en 1206', *Révue de l'histoire de religions* 151 (Paris 1957) pp 79–92.

[20] Thouzellier, *Catharisme et valdéisme* p 203.

[21] *PL* 215 (1855) cols 1510–14.

[22] Thouzellier, *Catharisme et valdéisme* pp 204–12.

[23] Useful reprints and new works on the albigensian crusade include P. Belperron, *La Croisade contre les Albigeois 1209–1249* (Paris 1967); J. R. Strayer, *The Albigensian Crusades* (New York 1971); [W. L.] Wakefield, *Heresy, crusade and inquisition [in Southern France 1100–1250]* (1974).

[24] R. Lejeune, 'L'évêque de Toulouse, Foulquet de Marseille et la principauté de Liège', in *Mélanges Felix Rousseau* (Brussels 1958) pp 433–48. Fulk was in Liège in 1211 or 1212, again between January and September 1213 and finally in 1217.

of the usefulness of the crusade in extirpating heresy he supported Simon de Montfort and thus came to be regarded as his accomplice in those acts committed under the pretext of the crusade. Fulk was perhaps not happy with the way things had developed and in 1217 he asked Honorius III to allow him to resign his see and return to his monastery.[25] Honorius would not allow this.

Although politically Fulk had not been happy, there were other related aspects of his crusade-preaching which were more rewarding. On his visit to Flanders, Fulk had marvelled at the group of beguines centred on the new saint, Mary of Oignies, which he found in Liège.[26] His interest in religious women's communities as a bulwark against heresy had led him earlier to support Dominic's foundation at Prouille in his own diocese.[27] It was now at his request that Jacques de Vitry wrote the *Life of Mary*.[28] Mary's vision of the massacre of northern crusaders at Montgey and her strong desire to take the cross herself were, Fulk felt, useful both as a manifestation of contemporary sanctity and as an *exemplum* to be used when preaching against heretics in his own province.[29] Fulk's role as protector and friend of these groups of religious women was of considerable importance both to the women and to Fulk's self-satisfaction in the value of his preaching. Similarly this was so in regard to his support for Dominic's preachers.

His success in the business affairs of the diocese, concurrent with his attack on usury in Toulouse may also have been another factor in reconciling him to Honorius's refusal to relieve him of his office. When he entered his see in 1206 he was immediately forced to deal with business affairs in an attempt to recover both episcopal rights and associated revenues. The diocese of Toulouse, referred to as the 'dead diocese' by William de Puylaurens, was in a deplorable condition.[30] Even the able bishop Fulcrand (1179–1200) had been forced to live as a humble townsman because he could not enforce the

[25] Devic and Vaissète, *Histoire générale* 6 p 502.
[26] Mary of Oignies, the child of rich and respected parents, was married at the age of fourteen but later separated voluntarily from her husband to live in a cell at the augustinian priory of St Nicholas of Oignies in complete poverty. She became the focus of female piety in the diocese of Liège. See my article '*Mulieres Sanctae*', SCH 10 (1973) pp 77–97.
[27] Grundmann, pp 209–11. See also [M.-H.] Vicaire, *Saint Dominic [and his Times]* (trans by K. Pond London 1964) and *Saint Dominic en Languedoc, Cahiers de Fanjeaux* 1 (Toulouse 1966).
[28] *ASB* 5 (1867) pp 542–72.
[29] *Ibid* p 556.
[30] Puylaurens, *Cronica* ed Beyssier p 125.

payment of tithes due to the see.[31] Fulk's predecessor, Raymond de Rabastens, had encumbered most of the demesne to pay for several lawsuits and to make war on his vassal. The diocese was thus largely in pledge to creditors and Fulk's new treasury contained ninety-six sous. Nor dared he allow the episcopal mules to move outside to drink lest they should be seized for debt.[32]

We have seen that Fulk's emphasis on apostolic poverty had led him to become a cistercian, and he would not have been concerned for himself at the state of the diocesan finances. This is aptly indicated by Robert de Sorbon who reported that Fulk was so highly critical of those who sought to please and praise him at a feast arranged to perform his songs that he interrupted his meal to partake only of bread and water.[33] It is also said of him that he wore a hair shirt as a demonstration of his lack of concern for his own comfort.[34] Nevertheless, it was essential for the power and respect for the office of bishop that this impoverished situation be remedied. Although this was one of the greatest periods of public charity in Toulouse, the church seemed unable to retain the economic means to support its spiritual mission.[35] The value of rents was fast diminishing and few new gifts and donations were coming in. Secular clergy and bishops alike had lost much of their temporal jurisdiction and direct coercive power to the more recent orders as well as to the consuls. Previous bishops had lacked property and the power to reform. Fulk had been sent to Toulouse with the specific task of reforming and this he was determined to do. Because of the financial state of his diocese, Fulk had to decide whether or not to continue to use money obtained for the diocese from usurers.

Usury had always presented a problem to the church.[36] Usury, money lending and commerce raised problems of conscience for those who participated in these activities. The gap between new social

---

[31] *Ibid* p 125; Mundy, *Liberty and Political Power* p 81.   [32] *Ibid* p 82.

[33] Stronski, *Folquet de Marseille* p 112*.

[34] Vicaire, *Saint Dominic* p 387.

[35] J. H. Mundy, 'Charity and Social Work in Toulouse 1150–1250', *Traditio* 22 (1966) pp 203–87.

[36] [J. W.] Baldwin, *Masters, Princes and Merchants:* [*the social views of Peter the Chanter and his circle*], 2 vols (Princeton 1970); J. T. Noonan, *The Scholastic Analysis of Usury* (Cambridge, Mass., 1957) and B. M. Nelson, *The Idea of Usury: from tribal brotherhood to universal otherhood* (2 ed Chicago 1969). A recent article by B. H. Rosenwein and L. K. Little, 'Social Meaning in the Monastic and Mendicant Spiritualities' *Past and Present* 63 (1974) pp 4–33, especially pp 29–31 gives a useful indication of the ways in which justifications for usury were appearing at this time.

realities and orthodoxy fostered many anxieties and this was nowhere truer than when applied to advancing commercial activity. In Toulouse the problems posed by usury coincided with the growth of heresy but usury was not a feature of heresy alone.[37] The form of social structure here led to a weak social control in regard to individuals. This certainly stimulated heresy and no doubt fostered usury. The social frictions characteristic of the town were due to the rise of business and commercial elements and to an accompanying decline in the wealth and influence of patrician families. Some patricians felt themselves so threatened by this loss of wealth and political leadership that their orthodoxy was reinforced. Other patricians especially those from the countryside became heretics. This division is best shown by the Capitedenario family. Its urban branch was a pillar of the orthodox church while the rural knightly branch was heretical and produced at least one usurer.[38] Similar divisions occurred among the artisans, some being perennial enemies of usury and others heretical *textores*. While catharism permitted usury and did not prescribe poverty for believers, other heretical poverty movements represented a strong expiatory reaction against wealth usuriously acquired. Distinctions here are blurred and I can only stress again that usury was not a feature of heresy alone nor even a feature of all types of heresy. Many of the orthodox also indulged in usurious practices and if, in the view of Weber, usury is regarded as incompatible with brotherly love, it may have been this which decided whether or not usury was practised rather than the holding of orthodox or heretical beliefs.[39]

Fulk attributed the state of his lands in part to lax usury laws and certainly his remedies attempted to tighten them. Nevertheless he may have been more influenced in these remedies by the preaching campaign of Robert de Courçon against usury than by the impoverishment of his episcopal estates, although such an example would have been a telling content in his own preaching.[40] He created a tribunal of two judges to hear complaints and charges of usury. This tribunal, active until 1215, was empowered to force usurers to make restitution. It succeeded for example in condemning the deceased

[37] Mundy, *Liberty and Political Power* pp 74–9.
[38] *Ibid* p 290 n 18.
[39] M. Weber, *The Sociology of Religion* (4 ed 1971) pp 215–16.
[40] Baldwin, *Masters, Princes and Merchants* 1, pp 296–7. This preaching campaign was conducted in northern France but was widely supported in other areas.

and orthodox Pons David and forcing the hospitallers, his heirs, to give restitution to the guarantor of a loan.[41]

We know from the chronicler William de Puylaurens that Fulk established or renewed a confraternity devoted to the destruction of heresy and usury.[42] During a period of intense factional strife, this was the agency which more than anything else stimulated trouble in Toulouse. This white confraternity, partly patrician and partly popular, had power to enforce and render judgements against usurers. Its armed bands of righteous citizens excited by a wave of popular enthusiasm destroyed the houses and goods of well-known usurers but found very few heretics. In considering why this should be so, Mundy advances the view that it was a simple question of fear. Usurers would not dare to be heretics also.[43] It is certainly difficult to demonstrate any inherent link between heresy and usury from this experience in Toulouse. The evidence would seem to point to Fulk pursuing heretics and usurers as two separate concerns of his own. Although a rival black confraternity was set up in opposition by the bourg of Toulouse and was probably dominated by the new urban patriciate of commerce and real estate, any success it may have had is uncertain. Under the existing pressure against usury, interest agreements tended to disappear at least from notarial records and merchants trying to avoid open usury resorted instead to fictitious deals. In practice, therefore, and in spite of Fulk's opposition, usury continued in Toulouse although it was driven underground.[44] However the ecclesiastical attack on usury and the popular enthusiasm which accompanied it were the first signs of the rebirth of episcopal authority in Toulouse. This rebirth, and the fact that Fulk's position despite wartime reverses was much strengthened and his office revivified by the end of the albigensian crusade, were not exactly what he appeared to want for himself. This is clear from his attempt to return to the monastery in 1217. With Honorius's refusal to allow this, he turned his energies to what he hoped would be more peaceful, more permanent and more effective ways of destroying heresy. For example in 1229 he established the university of Toulouse in an attempt to defeat heresy by intellectual means.[45] Perhaps he retained his desire

[41] Mundy, *Liberty and Political Power* p 83.
[42] Puylaurens, *Cronica* ed Beyssier pp 131–2.
[43] Mundy, *Liberty and Political Power* p 79.
[44] J. H. Mundy, *Europe in the High Middle Ages 1150–1309* (1973) p 180.
[45] *Ibid* p 466.

to return to the monastery but this was not to be fulfilled. He died in office in 1231.[46]

Thus Fulk who had entered the cistercian order precisely to escape from the world found himself thrust into politics because of the political character which this order had acquired as the leading crusade agency of the papacy. He was also thrust into business affairs because of the necessity of dealing effectively with the financial needs of the episcopal estates of Toulouse. He had consistently and vigorously opposed heretics and usurers by his own methods, achieving some success especially in reviving the episcopal powers in which the office had been previously lacking. It is ironic that Fulk's retreat from the world should in fact have meant for him a greater involvement with society.

University of London
Westfield College

---

[46] Chronicle of William Pelhisson, printed in Wakefield, *Heresy, crusade and inquisition* p 210.

JUDICIUM DEI: THE SOCIAL AND POLITICAL SIGNIFICANCE OF THE ORDEAL IN THE ELEVENTH CENTURY

by COLIN MORRIS

'CHURCH, Society and Politics' is a theme of great importance, and for most of the history of the church christians have been aware of the distinction between these three areas of human activity. They have differed about their relationship, and in particular about the extent to which political action and social order ought to be controlled directly by the christian ethic, but it has been widely recognised that the conduct of government, for example, was a field which had its own special requirements and expertise, in which God's personal intervention would be neither expected nor welcomed. 'Aid from heaven', went one nineteenth-century comment, 'aid from heaven you may have by saying your prayers, but no angel will come to name the junior lords of the Treasury'.

In the early middle ages, before (let us say) the twelfth century, there was no such awareness of a clear distinction between religion, politics and society. The fact that they had no word equivalent to our 'politics' or 'state' is no mere semantic accident. They lacked the word because they lacked the concept, and they lacked the concept because they had no idea of a natural or human sphere which was exclusively under the care of men. The involvement of God and of other spiritual powers in the political and social order was taken for granted. Some aspects of this sacral society, as it is often called, have been closely studied in recent years, especially the divine nature of royal authority and the position of the saint as lord and protector of his local church working mysteriously in human affairs through the power of his relics. Perhaps an even more striking illustration of the routine way in which divine intervention was expected was the institution of the ordeal, for here we have an instance in which God's guidance was not merely hoped for; it was required for the normal administration of justice. Men were convinced that they could not run a system of justice without securing specific rulings from God. We are here at the opposite end of the spectrum from the 'man come of age' who is the dream of twentieth-century writers, and it may be of interest to study the impact upon society and politics of an institution so completely different from our own way of thinking.[1]

Ordeals were unknown in the judicial practice of the roman and christian world until the germanic invasions, but from the sixth century onwards their use was widespread in western Europe. In spite of many local variations they showed some important common features. From the beginning, the standard term was *iudicium* or *iudicium Dei*. This meant that there was no technical expression for an ordeal, as distinct from any act of judgement in general, and the meaning of *iudicium* is often determined by the context. In this respect latin practice apparently echoed the vernacular, for this used words cognate with modern german *Urteil*, judgement.[2] This choice of language expressed the position of the ordeal as the most solemn possible act of judgement. Germanic procedure was sadly defective in its means of trying an accusation unless there were actual eye-witnesses to the crime. The defendant was therefore allowed to purge himself by means of a solemn oath, with the aid of a number of oath-helpers. It might be, however, that this defence by oath was not available. There were many reasons why it could not be used, and they varied from one region to another: the refusal of the oath-helpers to swear; the grave or the private character of the crime; or (most commonly of all) the low social standing of the accused. Although the details varied, the principle remained the same: when a defendant could not prove his innocence by oath, he could resort to the ordeal, and thus call God to witness. Ivo of Chartres, although he was no friend of this procedure, nevertheless defined it exactly: 'We do not deny that sometimes it is necessary to resort to divine testimony when, after an ordinary accusation, human testimony is wholly lacking'.[3]

Faced with practices so alien to those of the roman past, churchmen characteristically reacted in two different directions. A minority

---

[1] A good survey, with abundant references to the older literature, is [H.] Nottarp, [*Gottesurteilsstudien*] (Munich 1956) and our particular theme is explored in C. Leitmaier, *Die Kirche und die Gottesurteile* (Vienna 1952). Relevant material is usefully collected by [P.] Browe, [*De Ordaliis*] (Rome 1932–3). I am indebted to my colleague, Dr Paul Hyams of Pembroke College, Oxford, for supplying helpful references and comments.

[2] Vernacular usage is not well evidenced before 1100, but we can find bavarian *urteil*, frisian *ordeel* and anglo-saxon *ordal*. It seems that only in England was there a special word for 'ordeal', for *ordal* definitely had this sense, and the latinised form *ordalium* can occasionally be found here (for references, see Nottarp pp 16–17).

[3] *PL* 162 (1889) col 258c.

rejected the ordeal as superstitious and irrational. The tradition of criticism of the ordeal, which was clearly evident in the carolingian period, is interesting, and is also important, because during the twelfth century the weight of the attack was to increase until the fourth lateran council in 1215 declared against the participation of clergy in the ordeal. This, however, is not our present subject, for I am more concerned with the way in which the ordeal, as a living institution, operated in society and in political life. For this purpose the eleventh century is a good period to choose, because there is little sign of hostility to the ordeal until the very end, when Ivo of Chartres can be found expressing his reservations in a series of letters. It would be wrong to say that there was at this time no scepticism on the part of laymen or disquiet among scholars. William Rufus made clear, in a few well-chosen words, what he thought of the judgement of God when it freed a group of men accused of forest offences, and his views may (or may not) have found an echo among other free-thinkers.[4] In more respectable circles there is an important letter of Alexander II which roundly condemned judgement by cold water or hot iron as a 'popular practice (*lex*) devoid of canonical sanction', a view which may well indicate that the revival of canon law in gregorian circles had already produced some reservations about the ordeal as early as the ten-sixties, for in many of the older canonical collections ordeals were ignored, and had in one or two important earlier decretals been condemned.[5] But Alexander's comment remained an isolated one in that century, and it can fairly be said that the spirit of the eleventh century remained that of the carolingian capitulary: 'All shall believe without doubt the judgement of God'.[6]

The eleventh-century church accepted the ordeal as a normal part of judicial procedure, and at this point it is necessary to say something, however briefly, about the proofs employed in these ordeals. If we look at Europe as a whole, there was great variety, and some were frankly macabre, like the earth-ordeal in which the accused was buried alive for three days with a breathing-pipe in his mouth.[7]

---

[4] Ad hoc quoque lapsus est, ut Dei iudicio incredulus fieret iniustitiaeque illud arguens, Deum aut facta hominum ignorare aut aequitatis ea lance nolle pensare astrueret. Eadmer, *Historia Novorum* 2, PL 159 (1903) col 412c.

[5] PL 146 (1884) col 1406d. The absence of the ordeal from, or its condemnation in, the older collections was a major influence on the critics of the system from Ivo of Chartres onwards.

[6] ut omnes iuditium Dei credant absque dubitatione. *MGH, Leges* 2, 1 (1883) p 150.

[7] Evidenced in a Worcester manuscript of *c* 1025. F. Liebermann, 'Ein Ordal des Lebendig-Begraben', *ZRG, GA*, 19 (1898) p 140.

Certain procedures, however, became very common, and it is worth noticing what these were.

First, there was a group of trials by fire, in which the customer, if he may be so described, had to handle hot objects without being burned. He carried a hot piece of iron nine paces; retrieved a small object from a cauldron of hot water; or (less commonly) walked barefoot over nine ploughshares which had been heated in the fire. The hand or foot was then bound up and sealed to prevent interference, and the injuries were examined after three days. It seems that there were conventions about how long the iron and the water should be heated, and although hot, they were not impossibly so. Our one solitary source of statistical information, a hungarian register of the early thirteenth century, indicates that of those carrying the hot iron about half were found unburnt on inspection.[8]

Another common practice was immersion in cold water. The proband, bound and secured by a rope, was lowered into water, and declared innocent if he sank a specified distance, indicated by a knot on the rope.

A third, and quite different type, was the *duellum*, an ordeal by battle, favoured by the aristocracy and in disputes over land, but also fought with inferior arms to settle disputes among the peasantry.

All of these were accepted by the clergy as normal procedures. There were indeed reservations about the judicial duel, but it was frequently used by the clergy, especially in France, where several cases may be found in the eleventh century of monasteries who defended their rights in a duel fought by champions. Even Alexander II authorised his deputy in the bishopric of Lucca, which he retained while he was pope, to defend the rights of the bishopric by judicial combat.[9] Acceptance of this social practice did not mean, however, that the church fully sanctioned it as a part of its own practices. The oath by the combatants was taken in church, and they were encouraged to prepare themselves by confession and communion, but the weapons were not normally blessed, and clergy were not expected to participate in the combat. By the same token this ordeal

---

[8] [*Regestrum de*] *Varad*, printed S. L. Endlicher, *Rerum Hungaricarum Monumenta Arpadiana* (Sangalli 1849) pp 640–742, and discussed by R. Dareste, *Études d'histoire du droit* (Paris 1889) I, pp 259–64.

[9] res supradicti episcopatus per bellum et omnibus modis requirendi et excutiendi (Browe I, no 16). In this context *bellum* must mean judicial combat, in spite of the view of B. Schwentner, 'Die Stellung der Kirche zum Zweikampf', *Theologische Quartalschrift* III (Munich 1930) p 205n.

was rarely used in the decision of spiritual causes, although one must note one spectacular exception, when two champions fought a battle in 1077 to decide whether the roman rite should replace the mozarabic one in Spain.[10] On the whole, therefore, the process of sacralisation of the judicial duel was far from complete, and I do not intend to discuss it in detail. This, it must be confessed, is a large omission, because the warrior aristocracy looked to battle as the most obvious way of obtaining a *iudicium Dei*. It would, however, take us beyond the limits of our proper theme and would involve the re-examination of contemporary attitudes to warfare, and for this reason I propose to concentrate on the other ordeals, which were more completely taken into the life of the church.

For in these the hierarchy had gone far beyond their acceptance as a social institution, and saw them as means by which God's will was declared to men. Several distinctively christian ordeals had been devised. These either had been wholly developed within the tradition of the church, or were germanic ones adopted for sacred purposes. Thus the authenticity of relics could be tested by placing them in a fire.[11] A strange procedure occurring quite frequently in the liturgies of the time was trial by bread and cheese, in which the proband was required to swallow a large piece of bread and hard cheese. (A modern commentator has remarked, somewhat unnecessarily, that cream cheese would be unsuitable for use in this ordeal). Communion itself became an ordeal, a practice especially common in the tenth and eleventh centuries, and undoubtedly encouraged by the words of saint Paul: 'Let a man examine himself, and so eat of the bread and drink of the cup. For any one who eats and drinks without discerning the body eats and drinks judgement upon himself.' (1 Cor. 11, 28–9). Guilt might be shown by failing to swallow the consecrated elements, or by falling ill afterwards.

[10] The evidence for this duel and for the (probably legendary) ordeal by fire which is said to have followed, is discussed by P. David 'L'abolition du rite hispanique', *Études historiques sur la Galice et le Portugal* (Lisbon/Paris 1947) pp 400–2, and by R. Hitchcock, 'El rito hispánico, las ordalías y los mozárabes en el reinado de Alfonso VI', *Estudios Orientales* 8 (Colegio de México 1973) pp 19–41.

[11] Instances are given by [A.] Franz [*Die Kirchlichen Benediktionen im Mittelalter*] (Freiburg 1909) 2, pp 347–9. Examples in our period are the use of fire by abbot Gauzlin of Fleury in 1013 to test the *sudarium* of Christ—*Vita Gauzlini*, ed R-H Bautier (Paris 1969) p 60; the trial of relics of the anglo-saxon saints by abbot Walter of Evesham on the advice of archbishop Lanfranc—*Chronicon Abbatiae de Evesham*, *RS* 29 (1863) p 323; and the trial of the holy lance and of Peter Bartholomew with it, on the first crusade.

Besides sponsoring ordeals of its own, the church provided rituals for those in most common use, other than the duel. Such *ordines* were apparently introduced in the carolingian period, and are widely found in the eleventh century.[12] In them we see the ordeal fully christianised and brought within the ceremonial of the church. The ordeal was preceded by three days of fasting, and its liturgy took the form of a mass with special litanies, psalms and lections. The proband, having been exhorted not to go ahead unless he were innocent, made his communion, with the special formula of administration: *Corpus Domini nostri Iesu Christi fiat tibi hodie ad probationem.* The elements required were exorcised and blessed, and the ordeal itself was supervised by the clergy. The extent to which the whole thing was ecclesiastically controlled is vividly shown in two illustrations in a codex originating at Lambach early in the twelfth century, in which the position of the priest, blessing the ordeal, is very evident.[13] Everything was done to reinforce the religious character of the ceremony. The proband was given holy water to drink. The proof by hot iron was largely confined to cathedrals and greater churches and often took place inside the church itself. In 1082 the abbot of Saint-Wandrille of Rouen was put to the embarrassment of asking the archbishop of Rouen to consecrate a new ordeal iron because one of the monks 'out of ignorance and a certain simplicity' had transformed the old one to other uses.[14] The tools for the ordeal were supervised with the same care and jealousy as the sacred chrism itself.

These rituals give us a good idea of the theology which lay behind the ordeals. Men's confidence in them rested on their belief in the justice of God. This was the theme expressed in psalms and antiphons: *Iustus es, Domine, et rectum iudicium tuum.* The spirit is summed up in an English *ordo* of the tenth century 'Let there be no other speech there, except assiduous prayer to God the Father Almighty, that he should deign to manifest his truth'.[15] The true fulfilment of the ordeal came on those occasions when the truth was manifested in a complete

---

[12] The best edition of the *ordines iudiciorum Die* is that by [K.] Zeumer, [*MGH, Leges 5*] (1886) pp 599–725. Further material may be found in Franz 2, pp 307–98. Doubt has recently been expressed whether or not these liturgies were still in use. See W. Dürig, 'Gottesurteile im Bereich des Benediktinerklosters Weihenstephan (Freising) unter Abt Erchanger (1082–96)', *Archiv für Liturgiewissenschaft* 15 (Munich 1973) pp 101–7. I am not, however, convinced by the evidence that the ordeal had become a purely popular custom, unblessed by the ritual of the church.

[13] Zeumer p 672.

[14] Ed F. Lot, *Bibliothèque de l'École des Hautes Études* 204 (Paris 1913) pp 87–90.

[15] Zeumer p 711; Browe 2, no 5.

and marvellous way. Such a case was the dispute over the possession of certain vineyards, between the convent of Saint Mary, Angers, and a group of nearby nobles, who were represented in the ordeal by one of their men, Hernald. The judgement by hot water took place in the cathedral of Angers:

> Almighty God . . . made manifest by an appropriate judgement that they were claiming the vineyards unjustly. Mass was celebrated, and the aforesaid Hernald received communion of the body and blood, and took the usual oath upon the relics of the saints. He was thereupon deprived of the sight of his eyes, so that he could scarcely find his way to the cauldron into which he had to put his hand, as he subsequently told all those who were there. When he took his hand out again from the hot water, he confessed that he had been burned, not only on the hand, but inwardly to the very heart, and his sponsors, the aforesaid claimants, were obliged . . . to acknowledge their fault. When he was asked to let his hand be bound and sealed in the normal way, he said that he could not bear anything to touch his hand because of the pain. His hand was therefore left bare until the third day, when it proved to be swollen up, scalded and completely septic. Thus by divine power truth was shown forth and falsehood overthrown and the holy convent retained the vineyards which were justly theirs.[16]

If we ask by what mechanism this judgement was thought to operate, we encounter almost complete silence. The explanations which occur most readily to modern men are likely to be wrong. The ordeal was not designed (like the modern lie-detector) to discover if the accused was self-consciously guilty, nor was it a test of fortitude in face of pain. These aspects were rarely mentioned at the time, and in any case the the ordeal was frequently taken by a deputy. The assumption was that guilt was actually present, even in a deputy who might have come in good faith, and that it was almost physically embodied in him. As a twelfth-century glossator explained in another context, 'those things which concern the right are implanted in their bones, and are so attached to them that they cannot be separated from their bones'.[17]

[16] Browe 2, no 43. Other marvels are to be found in the narratives, especially in those connected with Leo IX discussed later. In 1172 a heretic was found burned by the ordeal of hot iron, not only on the right hand, but all over his body, *Annales Colonienses, MGH, SS*, 17 (1861) pp 784–5.

[17] E. Genzmer, 'Quare Glossatorum', *Gedächtnisschrift für E. Seckel, Abhandlungen aus der Berliner juristischen Fakultät* 4 (Berlin 1927) p 49, no 147.

This guilt could be discovered by God, as a litmus-paper will distinguish acid or alkali, through the holy communion, the sanctified water and the consecrated iron. That is why poor Hernald was burned to his very heart, and why it was so important to use physical means which had been properly sanctified. In the bread and cheese rituals, for example, the proband had a cross at his head and feet, and a prayer was written on the bread. It was *crustum panis carmine infectum*.[18] The explanation was exceedingly primitive, but it was the best they had achieved.

Contemporaries were well aware that something might go wrong with the ordeal, but they were not worried (or only a little worried) by the possibility of fraud in our sense. A more serious danger was that spiritual or magical powers might disrupt the course of justice. This was the way people tried to cheat, so that it was found that one accused, before picking up the hot iron, had taken the consecrated host out of his mouth and put it in his hand.[19] In particular, the prayers in the *ordines* were directed towards driving away Satan from any interference: 'I adjure thee, mighty dragon, ancient serpent, by the word of truth . . . that thy devices may impose no impediment, but that the right judgement of God may be set forth'.[20] It has recently been observed that, in a society which had no proper procedure of inquest and little capacity to use written proofs, the use of ordeals can be seen, if not as rational, at least as wholly understandable.[21] One might add that in a world populated not only by men but also by the malice of demons and the threat of malign and invisible powers, there is something heroic about this steady determination to appeal to the justice which could be found only with God:

> From this peril, if he is not guilty, deliver him, Lord.
> From the deceits of the devil, deliver him, Lord.
> From all witchcraft and magic arts, deliver him, Lord.
> For the trial of this affair, we beseech thee, hear us.
> That iniquity may not overcome justice, we beseech thee, hear us . . .[22]

---

[18] Cited from an eleventh–century french manuscript by H. Brunner, *Deutsche Rechtsgeschichte*, 2 (2 ed Munich/Leipzig 1928) p 544n.   [19] *Varad* no 332, p 723.

[20] Zeumer pp 697–8. Compare the oath of Liprand at Milan in 1103: Ego ad fiduciam maleficii, aut incantationis vel carminis non intro hoc iudicium, sic me Deus adjuvet, et ista sancta Evangelia in isto sancto iudicio: Landulf Junior, [*Historia Mediolanensis*] cap 10, PL 173 (1895) col 1466c.

[21] R. V. Colman, 'Reason and Unreason in early medieval Law", *Journal of Interdisciplinary History* 4 (1974) pp 571–91.   [22] Zeumer p 615.

Judicium Dei

Since the ordeal offered an appeal to the judgement of God, it was potentially important in public affairs, for it was by no means confined to exclusively judicial matters. By this means, men could seek to justify their actions or submit others to examination, and it was especially appropriate to the needs of great religio-political movements such as the gregorian reform and investiture contest. It is understandable that historians have paid only limited attention to the part played by ordeals in advancing the papal reform movement. The sustained theological and political arguments are of more interest to the historians of thought, and are very much better preserved. It would, however, be rash to conclude that trials by ordeal were unimportant to the men of the age, and enough material survives to give us some glimpse of the ordeal as a mode of political action and religious propaganda. That is not to say that its use was specially encouraged by the papacy. On the contrary, there is some slight evidence that the gregorians felt some reserves about it. It was, as we shall see, the resort of the enthusiastic and the perplexed in circumstances of particular tension.

It had a significant place in the initiation of the papal reform. The work of Leo IX rested in part, no doubt, upon legislation to remedy the ills of the church, but contemporaries were still more impressed by the charismatic leadership displayed on Leo's travels in 1049–51. His was a ministry consisting in the consecration of great churches, the humbling of prominent offenders, and the proclamation of God's judgement against simony. Udalric, provost of Rheims, later described the impression made on him by Leo's visit there:

> He admonished those who were present about the heresy of simony and the ministry of the church . . . and utterly terrified them. Then I and certain other colleagues, terrified by so great a threat of judgement, returned our offices to archbishop Guy, lest we should incur the divine vengeance which the lord pope was announcing.[23]

This proclamation of the *iudicium Dei* upon sinners was supported by miracles, by ordeals and by tests of guilt closely similar to the conventional ordeals. At the council of Mainz bishop Sibicho of Speier undertook to defend himself by the communion-ordeal, *terrifico sacramento Dominici corporis*. He not only failed, but his jaw was paralysed for the rest of his life. The *Vita Leonis* drew the moral: 'It is a fearful thing to fall into the hands of the living God'.[24] Bruno of

[23] *PL* 150 (1880) col 1547c.
[24] *Vita Leonis* 2, 5, *PL* 143 (1880) col 493b. This is the only source to report the miracle.

Segni tells how the pope required another accused bishop to purge himself by reciting the *Gloria Patri*, but as he was a simoniac his tongue failed him, and he was unable to pronounce the name of the Holy Spirit. This particular story became a favourite at the time, but was usually assigned, not to Leo himself, but to Hildebrand as papal legate in Gaul.[25] God's judgement was often manifested by his interventions in legal proceedings. At Rome, the bishop of Sutri defended himself with an oath with compurgators, and sensationally collapsed on the spot; at Rheims, the advocates of bishop Hugh of Langres found they were unable to speak a word.[26] The pope's opponents also called down God's verdict against themselves. Bishop Nizo of Freising, exasperated by Leo's policy in the dispute between Rome and Ravenna pointed to his own throat and said: 'May this throat be cut by a sword if I do not get you deposed from the papal dignity'. At that moment he felt a terrible pain in his throat, and died within three days.[27] Not all of these instances, as I have tried to make clear, were ordeals in the strict sense, but they were very close: *iudicia Dei* making manifest guilt or innocence by a clear outward sign, in a way which would appear compelling to an ordeal-minded age. One cannot say with confidence what was the factual basis of these stories, but it is interesting to observe that they were circulating among those close to the papacy and were being used to strengthen their resolve and to warn others against simony. Leo succeeded in integrating the ordeal into his spectacular proclamation of the judgement of God upon sinners, and perhaps only this could have opened the door to an effective campaign for reform. As later cases were to show, it was virtually impossible to prove simony against an accused who defended himself stubbornly, and the atmosphere of enthusiasm and divine intervention generated by Leo IX was exactly what was needed to initiate the papal reform.[28] Perhaps, we may speculate frivolously, Leo had ordeals in his blood, for his father and mother had taken the ordeal of cold water to ensure that they had paid their tithes in full.[29]

[25] W. Berschin, *Bonizo von Sutri* (Berlin/New York 1972) p 96n.
[26] *Vita Leonis* 2, 4, col 492c.
[27] *Ibid* 2, 7, col 495b.
[28] Compare the words of the priest Liprand before undergoing ordeal by fire at Milan in 1103: Nonne ille diabolus, qui suasit illum fieri simoniacum per pecuniam suadere potest ut adhuc majorem pecuniam daret, et veritatem occultaret et testes et judices mundanos mihi auferret? et non nescitis quia propter vitandam astutiam diaboli et pravorum hominum, ego elegi Deum judicem, qui neque per pecuniam, neque aliquo modo potest falli in iudicio? Landulf Junior, cap 10, col 1464c.
[29] *Vita Leonis* 1, 2, cols 467–8.

Judicium Dei

Our next example once again shows the ordeal being used in the service of enthusiasts against the entrenched interest of simony, but this time the circumstances are very different.[30] We are dealing with a local crisis, which had wide implications for the church at large. On the death of pope Nicholas II in 1061, he was succeeded in his original bishopric of Florence by Peter Mezzabarba. Peter was a Pavian, and a sympathiser with the imperialist pope Cadalus, but it seems that at first he was readily received at Florence. Near the city, however, were several vallombrosan houses, whose founder John Gualbert was a passionate opponent of simony. He laid extreme stress on the personal holiness required of priests, and held that no one should minister at the altar if he had been ordained by a simoniac, even if he himself had paid nothing.[31] The vallombrosans now accused bishop Peter of having obtained the see by simony. There followed at Florence a time of troubles not unlike the paterine disturbances in the much larger city of Milan. The monks persuaded considerable numbers of inhabitants to avoid any contact with the bishop, to the extent of giving up penance and communion, for fear of being contaminated by simony. The bishop's officers attempted to suppress the activity of the monks within the city, but their efforts merely aroused popular fury, and caused the vallombrosans to be regarded as martyrs. In the meantime, pope Alexander II, with the assistance of Peter Damian, was attempting to settle the dispute. The events of 1067–8 were so embarrassing to later writers, like Berthold, that they felt obliged to change them, but it is possible to reconstruct the main elements without too much uncertainty. It was probably at the lenten synod in 1067 that the reformers asked for a papal judgement against the bishop, and offered to prove their case by the most dramatic possible ordeal: walking through fire. They may well have had the support of Hildebrand, but Alexander II was not impressed. Although he had sympathies with the milanese reform, he always championed an orderly and legal procedure, and he refused either to depose bishop Peter or to authorise the ordeal by fire.[32] By this time, feelings at Florence were growing very intense, and in February 1068 there was a major tumult, with the populace shouting that Christ had been driven out of Florence. The

---

[30] For the following section, see the discussions by G. Miccoli, *Pietro Igneo* (Rome 1960) and [E.] Werner, [*Pauperes Christi*] (Leipzig 1956) pp 101–10.

[31] Andreas, [*Vita Gualberti*] cap 24, *MGH, SS*, 30, 2 (1934) p 1086.

[32] Andreas cap 73, p 1095: favebat enim maxima pars episcoporum parti Petri et omnes pene erant monachis adversi.

reformers decided that the chance had come to hold the ordeal, even without papal permission.

It was conducted on 13 February 1068 at San Salvatore a Settimo, in the presence of a huge crowd, and a vallombrosan monk Peter was appointed to walk through the fire. He later deservedly acquired the nickname Igneus. The liturgy for the ordeal was constructed so as to stress the vallombrosan position. It began with a litany for deliverance from simony, and after Peter had said mass, another monk addressed the people.

> Brothers and sisters, we are doing this, as God is our witness, for the salvation of your souls, so that henceforth you may be safe from the leprosy of simony, which has now contaminated almost the whole world. And you know that the contagion of this leprosy is so great that in comparison with its enormity, other crimes are almost nothing.[33]

The language of leprosy and contagion were well chosen to express the belief that simony is more than an individual sin, and contaminates the religion of all those who have any dealings with simoniacs. The emotional atmosphere was made even more tense when the crowd was asked how long Peter should stay in the flames for the proof to be complete. They replied that it was sufficient for him to walk through them. When Peter entered the fire, carrying a cross, the two piles of wood were blazing fiercely, so that the narrow path between them was filled with flames; he was in effect walking on fire and the flames were entering his clothing. Nevertheless, he emerged at the other side completely unscathed.

There is a tendency among modern scholars to treat the ordeal by fire at Florence as a disgraceful piece of fraudulent showmanship.[34] It is true that, in reading any narrative of an ordeal, the twentieth-century observer must keep in mind the probability of exaggeration and the possibility of fraud, but I see no grounds for being particularly suspicious about this occasion, and to treat the whole episode as a deception distracts attention from the real importance. It is a fascinating example of the politics of enthusiasm. The vallombrosans saw the situation as a desperate one, for the whole life of the city was being corrupted by the presence of a simoniac bishop, they themselves were being harried by his officers, and the pope—who did not share

---

[33] *Ibid* cap 75, p 1098.
[34] Werner p 106: Die ganze Zeremonie des Feuerwerkes war ein übles Bubenstück, aufgebaut auf Trug und der Leichtgläubigkeit der Zuschauer.

their more extreme views about simony—was not disposed to take action. In the circumstances, they appealed to God in the most spectacular way possible, and persisted with the ordeal even after Alexander II had refused it. There is certainly conscious management in the staging of the ordeal, but it was directed to inculcating the truth as the reformers saw it—the corrosive evil of simony, their own role as God's agents in the salvation of the people of Florence. The appeal to the *iudicium Dei* was a great success. Bishop Peter was at once expelled by the populace, and at the lenten synod in 1068 his deposition was proclaimed. It is a striking instance of the decisive power of an ordeal which, formally speaking, should never have been held at all.

The advent of the division between Gregory VII and Henry IV opened a different area for the use of ordeals: the direct question, which was right, the pope or the king? Lampert of Hersfeld has the story that after the reconciliation at Canossa, Gregory celebrated mass 'as a proof of his innocence'. He also offered the sacrament to Henry, who declined this ordeal, pleading that he was not properly prepared.[35] This needs to be regarded with scepticism, at least as far as Henry is concerned, because other sources specifically say that on this occasion he communicated with the pope. Nevertheless, the *Annals* of Berthold preserve another story from 1077 which makes it clear that the communion-ordeal was sometimes used for this purpose.[36] Bishop Embricho of Augsburg had joined Rudolf of Suabia, and then returned to Henry IV. He resolved to receive communion at Ulm 'as a proof and judgement (*iudicium*) of this, that the cause of his lord king Henry was just, and Rudolf's completely unjust.' However, he fell ill almost immediately and died shortly afterwards, thus demonstrating that the *iudicium Dei* was in favour of Rudolf. It is worth noticing that we have here an instance of attempting to arrive at the truth by ordeal before the pope had given his ruling on the merit of the two claimants.

There is no certain evidence about the attitude of Gregory VII himself to the judicial ordeal. He undoubtedly believed, however, that God manifested his judgements visibly in this world, and that one could prove from the events of history the rightness of one's cause.

---

[35] Ecce corpus dominicum, quod sumpturus ero, in experimentum hodie fiat innocentiae meae, ut omnipotens Deus suo me hodie iudicio vel absolvat obiecti criminis suspicione, si innocens sum, vel subitanea interimat morte, si reus, *MGH, SS,* 5 (1844) pp 259–60.
[36] *Ibid* pp 295–6.

Bonizo of Sutri tells us that, after excommunicating Henry IV in 1080, Gregory added: 'Let it be known to all of you that, if he has not repented by the feast of Saint Peter, he will have died or been deposed. If that has not happened, you ought to believe me no more'. Bonizo was obliged to explain that the reference was to Henry's spiritual death, as the pope's prophecy had apparently not been fulfilled, but he admitted that 'the stupid people did not understand the matter correctly'.[36a] In this belief Gregory unquestionably stood in the reformed tradition. Already in 1059 the papal election decree had threatened that those who broke its terms would suffer penalties in this life, and Peter Damian in 1062 had threatened Cadalus of Parma (the anti-pope Honorius II) with death within a year.[36b] This is not the ordeal as defined in germanic law, but theologically it is very little different. At least in cases of exceptional and special importance, God will make his *iudicium* evident and thus make plain who are his friends and enemies.

There is preserved in British Museum MS Arundel 390 a fragmentary description of a curious ordeal conducted on the orders of Gregory VII, apparently in 1083.[37] 'There are those', the writer remarks disapprovingly, 'who carried out an ordeal (*fecerunt iudicium*) about empire and papacy, but God, who is most merciful and faithful, provided what is just'. Abbot Desiderius of Monte Cassino supervised the ordeal, along with other important gregorians, on the instructions of the pope, by submitting a boy to the judgement of cold water. When the question was asked if the king had justice on his side, the boy disconcertingly sank, thus proving Henry to be right. After an unseemly wrangle about whether one of the party was pushing the boy under, they tried again with the same result. They then reversed the question: whereupon he floated instead, and vigorous attempts to push him down were unsuccessful. The group was finally reduced to taking an oath to keep the whole thing secret. This narrative is, to put it mildly, tendentious, for it shows a group of papalists, not merely failing to secure a favourable response from the ordeal, but going to ridiculous and even blasphemous lengths to cook the result. Yet one cannot escape the suspicion that there is some reality some-

[36a] Bonizo, *Liber ad Amicum* 9, MGH Lib 1 (Hanover 1891) pp 616–17. Bonizo is vague about the date, but circumstantial evidence fixes it in 1080 rather than 1076, and this is confirmed in the *Chronicle* of Sigebert. In view of Bonizo's comments there can be no doubt that this prophecy actually was delivered, and was widely known.

[36b] Peter Damian, *ep* 1, 20, PL 144 (1892) col 247b.

[37] Printed MGH, SS, 8 (1848) pp 460–1n.

where behind the propaganda. The narrative is nearly contemporary, probably excerpted from a letter, and it is circumstantial about dates and places. Moreover 1083 is a significant date, for at this time the solidarity of the papal supporters was beginning to give way to questioning and uneasiness. It would be characteristic of poor abbot Desiderius, who did not appear to good effect during this crisis in the papal fortunes, if he had tried to help with an ordeal and got the wrong answer.

The death of Gregory VII did not see the end of the use of ordeals in the investiture contest. Under Paschal II, for instance, we hear of one by hot iron which demonstrated the validity of orders conferred by bishops in the obedience of Clement III,[38] and of another by fire at Milan in 1103 which is in many ways similar to the triumph of Petrus Igneus at Florence.[39] Undoubtedly, too, there were many references to *iudicia Dei* of which we have no record—how many we can only guess, for the indications are ambiguous on this point. Perhaps enough has been said, however, to permit ourselves to widen our view and attempt some general conclusions.

If we look at the religious and political life of western Europe generally it is interesting to find that recourse to ordeals follows the lines which we have observed in the papal reform movement. It is natural that they occur in connection with political charges or accusations. The story went, for instance (although the facts are in doubt) that earl Godwin had cleared himself by ordeal of complicity in the death of the Confessor's brother. The ordeal was also used, again as in the investiture contest, at moments of crisis so acute that resolution was possible in no other way: the mozarabic liturgy in Spain, and the career of Peter Bartholomew on the first crusade, are examples of this. We must also remind ourselves of what has been left out so far. The natural way for kings and princes to seek the judgement of God was in battle, and there are examples where this was clearly and consciously being done. The hungarian campaign of Henry III in 1044 was at least written up after the event as a formal invocation of the judgement of God, and duke William and his followers saw the victory at Hastings in the same light. In the eleventh century, therefore, men did not merely use the ordeal for solemn judicial purposes. In political crises they also looked for the *iudicium Dei*, by battle, or by

[38] Reported in a letter of bishop Peter of Pavia to Henry IV preserved in the Codex Udalrici, ed P. Jaffé, *Monumenta Bambergensia, Bibliotheca Rerum Germanicarum* 5 (Berlin 1869) p 196.   [39] Landulf Junior, cap 11, cols 1462–6.

ritual, or by some appointed test. Yet this was an age which was beginning to be a little more critical and more open to change than earlier centuries had been. How does one account, then, for its remarkable attachment to the ordeal?

In the whole range of its uses, the function of the ordeal was to reveal the truth and to resolve perplexity. Is this man guilty of theft? Is this bishop guilty of simony? Is Henry the lawful king? Is Clement the rightful pope? Paradoxically, the very forces of change threw them back more heavily upon the old practices. Wider issues were now at stake, and much larger areas of society were involved in them. Some of the political or religious questions which we have seen going to the ordeal would not have been asked in the tenth century, and others would not have been anything like as acute or as controversial. As perplexities increased, the value of the accepted way of resolving them did not diminish. One can indeed go further than that, for the ordeal had a special value in an age of increasing change. It provided an appeal to God against the authority of the established order. Just as in the courts ordeals were especially the defence of the unfree, so in politics they could be used as the weapon of the innovator or of the weaker party: by Leo IX against the rooted position of the great regional churches, by the florentine reformers against even the papacy itself, by Peter Bartholomew when the princes and public opinion turned against him. These appeals to the ordeal by no means guaranteed success, but for men who were coming to believe that Christ is the Truth and not the Custom, it was important to have available this hot line to the divine judgement. Absurdly archaic as they seem to us, ordeals were by no means a wholly conservative force in the eleventh century.

They can only be understood as part of that world-view which it is fashionable to call romanesque. This was not an age of utility and management, but one in which man was caught up in a cosmic conflict among unseen forces: God against the devil, sacraments against magic arts, Simon Peter against Simon Magus. In this world of great issues and great perils, every man needed a protector, and to protect the innocent from injustice, God made known his judgement in the sacred rituals. After all, He always made Himself known to men: as Gregory VII remarked (or quoted) 'nothing happens on earth without a reason';[40] and the ordeals were God's special guarantee that justice would not fail to be done on earth.

[40] *Das Register Gregors VII*, ed E. Caspar, *MGH, Epp* 4, 2 (2 ed Berlin 1955) ep VIII 9, p 527.

Judicium Dei

As we approach 1100 the sacral status of the ordeals still seems unchallenged. It may be that there was criticism which remained unrecorded, but before Ivo of Chartres we know of almost none. It was around 1100 that a critique began which first removed the ordeals from the tribunals of the church, and then, in just over a century, led to the total withdrawal of clerical participation in them. It was to be one more sign of the ending of the sacral society; but that is another story, and one which cannot occupy us here.

University of Southampton

ECCLESIASTICAL ATTITUDES
TO NOVELTY *c.* 1100 – *c.* 1250

by BERYL SMALLEY

NOVELTY in this paper refers to a new idea or institution. I shall not distinguish between religious, social and political novelties, since medieval churchmen did not do so. The church concerned herself with every aspect of christian life: any change in men's way of living affected her either directly or indirectly and generally the former.

I shall begin by quoting four examples of attitudes to novelty. My first two come from the late eleventh and early twelfth centuries. One will illustrate an attitude to new ideas, the second to a new institution. The distinction is artificial, but convenient. Men normally think up ideas in order to justify or criticise institutions. First listen to an anonymous opponent of Manegold of Lautenbach. Manegold contributed an extremist theory to papal polemic in the gregorian reform movement in order to explain and justify Gregory's action in declaring the emperor Henry IV deposed and absolving subjects from their oath of allegiance (1085). His opponent cries:

O nova lex, O dogma novum, noviter fabricatum![1]

This anonymous imperialist uses 'new' as a smear word. Manegold's doctrine is *bad*, just because it is *new*. The phrase 'new and unheard of' rings through anti-gregorian polemic from the beginning of the investiture contest. My second example is hackneyed, but irresistible. The monk Guibert of Nogent describes how the townsmen of Laon rebelled against their bishop and attempted to set up a commune. Guibert calls 'commune'

> a new and detestable name for an arrangement whereby the people pay the customary head tax, which they owe their lords as a servile due, in a lump sum once a year; . . . and all other financial exactions which are customarily imposed on serfs are completely abolished.[2]

---

[1] *MGH Lib de lit,* 1, p 431. On Manegold see W. Hartmann, *Manegold von Lautenbach Liber contra Wolfhelmum, MGH Quellen zur Geistesgeschichte des Mittelalters* 8 (1972) pp 11–14; K. J. Leyser, 'The Polemics of the Papal Revolution', *Trends in Medieval Political Thought,* ed B. Smalley (Oxford 1965) pp 47–51.

[2] *De vita sua* iii, 7; trans by J. F. Benton, *Self and Society in Medieval France* (New York 1970) p 167. Guibert was born 1065 (?) and died *c* 1125.

Guibert sums up the conservative reaction to the communal movement in northern France in his own excited way. Here again, *new* means *bad*.

Passing to the mid-thirteenth century, I shall illustrate an attitude to new ideas from a sequence in honour of St Francis of Assisi, ascribed to friar Thomas of Celano, who died soon after 1260. The saint is praised for his novelty:

> Novus ordo, nova vita
> Mundo surgit inaudita.[3]

The words 'new and unheard of' here denote good instead of bad. Next comes Robert Grosseteste bishop of Lincoln, defending his mode of visiting his diocese at the curia at Lyons in 1250. His inquisitorial method of detecting abuses had raised a storm of protest. Such inquisition was 'new and unaccustomed', its victims complained. Grosseteste justified his reform programme to the pope and cardinals as follows:

> Every new measure which plants, fosters and perfects the new man, and which harms and destroys the old, is a blessed novelty, wholly pleasing to him who came in order to renew the old man by his own newness.[4]

The text of St. Paul, *to put off the old man . . . and put on the new* (Eph. iv, 22–24) underlies the argument. Grosseteste claims that any measure of ecclesiastical discipline which aims at correcting and improving fallen man will be pleasing to God, however novel it may be. He went on to the corollary: any measure which was not framed to achieve this end came from the devil. His strong language amounts to a provocative rephrasing of the canon law maxim that custom, however old and venerable, must give way to truth, as defined by the church.[5] The bishop assumed that Innocent IV and his cardinals would agree with his view that new institutions to promote reform came from God, while obstruction on grounds of custom was devilish.

---

[3] *Analecta Franciscana* 10, p 402.

[4] . . . Quibus ego respondi: Omne novum, quod novum hominem instituit, promovet et consummat, veterem hominem corrumpit et destruit, benedictum novum est et omnino acceptum ei qui veterem hominem venit sua novitate renovare. See S. Gieben, 'Robert Grosseteste at the Papal Curia, Lyons, 1250. Edition of the Documents', *Collectanea Franciscana* 41 (1971) p 376. On Grosseteste's visitations see J. H. Srawley, 'Grosseteste's Administration of the Diocese of Lincoln', *Robert Grosseteste Bishop and Scholar*, ed D. A. Callus (Oxford 1955) pp 151–5; on royal objections to his procedure see F. M. Powicke, *The Thirteenth Century* (Oxford 1953) pp 454–6.

[5] See especially G. B. Ladner, 'Two Gregorian Letters', *Studi Gregoriani* 5 (1956) pp 225–42.

Ecclesiastical attitudes to novelty

An emotional change has come about in some hundred and fifty years. *New* has ceased to be a dirty word. It may carry the sense of 'improvement'; in that case it is praiseworthy. God has changed sides; he is no longer safely conservative. The picture obviously needs shading. I have made it look too black and white. In the first place, defence of novelty began in the first stages of gregorian polemic. Gregory VII had two lines of defence for his policies: he was making no new decrees, but was merely repeating what had been ordered by the holy canons and the holy fathers; alternatively, he could devise new measures to correct new abuses by virtue of his authority as vicar of St Peter. But shading does not hide the contrast. The innovator defends himself as best he can. The burden of proof lies on him. His best line of defence is an appeal to the good old days before abuses arose. 'Novelty' looks better if he presents it as having been 'heard of' in the past. It is not his fault that wicked men have forgotten it in the present.[6]

My shading pencil goes to work again on the thirteenth-century welcome to novelty. Conservatives still attacked changes which struck them as 'new and unaccustomed', especially if the changes hurt vested interests. The new orders of mendicant friars ran the gauntlet of such attack. They undertook duties prescribed for both canons and monks, instead of obeying the statutes of the fathers, who allocated these duties to separate religious orders. So a bolognese rhetor complained about 1226, echoing a common criticism.[7] The antimendicant polemic led by William of St Amour in the fifties turned largely on the question of novelties in religion introduced by the friars.[8] But shading sets off the contrast again. The champions of novelty have moved from defence to attack. They glory in novelty and have no idea of sneaking it in under cover of a mere return to the past. The very concept of return to the past was presented differently. St Francis and his sons imitated Christ; but their imitation was novel, because no christian, not even the greatest saint, had ever set about it in the franciscan way. If they misread the past, they did so to stress their novelty, not to excuse it. St Bonaventure, among many other arguments, chose to defend the friars along lines similar to Grosseteste's apology for his inquisitorial procedure on visitations. In *De septem donis Spiritus sancti* (1268) Bonaventure answered the objection that

[6] *Ibid* pp 221–4 and the same author's *The Idea of Reform* (Cambridge, Mass., 1959).
[7] Quoted by J. Koudelka, 'Notes pour servir à l'histoire de S. Dominique II', *Archivum Fratrum Praedicatorum* 43 (1973) p 27.
[8] [M.-M.] Dufeuil, [*Guillaume de Saint-Amour et la polémique universitaire Parisienne 1250–1259*] (Paris 1972).

BERYL SMALLEY

mendicant religion was 'fictitious and of new institution'; we might translate the phrase as 'new-fangled'. He did not dispute the charge, not here at least, but held that however 'fictitious and new' it might be, the order was good, since it led men to follow Christ. That was found compatible with the view that the franciscan rule or way of life was not something new, but a renewal.[9]

A novelty could now be judged on its merits, instead of being 'presumed guilty'. How account for the change? The pace of events imposed it. Unprecedented phenomena sprang up like mushrooms. To observe is to evaluate, especially for men whose interests are affected and who have been trained to moralise. In some cases the novelty was accepted tacitly without any acknowledged *volte face*. No cleric to my knowledge stated that the communal movement was 'a good thing after all'. But towns gained privileges and became more or less self-governing corporations, with or without bloodshed, so extensively that communes and *bonnes villes* turned into a fact of life. A moralist like Stephen of Tournai complained that townsmen abused their privileges; he did not urge that the privileges should be withdrawn. Theologians and civil and canon lawyers settled down to analyse and classify the various kinds of corporations and 'universities' which they observed. Their studies were objective, penetrating and realistic, as the late Pierre Michaud-Quantin has shown in his book on thirteenth-century notions of *universitas*. The college, commune and *studium* ceased to be novelties to schoolmen; they were now data to be examined.[10]

Other new movements had such obvious usefulness for the regulation of christendom that their momentum could hardly be put into question. No member of society could escape the impact of canon law, least of all the lawyers who studied and helped to make it. The development had critics. St Bernard deplored the amount of legal business, which, as he thought, prevented the pope from attending to the more important duty of pastoral care. But even his reproach to Eugenius III in his *De consideratione* admits that the pope could do little

[9] *Opera* 5 (Quaracchi 1891) p 492: Dicit 'ordo fictitius est, de novo institutus . . .' . . . Carissimi! quantumcumque sit ordo fictitius et novus, est tamen bonus . . . *Ibid* 8 (1898) p 393, *Expositio super Regulam*: . . . Non est ergo haec Regula aut vita nova res, sed procul dubio renovata . . .
On the authorship of the *Expositio* see now S. Clasen, 'Bonaventuras Expositio super regulam Fratrum Minorum', *S. Bonaventura 1274–1974* (Grottaferrata, Rome, 1974) 1, pp 531–70, where the contested ascription to Bonaventure is rejected in Bonaventure's favour.
[10] *Universitas, expressions du mouvement communautaire dans le moyen âge latin* (Paris 1970).

Ecclesiastical attitudes to novelty

more than try to control the flood of appeals to Rome; there was no stopping them from coming in.[11] Canon lawyers were not allergic to the charge of novelty. Their work immunised them. No amount of *concordantia discordantium canonum* could cover up their innovations. A recent study of the twelfth-century canonists' attitude to the early church as a standard of righteousness has shown that they were well aware of its distance from the contemporary church. They saw many divergencies in discipline and in permitted practices from the arrangements of the early christians as described in the new testament. Changing times required new measures to meet new needs. Canonists did not feel guilty on that account.[12] Untroubled by nostalgia for the past, they saw the church as an expanding concern. Canon law was a growth industry, beneficial to christendom in general and to themselves in particular.

Heresy posed a new problem to defenders of novelty, and forced them to apologise. They had to find reasons for what canonists took for granted. Heretics, the waldensians in the forefront, reproached catholics for having departed from the customs of the early church. The wealth of the medieval church had brought abuses, laxity, litigation and a host of rules and practices which had no authority in scripture. An obvious answer to the sectaries' charge was *Tu quoque:* they, too, made new regulations for their members. It was true, since every religious organisation has to make rules to guide its faithful and keep them up to scratch. But the pendant to *Tu quoque* is that two blacks do not make a white. Catholic apologists went further and defended innovation as wholesome and God-given. I shall quote from two anti-heretical treatises to illustrate the type of argument put forward and to show how defence of novelty gained in depth and assurance. Neither of my writers was original in his ecclesiology. The interesting point is the way they deployed their arguments.

Master Prepositinus of Cremona (or Pseudo-Prepositinus; the authorship is still disputed) wrote probably in the early years of the thirteenth century. He met the heretics' objection: 'Ecclesiastical institutions are superfluous; Christians are bound to obey the ten commandments and the faith of Christ only, and not the institutions of men.'[13] Prepositinus answered that Christ's guidance to his church

[11] *S. Bernardi Opera* 3 ed J. Lerclercq and H. M. Rochais (Rome 1963) pp 435–9.
[12] G. Olsen, 'The Idea of the *Ecclesia Primitiva* in the Writings of the Twelfth-Century Canonists', *Traditio* 25 (1969) pp 61–86.
[13] *The Summa contra Haereticos ascribed to Praepositinus of Cremona*, ed J. N. Garvin and J. A. Corbett (Notre Dame, Indiana, 1958) pp 158–63. The chapter heading *Contra*

was a continuous process. He left his commandments to us in the gospels; he commanded other things through the apostles, and he now commands other things through the church. Taking a leaf from the canonists' book, the writer points out that masters in the schools recognise changes when they say: 'This *decretum* has been abolished, or its force is altered by the sequel or by a custom contrary to it.' He then makes a distinction between the various types of commandment. Ecclesiastical institutions are not precisely additions to the gospels; they prepare us to understand God's commands and to follow them more easily. The church of today fills in details, as though a master should order a servant to cross the sea and leave it to a friend to tell him when and where, and what provision to make for his journey. Prepositinus makes a far-reaching claim when he quotes the text: *He who is not with me is against me* (Mk. 9, 39). Therefore, what is not against Christ must be for him. In this light he interprets the role of doctors and prelates, who supply what the apostles failed to make plain when the church orders christendom by the revelation of the Holy Spirit. He allowed them a wide scope indeed. To put his view in modern language, he contrasted the static church of the sectaries with the dynamic church of the catholics; ecclesiastical institutions grow out of their originals by a healthy drive for survival.

The dominican inquisitor, Moneta of Cremona, working in Milan, wrote his *Adversus Catharos et Valdensienses* in 1241 or perhaps some ten years later.[14] He offers us a bolder sweep of history. The church has had a continuous existence since the time of Abel. Moneta uses this traditional theme against the heretics skilfully. A church which exists throughout time must necessarily change with the times. She has passed from the law of nature, through the written law to the law of grace. Continuity must include innovation. The jews themselves made good additions to their institutions, as when the Rechabites were established and when David recruited singers for divine service. We read in their *Acts* that the apostles altered some arrangements of the early church. How much more then must the church of today add her quota to the long history of changes, divinely ordained? Current

---

Passaginos is mistaken, since the *Passagini* believed in the obligation to keep both the Old and the New Law. On anti-heretical tracts *c*1185–1200 see C. Thouzellier, *Catharisme et Valdéisme en Languedoc à la fin du XIIe et au début du XIIIe siècle* (2 ed Louvain/Paris 1969) pp 49–129.

[14] G. Schmitz-Valckenberg, *Grundlehren katharischer Sekten des 13 Jahrhunderts* (Munich 1971) p 4.

abuses do not justify the heretics' action in leaving the church. Abuses simply show the other side of the coin; they are part of the church's history from the beginning. Moneta has absorbed innovation into his *Heilsgeschichte*.[15]

The sharpest polemic on innovation in the twelfth century centred on the rise of new religious orders. These proliferated: there were white monks, black and white canons regular, military orders and hermits, living singly or in groups. Traditionalists, including black monks and secular clergy, attacked their novelties; the innovators defended themselves. A satirical poem by a secular canon of Chartres called Pain Bolotin provides a forceful example of attack; Pain wrote *c*1121–36 (?). He criticised hermits in particular, but all the new religious orders were *visés*. His poem strikes a sinister apocalyptic note, anticipating the anti-mendicant polemic of William of St Amour. 'We all know this novelty in religion,' he writes: 'We cannot doubt that false hermits presage the coming of Doomsday, when we see so many religious monstrosities arise.' The four horsemen of the apocalypse signify the four types of enemies of the church: pagans, persecutors, heretics and finally hypocrites. Pain interpreted the 'pale horse' as presaging hypocrites and identified them with hermits and other self-righteous innovators. Hence novelty is not only bad in itself; it prophesies something worse, that is the coming of Antichrist; the new orders make ready for him.[16]

Most of the combatants in the battle of words had to wage a war on two fronts. The black monks, traditionalist as they were, had to defend themselves against the secular clergy. The latter objected to the priesthood of monks plus their right to minister to the people outside the monastery and to take tithes.[17] The priesthood of monks was nothing new in the twelfth century; but it came under fiercer fire than formerly. It was certainly novel if one took the *Rule* of St Benedict as a standard. The early monks had not received holy orders, as opponents of monastic priesthood were quick to point out. The black monks therefore had to defend the change in their status. On the other hand, they attacked innovators such as the cistercians, since the stricter religious orders showed up the black monks' decline from their

[15] *Adversus Catharos et Valdensienses* (Rome 1743) pp 408, 443, 446.
[16] J. Leclercq, 'Le poème de Payen Bolotin contre les faux hermites', *Revue Bénédictine* 48 (1958) pp 52–68; see especially pp 74, 84, 81.
[17] On the whole subject see G. Constable, *Monastic Tithes and their Origins to the Twelfth Century* (Cambridge 1964) and M. Chibnall, 'Monks and Pastoral Work' *JEH* 18 (1967) pp 165–71.

early standards. The canons regular had to meet attacks from both the secular clergy and black and white monks combined. Philip of Harvengt, abbot of Bonne Espérance, a house of praemonstratensian (white) canons, put it neatly when he wrote about 1158 that black and white monks quarrelled with one another, only to join forces against canons regular.[18]

The polemic gives us a birdseye view of changing attitudes to novelty. The first and commonest line of argument was to outbid tradition by seeking to prove that what looked novel really went back to antiquity. The combatants ransacked the old and new testaments for precedents. Success in finding them obviated the charge of novelty; failure would leave one's flank exposed. Both monks and canons claimed Christ and the apostles as their predecessors. The monks held that Christ and his apostles had lived as monks. Later on, they claimed, as the number of christians multiplied and decay set in, those who wished to maintain the early norm of life had separated themselves from the main body of christians in order to live as religious. Therefore monks had priority over other christians. The canons denied that Christ and his apostles had lived as monks. Monasticism was a later development in the church. Therefore canons had priority over monks. The old testament provided its quota of precedents. The levites prefigured christian priesthood; that was unquestionable in catholic tradition. Therefore all priests had priority over all other churchmen. Both secular priests and canons regular made capital out of the levites. The monks cashed in on them by claiming that all those who received holy orders, as monks now did, derived from the levitical priesthood as much as any other priests. They fell back on the old testament prophets as a second line of defence. The prophets and holy men of the old testament had lived as monks or hermits, thus forging a link between the monasticism of the old testament and the gospels.

The ingenuity which went into this search for biblical origins can be illustrated by two contrasting examples. The first is academic and scholarly. Professor Constable has edited the *Libellus de diversis ordinibus et professionibus qui sunt in Aecclesia*, composed by a canon who called himself 'R'.[19] He probably came from the diocese of Liège and wrote in the period 1121–61. His attitude to the diverse religious orders

---

[18] D. Roby, 'Philip of Harvengt's contribution on the question of passage from one religious order to another', *Analecta Praemonstratensia* 49 (1973) pp 69–100.

[19] Ed with transl. and notes by G. Constable and B. Smith (Oxford Medieval Texts 1972).

suggests that he was a canon regular, not of the strictest observance. 'R' set up as a peacemaker. His eirenic purpose was to justify diversity. The church had room for religious orders of all kinds, from the cluniacs and other black monks of milder observance, through the various branches of canons regular to the white monks. All of them enriched the church; all served christendom in their different ways. 'R' makes his point by finding precedents in both testaments for each and all of the orders in turn. His interest for us as an example is that his purpose gave him wider scope for precedent hunting than any other contestant, since he was justifying all ways of life and not one only. This collector of religions shows scholarly expertise. The editor's helpful table of concordances or parallels between biblical originals and the various orders brings it out at a glance. Each of the old testament tribes, whether dwelling in town or country, or centred on the capital city of Jerusalem, serves as a prototype for some present-day order, whose members commonly found their houses in towns or choose rural solitude. New testament characters offer a second set of prototypes. Hence all orders were needed and none was novel, if examined closely with an eye to the bible. Each one derived from an original whose function in ministry, prayer, contemplation and alms-giving corresponded to its own special brand of religion.

My second precedent hunter was an amateur enthusiast for antiquity. He leads us from the sphere of biblical scholarship to fantasy. The knights hospitallers of St John of Jerusalem had a strong incentive to make themselves respectable by disclaiming the charge of innovation. The military orders of knights templars and hospitallers grew in response to the needs of the crusades and of the latin colonists of Palestine. They broke with religious precedent in that their members were laymen, apart from their chaplains. Moreover, instead of taking vows of stability and expecting to remain in one house of the order, a novice put himself at the disposal of superiors who could send him anywhere at any time, to fight or to collect revenue or to rule over dependancies. He belonged to a supra-national network and his duties were fluid. The hospitallers at first served hospitals for the care of sick and poor pilgrims. They took over military service under pressure to help in the defence of Outremer. The resulting type of organisation was so new that even papal approval did not quench the knights' thirst for ancestors. And they owed it to themselves that the Hospital should rival the Temple.

The story, which took shape perhaps as early as 1140–1150, told that the Hospital had been founded by Judas Machabeus; a garbled version of an incident recounted 2 Machab. 12, 43 authenticated the claim. Then Zacharias, father of St John the Baptist, the order's patron, served the Hospital until divine command released him and he was followed by 'Julian the Roman'. Julian belongs to the realm of fiction. The emperor Augustus sent him, an honest Roman, to collect tribute from the jews. His companions on the journey all perished in a shipwreck; but Julian was saved by the Son of God and sent to serve the Hospital in succession to Zacharias. One version of the story is ascribed to the historian Josephus. The author of *The Jewish War*, widely read in its latin translation, cast his cloak over 'Julian the Roman'. Who was more likely to tell of his mission to Judaea? After this *tour de force*, it was child's play to put new testament scenes into a Hospital setting: here Jesus healed the sick; here lived his disciples and his mother after the ascension; St Stephen was the first Master of the order.[20]

Both canon 'R' and the unnamed fakers of the Hospital legend counter the charge of novelty by linking themselves to the past, much as a *nouveau riche* will pay genealogists to supply him with ancestors. In other words, they and their like admitted the blame attached to novelty, but parried it by stretching history like a piece of elastic in order to settle safely inside.

The cistercians had a readier answer. They were observing the *Rule* of St Benedict 'to the letter', stripping it of all those customs and relaxations which it had accumulated through the years. 'Innovator yourself!' they replied to their black monk critics. Customs added to the *Rule* were innovations, and bad ones, since they detracted from the primitive simplicity desired by the founder. The black monks defended changes, which they could not deny, on the grounds that christian charity obliged them to temper the wind to weaker brethren or that modern monks could not bear the rigours of old times; to insist on the primitive *Rule* would have meant excluding many potential religious from the path of salvation. Apologists for black monk institutions tended to be rather shamefaced. They could hardly defend the changes made to the *Rule* as good in themselves, much less evolve any theory in favour of change.[21] Tradition confronted tradition; so the earliest tradition would win.

[20] J. S. C. Riley-Smith, *The Knights of St John in Jerusalem and Cyprus 1050–1310* (London 1967) pp 32–59.
[21] M. D. Knowles, *The Historian and Character and Other Essays* (Cambridge 1963) pp 50–75; 'Peter the Venerable: Champion of Cluny', *JEH* 19 (1968) pp 213–17;

Ecclesiastical attitudes to novelty

The cistercian order, however, attracted men of intelligence as well as piety. The first breakthrough on the question of religious novelties came from cistercian circles, when white monks came to the rescue of other new orders. Novelties could be holy and blessed, without being hallowed by precedent. St Bernard's letter in praise of the knights templars springs to mind (1128–36). In *De laude novae militiae* Bernard stressed the newness of this military order. The crusade itself was a new movement and Bernard never doubted the righteousness of killing obstinate infidels. The holy war sanctified participants. God's holy places belonged to christians and cried out to be defended. Hence the templars represented a new and holy type of warrior, fufilling a new need. It is true that the abbot of Clairvaux cited biblical prophecies predicting the christian conquest of Jerusalem, which the templars helped to keep in latin hands. He fits the New Militia into God's plan of salvation; but the plan had room for novelties and indeed required them for its fulfilment.[22] The man who pitched into Abelard for his theological novelties justified a novel type of fighter.

Bernard's friend William of St Thierry defended the carthusians for their innovation in his *Golden Letter to the Brothers of Mont Dieu* (1144–8). William, former abbot of St Thierry, joined the cistercian order as a convert and wrote as a monk of Signy, to encourage the carthusians to persevere in their solitary way of life in spite of difficulties and criticism. This scholar monk had a keen awareness of the changes in all spheres of human activity which he observed. He saw them as a natural consequence of God's provision for mankind. God endowed man, even fallen man, with the natural wit he needed, not only for mere life, but for civilised living too. A sparkling passage in *The Golden Letter* describes the opportunities open to contemporaries. There were new discoveries in architecture, in sciences and arts and new varieties of positions and posts (choice of careers in the world). Such novelties could be exploited by good men and bad men alike. Their value depended on the purpose to which they were put by their users.

G. Constable, *The Letters of Peter the Venerable* (Cambridge, Mass., 1967) 1, pp 52–8, 2, pp 270–4; A. Wilmart, 'Une riposte de l'ancien monachisme au manifeste de Saint Bernard', *Revue Bénédictine* 46 (1934) pp 296–344; J. Leclercq, 'Nouvelle réponse de l'ancien monachisme aux critiques des Cisterciens', *ibid* 67 (1957) pp 77–94; C. H. Talbot, 'The Date and Authorship of the "Riposte",' *Studia Anselmiana* 40 (1956) pp 72–80.

[22] Ed cit 3, pp 213–39; on the date see *ibid* p 207. On criticisms of the templars see J. Leclercq, 'Un document sur les débuts des Templiers', *RHE* 52 (1957) pp 81–91.

William welcomed religious as well as secular novelties with the same proviso. The carthusian type was 'no empty pursuit of newness'. Novelty inhered in religion, and had done since the earliest times, from the prophets to Jesus and afterwards. He poured scorn on men who carped at 'the mere name of novelty': 'with their minds set in the old ways they do not know how to think new thoughts.'[23] This is an impressive attitude towards changes in both secular and religious affairs. I have to admit that William did not co-ordinate his ideas, but threw out his remarks in passing; he made no bridge between the two passages which I have quoted, though both must have sprung from the same process of thought.

To find a co-ordinated theory of religious change, we must turn to a white canon, Anselm of Havelberg. He certainly experienced changes in his own career. First a scholar, then a praemonstratensian canon, then bishop of Havelberg, a border diocese, a leader of the wendish crusade of 1147 as papal legate, an envoy to Constantinople, where he disputed with greek churchmen, he died as archbishop of Ravenna in 1158. Book 1 of his *Dialogues* (c1149) presents a theory of *Heilsgeschichte* specially designed to accommodate novelties.[24] Modern scholars have spilled rivers of ink on Anselm's theory. Briefly, he divided the history of the church into seven ages, corresponding to the seven 'states' of the apocalyptic prophecies. Elaborating on a traditional theme, he identified his own time with the fourth age, when the church was persecuted by hypocrites and false brethren. The hypocrites persecuted the church by decrying religious reform and new orders. Here he neatly reversed Pain Bolotin's identification of hypocrites as false hermits and other 'enthusiasts'. The whole history of the church, as Anselm told it, called for novelties as useful, indeed essential, to her well-being. He had already defended his own order of white canons against attacks on it by a black monk abbot on the score that the canons' mixed life of action and contemplation served a pressing need.[25] Now, in the *Dialogues*, he found a wider framework in which he could present novelties as a constant factor in the history of salvation and could praise variety. The diversity of

---

[23] On William of St Thierry see *DSAM* 6, pp 1241–63. I quote the English translation of *The Golden Epistle* by T. Berkeley, Cistercian Fathers Series 12 (Spencer, Mass., 1971) pp 32, 11–12; for the latin text see PL 184 (1858) cols 317, 310–11.

[24] *Dialogues 1*, ed with french translation and notes by G. Salet, *SC* 118 (1966); J. W. Braun, 'Studien zum Uberlieferung der Werke Anselms von Havelberg', *Deutsches Archiv* 27 (1972) pp 133–209.

[25] *Epistola ad Egbertum*, PL 183 (1858) cols 1119–20.

religious orders, including military orders, were beneficial to christendom. Anselm approved of diversity, as did canon 'R'. Unlike 'R', he saw no reason to defend it by searching for precedents; the old need not be good, nor the new bad in his view.

Anselm may perhaps have been influenced by Hugh of St Victor (d. 1141). The victorine master, too, saw the church's history as a continuous process through time. History provided the clue to his theology and to his account of the arts and sciences.[26] He does not come into the controversy on religious innovation as I have outlined it, since he never set himself to defend any particular novelty. It is significant that in his letter to the knights templars he differs from St Bernard in making no mention of their newness as an order; he simply encourages them to continue in the active religious life which they have chosen on the plea that the church needs them to fight for christians in the holy land.[27] Hugh was not a polemicist. He took for granted what his contemporaries picked on as a battlefield.

The debate on religious novelties has taken up a disproportionate amount of space. The reason is that they provoked more discussion than other kinds, because they touched *esprit de corps*. Individual writers sharpened their pens for the service of their orders. Rivalry, jealousy and competition for recruits and patronage made the argument a matter of bread-and-butter, as well as prestige. Genuine concern and perplexity on the question of where to find the perfect way of life raised the debate to higher levels. The 'crossroads' of religious life stirred seekers after perfection to agonising reappraisals.[28]

The anti-mendicant polemic and the friars' defence of themselves in the thirteenth century offers an anticlimax from the point of view of attitudes to novelty, although this pamphlet warfare has many other interesting features. Conservatives now fought with their backs to the wall. After the defeat of William of St Amour the friars' enemies aimed at restricting their privileges rather than at abolishing their orders. Perhaps the existence of so many 'bad' novelties in the crisis of christendom around 1200 in the shape of heresies and growing anti-clericalism called for 'good' novelties as a remedy. The rise of

---

[26] R. W. Southern, 'Aspects of the European Tradition of Historical Writing: 2. Hugh of St Victor and the Idea of Historical Development'. *TRHS*, 5 series, 21 (1971) pp 159–79.

[27] C. Sclafert, 'Lettre inédite de Hugues de Saint-Victor aux Chevaliers du Temple', *RAM* 34 (1958) pp 275–99.

[28] M.-D. Chenu, 'Moines, Clercs, Laïques. Au carrefour de la vie évangélique', *La théologie au XIIe siècle* (Paris 1957) pp 225–51.

populous cities and university towns, breeding grounds of heresy and of ignorance, as the parish system broke down, ensured a future for the friars They melted into the landscape with surprising speed.

We shall now turn to the schools. *De faire du neuf, d'etre des hommes nouveaux, les intellectuels du XIIe siècle en ont le vif sentiment.* This is professor Le Goff's impression of the scholars.[29] It is validated by their pushing self-confidence and by the titles which teachers of the liberal arts gave to their books: *Poetria nova, Rhetorica novissima.* Gerald of Wales, admittedly an individualist, prided himself on the novelty of his books on Ireland. Some even gloried in their claims to have discovered things new and unheard of, according to Hugh of St Cher, teaching at Paris 1230–1235[29a]

Theologians walked more warily. No theologian called his book *The New Theology.* There was much blame of 'overstepping the bounds set by the fathers in pursuit of vain curiosity'. Such blame served as a smokescreen, behind which the masters of theology produced new questions, new answers, and new attempts at synthesis. The proceedings against Abelard and Gilbert of la Porrée acted as a catalyst. From 1148 onwards the parisian theologians were left to censure themselves, without much interference from the hierarchy. Their language was so obscure, in any case, that few outside the élite really knew what they were at. Walter of St Victor's diatribe against new doctors and new doctrines (c1180) fell on deaf ears, as far as we know. The popes understood the usefulness of the schools to themselves and to christendom and protected them, as they did the mendicant orders. The pragmatic, optimistic attitude of the canon lawyers to novelty came into play; many of the popes had trained as canonists and depended on canon lawyers for advice and for business affairs. The 'new Aristotle' revived old fears; but the papal ban on the teaching of the *libri naturales* in the arts course did not prevent them from becoming set texts there. The monastic response to the rise of the schools illustrates how yesterday's novelty took its place as part of today's establishment: monasteries hired friars, trained in universities or *studia*, as lecturers to keep the brothers up to date on theology; both black and white monks founded houses of study for their members in universities. The monk student joined the seculars and friars as fellow academics.

It may be asked whether secular government had the same history

[29] J. Le Goff *Les intellectuels au moyen âge* (Paris 1957) p 14.
[29a]*Postilla in Bibliam* (Paris 1530–45) *ad* Eccles. i, 10.

of reaction to novelty as bad and final acceptance of it as possibly good. The modern historian sees developments in bureaucracy, law-making, and judicial and financial administration in the twelfth and thirteenth centuries which impress him just as much as innovation in other fields. My impression, as far as it goes, is that secular government gives us an exception to prove the rule. There were reasons for it. If we begin with churchmen at the receiving end of governmental development, we notice at once that novelties affected their pockets in the form of new exactions and new restrictions on clerical privilege. Governments continually laid new and heavier burdens on their subjects. Taxpayers, whether clerks or laymen, could hardly be expected to welcome royal and papal taxation as 'a good thing'; in fact they denounced it bitterly. Nor did their acceptance of it become less grudging as methods of assessment and collection gained in sophistication and efficiency, rather the reverse.

If we look at churchmen as participants in secular government, we might expect to find a more positive response. As chancellors, justices and counsellors or as lower-grade bureaucrats, churchmen helped to create and invent means by which power could reach out to wider areas. Bureaucrats are not given to speculation. It would have called for a gigantic effort of reappraisal to overcome the old notion that temporal power was punitive. Tradition presented it as a sad consequence of original sin, and 'good' only in so far as it quelled snatch-and-grab by keeping each man in his place in the social hierarchy. Appearances were for such a view: government in the twelfth and early thirteenth centuries concerned itself mainly with the repression of crime and rebellion and with warfare. Expenditure on warfare stimulated governments to devise new means of increasing their revenues more than any other demand on their budgets.[30] No amount of propaganda could avail in the long run to persuade victims of the new regulations that the wars would benefit them, when their rulers so often suffered defeat after pouring their subjects' money down the drain and then asking for more. It need not surprise us that civil servants kept off the task of justifying novelties. Their propaganda for the ruler, if it was entrusted to them, followed other lines. We hear of 'reforming the peace' and 'renewal of empire'. The best that can be done is to present the ruler as going back to the good old days. Again

[30] See for instance J. O. Prestwich, 'War and Finance in the Anglo–Norman State', *TRHS*, 5 series, 4 (1954) pp 19–44; J. M. Powell, 'Medieval Monarchy and Trade', *Studi medievali*, 3 series, 3 (1962) pp 420–524.

appearances and fact, too, explain why the very term 'novelty' was inapt to describe government measures, even those which we might now rate as constructive. They took place against a background of custom; they were often *ad hoc* and unspectacular. The practice of summoning representatives of estates or local communities to attend 'parliaments', which developed throughout most kingdoms of Europe, including the papal states, strikes us as significant and exciting. Contemporaries hardly noticed it, because they had been conditioned to the view that rulers should consult their free subjects at all levels.[31] The reforms of Henry II Plantagenet provide a litmus test of the civil service attitude to novelty. Richard Fitzneal in his *Dialogue of the Exchequer* and the author of *On the Laws of England*, ascribed to Glanvill, both take pride in the efficient working of angevin government. 'Glanvill' even calls the grand assize 'a royal benefit granted to the people by the goodness of the king acting on the advice of his magnates.'[32] But both writers aim at setting out how institutions work in practice. The question of novelty versus tradition does not come into it.

With that understandable exception novelty lost its stigma. Innovation could be beneficial in some cases. Nothing vague and general, like Bury's 'Idea of Progress' gained currency. Tradition was not devalued. It was simply that churchmen came to accept or even welcome efforts to improve and adapt out-dated institutions or invent new ones. The benefits of innovation are self-evident to us. They were not so in the early twelfth century, witness the mental labour expended on finding arguments to justify change. Some writers defended changes on the grounds that they were really antiquities in disguise, 'mutton dressed as lamb'; and that was a compliment, not an insult. Others defended them as useful to the church. The second was the more promising line. It expressed a view of the church in society and politics as a growing institution. The history of salvation showed that novelties formed part of the divine plan. Religion especially was presented as a process of incessant renewal; a tree puts out new shoots from the parent stem as the sap rises. St Thomas Aquinas normally tested institutions according to whether they conduced to 'the common good'. The way had been prepared for his attitude in the debates of his forerunners. The novelties themselves came first in time. They

[31] T. N. Bisson, *Assemblies and representation in Languedoc in the thirteenth century* (Princeton 1964) gives a general bibliography.
[32] Ed with notes and translation by G. D. G. Hall, *Medieval Texts* (London 1965) p 28.

battered on men's consciousness and forced them to take stock of new situations.

Finally, I shall raise a question which cannot be answered for lack of evidence. History would be a duller subject than it is if historians limited themselves to questions which admit of answers on the evidence available. My question here is whether current cosmological theories of change affected churchmen's attitude to changes on earth. Did physics and metaphysics have anything to do with reactions to novelty? To argue for this as a possibility one could begin with St Augustine. In his platonist or neoplatonist thought-world change meant decay. God punished fallen man by subjecting him to change together with the lower part of creation. Everything on 'our middle earth' tended to crumble and deteriorate. Man's foremost task in this life was to raise his eyes above earthly things and fix them on the eternal and un-changing, in so far as a sinful mortal could.[33] The individual could be converted and change for the better, as St Augustine had done, and could try to help his fellows; that was all. Readers of St Augustine and those educated in his tradition would tend to assume that changes must be from bad to worse. Granted that terrestrial institutions, however imperfect, saved man from the chaos brought about by original sin, then they were better let alone or else preserved from attack by would-be reformers. The divine order, adapted to an evil world, looked static and capable only of preservation, not of improvement.

The reception and study of the corpus of writings ascribed to St Denis the Areopagite offered an alternative picture of the universe, although medieval scholars often amalgamated the two traditions or attempted a synthesis.[34] The celestial and ecclesiastical hierarchies described by Pseudo-Dionysius (the ranks of angels corresponding to the ranks of prelates and priests and lesser orders) is static in that each creature, visible or invisible, has its own degree and must stay there. On the other hand, the members of each degree in the hierarchies must help those in the next lower degree to realise their potential and to move as far upward as their divinely fixed nature allows. Hugh of St Victor, who had a historical vision of the church proceeding through time, wrote an influential commentary on Pseudo-Dionysius. William of St Thierry drew on another greek patristic tradition in

---

[33] H. I. Marrou, *L'Ambivalence du Temps de l'Histoire chez S. Augustin* (Paris 1950).
[34] R. Roques, *L'Univers Dionysien: structure hiérarchique du monde selon le Pseudo-Denys* (Paris 1954).

latin translation. He based his religious and philosophical thinking on the theme of 'withdrawal and return'.[35] The whole of creation is in a state of flux, *egressus/regressus*. Creatures flowed from the Godhead and are returning to their source, thanks to the saving work of Christ and the Holy Spirit. It is not a pantheistic view, since the creatures retain their individualities. Motion implies change. We have seen that William observed both secular and religious changes in the world around him and welcomed them if they were rightly used. Did the influence of greek patristic writings impart a sense of movement into the more static picture of the universe handed down by the latins?

The concept of God as immobile mover went back to Boethius. It was known to medieval scholars through his *Consolation of Philosophy* and could serve as an argument to prove God's existence.[36] The reception of Aristotle's *libri naturales* in the late twelfth and early thirteenth centuries gave it new force and a significance which it had not had before. Aristotle directed his readers' attention to the phenomenon of motion and change, which was central to his philosophy. Hence 'generation and corruption' became scientific terms. The notion of agency, moving potency to act, entered into the scholars' view of their universe.[37] Change was a fact of life, not to be deplored as an evil, but to be registered and studied. If change became 'natural' in the teleological sense of the word, it lost some of its horror. It would be far-fetched to suppose that even Grosseteste, for all his interest in natural science, had it in mind when he praised 'good' novelties. But the *libri naturales* formed the climate in which educated men lived and thought. We are not always conscious of the way in which our schooling in one subject seeps into our ideas on something quite different.

A more down-to-earth suggestion comes from Walter Freund's study of the notion of *Modernus* in the middle ages. In an excursus on the meaning of *Novus* he points to use of the term in ancient and medieval literature. It often denoted 'surprising' or 'unexpected' and therefore 'frightening'. 'New' in this context expresses man's helpless-

[35] See above n 23. The theme of 'withdrawal and return' informs the *De divisione naturae* of John Scot Erigena; but this early ninth-century book was not widely read in the twelfth century; see *Iohannis Scotti Erivgenae Periphyseon*, ed I. P. Sheldon-Williams, 1 (Dublin 1968) pp 1–25, 32–3.

[36] P. Courcelle, *La Consolation de Philosophie dans la tradition littéraire* (Paris 1967) pp 179–89.

[37] On latin translations and their dates see *Aristoteles Latinus*, ed G. Lacombe and others, 1 (Rome 1939) pp 49–61; 2 (Cambridge 1955) pp 787–8.

ness in face of a strange situation, which he cannot control; he feels all at sea because he has no precedent to guide him.[38] It might be argued that in the period *c*1100–*c*1250 men gained more control of their environment. Production and trade reached a higher level, in spite of war and famines. Economic prosperity may have pushed back the zone of the terrifying unknown a little further. Although churchmen generally distrusted merchants and their new business techniques, thriving trade and industry with the opportunities to raise the standard of living which they brought may have induced a greater sense of security. Bonaventure suggested that famines were a thing of the past when disputing at Paris in 1255/6.[39]

My provisional dossier on churchmen's attitudes to novelty will have shown that they became more positive in the period *c*1100–*c*1250. Conservatives and reactionaries are a constant factor in history. Spokesmen in favour of novelties won a verbal victory at least in this century and a half. They won it after a long and painful battle of words, and more than words only. Builders of institutions went about their work and contributed novelties without making a fuss. Lawyers and scholars took novelties in their stride. After posing some unanswerable questions on the intellectual background to this change, I shall end with one more question, which could be answered by someone willing to sift the evidence available for the late thirteenth and fourteenth centuries. Did novelty shed its newly acquired respectability and slip backwards, to become a term of abuse? The crises of the later middle ages make it seem likely that this would happen. Perhaps so, or perhaps there is no simple answer.

University of Oxford

[38] *Modernus und andere Zeitbegriffe des Mittelalters*, Neue münstersche Beiträge zur Geschichtsforchung, ed K. von Raumer, 4, (1957) pp 107–8.
[39] Dufeuil pp 176, 183.

THE ALIEN PRIORIES AND THE
EXPULSION OF ALIENS
FROM ENGLAND IN 1378

by A. K. McHARDY

THE expulsion of aliens from England in 1378 forms one episode in the history of the alien priories, a story which began with the norman conquest and continued into the fifteenth century.[1] The alien priories—they may be defined as the english dependencies of foreign religious houses[2]—had been subjected to interference from the english crown since 1295, when Edward I's seizure of them on the outbreak of the anglo-french war became the precedent, both of occasion and method, for the future.[3] By 1378 the priories had been in crown hands during four periods of hostilities: 1295 to 1303, 1324 to 1327, 1337 to 1360, and again from 1369.[4]

The official position was that the alien priories had to be taken over in wartime because they were a security risk;[5] in fact the crown was motivated by a desire to gain control of their two assets: patronage and land.[6] The evidence for the equivocal nature of the crown's

---

[1] See C. W. New, *History of the Alien Priories in England to the Confiscation of Henry V* (Menash, Wisconsin 1916 privately printed); [Marjorie] Morgan, [*The English Lands of the Abbey of*] *Bec* (Oxford 1946); [Donald] Matthew, [*The*] *Norman Monasteries* [*and their English Possessions*] (Oxford 1962); for the fourteenth and fifteenth centuries, [Marjorie] Morgan, ['The Suppression of the] Alien Priories', *History* 26 (1941) pp 204–12.

[2] The term 'alien priories' was not ecclesiastical but political and became current in 1295. It included both priories with full conventual life and cells which were not strictly priories since they housed only one or two monks. The situation was further complicated when alien monks left the country and the status of small cells became doubtful. Cammeringham, Lincs, for example, was by 1395 described as 'the manor otherwise called the priory', *CPR*, 1391–6, p 579. The following discussion is not concerned with the manors and other pieces of property which had never had conventual status and which merely swelled the resources of a french house or cathedral.

[3] Morgan, 'Alien Priories', p 205.

[4] After 1369 they remained in crown hands until restored, under conditions, by Henry IV, 1399, *ibid* p 208, *CPR*, 1399–1401, pp 70–2.

[5] Morgan, *Bec* p 121.

[6] The commissions for keeping of alien priories were always careful to state that the king reserved to himself the advowsons which the priories possessed, and thus the amount of patronage at the crown's disposal was vastly increased. From 1369 to

attitude to alien religious takes several forms. The crown's definition
of the word 'alien' was selective; during the french wars the order
of Cîteaux was unmolested[7] while the property of the orders of
Cluny[8] and Bec was seized, as were the cells of the french benedictine
houses. Again, though the crown, on the outbreak of war, took the
alien priories into its possession, it subsequently handed them back
to the priors, but they had to give surety for their good conduct and
to pay a farm at the exchequer.[9] And despite the official policy of
hostility it is noteworthy that some alien priors were favourably
regarded by Edward III: John of Jancourt the french prior of Lewes
(Sussex) was used in Edward's diplomatic service,[10] and the prior of
Tickford (Bucks) was, on 25 July 1358, paid 100 shillings for expenses
incurred on a journey to Normandy as a messenger of the king.[11]

The priors who farmed their priories for the crown found their
legal position altered in two ways. They were, and always had been,
merely proctors of the french abbots, and this meant that theoretically
they could not engage in lawsuits without the abbots' consent. When,
during the french war, the priories were taken into the king's hand the
priors became the crown's proctors, a circumstance some priors fell
back on when hard pressed in the courts.[12] The second change in their
position during the war was that, as alien priories were now royal
property, debts owing to them became debts to the crown.[13] What is

1398, for example, the patent rolls record 223 presentations to benefices formerly in
the patronage either of alien priories of Lincoln diocese or to benefices within that
diocese in the direct patronage of foreign religious houses. The total amount brought
to the exchequer at any one time by the farming of the priories cannot be calculated
because some farms are not known and because rates fluctuated, see Morgan, *Bec*
p 121, Matthew, *Norman Monasteries* p 151.

[7] Morgan, *Bec* p 2.

[8] Though the cluniac nunnery of Delapré, Northants, was left undisturbed.

[9] Commissions to farm the alien priories are to be found in the C[alendars of] F[ine]
R[olls], *passim*.

[10] Rose Graham, *English Ecclesiastical Studies* (London 1929) p 49.

[11] PRO, Issue Roll, MS E403/392 m 28.

[12] The prior of Tickford, when sued by the dean and chapter of Lichfield for a debt of
100 marks, replied that he could take no action without informing the king; the
royal response was to issue two mandates to the justices of the common bench ordering
judgement to be made, despite the prior's objection, *CCR*, 1381-5 pp 29-30, 377-8.
The same excuse was made by the prior of St Andrew's, Northampton, in a lawsuit
concerning property, and it met with the same result, *CCR*, 1385-9 p 74.

[13] A series of eight writs concerning debts to Willoughton, Lincs, name the king as sole
creditor, L[incolnshire] A[rchives] O[ffice] *Lincoln Register 12B (Buckingham, Royal
Writs)* fols 19, 19v, 20, 21, 21v (2), 23 (2). Writs about debts to Lenton, Notts, and
Eye, Suffolk, make the king joint creditor with the prior, *ibid* fols 24v, 27r/v.

not certain, however, is whether the crown's interest in the priories' financial condition made the recovery of their debts more efficient.

The chief factor influencing the financial condition of the alien priories after 1295 was the high farm which the crown demanded. Initially this was based on an assessment of income, and Graham calculated that in the case of the cluniac house of Wenlock (Salop), for example, it was at the rate of twelve shillings in the pound.[14] Against this background of heavy farms and unfavourable economic conditions almost all the characteristics of the late fourteenth century had shown themselves by 1360: the selling[15] or leasing[16] of their english property by french religious corporations; the denization of priories;[17] and the petitioning of parliament for the expulsion of alien monks.[18] Only the employment of laymen as keepers was to come later, in 1373.[19]

Both factors, the ambivalent attitude of the crown to alien priories and the presence before 1378 of the features characteristic of the latter part of the century, should be borne in mind when considering the expulsion of 1378. This resulted from a commons' petition presented in the parliament which met on 13 October 1377, demanding the expulsion of all aliens from the realm. In reply the crown accepted this in principle, and it ordered aliens with but few exceptions to leave by candlemas from the port of Dover where they were to be searched to ensure that they carried no more money than was necessary for their expenses and no extra clothes or plate. Any foreigner found to be still in England without permission after that date, 2 February 1378, was to be arrested and held for ransoming and one third of his goods was to go to the person who had informed against him. But, provided they did not leave the country or receive messages from outside,

[14] Quoted by Morgan, 'Alien Priories', p 205.
[15] By the canons of Rouen in 1334, and 1335, and by the canons of Coutances in 1336, Matthew, *Norman Monasteries* p 104.
[16] Weedon Bec, Northants, was leased out to a layman in 1353, Morgan, *Bec* p 114.
[17] The first was the cluniac priory of Lewes in 1351, D. Knowles, *The Religious Orders in England* 2 (Cambridge 1955) p 159.
[18] 1346, *Rot[uli] Parl[iamentorum,]* ed J. Strachey (London 1767–77) 3 p 22.
[19] The first commissions to laymen were made in 1371 but these were only temporary: Panfield, Essex, *sede vacante*, and Burwell, Lincs, 'until the prior shall return from abroad', CFR, 1369–77 pp 135, 136. In 1373 seven houses were farmed to laymen 'for as long as the war with France shall endure', this being the usual form. These were Takeley, Essex, 3 June; Stratfield Saye, Berks, 20 June; Monks Toft, Norfolk, 6 October; West Mersea, Essex, 19 November; Sporle, Norfolk, 3 December; Minster Lovel, Oxon, 7 December; Panfield, 14 December; *ibid* pp 214, 213, 220, 222–5, 232.

priors of alien priories and certain others were to be allowed to stay.[20]

Meanwhile, a series of commissions was being issued for the farming of the alien priories. The commissions, their form, and their incidence since 1369 may be briefly rehearsed. Edward III resumed the title of king of France on 3 June 1369, and very shortly afterwards, on 11 June, commissions were issued to farm thirty-one priories, the priors to act as farmers in every case save one. Two more commissions were issued in August. On 6 October commissions were issued to the farmers of thirty-nine priories, only twelve concerned the same houses, setting out in detail the terms on which the houses were to be held. As before, the great majority of farmers were priors, thirty-five out of thirty-nine. Between that date, October 6 1369, and the second half of 1377 the commissions—anything from ten to thirty-three a year[21]—conform to no one pattern. They were issued throughout the year, and, where reasons for issuing a new commission are apparent, they are various: the priory is vacant,[22] the prior is abroad,[23] or sometimes a priory was the subject of an 'auction', the keepership going to the highest bidder.[24] The proportion of commissions issued to priors as farmers varied widely, from nineteen out of twenty-one in the first eight months of 1377 to two out of fifteen in 1375.[25]

But in the autumn of 1377 came a spate of commissions, comparable only with that of 1369. Between 4 October and 1 December fifty-five were issued for the farming of priories.[26] Most specify that the farmers were to hold office from the previous 22 June, that is, from the first day of Richard II's reign. Since the death of Edward III was no more unexpected than the renewal of war in 1369, and the reissuing of commissions in 1377 was far less of an administrative upheaval than that of 1369, the delay in issuing the commissions is noteworthy. So it may be asked who these commissaries were, whether they differed significantly from previous groups, and, in particular, whether the

[20] *Rot Parl* 3 p 22.
[21] The numbers of commissions are: 1370: 33; 1371: 21; 1372: 12; 1373: 10; 1374: 15; 1375: 15; 1376: 21; January-September 1377: 21.
[22] Frampton, Dorset, 6 April 1370, *CFR*, 1369-77 p 72.
[23] Burwell, 24 October 1371, *ibid* p 136.
[24] Monks Toft, prior, £20 plus £30 arrears, 1370; George Felbrugge king's esquire, £33-6-8d plus £30 arrears, 1373; prior, £60, 1376; prior, 100 marks, and tenths with the clergy, May 1377, *ibid* pp 81, 220, 358-9, 403.
[25] The numbers of commissions to priors compared with totals are 1370: 26/33; 1371: 16/21; 1372 9/12; 1373: 1/10; 1374: 5/15; 1375: 2/15; 1376: 17/21; January-September 1377: 19/21.
[26] Including two each for Brimpsfield, Gloucs; Minster Lovel, Oxon; and Takeley, Essex.

position of the priors as farmers was seriously weakened. The fifty-five farmers committed in the autumn of 1377 fall into various categories: priors acting alone numbered forty; one commission linked a prior with another monk and a layman;[27] two houses were farmed by alien monks, and a third by a local abbot;[28] seculars, ranging from a chaplain to a bishop,[29] received six commissions, and five were issued to laymen alone.[30] Thus over two-thirds of these commissions were issued to the priors of the houses concerned, a proportion lower than in the years 1370-2, 1376 and early 1377, but higher than in 1373-5. For thirty-seven priories these new commissions meant that there was no change in their farmer;[31] in some instances the prior's position was actually strengthened, either because he was made sole keeper after acting with outsiders[32] or because he supplanted another keeper.[33] Only in one case did the autumn of 1377 see the ousting of the prior as farmer by an outsider: at Throwley, where the new farmer was the sheriff of Kent.[34]

Since this spate of commissions began before the 'expulsion' parliament opened one must be wary of asserting that there was a connection between these commissions and the petition for the expulsion of aliens, but it is arguable that the crown, anticipating hostility to the french monks, was confirming their position as farmers of the priories. This contrast between public policy and private practice is explicit in some of the commissions given to priors in 1378. Custody of seventeen priories was given into the hands of their priors alone and four of these commissions—for Appuldercombe (Isle of Wight), Astley (Worcs), Wolston (Warwicks), and Holy Trinity, York—

---

[27] Hugh earl of Stafford, brother Michael Cheyne and the prior farmed Wootton Wawen, Warwicks, *CFR*, 1377-81 p 29.

[28] Hayling, Hants, and St Neots, Hunts, *ibid* pp 16, 19; the abbot of Barlings farmed Cammeringham, both Lincs, *ibid* p 30.

[29] Ellingham, Hants, Frampton, Dorset (Henry Wakefield, bishop of Worcester), Minster Lovel, Oxon (two commissions), Takeley (vacated, the keeping returned to the prior), Titley, Herefs, *ibid* pp 23, 48, 29, 19, 18-9, 30.

[30] Brimpsfield (two), Panfield, Throwley, Kent, Monks Kirby, Warwicks, *ibid* pp 22, 36-7, 22, 20-1, 27.

[31] Four of the priories, Bermondsey, Surrey, Brimpsfield, Kerswell, Devon, and St Neots appear in commissions for the first time since the resumption of war.

[32] As happened at Edith Weston, Rutland, and Hinckley, Leics, *CFR*, 1369-77 p 311, *CFR*, 1377-83 p 19; *CFR*, 1369-77 p 286, *CFR*, 1377-83 p 17.

[33] At Beckford, Gloucs, and Coggs the priors supplanted laymen, *CFR*, 1369-77 p 255, *CFR*, 1377-83 p 14; *CFR*, 1369-77 p 302, *CFR*, 1377-83 p 41. The prior of Loders, Dorset, displaced a king's clerk, *CFR*, 1369-77 p 217, *CFR* 1377-83 p 15.

[34] *CFR*, 1369-77 p 383, *CFR*, 1377-83 pp 20-1.

award custody to the prior 'notwithstanding the ordinance made in the last parliament for the expulsion of aliens'.[35]

Though priors acting alone account for less than half the 1378 commissaries, there are also six group commissions in which priors are named, and this is the pattern for the next three years—priors, usually alone, but sometimes with others—accounting for about half the commissaries.[36] Not until 1382 are the priors outnumbered by others,[37] and the new trend was never reversed.

It would seem, therefore, that the initial impact of the anti-alien petition upon the personnel of the keepers of alien priories was slight. The long-term effects of preventing recruitment of religious from France were more serious, and in the eighties and nineties of the century custody of priories tended to pass from the hands of priors. This happened for a variety of reasons, one being that an increasing number of priories became vacant—there were said to be thirty vacant by the end of the century.[38] Yet there were exceptions to the general trend. At Ravendale (Lincs) and St Neots the priors retained control of their property until the end of the century,[39] and at St Andrews, Northampton until 1395.[40] At three other houses, Long Bennington, Hough (both Lincs) and Tickford the priors regained the custody after losing it for a time; at Long Bennington the commission of 13 October 1383 to Robert Tidman of Winchcomb and Michael Rogers the prior[41] was revoked on 18 November 1388[42] in favour of an earlier grant of custody to the prior alone;[43] and at Hough the prior, Richard Beaugrant, secured, after a lapse of eight years, the position held by his predecessor.[44] And while the crown usually exercised the patronage of the priories during the war,[45] there are

[35] Ibid pp 75–6, 79–82.
[36] The figures are, 1378: 17+6/39; 1379: 11/23; 1380: 5/9; 1381: 9+2/22.
[37] 1382: 2+1/12.
[38] CPR, 1399–1401 pp 70–2.
[39] At St Neots this was due primarily to the longevity of William of Saint-Vaast, appointed prior of Ogbourne, Wilts, and proctor-general of the abbot of Bec in March 1364, who was still alive on 28 October 1404, Morgan, Bec p 126.
[40] 7 December, CFR, 1391–9 p 171.
[41] CFR, 1383–91 p 255.
[42] CPR, 1385–9 p 527.
[43] 23 October 1377, CFR, 1377–83 p 27.
[44] Commissions to outsiders were issued on 16 April 1386, CFR, 1383–91, p 137, and 7 November 1393, CFR, 1391–9 p 94. Beaugrant was appointed 26 January 1394, ibid p 109.
[45] See, for example, royal presentations to Stogursey, Somerset, 1374, Modbury, Devon, 1375, Barnstaple, Devon, 1376, CPR, 1374–7 pp 9, 93, 393.

instances when the normal peacetime procedure was followed. On 12 February 1380 a presentation to Coggs was made, not by the abbot of Fécamp himself, but by Philip Arnulph his proctor in England *potestatem habentem specialem ad prioratum de Cogges Lincoln' dioc' vacantem . . .,* and the presentee, brother Nicholas Coyn, was described as being a monk of Fécamp.[46] Even as late as 12 June 1386 one may see an example of patronage being exercised by a french abbot in the presentation of brother Giles Petri, priest, for he was presented to Hough by the abbot of Notre Dame du Voeu, Cherbourg.[47]

That the immediate impact of the expulsion order on the priors' hold of keeperships was slight need not surprise us, for the crown had no quarrel with the priors as a body. Provided that the money for the farms was forwarded regularly to the exchequer it mattered little who held the custody of the houses. The case of foreign monks, as distinct from priors, was different. While they remained in the houses provision had to be made for their maintenance, as commissions to outside farmers make clear,[48] and this diverted valuable revenue from the exchequer. If, however, the monks should die or go overseas, the money formerly assigned for their keep was added to the farm.[49] In seeming contrast to this there may be set the wish, expressed in a petition to parliament in 1376, that divine service in the priories should be maintained, works of charity continued, and founders' wishes respected.[50]

The 1377—expulsion of aliens—petition would seem to have had more serious effect on monastic life than on the farming of the priories. Matthew has printed a list of over one hundred monks who left the country in 1378, over against forty-two who are known to have remained; he also found reference to a further thirty-four alien religious who occur in England in the period 1378–99.[51] Some comments may be offered. Firstly, though it is not always possible to know from which houses some of the monks were expelled, it seems that there was some regional variation in the effects of the

---

[46] LAO, *Lincoln Register 10 (Buckingham, Institutions I)* fol 370.

[47] LAO, *Lincoln Register 11 (Buckingham, Institutions II)* fol 24.

[48] The usual sum set aside for maintaining a monk was £10 p.a., *CFR 1369–77* pp 220, 223–4, 232, 292.

[49] See, for example, the commission to farm Hayling, Hants, 1382, *CFR, 1377–83* p 284.

[50] *Rot Parl* 2 p 342.

[51] Eighteen priors also obtained permission to stay in 1378, Matthew, *Norman Monasteries* appendix III.

A. K. McHARDY

expulsion order. Thus only four monks who left in 1378 are known to have lived in Lincoln diocese, which contained twenty-one priories. Such dioceses as Salisbury and Norwich seem to have been more greatly affected. Secondly, the list of monks known to have been in England after 1378 is certainly not complete. Neither Nicholas Coyn, the monk of Fécamp who became prior of Coggs in 1380, nor Guillermus de Trenchefan, monk of St Vigor de Cerisy, prior of Monk Sherbourne (Hants) from 1397, nor Denys Chanon, monk of St Florent, Anjou who was prior of Andover (Hants) in 1385, is mentioned.[52] Further research would doubtless reveal more names. Thirdly, while conventual life certainly disappeared from some houses, others, for example, Prittlewell (Essex),[53] Folkestone (Kent),[54] Wenlock,[55] and Tywardreath (Cornwall),[56] had managed to recruit english monks, so that for them the loss of the foreign monks was less serious. Yet others maintained their complement by the transference of monks from one house to another.[57] Numbers actually increased at Hough where there were three alien monks in 1378 and four monks in 1381.[58] Occasionally recruitment from abroad was allowed,[59] and this continued into the fifteenth century, witness the succession of monks which came from St Mary's, St Pierre-sur-Dives to Modbury (Devon), which continued even after the priory had become part of the endowment of Eton College.[60] Finally, that the effects of the petition of 1377 were not as sweeping as had been hoped may be deduced also from the continuing agitation for the removal of alien priors in the parliament of 1379 and in the second parliament of 1380.[61]

[52] *Wykeham's Register,* ed T. F. Kirby, Hampshire Record Society (1896–9) 1 p 207, 2, p 354.
[53] *Registrum Simonis de Sudbiria,* ed R. C. Fowler, CYS 38, 2 (1938) pp 1–4, 23, 25, 34, 38, 58.
[54] *Registrum Simonis Langham,* ed A. C. Wood, CYS, 53 (1956) p 375.
[55] *Registrum Johannis Gilbert,* ed J. H. Parry, CYS, 18 (1915) pp 130, 166, 170.
[56] *The Register of Thomas de Brantyngham,* ed F. C. Hingeston-Randolph, 2 (London and Exeter 1906) pp 753, 756, 773, 776.
[57] This happened, for example, at Newton Longville, Bucks, when, on the death of the alien John Boys, a monk of St Andrew's, Northampton, William de Buckby by name, was given permission to replace him, CPR, 1381–5 p 329.
[58] Matthew, *Norman Monasteries* p 157; PRO, Clerical Subsidies, MS E179/35/16, m 3.
[59] John Rogger, monk of St Pierre-sur-Dives was admitted, at Richard II's nomination, as prior of Modbury in March 1399, on taking an oath of allegiance, Eton College Records, 1 (Modbury)/44.
[60] *Ibid* 1/130 (1432), 131 (1438), 132 (1442), 135 (1456), 79 (1470).
[61] *Rot Parl* 3 pp 64, 96.

The English alien priories in 1378

Thus it appears that the expulsion of 1378 was neither the beginning of a new situation nor did it lead to clearly-defined results. Already the inability of the french houses to collect their revenues from England and to have their members come and go freely on matters of business or discipline was forcing a severence of relations between the mother houses and their english dependencies. The trends in evidence before 1378, namely the denization of houses, the transfer of priories to the endowment of english foundations, the lease or sale of property, accelerated in the later fourteenth century and seem to have been unaffected either by the resumption of government by Richard II in 1389 or by the peace of 1395. In this process the 1378 expulsion acted as no more than a catalyst, 'aiding and speeding a reaction' already under way.

University of London
Royal Holloway College

CHURCH, SOCIETY AND POLITICS IN THE EARLY FIFTEENTH CENTURY AS VIEWED FROM AN ENGLISH PULPIT

by ROY M. HAINES

SOME may question the suitability of sermon material as a means of illuminating the thought and background of a specific period. If anything, preachers were even less original—though that is too modern a concept—than other categories of medieval author. Frequently the same material was recast and pressed into service on a variety of occasions; a practice familiar to preachers down the centuries, but one which effectively blurs the dates of initial 'publication' and the extent of an individual's contribution.

Much of this criticism is applicable to the collection of twenty-five sermons which occupies the first part of Bodley MS 649.[1] Yet, when all the customary quotations from classical and medieval authors have been abstracted, along with the time-worn exempla to be found in the works of Jacques de Vitry, Vincent de Beauvais, Jacques de Voragine, and a host of other compilers, acknowledged and unacknowledged, there remains a core of material which is both contemporary and in the manner of its handling, particular. As one reads the sermons there is an increasing awareness of atmosphere, the sense of a distinct historical period and its problems. A wealth of contemporary metaphor and apt proverbial phrase, the interpolation of arresting—albeit to our ears incongruous—passages in english, and the mention of specific events, together contribute to an impression of society which is both vital and convincing.

The individuality and homogeneity of these sermons becomes apparent on comparison with others, for instance the group of *De sanctis* sermons in the latter part of the same manuscript, or those of bishop Brinton delivered some forty or more years previously.[2] It

---

[1] I gratefully acknowledge the assistance of the Dalhousie research and development fund in the preparation of this paper. The MS has been described in my earlier communication: ' "Wilde Wittes and Wilfulnes" [: John Swetstock's Attack on those "Poyswunmongeres", the Lollards'], *SCH* 8 (1971), pp 144–5 nn.

[2] [*The Sermons of Thomas*] Brinton [, *Bishop of Rochester (1373–1389)*], ed M. A. Devlin *C Ser*, 3, 85–6 (1954).

is true that Brinton has much to say about the life of his day, but his measured words bear little resemblance to the vigorous and lively effusions of our author.

Bodley MS 649 is anonymous.[3] Internal evidence suggests that the author of the initial collection of sermons was a monk, probably a benedictine. Favourably disposed towards the friars,[4] he had received an Oxford education, presumably at Gloucester college, to which the black monks were sent. His exaltation of theology may or may not have specific reference to his own studies, but his claim that, if time allowed, he could expound (*congruenti racione et historia*) the doctrine of the spiritual and bodily assumption of our lady, argues a theological training.[5]

At least one of the sermons was preached at Oxford, and a midland context is also suggested by the location of two modern *exempla*, one in the vicinity of Oxford, the other in the county of Nottingham.[6]

The bulk of the sermons constitutes a lenten course[7] addressed mainly to a clerical audience. This, no doubt, accounts for the emphasis on penitence and confession. But despite this preoccupation and the solemnity of the season, the subject matter proves neither morbid

---

[3] Attributed in the 1602 MS catalogue (Bodleian Library, MS Rawlinson Q e 31, fol 117ᵛ) to a John Swetstock, who was seemingly the scribe. See 'Wilde Wittes and Wilfulnes', p 144 nn 3–4. The script is anglicana with some secretary forms, for example 'a', 'r' and final 's'. The hand is not unlike that described by M. B. Parkes, *English Cursive Book Hands 1250–1500* (Oxford 1969) p 17 no i, as a 'typical Oxford hand of the period 1425–50', though the writing, not being in double columns, is better spaced and of more regular appearance. A single hand is responsible for the whole MS.

[4] Sermon 24, fol 124ᵛ, In ista prece et in speciali venerabile collegium et capitulum Sancti Francisci sacre professionis qui liquerunt divicias, vanitates, pompam et iactanciam huius mundi pro Dei amore et clauserunt se voluntarie infra custodiam paupertatis et alte perfeccionis, quod Deus ex sua bonitate det eis graciam sic servare et defendere castellum sue sacre et approbate religionis . . . Both here and later in the same sermon he speaks of the friars in the third person.

[5] He identifies himself with the *possessionati*, for example sermon 24, fol 125ʳ (compare 6, fol 35ʳ), speaking of 'our' possessions and food. In sermon 8, fols 48ʳ–49ʳ (the *exordium*), he talks of Oxford as of his *alma mater* and alludes to his 'master', 'Ut honorabilis meus magister told ȝow on Sonday last' (fol 49ᵛ). Elsewhere (sermon 25, fol 132ᵛ) he lauds the multitude of saints 'qui vixerunt et moriebantur ob [for 'sub'?] vexillo sancti Benedicti'. The reference to the doctrine of the assumption of our lady comes in sermon 24 (fol 124ʳ–ᵛ) preached on that festival.

[6] Sermon 8; sermon 14, fols 89ᵛ (non longe ab Oxon'), 90ᵛ (in Notyngham' comitatu).

[7] The theme of sermon 1 is from the epistle for the first Sunday in lent. Themes for sermons 2–13 are from the gospels for the Sundays in lent (in order) down to passion Sunday. Sermon 14 was presumably preached on palm Sunday, sermon 15 during holy week and 17 on Good Friday.

nor monotonous, though the author does have a habit of transferring his metaphors and allegories from one sermon to another, adapting them to a variety of situations.

He is particularly partial to the allegory of war, displaying an unclerical knowledge of military matters, although his usage is, as expected, literary rather than technical. The whole of life is envisaged as a time of battle, of great peril and fear.[8] Penance is conventionally analysed in terms of the sword of confession, the lance of contrition, and the shield of satisfaction.[9] Christ appears in the guise of the celestial knight,[10] jousts for us on the cross,[11] and bears the arms 'silver w^t five roses of gowles'.[12] At one stage we are led to imagine the opposed cities of 'Mercy' and 'Sin', with their curtain walls, towers and ditches,[13] at another, with an obvious pun on Sir John Oldcastle's name, the 'Castellum peccati et miserie, castellum diaboli Oldcastell'.[14] Lollards undermine the tower of the *possessionati*,[15] while the walls of Jericho fall merely by priestly trumpeting and the shouts of the people 'sine schot of gun vel engyne sine ictu aut undermyn'.[16] Adam figures as captain of Paradise Castle,[17] Wycliffe as leader and captain of the devil's host.[18]

Allegorically the alternative to life as a battle is life on the ever restless sea, full of the tempest and storm of labour, tribulation, misery and woe,[19] and fraught with that frightful hazard the bottomless whirlpool of avarice or of ill-faith and desperation.[20] Tossing on the sea of life is the ship of state[21] or, as a variation, the ship

---

[8] Sermon 1, fol 1^r. The image is used elsewhere, for example sermons 4, 10, 16, 23; fols 22^r, 60^v, 97^r, 121^r.

[9] Sermon 1, fol 7^v.

[10] Sermon 6, fol 35^r.

[11] Sermon 5, fol 30^r, Spiritualiter quando placuit digno principi Jhesu hastiludiare pro nobis super crucem contra diabolum he disgisid se in extraneis armis . . . gestabat ex argento cum 5 rosis of goles.

[12] Sermons 5, 17; fols 30^r, 100^v.

[13] Sermon 2, fols 8^r *et seq*, Sic civitas misericordie est summe commendabilis quia alte muratur profunde fossatur et situatur super pulcherrimum flumen quod unquam fluxit in terris. For the 'maledicta civitas' figured by Jericho see fols 10^v–11^r.

[14] Sermon 14, fol 125^r. Compare 22, fol 113^r, Per castellum quod erat in fiendo et non potuit stare interpreto castellum demonis inferni Oldcastel et eius sectam.

[15] Sermons 6, 24; fols 35^r, 125^r.

[16] Sermon 2, fol 10^v.

[17] Sermon 5, fol 28^r.

[18] Sermon 6, fol 35^r.

[19] Sermons 4, 10, 23; fols 22^r, 60^v–61^r, 121^{r-v}.

[20] Sermons 4, 10, 23; fols 22^{r-v}, 61^v, 123^v.

[21] Sermons 4, 10, 25; fols 22^r, 61^r, 129^v.

of our mortal life with its tripartite division into youth, middle and old age.[22]

Other facets of medieval life are conjured up by the metaphors of chancery: the *articuli* of faith, the *clausulae* of the creed, Christ's *carta* for mankind sealed with his blood and with the red wax of glorious martyrdom.[23] Or in manorial terms, all men are named on the devil's court roll, thralls of the fiend, doing him suit and service. For them Christ brought manumission through faith.[24]

The bestial world is represented by a whole menagerie of animals, factual and fabulous—wolves, serpents, mantichorae and dragons. Exotic creatures, such as the chameleon, the hyena, the lion and the eagle, some ostensibly from the folios of Solinus,[25] mingle with others of the preacher's everyday experience, the ox, the horse, the swan and the fox.[26] The horse is introduced by a quotation from the apocalypse: 'And there as I looked, was another horse, sickly pale; and its rider's name was death'.[27] This 'pale huyt hors' is to be interpreted as our mortal nature. It is not, the preacher contends, the 'pomely gray' of duplicity and flattery, nor the 'colblack' of hatred or vicious living, but the 'pris hu' of all, the noble bay of original justice.[28]

The domestic swan serves for a pointed analogy. It enjoys having its back stroked, says the preacher, but touch the front of its neck and it ruffles its feathers—just like the magnates. Speak to them of their virtues, commend their life and deeds, look up to them and make much of them, and you will be held dear; but touch their gorge with talk of vices, take them to task for their evil life, tell them the

---

[22] Sermon 23, fols 120v *et seq.* This is the division used in the poem 'The Parlement of the Thre Ages'.

[23] Sermon 3, fols 15r-v, 19r-v. At fol 19r the preacher uses a testamentary metaphor, Misericors pater celi legavit nobis suam hereditatem; and at fol 101r that of the 'patent eterne vite' likened to royal letters patent 'quia sicut in patente . . . in una parte est ymago regia in altera impressio armorum et est sufficiens warant pro tua vita'.

[24] Fol 15r, Omnes erant rotulati in diaboli court rolle, omnes erant þral deaboli and dide him sute and service.

[25] For example, sermon 4, fols 24v, 25v. He cites Solinus [De mirabilibus mundi] to the effect that the mantichora 'generatur et educatur in India et est a parlous best eciam stupenda, habet 3 ordines dencium in ore, habet faciem similem homini et caudam similem scorpioni et precipue desiderat vesci de humanis carnibus'.

[26] The ox [sermon 15, fol 95r] ut novistis est grande cornutum animal et forte ad tractum et designat þes helberes, ringleders et extorcionatores qui trahunt patriam totalem post se, agunt secundum libitum non secundum legem. For the other animals, see below.

[27] Rev. 6. 8.

[28] Sermon 11, fol 72v.

truth, and they will knit their brows. There will be a 'groyne'[rebuke] for your labour and you will be sent packing without a drink.[29]

As for the fox; why, he asks, cannot the *generosi* concentrate on hunting and destroying those foxes nearer home—'billeberers' and flatterers—for the woodland variety never caused such harm to the realm?[30]

He makes similar use of familiar flora. The herb garden of paradise is said to have grown a perfect rose, finer in colour than the primrose or the peone, more sweet-smelling than the lily or rosemary.[31]

There is frequent mention of games. Remember, warns the preacher, that death must come. However robust or handsome you may be, you must draw that lot. Your game may be a strong one, but at length by death's move comes 'chek mate'.[32] Elsewhere the fortunes of this fleeting world are likened to a boy chasing his shadow on a wall. When he believes it to be within his grasp, it suddenly vanishes. So is it with lordship in this world; when men put too much faith in it and think themselves secure, some misfortune or mischief causes it to dissolve.[33]

Another game illustrates the activity of the gluttonous. He who runs round a dish to which a lighted candle is affixed becomes so giddy that when he tries to move towards the flame he falls into the fire on the way, bangs his head on a bench, or clutches at his shadow.[34] Such is the fate of those who think to capture the light of happiness by the life of pleasure. To feed their bodies they rush from cook to cook, tavern to tavern, encircling the dish so often that for each candle they see two.[35]

Blind Man's Buff or—as the preacher calls it—'þe bobbid ludus',

[29] Sermon 13, fol 84^r, Volunt agitare supercilia super te, habebis a groyn pro tuo labore et ibis antequam potaveris.

[30] Sermon 3, fol 16^v. Elsewhere [sermon 9, fol 55^v] there is a reference to the 'wile fox'.

[31] Sermon 11, fol 71^v.

[32] Sermon 1, fol 3^r.

[33] Sermon 4, fol 23^v.

[34] Sermon 9, fol 56^v. Hit fareth de istis [gulosis] sicut de ludentibus perdicem sub disco. Videmus quod si quis currat sepius rond circa discum ubi figitur candele lumen caput wext so gidi cerebrum ita evertitur quod quando credit se optime procedere versus lumen vel cadit in ignem per viam vel frangit caput ad scabellum vel abit awayward et capit tuam umbram. Sic est de istis gulosis que [sic] credunt capere lumen felicitatis sua delicata vita . . .

[35] *Ibid*, . . . currunt a cocis ad cocos a taberna ad tabernas ad pascendum cadaver adeunt ita frequenter circa discum, ciphus rowt so longe inter ipsos, donec quelibet candela appareat due.

exemplifies the sinner who must blame anyone but himself. The game, it is said, was played by the soldiers with Christ during his passion. The players run round their blindfold comrade shouting

a bobbid, a bobbid, a biliried (byrlyryhode)
smyte not her bot þou smyte a god[36]

and he tries to guess who has struck him. In like manner the devil blindfolds the sinner, who blames his fate, God's ordinance, the fact that he was born under such and such a planet, or the devil himself. But the sinner must accept that it is he who has sinned and wounded his own soul. He has to 'pley fere', remain blindfold, and put the blame on himself.[37]

These instances by no means exhaust the vigorous world of the preacher, peopled by men and demons, illuminated by classical or more homely illustration; a bewildering amalgam of fable and fact, social comment and theological assertion. But the picture which emerges is impressionistic. By extracting his basic ideas from their diverse contexts it is possible to arrive at an overall pattern of thought, admittedly too systematic, but not altogether misleading.

The preacher exhibits a keen sense of recent history. There are no dates, of course, but the events are generally identifiable. Causation is for him a simple matter: lollardy lies at the root of all social and national ills, which cannot be rectified until it is extirpated.[38] Like many others of his day he casts a regretful glance at the supposedly settled times of Edward III, when english arms were successful abroad and heresy had not yet raised its head;[39] unrest and decline date from Wycliffe's time.[40] Hence he speaks approvingly, though not by name, of the statute *De heretico comburendo* (1401)—a 'sharp sentence' against lollards and the means whereby they are handed over to the fire.[41]

---

[36] This is quoted—from [G. R.] Owst, *Literature and Pulpit* [*in Medieval England,*] (Cambridge 1933, 2 ed Oxford 1961) p 510—in *Middle English Dictionary*, ed H. Kurath and S. M. Kuhn (Ann Arbor 1956–) see under 'bobet'. But the marginal 'byrlyryhode' is better for the rhyme than the 'biliried' of the text.

[37] Sermon 13, fol 82ʳ.

[38] For example, sermons 2, 3, 9, 16; fols 13ʳ, 17ʳ, 55ʳ, 99ᵛ.

[39] Sermon 25, fol 130ᵛ. Navis Anglie claudebatur infra pluribus annis a tempore Edwardi ultimi ad tempus nunc regis nostri. As Owst suggests, this could represent the preacher's own life-span.

[40] Sermon 6, fol 35ʳ, Ista guerra non duravit per unum vel duos dies sed a tempore Wiclif qui fuit armatus in heresi.

[41] *Ibid*, fol 35ᵛ, Per lanceam quam miles vibravit in manu interpretatur acuta sentencia contra lollardos per quam traduntur igni et morti.

In past time the english ship of state had been familiar with many and great dangers: when the commons rose against the lords (1381),[42] when the lords litigated among themselves—presumably a reference to Suffolk's impeachment (1386),[43] at the 'scharp schowre' of Shrewsbury—Northumberland's rebellion (1403),[44] when the lords rebelled—possibly the 'Southampton Plot' (1415),[45] and when the lollards rose against God and the king (1414) 'to a distroyed him and holichurch',[46] not to mention the hazards of Henry V's campaigns in Normandy and France.[47]

An intense nationalism pervades the sermons. For the preacher the ship of state—like that of our mortal life—comprises three integral parts: the forecastle is occupied by the clergy, the *corpus navis* by the commonality, and the hindcastle by the baronage—the king and his lords.[48] In the topcastle are the saints at rest in the realm, by means of whose alms, merits and prayers the ship is often saved from perils, and victory is gained over the nation's enemies. At one time the forecastle was set up 'w^t perfeccioun and heliness', the baronage in the hindcastle exhibited 'a stondard of bodile my3t and hardines', while the body of the ship was 'ful frawt magna copia diviciarum'.[49] When fully tackled, her three castles 'ful apparailid w^t stremores and pavys', she was a fair vessel to look upon.[50] So powerful was she that

---

[42] Sermons 16, 25; fols 97^v, 130^r.

[43] *Ibid*, Quando domini litigabant inter se.

[44] *Ibid*, At þe scharp schowr Salopie. 'Sharp shower' was a favourite expression: see, for instance, fols 61^r, 71^r, 106^r, 131^r.

[45] Sermon 6, fol 35^{r-v}, Fuisset triset inter rebelles dominos et lollardos qui insurrexerunt contra ipsum. I am assuming that this refers to two separate incidents (close in time), though they are conflated in the similar passage at fol 130^r (see next note).

[46] Sermon 25, fol 130^r. 'Fuit eciam in grandi periculo quando lollardi rebellabant et surrexerunt contra Deum et regem to a distroyed him . . .'. Compare sermon 22, fol 113^r, where the lollards are likewise set in opposition to God, the king, and the church's ministers.

[47] For instance, fol 35^v. 'He was schaply to ha be ded in campo aut capi ad bellum de Agyncourt nisi secure fuisset armatus armis gracie, non posset durare in yeme guerras Normannie nisi quod armatur aureis gracie armis'.

[48] Sermon 4, fol 22^r; repeated at fol 129^v (sermon 25). Compare sermons 10, 16; fols 61^r, 97^r. Owst, *Literature and Pulpit* pp 68 *et seq.*, considers the 'symbolic ship' and renders parts of the present sermons in english.

[49] Fol 129^v. At fol 61^r (sermon 10) it is the preacher himself who stands in the topcastle 'ad premuniendum vos de hostibus supra mare'. The steersmen are the clergy who rule the whole ship: 'þe rothir per quod tota navis is stirrid bi est predicacio et doctrina' (fol 62^v).

[50] Fol 129^v. Owst, *Literature and Pulpit* p 72 & n, has 'pavys' (with a palisading of shields), but it is just possible that the preacher may have intended 'streamers and pennons'. He uses 'pavysid' (with a 'v' form) earlier in the passage.

the strongest ship of Tours [?] dared not await her, the swift galleys of Spain on sighting her took flight, while the lusty coracles of Scotland struck sail and did her honour.[51] All christian realms once feared and honoured the english for their fortitude, their good government and virtuous life.[52] A ship thus ruled by virtue sailed on the sea of prosperity. Only when virtue decayed and vice held sway did fortune change and honour fall away. Then the craft became so enfeebled that it was in danger of being outsailed by the little fishing boat of Wales.[53]

The situation is not without remedy; a saviour has arrived in the person of Henry V whom the preacher—in apocalyptic imagery— sees as the celestial warrior[54] or the column which supports the whole temple.[55] In naval allegory he is the master mariner.[56] It is Henry who has been sent to smite lollards at home and frenchmen abroad.[57] There is a churchillian ring in his estimate of the king's greatest triumph: 'Nullus cum tam parva plebe passid so terful bellum cum palma victorie sicut ipse ad acerbam procellam de

---

[51] *Ibid.* Owst reads 'of toure' (a towered ship? and 'turyeres (or curyeres)'. The regular use of place-names in these passages points to a proper name, though 'tour' itself does not occur elsewhere. Tours, admittedly far inland, was on the Loire, and its merchants well known in England. 'Curyeres' is confirmed by 'krayir' in two other places (fols 22ʳ, 97ʳ). The *Scottish National Dictionary* ed W. Grant and D. D. Murison (Edinburgh 1941–), gives 'coracle' under Currach, Curragh. See also sermons 4, 16; fols 22ʳ, 97ʳ (where the 'great cog' of France and Normandy is added).

[52] Sermon 4, fol 22ʳ. 'Omnia Christiana regna olim timebant et venerabantur Anglicos propter fortitudinem et bonam gubernacionem que fuerat inter ipsos'. The phrase is omitted from fol 97ʳ, but it is repeated at fols 129ᵛ–130ʳ. Corresponding to the naval boast is a military one: 'Omnia Christiana regna honorabant et timebant Anglicos in tantum quod a litel penown Anglici militis sculd aferayed in campo totum exercitum regium'. Sermon 8, fol 50ʳ, repeated in sermon 11, fol 69ᵛ.

[53] Sermon 25, fol 130ʳ. Compare fol 22ʳ (sermon 4) where there is a similar passage with a gap in the MS after 'modica fischers bote'. Owst, *Literature and Pulpit* p 72 n 8, suggests that this is a reference to Owain Glyn Dŵr's successes against Henry IV.

[54] For example, sermon 6 fol 35ʳ. 'Iste celestis miles est qui celice vivit ligius dominus nostri [*sic*] rex quem Deus misit nobis in defensionem ecclesie et salvacionem tocius regni'. In sermon 5 (fol 29ᵛ) Christ himself figures as the celestial knight sent by God for man's salvation. See 2 Macc. 11.8.

[55] For example, sermon 15 fol 95ᵛ. 'Sed misericors et miserator dominus videns ruinam et miseriam sui templi huius regni quod erat in puncto corruendi et destruendi ex sua gracia et misericordia erexit fortem columpnam in medio templi ad sustinendum totum opus nostrum ligium dominum graciosum regem, qui nunc est, Deus fortificet ipsum in virtute et augeat ipsius honorem'. See Rev. 3.12.

[56] For example, sermon 25 fols 132ʳ, 133ʳ.

[57] For example, sermon 15 fol 96ᵛ. 'Noster graciosus rex suos *is*tomodo vicit hostes intus et ex[t]erius.' The recent (tarde) death of Oldcastle (1417)—the captain of the lollards— is mentioned at fol 38ʳ.

Achyncourt'.[58] It is the love which Henry bears towards God and the church—the *spiritus vite*—which has caused the wheel of fortune to turn upwards once more.[59] As he has increased the worship of God by the foundation of holy places,[60] so God has increased his honour and by grace saved him from many dangers, giving him victory over his enemies.[61]

If only, laments the preacher, the lords and commons could live virtuously as they had formerly done, honouring God and the church —witness the great monasteries, colleges and hospitals. At such time there was a 'spring flod' of wealth, great supply of goods, peace at home, victory over enemies abroad. His final sermon concludes with a prayer that God may preserve Henry on land and sea, in peace and war, and that all may live righteously. Thus can the king say: 'Of alle þe londes aboute me I am sovereyn lord'.[62]

The same notion of national superiority is expressed in the exordium of another sermon, in a quite different context. Although other universities shine in the firmament of the church they are, asserts the preacher, as little stars in comparison to 'our' sun, Oxford.[63] Other studia excelled in some branch of learning—Paris in theology, Bologna in law, Salerno in medicine, Toulouse in mathematics—but Oxford, the fount of wisdom, excelled in all. Its bright sun gave light to the whole realm, the beams of its wisdom spread throughout the world. All other studia sought her opinion, other realms honoured her, 'as fer as God hay lond Oxon habuit nomen'. But now the situation has changed. The sun has been eclipsed by the moon of evil living, the seven mortal sins are fostered, there is 'gettinge and feʒtinge', robbery and homicide. By common report scholars waste the goods of their friends in dishonest and unclean living. The cause of all this is

[58] Sermon 25, fol 132^r.
[59] *Ibid.* 'Et quare credis rota sui honoris rotatur versus sursum? Certe spiritus vite ascendit qui movet istam rotam. Quid est iste spiritus vite? Bonus zelus altus amor quem habet erga Deum et ecclesiam.'
[60] In pursuance of his father's vows Henry V founded the carthusian house at Sheen and the nearby bridgettine house of Syon. E. F. Jacob, *The Fifteenth Century* (Oxford 1961) p 196; and for Syon's foundation, *The Incendium Amoris of Richard Rolle of Hampole* ed M. Deanesly (Manchester 1915) pp 91–144.
[61] Fol 132^r, Sic ipse augmentavit cultum Dei per fundacionem locorum sacrorum et destruccionem lollardorum. Sic Deus auxit honorem ipsius, salvavit eum per graciam a multis periculis and sent illi victoriam de suis inimicis.
[62] Fol 133^r. See Ecclus. 24.8–11. This may well have been a valedictory sermon for Henry's final journey to France.
[63] Sermon 8, fols 48^r–49^r.

that the university has become a breeding ground of heretics and lollards.[64]

The preacher's enumeration of current misfortunes is commonplace: dissensions at home, lack of success abroad—prior to Henry V's reign, murrain of animals and pestilence. The underlying causes, lollardy apart, are lack of faith, a decline of charity, and reliance on sorcery, witchcraft and diabolic intervention.[65]

A sermon on confession with its conventional subdivision into the seven mortal sins—allegorically the seven towers of the city of Jericho—permits expansion on the sickness of the times.[66] Elements of this catalogue of faults recur elsewhere: ostentation in dress even *inter vulgares*,[67] the falsifying of weights and measures and oppression of the poor,[68] the spreading of dissension and discord,[69] the malice which forces men into the Marshalsea prison,[70] and drunkenness—the first step in a descent through lust, theft, homicide and desperation, to the pit of hell.[71]

As might be anticipated the preacher's stance with respect to the church and its role in society is traditional and conservative. His concept of reform—to put an idea into his head—was simply a return

---

[64] Fol 49ʳ, Sicut hec universitas fuit olim verus fons fidei et virtutis sic reputatur iam a chef . . . [gap in MS] hereticorum et lollardorum. Istomodo mater nostra scandalizatur. Non est meum verbum, est communis clamor in patria.

[65] For example, sermons 3, 18; fols 18ʳ, 103ʳ. For lollardy see, for instance, sermon 9 fol 55ʳ, Sed que est causa istius tocius doloris creditis? Certe serpentinum venenum inferni execrata lollardria que flatur inter nos.

[66] Sermon 1, fols 11ᵛ–12ʳ.

[67] Sermon 4, fol 23ᵛ, Quia ut dicitur peccatum luxurie non tantum fuit usitatum ante ista tempora inter vulgares sicut iam in diebus. He frequently returns to this theme of ostentatious dress, for example in sermons 2, 22; fols 10ᵛ–11ʳ, 114ᵛ–115ᵛ.

[68] Sermon 1, fol 11ᵛ, see under 'Avaricia'. Si pauperem iniqua extorcione oppresisti . . . Si aliquem defraudasti in mercimoniis per falsas ulnas et mensuras. Compare fols 94ᵛ–95ʳ. In sermon 7 (fol 45ʳ) the preacher, using a musical analogy, castigates the victuallers of his day. See also fol 57ᵛ.

[69] Fol 12ʳ see under 'Invidia'. Vide si peiorasti aut deprivasti si diffamasti aut scandalizasti proximum, si falsas fabulas finxisti ex proprio capite ab uno ad alium portasti discenciones et discordia in Christi plebe seminasti.

[70] *Ibid*, see under 'Ira'. Vide si gessisti rancorem aut odium adversus aliquem si prosecutus es ipsum per brevia si imbillasti eum in Marchesiam magis ex malicia quam ex iusticia, for to undo þi self for to undo him. Compare fol 41ᵛ. On the use of the name 'Marshalsea' see R. B. Pugh, *Imprisonment in Medieval England* (Cambridge 1968) pp 120–1.

[71] Fol 12ʳ see under 'Gula'. Also sermon 10, fol 62ʳ, Vis videre hoc aperte þes riotours qui cadunt cotidie in ebrietatem, iactantur de gula in luxuriam, de luxuria in furtum, de furto in homicidium, de homicidio in desperacionem, de desperacione in puteum inferni.

to order, deviation from which had brought the chaos of misbelief and heresy.[72]

Ostensibly the church is conceived in national terms as an integral part of the english realm. Its virtues and vices are those observed by the preacher himself. The pope is peripheral, though he merits a word of defence against lollard rejection.[73]

Within english society the church, like the other two elements— the nobility and the commonality—has its appropriate function. In the allegories of the tree and of mount Sinai it is the clergy—the 'heavenly birds'—who occupy the branches of the tree and the heights of the mountain; the laity—terrestrial beings—keep place at the foot.[74] *Clericus* is regularly used as a synonym for *literatus, laicus* for *illiteratus*. This distinction in its extreme form was anachronistic, as the preacher knew well enough; both lettered and unlettered laymen were tinkering with theology.[75] But for him there was only one solution; the church must reassert its monopoly of exposition. Consequently, the sermons have a strong doctrinal undercurrent. Against a background of heresy and 'novel intoxications'[76] they vindicate the traditional *via salvacionis*. People must shun the seven mortal sins, perform the seven works of mercy, keep the ten commandments and all the approved usages of the church—veneration of images, pilgrimages, fasting and oblations.[77] Eucharistic doctrine— rejected by the lollards—is stoutly affirmed, but with the warning

---

[72] This and other assumptions to be gathered from the sermons were doubtless commonplace. At many points there are echoes of the thought of Jean Gerson. See, for instance, Louis B. Pascoe, *Jean Gerson: Principles of Church Reform* (Leiden 1973), and for the methodology which Pascoe adopted: G. B. Ladner, *The Idea of Reform* (New York 1967).

[73] Sermon 15, fol 91ᵛ, Speciale templum et habitacio quod Christus filius Dei superni habet hic in terris est multitudo et congregacio fidelium angligenarum concordat scriptura 2ᵃ ad Corinthios vi. The pope occurs in a phrase which is transferred from one sermon to another: sermons 6, 24; fols 35ʳ, 125ʳ.

[74] Sermon 3, fols 14ʳ ff; nos 13, 24; fols 79ᵛ ff, 124 ff. See 'Wilde Wittes and Wilfulnes' pp 148–9.

[75] For example, sermon 13 fol 80ᵛ, Isti laici qui nesciunt litteras volunt se smater de profundissima clerimonia, movebunt altas materias, petent arduas questiones difficiles alicui clerico ad solvendas. Compare sermon 16, fol 98ʳ, Ideo tu qui es laicus et licet bene litteratus tene te deorsum ad pedem montis. But clergy also had to recognise their limitations, Minimus punctus fidei est supra humanum sensum, transcendit naturalem racionem. Nullus clericus potest ipsum attingere nisi Deus ad ipsum descendat per specialem inspiracionem (fol 80ʳ). A similar statement is to be found at fol 97ᵛ.

[76] Sermon 10, fol 64ᵛ.

[77] See fol 64ʳ and compare fol 113ᵛ (sermon 22).

that laymen should not attempt to reason it. Such subtleties are for clerks, although in any case the least point of the creed transcends the limits of natural reason.[78] One contemporary trend receives the preacher's approbation, that of mysticism (*contemplacio divina*), but whether he had in mind its practice by the clergy alone or by people in general is not clear.[79]

Expectedly the preacher is utterly opposed to the secularisation of church property; a suggestion fostered by the rumour that an infinite treasure lay beneath the 'column' of the religious. The idea is divisive; an invitation for temporal lords to despoil God's temple.[80] But earthly goods must be shared, one half being retained for one's own physical support, the other for division among the poor, the blind, the halt, the sick and the bedridden.[81]

The preacher directed a scourging tongue at the lack of lay devotion. Disrespect in church, especially at mass, is a recurrent plaint. People traipse from one end of the building to the other and tittle-tattle with everyone they meet. If there is trade or business to be done, they proceed to transact it. At the elevation of the blessed body they only go on one knee for fear of cracking their shoes. As soon as the sacrament is over they take holy water and say *sancti Amen*;[82] they will not wait a moment longer. Traditional practices have declined: pilgrimages are virtually at an end, meritorious offerings to saints and their images have fallen off.[83]

The laity must turn to the priest with cure—the spiritual doctor, the celestial armourer.[84] At the same time, the preacher does not

---

[78] Sermons 3, fol 18ᵛ, Oportet te scire, non potes iudicare hic secundum gustum vel visum quia hic deficit naturalis racio, omnes sensus tui decipiuntur. Compare fols 90ʳ, 98ʳ, Quod Christi corpus caro videlicet et sanguis est in altari sub specie panis et vini per virtutem verborum Christi que sacerdos recitat in missa . . . sed subtilitatem et circumstancias istius puncti, quomodo sapor et color remanens panis et vini absque substancia panis et vini et alias circumstancias quas non expedit hic recitare, non teneris cognoscere, non pertinet ad te (fol 98ʳ).

[79] See sermon 22, fol 117ᵛ, Et sicut per speculum concavum capitur ignis a sole, sic per visum speculi misericordie per contemplacionem ignis devocionis et amoris accenditur in nobis erga Deum. This suggests Rolle, but I have not found this passage in his *Incendium Amoris*. Compare fol 14ᵛ, addressed to the clergy, tenete vos in altis ramis fidei, date vos contemplacioni divine.

[80] Sermon 15, fols 93ᵛ–94ʳ.

[81] Sermon 4, fol 23ʳ. This advice is apparently directed specifically to the clergy.

[82] Sermons 13, 17; fols 83ʳ, 101ʳ. In the later version this refers to the beginning of the mass, Vix assumet aquam benedictam et dicere 'Sancti Amen' ut veniunt, capiunt consortes, transith ecclesiam up and doune. Compare fol 30ʳ.

[83] Sermon 5, fol 30ʳ.

[84] Fols 31ᵛ, 39ᵛ.

ignore clerical shortcomings. Clerks ought to be the mirror of holiness, but they are so engaged in worldly matters that they neglect their sheep, allowing them to remain uncorrected.[85] The extravagance of clerical attire merits specific condemnation,[86] as does the avarice attributed to ecclesiastical courts.[87]

Our preacher, then, echoes the hopes and fears, the woes and aspirations of a man of his particular time and place. He sees himself confronted by a society which is losing its faith and turning to other gods; a society lukewarm in religion, oblivious to the needs of the poor, and riddled with lollardy. Detraction and backbiting, 'pop-holiness' and hypocrisy are abroad.[88] His expressed aspirations are confined to the english people and may be summed up as victory over enemies without, and the eradication of heresy and irreligion within. The necessary combination of military prowess and religious zeal is to be found in that apocalyptic warrior-king, Henry V, sent from heaven to vanquish Antichrist.[89]

The preacher invokes Boethius's wheel, turned by the blindfold Dame Fortune,[90] to illustrate the transience of this world's glory and the levelling influence of fate—'hodie dominus, cras a lost man'.[91] Death was likewise a great leveller. Yet the preacher's emphasis on

---

[85] Sermon 4, fol 22^v, Indulgent parochianis suis et omnium pessimum lucro modici auri paciuntur subiectos suos iacere in peccatis et non corrigunt ipsos. Or again (fol 2^r), Et nulla fit correccio vel modica. Moreover, according to the preacher there might be some danger in making correction because of the spread of lollardy, Suus ordinarius ipsum non audebit corrigere pre mortis timore (*ibid*).

[86] For example, fol 10^v (sermon 2), Sacerdotes prankyt [and] pinchet in togis suis sicut seculares. Compare fol 115^r (sermon 22), þi goune is pinchet and prankid retro w^t goteris enowe, apparently a specific reference to the clergy.

[87] Sermon 22, fol 116^r, Lex et avaricia connectuntur, rectum non habet exitum nisi moneta ostendatur. Avaricia regnat communiter in omni curia et adhuc Christiana curia est pessima ut noscitur per experienciam.

[88] See, for example, fol 93^v.

[89] Norman Cohn, *The Pursuit of the Millennium* (rev ed Oxford 1970) has demonstrated the influence of apocalyptic writings on medieval and later heretical movements. For some animadversions see R. E. Lerner, *The Heresy of the Free Spirit in the Later Middle Ages* (Berkeley 1972). As our preacher shows, the orthodox also invoked apocalyptic imagery. Antichrist, Antiochus Epiphanes, the celestial knight, the pillar of the temple, the great portent in the sky and the pale white horse all figure in his sermons.

[90] Sermon 11, fol 69^v, for instance. Boethius's wheel was a commonplace of the fifteenth century. A contemporary illustration of it aptly serves as the cover for F. R. H. Du Boulay's, *An Age of Ambition* (London 1970). Our preacher also used Ezechiel's wheel—within which moved the 'spiritus vite'—to represent the 'honor istius seculi'. See fols 70^r, 131^r.

[91] Sermon 25, fol 131^r. Compare fols 49^v, 69^v.

death does not proceed from morbid preoccupation, but from an anxiety to balance the extravagant love of life he saw all around him by a proper concern for the welfare of man's immortal soul. Though he condemns extravagance and ostentation, he does not accept poverty as desirable—except for the friars who sought 'high perfection'.[92] Involuntary poverty involves failure, the opposite of worldly success. Honour and wealth are signs of God's favour to right-living men: it is evil living that excites God's anger and brings the retribution of poverty and ill-fortune.[93] This is the familiar old testament view, with the english taking the place of the israelites as the chosen people of God.

In short, the preacher's message is that for peace and security to be reinstated in the english realm, people must turn from heresy to the church's teaching, from sin to a life regulated by charity—the love of God. Only thus can the natural order be reconstituted, the unity of the nation restored,[94] and the wheel of fortune made to revolve to England's advantage by the eponymous hero, Henry V.[95]

Dalhousie University

---

[92] Sermon 15, fol 124[v].

[93] For medieval notions of poverty see *Études sur l'Histoire de la Pauvreté*, ed Michel Mollat (Paris 1974). Cahier no 2 (1963–4 roneotype) contains a paper by Mollat (not included in the above and which I have not yet seen) entitled: 'La pauvreté dans la pensée de Thomas Brinton, évêque de Rochester, au temps de soulèvement des travailleurs'. See *Brinton*, intro, pp xxiii–xxiv, xxvii–xxviii.

[94] The preacher frequently stresses national unity and its necessity. For example, fol 103[r] 'Nostrum regnum quod est unum corpus'. He harks back nostalgically to a time when 'clerus and þe laife huius terre wer knet to gedur in uno fagot and brenden super istum ignem [perfecte caritatis]' (fol 50[v]). The most extravagant eulogy of Henry V is in sermon 6, fol 35[r–v], but sermon 25 is notably jingoistic. The latter is shortly to be printed in *Mediaeval Studies*. For a brief discussion of fifteenth-century 'nationalism' see L. R. Loomis, 'Nationality at the Council of Constance: an Anglo-French Dispute', *Change in Medieval Society* ed S. L. Thrupp (New York 1964) pp 279–96. Denys Hay, 'The Church of England in the later Middle Ages', *History* 53 (1968) pp 35–50, rightly argues that it can be appropriate to speak of the 'Church of England' at this time.

[95] Since reading this paper I have received pertinent information from Patrick Horner who is working on some english sermons in another Bodleian MS, Laud misc. 706. I have made a preliminary examination of this MS, which contains just over thirty sermons. Four of them, as Horner points out, are to be found in Bodley MS 649 (nos 5— inchoate in Laud, 12, 15 and 19). The Laud MS has ornamental capitals reminiscent of those in the Bodley MS and the initial hand, which recurs from time to time, is similar to (and possibly the same as) the hand of the latter—attributed to John Swetstock. A rubric (fol 13[r]) declares that John Paunteley preached one of the sermons at the funeral of Walter Froucester, abbot of Gloucester, 3 May 1412. But although some of the Laud MS sermons have characteristics recalling those of the Bodley material, it is

probable that closer scrutiny will show that the former constitute a collection which is, as the numerous hands suggest, far from homogeneous. The Laud MS was in the possession of John Paunteley, a monk of St Peter's abbey, Gloucester. He was ordained deacon and priest in 1392—*Registrum Johannis Trefnant Episcopi Herefordensis,* ed W. W. Capes (London 1916) pp 201, 203; *Bodleian Library Quarto Catalogues II, Laudian Manuscripts,* ed H. O. Coxe (repr Oxford 1973) pp 505–6. The Paunteley of the Worcester *sede vacante* register, who was ordained priest in 1375, see *A Biographical Register of the University of Oxford,* ed A. B. Emden (Oxford 1957–9), must be a different man. According to Emden (citing PRO C47/127/5, now C258/38 no 30), Paunteley was (in 1410) a doctor of theology and (by inference) from Gloucester College. What we know of Paunteley suggests that he would fit very well as the author of the Bodley MS 649 sermons, the first twenty-five that is. He must have been born about 1367, which would make him roughly 55 years of age in 1422. I am most grateful to Horner for placing his information about Paunteley at my disposal.

LUTHER AND THE RIGHT OF
RESISTANCE TO THE EMPEROR

by W. D. J. CARGILL THOMPSON

L IKE most problems connected with Luther, the question of his attitude to the right of resistance to the emperor is one that has attracted a great deal of attention from german scholars. Sixty years ago, at the height of the first world war, Karl Müller published his pioneering essay, *Luthers Äusserungen über das Recht des bewaffneten Widerstands gegen den Kaiser*, in which he provided the first detailed analysis of the development of Luther's views:[1] since then the problem has been extensively debated by a succession of german historians and theologians.[2] Yet it is perhaps typical of the insularity of so much english historical writing on the continental reformation that these debates have largely been ignored on this side of the Channel. Even to-day there is no adequate study of the problem in english. It is, of course, common knowledge that Luther changed his views on the question of resistance to the emperor after the diet of Augsburg under pressure from the protestant princes; but one will search most english biographies of Luther in vain for more than a

---

[1] [Karl] Müller, [*Luthers Äusserungen über das Recht des bewaffneten Widerstands gegen den Kaiser*], Sitzungsberichte der Königlich Bayerischen Akademie der Wissenschaften, Phil.-hist. Klasse, Jahrgang 1915, Abhandlung 8 (Munich 1915).

[2] Among the most important contributions to the discussion of the problem since Müller are: [Fritz] Kern, ['Luther und das Widerstandsrecht',] *ZRG*, 37, *KA* 6 (1916) pp 331–40; [Johannes] Heckel, *Lex Charitatis* [*: Eine juristische Untersuchung über das Recht in der Theologie Martin Luthers*], Abhandlungen der Bayerischen Akademie der Wissenschaften, Phil.-hist. Klasse, N.F. 36 (Munich 1953), 2 rev ed, ed Martin Heckel (Darmstadt 1973), App I 'Luthers Lehre vom Widerstandsrecht gegen den Kaiser', pp 295–306; [Hermann] Dörries, ['Luther und das Widerstandsrecht'] in *Wort und Stunde,* 3 (Göttingen 1970) pp 195–270, which has now replaced Müller as the standard work on the subject. [*Das*] *Widerstandsrecht* [*als Problem der deutschen Protestanten 1523–1546*], ed [Heinz] Scheible, Texte zur Kirchen- und Theologiegeschichte 10 (Gütersloh 1969), contains a valuable selection of documents relating to the problem, including several of Luther's most important *Gutachten*. For detailed bibliographies of the modern literature on the subject, see Heckel, *Lex Charitatis*, p 295 n 1441; Scheible, *Widerstandsrecht*, pp 9–13; *Luther und die Obrigkeit*, ed. [G.] Wolf, Wege der Forschung 85 (Darmstadt 1972) pp 469–82. The latter contains a selection of articles published in the 1950s and 1960s, several of which relate to the question of Luther and the right of resistance to the emperor (see especially those by K-F. Stolzenau, pp 196–302; E. Weymar, pp 303–34; and G. Wolf, pp 335–40).

passing mention of this episode[3] or for a clear analysis of what the change involved, while the subsequent evolution of Luther's ideas in the later 1530s has escaped notice almost entirely. If, therefore, I am only too conscious that in choosing to discuss this subject I am venturing into territory that has already been intensively explored, I may perhaps be allowed to justify my choice on three grounds: first, that it is particularly germane to the theme of this volume; secondly, that it is a topic which has hitherto received too little attention from english historians; and thirdly, that even to-day there is considerable disagreement among german scholars over the way in which Luther's development should be interpreted, so that it is perhaps worth making a fresh attempt to draw the strands of the story together.

A study of the development of Luther's views on the question of resistance to the emperor enables us to explore the theme of 'the Church and Politics' from a number of different angles. In the first place, it provides an opportunity to see how Luther, who has so often been accused—quite wrongly—of being indifferent to politics, attempted to deal with a concrete political issue. Secondly, it brings out very clearly the tensions which existed within the reformation almost from the beginning between the conflicting demands of religious principle and political necessity. No issue of practical politics presented the first generation of german reformers with such acute moral problems and it was one with which Luther was continually concerned throughout the last twenty-five years of his life. During these twenty-five years his ideas changed slowly but radically, largely in response to the pressure of political events. A study of the problem therefore reveals not only the strains to which Luther's teaching was exposed but also the extent to which his thinking was influenced, both consciously and unconsciously, by external factors. In addition, it has important implications for the general history of political thought in the sixteenth century: for the debate over the right of resistance to the emperor in Germany gave rise to the later protestant doctrine of the right of inferior magistrates to resist their superiors.

From the publication of the edict of Worms in 1521 until the outbreak of the schmalkaldic war in 1546 the german protestants had to face the continual possibility that Charles V would at some time or another take active measures to suppress the reformation. It was a threat which varied in intensity at different times. Throughout the

[3] An exception is [James] Mackinnon, *Luther and the Reformation*, 4 (London 1930) pp 24–8.

greater part of the 1520s the prospect of imperial intervention remained fairly remote. But the question was always there in the background—even if it did not become acute until after 1529—what action, if any, should the protestants take if the emperor were to try to enforce the edict of Worms against them? In practice, the issue with which the protestants were concerned was whether it was lawful for the estates of the empire (*die Reichsstände*)—the princes and the imperial cities—to resist the emperor in defence of the gospel. At this period it was taken for granted that the common people did not possess the right to resist their superiors: the only question that was seriously considered was whether the princes and the cities had the right to defend themselves if attacked by the emperor in the cause of religion.

It was a question that involved a number of different issues—political, legal, moral and theological—all of which tended to cut across one another, but which need to be distinguished. On the political plane, there was the practical question of whether the princes and cities were prepared to take up arms against the emperor and under what circumstances. On this issue there were marked differences between the attitudes of the leading protestant estates, especially in the 1520s.[4] Philip of Hesse, for example, never appears to have had any scruples about the concept of resistance; Saxony, on the other hand, while supporting the idea of a defensive league against the catholic princes, vacillated for a considerable time before accepting the principle that the emperor might be resisted; while a few states, of which Nuremberg is the outstanding example, ended by repudiating the principle of resistance to the emperor altogether, partly on theological grounds but also for reasons of state. Closely bound up with the political question was the legal question, whether the estates of the empire possessed a constitutional right to resist the emperor under certain circumstances? Here, however, once the political will to resist existed, the jurists attached to the saxon and hessian courts found little difficulty in producing an array of arguments from roman

---

[4] The most comprehensive modern study of the policies of the protestant princes and cities in the 1520s and early 1530s is [Ekkehart] Fabian, [*Die Entstehung des Schmalkaldischen Bundes und seiner Verfassung 1524/29–1531/35: Brück, Philipp von Hessen und Jakob Sturm*], Schriften zur Kirchen- und Rechtsgeschichte 1 (2 ed Tübingen 1962). Older but still useful is [Hans von] Schubert, *Bekenntnisbildung[und Religionspolitik 1529/30 (1524–34): Untersuchungen und Texte*] (Gotha 1910). Both books contain important chapters dealing with the political history of the debate over the right of resistance to the emperor.

and canon law, and from the laws and customs of the empire, to justify the right of resistance, arguments which eventually exercised a considerable influence on the views of the theologians.

Finally, there was the moral and theological question, was resistance compatible with the teaching of the gospel? Luther had always taught that resistance to properly constituted authority was forbidden by divine law. 'The powers that be are ordained of God. Whosoever therefore resisteth the power, resisteth the ordinance of God: and they that resist shall receive to themselves damnation' (Rom. 13: 1-2). It was the christian's duty to endure oppression, however tyrannical his rulers might be. If his ruler commanded him to do something that was contrary to divine or natural law, then he must refuse obedience and be prepared to suffer the consequences.[5] *Leyden, leyden, Creutz, creutz ist der Christen recht, des und keyn anders,* as he admonished the peasants in 1525.[6] The question was whether this principle extended to the estates of the empire in their relations with the emperor. Initially Luther held that it did, and he repeatedly advised the elector Frederick the Wise and his successor, the elector John, against engaging in any form of opposition to the emperor. But after the diet of Speyer of 1529 he came under increasing political pressure to modify his position, and eventually at the end of 1530 he did so, at first reluctantly and equivocally, but later at the end of his life with increasing enthusiasm.

Thus there are, in fact, three stages in Luther's development with which we shall be concerned in this paper. First, the period down to 1530, when he opposed resistance to the emperor under all circumstances; secondly, the period after the declaration of Torgau in October 1530, when he conceded with extreme reluctance that there might possibly be a valid legal right of resistance, although as a theologian he refused to pronounce on the question which he insisted was a matter for the lawyers. Finally, there is a period at the end of his life, in the late 1530s, when he reversed many of his earlier views and emerged as an outspoken champion of resistance to the emperor on theological as well as on legal grounds.

The possibility of a confrontation between the princes and the emperor—and with it the problem of how the princes should act in

[5] For a classic statement of Luther's teaching on non-resistance and the limits of obedience, see *Von weltlicher Oberkeit, WA* 11, esp pp 265-8.
[6] *WA* 18, p 310.

such a situation—was first raised by the publication of the edict of Worms in 1521, although initially only in a limited form. In the long term the edict was to provide the main legal justification for Charles V's later moves against the protestant estates and the question of its enforcement was to become one of the most divisive issues of german politics of the next twenty-five years. But in 1521 this still lay in the future. At the time the edict was promulgated there were no protestant estates. Consequently, the question of whether the estates had the right to resist the emperor for the sake of religion did not arise directly. Nevertheless, the edict raised one immediate issue which was a potential source of conflict. This concerned the fate of Luther himself. The edict was addressed to the electors, princes and other ruling authorities of the empire. Under clause 27 it was laid down that after the expiry of Luther's safe-conduct no one was to harbour him, 'but in whatever place you'—that is, the recipients of the edict—'shall find him, if you have sufficient power, you shall take and bind him and bring him or cause him to be brought to us in close custody, or at the least you shall instantly notify us where he may be taken, and in the meanwhile you shall guard him carefully in prison until you receive our instructions as to how he shall be dealt with further'.[7] This clause posed a potentially acute problem for the elector of Saxony. Up until the diet of Worms Frederick the Wise had been able to justify his refusal to surrender Luther with strong legal arguments[8] and Charles V had tacitly acknowledged the strength of Frederick's position when he agreed to summon Luther to Worms. The publication of the edict of Worms altered the situation radically. Luther had now been formally placed under the ban of the empire— even though he had challenged the validity of his excommunication by appealing to a general council—and Frederick would have been put in a difficult legal position, if Charles had proceeded to call upon him to surrender Luther. In fact, Charles appears to have been as anxious as Frederick to avoid an open confrontation and he secretly took steps to ensure that a copy of the edict was never officially sent to the elector.[9] But it was largely in order to find a way around this

[7] *Documents Illustrative of the Continental Reformation*, ed B. J. Kidd (Oxford 1911) no 45, pp 87–8.
[8] For a detailed study of Frederick's role in the Indulgences controversy and the legal arguments which he employed on Luther's behalf, see [Wilhelm] Borth, [*Die*] *Luthersache [(Causa Lutheri) 1517–1524; Die Anfänge der Reformation als Frage von Politik und Recht*], *Historische Studien* 414 (Lübeck/Hamburg 1970).
[9] *Ibid* pp 129–31.

dilemma that Frederick arranged for Luther to be kidnapped on his
way back from Worms and concealed in the Wartburg, and it is clear
that Luther was only persuaded to acquiesce in this arrangement in
order to rescue the elector from an embarrassing situation, and not
from any fears for his own safety.[10]

Luther outlined his own views on the question, some months later,
in the famous letter which he wrote to Frederick the Wise on 5 March
1522,[11] in which he announced his decision to leave the Wartburg
and return to Wittenberg without the elector's permission in order
to deal with the religious disturbances that had arisen there during
his absence. This letter is best known for the forthright manner in
which Luther justified his decision to disobey the elector's commands
on the grounds that his duty to God must override his obligations to
his temporal sovereign. But in the concluding paragraphs he went on
to advise Frederick on how he should proceed in the difficult
situation that Luther's return would create for him. In fact, his advice
was that the elector should do nothing, since he had already done too
much, and he should on no account take any steps to protect Luther
from the imperial authorities. 'Because I will not obey your Grace,
your Grace is excused before God if I am captured or put to death.
Before men your Grace should conduct himself thus: namely, as an
elector you should be obedient to the magistrate and allow his
Imperial Majesty to exercise authority over life and property in your
Grace's towns and lands, as he is entitled to do according to the
constitution of the Empire, and you should not defend nor resist
nor require anyone to resist or hinder the [imperial] power, if it wishes
to arrest or kill me. For no one should destroy or resist the power
except only he that has ordained it, otherwise it is rebellion and
against God'. On the other hand, Luther insists, there is no obligation
on the elector to become his executioner. It is enough if he permits
the envoys of the imperial government to enter his lands and arrest
Luther, in which case Luther will allow himself to be taken without
causing any trouble or danger to the elector—'For Christ has not
taught me to be a Christian at another's expense'. But should the
imperial authorities be so unreasonable as to require the elector himself
to lay hands on Luther, then Luther will give the elector further
advice at the appropriate time on what he should do; but he

[10] See Luther's letter to elector Frederick, 5 March 1522, *WA Br.* 2, no 455, p 455.
[11] *WA Br.* 2, no 455, pp 454–7.

undertakes that, whatever happens, the elector will come to no harm in body, estate or soul for his sake.[12]

Here in a nutshell is a classic statement of the basic principles of Luther's original position on the question of resistance to the emperor. As far as he personally is concerned, he is ready to suffer arrest and the elector must not intervene to protect him. The princes of the empire have no right to resist the emperor, however just the cause. For within the empire the emperor represents the powers that be that are ordained of God. In relation to the emperor the princes are merely subjects: for them to oppose his commands is to be guilty of rebellion, which is itself a sin against God. On the other hand, the princes are not obliged to assist the emperor in the performance of ungodly acts. Provided that the elector does not prevent the emperor's representatives from entering his territories, he is under no moral obligation to take active steps himself against Luther. Luther leaves open the further question of what is to be done if the imperial authorities should order the elector to arrest him—probably deliberately, because he did not want to trouble Frederick's conscience any further, but also perhaps because he was confident that the issue would not arise.

The letter also contains certain other ideas which are fundamental to the understanding of Luther's attitude to the question of resistance to the emperor in the 1520s. First, there is his strong moral conviction that the gospel ought not to be defended by force, an idea which he was to develop more fully in his treatise *Of Temporal Authority* of 1523; closely associated with this there is, secondly, his confident belief that God will protect and promote the gospel without any human assistance.[13] Both these ideas were among Luther's most deeply-held convictions during the first decade of the reformation and together they do much to explain the emotional fervour with which he initially opposed the idea of resistance to the emperor. It was a basic axiom of Luther's thought in the 1520s that the battles of the spirit could only be fought with spiritual weapons, with prayer and preaching, and this led him to condemn the use of force in support of the gospel under any circumstances.[14] Equally he believed passionately that God would never allow his cause to fail, but would

---

[12] *Ibid* p 456.
[13] *Ibid* pp 455–6: 'Dieser Sachen soll noch kann kein Schwert raten oder helfen, Gott muss hie allein schaffen, ohn alles menschlich Sorgen und Zutun'.
[14] Compare *Von weltlicher Oberkeit*, *WA* 11, pp 268–9.

always intervene to defend the gospel in ways which man could not foresee; consequently, he tended later in the decade to interpret any moves on the part of the protestant princes to form a defensive alliance on behalf of the gospel as evidence of lack of faith, since it indicated that they were not willing to put their trust in God alone.[15] Significantly, it was when Luther's faith in these two concepts began to weaken, as it did in the 1530s, that his attitude to the question of resistance to the emperor also underwent a change.

As it turned out, Frederick the Wise was never called upon to face the decision whether or not to surrender Luther. Following Charles V's return to Spain in the summer of 1521, the imperial governing council (*das Reichsregiment*), which was responsible for the administration of the empire in Charles's absence, showed extreme reluctance to enforce the edict of Worms and for the next eighteen months it successfully side-stepped the issue. However, the question of the enforcement of the edict could only be postponed; it could not be avoided altogether, and it re-emerged as a critical issue at the second diet of Nuremberg which sat from November 1522 to February 1523.[16] At the diet the papal legate presented the estates with a formal request from the new pope, Adrian VI, calling on them to implement the papal bull and the edict of Worms against Luther and his followers. At the same time, a group of catholic princes, led by Frederick's dynastic rivals, the elector Joachim I of Brandenburg and duke George of Albertine Saxony, began to press for active measures to be taken against electoral Saxony. In the end the crisis blew over. The estates finally resolved not to enforce the edict until the abuses in the church had been dealt with and they called instead for a new general council to be summoned within a year—although as a sop to the papal legate it was agreed that Frederick should be required to prevent Luther and his followers from writing or publishing any new works—a demand with which Luther not surprisingly refused to comply.[17] However, in the weeks before the diet reached its decision, the outlook for Saxony appeared so threatening that Frederick took the step of consulting the Wittenberg theologians on whether he might lawfully engage in a defensive war if he were to be

---

[15] Compare his letters to elector John of Saxony, 22 May 1529, *WA Br.* 5, no 1424, pp 76–7; 18 November 1529, *Ibid* no 1496, pp 181–3; 24 December 1529, *Ibid*, no 1511, pp 209–11.

[16] For the proceedings of the diet of Nuremberg in regard to the edict of Worms, see Borth, *Luthersache*, pp 135–43.

[17] See Luther's letter to elector Frederick, 29 May 1523, *WA Br.* 3, no 618, pp 75–7.

attacked for Luther's sake. It is to this crisis that we owe the first formal *Gutachten* that we have on the subject of resistance. These consist of four short statements by Luther, Melanchthon, Bugenhagen and Amsdorf, which were drawn up at the beginning of February 1523 at the request of the elector's secretary, Georg Spalatin.[18]

Because of their early date these *Gutachten* are of particular interest, but they also present problems of interpretation. The difficulty arises from the fact that Spalatin's original letter to the Wittenberg divines does not survive and we do not know the precise form of the questions that he put to them.[19] As a result, most historians have tended, in practice, to treat these statements as if they represented opinions on the question of whether it was lawful to resist the emperor.[20] But it is clear from the answers of Luther's colleagues—though not from that of Luther himself—that Spalatin's questions were couched in more general terms and that the problem with which the elector was immediately concerned was not whether he might resist the emperor, but whether he might offer any resistance in the event of his being attacked on Luther's account by an alliance of catholic princes. This problem was particularly pressing at this juncture for two reasons: first, because of Luther's previously-declared opposition to the use of force in defence of the gospel; and secondly, because of the real, if short-lived, threat that the elector of Brandenburg and duke George might attempt to invade Saxony under the pretext of enforcing the edict of Worms.

Luther's answer is terse to the point of ambiguity and it presents the most problems of interpretation. He begins by insisting that so long as the elector maintains his present position of neutrality in regard to Luther's cause[21] he should not go to war on account of it, but 'ought to yield to the imperial power' and permit it to 'arrest and proceed

[18] All four statements are printed, with a useful historical introduction, in *WA Br.* 12, no 4222, pp 35–45; also (without introduction) in Scheible, *Widerstandsrecht*, nos 1–4, pp 17–19.
[19] See *WA Br.* 12, no 4222, Introduction, p 36. Some of the specific points raised by Spalatin can be deduced from the answers of Melanchthon, Bugenhagen and Amsdorf—for example whether it is wrong for a prince to go to war without the consent of his people (see below pp 169–70).
[20] Compare Müller pp 4, 6–9; Dörries, 3, pp 196–8.
[21] For Frederick's position at this period, see Paul Kalkoff, 'Friedrich der Weise und Luther', *HZ* 132 (1925) pp 41–2. Frederick officially maintained in his dealings with the imperial authorities that he was in no way committed to the truth of Luther's teaching, but that his only concern in the matter was to ensure that *dieser nicht ungehört vergewaltigt werde.*

against those whom it wishes in his territories, since the emperor is his lord by the consent of God and of men, even though they be ungodly'. However, he then goes on to concede that 'if the elector wishes to undertake war for the sake of this cause' (*si autem vellet bellum suscipere pro tuenda ista causa*) he may do so under strictly defined conditions. In the first place, he must publicly acknowledge that Luther's cause is just and abandon his previous attitude of neutrality. Secondly, he may not go to war for the reason that these people are his subjects, 'but he may as a foreigner coming from a foreign land go to the assistance of foreigners' (*sed tanquam alienus alienis ex aliena terra veniens succurrat*).²² Thirdly, he may act if he has a special divine calling (*vocante singulari spiritu et fide*). Otherwise he must yield to the superior sword and die with those whom he acknowledges to be christians. Fourthly, provided that the dispute is between him and his equals—if, for example, duke George or the elector of Brandenburg or some one else should attack him 'not with the emperor nor at the emperor's command, but out of their own arrogance'—then he may act in the same way as in wars involving secular causes; in other words, he should first offer justice and peace; then, if that is refused, he may 'resist force by force on behalf of his subjects'.²³

This document has usually been interpreted as meaning that Luther was prepared to concede the possibility that the emperor might be resisted under certain hypothetical conditions, but these conditions were so stringent that, as Karl Müller put it, it was unthinkable that they could be fulfilled.²⁴ Consequently, Luther may effectively be said to have ruled out the idea of resistance to the emperor in practice, while admitting it in theory. Certainly, Luther's answer can be read in this sense, if one starts with the preconception that the only question he was discussing throughout the paper was that of resistance to the

²² The meaning of this obscurely worded passage appears to be that, while it is wrong for a prince to defend his own subjects if they are attacked for the sake of religion, it is permissible for him to go to the assistance of foreigners who may be attacked. To illustrate Luther's meaning, Müller cites the example of Gustavus Adolphus coming to the aid of the german protestants in the thirty years war (Müller p 7 n 2).

²³ *WA Br.* 12, pp 39-40.

²⁴ Müller p 7. Dörries describes these conditions as being 'not only . . . difficult to fulfil, but incapable of fulfilment'; he suggests—somewhat implausibly—that Luther deliberately couched his rejection of resistance to the emperor in oblique language, leaving the elector to draw his own conclusions, since he was confident that Frederick would understand how his remarks were intended to be interpreted, even though they avoided giving a direct negative (Dörries, 3 pp 197-8).

emperor. But this interpretation is impossible to reconcile with Luther's other statements at this stage of his career. On no other occasion in the period down to 1530 did he concede that it could be lawful to resist the emperor under any circumstances and it is difficult to believe that he was prepared to do so, even momentarily, in 1523. If, however, one sees the paper as being concerned not with the specific question of resistance to the emperor, but with the more general question of whether it was lawful for the elector to go to war if he were to be attacked on Luther's account, then Luther's answer emerges in a different light. For it becomes clear that the conditions that Luther laid down in the second part of the paper do not relate to the question of resistance to the emperor but rather to the circumstances in which the elector might take up arms for the protestant cause[25]— a very different matter.

That Luther's paper was not primarily concerned with the question of resistance to the emperor is also suggested by the answers of his colleagues. All three answers are concerned simply with the general question of whether the elector might defend his people, if attacked for Luther's sake, and none of them makes any mention of the emperor. Melanchthon went a step further than Luther in insisting that it was wrong for the elector to undertake war 'in any cause', unless he was convinced that the cause was just and that it was pleasing to God that it should be defended by war. Apparently in answer to points raised by Spalatin, he also put forward two other arguments against armed intervention by the elector. First, he insisted that if it was wrong for a prince to go to war 'without the consent of his people, from whom he receives his authority' (*nisi consenciente populo, a quo accipit Imperium*),[26] then it must follow that the elector ought not to

[25] The words Luther uses at the beginning of this section, *Si autem vellet bellum suscipere pro tuenda ista causa* are ambiguous and it is possible to interpret them as referring to war against the emperor: but, in view of the context in which the paper was written, it seems more probable that Luther was using them here in a wider sense to refer to war in general.

[26] This passage is often interpreted as meaning that Melanchthon held the view that princes derived their authority from the people (compare Müller p 6; Dörries, 3 p 199). But it is probably wrong to read too much into this passage. The form of words used by Melanchthon suggests that he was not so much expressing his own thoughts as commenting on a point raised by Spalatin: in other words, what he appears to be saying is that, *if* it is the case that rulers should not go to war without the consent of their subjects, from whom they derive their authority, then clearly the elector should not go to war in this instance, since his people do not support Luther's teaching. H. Lüthje states that this is the only passage in Melanchthon's writings in which the idea that the prince holds his authority from the people is to be found; see [Hans]

go to war in this case. For it was evident that the people of Saxony would not wish to go to war for the sake of the gospel, since they did not believe—a clear-sighted, if perhaps unexpected comment on the small progress the reformation had made in Saxony at that date. Secondly, he dismissed as irrelevant the precedent of the old testament kings of Judah: for whereas the people of Judah were expressly commanded by God to wage war in defence of the faith, 'our people have no command to defend themselves, but those who are Christians ought to give up their lives for the Gospel, not wish to be defended by others'.[27] Bugenhagen's answer reveals most clearly the moral dilemma which the issue posed for the Wittenberg reformers: for after tying himself up in knots in an agonised attempt to reconcile the christian's duty to suffer with the magistrate's duty to defend his subjects, he finally gave up the struggle and referred the issue to God, with the prayer that he would guide their consciences to act aright when the time came.[28] By contrast, Amsdorf argued unequivocally that although in his private capacity as a christian the prince ought not to wage war on account of the gospel, he is also a 'public person' and bears the sword. Consequently, it is his duty to defend his subjects against attack. Amsdorf, therefore, had no hesitation in saying that the elector might lawfully resist, if attacked, even without the consent of his people—for, as he pointed out with a side-glance at Melanchthon's reply,[29] the prince does not bear the sword by the will of the people. All that is necessary is that he should act with a secure conscience, strengthened and confirmed by the pure word of God.[30] Taken together—despite their differences—these three answers demonstrate that resistance to the emperor was not the question on which the Wittenberg theologians were asked to give their advice in February 1523. That Luther alone should have felt it necessary to touch on the matter in his reply is perhaps not surprising in view of his earlier advice to Frederick on the subject; but there can be little doubt that Luther,

---

Lüthje, ['Melanchthons Anschauung über das Recht des Widerstandes gegen die Staatsgewalt'], Z[eitschrift für] K[irchen] G[eschichte], 47, N.F. 10 (Gotha 1928) p 516.

[27] WA Br. 12, p 41.

[28] Ibid pp 42–3.

[29] Amsdorf had been entrusted with the task of collecting the opinions of his colleagues and forwarding them to Spalatin and his own answer, which is dated 8 February 1523, was evidently written after he had received the replies of the others.

[30] WA Br. 12, p 44. For a fuller discussion of the views of Melanchthon, Bugenhagen and Amsdorf, see Dörries, 3, pp 199–202; for Melanchthon's paper, see also Lüthje pp 515–16.

like his colleagues, was primarily concerned on this occasion with whether the elector might resist an attack by his enemies and it is almost certainly wrong to interpret his paper as conceding a hypothetical right of resistance to the emperor.

For an unambiguous statement of Luther's views at this period it is only necessary to turn to his treatise *Of Temporal Government*, which was published in March 1523 barely a month after he wrote his memorandum for the elector. There he states categorically, in language which echoes some of the phrases of his memorandum,[31] that for princes to resist their superiors is always wrong:

> I say that to act here in a Christian manner no prince should wage war against his overlord, be he king, emperor or other liege lord, but should let him who takes take. For no one should resist the magistrate with force, but only with confession of the truth. If he is converted thereby, it is good; but if not, you are excused and suffer wrong for God's sake. But if your opponent is your equal or inferior to you or a foreign ruler, you should first offer him justice and peace, as Moses taught the children of Israel. But if he will not accept it, then do your best and defend yourself with force against force; as Moses has so well written, Deut. 20.[32]

In practice, because of the reluctance of the diet and the imperial governing council to take any steps to enforce the edict of Worms, the threat of direct intervention by the imperial authorities gradually receded and it remained a relatively remote contingency until after the diet of Speyer of 1529. On the other hand, the protestants had to face the continued possibility of an attack by the catholic princes and this danger became increasingly acute after 1525 as a small but growing number of princes and cities began to adopt the reformation officially—some, though by no means all, of whom were eager to take active counter-measures against the catholics. In consequence, during the second half of the 1520s the question of the right of resistance to the emperor, although it could not be ignored completely, tended to be subordinated to the more immediate issue which confronted and divided the protestant estates—the question of whether, and under

[31] The treatise was apparently finished in December 1522 (the preface is dated 'New Year's day 1523'—that is, Christmas day 1522) and it is likely that Luther borrowed from it, consciously or unconsciously, when he came to write his *Gutachten* for the elector.

[32] *WA* 11, pp 276–7.

what conditions, it was lawful for them to engage in a defensive alliance against the catholic princes.

In so far as Luther discussed the question of resistance to the emperor between 1525 and 1529 it was largely in the context of the debate over the formation of a protestant league. Thus in an opinion which he wrote for count Albrecht of Mansfeld, probably early in 1525 at the time when the possibility of an alliance between Saxony and other princely states was first being mooted, he insisted categorically that no league could be lawful which was directed against the emperor. 'Your Grace knows well', he wrote, 'that against the magistrate [the emperor] no alliance is valid. For God requires that the overlords be honoured, be they evil or good, Rom. 13 and I Pet. 3.' On the other hand, he was prepared to allow that a general defensive league might be permissible, provided that no attempt was made to specify its objectives and it was directed solely against some 'unnamed mischance', in which case it might usefully serve as a deterrent to the catholic princes.[33]

Luther reaffirmed his fundamental opposition to resistance to the emperor in his tract, *Whether Soldiers too can be saved?* of 1526, in which he argued at length that it was always wrong for inferiors to wage war against their superiors, however tyrannical they might be. This maxim, he insisted, applied equally to 'peasants, townsmen, noblemen, counts and princes. For all these also have overlords and are underpersons in relation to some one else. Therefore just as one cuts off the head of a rebellious peasant, so one should cut off the head of a rebellious nobleman, count or prince, the one like the other, and no wrong is done to anyone'.[34] Some of the arguments that Luther used in this tract are of particular interest in view of the subsequent development of the controversy. For example, he refused to accept the validity of any historical precedents for rebellion, whether taken from classical antiquity, or from the old testament, or from more recent historical events, such as the revolt of the swiss against the hapsburgs or the danes against king Christian II, arguing that what matters is not what has been done in the past, 'but what one should and can do with a good conscience', and that even if rebellion seems to prosper to begin with God will always punish it in the end.[35] He also

---

[33] *WA Br.* 3, no 814, pp 416–17. For the problem of the date of this letter, see *Ibid*, Introduction, p 415.

[34] *Ob Kriegsleute auch in seligem Stande sein können*, *WA 19*, p 643.

[35] *Ibid* pp 633–6.

specifically rejected the argument that where a king or lord has bound himself by a formal oath to his subjects to observe certain articles of government, he may legitimately be resisted if he breaks his oath; for God alone has the right to punish tyrants.[36] On the other hand, he did not dispute that war might be justified between equals, but only under certain conditions. Above all, he insisted that a prince must not go to war unless he is attacked first, in which case 'war may be called not only war, but a necessary protection and self-defence';[37] and secondly, that a prince must always fight in the fear of the Lord and not put his trust in his own might, however just his cause; for it is God who decides the outcome of wars and he will punish those who, in their arrogance, believe that they can win by the strength of their own resources alone without his aid.[38]

From 1528 relations between the catholic and protestant estates became increasingly strained, at first largely because of the aggressive policies of Philip of Hesse, later because of the renewed threat of imperial intervention after the diet of Speyer of 1529. In consequence, a new impetus was given to the negotiations over the formation of a protestant league, although in practice the protestant estates proved to be so deeply divided over the issue that it was not until nearly three years later, when the political situation had become much more threatening after the diet of Augsburg, that the league of Schmalkalden was finally concluded.[39] During these three years Luther and his colleagues were frequently consulted by the elector John on the moral implications of taking part in such a league and some of Luther's most important *Gutachten* both on the question of a protestant league and the related question of resistance to the emperor date from this period. In general down to the closing months of 1530 there is little discernible alteration in Luther's position except on one issue. By 1529 he appears to have quietly abandoned his earlier insistence that the reformation should not be defended by force. In other respects his views remained unchanged. While he accepted that a defensive alliance was not in itself unlawful, he continued to insist that it must not be directed against the emperor and that it must be purely defensive. Throughout this period he repeatedly emphasised

---

[36] *Ibid* pp 640–1. As examples of rulers who are said to be bound by such an oath, Luther cites the cases of the kings of France and Denmark.

[37] *Ibid* pp 647–8.

[38] *Ibid* pp 649–51.

[39] For a detailed history of these negotiations, see Fabian, pt A.

that the protestant estates must on no account embark on a preventive war: they must wait to be attacked before attempting to defend themselves; otherwise they would be breaking God's law and God would surely punish them. At the same time he remained firmly convinced that the truly christian course of action which the protestants ought to follow was not to take defensive measures of any kind, but to put their trust in God who had protected them in the past and who would continue to do so provided that they did not let their faith fail. Thus although Luther's attitude tended to fluctuate with the political situation, on balance he viewed the idea of a protestant league with considerable reservations and this is clearly reflected in his letters of advice to the elector.

In March 1528 Luther was called upon to advise the elector at the time of the so-called 'Pack affair', when it was widely believed by the protestants on the strength of a forged document passed on to Philip of Hesse by Otto von Pack, a former councillor of duke George of Albertine Saxony, that the leading catholic princes had made a secret treaty the previous year to launch an attack on the protestants.[40] Luther, like the saxon government, was at first convinced that the secret treaty was genuine and in a memorandum, which he drew up for the elector's chancellor, Gregor Brück, on 28 March 1528, he had no hesitation in recommending that the elector might defend himself with a good conscience if he were attacked by the catholic princes, since 'as an elector of the Empire he has no overlord who has the right and power to punish or judge his Grace except only his Imperial Majesty himself'. The elector, he advised, could safely disregard any claims by the catholic princes to be acting in the emperor's name, since it was evident that this was only a pretext and that they were acting 'without his Imperial Majesty's knowledge, will and command'. On the other hand, as he was to do again and again over the next three years, he warned the elector in the strongest terms that he must on no account take part in a preventive war against the catholics. If the

---

[40] For the details of the 'Pack affair', see Kurt Dülfer, *Die Packschen Händel. Darstellung und Quellen*, Veröffentlichungen der Historischen Kommission für Hessen und Waldeck, 24, 3 (Marburg 1958), and Fabian, pp 33–6 and Excurse 11–14, pp 338–42. Fabian argues against Dülfer that the real instigator of the whole incident was Philip of Hesse who used Pack's revelations to further his plans to attack the ecclesiastical principalities of Mainz and Würzburg. Fabian demonstrates conclusively that Philip was already planning his campaign against Mainz and Würzburg before Pack made his revelations about the 'Breslau treaty' and he makes out a strong case for suggesting that not only was Philip not Pack's dupe, but that it was he who inspired Pack's revelations (see especially Excurse 12 and 14, pp 339–42).

protestants were to attack first, they would immediately put themselves in the wrong, while the catholic princes would be able to claim that they were acting in self-defence. 'No greater dishonour could befall the Gospel; for the outcome would be not a peasants' uprising, but a princes' uprising *(nicht ein Bauraufruhr, sondern ein Fürstenaufruhr)*, which would destroy Germany utterly, something which also Satan would gladly see'. He therefore urged that if Philip of Hesse refused to follow this course of action and persisted with his plans for attacking the catholics, the elector should stand aside; for he was not bound to hold to the alliance, if it would involve him in breaking God's laws.[41] A few days before this memorandum was written Luther had expressed himself even more forcibly on this point at a private interview with the elector, at which he had warned John that if he and Philip were to proceed with the idea of launching a preventive attack against the catholics, then Luther and his colleagues would feel obliged to leave Saxony in order to protect the good name of the gospel from the scandal which would inevitably ensue.[42] In the end, after considerable hesitation, the elector was persuaded to withdraw his support from Philip; and Philip, whose troops had already begun to invade the territories of the archbishop of Würzburg, was forced to call off his planned campaign against the prince bishoprics of the Main. Shortly afterwards, the crisis was defused when Pack's revelations were exposed as fraudulent. But the whole incident left Luther with a lasting suspicion of Philip's intentions and it served to reinforce his reservations about the idea of a protestant league.

Luther's distrust of Philip and his reluctance to support Philip's schemes for a protestant league is reflected in the series of letters which he wrote to the elector in the months that followed the second diet of Speyer of 1529. The decision of the catholic majority at the diet to annul the recess of the 1526 diet of Speyer, coupled with the announcement that Charles V was planning to return to Germany before the next diet, provoked a new crisis for the protestants and it once again made the question of a protestant league a matter of urgency. The first steps were taken at Speyer itself. Before they left the diet, five of the leading states which had signed the protestation against the recess— Saxony, Hesse, Nuremberg, Ulm and Strassburg—agreed in principle to the formation of a new protestant league, although the details were

[41] *WA Br.* 4, no 1246, pp 421–4.
[42] See the letter from Luther and Melanchthon to elector John, 1 or 2 May (?) 1528, *WA Br.* 4, no 1258, p 449.

left to be settled later. Luther's reaction was immediate and hostile. As soon as news of the Speyer agreement reached him in Wittenberg, he wrote to the elector to express his vehement disapproval of the proposed league. 'Such an alliance', he protested, 'is not of God, nor is it based on trust in God, but on human wisdom and the desire to seek and trust in human help alone'; as such, it 'has no good foundation and therefore may bring forth no good fruit'. He warned the elector against becoming involved in any new alliance with Philip after his experiences of the previous year; for the landgrave is 'a restless young prince' *(ein unrugig junger Fürst)*, who could not be relied upon to keep the peace but would endeavour to find some excuse to attack their enemies.[43]

In fact, the unity which the protestant states displayed at Speyer turned out to be short-lived. Almost as soon as the diet was over, splits began to appear in their ranks and although the negotiations for a league continued until the beginning of the following year it proved impossible for them to reach any definite agreement on the form the alliance should take.[44] The two major issues which divided the protestant estates were, first, the question of who should be admitted to membership of the league, and, secondly, the question of whether it should be directed against the emperor as well as against the catholic princes. The initial agreement at Speyer in April 1529 had been signed by the representatives of two cities with zwinglian leanings, Ulm and Strassburg. It soon became clear that Philip of Hesse's aim was to construct a comprehensive anti-catholic and anti-hapsburg alliance that would include not only the zwinglian cities of southern Germany, but also some of the swiss cities as well. By contrast, Saxony for both political and theological reasons favoured a more cautious policy and, as the summer wore on, it began to insist that membership of the league should be restricted to those states that accepted the lutheran doctrine of the eucharist. This policy was strongly supported by the Wittenberg theologians. Both Luther and Melanchthon had been deeply disturbed by Philip of Hesse's plans to include the zwinglians in the league and in his letter of 22 May 1529 Luther had advanced as one of his principal objections to the Speyer agreement the fact that it

---

[43] Luther to elector John, 22 May 1529, *WA Br.* 5, no 1424, pp 76–7. Significantly, this letter was written by Luther on his own initiative and not in answer to a request for advice from the elector.

[44] The league negotiations of 1529 and the reasons for their collapse are examined in detail in Fabian, pt A, I, 2, 'Das Scheitern der Speyerer Bündnispolitik am "Bekenntnis"', pp 44–92; see also Schubert, *Bekenntnisbildung*, esp cap 5.

would have involved the lutherans in allying themselves with those who 'strive against God and the Sacrament'.[45] He repeated these views in a formal opinion which he wrote at the end of July or the beginning of August on behalf of his Wittenberg colleagues, in which he insisted that any alliance must be based on unity of faith. In this paper he specifically condemned the inclusion of the zwinglians in the league on the ground that this would mean lending support to their heresies, while he once again warned the elector against the dangers of taking part in an alliance with Philip of Hesse.[46] During the coming months Saxony's intransigent demand that the members of the league should subscribe to a common statement of faith was to become one of the principal factors which prevented the negotiations from making any progress.

The other major issue on which the negotiations eventually stalled was the question of resistance to the emperor, although this did not become a serious point of controversy until the autumn. At an early stage in the negotiations a proposal had been put forward by Lazarus Spengler, the city secretary of Nuremberg, that the treaty should include a clause specifically excluding resistance to the emperor from the terms of the league. But this proposal was initially rejected not only by Philip of Hesse but also by the elector of Saxony and the margrave of Brandenburg-Ansbach without serious opposition from the other states.[47] At this stage there appears to have been little public discussion of the issue. Perhaps deliberately the elector did not consult Luther, although he did consult Bugenhagen in September 1529 at a time when Luther and the other leading Wittenberg theologians were absent at the colloquy of Marburg. Bugenhagen replied in a letter, dated 29 September, in which he tentatively agreed that the elector might lawfully defend his people if they were unjustly attacked by the emperor, although he insisted that this was only his personal opinion and he begged the elector to keep his advice secret until his colleagues had had the opportunity to consider the matter.[48] In this situation the question might have been allowed to go by default, especially since the legal councillors of Saxony and Hesse were agreed that resistance to the emperor could be justified on grounds of natural and positive

---

[45] *WA Br.* 5, p 77. For the part played by Melanchthon in organising opposition to the Speyer agreement, see Fabian, pp 46–50.

[46] *WA Br.* 5, no 1424, Beilage, pp 78–81.

[47] See *WA Br.* 5, no 1496, Introduction, pp 180–1; Schubert, *Bekenntnisbildung*, pp 184 *et seq.* For Philip of Hesse's opposition to the clause, see Fabian, p 54.

[48] Scheible, *Widerstandsrecht*, no 7, pp 25–9.

law.[49] That this did not happen was largely due to Lazarus Spengler.[50] At the beginning of November Spengler produced a long and carefully reasoned memorandum for the city council of Nuremberg, in which he argued that resistance to the emperor was absolutely forbidden by divine law.[51] Spengler succeeded in winning over both the council of Nuremberg and the margrave of Ansbach to his views and this had the effect of reopening the debate among the protestant estates. While Nuremberg and Ansbach now came out against any alliance that was directed against the emperor, Philip of Hesse, not surprisingly, championed the opposite point of view and insisted that the princes of the empire possessed both a moral and a constitutional right to defend themselves if the emperor were to attack them without just cause.[52] The issue came to a head at a meeting of the lutheran estates held at Nuremberg in January 1530 to discuss the future of the league, following the withdrawal of the south german cities from the negotiations because of their refusal to accept an alliance based on the Schwabach articles. At this meeting the question of resistance to the emperor emerged as the dominant issue. While the chancellor of Saxony expressed himself in favour of resistance, the representatives of Nuremberg and Ansbach refused to take part in any alliance against the emperor, with the result that the meeting ended without any agreement.[53]

[49] For the arguments of the saxon jurists, see Schubert, *Bekenntnisbildung*, pp 186–7.

[50] *Ibid* pp 189–90; see also *WA Br.* 5, no 1496, Introduction, p 181.

[51] Scheible, *Widerstandsrecht*, no 8, pp 29–39. For similar views expressed by Johannes Brenz, see the letter from Brenz to margrave George of Brandenburg-Ansbach, 27 November 1529, *Ibid* no 9, pp 40–2.

[52] See the letter from Philip of Hesse to margrave George of Brandenburg-Ansbach, 21 December 1529, *Ibid* no 10, pp 43–7. Among the arguments which Philip put forward in this letter are: (i) that the emperor and the princes have mutual obligations towards each other and the emperor has bound himself by oath (namely, in his election capitulation) to observe the laws of the empire, therefore the princes only owe the emperor a conditional obedience and may resist him if he breaks his obligations to them; (ii) the position of the german princes is altogether different from that of the officials of the roman empire in the time of the apostles, in that the latter were not hereditary rulers, *sunder schlechte landtpfleger* whom the roman emperors could remove at their pleasure, therefore Paul's prohibition of resistance does not necessarily apply in the same way to the german princes (compare Philip's letter to Luther, 21 October 1530, *WA Br.* 5, no 1737, pp 653–5, see below p 184); (iii) the princes have a christian duty to protect their subjects against all unjust force not only in temporal but also in spiritual matters *(wir als die dorzu unsern unterdanen eingesezte obrigkait dieselben unsere unterdanen vor unrechtem und unpillichem gewalt in zeitlichen und vil meher in geistlichen, doran die eher Gottes und die seligkait gelegen ist, zu beschirmen schuldigk)*.

[53] Schubert, *Bekenntnisbildung*, pp 223–4; *WA Br.* 5, no 1522, p 224 n 3. In arguing for resistance, the saxon chancellor, Christian Beyer, claimed to be speaking only in his

Luther and the right of resistance to the emperor

Following the Nuremberg meeting the elector of Saxony decided to refer the matter to the Wittenberg theologians. Up to this point he appears to have been unwilling to seek Luther's advice on the question, preferring instead to rely on Bugenhagen's opinion of September 1529,[54] partly no doubt because he was afraid of what Luther's answer might be. Thus it is almost certainly no accident that neither of the two *Gutachten* which Luther wrote for the elector on 18 November and 24 December 1529 is concerned directly with the moral question of resistance to the emperor, although on both occasions he advised the elector very strongly against taking part in an alliance with Philip and in the second letter he advanced a number of practical reasons why the elector should not accede to Philip's latest suggestion that the protestants should mobilise their forces in readiness to meet an attack by the emperor.[55] It is clear from the content of Luther's answers that he was not asked to discuss the principle of resistance to the emperor and there can be little doubt that at this stage the elector did not wish to have the matter raised. The reports of the debates at Nuremberg, however, unsettled the elector and on 27 January 1530 he wrote to Luther to ask him to consult with Justus Jonas, Bugenhagen and Melanchthon and to present their considered opinion on whether the emperor might lawfully be resisted if he were to attack the protestants while their formal appeal to a general council was still pending, especially since such an attack might be regarded as a breach of his election capitulation by which the emperor had bound himself to observe the due process of law in all his dealings with the estates.[56] The form of the question is

---

personal capacity and not on behalf of the elector, but it is clear that his views were those of the saxon government.

[54] See his letter to Luther, 27 January 1530, *WA Br.* 5, no 1522, pp 223–4, from which it is evident that he had not consulted Luther directly on the question since receiving Bugenhagen's opinion. For John's attitude at this period, see Dörries, 3, pp 208–9.

[55] *WA Br.* 5, no 1496, pp 181–3; no 1511, pp 209–11. Karl Müller argued that Luther's letter of 24 December 1529 marked a significant turning-point in the development of his attitude to the question of resistance to the emperor in that in it Luther appeared no longer to be opposing resistance to the emperor in principle, but only on the grounds that it was inopportune at the present time (Müller pp 20–2, 24–9). But this view has rightly been rejected by modern scholars: compare G. Wolf in Wolf, *Luther und die Obrigkeit*, pp 337–9; Dörries, 3, p 215 n 42. As Dörries points out, Müller's interpretation is impossible to reconcile either with Luther's letter of 6 March 1530 or with his position at the time of the Torgau meeting in October 1530, and it is clear that too much should not be read into the language of the letter of 24 December 1529, which is concerned with opposing a specific proposal by Philip of Hesse rather than with the general question of resistance to the emperor.

[56] *WA Br.* 5, no 1522, pp 223–4.

179

particularly interesting, since it encapsulates two of the main arguments which the protestant lawyers were beginning to develop as the basis of their case for resistance—first, the claim that it was unlawful for the emperor to proceed against the protestants until their appeal to a general council had been heard, and, second, the claim that the estates were entitled to resist the emperor if he failed to observe the promises he had made in his election capitulation.[57]

Luther replied on behalf of his colleagues on 6 March 1530 in a long and carefully composed letter which later came to be regarded as one of his most important pronouncements on the question of resistance to the emperor.[58] In this letter he reviewed the principal arguments that had been put forward in support of resistance and rejected them in turn, taking his stand, as he had always done, on the principle that resistance to superiors was absolutely forbidden by divine law. He began by examining the claim that the emperor might be resisted if he broke the terms of his election oath. While he was prepared to accept that a case could be made out for this on the basis of imperial and temporal laws, he insisted that it was entirely contrary to the plain teaching of scripture. 'According to the Scripture it is in no way meet that anyone who would be a Christian should resist his ruler, irrespective of whether he acts justly or unjustly, but a Christian should suffer force and injustice, especially from his ruler'. However unjustly the emperor acts, he still remains emperor and 'neither his imperial authority nor his subjects' duty of obedience is abrogated so long as the Empire and the electors still acknowledge him as emperor and do not depose him'. This is so, even if he transgresses God's laws: otherwise there would be chaos, since subjects would always be able to justify any act of resistance by claiming that their ruler had broken God's laws. But if the emperor may not be resisted, 'even if he breaks all of God's commandments simultaneously, yea, even if he were a heathen', then it must follow that 'until he is removed or is no longer emperor' he may not be resisted if he breaks his oath to his subjects;

---

[57] The first argument had been used by the saxon jurists in the joint memorandum drawn up by Saxony and Brandenburg-Ansbach for the Schwabach meeting of the protestant estates in October 1529, Schubert, *Bekenntnisbildung*, pp 186–7. Similarly, Philip of Hesse had used the second in his letter to margrave George of Ansbach of 21 December 1529, see above, p 178 n 52.

[58] *WA Br.* 5, no 1536, pp 258–61; Scheible, *Widerstandsrecht*, no 14, pp 60–3. The letter was reprinted on several occasions in the sixteenth century, see *WA Br.* 5, no 1536, Introduction, pp 251–8. The letter is discussed in Müller, pp 22–4; Dörries, 3, pp 209–12.

for the duty he owes to God is of a far higher order than the duty he owes to men. At this point in his argument, however, Luther introduced an important distinction: for he suggested that although sin did not abrogate the emperor's authority, punishment did—in other words, he could be deprived of his authority, if he were unanimously deposed by the empire and the electors. In that case he might lawfully be resisted since he would no longer be emperor. 'Otherwise, so long as he is unpunished and remains emperor, no one may withdraw his obedience from him or resist him. For that is to initiate mob-violence and rebellion and discord'.[59]

Having disposed of the argument of the emperor's election oath, Luther then proceeded to deal more briefly with two other arguments that had been put forward to justify resistance. The first was an argument which was strongly favoured by Philip of Hesse's lawyers, that resistance to the emperor could be justified on the basis of the natural law right of self-defence. Luther rejected this out of hand. He pointed out that the natural law maxim *vim vi repellere licet* which the lawyers cited, only applied, if at all, to cases in which one was attacked by one's equals: it did not give inferiors the right to defend themselves against their superiors. To drive the point home with a local example, he insisted that, since all the princes' subjects were also the emperor's subjects the princes had no more right to defend them against the emperor than the burgomaster of Torgau had to defend his townsmen against the princes of Saxony. He gave even shorter shrift to the argument that resistance was justifiable on the grounds that the emperor intended to ignore the protestants' appeal to a general council. With cold common sense Luther pointed out that it made no difference whether the emperor allowed the protestants' appeal to be heard or not, since both he and the protestants knew perfectly well that, even if the appeal were heard, the protestants would certainly be condemned, so that in ignoring the appeal the emperor would merely be treating them as if they had already been condemned.[60]

As in 1522, Luther advised that the proper course of action for the princes to follow was to 'let their land and people stand open to the

[59] *WA Br.* 5, no 1536, pp 258–9.
[60] *Ibid* p 259. Both these arguments and the argument from the emperor's election capitulation were also rejected equally emphatically by Melanchthon in a separate *Gutachten*, dating from the same period, which covers many of the same issues, Scheible, *Widerstandsrecht*, no 13, pp 57–60. Scheible considers that in view of the obvious parallels between the two documents Melanchthon's *Gutachthen* represents a preliminary study which he prepared for the joint letter of 6 March 1530, *Ibid* p 57 n 182.

emperor, since they are his, and entrust the matter to God'. No one, he maintained, should expect the prince to do otherwise: for each person ought to stand up for his own faith and be prepared, if necessary, to lay down his life for it without bringing his prince into danger by seeking his protection. On the other hand, if the emperor were to go further and require the princes to attack and persecute their subjects for the sake of the gospel, they should refuse to obey: for it is enough if they leave their lands and people undefended and they should on no account cooperate with the emperor in doing evil. In the meanwhile, Luther urged, as he had done in all his letters in 1529, that the protestants ought to put their trust in God and not seek to anticipate events, for God would find ways to help them and to protect his Word as he had done ever since the foundation of the Church. To do otherwise was to show a lack of faith in God.[61]

Luther's arguments and even some of his phrases are strikingly reminiscent of his letter to Frederick the Wise of March 1522. The one novel element in this letter—which does seem to mark the beginnings of a shift in his position—is that he was now apparently prepared to recognise the possibility that the emperor might be deposed by the unanimous judgement of the electors and the estates.[62] But the shift—if it can be counted as such—was essentially academic; for it did not affect the existing situation. As Luther was at pains to point out, Charles V was still recognised as the lawful emperor by the empire and so long as this remained the case the protestants had no right to resist him, however unjustly he might behave towards them. Moreover, given the existing divisions within Germany, it was inconceivable that Charles could ever be removed by a unanimous decision of the electors and estates, so that the situation could never arise in which it would be lawful for the protestants to resist him.

In March 1530, in other words, Luther's position and that of his colleagues was still in essentials what it had always been: they remained convinced that resistance to the lawful emperor was absolutely prohibited by scripture and they refused to allow that there could be any exceptions to this rule. Yet only seven months later they were to abandon their uncompromising stance and were to concede—

---

[61] *WA Br.* 5, pp 259–60.

[62] *Ibid* p 259: 'Sunde hebt oberkeit und gehorsam nicht auff, Aber die straffe hebet sie auff, das ist, wenn das Reich und die kurfursten eintrechtiglich den keiser absetzten, das er nimer keiser were'. By *das Reich* Luther presumably meant the estates of the empire assembled in the diet.

admittedly with the greatest reluctance—that a legal right of resistance might exist. How did this change come about and what did it involve?

The answer to the first part of the question lies in the outcome of the diet of Augsburg of 1530. The diet altered—or, perhaps it would be more accurate to say, appeared to alter—the political situation in Germany dramatically. The return of Charles V to Germany, his rejection of the Augsburg confession and the subsequent recess of the diet, which called for the strict enforcement of the edict of Worms, faced the protestants once more with the threat of direct intervention by the emperor. In practice, the recess was to prove no more enforceable than that of 1529, but its effect was to reunite the protestants and steps were immediately taken to resume the negotiations for a protestant league which had been suspended since the failure of the Nuremberg talks in January.[63] The seriousness of the threat of imperial intervention removed any lingering doubts that the elector of Saxony still had on the question of resistance to the emperor and from this time on the policies of the saxon and hessian governments were in close accord on this issue.[64] The one major difficulty remained the attitude of the Wittenberg theologians, who now came under increasing pressure both from the electoral government and from Philip of Hesse to accept the legality of resistance to the emperor.

So seriously did the elector regard the situation that in October 1530, shortly after his return from the diet, he summoned Luther together with Melanchthon and Justus Jonas to a meeting at Torgau to discuss the matter with his legal councillors. At this meeting they were presented with a paper drawn up by Gregor Brück, the elector's principal councillor and former chancellor, and several of the jurists attached to the saxon court, in which a case was made out for resistance on the basis of arguments drawn from roman and, rather surprisingly, canon law.[65] At about the same time—apparently while he was

---

[63] For a detailed account of the negotiations between the protestant estates following the diet of Augsburg, see Fabian, pt A, II 'Der Augsburger Reichstag von 1530 und der Abschluss des Schmalkaldischen Bundes', pp 92–183.

[64] For the attitude of the Saxon government after Augsburg, see *Ibid* pp 114 *et seq.*

[65] The text of this paper is printed in Müller, Beilage 2, pp 89–92; Scheible, *Widerstandsrecht*, no 15, pp 63–6. For the authorship of this paper, which is cited in Müller p 89, simply as an 'anonymous legal opinion' *(Anonymes Rechtsgutachten)*, see Fabian, pp 117–18. There is some disagreement among scholars as to whether Luther and his colleagues were presented with the full text of the jurists' memorandum or with a paper summarising its main conclusions; the arguments on both sides are discussed in Dörries, 3, p 217 n 45.

actually at Torgau[66]—Luther received a letter from Philip of Hesse in which he advanced a number of reasons why resistance might be considered lawful. In particular, Philip argued that the constitutional position of the german princes was quite different from that of the magistrates of the roman empire in the time of the apostles, since they were not appointed officials of the emperor but hereditary rulers who possessed rights which the emperor—who was himself not hereditary, but elected—was bound to observe: in consequence, if the emperor exceeded his jurisdiction, or failed to keep his oath to the princes, they were fully entitled to resist him, since he automatically forfeited his authority and made himself 'a common person', who could 'no longer be regarded as a true emperor, but as a peace-breaker'.[67] However, it is noteworthy that, although the argument that the princes possessed constitutional rights against the emperor later came to play an important part in protestant political theory, it was not used by the saxon jurists in their memorandum[68] and there is no evidence that it was accepted by Luther at this stage. Instead the saxon councillors relied on the much narrower legal argument, which Luther had previously rejected in his letter of 6 March 1530, that if the emperor were to attack the protestants for the sake of religion, while their appeal to a general council was still pending, he would be guilty of *notoria iniuria*, since he would be acting in a matter in which he had no powers of jurisdiction, and that therefore, according to the views of both roman lawyers and canonists, he might lawfully be resisted.[69]

We do not have a full report of the Torgau meeting, but the discussions continued over three or four days[70] and we know from subsequent letters by both Luther and Melanchthon that the matter was hotly debated.[71] From these letters two points are clear: first, that

[66] See Fabian p 119.

[67] Philip of Hesse to Luther, 21 October 1530, *WA Br.* 5, no 1737, pp 653–5. Luther's reply, which was dated from Torgau, 28 October 1530, is in *ibid* no 1740, pp 660–1. In it Luther avoided giving Philip a direct answer on the question of resistance, stating merely that he had declared his opinion on the matter to the elector (that is, in the Torgau declaration), *Welche on zweivel E.f.g. unverborgen sein wird.*

[68] Contrary to what is suggested by [Hans] Baron in ['Religion and Politics in the German Imperial Cities during the Reformation'], *EHR*, 52 (1937) p 423. Baron attributes to the saxon jurists the arguments used by Philip of Hesse in his letter to Luther of 21 October.

[69] Müller pp 90–2.

[70] 25 or 26 October to 28 October.

[71] Luther to Wenceslas Link, 15 January 1531, *WA Br.* 6, no 1772, pp 16–17; Luther to Lazarus Spengler, 15 February 1531, *ibid* no 1781, pp 36–7; Luther to Spengler, 18 March 1531, *ibid* no 1796, pp 56–7; Melanchthon to Joachim Camerarius, 1 January

the talks were not confined to the issues raised in the jurists'
memorandum, and, secondly, that initially the Wittenberg theologians
refused to make any concessions. In particular, Luther resolutely
refused to go back on the opinion, which he had expressed in his letter
of 6 March, that resistance to the emperor could not be justified on
the basis of the natural law right of self-defence *(vim vi repellere licet)*.[72]
In the end, however, without formally retracting their belief in the
principle that resistance to superiors was forbidden by scripture, they
were persuaded to withdraw their opposition to the arguments used in
the jurists' paper and they agreed to the famous statement known to
historians as the Torgau declaration. This statement was presented in
the names of Luther, Jonas, Melanchthon, Spalatin 'and certain other
theologians', whose names are not recorded, although it is usually
assumed that the text was drawn up by Luther.[73] Although its
grammar is rather tortuous and it shows signs of having been written
in haste, the declaration was worded with considerable care and it is
therefore necessary to quote the greater part of it verbatim:

> A paper has been presented to us, from which we observe what
> the doctors of law conclude in regard to the question, in what
> cases it is lawful to resist the magistrate. If now this has therefore
> been established by the said doctors or experts in the law, then
> seeing that we are certainly placed in such a situation in which
> (as they show) the magistrate may be resisted, and [secondly] that
> we have at all times taught that one should accept and uphold the
> validity of temporal laws in what concerns them so long as
> *(weil)*[74] the Gospel does not teach anything contrary to the

1531, C[orpus] R[eformatorum], 1–28, *Philippi Melanchthonis Opera*, ed C. G.
Bretschneider and H. E. Bindseil (Halle and Brunswick 1834–60) 2, no 955, cols 469–
70; Melanchthon to Camerarius, 15 February 1531, *ibid* no 957, col 471.

[72] See esp *WA Br.* 6, no 1781, p 36, no 1796, p 56.

[73] The original manuscript in the Weimar archives is in Luther's hand. Müller considered
that Luther was the sole author of the declaration (Müller p 32 n 2). This view has
recently been criticised by Fabian on the grounds that the paper was presented in the
joint names of Luther and his colleagues and that they must therefore be regarded as
co-authors of the statement (Fabian p 121 and n 616). But while he is undoubtedly
right to emphasise the collective character of the declaration, there is no reason to
suppose that Luther was not responsible for the actual wording of the document.

[74] In the sixteenth century *weil* could be used both in the causal sense of 'because' and in
the temporal sense of 'so long as': see J. and W. Grimm, *Deutsches Wörterbuch* (Leipzig
1854–1971) 14, I, cols 762 *et seq*, which cites numerous examples of both usages from
Luther's writings. In general, historians have tended to assume that Luther was using it
here in its modern sense of 'because'; in other words, that he was saying that the
theologians would not oppose resistance if it was permitted by the temporal laws,

temporal law, we cannot oppose it with the Scripture if in this case it is necessary to defend oneself, whether it be against the emperor in his own person or anyone acting in his name . . .
With regard to the fact that we have hitherto taught that the magistrate should on no account be resisted, this is because we did not know that the magistrate's law itself permitted this—which law we have always diligently taught should be obeyed.[75]

Hedged about with reservations as this statement is, the theologians then proceeded to qualify their remarks still further by submitting a supplementary memorandum to the elector in which they presented their advice as to how the protestant estates should act in the present crisis. Far from lending their support to the idea of resistance, they recommended that the protestants should continue to seek peace from the emperor and that they should send him an embassy to explain why they could not in conscience accept the recess. If, however, he persisted in his determination to enforce the recess, they should inform him that in order to avoid causing bloodshed they would not offer any resistance to the restoration of catholicism, but that they would not cooperate in any way. If this course of action were followed, the divines concluded hopefully, the reintroduction of catholicism would take place without the use of military force or bloodshed and it would probably collapse of its own accord within one or two years.[76]

The Torgau declaration is rightly regarded as a crucial turning-point in the development of lutheran political theory,[77] since from this time on the Wittenberg theologians abandoned their outright opposition to resistance to the emperor. But it is important not to exaggerate the nature of the change in their views at this period. While

---

'because the Gospel does not teach anything contrary to the temporal law': compare Müller, p 33; Kern, p 334; Mackinnon, Luther and the Reformation, 4, p 28. But although both usages are to be found in Luther, it is clear that weil must mean 'so long as' in this passage: this view is supported, though more tentatively, by Gottfried Krodel in Luther's Works, American Edition (St. Louis and Philadelphia 1955–) 49, Letters II, ed and trans Gottfried G. Krodel, p 432 and n 29. In practice, Luther never had maintained that temporal laws could not be in conflict with divine law and it would have been contrary to his basic principles to do so.

[75] WA Br. 5, Beilagen, p 662; Scheible, Widerstandsrecht, no 16, p 67.

[76] WA Br. 5, p 662; Scheible, Widerstandsrecht, pp 67–8. For the importance of this supplementary advice, see Dörries, 3, pp 218–21. In the subsequent negotiations over the formation of the Schmalkaldic league, the saxon government apparently relied exclusively on the Torgau declaration and deliberately suppressed all mention of the theologians' second paper (ibid pp 220–1).

[77] For discussions of its significance, see Müller pp 32 et seq; Dörries, 3, pp 216 et seq.

the practical implications of the declaration were far-reaching, the shift in the intellectual position of Luther and his colleagues was at first relatively small. As the wording of the declaration makes clear, they did not positively assert the existence of a right of resistance nor did they abandon their basic belief that resistance to superiors was forbidden by scripture. The most they were prepared to concede was the possibility that positive law might permit resistance in certain circumstances, in which case they declared that they would not oppose it on scriptural grounds. But even this concession was strictly qualified. In the first place, they refused to commit themselves as to whether such a right of resistance did exist, insisting that it was a matter for the lawyers to decide. Secondly, they did not state, as some historians have suggested through a misunderstanding of Luther's use of the word *weil*, that scripture did not contradict temporal laws: they merely said that temporal laws were to be regarded as valid in their own sphere *so long as* they did not conflict with the teaching of the gospel.[78] Thus it was in accordance with this principle that in the course of the debate they rejected the argument that resistance to the emperor could be justified on the basis of the natural law right of self-defence as being contrary to Christ's teaching.[79] In practice, it is clear that the only legal argument that they were prepared to consider at this stage was the one put forward by the saxon jurists in their memorandum, that grounds for resistance might exist if the emperor exceeded his powers of jurisdiction by attacking the protestants for the sake of religion while their appeal to a general council was still pending. Significantly, it was not until several years later that they came to accept Philip of Hesse's argument that the princes of the empire were not mere 'private persons', but possessed constitutional rights in virtue of the nature of their office which entitled them to resist the emperor if he acted tyrannically.[80] Equally, it is clear from their second paper, which needs to be read in conjunction with the first, that in October 1530 Luther and his colleagues were still opposed

[78] See above, p 185 n 74.
[79] See *WA Br.* 6, pp 36, 56.
[80] See below, pp 195, 198. In a passage in the *Table Talk*, dated between 18 August and 26 December 1531, Luther specifically rejected the argument that the princes were public persons, insisting that they were private persons in relation to the emperor, though he added that the matter should be discussed by the lawyers. *WA TR* 2, no 2285a, p 404: 'Principes Germanicos esse publicas personas dicunt, ideo ipsos adversus caesarem defendere posse suos, si post concilium executio fuisset caesari a papa mandata. Ego autem dico: Nequaquam. Principes enim erga caesarem dico esse privatas personas. Sed iuristis afferamus illa discutienda'.

to resistance in any form and that they would have preferred to see the protestants submit to the emperor if he attempted to enforce the edict of Worms against them. Thus the Torgau declaration is an equivocal document. It represents not so much a change of front on the part of the Wittenberg theologians as an abdication of responsibility. They withdrew their formal opposition to the lawyers' arguments; but instead of coming out openly in support of resistance themselves, they took up a position of guarded neutrality, declaring that it was not for them as theologians, but for the lawyers to determine what the law allowed. As Luther wrote in a letter to Wenceslas Link in Nuremberg in January 1531, 'I may not advise nor judge concerning that law itself, but remain in my theology.'[81]

How little Luther was prepared to admit that his views had changed is shown by this letter and two others which he wrote to Link's associate Lazarus Spengler, the city secretary of Nuremberg, in the early months of 1531.[82] As in the previous year, the two franconian states, Nuremberg and Ansbach, had continued their policy of total opposition to the principle of resistance to the emperor, even after the diet of Augsburg. While the motives of the Nuremberg city council were as much political and commercial as religious,[83] this stance was strongly supported on theological grounds by Wenceslas Link and Lazarus Spengler.[84] When, therefore, rumours began to circulate after the meeting of the protestant estates at Schmalkalden in December 1530 that Luther had changed his mind on the issue of resistance, both Link and Spengler wrote to him to express their concern. Luther's replies throw a revealing light on his attitude. In these letters he indignantly repudiated the charge that he had altered his views and insisted that neither he nor his colleagues had advocated resistance—indeed, they had continued to argue against it. What had happened at Torgau, he wrote, was that after a sharp debate, in which they had reaffirmed their opposition to resistance, they had been presented with the argument that the 'imperial law' *(das Kaiserliche Recht*—that is roman law) permitted the emperor to be resisted in cases of notorious injustice *(in notorie iniustis)*. In this situation they had

---

[81] *WA Br.* 6, no 1772, p 17.

[82] See above, p 184 n 71.

[83] For the politics of Nuremberg during the Reformation, see Baron, esp pp 415–22, pp 614–21.

[84] The Nuremberg pastors appear to have been divided on the issue, Andreas Osiander being in favour of resistance *(ibid* pp 421–2). Baron's account underestimates the strength of the theological opposition in the city to resistance to the emperor in 1529–31.

concluded that they could not oppose resistance, if it was permitted by the law, since they had always taught that the laws should be obeyed.[85] Thus, as he put it in his first letter to Spengler the issue could be reduced to a syllogism:

'Whatever the emperor or the emperor's law has laid down is to be obeyed; but the law has laid down that he is to be resisted in such a case; therefore he must be resisted, etc.' Now we have hitherto taught the major: that the sword is to be obeyed in political matters. But we neither assert nor know the truth of the minor. Wherefore I may not draw any conclusions, but we have referred this wholly to the jurists, that they may judge. We wish neither to lay down nor advise nor assert nor urge anything except this major: the emperor is to be obeyed. But if they prove the minor, which does not pertain to us, we cannot deny the conclusion, since we teach the major.[86]

In his letter to Link Luther displayed an even more casuistical attitude. 'I console myself', he wrote in conclusion after admitting that his advice was likely to go unheeded, 'that if they altogether decline to accept our advice, they sin less or act more safely, if they have acted in accordance with the civil law than if they have acted directly against conscience and in clear and voluntary opposition to the scriptures. In the meantime they themselves believe that they are not acting against the scriptures, since they are not acting against the civil law. So I let them act. I am free'.[87] Disingenuous and even complacent as these arguments are, they indicate that even after the Torgau declaration Luther remained anxious to dissociate himself from the idea of resistance and he declined to take any responsibility for what the lawyers and politicians might decide.

Nevertheless, as Mme de Deffand remarked in another context, *il n'y a que le premier pas qui coûte*. Having once taken the step of admitting the possibility that a right of resistance might exist, the Wittenberg reformers found it difficult to resist the temptation to go further and in the course of the next few years they quietly abandoned the cautious position they had adopted at Torgau and began to emerge as active exponents of the necessity of resistance. Precisely when this conversion took place is uncertain. Most probably it was a gradual process which occurred almost unconsciously as the reformers became

[85] *WA Br.* 6, pp 16–17, 36–7.
[86] *Ibid* p 37.
[87] *Ibid* p 17.

increasingly acclimatised to the idea of resistance. Such evidence as there is suggests that throughout 1531 Luther continued to maintain his position of ambivalent neutrality, neither supporting nor condemning resistance to the emperor, but insisting that it was a matter for the lawyers;[88] while after the Nuremberg standstill of the following year the issue became for a time less urgent, as the threat of imperial intervention was once again postponed. However, from the mid-1530s there is a marked change in the attitude of the Wittenberg theologians which is apparent both in the formal *Gutachten* which they prepared for the electoral government at times of renewed political crisis and in some of Luther's later writings.

The first clear signs of this change are to be found in an official opinion, dated 6 December 1536, which was signed by all the leading Wittenberg theologians—Luther, Jonas, Bugenhagen, Amsdorf, Caspar Cruciger and Melanchthon.[89] This opinion represents a radical break not only with their earlier views but also with the position they had taken up at Torgau. It was written at the request of the elector John Frederick at a time when the protestants were facing a new crisis as the result of pope Paul III's decision to summon a general council to meet at Mantua the following year and it was widely feared that the council would proceed to pass judgement against the protestants' appeal, thus providing the emperor with a fresh excuse for attacking them.[90] The opinion is concerned with two issues: first, what attitude the protestants should adopt towards the forthcoming council, and second, the question of resistance. On the first question the Wittenberg divines urged a policy of caution and they strongly attacked the proposal, which had been put forward by the elector, that the protestants should summon a rival council of their own on the

---

[88] Compare *WA TR* 2, pp 404–6, nos 2285a, part of which is quoted above, p 187 n 80, and 2285b. Equally ambiguous is Luther's attitude in his *Warnung an seine lieben Deutschen* (*WA* 30, 3, pp 276–320) which was published about March or April 1531 but was begun, if not finished, the previous October. It is sometimes claimed that in this tract Luther came out openly in support of resistance: but although he states that he will not blame those who resist if war should break out, since it is the catholics, not the protestants, who will be responsible for causing the war, he studiously refrains from actually advocating resistance, insisting that it is his duty as a preacher not to counsel war, but rather to advise men to seek peace and avoid war, as he has always done in the past, see esp pp 278–83.

[89] *CR* 3, no 1458, cols 126–31. Scheible prints only the second part of the paper which deals with the question of resistance to the emperor, *Widerstandsrecht*, no 20, pp 89–92.

[90] For the political background to this memorandum, see [Franz] Lau and [Ernst] Bizer, [*A History of the*] *Reformation in Germany to 1555*, trans B. A. Hardy (London 1969) pp 123 *et seq*.

grounds that this would lay them open to the charge of schism which it would be difficult for them to rebut.[91] By contrast, on the second question they now abandoned their earlier neutrality and came out openly in favour of resistance to the emperor.

This section of the paper is remarkable for the number of points on which the Wittenberg divines reversed opinions that they had held earlier. They began with what might appear at first sight to be a conventional restatement of the principles of the Torgau declaration, insisting that the gospel is a purely spiritual doctrine which 'does not concern external, temporal government, but rather confirms it and values it highly'. But they immediately proceeded to give this principle a new and much more far-reaching significance by adding 'therefore it follows that the Gospel permits all natural and equitable protection and defence that is authorised by natural laws or else by temporal government'—a phrase which can only be interpreted as meaning that they were now prepared to accept the validity of the natural law argument for resistance *(vim vi repellere licet)* which they had so strenuously opposed in 1530.[92] Even more striking is the change in their conception of the duties of temporal rulers. Whereas in the 1520s Luther had repeatedly affirmed that the magistrate, in his capacity as magistrate, was not concerned with matters of faith and that the gospel must not be defended or promoted by force, they now stated categorically that it was the duty of each prince 'to protect and maintain Christians and the external worship of God against all unjust force'. This duty, they insisted, was enjoined on princes by scripture, both by the example of the godly kings of the old testament and by the teaching of the second commandment, 'wherein the rulers are commanded that they should preserve God's name from being dishonoured . . . Therefore the princes are bound to plant and uphold true doctrine in their territories, and as God threatens those who dishonour his name so also will he help those who abolish idolatry and protect pious Christians'. On the strength of this argument they had no difficulty in

---

[91] *CR* 3, cols 126–8.

[92] *Ibid* col 128. The natural law argument had been used as early as 1532 by Melanchthon (despite his rejection of it in 1530) in a letter to Heinrich von Einsiedel, 8 July 1532, *CR* 2, no 1066, cols 603–4. After 1536 it was used quite explicitly by the Wittenberg reformers in several of their individual or collective *Gutachten* justifying resistance; see, for example, *CR* 3, no 1067, cols 631–2 (1537 or 1539, Melanchthon only); Scheible, *Widerstandsrecht*, no 21, pp 92–4 (November 1538); *WA Br.* 8, no 3369, pp 515–17 (July ? 1539). In the later 1530s this argument seems to have been particularly favoured by Melanchthon, who was responsible for drawing up most of the collective *Gutachten* on resistance of these years, see Lüthje, pp 530–3.

concluding that it was the duty of every prince to defend his christian subjects and true religion not only against attacks by princes of equal rank or by private persons but also against the emperor. How far the ideas of Luther and his colleagues had changed since 1530 is shown by the fact that they now unhesitatingly accepted the legal argument, which the saxon jurists had put forward at Torgau, but which at that time they had regarded as unproven, that if the emperor were to attack the protestants, while their appeal was still pending, he would be guilty of *notoria iniuria* and therefore might lawfully be resisted.[93]

The pope's decision to summon a general council raised the further question of how the protestants should act if the council were to pronounce judgement against their appeal, thereby enabling the emperor to proceed against them with the semblance of law. Here too the Wittenberg divines had no hesitation in declaring that resistance would be permissible: for, even if the council were to condemn the protestants in accordance with the procedures of canon law, the decision would have been reached unjustly and the whole process could therefore be regarded as void, since it was 'contrary to natural equity'. Similarly they argued that, if the pope by his sentence were to confirm public idolatry, the princes would be entitled to oppose him and to protect their subjects; just as they would have the right—and, indeed, the duty under the second commandment—to oppose the turks, if they attempted to establish the religion of Mahomet in their territories, in the same way that Judas Machabaeus opposed Antiochus.[94]

Unlike the opinions of the 1520s this paper was not drawn up by Luther, but by Melanchthon,[95] and it is arguable that some of its ideas are more typical of Melanchthon's thinking than of Luther's. In particular, the emphasis which is placed on the prince's duty to protect and uphold true religion and the appeal to the second commandment and the precedents of the old testament kings are characteristic of Melanchthon's doctrine of the *ius reformandi* of the magistrate which he was beginning to develop at this period in order to justify the princes' role in the church[96] and which went considerably further than

[93] *CR* 3, cols 128–9.
[94] *Ibid* cols 129–30.
[95] Müller p 68.
[96] See his treatise, *De officio principum, quod mandatum Dei praecipiat eis tollere abusus Ecclesiasticos* (1539), printed in *CR* 3, no 1520, cols 240–58, under the year 1537, and the *Gutachten* of the Wittenberg theologians of 1536, also composed by Melanchthon, *CR* 3, no 1511, cols 224–9.

Luther's limited concept of the prince as *Notbischof*. Nevertheless, if the ideas are Melanchthon's and it cannot necessarily be assumed that Luther accepted them in entirety, there can be no doubt that the main conclusions of the paper had his support. At the beginning of the section on resistance it is expressly stated that the theologians 'have today concluded unanimously' on what follows, while Luther not only signed the document, but he added the flamboyant endorsement—*Ich Martinus Luther will auch dazu thun mit Beten, auch (wo es seyn soll) mit der Faust.*[97] Over the next few years the Wittenberg divines were to reaffirm their support for resistance in a number of other opinions.[98]

As far as Luther himself is concerned, the main evidence for his later views comes from a series of pronouncements which he made in the early part of 1539. During the winter of 1538/39 the relations between the catholic and protestant estates in Germany had once more reached a point of crisis and for several months it looked as if the war, which had been so long delayed, was finally about to break out. In the end—as so often in the past—the crisis subsided and a new religious truce known as the Frankfurt standstill was arranged in April 1539.[99] But in the period before the truce was signed, when the danger was at its height, Luther succumbed to the general war hysteria which infected the protestants and he began to assert the necessity of resistance to the emperor and the pope more vehemently than he had ever done in the past.

The two most important statements of Luther's position at this period are his letter to Johann Ludicke of 8 February 1539 and the theses which he drew up for the *Zirkulardisputation* of April/May 1539. Luther's letter to Ludicke may be classed as a semi-official *Gutachten*. Its recipient was a lutheran preacher in Brandenburg, who had apparently been asked—or was expecting to be asked—to advise the elector of Brandenburg, Joachim II, on the question of resistance, and Luther's letter was written to give him guidance on the form his reply should take.[100] In it Luther began by stating that it was too late to

[97] *CR* 3, cols 128, 131.

[98] Scheible, *Widerstandsrecht*, no 21, pp 92–4, Luther, Jonas, Bucer and Melanchthon to elector John Frederick and Philip of Hesse, 13/14 November 1538 (written by Melanchthon); *WA Br.* 8, no 3369, pp 515–17, Luther, Jonas and Bugenhagen to elector John Frederick, July ? 1539 (probably written by Bugenhagen or Jonas); Scheible, *Widerstandsrecht*, no 23, pp 98–100, Bugenhagen, Cruciger, Maior and Melanchthon to the heads of the Schmalkaldic league, May/early June 1546.

[99] For the political background, see Lau and Bizer, *Reformation in Germany to 1555*, pp 141 *et seq.*

[100] Müller pp 69–70; *WA Br.* 8, no 3297, Introduction, pp 364–5.

discuss the question of whether it was lawful for 'our princes' to resist the emperor, since they had already made up their minds to resist, and that it was lawful for them to do so, and they were unlikely to be influenced by anything further that he might say. Nevertheless, while protesting that he still hoped that Christ would render his advice unnecessary by intervening to prevent the emperor from embarking on 'such a mad war', he now declared that he had 'the gravest reasons' *(gravissimas causas)* for not opposing the plans of the princes.[101] The remainder of the letter is devoted to outlining some of these reasons.

As his principal argument Luther now took over the claim, which had been developed by the propagandists of the Schmalkaldic league[102] but which had not figured at all in the Wittenberg theologians' opinion of December 1536, that if the emperor were to attack the protestants, he would not be acting on his own account, but simply as the agent of the pope, and therefore might lawfully be resisted. For it was the pope and the bishops who were the real instigators of the war against the protestants and who wished to use the emperor 'as their soldier' *(velut milite)* for defending 'their horrible tyrannies and diabolical crimes' against the truth. Now the pope may undoubtedly be resisted: for 'if it is lawful to wage war or defend oneself against the Turk, how much more so is it to do so against the pope who is worse'. In consequence, if the emperor who has no grounds of his own for attacking the princes chooses to involve himself in the pope's war, he must expect the same fate. 'For these reasons', Luther informed Ludicke, 'our princes judge that in this case the emperor is not emperor, but the soldier and robber of the pope' *(militem et latronem papae)*—for it is the pope who is the true emperor in this war. However, Luther was clearly conscious that in adopting this argument he was laying himself open to the charge of contradicting his earlier views, for he hastily added by way of extenuation that, while this was the opinion of the princes, he himself had not previously given any advice on the position of the emperor as 'the soldier of the pope'. In an attempt to underline the consistency of his attitude, he went on to suggest that it was only because the pope and his followers were guilty of blasphemy in claiming to be acting in the name of Christ that it was lawful to resist them: if they were to

---

[101] *WA Br.* 8, no 3297, pp 366–7.

[102] Dörries, 3, p 246 n 117. Dörries points out that the argument that the emperor may be resisted since he is not acting as emperor, *sonder als ain geschworner und hauptman des bapsts*, appears in an anonymous theological *Gutachten*, printed in Scheible, *Widerstandsrecht*, no 18, p 80. Scheible dates this paper as *c*1530, but the date is uncertain.

lay aside the name of Christ and confess themselves to be the servants of Satan, he would continue to urge the necessity of submitting to 'heathen tyrants' *(gentilibus tyrannis)*, as he had done in the past.[103]

In addition to the concept of the emperor as *miles papae*, Luther cited two other arguments in this letter which he did not develop in such detail. First, he appealed briefly, as he and his colleagues had done in 1536, to the example of Judas Machabaeus and various old testament precedents. Secondly, he now adopted the constitutional argument that Philip of Hesse had put forward in 1529 and 1530, but which at that time he had declined to accept, that the empire was not an absolute monarchy and that the princes of Germany possessed the right to resist the emperor if he failed to observe the laws and customs of the empire: for they 'govern the Empire in association *(communi consilio)* with the emperor: the emperor is not an absolute king *(monarcha)*, neither can he alter the form of the Empire against the will of the electors, nor should it be endured, if he were to try'. If this principle applies in civil matters, it must apply equally, Luther insisted, in cases where the emperor seeks to subvert the constitution of the empire in the cause of the pope and the devil.[104]

The concept of the emperor as *miles papae* also plays an important part in Luther's theses for the *Zirkulardisputation* on Matt. 19:21,[105] where it took on a new significance by being coupled with Luther's eschatological conception of the pope as the beast of the book of Daniel. These theses were drawn up early in April 1539 for a regular academic disputation at the university of Wittenberg, at a time when the prospect of war between the catholics and protestants seemed inescapable. In the event the Frankfurt standstill was signed before the

[103] *WA Br.* 8, p 367.
[104] *Ibid* pp 367–8. Virtually the same arguments as Luther used in this letter appear in a passage in the *Table Talk*, dated 7 February 1539 (that is, the day before the letter to Ludicke): but there the order is reversed and Luther places his main emphasis on the constitutional position of the princes and he appears to attach rather less importance to the argument that the emperor is not acting *pro sua persona* but as the *feudatarius* of the pope, *WA TR* 4, no 4342, pp 235–9; see also Müller pp 75–6; Dörries, 3, pp 253–4. For his comment on the relationship of the princes to the emperor see *WA Br.* 8, p 367: Nam Principes Germaniae plus iuris habent contra Caesarem, quam illic populus contra Saul, vel Ahikam contra Joiakim, ut qui communi consilio gubernent imperium cum Caesare, et Caesar non sit monarcha nec posset deiectis Electoribus mutare formam imperii, nec esset ferendum, si tentaret.
[105] *WA* 39, 2, pp 39–44. Luther's theses are discussed in detail in Rudolph Hermann, 'Luthers Zirkulardisputation über Mt 19, 21' in *Gesammelte Studien zur Theologie Luthers und der Reformation* (Göttingen 1960) pp 206–50. See also Müller pp 73–5; Dörries, 3, pp 241–6.

disputation was held and Luther subsequently added a further twenty-one theses attacking the validity of ecclesiastical laws made by the pope.[106] The original seventy theses—with which we are concerned—fall into two sections: theses 1–50, dealing with the christian's position in the world; and theses 51–70 on the pope. In theses 1–50 Luther put forward what was, in essentials, his conventional teaching on the place of the christian in the world, his duties under the first and second tables of the law and his obligations to secular rulers. He insists that the christian has a dual role as a christian and as 'a citizen of this world' *(civis huius mundi)*. As the latter, he is bound to do and suffer everything that is required of him according to the second table of the law (Th.30). Thus as a pious citizen of the world, you may lawfully resist a robber who attacks you, even if he seeks to kill you on account of Christ: for the magistrate has commanded that robbers are to be resisted and this is therefore in accordance with the second table of the Law (Th. 31–35). On the other hand, if the magistrate persecutes you for Christ's sake—whether he be a heathen magistrate or a bad christian—it is your duty to suffer and offer no resistance. For the magistrate is not a robber, but is instituted by God to preserve law and order. Therefore, even if the magistrate breaks the first table of the law, he is not to be resisted; for we are forbidden to destroy the magistrates and governments which God has ordained on account of human wickedness (Th. 36–50).[107]

Such statements are entirely in accord with the views that Luther had expressed in the 1520s and, taken on their own, they might suggest that he had reverted to his earlier standpoint. But in theses 51–70 Luther turned to deal with the position of the pope and in the process of attacking the papacy he reaffirmed, but in more passionate language, the arguments of the letter to Ludicke. He began by insisting that the pope is not a magistrate of any kind, either ecclesiastical or civil, since he does not belong in any of the three divine hierarchies which God has ordained against the devil—the family, civil government or the church[108] (Th. 51–55). Rather he is the monster foretold in the book of Daniel. He is what 'we Germans call a *Beerwolf*, what the Greeks, if perchance it had been known to them, would have called *arktolukos*' —a wolf which is possessed by a demon and which destroys everything

---

[106] *WA* 39, 2, *Zirkulardisputation*, Introduction, pp 34–5.

[107] *Ibid* pp 40–1.

[108] For Luther's concept of the three divine hierarchies, see Harald Diem, *Luthers Lehre von den zwei Reichen*, Evangelische Theologie, Beiheft 5 (Munich 1938) pp 56–61; Gustaf Törnvall, *Geistliches und weltliches Regiment bei Luther* (Munich 1947) pp 38–40.

in its path (Th. 56–59). Such a monster can only be destroyed if all the people from the surrounding countryside and towns gather together to hunt him down. Nor is it necessary to wait for orders from the magistrate before attacking him for present necessity is enough (Th. 60–61). So likewise, if the pope provokes war, he must be resisted 'like a furious and possessed monster or a true *arktolukos*: for he is not a bishop nor a heretic nor a prince nor a tyrant, but the beast who lays everything waste, as Daniel declares' (Th. 66–67). But equally— and here Luther returned once again to the theme of the emperor as *miles papae*—whoever fights for the pope must be resisted, regardless of whether they be princes, kings or even emperors: for whoever 'fights under a robber (whoever he may be)' has to face the risks both of war and of eternal damnation. 'Nor will it save kings, princes, or even emperors that they claim to be acting as defenders of the Church, since it is their duty to know what the Church is' (Th. 68–70).[109] By identifying the pope with the beast of the book of Daniel and by insisting that any ruler who went to war on his behalf must be resisted, Luther had effectively undermined the conclusions of the first fifty theses.

By the time the disputation was held on 9 May 1539 the immediate threat of war had been removed. But it is clear from the three anonymous reports of the disputation which survive[110] that the news of the Frankfurt standstill had in no way diminished Luther's obsessive horror of the papacy and, despite the wide-ranging character of the original theses, the greater part of the debate seems to have been taken up with the discussion of the twin questions of whether it was lawful to resist the pope and the emperor. In the course of the disputation Luther repeatedly reaffirmed his apocalyptic view of the papacy in language which appears from the reports to have been even more extreme than that of the theses. In passage after passage, he reiterated his belief that the pope was not 'a legitimate magistrate',[111] nor even a tyrant in the conventional sense of the term,[112] but 'a monster',[113] an '*arktolukos*',[114] 'a minister of the devil who is possessed by the devil',[115] a creature who is worse even than the turk since he

---

[109] *WA* 39, 2, pp 42–3.
[110] Printed in *WA* 39, 2, pp 52–89.
[111] *Ibid* pp 56–7.
[112] *Ibid* p 60.
[113] *Ibid* p 59 and *passim*.
[114] *Ibid* p 60 and *passim*.
[115] *Ibid* p 74.

destroys men's souls.[116] Consequently, he is to be resisted at all costs.[117] So equally are those who seek to defend him, including the emperor.[118] But Luther did not stop there. To the question whether it was lawful to resist the emperor *propter doctrinam Dei*, if he were to act as an ordinary tyrant by persecuting christians on his own initiative, and not at the behest of the pope, Luther replied just as emphatically, 'This evil is to be resisted. For we ought to leave to our descendants this doctrine and the church well established'.[119] In answer to another question he also repeated the argument, to which he had alluded briefly in his letter to Ludicke, that the constitution of the empire gave the princes the right to resist the emperor. The prince electors, he now maintained, in striking contrast with the view he had so often expressed in the 1520s, were not private persons. Rather, the seven electors were the equals of the emperor, since they were a constituent part of the empire, of which the emperor was the head.[120] Moreover, since the magistrates were now christians, not heathens *(gentiles)*, they all had an equal duty along with the emperor to prevent blasphemy and they therefore might resist him in defence of the first table of the law.[121]

Fate was kind to Luther, for he died before the Schmalkaldic war broke out and he was spared the disaster of Mühlberg and the dismemberment of Ernestine Saxony. As a result, we cannot know for certain how he would have reacted to these events. But in view of his attitude in the late 1530s there can be little doubt that, had he lived a few months longer, he would have joined Melanchthon and the other Wittenberg theologians in their support for the war. Certainly, Melanchthon was to make extensive use of Luther's writings to justify the position which the Wittenberg divines adopted in 1546 and the theses for the *Zirkulardisputation*, in particular, were reprinted several times in both latin and german in the early months of the war.[122] It is interesting to speculate how Luther would have

---

[116] *Ibid* p 58–9.

[117] *Ibid* pp 56–62, 64–5, 74–6.

[118] *Ibid* pp 56 *et seq*, 65, 74 *et seq*.

[119] *Ibid* p 77.

[120] *Ibid* p 78. The phraseology attributed to Luther here, especially in report A, is very similar to that of the *Table Talk* of 7 February 1539, *WA TR* 4, no 4342, pp 236–7, where the argument that the emperor shares his authority with the electors is developed at greater length. See also *Table Talk*, 8 and 9 May 1539, *Ibid* no 4582, p 388.

[121] *WA* 39, 2, p 78.

[122] See *Ibid* Introduction, pp 35–8. For the posthumous use made of Luther's writings during the Schmalkaldic war, see Dörries, 3, pp 261–4.

reacted to the defeat of Mühlberg. Twenty years earlier he would have treated such a defeat as divine retribution on the protestants for the sin of rebellion. One can only conjecture that, had he been alive in 1547, he would have rationalised it as the triumph of anti-Christ.

In Luther's later pronouncements and the opinion of 1536 one finds three main lines of argument which represent a radical departure from the views he had held in the 1520s. First, there is the idea, which is developed more fully in the 1536 opinion than in Luther's own writings, that the christian magistrate has a duty to uphold true religion and suppress idolatry, and that it is therefore incumbent upon the german princes to defend the gospel and their christian subjects against all attacks, whether from other princes or from the emperor—an idea which is utterly at variance with the principle which figures so prominently in Luther's writings of the early 1520s that the gospel is a purely spiritual doctrine which must not be defended by force. Secondly, there is the constitutional argument, which Philip of Hesse had first put forward in 1529 and 1530, that the princes of the empire are not mere 'private persons' in relation to the emperor, as Luther had maintained throughout the 1520s, but are associated with him in the government of the empire and are therefore legally empowered to resist him if he acts tyrannically—an argument which Luther had initially opposed, but which by 1539 he had quietly come to accept. Thirdly, there is the claim that the emperor may be resisted if he attacks the protestants for the sake of religion, since he is not acting as emperor, but merely as the agent of the pope, as *miles papae*. This argument too did not originate with Luther, but with the theorists of the Schmalkaldic league. But, in taking over the idea, Luther radically transformed it: for, by combining it with his doctrine of the pope as the beast of the book of Daniel, the *Beerwolf* who must be resisted at all costs, he turned what had originally been a purely legalistic argument into an apocalyptic call to arms. The fanaticism of Luther's language in the *Zirkulardisputation* is not in itself surprising: for it is in keeping with his increasingly obsessive hatred of the papacy which is to be seen in so many of his writings of the period.[123] But it is perhaps indicative of the idiosyncratic character of Luther's later views that he should have chosen in both the *Zirkulardisputation* and the letter to Ludicke to place his main emphasis not on the

---

[123] Compare his preface to the german translation of *Consilium delectorum cardinalium et aliorum prelatorum de emendanda ecclesia* (1538), *WA* 50, pp 288–91.

constitutional claims of the princes, but on the concept of the emperor as *miles papae*.[124]

Historically, however, it was the first two arguments which were to prove to be the most influential for the subsequent development of protestant political thought. For it was out of a fusion of these two sets of ideas that there evolved the standard protestant theory of resistance of the mid-sixteenth century—the doctrine that the inferior magistrates (though not the common people) had not only the right but the duty to resist the supreme magistrate in defence of true religion. This doctrine is popularly associated with calvinism rather than with lutheranism. But it is important to note that it originated in Germany in the confessional conflicts of the 1530s and 1540s and that Calvin, Beza[125] and the english marian exiles who amplified the doctrine in the 1550s were not propounding a new political theory, but were building on foundations that had already been laid by the german lutherans. As will be clear from what has been said, Luther's personal contribution to the development of this theory was relatively small. He did not originate either the idea that the german princes had the legal right to resist the emperor or the more general claim that the christian magistrate had an ex officio duty, which was laid down in scripture, to defend the faith by force against all attacks, although he later endorsed both these arguments and by so doing helped to popularise them. So far as I have been able to discover, the main credit for introducing into protestant political thinking the principle that it was lawful for inferior magistrates to resist their superiors in defence of religion must go to Philip of Hesse and his advisers; for it was they who first developed the main outlines of the theory in relation to the german princes, although it was not perhaps until the appearance of the Magdeburg *Bekenntnis* in 1550 that the doctrine was fully worked out in its classic mid-sixteenth century form.[126]

---

[124] A fourth line of argument which appears in several of the collective opinions presented by the Wittenberg theologians at this period, especially those written by Melanchthon, is the claim that resistance to the emperor is justified on the basis of the natural law principle of self-defence (see above, p 191 n 92)—a claim which again involves a reversal of Luther's earlier views. But although Luther signed the joint *Gutachten* of 1536, 1538 and 1539, he did not make use of the natural law argument in any of his own writings and, in my view, it must be considered doubtful whether he ever fully accepted it in his own mind.

[125] For Beza's early views, see [Robert M.] Kingdon, ['The First Expression of Theodore Beza's Political Ideas',] *A[rchiv für] R[eformations] G[eschichte]*, 46 (Gütersloh 1955) pp 88–99.

[126] For an analysis of the arguments of the Magdeburg *Bekenntnis*, see J. W. Allen, *A*

Luther and the right of resistance to the emperor

At the same time, it is equally clear that the conventional picture of Luther as acquiescing in the idea of resistance only with the greatest reluctance under pressure from the princes needs considerable modification. While this is true of his position in 1530 at the time of the Torgau declaration, by the end of the 1530s a profound change had taken place in his attitude and he had emerged as a passionate advocate of the need to resist both the pope and the emperor. Contrary to the popular image of the two reformers, the later Luther was far more outspoken than Calvin ever was in his support for resistance. Indeed, it could be argued that in the *Zirkulardisputation* he came close to anticipating the views of John Knox. For, although it is probable that Luther did not fully understand where his remarks were leading, the logical conclusion to be drawn from the *Beerwolf* analogy is that it is not only the princes but the common people who have the right to resist the pope, and therefore by implication any secular ruler who fights on his behalf—a claim which most mid-sixteenth century supporters of the rights of inferior magistrates would have repudiated with horror.

In general, the tendency among historians has been to stress the contradictions between Luther's earlier and his later views. It should be said, however, in conclusion that in recent studies of the problem there has been something of a reaction against this approach. Both Johannes Heckel and, in a different fashion, Hermann Dörries have attempted to qualify the charges of inconsistency which have usually been levelled against Luther: Heckel, by claiming that most earlier writers had failed to take sufficient account of the theological and juristic assumptions underlying Luther's thought and that, if this is done, there is a greater degree of unity to his pronouncements than might appear at first sight;[127] Dörries, more convincingly, by pointing out that even at the end of his life Luther did not so much abandon his earlier principles as allow them to be overshadowed by new ideas, and

---

History of Political Thought in the Sixteenth Century (London 1928) pp 103–6. Allen, however, tends to exaggerate the revolutionary significance of the arguments of the Magdeburg *Bekenntnis*, largely because he virtually ignores the previous development of resistance theory among the german lutherans. He also suggests that there is no causal connection between german resistance theory and the later ideas of the english marian exiles and the french huguenots (pp 104, 106). But, as Kingdon points out (pp 92–4), Beza in his *De haereticis a civili magistratu puniendis* (1554) refers specifically to the example of Magdeburg; and there can be little doubt that Calvin, Beza and the english marian exiles were drawing on a well-established lutheran tradition when they propounded the theory of the right of inferior magistrates to resist their superiors.
[127] Heckel, *Lex Charitatis*, App I, pp 295–306.

that even in his 1539 writings there are elements in his thinking that go back to the early 1520s.[128]

Nevertheless, while there is some substance in these arguments and it is clear that there is more continuity in Luther's thought than has sometimes been allowed, the fact remains that in the 1530s he did alter his position radically and for reasons that had more to do with politics than with religion. The years after 1529 were a period of intense and continuing crisis for the german protestants and, even though war did not finally break out until 1546, the psychological pressures on Luther and his colleagues to abandon their earlier opposition to resistance to the emperor were very strong. It is therefore hardly surprising that, having once taken the initial step at Torgau of conceding that resistance might be permitted on legal grounds, they should gradually have given up their attempt to maintain a position of neutrality and identified themselves completely with the policies of the Schmalkaldic league. In this sense the evolution of their views is exactly paralleled by that of the more radical english exiles in the 1550s and the french huguenots in the 1570s. But it means that, if one wishes to understand the transformation which took place in the attitude of the Wittenberg divines in the 1530s, it is more important to look at the political and psychological factors which influenced them than at the intellectual arguments which they used to justify the change. There is undoubtedly a logic to the development of Luther's views on the question of resistance to the emperor, but it is a logic deriving from events rather than from the underlying principles of his theology.

University of London
King's College

[128] Dörries, 3, pp 265–6. See also pp 245 et seq.

WAS THE PROTESTANT REFORMATION
A REVOLUTION?
THE CASE OF GENEVA*

by ROBERT M. KINGDON

THE problem which I wish to consider is the problem of deciding whether the protestant reformation was a revolution. The problem should be of interest to a number of different scholars. There is no obvious reason, however, why it should interest those who define themselves primarily as ecclesiastical historians. I believe, however, that there is an ecclesiastical dimension to this problem and that earlier work upon it is flawed by a failure to recognize that fact. I see these flaws even in the work which has most stimulated my own recent thinking on the problem. This is the work of a number of modern english historians and above all a book published by that great english contribution to the american community of historians, Lawrence Stone, titled *The Causes of the English Revolution, 1529–1642*.[1] I found particularly useful Stone's lengthy analysis of the phenomenon of revolution, borrowing extensively from the recent work of political scientists, sociologists, and other behavioral scientists. And I found persuasive his application of that analysis to the puritan revolution. I found his ultimate conclusion, however, 'that the crisis in England in the seventeenth century is the *first* "Great Revolution" in the history of the world,'[2] to be nonsense. It is nonsense partly because he has ignored the illumination which can be shed on this topic by a consideration of ecclesiastical history. I shall argue that the protestant reformation of the early sixteenth century was also a revolution, anticipating Stone's by more than a hundred years. And I shall seek to demonstrate this argument with evidence drawn from ecclesiastical history.

Very few men at the time of the protestant reformation would have

---

* This essay is a revised version of one originally published in Robert M. Kingdon (ed) *Transition and Revolution: Problems and Issues of European Renaissance and Reformation History* (Minneapolis, Minnesota: Burgess Publishing Company, 1974). This version is published with the permission of the Burgess Company.
[1] New York 1972. Originally published in London 1972.
[2] p 147, italics mine.

called it a revolution.[3] In those days the term did not normally possess a political or social meaning. It was basically a scientific term, used primarily by astronomers. Its best known usage was in the title of the famous treatise in which Nicolaus Copernicus advanced his radical new heliocentric theory, *On the Revolution of the Heavenly Bodies*, first published in 1543. In this context the term 'revolution' referred to the motions of heavenly bodies in orbits around either the earth or sun.

There are obvious ways in which this astronomers' term can be applied, by analogy, to certain political and social changes. One can find a few scattered examples of such applications during the sixteenth and seventeenth centuries, but they are rare and ambiguous.[4] Only in the eighteenth century did the term 'revolution' come to be used in a way we would recognize. It was applied then to the two great upheavals we know as the american and french revolutions. At first these revolutions were conceived of as primarily dramatic political changes. Soon, however, they were interpreted as fundamentally social upheavals. The social interpretation, as developed by Marx and his disciples, has tended to prevail in the twentieth century. And the recent marxist revolutions, in Russia and China, tend to supply the type to which most modern usage of the term refers.

Modern behavioral scientists have tried to refine definitions of revolution still further. There are surely some who have tried to reduce them to mathematical formulae. I shall not try to follow them. I shall rather stop with a common-sense definition developed by Sigmund Neumann, an eminent and sensible and somewhat old-fashioned political scientist, imported to the United States from Germany. In this I follow Stone who, in spite of his enthusiasm for the most modern social sciences, also really stops at this point. Neumann defined revolution as 'a sweeping, fundamental change in political organization, social structure, economic property control, and the predominant myth of a social order, thus indicating a major break in the continuity

[3] On the history of the word revolution, see Hannah Arendt, *On Revolution* (New York 1965) cap I esp pp 34–40; Jacques Ellul, *Autopsie de la révolution* (Paris 1969) pp 51–2.
[4] For example Philippe du Plessis-Mornay, *Remonstrance aux Estats pour la paix* of 1576, repr *Mémoires et Correspondance de Duplessis-Mornay*, 2 (Paris 1824) p 75, in speaking of the evils brought to France by the catholic league, says: 'Les villes, qui de neutralité seront venues à liberté, de ceste liberté viendront à une licence populaire, de la licence retomberont à la tyrannie de quelqu'ung, et toutes les semaines par sedition auront nouvelles revolutions.' An even earlier example, drawn from a 1525 description of the revolt of the Comuneros in Spain is cited by [J. H.] Elliott, ['Revolution and Continuity in Early Modern Europe,'], *PP* no 42 (1969) p 40.

of development.'[5] This formula seems to me to sum up modern opinion reasonably enough so that we can use it. Armed with this definition, we can now return to the original problem: was the protestant reformation a revolution?

At this point some scholars would object that to use the term 'revolution' in speaking of the reformation era, is to adopt an anachronism, the greatest sin any historian can commit. It seems to me that this objection is specious. In order to understand a period one need not restrict oneself to the language of that period. Indeed it is often possible to understand some aspects of a period in history even better than the men who lived through it, by use of concepts developed and refined since they died. Modern economic historians, for example, understand far more about the development of the european economy during the fifteenth and sixteenth centuries than did businessmen who participated in that development. Their superior understanding is based in part on the use of concepts derived from modern economics and mathematics, unknown to the sixteenth century. These scholars, for example, can construct price indices which show exactly what and where and how prices increased or decreased during the reformation. Men of that period often complained bitterly of rising prices but not even the best educated of them would have been able to construct a price index. That does not prevent modern scholars from creating price indices and then using them to explain many facets of the economic and social development of the period only imperfectly understood by contemporaries. These indices, for example, help us to explain more fully than ever before many of the food riots of the sixteenth century. I would argue that the concept of revolution is like the concept of a price index. If it is used with care, by someone who knows both what it means and what happened in the earlier period, it can be enormously illuminating.

A far more weighty objection to the suggestion that the protestant reformation was a revolution comes from specialists in the period itself. Many of them would argue that the reformation did not involve changes in political organisation, social structure, economic property control, and social myths which were fundamental enough to be fairly labeled revolutionary. It was not a revolution in Neumann's sense. One thoughtful expression of this point of view can be found in the writing of J. H. Elliott. He sums up his argument in these words:

[5] Sigmund Neumann, 'The International Civil War,' *World Politics*, I (1948–9) p 333, n 1, quoted and used by Stone p 48.

The sixteenth and seventeenth centuries did indeed see significant changes in the texture of European life, but these changes occurred inside the resilient framework of the aristocratic-monarchical state. Violent attempts were made at times to disrupt this framework from below, but without any lasting degree of success. The only effective challenge to state power and to the manner of its exercise, could come from within the political nation—from within a governing class whose vision scarcely reached beyond the idea of a traditional community possessed of traditional liberties.[6]

Elliott, to be sure, advanced this argument in the course of a debate on the meaning of early seventeenth-century political uprisings and in that context it constitutes a useful rejoinder to arguments about the depth and pervasiveness of an alleged general european crisis. He has not considered with equal care the uprisings which accompanied the beginnings of the protestant reformation, early in the sixteenth century. Still he seems to believe that his conclusion applies to the entire early modern period in european history.

I would argue that this conclusion is defective as an explanation of reformation changes because it overlooks one crucial fact: it ignores the role of the clergy in pre-reformation european society. A revolution does not have to be aimed at the power of kings and aristocrats or at the bourgeoisie to be a true revolution. It can also be aimed at other ruling classes. The class against which the protestant reformation was aimed was the roman catholic clergy. In most of Europe before the reformation, the catholic clergy did constitute an important element in most political organization and in social structure, did control a good deal of the property, and were custodians of the predominant social myth. A challenge to the clergy thus had to be a radical challenge, calling for a revolutionary change in european society. It is my contention that the protestant reformation was such a challenge.

Protestants, of course, were not the only enemies to clerical power. Much of the power of the clergy had been attacked and eroded in many parts of Europe well before the reformation, during the renaissance and even earlier. Furthermore clerical power survived the reformation in many areas and in many ways. In some instances it even grew in strength. However protestants, wherever they were active, invariably

[6] Elliott p 55.

opposed the catholic clergy, often with considerable vehemence and insistence. The protestant reformation can fairly be called, I believe, an anti-clerical revolution.

To document this conclusion fully would require massive empirical studies of the growth and nature of anti-clericalism all over western Europe during the reformation. That is clearly beyond my present capacity. I would like to provide some indication of the plausibility of my conclusion, however, by presenting one case study. The case I have selected is of the european community in which I have lived and worked the longest and whose history I know best, the canton of Geneva.[7]

Before the reformation Geneva was an episcopal city, part of an episcopal principality.[8] Her temporal and spiritual ruler was a bishop. Occasionally, especially in the early middle ages, she claimed to be a part of the Holy Roman Empire, but as an ecclesiastical principality rather than as a free imperial city. More important by the sixteenth century was the fact that she was then closely connected to the duchy of Savoy. Many of the rural areas and villages surrounding Geneva belonged directly to the dukes of Savoy or their vassals. For several decades before the reformation the bishop of Geneva had always been attached to the court of Savoy. Often he had been a younger son or brother of the duke himself. This arrangement had the advantage for Geneva of securing savoyard support for the city. She could call on the ducal army for defense and her merchants could trade more freely throughout the duchy. It also meant, however, that the bishop was seldom in actual residence within the city. He had to spend a good deal of time at the ducal court. Some of the bishops also acquired charges

---

[7] A good introduction to the early history of Geneva is supplied by the symposium volume edited by [Paul-E.] Martin, *Histoire de Genève [des origines a 1798]* (Geneva 1951). A fine guide to more intensive studies is supplied by Paul-F. Geisendorf, *Bibliographie raisonnée de l'histoire de Genève*, vol 43 in the series *Mémoires et documents [publiés par la Société d'histoire et d'archéologie de Genève]* (Geneva 1966). An important recent contribution to our knowledge of medieval genevan ecclesiastical history is provided by [Louis] Binz, [*Vie religieuse et réforme ecclésiastique dans le diocèse de Genève pendant le grand schisme et la crise conciliare (1378–1450)*], first of a projected two volumes, published as vol 46 in the same series (Geneva 1973). For an excellent introduction in english to the history of Geneva during the reformation, see [E. William] Monter, [*Calvin's Geneva*] (New York 1967).

[8] An interesting contemporary description of pre-reformation Geneva is provided by [François] Bonivard, [*Advis et devis de l'ancienne et nouvelle police de Genève*.] . . . (Geneva 1865). An excerpt, translated by Raymond A. Mentzer, Jr., is appended to the Burgess Press version of this essay. See also Binz, part 2 of the Martin *Histoire de Genève*, and vol 1 of [Henri] Naef, [*Les origines de la Réforme à Genève*] (Geneva/Paris 1936).

outside of Savoy. Many acquired ecclesiastical property with attendant responsibilities in France. A few received administrative assignments from Rome. Still the power of the bishop was always felt within Geneva. That power was symbolised graphically by the cathedral of St Pierre on the top of the hill in the center of the old city. It had been splendidly rebuilt and redecorated in the course of the fifteenth century, when the commercial fairs for which the city was famous in that part of Europe were flourishing. It was visible for miles around, even from the high mountains which enclose three sides of the city from a distance. It easily dominated the city physically.

Within Geneva, the bishop's power was exercised by an episcopal council. The most important members of this council were the vicar, who was the bishop's chief representative in the city and presided over the council in his absence, and the 'official,' who supervised the administration of justice, both civil and criminal, for all clerics. This council acted as both an administrative body and an ecclesiastical court. The bishop was further assisted in his rule of Geneva by a cathedral chapter of thirty-two canons. Almost all of them came from prominent savoyard noble families. Each of the canons was assigned a luxurious house near the cathedral. Vacancies in the chapter were filled by the canons themselves, through co-option. Their most important single function was to elect a new bishop on the death or resignation of an incumbent. However they often saw their choice set aside by the pope. Not only did he retain the right to confirm any election of a bishop, but in the case of Geneva he also reserved to himself the right to make his own final selection. Both the chapter elections and the final papal selections reflected heavy political pressure from neighboring secular authorities. This pressure came primarily from the dukes of Savoy but it could also come from the french royal house or the swiss cantons.

For the exercise of his spiritual responsibilities, the bishop depended upon ordained clergymen. There were several hundred of them in pre-reformation Geneva, out of a total population of about ten thousand.[9] They included secular priests, most of whom were attached to one or another of seven city parishes. They also included regular clergy, mostly of the mendicant orders, housed in some seven convents. The newest of these convents had been built in the century before the

[9] See Naef, 1, pp 22-5, for a careful estimate that there were four to five hundred clergymen resident in Geneva. See Monter p 2, for an estimate that the total population in 1537 was 10,300.

208

reformation for communities of augustinian hermits and Poor Clare sisters.

For the exercise of his temporal responsibilities, the bishop delegated some of his powers to laymen. Justice for laymen, in both civil and criminal cases, was supervised by an officer with the unusual title of 'vidomne.' Some time before the reformation, a bishop of Geneva had ceded the right to choose this officer to the ducal government of Savoy. The vidomne and his staff lived in a castle on an island in the middle of the river Rhone which cuts Geneva in half. That castle symbolised graphically the power of Savoy within the city. The bishop further allowed the lay population of Geneva to elect certain other officers to share in local government. The most important of these elected officers were four syndics, chosen once a year by the entire body of male citizens in an assembly called the general council. These syndics had the right to act as judges in the more important criminal trials initiated by the vidomne. That right, along with many others, had been spelled out in writing in a charter of liberties of the citizens of Geneva promulgated by a bishop in 1387. Every subsequent bishop was expected to swear to uphold these liberties at the time of his installation. The syndics also chose a small or ordinary council, of twelve to twenty-five men, who met at least once a week to handle local civic problems. They had to see to it that the walls and moats which fortified the city were maintained in good condition, that adequate food supplies were regularly brought into the city and stored with care, that the streets were kept clean. They also had to direct the collection and expenditure of much of the city's money. And they supervised a variety of educational and charitable institutions.

At this last point ecclesiastical and temporal authority overlapped. For most of the educational and charitable institutions were staffed by clergymen. The education of the clergy had been handled within the cathedral establishment for a long time. In the fifteenth century, an independent school for laymen had been established, financed and supervised by the city council, but normally staffed by clergymen. Charity was handled primarily by seven 'hospitals'.[10] Most of them had been founded by the gifts or legacies of wealthy individuals, to provide both for the repose of their own souls and assistance to the poor. A typical 'hospital' would be a converted house, perhaps itself part of the original bequest. Resident in it would be a priest, who would be in

---

[10] See J.-J. Chaponnière and L. Sordet, *Des hopitaux de Genève avant la réformation*, vol III/2 in *Mémoires et documents* (1844).

charge and would say masses for the souls of the founder and his family. He would be assisted by a *hospitallier* or administrator, who would help the poor. Usually there would be a dozen or so of the poor in residence, a mixture of orphans, the handicapped, and the very old. From the middle of the fifteenth century, many of these hospitals were supervised by a municipal foundation, controlled by the council, which also had supplementary funds to assist the poor who could remain in their own homes. In addition the city maintained a pestilential hospital, outside the walls and near the cemetery, for the victims of serious contagious diseases. It was staffed by a priest, a doctor, and several servants. The city also maintained two small *leprosaria* outside its walls.

The control of public morals should have been the responsibility of the bishop, but he was seldom interested.[11] There were always a good number of prostitutes in pre-reformation Geneva, to service the visiting merchants and clergymen. Seldom was any effort made to drive prostitutes from the city. Instead they were regulated by the city council. At one point they were asked to organise themselves into a kind of guild and elect from their number a 'queen' who would represent them in dealings with the government. The prostitutes were also expected to live within an assigned quarter of the city, wear distinctive kinds of clothing, and limit their solicitation to specified times and places. If a sexual or marital problem required legal intervention, of course, the courts were prepared to act. Most cases of this sort were handled by the court of the bishop.

Geneva's ecclesiastical establishment was supported materially from a variety of sources. Taxes and church property within the city provided some income. A great deal of additional income came from a patchwork of rural properties scattered over the countryside around Geneva and belonging directly to the bishop. These were superintended by episcopal officers who saw to it that order was maintained in each rural village, that local priests served the spiritual needs of the peasants, and that all the rents and taxes due the bishop were regularly paid.

After the reformation Geneva was a secular city-state. The bishop and all his officers had been evicted, including the ones appointed with his permission by the dukes of Savoy. The clergy had all, without exception, been forced either to leave the city or abandon clerical careers. Almost all of the ecclesiastical property, both within the city and in the countryside, had been confiscated by the new government.

[11] See Naef, I, cap 5, section I.

Reformation and revolution: the case of Geneva

Many of the social services provided by clergymen had been secularised. A new reformed church had been created to minister to the spiritual needs of the population, but it was completely under the control of the city government. All of this had been engineered by the lay merchants and professional men of Geneva, led by their elected syndics and council members. These changes began in the 1520s, with the whittling away of the bishop's powers. They reached a climax in 1536, with a formal vote by the entire male population to adopt the protestant reformation. They were not fully consolidated until 1555, when John Calvin, the new director of Geneva's spiritual life, finally won a definitive triumph over all local opposition.[12]

It all began as a rebellion against the government of the bishop and his savoyard allies. Step by step the syndics and the city council seized powers that had heretofore been held by the episcopal government as parts of its sovereign prerogatives, until finally nothing remained for the bishop. The first powers to go were those of control over foreign affairs. This crucial attribute of sovereignty had naturally been claimed by the bishop. Now, however, the syndics and city council, on their own initiative, opened formal negotiations with other governments, particularly with those of free city-states within the swiss confederation. These were states with which genevans had long had commercial relations. A struggle developed within the city between merchants with savoyard and swiss interests. When the latter faction won the upper hand, it tried to consolidate its power by negotiating formal alliances with two of the more powerful neighbours to the north, Fribourg and Berne. Fribourg soon withdrew but Berne remained as Geneva's staunchest ally. That alliance was important, for Berne was one of the greatest military powers in the area.

The savoyards protested vehemently against these alliances, arguing that they amounted to usurpation by the city council of a sovereign

12 There is an excellent but unfortunately incomplete account of these changes in Naef, 2 (Geneva 1968), published posthumously, carrying the story only to 1534, without any documentation for the period 1532–1534. To complete this narrative, the best accounts remain those of Jean-Antoine Gautier, *Histoire de Genève des origines à l'année 1691*, 9 vols (Geneva 1896–1914), esp vol 2 (1501–1537), and [Amédée] Roget, [*Histoire du peuple de Genève depuis la Réforme jusqu'à l'escalade*,] 7 vols (Geneva 1870–1883) which covers the period 1536–1567. See also the contemporary accounts of Michel Roset, *Les chroniques de Genève*, ed by Henri Fazy (Geneva 1894) and Jeanne de Jussie, *Le levain du calvinisme ou commencement de l'hérésie de Genève*, ed Ad.-C. Grivel (Geneva 1865). Excerpts from both of these chronicles translated into english by Raymond A. Mentzer, Jr. can be found following the Burgess Press version of this essay. I have been told that the Grivel edition of the Jeanne de Jussie chronicle is based on an inferior manuscript and that a new edition is consequently needed.

power belonging to the bishop. The incumbent bishop, however, did not support this protest. He had become alienated from the duke, despite the years he had spent in the ducal entourage, and was trying to play an independent game. In 1527, he conceded to the city council the right to sign alliances and tried to make himself a party to the alliance with Fribourg and Berne. The bernese refused to admit the bishop to the alliance and the bishop tried to revoke his concession to the Geneva council. But it was too late.

The next episcopal powers to be seized by the city council were the rights to control justice, another crucial attribute of sovereignty. The syndics had already won much earlier, under the terms of the 1387 charter, the right to sit as judges in certain criminal trials. The council now moved, during the 1527 negotiations with the bishop, to gain control over all civil cases. In granting this request, the bishop was surrendering powers previously exercised by his 'official' and by the vidomne. His cession of the vidomne's powers made the savoyards furious, since the vidomne was appointed by their government. Again the bishop changed his mind and tried to retract the concession, but again he was too late. Instead the city council proceeded to take over even more judicial powers. It blocked all appeals to superior courts outside of Geneva. It transferred to the syndics the right to execute criminal sentences. Finally a new elective magistracy was created, the office of the lieutenant, charged with supervising all criminal justice. By 1530 all the judicial powers once belonging to the bishop and his agents had been transferred over to the elective government of the city. In 1533 the bishop paid one last visit to the city, then left it for good. He soon transferred his entire court to the small neighbouring town of Gex. A number of canons also left Geneva during these years of turmoil.

Meanwhile protestantism had begun to penetrate Geneva. It was introduced with powerful encouragement from Berne, which had itself formally adopted zwinglianism in 1528. The leader of the campaign to convert Geneva to protestantism was Guillaume Farel, who repeatedly visited Geneva during these years in spite of fierce opposition from the local clergy. His inflammatory sermons and public appeals plunged the city into further turmoil. Iconoclastic riots began and catholic services were repeatedly disrupted. Protestants seized certain of the church buildings, most notably the franciscan convent, and began holding services and administering sacraments, in competition with the local priests. Finally a public debate was held in 1535 between a group of protestant pastors and a few of the local priests. The protestants claimed that the debate had resulted in a decisive victory for them, and that the population was now generally convinced of the truth of their point of view. They demanded that the city adopt legislation to establish firmly a truly reformed service of worship. The council responded cautiously by ordering a suspension of the catholic mass.

That step convinced most of the catholic clergy who were still in the city that they could no longer remain. A number had already left. A few had abandoned their religious vocations, had publicly converted to protestantism, had turned to secular occupations, and had even married. In 1535, after the great debate, practically all the remaining catholic clergy left Geneva. This included the bishop's vicar, the remaining canons, most of the parish priests, and most of the friars and sisters. A handful of priests who tried to remain were ordered by the council either to leave or to conform. The few who conformed were relieved of all clerical duties.

Once most of the clergy had left the city, the council seized control over all church property, both within the city and in the country districts heretofore controlled by the bishop's officers. Some of this property was used to pay off a substantial debt to Berne. The rest was allocated to charity. All of the hospitals created during the middle ages were closed. A new hospital-general was established in the building which had been the convent of the Poor Clare sisters. A civilian staff, including a *hospitallier* or administrator, a teacher, a doctor, and servants was assembled and housed in the building. A special committee of the government was created to supervise the activity of this staff. The administration of charity was thus thoroughly laicised and rationalised in Geneva.[13]

As a final assertion of sovereignty, the city council authorised and supervised the coining of money. The new coins carried a slogan which was to become a rallying cry for the reformation: *Post tenebras lux.*

Naturally all of these changes increasingly alarmed the bishop, the ducal government of Savoy, and the savoyard noble families of the area surrounding Geneva. The bishop could see his power and wealth evaporating, the duke could see his claim on the city withering away, the nobles could see their relatives among the canons insulted and exiled. Considerable military pressure was brought to bear upon

---

[13] See [Robert M.] Kingdon, 'Social Welfare [in Calvin's Geneva,'] *AHR*, 76 (1971) pp 50–69.

Geneva to stop this course of events. Armed bands of savoyard noblemen, encouraged by the duke and the bishop, ravaged the countryside, interdicting much of the trade so vital to the city's economy and making it hard for the city to gather in essential food on a regular basis. By 1535 the city was virtually under siege. Geneva persuaded its bernese ally to come to the rescue. A large swiss army came pouring down from the great plain to the north. This army commanded by the bernese effectively conquered all the savoyard and independent territory surrounding Geneva. It even tried to take over the city itself, but the genevans were able to resist that pressure.

With a ring of bernese dependencies around her, Geneva was now free to go all the way to reformation. In a special meeting of the general council held in May of 1536, the final step was taken. It was voted that the city would henceforth live by the gospel and the word of God as it had been preached in Geneva since the suspension of the mass. It was further voted that the 'masses, images, idols, and other papal abuses' would no longer be permitted in the city.[14]

That decision ended the power of the catholic clergy in Geneva. But it did not immediately create a reformed church. It really only left a vacuum, which was unstable and dangerous in an age when almost all europeans felt it necessary to build their lives and their communities around some form of religious ideology. Farel desperately tried to fill this void. He had the great good luck to recruit as his principal assistant a brilliant young french humanist lawyer who happened to be passing through Geneva only a few months after its fateful decision to become protestant. This was John Calvin. He had only recently converted to protestantism and fled from religious persecution in his native country. He was now appointed a public lecturer in theology. For two years, Farel and Calvin worked together to announce the christian truth as they saw it and to give that truth reality within Geneva by developing reformed services and ecclesiastical institutions. They were frustrated at every turn, however, by genevans who did not want to trade catholic clerical tyranny for a new protestant yoke. Finally they were both rather unceremoniously ejected from the city.

Now Geneva was really drifting, without any clerical leadership it could respect. Some thought the city might return to catholicism. Others expected it to drift into some wild and eccentric religious experiment. This period of indecision ended when Calvin, alone, was

---

[14] See [*Ioannis*] *Calvini Opera* [*quae supersunt omnia*], ed by Baum, Cunitz, & Reuss, 21 (Brunswick 1879) cols 201–2, for the full text of this decision of 21 May 1536.

invited back to take charge. He was reluctant to return to Geneva and he posed strict conditions, but they were accepted. Finally in 1541 he came back. He remained in Geneva until his death in 1564, and created there a reformed church which proved to be a model for protestants in much of Europe and America.

Calvin accomplished this feat solely by moral suasion. He never possessed even a fraction of the legal power of the deposed catholic bishop. He never commanded even a fraction of the material resources owned by the bishop, or for that matter by any one of the canons. Political power remained solely within the hands of the elected council and syndics. Calvin and the other pastors were only employees of the municipal government, living on salaries paid by the city,[15] most of them in houses owned by the city. They were far fewer in number than the catholic clergy whose places they took. Altogether there were only nine pastors in 1542. The number had risen to only nineteen by 1564, the year of Calvin's death.[16] A few additional men with protestant theological training secured positions as chaplains, teachers, or tutors. But the total of all these men was far short of the hundreds of catholic religious who had served Geneva under the bishop. Furthermore none of these protestant clergymen was allowed to become a full citizen of Geneva. The city had become so suspicious of foreign pressures that it reserved citizenship, with full rights to vote and hold office, to certain native-born residents. All the pastors were immigrants, most of them from France, like Calvin. No native genevan had secured the type of advanced education the council now decided was essential for the position. A few of the pastors became 'bourgeois' of Geneva, an intermediate status which gave a man many political and legal rights, but not full citizenship. Calvin himself was granted the status of *bourgeois*, but only toward the end of his life, in 1559.[17]

This does not mean that Calvin and the other pastors did not

---

[15] See the excellent study of Jean-François Bergier, 'Salaires des pasteurs de Genève au XVIe siècle,' in *Mélanges [d'histoire du XVIe siècle offerts à Henri] Meylan*, vol 43 in *Bibliothèque historique vaudoise* (Lausanne 1970) pp 159–78. The salaries consisted of both payments in cash and large allocations of grain and wine from the municipal supplies.

[16] There are lists of all the pastors employed by the city in each year from 1542 on, in Roget at the end of each volume.

[17] *Le livre des bourgeois de l'ancienne république de Genève*, ed by Alfred L. Covelle (Geneva 1897) p 266, two variant entries for 25 December 1559. For the distinction between the status of citizen and that of bourgeois, see Bonivard p 25. On the significance of the appointment of foreigners as pastors, see Monter esp pp 126, 221.

exercise considerable political power in Geneva. But their power was always exercised indirectly, usually through preaching or consulting. Calvin used both means effectively. He became an eloquent preacher, who clearly commanded the respect, if not always the affection, of his audience. This was in marked contrast to many of his predecessors both in the catholic clergy and among the earliest protestant preachers. He also became an active consultant to the city government. The council found his skill as a trained lawyer and his first-hand knowledge of the greater world of international politics to be extremely useful. He was often called in for consultation and his advice was usually accepted.[18]

One of the first things Calvin did on returning to Geneva in 1541, was to draft a set of ecclesiastical ordinances, to give institutional shape and legal standing to the newly reformed church. His right to do this had been part of the bargain that led to his return. After some discussion and a few minor amendments, these ordinances were enacted into law by the government.[19] This famous settlement organised the genevan church by creating four categories of ecclesiastical officials and then building institutions through which the work of each could be channelled. The categories were, (1) the pastors who were to preach the word of God and administer the sacraments, (2) the doctors who were to study the word of God and teach, (3) the elders who were to maintain discipline within the community, (4) the deacons who were to supervise the administration of charity.

The pastors were distributed among the parishes created before the reformation both within the city and in the country villages it controlled. There were seldom enough men to staff all of these parishes fully, but arrangements were made so that everyone had access of some sort to a pastor. For organisational purposes, the pastors were grouped into a company, which met once a week to handle routine church business, to discuss theology, and to engage in criticism of

[18] Records of many of these consultations can be found in the *Annales Calviniani* in vol 21 of the *Calvini Opera*. Several of them are discussed further in Robert M. Kingdon, *Geneva and the Coming of the Wars of Religion in France, 1555–1563* (Geneva 1956) for example pp 34–5.

[19] There is a good recent critical edition of these ordinances by Jean-François Bergier in the *Registres de la Compagnie des pasteurs de Genève, au temps de Calvin*, 1, *1546–1553* (Geneva 1964) pp 1–13. There is an english translation, without most of the critical apparatus, in *The Register of the Company of Pastors of Geneva in the Time of Calvin*, ed and trans by Philip E. Hughes (Grand Rapids, Mich, 1966) and a fresh translation of some of them by Raymond A. Mentzer, Jr., appended to my essay in the Burgess volume.

themselves and their colleagues.[20] Calvin served as moderator, or presiding officer, of this company until his death. That was his only position of pre-eminence in Geneva. He also served as one of the pastors in the cathedral parish of St Pierre, and occasionally also preached in the nearby parish of the Madeleine. The pastors were all chosen by co-optation, with the existing company deciding on each new appointment. No choice could become final, however, until the candidate had been approved by the city council and presented to the parish in which he was to serve. The council reserved to itself the right to dismiss without notice any pastor who displeased its members. Over the years a number were in fact dismissed, most commonly because they had offended council members by things they said in sermons.[21]

At first Calvin was the only doctor. In addition to his pastoral duties, he spent a good deal of time in writing and lecturing on the bible. His lectures attracted hundreds of eager young intellectuals from all over Europe. This teaching did not get formal institutional shape, however, until 1559, fairly late in Calvin's life. In that year Geneva created a new academy, providing both secondary and university-level training in theology.[22] Calvin, of course, was the star of this faculty. He was joined by a number of his disciples who had been teaching in neighbouring Lausanne but who had recently been driven out by Berne. Material support for this new academy was provided primarily from property confiscated by the council from native genevans who had been expelled from the city in a number of internal upheavals ending in 1555.[23] These ejections had the net effect of eliminating all opposition within Geneva to Calvin and fully consolidating his authority.

The other two orders of ecclesiastical officials, elders and deacons, were laymen, most of whom served in this capacity only on a part-time basis. They were drawn from the same pool of wealthy merchants

---

[20] For a full critical edition of the rather casual records of this body, see the *Registres de la Compagnie des pasteurs de Genève, au temps de Calvin, 1546–1564*, 1 and 2, ed by R.-M. Kingdon and J.-F. Bergier (Geneva 1962–1964); 3, *1565–1574*, ed by Oliver Fatio and Olivier Labarthe (Geneva 1969); 4, *1575–1582*, ed by Olivier Labarthe and Bernard Lescaze (Geneva 1974).

[21] There are several examples of dismissals discussed in Robert M. Kingdon, *Geneva and the Consolidation of the French Protestant Movement, 1564–1572* (Geneva/Madison, Wisconsin 1967) cap I.

[22] The standard account is Charles Borgeaud, *Histoire de l'Université de Genève*, vol I, *L'Académie de Calvin, 1559–1798* (Geneva 1900).

[23] E. William Monter, *Studies in Genevan Government (1536–1605)* (Geneva 1964) pp 25 *et seq.*

and professional men as the members of the city council and the city's various governing committees. Near the beginning of every year, a meeting of the general council was called to elect the syndics and council members for the coming twelve months. At the same time members of a number of governmental committees were elected, from slates prepared by the outgoing government. These committees included ones to maintain the city's fortifications, control its grain supply, keep the streets clean, act as courts to judge certain legal cases. Calvin's ecclesiastical ordinances added two new committees to the list: a committee to maintain christian discipline, staffed partly by elected elders; a committee to assist the poor, staffed by elected deacons.

The committee to maintain discipline was called the consistory.[24] It was made up of all the elders and city pastors, with one syndic added as its presiding officer. It acted as a court and met once a week. The elders were chosen so as to represent all of the districts into which the city was divided. They reported to the consistory names of residents whose religious ideas were suspect, who still clung to catholic practices, and who did not behave properly. A high percentage of their cases were of people accused of sex crimes—fornication, adultery, sodomy, rape. The consistory examined each case. If the fault was minor and the accused penitent, he might be let off with a scolding. If the fault was more serious and the accused stubborn, he could be excommunicated. If the accused had done something of a criminal nature that required further punishment, he would be referred to the city council.

This was the most controversial single institution established by the reformation in Geneva. Calvin insisted on its creation when he returned in 1541, and threatened to resign when its power to excommunicate was challenged in later years. Calvin ultimately had his way, the opponents of consistorial excommunication were discredited and driven out, and a moral 'reign of terror' followed.[25] All of this helped to create that particularly austere pattern of behaviour which has come to be labelled 'Puritan.'

[24] See Robert M. Kingdon, 'The Control of Morals in Calvin's Geneva,' in Lawrence P. Buck and Jonathan W. Zophy, *The Social History of the Reformation* (Columbus 1972) pp 3–16, and the works there cited, particularly [Walther] Köhler, [*Zürcher Ehegericht und Genfer Konsistorium,*] 2 (Leipzig 1942). The registers of the consistory have never been edited and merit further study.

[25] For statistics of the dramatic increase in excommunications following Calvin's definitive triumph in 1555, see Köhler p 614, n 544.

The deacons worked with the hospital-general.[26] Their positions had actually been created before Calvin's arrival, in the series of events which led up to the final break with catholicism. Calvin simply made room for them in his ecclesiastical ordinances and found biblical warrant for their assignments. In effect he sanctified this office, gave it a special religious character, and in so doing made it a more highly valued and respected feature of genevan society.

The ecclesiastical ordinances required the council to consult the pastors every year when it drew up its slates of nominations for elders and deacons before the elections. This rule, however, was not followed invariably. It was followed more often in the choice of elders than of deacons, and was followed quite scrupulously in the selection of both only after Calvin's power had been fully consolidated toward the end of his life.

This ecclesiastical structure was an outstanding success in consolidating the reformation in Geneva. Much of it persists there down to the present. It helped win for the city its international reputation as a centre of reformed protestantism.

Taken all together, it seems obvious to me that the changes in Geneva between 1526 and 1559 constitute a genuine revolution. They meet every requirement of the definition of a revolution laid down by Neumann which I described earlier. There was a fundamental change in political organisation: a government run by a bishop assisted by canons, chosen according to church law, was overthrown; a new government run by a council of local laymen elected by the people took its place. There was a fundamental change in social structure: several hundred catholic clergymen, a number of savoyard noblemen, and ordinary laymen hesistant to go all the way to calvinism were all driven out of the city; their places were taken by hundreds of immigrants, most of whom were artisans and merchants and most of whom came from France, as had Calvin. There was a fundamental change in economic property control: large amounts of property were confiscated from the old church and its supporters and in effect socialised, put at the disposition of the entire community as represented by its government, rather than being distributed to private individuals. All of these changes were justified and sanctified by the

---

[26] See Robert M. Kingdon, 'The Deacons of the Reformed Church in Calvin's Geneva,' in *Mélanges Meylan*, pp 81–90; also Kingdon, 'Social Welfare' and the works there cited, particularly Léon Gautier, *L'Hôpital Général de Genève de 1535 à 1545 et l'Hospice Général de 1869 à 1914* (Geneva 1914).

most obvious change of all, in the predominant myth of social order. Roman catholic theology was brutally rejected and a new variety of protestant theology was created to take its place.

There remains one final problem that must be explored, however, before we can resolve our problem satisfactorily. We must consider the extent to which the reformation in Geneva was typical. Even if the reformation clearly meant revolution in this particular city-state, it may not have had the same meaning elsewhere. Geneva may have been unique, and thus not a case upon which generalisations should be built.

To resolve this problem would require extensive comparative studies. Even some tentative and preliminary consideration, however, does make one thing clear: the reformation in Geneva was clearly more radical than in many communities. In few places had the power of the catholic clergy remained as strong and as pervasive as it was in pre-reformation Geneva. Cities all over Europe had once been controlled directly by bishops. For example in Germany most cities had been ruled by bishops back in the tenth century. Since that period, however, new secular cities had been founded and many old cities had broken loose from episcopal control. By the time of the reformation only a few german cities remained under the effective control of bishops. Most of the cities of importance had become free imperial cities, acknowledging allegiance to only one sovereign—the holy roman emperor. Remnants of episcopal power remained in most of these cities, but most temporal power was concentrated in elected city councils like those of Geneva.[27]

Furthermore, in many cities services that had previously been performed by the clergy had been turned over to secular institutions well before the reformation. This was particularly true of educational and charitable services. The move to secularisation of these services was especially pronounced in the great italian city-states of the late middle ages. In fact it can be argued that the celebrated culture of the italian renaissance was made possible by the creation of secular schools and academies supported by municipal governments and wealthy laymen in communities like Florence. Similarly the administration of charity had been laicised and rationalised in

[27] Hajo Holborn, *A History of Modern Germany: the Reformation* (New York 1959) makes a special point of noting the remnants of episcopal powers in the free imperial cities for example pp 23, 183. See also Bernd Moeller, *Reichsstadt und Reformation* (Gütersloh 1962) also in french translation (Geneva 1966), and english (Philadelphia 1972).

communities like Milan which built and endowed large municipal hospitals for this purpose.[28] Clergy still staffed some of these institutions. But clerical control was gone and clerical participation was reduced if not ended. It can thus be argued that Geneva in the sixteenth century was socially retarded and that she used the reformation to catch up, to introduce changes which had already occurred in other communities.

It is also clear that in few places did the reformation go as far as it did in Geneva. It was not common for the entire body of the clergy in a community to be deposed or ejected. More often catholic parish priests were simply converted to protestantism, with a greater or lesser appreciation of what that meant, and allowed to remain at their work. Only slowly was a body of clergymen fully trained in protestant doctrine developed. This seems to have happened in most of the lutheran principalities in Germany and in England.

Even if the changes accompanying the reformation were seldom as abrupt and as far-reaching as in Geneva, however, there were always some changes. In every single instance, to begin with, a community adopting protestantism rejected the authority of the pope and broke all ties with Rome. And this was not a trivial move. The papacy had long symbolised in a concrete institutional way the unity of all western european civilization. Rejection of its power meant a move to some sort of particularism, often to some type of nationalism, with great consequences for the future.

Another change that almost always came with the reformation was the closing of all monastic communities and the confiscation of their often considerable property. On rare occasions convents or monasteries were simply not allowed to recruit new members, thus going out of existence when all existing members died.[29] But more commonly all the monks and nuns, friars and sisters, were required either to leave or find new occupations. And they lost all of their community property. There is, to be sure, a good deal of debate as to how significant were the resulting massive transfers of property, as english scholars of the period know very well.[30] In many areas

---

[28] See Giacomo C. Bascapè, 'L'assistenza e la beneficenza a Milano dall'alto medioevo alla fine della dinastia Sforzesca,' part 4 in *Storia di Milano*, vol 8 (Milan 1957) esp pp 405 *et seq* re establishment in 1456 of the Ospedale Maggiore.

[29] For example the two convents of St. Clara and St. Catherine in Nuremberg. See Gerald Strauss, *Nuremberg in the Sixteenth Century* (New York 1966) pp 158, 178.

[30] For a useful summary, see A. G. Dickens, *The English Reformation* (New York 1964) cap 7.

noblemen who already controlled much of a monastery's activities were no doubt able simply to control this property more directly. But changes of some sort had to occur. And they could be brutal and of far-reaching impact.

Yet another change that usually came with the reformation was the collapse of the system of church law and church courts. Appeals to Rome, of course, were always stopped. So at least that element in the catholic legal system invariably disappeared. But a good many further changes usually followed. Church courts were either abandoned completely or their powers and the range of their jurisdiction were sharply reduced. New protestant ecclesiastical bodies were seldom given many legal functions. In at least one aspect of legal practice, most protestant communities went further than Geneva. Before the reformation cases involving marital and sexual problems were normally tried before church courts. Geneva assigned these cases to a semi-ecclesiastical court, the consistory. This court did not, to be sure, use catholic canon law to settle these cases, turning instead to civil law and the relevant parts of the bible as interpreted by Calvin. But clergymen were at least involved in this part of the judicial process in Geneva. In most protestant communities they were not granted this right, and jurisdiction over marital and sexual offences was jealously reserved to secular courts.[31] Both catholic law and the catholic type of court were abandoned.

These three changes—the renunciation of papal authority, the closing of the monasteries, and the dismantling of the catholic legal system—were all of considerable significance. They required some modifications in political organisation, in the social structure, and in the predominant myth of the community. It seems to me that these changes can fairly be called revolutionary. Their full implications, to be sure, become obvious only when one examines an extreme case like Geneva. But they were always present. I would therefore conclude that the protestant reformation was indeed a revolution.

University of Wisconsin

---

[31] For example in Württemberg. See James M. Estes, 'Johannes Brenz and the Problem of Ecclesiastical Discipline,' *Church History*, 41 (1972) pp 464–79. See also Köhler.

JEAN DE SERRES AND THE POLITICS OF RELIGIOUS PACIFICATION, 1594-8

by W. B. PATTERSON

L
IKE most other rulers of his time, king Henry IV of France wished to see a single religion practised within his realm. But in the late sixteenth century, as is well known, the state of France was such as to make this objective singularly difficult to achieve. The protestants, of whom Henry had been until his accession the political leader, were a sturdy minority, with a well-developed system of church courts for the definition of doctrine and the administration of discipline. The catholics, who adhered to the centuries-old established church of the kingdom, had no doubt become much more aware of their own religious heritage by the thirty years of civil and ecclesiastical strife they had had to endure. Henry himself, who announced his second conversion to catholicism in the summer of 1593, was never able to shed a certain aura of denominational ambivalence; he himself said, in a famous anecdote, that his own religion was one of the mysteries of Europe. Yet some measure of religious pacification and conciliation was clearly essential for France in the 1590s, both for the health of the country and for the security of the man who was her sovereign ruler.[1] And under the circumstances existing in France, new initiatives and fresh ideas were needed. As an english historian observed, some years ago, for Henry to be accepted by the french as their 'Most Christian King and eldest son of the Church, a new definition of Church and Christian would be required.'[2]

From the catholic side these new initiatives were chiefly elaborations of the constitutional doctrines of gallicanism, a body of ideas which had long enjoyed the support of french jurists and of a significant proportion of the french clergy. These ideas had recently been given

---

[1] Roland Mousnier, *The Assassination of Henry IV: The Tyrannicide Problem and the Consolidation of the French Absolute Monarchy in the Early Seventeenth Century*, trans Joan Spencer (London 1973) pp 106–16, 138–83; [Georges] Livet, *Les guerres de religion* [*(1559–1598)*] (2 ed Paris 1966) pp 28–50; Hardouin de Péréfixe, *Histoire du roy Henry le Grand* (rev ed Amsterdam 1664), pp 116–257.

[2] Stanley Leathes, 'Henry IV of France,' *CModH* 3 (Cambridge 1907) p 657.

enhanced stature as the result of the researches of french antiquaries in the late sixteenth century, who were intent upon finding the historic roots of french culture and institutions.[3] As the gallican writer Pierre Pithou expressed the matter, in a book dedicated to Henry IV and published in 1594, the king of France possessed the authority to regulate both the temporal affairs and the disciplinary procedures of the church within the borders of his kingdom. He exercised supervision over religious communities, over appointments to office, and over ecclesiastical property in general. Of special relevance to France in the last decade of the sixteenth century, the king, it was asserted, had the authority to assemble a national council of the french church to settle the ecclesiastical affairs of the kingdom under his jurisdiction. The spiritual primacy of the see of Rome was not disputed, though the exercise of papal authority in France was conceived to be strictly circumscribed within the framework of the laws, canons, and conciliar decrees which were accepted in the kingdom and had long governed the relations between France and the papacy.[4] Implicit in the theories of Pithou and other gallicans was the idea that french political and ecclesiastical leaders, acting under the authority of the king, could act to resolve the religious crisis of the 1590s along lines which were appropriate to, and even unique to, France. From the gallican point of view, the means for a settlement lay ready at hand.

Among the specific plans for a settlement which were advanced during these years was the set of proposals by the french calvinist theologian and historian Jean de Serres, whose ideas were theologically audacious yet never far removed from concrete political and ecclesiastical problems. Though now little known, the proposals were, in their time, very widely discussed, especially among the members of de Serres's own religious communion, and they were examined in detail by a number of official ecclesiastical bodies. The proposals seem to have been developed under the king's patronage, and to have emanated, at least in part, from his own court, circumstances

---

[3] [Corrado] Vivanti, *Lotta politica e pace religiosa* [*in Francia fra Cinque e Seicento*] (Turin 1963) pp 132–86 and *passim*; Donald R. Kelley, *Foundations of Modern Historical Scholarship: Language, Law and History in the French Renaissance* (New York 1970) pp 222–98.

[4] Pierre Pithou, *Les libertez de l'Eglise gallicane* (1594), in *Traitez des droits et libertez de l'Eglise gallicane*, ed P. Dupuy, 2 vols (Paris 1639) I, pp 1–22; see also, for other treatises, I, pp 275–398, 405–44. The development of gallicanism is dealt with in Victor Martin, *Les origines du Gallicanisme*, 2 vols (Paris 1939) and *Le Gallicanisme et la réforme catholique* (Paris 1919).

which strongly suggest that they constituted one not unimportant strategy being considered by Henry and his advisers during the troublous first decade of the new king's reign.

Jean de Serres, born about 1540 of a french family with lands near Villeneuve, was educated at Lausanne and at Geneva, where he was a member of the first group of students who, in 1559, 'made up the new academy founded by Calvin.'[5] After studying theology there, under both Calvin and Théodore de Bèze, he became, in 1566, minister of Jussy, not far from Geneva. Three years later he married Margaret Godary, of a family from Lorraine which had taken refuge in Geneva, a union which was ultimately to produce nine children.[6] About the time of his marriage de Serres began the historical work which was to be the most lasting source of his scholarly reputation. This was the latin history of the french religious wars, entitled *Commentariorvm de statv religionis et reipublicae in Regno Galliae*, which, as its title suggests, was conceived in the pattern of Sleidan's celebrated account of the opening years of the reformation in Germany. The first three volumes, taking the story to 1570, were published in Geneva, beginning in 1571; two other volumes followed, published elsewhere, continuing the narrative to the edict of May 1576.[7] Intended for a european audience, the work brought to light, by letters, documents, and de Serres's own observations, the sufferings of those, particularly of his own party, who were the victims of war and persecution.[8]

De Serres's ecclesiastical career was marked at an early stage by a rebuff from the authorities in Geneva, giving him a taste of calvinist

---

[5] [Charles] Dardier, 'Jean de Serres, [historiographe du roi, sa vie et ses écrits d'après des documents inédits, 1540-1598'], *R[evue] H[istorique]*, 22, 2 (Paris 1883) p 298. Dardier's work, which appeared in two parts in the *Revue Historique* (22, 2, pp 291–328; 23, 3, pp 28–76) supplements and, in some instances, corrects the account in [E. and E.] Haag, *La France protestante*, 9 (Paris 1859) pp 253–68. For a recent assessment of de Serres, see Vivanti, *Lotta politica e pace religiosa*, pp 246–68. I am very grateful to professor Robert M. Kingdon for directing me to manuscript sources in Geneva which throw additional light on de Serres's career.

[6] State Archives, Geneva, MS Notary Records, Jean Ragueau, vol II, fols 232–6: the marriage contract between Jean de Serres and Margaret Godare.

[7] Jean de Serres, *Commentariorvm de statv religionis et reipublicae in Regno Galliae [primae partis libri III]* (Geneva 1571); other volumes followed in 1575 and 1580. According to a recent article, de Serres's history first appeared in 1570 as *Rervm in Gallia ob religionem gestarum libri tres*. See B. A. Vermaseren, 'La première édition des *Commentaires* de Jean de Serres,' *Bibliothèque d'Humanisme et Renaissance*, 23 (Geneva 1961) pp 117–20.

[8] For de Serres's historical achievement, see Henri Hauser, *Les sources de l'histoire de France: XVIe siècle (1494–1610)* 4 vols (Paris 1912) 3 pp 68–70, and J. W. Thompson and B. J. Holm, *A History of Historical Writing* 2 vols (New York 1942) 1, pp 561–2.

rigorism. In August 1572 he had applied to Théodore de Bèze for a leave of six weeks from his charge at Jussy, having been there by then for six years. On his appearance before the company of pastors, however, his request was denied, and to his plea that he had been ill and needed to recuperate, it was replied that God had sent this malady upon him to warn him to amend his ways.[9] Not long afterwards de Serres chose a more academic mode of life as principal of the college of arts at Lausanne, a city in which he took up residence in late 1572. While there, de Serres translated the dialogues of Plato into latin, a work which was eventually published in three volumes by Henri Estienne in Geneva.[10] Having established himself securely as a historian and classicist, de Serres was named in 1578 as pastor and professor at Nîmes, for the purpose of reviving the college there. De Bèze gave him a testimonial assuring the authorities in Nîmes that de Serres had been fully reconciled to the church in Geneva; de Serres, on his part, endeavoured throughout the rest of his career to stay in touch with and to be in the good graces of de Bèze and his fellow pastors in the spiritual center of the french reform movement.[11]

At Nîmes de Serres became known as a staunch defender of the reformed doctrines concerning the authority of the church and the nature of Christ's presence in the eucharist against the attacks mounted against these doctrines by members of the society of Jesus. In disputations with the scottish jesuit John Hay, of the university of Tournon, de Serres argued that their disagreement was basically over the definition of the church: whether it was that body of christians whose earthly head was the pope at Rome, or whether it was that body of christians whose authority was the bible, which the church had the duty of preserving and obeying. In the course of his discussion de Serres examined the teachings of Irenaeus, Tertullian, Chrysostom, Augustine, and Hilary, and stated his claim that his own teaching, like Calvin's, was in conformity with that of Cyprian and other

[9] Dardier, 'Jean de Serres,' RH 22, 2 (1883) pp 309–10.

[10] Jean de Serres, Πλάτωνος ἅπαντα τὰ σωζόμενα: Platonis opera quae extant omnia, ex nova Joannis Serrani interpretatione, perpetuis ejusdem notis illustrata, 3 vols (Geneva 1578).

[11] Dardier, 'Jean de Serres,' RH, 22, 2 (1883) p 314. The relationship between de Serres and de Bèze may be traced in Univ[ersity] Lib[rary], Gen[eva], MS Arch[ives] Tron[chin] 5, fols 4–10, 21–3, 25–6, 31, letters between de Serres and Geneva, 1580–96. For the often complicated relations between Geneva and the reformed church in France, see Robert M. Kingdon, Geneva and the Coming of the Wars of Religion in France, 1555–1563 (Geneva 1956) and Geneva and the Consolidation of the French Protestant Movement, 1564–1572 (Geneva 1967).

fathers of the church.[12] Unwritten traditions, such as those claimed as authoritative by the roman church, strained the credulity of christians, and were in many cases inconsistent with the word of God and the witness of ancient writers; such traditions ought, therefore, to be repudiated.[13] In these disputations, published in the 1580s, de Serres seemed to put a considerable distance between the roman catholic and the reformed points of view, but in a new edition of his work on the church, published in 1594, he held out some hope for a reconciliation. In the dedication of the volume to the great huguenot military leader François de Bonne, duc de Lesdiguières, de Serres wrote that the papal usurpation of authority in the church was a danger to christians and to the french monarchy. But he thought there were grounds for agreement among christians of different persuasions in the doctrines which could be drawn from the scriptures and from the christian writers of antiquity.[14]

It was also in Nîmes that de Serres became more closely associated with the political and religious struggle under way in France, and became acquainted with Henry of Navarre, the head of the huguenot party. As early as October 1579 he was sent by the churches of Languedoc to Henry to represent to him their situation. The king of Navarre was obviously pleased with their spokesman, sending him on to the maréchal de Montmorency with the commendation: 'I have found his discourse tending above all to fashioning a good peace and to alleviating and extinguishing all differences and dissensions.'[15] Henry asked his marshal to provide de Serres with the passports and support he needed to carry out his work of fostering harmony among the protestant churches. A year later Henry informed the protestant churches of France that he had sought the support of the Rhineland prince Jean Casimir, count palatine, from whom 'the sieur de Serres,' evidently sent as Henry's emissary, 'has reported to me a good enough

[12] Jean de Serres, *Qvartvs anti-Iesvita, siue, Pro Verbo Dei Scripto et vere Catholica Ecclesia, aduersus Ioannis Hayi monachi Iesuitae commenta & conuitia*, in *Doctrinae Iesviticae praecipva capita, tomus quartus* (La Rochelle 1586) pp 28–32, 153, 246, 301, 309, 375. For John Hay's career, see the account by Thompson Cooper, *DNB*, 9, pp 267–8.

[13] Jean de Serres, *Qvarti anti-Iesuitae, siue De vera verae Ecclesiae autoritate, aduersus Ioannis Hayi monachi-Iesuitae commenta & conuicia, responsionis posterior pars*, in *Doctrinae Iesviticae praecipva capita, tomus sextus* (La Rochelle 1588) pp 276–7.

[14] Jean de Serres, *Pro vera Ecclesiae Catholicae autorite, defensio: Aduersus Ioannis Hayi Iesuitae disputationis, sacrae antiqvitatis iudicio simplicissime explicata* (Geneva 1594) Sig *iii verso–*v.

[15] Henry IV, *Recueil des lettres missives [de Henri IV,]* ed Berger de Xivrey, 9 vols (Paris 1843–76) 1, p 256 (letter dated 4 November 1579).

response.'[16] De Serres undertook further missions in 1580 and 1583 in support of the huguenot cause. These seem also to have been years when de Serres was in undiminished favour with his fellow pastors and other leaders in the reformed church, as is suggested by his membership in many of the assemblies and synods of the reformed community in France.[17]

When Henry of Navarre ascended the french throne in 1589, upon the assassination of Henry III, de Serres came to be associated even more closely with him, but at the same time the pastor's relations with the churches of Languedoc showed signs of strain. Though he was chosen by the colloquy of Sommières in October 1589 to go to court to congratulate the new king, the consistory of Nîmes took offence at his absence and dismissed him as pastor. To make matters worse the consistory of Montpellier complained, in 1591, that de Serres had mishandled funds entrusted to him for the work of the churches.[18] These were the very years, however, when he was formulating those ideas on religious unity which were to prove so lively an issue in the councils of the reformed faith. In defending those ideas he probably had also to contend against suspicions which continued to cling to him because of supposed irregularities in the conduct of his career as a pastor. He did, in any case, continue to exercise his ministry after his departure from Nîmes, becoming, soon afterwards, pastor of the church in the principality of Orange.

The earliest mention of de Serre's irenic writings in any public forum was an announcement by de Serres himself, couched in the language of polemical theology, in a letter addressed to the thirteenth national synod of the reformed churches of France, meeting at Montauban in June 1594. According to the records of the synod, de Serres asked that 'some learned persons be appointed' to oversee the collection of ancient writings which he had begun to make for the purpose of proving that 'our Religion' was ancient and catholic, whereas that of the papists was new and particular. The synod ordered in response that de Serres make three copies of his work, one of which was to be sent to Bas Languedoc, from whence it would be sent to

---

[16] Henry IV, *Recueil des lettres missives*, I, p 324 (letter dated beginning of November 1580).

[17] Haag, *La France protestante*, 9, pp 264–5; Dardier, 'Jean de Serres,' *RH*, 22, 2 (1883) pp 316–19; [Jean] Aymon, *Tous les synodes [nationaux des églises reformées de France]* 2 vols (The Hague 1710) I, p 156.

[18] Haag, *La France protestante*, 9, pp 265–6; Dardier, 'Jean de Serres,' *RH*, 22, 2 (1883) p 320.

other churches in that area of France, a second to Saintonge, which would send it on to churches near there, and a third to Geneva, in preparation for its eventual publication. He was, however, warned not to have any of its contents published before it had been formally reviewed in this fashion.[19] It was evidently this same work to which de Serres referred in a letter to Théodore de Bèze in Geneva, on 27 March 1594, in which he commented that he had amassed the material for his *Harmonie*, and declared his indebtedness to de Bèze for the ideas that lay behind it.[20]

The book described in these documents was ultimately to appear in printed form in latin, but meanwhile, in the same summer of 1594, another writing attributed to de Serres, in french but with a clearly irenical purpose, was circulating in manuscript. This piece was the subject of a letter written to de Serres by the pastor Daniel Chamier on behalf of the colloquy of Valentinois, meeting at Montélimar, which conveyed that assembly's sharp disapproval of the manuscript's contents. The colloquy, it seems, had received word from several places that a writing bearing de Serres's name was passing through the hands of the nobility of the area, 'as much of one as of the other religion.'[21] Having obtained a copy of this discourse, the members of the colloquy had decided to send it to the consistory of de Serres's church at Orange, in order that de Serres could examine it and, if appropriate, acknowledge it as his own. This was necessary, in their view, since there was much about the discourse which was 'other than good.' They speculated as to whether 'the confusions of the times or the love of the world' had led de Serres away from his duty. It was, in any case, incumbent upon the pastor of Orange, if he was indeed the author, to offer a satisfactory explanation for what was in the discourse.[22]

The discourse to which the pastors and elders of Montélimar took such exception is a list of fifty-seven propositions, without title, introduction, or ascription of authorship. The first eight of the propositions describe the historical situation in France in brief, but pungent terms. 'Experience has shown in this Realm,' they begin, 'that neither

[19] Aymon, *Tous les synodes,* 1, pp 186-7; [John] Quick, *Synodicon in Gallia Reformata* [*:Or, The Acts, Decisions, Decrees, and Canons of Those Famous National Councils of the Reformed Churches in France*] 2 vols (London 1692) 1, p 166.
[20] Univ Lib Gen MS Arch Tron 5, fol 9v: Letter of de Serres to de Bèze, Dauphiné, 27 Mar. 1594.
[21] Univ Lib Gen MS Fr 412, fol 32: Copy of the letter of the colloquy of Valentinois to de Serres, Montélimar (1594).
[22] Univ Lib Gen MS Fr 412, fol 32.

arms nor bitter disputes are efficacious in composing the existing differences in religion.'[23] The clash of arms had not won over the people to God, but had produced, instead, a flood of impiety. Nor had the theological disputes of the age made men wiser. The reason that all discussion of theological differences had ended in rancour and had failed to resolve the issues in dispute seemed evident: all conferences had dealt in the beginning with differences instead of those matters on which there was agreement. Thus, instead of reaching grounds of understanding, the parties had only become increasingly embittered. The truth which all parties sought could not be obtained by force but yielded to gentleness. As a practical matter, forbearance was a preferable policy to repression: 'experience has made us recognise that those have been wisest who have held the people during our uncivil tempests in the free exercise of both religions, finding it better to bear with one another than to rebuild some combustion after so many distresses.'[24]

The memorandum then invited those who read it to search step by step 'for the remedy for our dissensions,' by coming together in amicable fashion for a peaceful conference.[25] The necessity for such a conference seemed almost beyond dispute; after such a long and furious conflict, could there be any greater necessity than that of finding peace? The parties in the struggle could at last, perhaps, recognise what they had in common:

> We all recognise the same God for our father, the same Catholic Church for our mother, the same Scriptures for our infallible rule of truth and the foundation of our salvation. We are all interested in being saved in the bosom of our common country.[26]

The memorandum then dealt in some detail with the problem of the 'arbitrators' of this discussion. It is clear that the author was struck by legal analogies in the case of the long contention between parties in France. It was as if, as so often happened in the law, 'a long and ruinous case would be composed and terminated by arbitration.'[27] He observed that in legal cases it was necessary to ascertain the intention of the testator, 'the wish of whom is law,' and that for this purpose a close examination of the testament was required. In the event the terms of the testament needed to be explained or clarified, the principles of natural equity were employed. Finally, if there were circumstances

[23] *Ibid* fol 28: Copy of a memorandum on a union between catholics and protestants.
[24] *Ibid.*
[25] *Ibid.*
[26] *Ibid.*
[27] *Ibid.*

which still presented difficulties, recourse was had to 'the practice of civil law or custom.' In a similar way there were, in the religious controversies so long pursued, a 'common testament of Christians,' certain undoubted principles of truth, and a 'perpetual succession' of that truth in the Church in which 'alone there is salvation.'[28] The crucial problem, however, was that of finding arbitrators who could help to lead men to the truth.

The solution to this problem, vitally important for any discussion between the two parties, was provided in the central portion of the propositions. Since the arbitrators 'ought to be the advocates for and ought to be agreeable to all Christians, one could not choose more worthy nor more acceptable ones than the apostles; and then, as interpreters and expositors of their will, the doctors of the ancient and Catholic Church.' The latter, the memorandum added, 'who approach nearest to the time of the apostles, were better instructed about their intention and have always had authority and credence in the Church.'[29] It was clear, however, that the authority of these doctors was derived from and was dependent upon the authority of the scriptures. They 'could not better show the intention of the testator than by his testament, expounding the testament by the testament, namely, Scripture by Scripture, insofar as God has wished to declare his will concerning our salvation.' In obscure places, these arbitrators found their way by the compass of certain principles of truth, regarding as authentic what was ancient and what was catholic, that is, 'believed by a common consent of all Christians.'[30] The principal purpose of the arbitrators, then, would be 'to show the truth, and by it to mediate the Concord of the Church, removing abuses and establishing the practice of the true religion among Christians.'[31]

The memorandum specified some of the things which were ancient and catholic, had been approved in the church at all times, and enjoyed the common assent of christians. Not surprisingly, these doctrines were found to be largely contained in the *Symbols*, or ancient creeds, considered here to be apostolic in their contents as well as ecumenical. The great themes of the creeds were briefly summarised:

That there is one God, the Father, the Son, the Holy Spirit; that the Son of God, our Saviour Jesus Christ, is true God and true man,

[28] *Ibid* fol 28v.
[29] *Ibid.*
[30] *Ibid.*
[31] *Ibid* fol 29.

conceived by the Holy Spirit, born of the Virgin Mary, Virgin before and after childbirth, that is redeemer, mediator, head and sovereign pastor in the Church; that he shed his precious blood for the remission of our sins, and offered a perfect sacrifice by his death and passion; that his blood is the purgation of our souls.[32]

The memorandum gave some attention, moreover, to theological issues then current. Christ, it was stated, had instituted two sacraments, baptism and the eucharist, or what Paul had called the supper of the Lord. In the eucharist, 'the flesh is truly meat, and his blood truly drink . . . we truly eat this flesh, and truly drink this blood: and thus we receive in the Holy Supper or Holy Eucharist his body really and not by imaginary or fantastic signs.'[33] The doctrine of justification was briefly dealt with in a sentence which stated that 'we are justified and saved by the grace and mercy of God, which we enjoy by faith.' That faith, however, was 'opened by charity,' and was 'necessarily accompanied by good works.'[34] On these matters, the memorandum suggested, little fundamental disagreement could be expected. Dissensions, of course, would remain, but they were, to a large extent, over matters which were accessory to rather than central to the christian faith. For such outbuildings, 'one ought not to trouble the Church and the Realm.'[35]

Since both parties shared a common faith, preachers should proclaim 'Jesus Christ and him crucified; exhorting Christians to charity, concord, modesty, and to all good works,' not having any subject for their 'invectives' than the evils and corruptions which had become so widespread during the furious contests of arms.[36] Political themes, however, were evidently not to be completely eschewed, since one of the final propositions stated: 'as it has been strongly urged to obey the Prince for conscience's sake . . . it is also necessary that the French be persuaded that the most dangerous heresy is to disobey the King.'[37] Zeal for religion had been common to both sides, but this zeal needed to be matched by other qualities, namely 'charity and concord' between kinsmen and patriots of all parties. 'Necessity constrains us to wish for this remedy; reason, to search for it; religion, to hope for it,' the

[32] Ibid.
[33] Ibid.
[34] Ibid.
[35] Ibid fol 29v.
[36] Ibid.
[37] Ibid.

memorandum concluded, adding that nothing was impossible or un-obtainable which was 'to the glory of God, the health of the Church and the repose of the Realm.'[38]

In the months which followed, de Serres was several times called upon to defend the contents of the memorandum. His own consistory seems to have referred the matter to the colloquy which was due to meet in Orange. When the colloquy met, however, de Serres seems not to have been present, and that assembly, supposing his absence to have been a deliberate breach of discipline, suspended him from his duties.[39] The matter went next to the colloquy of the baronies, which met at St Paul-Trois-Châteaux, in Dauphiné, in mid-November 1594. In the report which the pastors and elders of this assembly sent to the company of pastors at Geneva, they stated that monsieur de Serres had appeared before them and that the controversial memorandum had been examined there in his presence. They asked the genevans for their guidance.[40]

In the meantime de Serres had written to Théodore de Bèze, in Geneva, asking for that venerable theologian's help and advice. In his letter de Serres protested strenuously against the idea that he had be-come tainted with heresy or had become a 'mixer of religions,' while he had been serving his prince; his faith, he declared, was still that which he had learned from de Bèze. He cited, in this connection, his writings against the papists, which had just been reprinted in Geneva. He was working night and day to finish the work which he had promised to send to de Bèze and which the national synod, on his own request, had authorised him to undertake. That work would be a sufficient defence and would show him to be loyal to the doctrines of his church. The essay which was attributed to him and had been sent to de Bèze was inaccurate and contained expressions which de Bèze would be bound to regard as unworthy of his disciple.[41] He wished to assure his 'most honoured father' and his brethren at Geneva that he had not changed in doctrine or in zeal, and he expressed the hope that his integrity would soon be recognised.[42]

All of this prepared the way for what was evidently a special

[38] *Ibid.*
[39] This, at least, is the order of events implied by the opening paragraph of MS Fr 412 fol 33. Compare Dardier, 'Jean de Serres,' *RH*, 23, 3 (1883) p 39.
[40] Univ Lib Gen MS Fr 412, fol 18: letter of the colloquy of baronies to the company of pastors, 16 November 1594.
[41] Univ Lib Gen MS Arch Tron 5, fol 13: letter of de Serres to de Bèze, 20 October 1594.
[42] *Ibid* fol 13ᵛ.

meeting of the colloquy, held again at St Paul-Trois-Châteaux, 14–16 December 1594. This colloquy proceeded, first of all, to lift de Serres's suspension, an action which they saw as having been taken at Orange 'out of great zeal,' but under the mistaken impression that de Serres had deliberately absented himself from that meeting.[43] De Serres was then asked to avow or disavow the discourse which had been such a cause of dispute. If he avowed it, then there were to be read to him 'the advisories on the matter by messieurs the ministers of this assembly and the same of messieurs the ministers of Geneva, Basle, and Languedoc.' But de Serres declared that he disavowed

> and disavows from now on this discourse, having escaped from his hands like an abortion, which, he says, has been adjusted, diminished, changed, and falsified in words and in substance, so that this summary being too general can only be confused and ambiguous and in this regard subject to many interpretations entirely contrary to his Intention.[44]

His intention was the subject of a wide-ranging discussion reported in considerable detail in the acts of the colloquy, an extract from which was sent to the company of pastors at Geneva.

De Serres's corrected copy of the memorandum, which also found its way to Geneva,[45] contained an inscription evidently intended to establish the document's authenticity. At the conclusion an appended note reads:

> I submit this my advice to the judgement of the Reformed Churches, which I believe to be the true Church of God, and the doctrine contained in its confession to be the ancient and Catholic. . . . 4 December 1594. Jean de Serres.[46]

The text of this version differed from that examined by earlier assemblies chiefly in that here a number of sharp distinctions were made between the doctrines held in the reformed church from those held in the roman church. Nevertheless, the outline of the argument in this second document is close enough to that of the first to suggest that, while the first may have been an 'abortion,' it did embody a good deal of de Serres's own thought.

In the course of de Serres's defence before the colloquy at St Paul-

---

[43] Univ Lib Gen MS Fr 412, fol 33: extract from the acts of the colloquy held at St Paul-Trois-Châteaux, 14–16 December 1594.

[44] *Ibid.*

[45] *Ibid* fols 21–7: copy of the memorandum of Jean de Serres on the possibility of a union between catholics and protestants.

[46] *Ibid* fol 27.

Trois-Châteaux,[47] he cited as evidence of his intention a part of the preface to the *Harmonie* which he was engaged in writing. This draft provides not only an indication of de Serres's motives but of the situation in which the reformed church found itself in France. De Serres observed that he wished, after the example of Paul, to win over the weak and the infirm. After, however, the 'scandalous confusions of our uncivil wars,' this was a matter of great difficulty.[48] The very names of the doctors of the reformed church were distasteful to those he would reach. It was necessary, therefore, to introduce them to the faith by leading them to the doctors of the ancient church, 'who, without doubt, taught the same doctrine as is contained in the Confession of our Churches in France.'[49] He did not, however, consider the ancient doctors to be more than interpreters of and witnesses to the truth as contained in the scriptures. Their writings were always to be submitted to that tribunal for judgement. The harmony which he sought was, in short, that which was founded upon the scriptures and the teachings of the fathers, and which would facilitate bringing those lacking in faith to the knowledge of God.

The proceedings of this colloquy did not mark the end of the dispute, but de Serres's rehabilitation did proceed steadily in the months which followed his appearance at St Paul-Trois-Châteaux. At the provincial synod of Bas Languedoc and Cévennes, held at Anduze in April 1595, he again explained himself and described his work on ancient doctrines which was still in progress. Evidently the members of the synod were fully satisfied; their letter to the pastors of Geneva, reporting on the work of the synod, was full of praise for the accused pastor of Orange.[50] By the time of the national synod of the reformed churches of France, which met at Saumur, 3–15 June 1596, de Serres seemed to be fully reconciled with his co-religionists. He attended the synod himself as a delegate from Dauphiné, Provence, and Orange, and the synod heard letters read from king Henry IV and from the constable of France with commendations of his services. His colleagues showed their confidence in him as a theologian by commissioning him to answer the writings of Pierre Cayet, a former protestant who had

---

[47] *Ibid* fols 33v–6v.
[48] *Ibid* fol 20v Jean de Serres to the reformed churches, from the preface to his *Harmonie*.
[49] *Ibid*.
[50] *Ibid* fols 41r/v: letter to the pastors of Geneva from the synod of Anduze, 17 April 1595.

defected to Rome. De Serres asked if he could proceed to have his *Harmonie* published, without having three transcriptions made and circulated, as had previously been specified. The reply was that he could, providing only that he have it examined first by the pastors and deputies of that province 'where the said printing will take place.'[51]

The following year was a time of rich fulfillment for de Serres as a writer and scholar, though he was imprudent enough not to go through with the prescribed procedures in having his irenic works approved before their publication. De Serres had evidently continued his historical researches during these years of personal and national turmoil with the objective of producing a general history of France. The result was his *Inventaire*, which traced the course of French history from the beginning to 1422, a narrative which he hoped to be able to continue to his own day.[52] De Serres spoke feelingly of king Henry IV's political rôle in France in a part of his dedication of the book to the king:

> I would add, Sire, that as God has made you pass through the sieve of many great difficulties since your youth, you will find here the image of all that you have courageously suffered and happily surmounted during the tempests among which you have kept the Ship of State from a cruel shipwreck.[53]

He expressed also a sense of 'particular obligation' to the king for his kindnesses and vowed to spend the rest of his life in the king's service.[54] The work touched only indirectly upon the difficulties of France in de Serres's lifetime, though the underlying theme was the importance of the french monarchy in preserving the nation in times of domestic difficulties and foreign wars. De Serres's vision, like that of Popelinière and several other contemporary historians, seems to have been that of a political régime so firmly established and so free of fanaticism as to bring civil and religious peace to France.[55] De Serres had, by this time,

[51] Aymon, *Tous les synodes*, 1, pp 195, 200–1, 206, 209; Quick, *Synodicon in Gallia Reformata*, 1, pp 175, 180, 185, 187.

[52] Jean de Serres, *Inventaire général de l'histoire de France, illustré par la conférence de l'Eglise et de L'Empire* (Paris 1597). The work was continued to the end of the sixteenth century by Jean de Montlyard and published as *Inventaire [général de l'histoire de France depuis Pharmond jusque à present]* 3 vols (Paris 1600). The latter is the edition used here.

[53] De Serres, *Inventaire*, 1, Sig. a vi.

[54] *Ibid.*

[55] *Ibid*, Sig. e iv–e viiiv. Compare Corrado Vivanti, 'Alle origini dell'idea di civiltà: le scoperte geografiche e gli scritti di Henri de la Popelinière,' *RSI* 74, 2 (1962) pp 231–2.

been signally honoured by his prince. In November 1596 he had been named royal historiographer of France.[56]

Of the three writings which appeared in print in 1597 the shortest by far was a pamphlet of half a dozen pages entitled, *Aduis povr la paix de l'Eglise & dv royavme*, published by the king's printers.[57] Here de Serres developed several of the leading ideas which had been a part of his memorandum on a religious peace in France. 'The experience of our long unhappiness,' he began, showed clearly the effects of religious prejudice:

> It has divided hearts, formed parties in the State, set altar against altar in the Church, and incited war by all; with danger of worse, if there is no end of it provided by some good and opportune remedy.[58]

The way of violence had been shown to be worse than useless in dealing with religion. Under the mask of religion men had acted from motives of ambition and avarice, giving vent to furious passions. Only reason provided a remedy for so perilous a malady. De Serres went on to declare that it was his intention to show 'how we are all Christians and that there is no other true religion than the Christian: also that we are all together in fundamental accord concerning this truth.'[59] He proceeded to enumerate the leading features of this accord: 'a common Baptism, the same Symbol of faith, the same Prayer, the same rule of virtuous living,' and faith in the same Saviour and Redeemer. From this it followed that christians had no reason to debate with one another on these issues, much less 'to tear each other apart by furious arms, as capital enemies,' causing chaos in families, the church, and the state.[60] De Serres believed that with the aid of God, without whom men's works were in vain, the concord of the church and the peace of the kingdom could be found. What he had provided was only a sketch, but he would be happy to supply the learned with a

---

[56] Dardier, 'Jean de Serres,' *RH*, 23, 3 (1883) p 59. De Serres's continuing association with the king is suggested by letters of Henry IV in 1596 and 1597. See Henry IV, *Recueil des lettres missives*, 8, p 611, and 9, p 227.

[57] Jean de Serres, *Aduis povr la paix [de l'Eglise & dv royavme]* (Paris 1597), published by Iamet Mettayer and Pierre l'Huillier, printers to the king. This edition is rare; the copy used here is to be found in Univ Lib Gen MS Arch Tron 143, fols 145–9. The tract was republished as one of the *Deux advis par souhait pour la paix et l'Eglise et du royaume* in François Hotman, *Opuscules françoises des Hotmans* (Paris 1616) fols 192–3ᵛ.

[58] De Serres, *Aduis povr la paix*, p 3.

[59] *Ibid* p 4.

[60] *Ibid* pp 5–6.

more complete description of the remedy, 'when it will please His Majesty to give commandment for it.'[61]

De Serres's ideas for an accord were, in fact, presented to the learned in the same year in a latin treatise entitled *De Fide Catholica*, published, as the title page indicated, by permission of the king. The subtitle described the contents of the book as having been drawn from 'Holy Scripture, the orthodox fathers, the holy Councils and canons, and other commentaries of the Catholic Church' for the purpose of 'illustrating the Truth and promoting Concord.'[62] The running title of the book, by which it was subsequently known, was *Apparatvs ad Fidem Catholicam*, an introduction to the catholic faith. The argument of the book reveals very clearly, however, that the catholic faith which the author knew and to which he was committed was that system of belief based upon the precepts of Paul and Augustine which Calvin and other reformed theologians had developed and systematised in de Serres's own lifetime. As de Serres presented this system of thought, however, it was remarkably free from dogmatism, bias, and rancour. It was the reasonableness of these theological propositions which he stressed and the degree of support which they enjoyed, as indicated by the evidence of the scriptures and the ancient christian writers.

De Serres began with a personal attestation which acknowledged, in effect, that his ideas had been the object of suspicion, but in which he pled that his readers would read and seriously consider the treatise which followed before passing judgement on his proposal.[63] The preface to the work, addressed to 'the Pious and Christian Reader, Zealous of truth and concord,' stressed that he had been moved, even driven to this undertaking, by the promptings of his conscience, even while he was wavering in his resolve. What he wished to propound to his readers was that there was a way of concord which could be travelled by all christians, based upon common principles and supported by reason. What was needed was to discover that truth which all christians embraced.[64] For the discovery of truth, persecution was clearly of no value, nor was war, which was the cruellest form of persecution. War had, in fact, led only to an increase in faithlessness and vice. Disputations constituted a more fruitful approach,

---

[61] *Ibid* pp 7-8.
[62] Jean de Serres, *De Fide Catholica*, [*siue principiis religionis Christianae, communi omnium Christianorum consensu semper et vbique ratis*] (Paris 1597); the work was reprinted under the same title in 1607. The latter is the edition used here.
[63] De Serres, *De Fide Catholica*, Sig. A iv.
[64] *Ibid* pp 3-5.

but there could be harmful as well as beneficial disputations. The former were garrulous, noisy, violent, and quarrelsome. The latter, however, which proceeded quietly, modestly, and reverently in pursuit of truth, could be profoundly illuminating.[65] Why not, then, 'a sane council to aid us opportunely'? By a friendly coming together in recognition of the common faith which Christians possessed, those who had endured 'so many and such great storms' could find the way of peace. The light of concord would shine on them 'as if after the deepest darkness of a long night.'[66]

The main body of the treatise was in ten parts, each of which dealt with a component of the faith which all christians were presumed to share. De Serres began with the central christian affirmation that there was 'One God, one Truth, one Faith.' Concord was, therefore, to be found in that truth. Since God was the author of all truth, his Word must be the expression of that truth for men; his Word, moreover, resounded powerfully in the divinely inspired scriptures.[67] In order to understand the scriptures recourse must be had to the whole body of revelation in scriptural books. But the catholic church itself, 'the column and support of Truth,' resolved issues in dispute by its own orderly procedures. The church judged according to certain criteria, including antiquity, certainty and evidence, catholic or universal consent, and perpetual succession in the church. Only if a belief could meet these criteria could it be considered a part of the catholic faith.[68] Some of de Serres's most interesting remarks are concerned with the value of early christian writers and of church councils in ascertaining the principles of the true faith. The fathers of the church had an importance second only to the apostles themselves in interpreting the scriptural revelation, but they were to be read critically and in full recognition of the circumstances under which they had composed their works. Moreover, the question of the integrity of the text was to be examined carefully, to see whether what was attributed to the writer truly represented what he had written. The training and equipment of the humanist scholar thus emerge as of considerable importance in theological studies.[69] Concerning councils, de Serres found that they had been extremely useful in defining those theological principles on which the edifice of the church had been built. From the apostles' own

[65] *Ibid* pp 6–9.
[66] *Ibid* pp 10–12.
[67] *Ibid* pp 29–56.
[68] *Ibid* pp 70–116, 126–76.
[69] *Ibid* pp 89–106. Compare Vivanti, *Lotta politica e pace religiosa*, pp 262–6.

time, synods and councils had been an important means of arriving at
the apprehension of truth; it was here that the Holy Spirit helped to
guide the minds of those representing the church at large.[70] De Serres
closed his treatise by affirming that as there was One God, one truth,
and one faith, so there was 'one Baptism and one Catholic Church,'
and that the latter was 'the Mother of all Christians.' Finally, he
contended that for the truth to be established among the faithful it
was necessary that it be granted and sealed expressly by the Holy
Spirit.[71]

De Serres's latin treatise was thus a plea for a conference of christians
in France, and paralleled the proposals being made for a national
council by gallican writers. The theological propositions he discussed
could be considered a kind of agenda for such a conference, which
would provide a basis for a broad agreement among all french
christians. There would be practical problems in working out the terms
of a mutual toleration or the organisational structure of a united
church, if this were to be attempted.[72] But the way towards a
religious reconciliation could be found, in de Serres's opinion, if the
parties assembled in full recognition of their shared beliefs and
practices. Among the initiatives taken in the sixteenth century towards
religious unity, de Serres's was surely one of the best-conceived as
well as one of the most ambitious. He saw with painful acuteness the
need for such an initiative in France, and he offered a plan which, at
least in its final version – the culmination of his plan for a *Harmonie* –
was at once theologically articulate and yet remarkably free of the kind
of language which would offend the sensibilities of christians of the
two contending parties.

De Serres's co-religionists, however, did not, for the most part,
respond favourably to his proposal. The colloquy of Nîmes, at its
meeting of 13 November 1597, called de Serres before the assembly
to answer questions about the *Aduis* and the *Apparatus*, which some
of its members felt had caused a scandal. In spite of a long and
detailed discussion with him the members were far from satisfied with
de Serres's defence. Strong exception was taken to the fact that de

[70] De Serres, *De Fide Catholica*, pp 106–13.
[71] *Ibid* pp 176–87.
[72] Proposals are advanced for solving some of the structural problems of a united church
in France in a manuscript included among materials relating to de Serres. Univ Lib
Gen MS Fr 412, fols 30–1: Project for the reunion of the two religions in France.
For discussions of the contents of this document, see Vivanti, *Lotta politica e pace
religiosa*, pp 266–67, and Livet, *Les guerres de religion*, pp 48–50.

Serres's writings had not undergone the required examination before being published.[73] The affair was scheduled to be discussed at the next national synod, due to meet in May 1598. Before that meeting, however, the company of pastors took a direct part in the controversy by sending a circular letter to the churches of several swiss, german, and dutch cities, warning them of an attempt being made to reconcile light and darkness, 'that is to say, Christianity and papism,' and entreating them to come to the aid of the reformed churches of France 'with a deputation and with counsel.'[74] Jean de Serres did not live to find out the decision of the national synod of his church, as he died on 19 May 1598, after a few days of illness.[75] The fifteenth national synod of the reformed churches of France, meeting at Montpellier, 26–30 May 1598, proceeded, nevertheless, to take up the question of a religious reconciliation, as set forward in de Serres's two books. On the general question, they exhorted pastors to warn their flocks not to lend an ear to those who 'make a semblance of uniting and mixing the two Religions,' as there was no possibility of communion 'between the Temple of God & that of Idols.'[76] The members proceeded to condemn de Serres's recent writings without naming their author directly:

> On the complaint of the Churches of Geneva, Berne, Basle, the Palatinate and others, concerning some writings which have appeared under the pretext of a Reunion of Christians in the same Doctrine, to the prejudice of the Truth of God & among others of a work entitled *Apparatvs ad Fidem Catholicam,* & another with this Inscription, *Avis pour la Paix de l'Eglise & du Roiaume de France;* the Synod, after having read and examined the said writings, & heard the Advice of the Colloquy of Nîmes, assisted by Deputies of another Colloquy of the same Province, together with the Censures of Churches named to examine the matter, has condemned them, as containing some erroneous propositions. . . .[77]

Among the condemned propositions was that 'the truth of Doctrine has always remained in its entirety among those who call themselves

---

[73] Univ Lib Gen MS Fr 413, fols 55–9: letter to the pastors of Geneva from the church of Nîmes, 22 March 1598, containing extracts from the acts of the colloquy of Nîmes, 13 November 1597, relative to the two publications of Jean de Serres.

[74] *Ibid* fols 61–2: letter to the pastors of Berne, Zurich, Schaffhausen, Basle, Heidelberg, the Hague, Amsterdam, 'for the affair of the Synod of Montpellier,' from the company of pastors at Geneva, 3 April 1598.

[75] Dardier, 'Jean de Serres,' *RH*, 23, 3 (1883) p 70.

[76] Aymon, *Tous les synodes,* 1, p 219; Quick, *Synodicon in Gallia Reformata,* 1, p 196.

[77] Aymon, *Tous les synodes,* 1, p 222; Quick, *Synodicon in Gallia Reformata,* 1, pp 196–7.

Christians,' that the roman church shared the same articles of faith, commandments, and means of salvation as the reformed church, and that 'the Ancient Councils and writings of the Fathers ought to be made the arbiters of our differences.'[78]

The opinions of roman catholics are more difficult to recover, though one of them, Pierre de l'Estoile, a layman and a moderate, is known to have been sympathetic to de Serres. L'Estoile noted in his *Journal*, under May 1598:

> M. de Serres, author of the *Inventaire de l'Histoire de France*, a learned person and a great zealot for the reunion of the Church, died in Orange in this month. The zeal with which he was mis-interpreted and his actions condemned was that which men of good will ordinarily receive. There was even a rumour current that he died a Roman Catholic, which was false, as his testament shows. It is said that his wife had died the same day as he. Thus, before the year was half over and in less than six months, three great persons died in France, Henri Estienne, Commelin, and Serres.[79]

Some years later, in November 1609, he came into possession of a letter 'from M. de Serres to M. Du M.', in defence of his *Apparatvs*. L'Estoile, no doubt influenced by de Serres's own words, called the book 'a simple and unadorned crayon sketch of the truth, drawn by a good man, condemned only by the badly informed or ill affectioned, who judge what they have never known.'[80]

The conclusion of Jean de Serres's career in the years from 1594 to 1598 poses an important question. How was it that a man whose career had been dedicated to teaching and defending the reformed doctrines which he had learned from Calvin and de Bèze themselves suddenly began to search for grounds of agreement between catholics and protestants and to devise strategies for negotiating some kind of

---

[78] Succeeding national synods were concerned lest the condemned propositions were not actually to be found in de Serres's works. At Gergeau in 1601, the church at Paris was asked to re-examine de Serres's writings to ascertain whether he had actually made the statements cited at Montpellier. But the church at Paris evidently declined to act; at Gap in 1603 that church was censured for not having carried out its work. Nothing further was heard of the matter. Aymon, *Tous les synodes*, 1, pp 246, 265; Quick, *Synodicon in Gallia Reformata*, 1, pp 218, 232.

[79] [Pierre de] l'Estoile, *Journal* [*de L'Estoile, pour le règne de Henri IV,*] ed Louis-Raymond Lefèvre, 3 vols (Paris 1948–60) 1, p 521. Henri Estienne was a well-known printer in Geneva; Jérôme Commelin, of Douai, was a printer, scholar, and classicist who lived in Heidelberg, where he had taken refuge for his religion.

[80] L'Estoile, *Journal*, 2, p 554.

agreement between the two major religious parties in France? The colloquy of Valentinois remarked, rather unkindly, that it might have been 'the confusions of the times or the love of the world' which had led de Serres astray in the summer of 1594. By the first, they presumably meant that de Serres's experiences as an observer of and perhaps as a participant in the political struggle in France had induced in him an earnest desire for peace.[81] De Serres's own letters to de Bèze in 1593 and 1594, in which he described the deprivations of an imprisonment he had suffered at the hands of the opposing party, certainly gave him a bitter taste of the civil war. No doubt the experience reinforced his desire to find a solution to a conflict whose long course he had traced in his historical writings.[82] Coupled with this, however, was another motive which was probably of even greater importance. One thing the pastors and elders at Montélimar may have meant by the phrase 'love of the world' was that de Serres was being urged to his task by the rich and powerful in return for their favour. King Henry IV, we know, was searching anxiously and with considerable ingenuity for a solution to the perilous situation in which his country found itself in the early 1590s – catholic and protestant armies still in the field, spanish troops making incursions into France, Paris itself, until 1594, under a revolutionary régime.[83] De Serres's plan has all the earmarks of having been fostered under the auspices of a court which had the pacification of the kingdom as one of its primary objectives. Yet there are many indications that de Serres was not working for an amelioration of religious differences simply to gain favour with the king. Rather, his work fairly crackles with the fervour of patriotism for his native land, and is often combined with his deep longing to see all men at one in the service of their Saviour. As he said in the memorandum of 1594, 'Who is a Christian and does not hope for salvation in Jesus Christ? And French, who does not desire peace for France?'[84] De Serres enjoyed the patronage and good will extended to him by Henry IV. He saw Henry, however, not as just another king of France, but as a remarkable political leader who could reunite and revive his kingdom.

De Serres's own experiences, however, suggest some of the difficulties which lay in the way of anyone's working for ecclesiastical

[81] Univ Lib Gen MS Fr 412, fol 32.
[82] Univ Lib Gen MS Arch Tron 5, fols 8–10ᵛ.
[83] See J. H. M. Salmon, 'The Paris Sixteen, 1584–94: The Social Analysis of a Revolutionary Movement,' *JMH*, 44 (1972) pp 540–76.
[84] Univ Lib Gen MS Fr 412, fol 28.

unity in France from the protestant side. At the same time de Serres was offering to catholics the substance of the ancient catholic faith, transmitted through the scriptures, the apostles, and the early christian writers, as the basis for an agreement, he had constantly to be assuring his co-religionists that it was this faith which they held to in its original purity, in contrast to that of the papists, who had altered and corrupted their spiritual inheritance. This rather tended to blunt the irenic thrust of his argument. Furthermore, de Serres's very freedom to express his ideas, whether in manuscript or in printed works, was sharply confined by the elaborate system of church courts in the french reformed church, as well as, indirectly, by the spiritual oversight exercised in France by the company of pastors in Geneva. The prevailing climate of opinion throughout this church, moreover, seemed to be hostile to any compromise with Rome. Once this fact had become inescapably clear, the political and ecclesiastical advisers to Henry IV must have concluded that only a settlement allowing for the existence of the reformed church as a kind of dispersed republic within the kingdom of France was likely to bring the long civil war to an end and make a reconstruction possible.

Davidson College
North Carolina

THE RESOLUTIONERS
AND THE SCOTTISH NOBILITY
IN THE EARLY MONTHS OF 1660

by JULIA BUCKROYD

ONE of the difficulties in the way of understanding the establishment of episcopacy in Scotland which followed upon the restoration of Charles II,[1] is that of accounting for the apparent willingness on the part of the politically active nobility to co-operate in such a change, when that nobility had previously taken a leading part in abolishing episcopacy and setting up presbytery. Some light can, I believe, be thrown on this problem by considering the relations between the resolutioner ministers and the scottish nobility in the early months of 1660. In particular I should like to consider the correspondence between Robert Douglas and the earls of Crawford, Lauderdale, Glencairn and Rothes. An examination of the letters reveals, it seems to me, a disposition on the part of the resolutioners to perpetuate ministerial control and direction of the nobility. This attitude may well have prompted an answering disposition on the part of the nobility to take back into their own hands as quickly as possible the conduct of political and religious negotiations in order to reduce ministerial pretensions to the direction of public affairs.

Since the history of this period of ecclesiastical history in Scotland has not been at all widely explored it may be necessary, in order to develop this subject, to recapitulate some of the principal developments in Scotland during the 1650s. It will be recalled that the revolution in Scotland in the years following 1637[2] had resulted in the establishment of presbyterian church government. In the 1650s however there had developed in Scotland, under the pressure of political developments, two parties within the church. One of these, the protestors, stood, generally speaking, for sympathy towards independency and the protectorate, and antagonism towards the stuart monarchy. The other

---

[1] By far the best analysis of this subject is G. Davies and P. Hardacre, 'The Restoration of the Scottish Episcopacy, 1660–1661', *JBS*, 1, ii, (1962) pp 32–51.

[2] The only major study of this period is D. Stevenson, *The Scottish Revolution, 1637–1644* (Newton Abbot 1973).

party, the resolutioners, stood for presbyterian church government and the return of the stuarts, provided that they implemented the solemn league and covenant. Throughout the 1650s these two parties had contended in the absence of the scottish nobility. They, the 'natural rulers', had been imprisoned or exiled after Worcester, and in their place was only the government of the cromwellian military occupation which had suspended all traditional assemblies and legislatures. The struggle was overtly for the two parties' respective forms of church government, but in the power vacuum in Scotland it carried much wider implications. Whichever party won the struggle would, it was clear, control not only the religious but the political and to some extent the economic life of the country.

In the event the struggle was still unresolved when in late 1659 political developments in England began to point towards a major upheaval. It soon became clear that whatever the nature of the final settlement, it would be unlikely to favour independency or a commonwealth, and so correspondingly the star of the protestor party fell while that of the resolutioners began to rise.

Meanwhile during the 1650s the scottish nobility imprisoned in England had not been forgotten in the party struggle within the church. Their likely adherence was to the presbyterian, pro-stuart resolutioners and in fact the resolutioner agent in London, James Sharp, found little difficulty in securing their support.[3] When therefore in 1660 the prisoners were about to be released, the resolutioners felt justified in making some effort to keep them on their side.

The resolutioners' first move was to be seen to be instrumental in effecting the release of the prisoners. It was, I think, clear in the event of the decline of the power of the commonwealth that the traditional hereditary rulers of Scotland must be released to resume their normal function and bring an end to the military government of an army of occupation. The resolutioner strategy was to be seen to be active in securing what must eventually in any case have taken place.

The first sign of resolutioner concern with the issue appears in a letter from Robert Douglas, the most prominent of the group of Edinburgh ministers who had taken upon themselves to promote the resolutioner cause. Douglas wrote to James Sharp, the resolutioner agent in London, almost as soon as Sharp arrived there in February

[3] *Registers of the Consultations of the Ministers of Edinburgh,* ed W. Stephen, 2 vols (Edinburgh 1921, 1930) 2, pp 35–6, 37–8, 98, 151. *Lauderdale Papers,* [ed Osmund Airy], 3 vols (London 1884–5) 1, pp 285–9.

1660, reminding him of their discussions of what can only have been the subject of the release of the prisoners, and offering to help to achieve that end by writing to Monck.[4] Sharp had not forgotten however and forecast their early release.[5] By 1 March Sharp was able to give Douglas a full report of his activities in that cause and of the steps he had taken to have the prisoners released:

> I had spoken to the General before the readmission of the secluded members concerning them, telling his lordship I had a commission from you so to do. I spoke also with divers of the members [of Parliament] and after the pressing of the most[?] of the House relating to them, I went to Windsor and advised their writing a letter signed by all their hands to the General, showing to them that by you I was particularly ordered to lay myself forth for their releasement. Their letter I carried and delivered to his Excellency who promised me to return them an answer. All this week every day I have been with some of the most considerable of the House who have promised me effectually to move for their coming to London [from Windsor], and this day I am hopeful it may be done.[6]

Sure enough three days later Sharp was able to report to the Edinburgh ministers that the prisoners were indeed free.[7]

It is important to consider at this point exactly in what Sharp's activities concerning the prisoners had consisted. He had spoken to Monck and various MPs about them; he persuaded the prisoners themselves to write a letter to Monck which he then delivered; and he had conveyed the good will of the resolutioners to the prisoners. Sharp and his brethren may just possibly have believed that these actions were crucial to their release; they certainly intended that the prisoners should think so, but it seems quite evident that the actions of a one man lobby and messenger boy would not have been effective had the release of the prisoners not already been intended and thought desirable. In fact it will be recalled that the return of the secluded members to the rump had brought about a general release of those sympathetic to the presbyterian cause.

The second part of the resolutioner strategy was to procure for Crawford and Lauderdale, the most important of the prisoners, status

---

[4] G[lasgow] U[niversity] L[ibrary] MS Gen 210 p 7.
[5] *Ibid* p 11.
[6] *Ibid* p 14.
[7] *Ibid* p 16.

as political negotiators, a formal commission as scottish representatives in London. Here again they were making themselves appear responsible for a development that was in any case likely and obvious. Crawford and Lauderdale were in London, members of the scottish political nobility; what was more likely than that they would negotiate for Scotland, especially in what looked more and more like the imminent restoration of the king?

Sharp had begun by introducing the nobility to his political contacts, and it was he who suggested that they should have more formal powers:

> I think our nation cannot do themselves more right and advantage than by sending up immediately a commission to the Earls of Crawford and Lauderdale to act here in the capacity of commissioners for the kingdom of Scotland.[8]

Douglas replied saying that he had had the same idea but was having difficulty in putting it into effect. The problem was that because of the suspension of normal government during the interregnum the bodies which might have been thought competent to commission representatives – parliament, the privy council, or even the general assembly – no longer met. The sole continuing assemblies, the conventions of shires and burghs, had already met at Monck's pleasure,[9] and in order to meet again required fresh authorisation. Douglas therefore requested that Sharp ask Monck for such a warrant.[10]

This activity on the part of the ministers did not please Monck, who soon squashed as firmly as he could all attempts to commission an official delegation from Scotland,[11] but nevertheless the resolutioners had acted in such a way as to convey to Lauderdale and Crawford in particular that they owed their freedom and their status in political negotiation to their efforts.

Douglas now took it upon himself to explain to Crawford and Lauderdale that in return he expected them to favour the resolutioners and not the protestors, and the public interests of the kirk and kingdom above their own private interests. In a letter of 20 March he congratulated them on their release and then indicated that he hoped to see a becoming gratitude in their behaviour: 'I am not doubtful but both of you will endeavour to be forthcoming in your stations to the service of the Lord who had remembered you in all your afflictions.'[12]

---

[8] *Ibid* p 18.
[9] *Ibid* p 20.
[10] *Ibid* pp 24, 22.
[11] *Ibid* pp 61, 63, 65, 75, 80, 82, 84.
[12] *Ibid* p 30.

The resolutioners and the Scottish nobility

This exhortation Douglas then makes plain does not only refer to their personal conduct, but also to their attitude to the protestors. He begs them:

> not to suffer yourselves to be befooled again by the fair pretences and promises of our countrymen to admit unto your councils and public employments them that never loved, nor yet do, your Master, the country, you, nor the cause wherein you suffered.[13]

He then goes on to express the hope that they will neglect their own ends and ambitions, and that they have learned 'one lesson more: to deny yourself and all your own interests and relations of blood and allegiance in comparison of the public interest of the kingdom of Christ and of this ancient kingdom.'[14] This public interest to which they should devote themselves, Douglas goes on to point out, is the putting into force of the solemn league and covenant:

> You should improve yourself unto the utmost of your ability upon all occasions and with all whom you have any interest there [in London] toward the furtherance of the solid settling of these nations according to our obligations by the solemn oaths of God.[15]

Finally in all these matters Crawford and Lauderdale should be prepared to be guided, Douglas tells them, by the resolutioner ministers and their supporters: 'Have a care to take the advice of these who have been firm to the cause and to yourselves.'[16]

When this letter is considered together with the earlier activities of the resolutioners it can hardly be doubted that the ministers aspired still to direct public affairs. Nevertheless the fact that Lauderdale and Crawford had both been prominent covenanters perhaps makes the attitude of the resolutioners more comprehensible. However since they also attempted to exert control over the earl of Glencairn who had an anti-covenanting, cavalier background, and had led the royalist rising in Scotland in 1654, the conclusion that the ministers were above all interest in political control of the nobility can hardly be escaped.

The ministers had failed to have Crawford and Lauderdale made scottish commissioners because of Monck's refusal to co-operate. Nevertheless earlier meetings of both the shire and burgh commissioners had chosen their own representatives among whom was Glencairn.

[13] *Ibid* p 31.
[14] *Ibid.*
[15] *Ibid.*
[16] *Ibid.*

These men now proposed to go to London, without any approval from Monck, as self-styled scottish commissioners. They were not of a type amenable to direction by the ministers[17] but nevertheless, as soon as it looked as though they would take matters into their own hands and go to London, with or without permission, Douglas entered into negotiation with the most important of them, Glencairn. In a very short time he pronounced himself satisfied with the way the talks were going: 'These two nights bygone I have had two hours each time with Glencairn, who after reasoning and debate hath given such satisfaction as I have reason to rest upon, [he] being a man of honour.'[18]

These negotiations apparently continued, since quite soon thereafter Douglas wrote to Sharp noting that Glencairn was coming to London and assuring him that Glencairn could be trusted to act for the independence of Scotland and the interests of the solemn league and covenant. Douglas also hoped that Glencairn would establish good relations with Crawford and Lauderdale so that the three of them could work together to use their influence to achieve these ends. In return for Glencairn's assurances of cooperation and assistance Douglas had apparently modified his negative attitude to the journey of the self-styled commissioners to London. He now required Sharp, as resolutioner agent, to use his influence with Monck to ensure that they were well received in London:

> I told you however my judgment was against their coming . . . yet seeing they are now come I entreated you to deal with the General that he would put respect upon them. Seeing now I hear that my lord Glencairn is following I entreat that he may be kindly used and that there may be a good correspondence between him and our noble lords. I am engaged to believe that he will do anything that may be for the liberty of the nation and for our covenanted interest here. I have so much from himself.[19]

It is no doubt true that Glencairn was prepared to urge Scotland's restoration to independence, but it is inconceivable that he would now turn into a covenanter. He wanted above all to get to London, which Douglas may have recognised,[20] and he was apparently therefore willing to say anything in order to get a measure of support from the

[17] *Ibid* pp 53–4, 77–8.
[18] *Ibid* p 59.
[19] *Ibid* p 83.
[20] *Ibid.*

ministers. Douglas does not seem to have realised there was any danger of being let down.

What is most relevant to our argument however, is the fact that Glencairn had found it necessary to engage in such negotiations with Douglas, and to submit to giving promises and assurances in order to gain his support. Moreover it is clear that ministerial support must have seemed to him a necessary condition of success in London. There can be no doubt that as far as Glencairn was concerned the resolutioners were very much involved in the direction of affairs.

Finally let us consider the case of the earl of Rothes who illustrates a rather different aspect of resolutioner activities. Rothes's parents had both died while he was still a child, and he was placed under the care of the earl of Crawford by whom his education seems to have been seriously neglected. The result was a man virtually illiterate, interested in soldiering and informed on no other subject, and with a reputation for drunkenness and fornication.[21] Certainly he had been imprisoned after Worcester for more than five years, but he had made no figure in ecclesiastical affairs despite being the son and ward respectively of two of the most eminent of the first generation of covenanting nobility. That the resolutioners should write to such a man in May 1660 and commission him, as they did, to represent their case to the king demonstrates, it seems, a willingness to use extremely weak vessels, and a determination to exploit whatever influence Rothes might have, to the best of their ability.

The letter in question first of all asks Rothes to use his influence towards a peaceful civil settlement, but then asks him to ensure the continuance of presbytery: 'We do humbly presume to entreat your lordship to put forth yourself for the good of this church, that we may enjoy these liberties allowed to us by law with his Majesty's royal consent.'[22] It goes on to remind Rothes how loyal to the king the resolutioners have been and that presbytery is generally acceptable in Scotland. In consequence, they point out, Rothes can safely assert to the king that there is no need for any sort of toleration in Scotland such as the declaration of Breda had proposed. Finally the letter indicates to Rothes that the resolutioners anticipate and hope for the implementation of the solemn league and covenant, and asks him to voice this desire to the king.

Thus we have a letter which consisted of a comprehensive

[21] *Lauderdale Papers, passim.*
[22] GUL MS Gen 210 p 99.

statement of the resolutioner position: their desire for the return of the king, the implementation of the solemn league and covenant, and above all their over-riding concern that at the very least presbyterian church government should be confirmed in Scotland. It is extremely hard to believe that Rothes was at all interested in the resolutioners' views, and even harder to believe that he was a competent or appropriate person to represent them to the king. There can be little doubt that the ministers, moved perhaps by desperation, were using their continuing influence to overawe an ignorant young man in order to get him to do their bidding.

In four cases the resolutioners had attempted to use their influence with the nobility to get their own way. In each case they became important members of the scottish administration after the restoration. Lauderdale became secretary of state for Scotland, Crawford became treasurer, Glencairn chancellor, and Rothes president of the privy council.

Godfrey Davies in his *Restoration of Charles II*, made a heroic attempt to analyse Scotland's part in that restoration. He confessed that 'the maintenance of a form of Presbyterianism [in Scotland after the Restoration] seems today to have been so natural that satisfactory explanations for the establishment of episcopacy are hard to find.'[23] While the attitude of the resolutioners to these four members of the nobility and of the post-restoration government does not provide by any means a complete explanation of that puzzling development, it is perhaps a contribution towards the understanding of it.

University of Cambridge

[23] G. Davies, *The Restoration of Charles II* (London 1955) p 231.

JANSENISM AND POLITICS
IN THE
EIGHTEENTH CENTURY

by JOHN McMANNERS

'ALL the gold in the world and all the promises of heaven'[1] could not persuade Sainte-Beuve to carry on his study of jansenism into the eighteenth century. The spirit of Port-Royal was not there, 'or at least it was only found in traces, dried up like a branch of a river that has turned aside into the sands and lost itself among the rocks . . . It is found even less in the entirely political Jansenism which was, or which appeared so considerable for a moment in the eighteenth century, and which allowed many to be of the party, without being of the dogma, or indeed, of religion at all'.[2] The story of jansenism after the death of Louis XIV is indeed a story of the war of the parlements against the crown – remonstrances, exiles, writs, denunciations, pamphlets; of the rising discontent of the lower clergy, demanding economic justice and a share in the government of the church; of the convulsionist movement, a strange spiritual underworld of masochism and miracles. Upon this barbarous scene of political and social strife and crude illiterate spirituality Sainte-Beuve turned his back, and those who have walked with him through the magic world of Port-Royal will understand his bitterness. The *journée du guichet* when Angélique Arnauld renounced human affections, the night of fire of 23 November when Pascal wept tears of joy, the cold ethereal beauty of the paintings of Philippe de Champaigne,[3] the intellectual adventure of the alliance with cartesianism, the grammar, the logic, the translation of the new testament, the plays of Racine and the *Pensées* of Pascal – the eighteenth century can offer nothing like this.

But Port-Royal was a moment of unique perfection, which was necessarily transient. It was a coincident flowering of spirituality and

---

[1] Sainte-Beuve, *Port-Royal* 6 (7) (8 ed Paris 1912) 7 vols, 5 p 483.
[2] *Ibid* 6 (13), in 8 ed 6 p 242.
[3] For the fusion of jansenist and classical inspiration in his work see L. Marin, 'Philippe de Champaigne et Port-Royal', *Annales* 25 (Paris 1970) pp 9 *et seq*.

genius which would wither when death removed the élite souls whose conjunction formed its greatness. Before Louis XIV's demolition squads and drunken grave-diggers moved in, before d'Argenson's police removed the last twenty-two courageous old nuns, Port-Royal was ended. 'The Earth is becoming empty of saints, while Heaven is filling up', said a jansenist letter of 1695.[4] Arnauld and Nicole had just died and of the great generation Racine only remained, and only for four years more, a Joseph of Arimathea presiding over the obsequies of a decaying community. Port-Royal ended with the death of Racine, in the last year of the seventeenth century. With Sainte-Beuve, we mourn its passing, but unlike him, we move on into the new century where, in spite of all he says, high principles were at stake and good men were willing to suffer for them, even though their spirituality lacked the illumination of intellectual and literary genius. The object of this study will be to disentangle the nature of these principles and to get rid of the stereotype of 'political jansenism' as a sort of sinister eighteenth-century degradation of the original jansenist ideal.

One thing we cannot do is to define 'jansenism'. Everyone knows (or at least Macaulay's schoolboy does) about Cornelius Jansen, bishop of Ypres, who read all the works of Augustine ten times and the works on Grace twenty-nine times, and died of a disease from the dust of old books, leaving behind him the *Augustinus* for posthumous publication – a volume proclaiming the uncompromising doctrine of pre-destination as against the jesuit Molina's insistence on free will. For long, orthodox roman catholic historiography sought to identify those who came to be called 'jansensits' with the strict acceptance of what is in – or was supposed to be in – the *Augustinus*. 'A Jansenist is a Calvinist saying the mass', is Carreyre's definition,[5] making the heretical accusation more certain. This unsophisticated technique was rejected by Bremond, who used as much ingenuity readmitting distinguished jansenists to the fold as had originally been employed to exclude them; he wanted to rescue Pascal and Racine (and others in proportion to their literary greatness) for orthodoxy – 'we must reclaim our property'.[6] As Bremond did, though not for the same

---

[4] Ruth Clark. *Lettres de Germain Vuillart, ami de Port-Royal à M. Louis de Préfontaine, 1694–1700* (Paris 1951) p 162.

[5] J. Carreyre, *Le Jansénisme durant la Régence*, 3 vols (Paris 1929–33) 3, p 391.

[6] H. Bremond, *Histoire littéraire du sentiment religieux en France* 4 (Paris 1920) p 244. On Bremond generally see *Henri Bremond, 1865–1933, Actes du Colloque d'Aix, 1966* (Fac. Lettres Aix-en-Provence 1967).

reasons, a modern description of jansenism must break free from the guilt-by-association procedures of the seventeenth century which made 'jansenists' out of people even when they had renounced the unorthodox doctrines which were ostensibly the subject of dispute. Indeed, the standard counter-argument was (and it lives on in the writings of Gazier)[7] that jansenism was a 'phantom heresy' invented by the jesuits as a sort of portmanteau device into which they could cram all their diverse opponents for more convenient condemnation. 'The Jesuits have a phantom that they call Jansenius' wrote Mme de Sévigné in 1680, 'upon whom they pile a thousand insults . . . This seems to me like when the Comte de Gramont said it was Rochefort who had trodden on the king's dog, though Rochefort was a hundred leagues away'.[8] As between these two extreme views of what jansenists were – a picture, on the one hand, of a conspiracy of crypto-calvinists, and on the other of a group of diverse and respectable catholics whom the jesuits unjustly tarred with the brush of heresy – modern researchers (led by M. Orcibal), insist that there were different kinds of jansenism – that of Louvain, of Saint-Cyran, of Arnauld, of Quesnel, of various bishops, and so on.[9] This is the only way to analyse a fantastically complex theme, though the question remains, what lies at the core of these diverse manifestations? It is still open to us to say (and in fact, there is something in this), that everything arose, like Rochefort's treasonable cruelty to animals, from a libellous accusation.

Attempts from the left to provide a sociological basis for jansenism do not help us. Lucien Goldmann's proposal[10] to make it the ideology of the declining nobles of the robe has won little favour; indeed, this is an exercise like explaining why so many cabinet ministers of our century have been educated at Oxford – where else would you

[7] A. Gazier, *Histoire Générale du mouvement Janséniste*, 2 vols (Paris 1922–4).

[8] Mme de Sévigné, 9 June and 31 July, 1680, *Lettres*, 3 vols (Pléiade 1960) 2 pp 734, 805. Compare the Maréchal d'Harcourt's observation, 'Un Janséniste n'est souvent autre chose qu'un homme qu'on veut perdre à la cour', G. Frêche, *Un chancelier gallican: D'Aguesseau*, Trav. et recherches, Fac. de droit et des sciences écon. Paris (1969) p 40.

[9] [J.] Orcibal, *Louis XIV contre Innocent XI[: les appels au futur concile de 1688]* (Paris 1949) p 81. An example of the refinement of definition needed is Bruno Neveu, *Sébastien-Joseph du Cambout de Pontchâteau, 1634–1690. et ses missions à Rome* (Paris 1969) p 46—'Plutôt que Janséniste, nous qualifierions . . . Pontchâteau de port-royaliste'. For Jansenism in Louvain, see M. Nuttinck, *La vie et l'œuvre de Zeger-Bernard van Espen, un canoniste janséniste, gallican et régalien à l'Université de Louvain, 1646–1728* (Louvain 1969).

[10] L. Goldmann, *Le Dieu caché: étude sur la vision tragique dans les Pensées de Pascal et le théâtre de Racine* (Paris 1959).

JOHN McMANNERS

expect them to come from? Kolakowski,[11] the polish historian of seventeenth-century spirituality, rejects Goldmann's oversimplified explanation and transfers the analysis of the sociology of power into the purely ecclesiastical field. Just as the jesuits were trying to extend the scope and influence of catholicism by assimilating to it the naturalist humanism of the renaissance, so the jansenists were attempting 'to assimilate and integrate certain values of calvinism which could have given that religion an advantage in the rivalry with the catholic church which followed the edict of Nantes'. This is an interesting interpretation of the inner logic of an ideological clash, and an insight into the possibilities of subconscious motivation; as sometimes happens, however, with patterns deduced from the specialist study of ideas, it does not bear a close relationship to the actual thoughts in the conscious minds of the men of the warring factions. No doubt the strangely diversified jansenist movement had its connexions with the rivalry of social groups for power, and of the churches for men's allegiance, but the actual historical form taken by the movement and the alliance of forces that gathered under its banner need a more precise explanation. There was a 'jansenist' current in theology, thought and devotion, and a 'jansenist' reforming spirit in the church, of which Cornelius Jansen's vast latin treatise[12] was only one manifestation, which ought to have remained of limited importance, a footnote to intellectual history. Between the exponents of these views and aspirations and the jesuits there were divergencies and hatred, and ever since Antoine Arnauld's three-fold onslaught of 1643–4 (to defend Jansenius and to attack the casuistry and lax doctrines of communion of the jesuits) the issue had been joined.[13] This episodic guerilla

[11] J. Kolakowski, *Chrétiens sans Eglise*, French trans A. Posner (Paris 1969) pp 350–62.

[12] A modern historian favourable to jansenism describes Jansenius as over-systematising Augustine, as Augustine had over-systematised Paul. Thus Jansenius was wrong, but Augustine was wrong before him, which neither side could admit in the seventeenth and eighteenth centuries— J.-F. Thomas, *Le problème moral à Port-Royal* (Paris 1963) pp 166–7, 175. Though a friend of Jansenius, Saint-Cyran was not enthusiastic about the *Augustinus*, J. Orcibal, *La spiritualité de Saint-Cyran* (Paris 1962) p 81; and it was Saint-Cyran who gave the decisive imprint to the movement which was to be called 'Jansenism', J. Orcibal, *Jean Duvergier de Hauranne, abbé de Saint-Cyran, 1581–1638*, 2 vols (Paris 1947) p 682. Arnauld in turn derived his theology from Saint-Cyran and Augustine, not from Jansenius, J. Laporte, *La doctrine de Port-Royal* (Paris 1927) 1 (I) p xv, and Arnauld's *Apologie de M. Jansenius* (Paris 1644) was more read in France than the *Augustinus* itself, N. Abercrombie, *The Origins of Jansenism* (Oxford 1936) p 214.

[13] In *Du Mysticisme à la révolte. Les Jansénistes du XVIIe siècle* (Paris 1968) A. Adam heads his chapter on this point: 'The Birth of a Party'. For the importance of the

skirmishing was transformed into a permanent war with precise battle-lines – bastions and trenches, ramparts and redoubts – by the manipulations of politicians, secular and ecclesiastical, who cared only about power. Before averting one's eyes from the sordid worldly involvements of eighteenth-century jansenism, it is as well to reflect that the whole great confrontation was a creation of seventeenth-century political cynicism.

We may leave aside Richelieu's hatred for Jansenius and Saint-Cyran, and start with Mazarin and the bull *Cum occasione* of 1653.[14] Pope Innocent X was a gouty octogenarian, green in colour as the painters honestly record, run by a sister-in-law who took all his money and would not even pay for his coffin. But he was a man of common sense; he noted that some of the 'qualificators' examining the *Augustinus* had not been able to find the five heretical propositions (or at least, four of them) in the actual book, so he took care to make the bull ambiguous. Indeed, to Mazarin's agent in Rome he insisted that the words *Cum occasione* were vital; Jansenius' volume was just 'the occasion' for the condemnation of the propositions. But Mazarin would not publish this. The pope was hostile to the french alliance with the english and dutch against Spain; he must therefore be driven into a dependence upon the french crown which alone could enforce obedience on the clergy. So the french bishops declared the five propositions were actually in the *Augustinus* and the pope was brought to connive with the statement. His successor, Alexander VII, not loath to demonstrate papal authority, in 1656 affirmed on his own authority that the propositions were in Jansenius and that they were condemned in the sense their author gave them. (Isaac Barrow, the anglican divine, reflected how the church would have been saved a lot of trouble if the pope had been able to give the page references,[15] and there was a story that the jesuits had printed a special copy of the *Augustinus* for the pope which had the propositions inserted).

Thus, tragically, the papacy was committed. When the crafty Mazarin was gone, Louis XIV committed the french crown also. He had been brought up to believe (as Saint-Simon said) that the jansenists 'were a republican party in Church and State'. This allegation

---

communion issue see the local example in J. Gallerand, 'Le Jansénisme en Blésois', *RHEF* 55 (1969) pp 30–45; for the issue of casuistry, L. Cognet's edition of the *Provinciales* (Paris 1965) pp viii–x.

[14] P. Jansen, *Le Cardinal de Mazarin et le Jansénisme* (Paris 1967) pp 45–53, 72–5, 84–8.

[15] C. B. Moss, *The Old Catholic Movement* (London 1948) p 78.

was easily refuted, both then and since,[16] but the point can be stated more subtly. Civil wars could arise from ostensibly religious causes; there were powerful *frondeurs* who would make capital out of any sort of rift in the established order. According to an english agent, Louis regarded jansenism as 'a . . . faction fomented by the princes and great nobles to regain their power'.[17] For the 'security of the State' therefore, in 1661, the king got the assembly of clergy to impose a formulary condemning the five propositions and explicitly stating that they were in the *Augustinus*. Four years later, Rome, reaffirming its authority in circumstances when it was certain of support from the secular arm, imposed its own formulary, making no mention of the king's, and this formulary was repeated in the bull *Vineam Domini* of 1705. Jansenists were prepared to condemn the five propositions but only to remain silent on the notorious problem of 'fact' – how could one swear to the presence of propositions in a volume when diligent search had failed to find them? It was no longer a question of efficacious grace or opposition to the jesuits: it was a question of intellectual veracity and of the limits of authority. What is truth? In the abbé Le Roy's opinion a man could not commit his word to the obscure and unverified. 'When a thing is honest and fair, this is evident, it shows up by a self-generated light without any need for demonstration or proof'[18] – not for nothing were the jansenists drawn to cartesianism. What is truth worth? Claude de Sainte-Marthe, the confessor of Port Royal, denounced the signature of the formulary, for this was 'to take from us the means to suffer for truth'.[19] The word truth, *vérité*, became the jansenist key word. Another jansenist of the uncompromising school, Nicolas Perrault, urged his friends not to be blackmailed by those who talked of the wickedness of schism, by those who crucified Christ then demanded sacrifices from others to keep his seamless robe undivided. To sign was to throw away ecclesiastical liberties[20] – liberty, together with truth, the other key word of the jansenist position.

[16] J. A. C. Tans, 'Les Idées politiques des Jansénistes', *Neophilogus* (Groningen Jan 1956) pp 1–8.
[17] Ruth Clark, *Strangers and Sojourners at Port-Royal* (Cambridge 1932) p 131. A *frondeur* using the plea of religion to oppose the crown would not necessarily be insincere— for example the pious bishop of Agde became an ardent jansenist after his brother had been destroyed by the king; see X. Azema, *Un prélat janséniste: Louis Foucquet* (Paris 1963) pp 38–47.
[18] G. Namer, *L'abbé Le Roy et ses amis: essai sur le Jansénisme extrémiste intramondain* (Paris 1964) p 59.
[19] *Ibid* p 102. [20] *Ibid* pp 44–52.

Jansenism and politics in the eighteenth century

While king and pope were busy affirming their authority (and nothing does this more spectacularly than obliging people to trample on their common sense), the question of intellectual veracity and of the limits of authority became the central issue of the jansenist dispute. Yet so far, only the few had faced the challenge. The five propositions represented a grim theological tendency little worthy of sympathy, and the *Augustinus* was unreadable; a man might be forgiven for refraining from a high serious line, and assuming that the propositions must be in the book, hidden there like thorns in a great knotty faggot. Then, in 1713, came the bull *Unigenitus*, which no one could ignore. It condemned 101 propositions which anyone could read (and some recognisable as the actual words of scripture)[21] taken from the jansenist Quesnel's *Réflexions morales sur le Nouveau Testament*, a work which for forty years had been regarded as a masterpiece of edification.[22] It was a political bull, the outcome this time of ecclesiastical politics, a plot of Fénelon and the jesuits to discredit their enemy cardinal de Noailles, the archbishop of Paris who had given his approval to Quesnel's volume. To sensitive consciences truth and liberty were already at stake over the issue of 'fact' concerning the five propositions. *Unigenitus* flouted truth and liberty before the whole world.[23] The aged and devout Quesnel (referred to in the bull as a 'wolf in sheep's clothing', a 'false prophet', an 'artful seducer' and 'master of lies') had not been allowed to appear to defend himself,[24] his book had been examined by a commission of which only one member knew french, and in a latin translation which had not been brought up to date with the revisions of later editions.[25] The bull accused Quesnel of renewing the propositions of Jansenius, whereas he specifically contradicted some of them – according to him men can resist grace, God does not command the impossible and Jesus is the Redeemer of all. Some of the 101

---

[21] An opponent of jansenism expressed horror at the condemnation of scriptural phrases—'Qui n'en eut été effrayé?'. *Mémoires de l'abbé Le Gendre*, ed M. Roux (Paris 1863), p 303.

[22] For the story of the magistrate of Grenoble who persuaded an opponent of jansenism to use the book as a devotional manual by having it bound up with the title page of a jesuit work, see E. Esmonin, 'La société grenobloise au temps de Louis XV d'après les miscellanea de Letourneau', *Etudes sur la France des 17ᵉ et 18ᵉ siècles* (Paris 1964) pp 484–5.

[23] See J.-F. Thomas, *La querelle de l'Unigenitus* (Paris 1950). He admits, however, that propositions 5, 38, 39, 59 and 61–3 deserved condemnation.

[24] A later pope, Benedict XIV, conceded that this was wrong.

[25] [J.] Parquez, [*La Bulle Unigenitus et le jansénisme politique*] (Paris 1936) pp 38–9.

propositions are blameable, but some are manifestly orthodox in themselves: all must read scripture, fear of an unjust excommunication ought never to prevent us doing our duty, grace is necessary for all good actions. How then was it possible to condemn them? A simple device achieved this tour de force; no less than twenty-four adjectives or adjectival clauses were listed and said to be applicable 'respectively' – 'false', 'captious', 'offensive to pious ears', 'harmful to the Church', 'sacriligious', 'impious', 'blasphemous', 'heretical'. (Some were nets to catch any fish – presumably there were pious ears which could be offended even by the mention of the possibility of an unjust excommunication.)[26] An intelligent man who was determined to accept the bull had to begin by accepting what was to be proved, that is, Quesnel's pious book was a suspect document written with some dark design in mind, and from thence proceed to hunt among the twenty-four epithets for something to fit each proposition, saving up 'captious' and 'offensive to pious ears' to hammer scriptural and orthodox statements.[27] And this was the age of reason, of cartesian clarity! 'When a thing is honest and fair', the abbé Le Roy had said, apropos of the formulary, 'this is evident; it shows up by a self-generated light without any need for demonstration or proof'. *Unigenitus* was not just another incident in the repression of jansenism: it was an insult to the intellectual standards of the enlightenment.[28]

More than ever, the jansenists used their key word *vérité*. It summed up precisely what was at risk – truth; and a man has a duty to 'witness' to truth. In August, 1714, père Vivien de La Borde published the *Témoignage à la vérité*. In a pastoral letter of 1718 the

[26] For the global condemnation as the stumbling block, see the opinion of the benedictines of Tronchet in 1718 in L. M. Raison, *Le Mouvement janséniste au diocèse de Dol* (Rennes 1931) pp 59–60.

[27] This is the line taken by apologists for the bull (Carreyre, 2 xx pp 59, 160; 3 pp 341–4, 347–8). John Wesley was exaggerating when he spoke of 'that diabolical bull *Unigenitus*, which destroys the very foundation of Christianity'. It was possible to accept the bull, but by intellectual procedures that were hardly straightforward.

[28] The connexion between jansenism and the enlightenment needs a major study— 'Ce Jansénisme des Lumières, si riche et si méconnu, mais si multiple et divergent', H. Himelfarb, 'Saint-Simon et le jansénisme', *Studies in Voltaire and the 18th Century* 87 (Geneva 1972) pp 749–68. R. Shackleton discusses two *philosophes* with jansenist backgrounds and suggests the possibility of an alliance between *philosophes* and jansenists—until convulsionism made this impossible—in 'Jansenism and the Enlightenment', *Studies on Voltaire and the 18th Century* 57 (1967) pp 1388–96. The jansenist priest Gordon is one of Voltaire's more attractive characters. But his kindness to l'Ingénu is repaid by his being converted to more sensible beliefs—he forgets efficacious grace for ever (*L'Ingénu* in *Romans et Contes*, ed H. Bénac (Paris 1958) pp 248, 262, 283).

bishop of Castres, a protector of jansenists, apologised for accepting
Unigenitus himself, in the interests of the peace of his diocese: *nous
laissons à d'autres le soin d'éclairer et de défendre la vérité*.[29] Colbert
bishop of Montpellier, dying in 1738, under official displeasure, his
revenues confiscated, looked back on his rejection of *Unigenitus*: 'I
rank as the happiest days of my life', he said, 'those in which I had
the good fortune to offer such a necessary witness to the truth'.[30] And
Nicolas Petitpied, the doctor of the Sorbonne who drafted the
remonstrances of the *curés* of Paris in 1727, hit upon the superb,
decisive formula for refusing to accept the bull: *Il ne suffit pas d'être
Catholique pour être sauvé, il faut encore rendre témoignage à la vérité*.[31]

By labyrinthine procedures, it was possible to explain *Unigenitus* to
the point of accepting it, but nothing could make the bull intellectually
respectable or the obligation to accept it morally just. It was 'a
mockery of good faith', said bishop Colbert, to go through the
necessary intellectual contortions, 'unworthy of the gravity of
bishops and entirely opposed to the simplicity of the Church'.[32] It
was a question of authority versus reason; in the first place, the
authority of the pope, and in the second, of the king. Some bishops,
episcopal gallicans, wished to be recognised as judges of the faith 'with'
the pope, not after him, and in promulgating a bull like this would
naturally wish to give their explanations. But the chief jansenist reply
was an appeal to a general council of the church. From the start, the
notion of an appeal against all the authorities of this world was
inherent in jansenism; when the *Provinciales* were condemned in
Rome, Pascal took refuge in Saint Bernard's defiant words, *Ad tuum,
Domine Jesu, tribunal appello*.[33] More prosaically, the gallican
tradition cherished the idea of the superiority of general council to
popes,[34] and in 1717, four bishops (joined eventually by thirteen
others), the doctors of the Sorbonne, the *curés* of Paris and three
thousand other ecclesiastics signed the appeal to a future general
council. In orthodox catholic historiography it is customary to describe

[29] E. Appolis, 'Un prélat philojanséniste?'. *La Régence* (Centre Aixois d'Etudes 1970)
p 243.
[30] [V.] Durand, [*Le Jansénisme au XVIII*e *siècle et Joachim Colbert*] (Toulouse 1907)
pp 348–9.
[31] Carreyre, 2 p 102.
[32] *Ibid* 1 p 142.
[33] The parallel between Pascal's words and the appeal to a general council is drawn by
Le Roy, *La France et Rome de 1700 à 1715* (Paris 1892) p xix.
[34] In 1688, Louis XIV had initiated such an appeal, see Orcibal, *Louis XIV contre
Innocent XI*.

the appeal movement as a gallican manifestation, which, of course, it was. But it was more. Though in their faith and belief the appellants had no sympathy with free thought as seventeenth-century *libertins* and eighteenth-century *philosophes* understood it, obliquely and in an ecclesiastical context they were upholding the ideal of liberty within the traditions of the enlightenment. Benoît Fourgon, of a rich merchant family of Lyon, was arrested in 1714 as a jansenist agent (he had been betrayed by the indiscretion of a seventy-four year old priest, a brother of Quesnel, who in prison had recounted his jansenist contacts to a fellow prisoner, a stool pigeon). From the dank and airless dungeons of the Château Pierre en Cize Fourgon was taken for interrogation before the archbishop and his legal adviser, the *officiel*. Fourgon said a general council was the final authority in the church. Asked by the archbishop if a national council would do as well, he replied – yes, if it was assembled in accordance with 'due forms' and 'liberty'. 'What is it, this liberty that you demand?' cried the prelate, 'To hear these gentlemen talk, we are not free, everything is done by plots and violence, and you'd imagine we were ruled by a tyrant.' Liberty, Fourgon explained, meant that the bishops would be able to attend such a council 'free from fear and hope alike'. The *officiel* interrupted: 'You believe that you will be damned by blind obedience?' 'Yes, Monsieur, that's what I believe'.[35]

No one can regret the condemnation of the five propositions; indeed, in the seventeenth and eighteenth centuries, hardly anyone wished to defend them. But by 1714, a proper censure of a dark theological tendency had become an issue of reason versus authority. This was the outcome of political manoeuvring – by the jesuits to defeat their enemies and to ensure the survival of their order, by Mazarin in the interests of french national security, by Fénelon to strike back at the friends of Bossuet, by Louis XIV in his determination to crush dissent, lest religious confusion become an arena for a new fronde, by the popes, unwilling to act and fearful, yet in the end lured on by the opportunity of being able to register a major exercise of authority with the rare and unusual support of the secular power. The politics of the seventeenth century created an issue of high principle for the eighteenth, and as is the way in human affairs, lofty issues were fought out by unprincipled means and by strange alliances.

Unigenitus reached Louis XIV on 23 September 1713, and the king

[35] [J.] Godart, [*Le Jansénisme à Lyon: Benoît Fourgon, 1687–1773*] (Paris 1934) pp 199–206.

Jansenism and politics in the eighteenth century

died on 1 September 1715. His last act of unreasoning force had been to compel the parlement of Paris to register the bull. His death released the forces of protest; for the first time, jansenism became a popular cause. 'The acceptants [of the bull] were the hundred bishops who had adhered under Louis XIV, with the jesuits and capuchins', said Voltaire, 'those refusing were fifteen bishops and all the nation'.[36] In 1727, according to the diarist Barbier (a sardonic anticlerical with no sympathy for religious disputers), all the second order of clergy, the greater part of the bourgeoisie, of the magistrates, of women and the common people, were on the jansenist side.[37] The *frondeur* mentality, gallicanism, hatred of the jesuits, reaction against royal absolutism – these in themselves are not enough to explain this surge of feeling. *Unigenitus*, with its defiance of lucidity and intellectual fair play, was the necessary catalyst. As opponents of the bull were gradually ousted from the French Church, or died, or were prevented from entering it, this popular feeling took new forms; it passed into support of the parlement of Paris in its resistance to the crown on strictly political issues on one hand, and on the other into the convulsionist movement.

Perhaps the acid test of any explanation of eighteenth-century jansenism lies here – is there some clause in it which can make sense of convulsionism? It is a subject that can hardly be looked at without either laughter or revulsion – the girls, (according to a pop-eyed police spy, *assez jolies et bien faites*) who waved their legs in the air on the tomb of the deacon Pâris,[38] the abbé Bécheran de la Motte leading an acrobatic troupe and, according to a comic *affiche*, doing 'the new perilous leap supporting himself on no more than two legs and aided by no more than three people',[39] the strange sects engaged in sinless or symbolic activities, the vaillantists (following canon Vaillant who expected Elijah's fiery chariot to be sent down for him, and thought it had come when some straw caught fire in his cell in the Bastille),[40] the decorous gatherings to watch the *grand secours*, in which women

---

[36] Voltaire, *Siècle de Louis XIV* cap 37. 'On parle du feu roi et de la Constitution (Unigenitus) avec une liberté étonnante', letter of 16 October, 1715 in D. P. Denis, 'Dom Charles de l'Hostellerie, 1714–20', *Revue Mabillon* (Liguge 1909) p 376.

[37] Barbier, *Chronique de la Régence et du règne de Louis XIV, 1718–63* (Paris 1857) 2 p 21, October 1727 (compare p 54).

[38] [A.] Mousset, [*L'Etrange histoire des convulsionnaires de Saint-Médard*] (Paris 1953) p 55.

[39] *Ibid* p 63; Barbier 2 p 199.

[40] Mousset, pp 147–76; Ph. de Félice, *Foules en délire: essai sur quelques formes inférieures de la mystique* (Paris 1947) pp 247–8.

endured tortures uncomplainingly, culminating in the 'fifth stage' in crucifixion.[41] Yet, sane and rational men vouched for miracles of healing, beginning in the provinces before the cemetery of St Médard became famous;[42] there were mystical writings of a kind,[43] and there were ecstatic seizures not entirely unlike the manifestations at Wesley's sermons. Some jansenists repudiated the whole convulsionist movement, some distinguished the miracles of healing from ecstatic or pathological phenomena. Bishop Colbert, in a pastoral letter of 1733, ascribed the outbreak of miracles to the suppression of the truth. 'When la *vérité* no longer has freedom to appear and men no longer speak of truth', he says, repeating the key word, 'then truth must speak of itself directly to men . . . Here is the cause of the marvels that are taking place before our eyes'.[44] In a way Colbert would have abhorred, it is possible to agree with him: persecution can have strange effects on its victims, and the outbreaks of 'prophesying' among the protestants of the Cévennes in the late seventeenth century are a parallel to some of the jansenist phenomena.[45] One may go further, and suggest that there could have been a movement in the eighteenth-century french church connected with jansenism – a movement for deeper personal piety, for liturgical reform (we know of half a dozen jansenist *curés* saying mass in an amended form as delegates of the worshipping community),[46] for lay participation in the leadership of religious worship, including the participation of

[41] Gagnol, [*Le Jansénisme convulsionnaire et l'affaire de la Planchette*] (Paris 1911). A case of 1787 in H. Pensa, *Sorcellerie et religion* . . . *au XVIIe et XVIIIe siècles* (Paris 1953) p 245—but is this really jansenist?

[42] In 1727, L. Paris, *Histoire de l'abbaye d'Avenay* (Reims 1879) 1 pp 491–2; in 1728, [P.] Dayon, [*Amiens, capitale provinciale: étude sur la société urbaine du XVIIe siècle*] (Paris 1967) p 423; in 1729, Godart, pp 112, 117. The Saint-Médard healings began in the early thirties, R. A. Knox, *Enthusiasm* (Oxford 1950) p 376.

[43] Mousset, p 129; Gagnol, pp 120, 126. It is easy to ridicule these examples—but compare them with what Bremond accepts as genuine spirituality in *L'ascension mystique d'un curé provençal*, 2 vols (Fontenelle 1951).

[44] Durand, p 317.

[45] Fleury held that the convulsionists were imitating the protestant manifestations in the Cévennes, E. Appolis, 'L'histoire provinciale du Jansénisme au XVIIIe siècle', *Annales* 7 (1952) p 91. Sainte-Beuve describes how, under persecution, collective hallucinations can begin, as in the mysterious singing at Port-Royal in 1706, when the abbess lay dying: 'Le délire commence, mais sur un ton assez doux; les Convulsions, qui viendront vingt et un ans plus tard, seront moins mélodieuses', *Port Royal* 6 (12), in 8 ed 6 p 188.

[46] E. Préclin, *Les Jansénistes au XVIIIe siècle et la Constitution civile du Clergé* (Paris 1929) pp 180–97. Another case in Ch. Bost, 'Documents: la conversion de Pierre de Claris', *Bulletin de la Société de l'histoire du protestantisme français* (Paris 1924) pp 33–42.

women.[47] Instinctive forces, deprived of a more respectable outlet and of intelligent leadership, found expression in convulsionism.

The appeal, and the renewed appeal to a general council raised the theoretical problem of authority in the church. (In 1722 a jansenist controversialist asked the ultimate question: who rules in the council? His answer was, priests and doctors must join the bishops in voting, and the laity have to give their approval, not, it is true, as 'judges' of the faith, but as *témoins*, witnesses.[48]) With the idea of an appeal in the air like the sound of distant thunder, the tyrannical measures of many bishops to enforce the acceptance of *Unigenitus* raised the question of authority in the church at the episcopal level. When the bishop of Amiens excommunicated appellants, canon Masclef of the cathedral issued an open letter to him: 'You published the constitution *Unigenitus* in your diocese, but was this done in full synod, at the head of your chapter and your *curés*? Have you asked for their votes and have you allowed them liberty of discussion?'[49] The claim of the lower clergy to share in the government of the diocese was not a new idea, but it was put forward with a new fervour. The jansenist periodical, the *Nouvelles Ecclésiastiques* (running from 1728) and jansenist propagandists like Travers, Le Gros and Petitpied put forward the claims of the *curés* to be descendants of the seventy-two disciples commissioned by Christ independently of the twelve apostles, and thus entitled to their share in the administration of the church. This movement has been studied by M. Préclin in a famous monograph, *Les Jansénistes du XVIIIe siècle et la Constitution civile du clergé* (1929). Though this work has stood the test of time, in one respect its conclusions need revision: the jansenist-richerist movement among the lower clergy became a force earlier and was more widespread than Préclin believed. The aristocratic domination of the episcopate was challenged and the rights of the lower clergy – and, indeed of the laity – were put forward in uncompromising terms by Jean Le Noir in *L'Evesque de cour opposé à l'évesque apostolique* in the heyday of the

---

[47] For the rôle of women in eighteenth century popular jansenism see the complaints of Massillon and Languet—in Blampignon, *L'Episcopat de Massillon* (Paris 1884) pp 254–7, and Carreyre, 2 xx p 56. Seamstresses were supposed to be especially inclined to jansenism. See the observations of a curé of Orleans in 1752 in C. Marcilhacy, *Le diocèse d'Orléans au milieu du XIXe siècle* (Paris 1964) p 427, and the phrase 'plus janséniste qu'un valet ou une lingère' cited by E. P. Shaw, *The Case of the Abbé de Moncrif* (New York 1953) p 34.

[48] Carreyre 2 xx p 285.

[49] Dayon, p 373.

absolutism of Louis XIV,[50] and after the royal edict of 1695 which gave bishops new powers to discipline their *curés*, a movement of protest among the lower clergy was inevitable. The maldistribution of ecclesiastical wealth, the inadequacy of the *congrue*, the honorific precedences of chapters and monasteries, the injustices of clerical taxation – all these were to be issues in the revolt of the *curés* at the end of the *ancien régime*. The exaction of the formulary of 1705 and the persecution of jansenist clergy, monks and nuns crushed jansenism as a theological and reforming movement in the french church (this is a persecution we tend to forget – a story of humiliations, *lettres de cachet*, confinements in seminaries and monasteries, deprivations of communion, exiles;[51] perhaps we have concentrated too much lately on Appolis' moderate bishops of the *Tiers parti*[52] and given too little attention to the ruthless ones). What was left was the jansenist-richerist drive for economic justice, enhanced status and increased powers to parish priests, a movement that was to have a decisive importance in the balance of political forces at the crisis of the *ancien régime*.

There were few genuine jansenists among the magistrates of the parlements; in the parlement of Paris there were not many more than half a dozen in the first half of the eighteenth century;[53] in the parlement of Brittany, the Huchet de la Bédoyère of Rennes and the Charette de la Gascherie of Nantes were the only significant jansenist

[50] There is an excellent Cambridge thesis by Dr N. W. McMaster on Jean Le Noir ('The extremist jansenists, 1660–1703, with special regard to Jean le Noir and Gabriel Gerberon'). It has become customary to refer to the arguments in favour of the *curés* as 'richerist'. Edmond Richer published a gallican treatise in 1611 claiming that power in the church should reside in the hierarchy of bishops and priests—by including the priests he gave his theory a democratic nuance, an indication that, alongside episcopal gallicanism, there was room for a 'gallicanisme parochiste'. See E. Préclin, 'Edmond Richer', *Revue d'histoire moderne* 29 (1930) pp 242–69.

[51] Fleury's 'avalanche' of *lettres de cachet* did much to discredit this weapon of royal power, M. Antoine, *Le Conseil du roi sous la règne de Louis XV* (Paris 1970) pp 505–6. Examples of *curés* in prison or confined in monasteries in Mgr [Martial] Levé, [*Louis-François Gabriel d'Orléans de la Motte, évêque d'Amiens 1683–1774*] (Abbeville 1962) pp 97–9, 100 and J. Charrier, *Histoire du Jansénisme dans le Diocèse de Nevers* (Paris 1920) pp 99–100. For humiliations inflicted on curés see *Journal de Dom Pierre Chastelain*, ed M. Jadert (Reims 1902) pp 45, 50, and J.-B. Bergier, *Histoire de la Communauté des prêtres missionaires de Beaupré et des missions faites en Franche-Comté, 1676–1850* (Besançon 1853) pp 168–9.

[52] E. Appolis, *Entre Jansénistes et Zelanti: le Tiers Parti Catholique au XVIIIᵉ siècle* (Paris 1960). R. Taveneaux, *Le Jansénisme en Lorraine, 1640–1789* (Paris 1960) p 356, adds bishop Coislin of Metz to the *Tiers Parti*, an important addition as he was one of the first.

[53] Gazier, 1 p 297, found only half a dozen all told in the jansenist necrologies.

Jansenism and politics in the eighteenth century

families.[54] Numbers on this scale suggest a religious inspiration working in accordance with the law of averages rather than a predilection of the robe for a particular theological outlook. The inspiration could, in individual cases, be convulsionist; Carré de Montgeron was one of the enthusiasts of the cemetery of St Médard who presented his book in defence of jansenist miracles to the king; from 1734 the château de la Bédoyère became a convulsionist centre, while some of the women of the Charette de la Gascherie clan went on a pilgrimage to the tomb of the deacon Pâris and were even heard preaching sermons. The magistrates, of course, were essentially gallican, rather than jansenist, ever ready to flourish their legal weaponry to defeat roman pretensions (they were particularly concerned, in the bull *Unigenitus*, with the condemnation of the proposition exhorting to courage in the face of an 'unjust excommunication').[55] They were also members of a proud corporation which regarded itself as the last national barrier remaining against the excesses of despotism; since the king had abandoned the gallican tradition of France by becoming the pope's accomplice in the jansenist quarrel, they were able to seize upon a popular cause in which they could justify their defiance of the monarch by reference to the true interests of the crown. The political struggle waged by the parlement of Paris, with popular support, against pope and crown culminating in the triumphant destruction of the jesuits, was no more cynical than political struggles normally are. *Unigenitus* was imposed on the parlement by Louis XIV, and finally, in 1730, was made into a law of state by Fleury. Was it possible for magistrates to do other than oppose a bull which was so unjust in its demands, so irrelevant to the true interests of the church and the country, lacking alike in clarity and charity, foisted on them by a misuse of secular authority?

For long dismissed as reactionaries, the magistrates of the parlement of Paris have recently been receiving more favourable treatment from historians:[56] they saw through Law's scheme and warned the public; their opposition to taxes was not limited to those which fell most heavily on themselves; they had a genuine sense of the national interest in times of crisis. Gallicanism and opposition to despotism

[54] J. Meyer, *La Noblesse bretonne au XVIIIe siècle*, 2 vols (Paris 1966) 2 pp 993–4, 998.
[55] Barbier 2 pp 115–16 (April 1730).
[56] J. Egret, *Louis XV et l'opposition parlementaire 1715–1774* (Paris 1970); J. H. Shennan, *The Parlement of Paris* (London 1968), and on Law's Scheme, Shennan in *HJ* 8 (1965); W. Doyle, 'The Parlements of France and the Breakdown of the Old Régime, 1771–8', *French Historical Studies* 6 (Raleigh, N. Carolina 1970) pp 415–58.

(respectable motives in any case) were not their only inspiration for their rôle in political jansenism. The parlements were, essentially, law courts, and the magistrates took seriously their duty to prevent injustice to individuals and insults to families, and to ensure the observance of legal forms. The legal procedure of the *appel comme d'abus* was, no doubt, a resort for gallican and anticlerical enterprises, but it was also a necessary device to prevent powerful churchmen from exceeding their rights or falling short in the performance of their duties. A priest deprived of his liberty by an ecclesiastical superior could resort to the secular courts; hence in 1716 the parlement of Paris acted against the archbishop of Reims who had sent half a dozen of his clergy to his seminary because they refused to publish his pastoral letter on *Unigenitus*. The laity could not be excommunicated without due process; that was why the parlement suppressed the roman letters *Pastoralis Officii* in 1718 (which declared the bull clear to the eyes of the true faithful and separated from the church all refusing to submit to it), and why provincial parlements suppressed the pastoral letters of bishops which flourished threats of excommunication.

The two great battles of parliamentary jansenism were in 1731–3 against Fleury's policies, ending inconclusively because of the outbreak of the war of the polish succession, and the crisis of 1749–54 over the refusal of sacraments, ending in the victory of the parlement. The story of remonstrances and tumults, strikes and collective resignations, *lits de justice* and *lettres de cachet* is all political, a spectacle from which Sainte-Beuve would have averted his eyes. But what were the issues? On 24 March 1730, Fleury[57] produced a royal declaration making *Unigenitus* a law of the kingdom; attacks on the bull were forbidden, and the *appel comme d'abus* was not to be used in questions concerning its enforcement. A prelude to this declaration had been the provincial council of Embrun, at which the bishops of that ecclesiastical province, under the presidency of their archbishop, the notorious Tencin,[58] had met to try and depose the pious old

---

[57] Fleury had been diplomatic in his own diocese on the jansenist issue, P. Ardoin, *Le Jansénisme en basse Provence au XVIIIᵉ siècle*, 2 vols (Marseille 1936) 1 pp 90–3. Probably, he had no real respect for the bull but was concerned only with authority in church and state (see his words in Gazier 1 p 300). He manoeuvred cautiously when he first came to power, but was utterly ruthless in enforcing orthodoxy— he was a 'chef de parti' not a national statesman, G. Hardy, *Le Cardinal de Fleury et le mouvement janséniste* (Paris 1925) pp 17–18.

[58] For Tencin see J. Sareil, *Les Tencin* (Geneva 1969). For Soanen, bishop of Senez, M. Vovelle, *Piété baroque et déchristianisation en Provence au XVIIIᵉ siècle* (Paris 1973) pp 463–97.

jansenist bishop of Senez. A consultation of *avocats* had been published censuring the injustice of the Embrun procedures, partly on technical grounds, partly because an appeal to a general council was pending. (This consultation was a good example of the combination of legal and scriptural arguments available to political jansenism. Cardinal de Bissy fell ill while writing a rejoinder to it and his valet was heard to curse the *avocats*: '*Ces bougres-là* are the cause of my master's illness. It's easy for them to write as they do; they find all they say in the bible, but what monseigneur writes he has to make up out of his own head').[59] From the Embrun scandal arose another affair of injustice to the individual; six *curés* of Orleans were deprived by their bishop for refusing to publish his pastoral letter against the bishop of Senez, and their case came to parlement by way of the *appel comme d'abus*. Efficacious grace and the appeal to a general council were now in the background. What mattered was, firstly, the gallican question – the parlement challenged the wisdom of the french crown committing its full authority to the support of an unsatisfactory papal bull; secondly, the question of the *appel comme d'abus*, the right of the law courts to protect ecclesiastics from the tyranny of their superiors.

The Embrun affair tied together the forces of protest constituting the political jansenism of the eighteenth century; it marks the decisive entry of the parlements and the lawyers into the jansenist debate.[60] The magistrates developed their theories of a monarchy subject to fundamental laws of which the parlements were the interpreters, and of a national will whose institutional embodiment was their own assembly. There were jansenist writers who found a political theology to suit the parliamentary alliance. In the government of the church, jansenist propagandists were proclaiming the rights of the whole community of pastors as a counterweight to the oppression of bishops; in the government of the state, it was natural to seek to justify the claims of the parlements to act as a barrier against arbitrary actions by the crown. In the writings of Nicolas Le Gros (1716) and Jérôme Besoign (1737) is found the idea of an underlying national community, older and more permanent than the monarchy: 'when the form of government changes,' said Le Gros, 'the basis of authority does not change, and the republic is not overthrown.' The abbé Barral, in a

[59] Barbier 2 p 39 (March 1738).
[60] R. Taveneaux, *Jansénisme et politique* (Paris 1965) p 41. For what follows see also B. Plongeron, *Théologie et politique au siècle des Lumières, 1770–1820* (Geneva 1973) pp 102–8.

significant work, the *Manuel des Souverains* (1754), rejected the grim old view that fallen man, in his rebellious state, was a suitable subject for tyrannical government; on the contrary, despotism is the most detestable of all assertions of rebellion against God. The universe itself is not ruled in an arbitrary fashion, for God has chosen to work through pre-determined laws; this being so, kings cannot justly aspire to be absolute – they must be under the law, the law God has prescribed, a law anterior to all contract and inherent in the natural order. Barral does not press his argument to startling conclusions (this was true of practically all eighteenth-century political theorising before the revolution). He says, simply, that the registration of laws by the parlements is not 'a vain ceremony', but is 'inseparable from the legitimate usage of legislation.' Though this was a cautious practical inference, it nevertheless went far beyond the political theories of jansenism before *Unigenitus*; Arnauld had gone further than the rest, yet he had merely allowed passive resistance.

The mid-century crisis, when parlement and crown met in a confrontation which made contemporaries think revolution was near, and when anticlerical feeling became so intense in Paris that priests dared not show themselves in the streets, was disproportionately simple in origin. Christophe de Beaumont,[61] archbishop of Paris, decided on the strictly logical and uncharitable course of refusing the last sacraments to dying jansenists. According to the law books, the temporal courts had a duty to act against a *curé* who refused the sacraments to a duly shriven parishioner – on grounds of neglect of priestly duty, of conduct prejudicial to public order, and of defamation of character. Only in the case of someone under formal sentence of excommunication would the courts be precluded from intervention.[62] Some ecclesiastics argued, however (though the magistrates never accepted this) that the viaticum, being privately administered, could not give rise to questions of defamation or disorder, and in fact, in the first half of the eighteenth century, there were cases in various dioceses of the last sacraments being withheld from dying jansenists.[63] There were precedents too, though slender

[61] *Life* by [E.] Régnault, 2 vols (Paris 1882). He was a combination of the slack aristocratic prelate, the fanatically orthodox churchman and the recklessly generous man of charity.

[62] P.-J. Guyot, *Répertoire universel et raisonné de jurisprudence*, 64 vols (Paris 1775–83) and suppl 14 vols (1786) 57 pp 121–31.

[63] Paris 1721, *Journal et mémoires de Mathieu Marais, 1715–37*, ed De Lescure, 4 vols (Paris 1863) 2 pp 177–8; Nantes 1729, Bachelier, *Le Jansénisme à Nantes* (Angers 1934)

ones, for bishops ordering their curés to demand a *billet de confession*, signed by an approved confessor, before administering the viaticum.[64] Christophe de Beaumont made this the general rule of his diocese. In June 1749, Charles Coffin, a former *recteur* of the university of Paris, whose latin hymns were sung daily in the cathedral of Notre Dame, died without the sacraments, and the scandalous dispute, outrageous in macabre incident, popular tumult and legal severities against the clergy, began. By June, 1754, d'Argenson considered that the war of jansenists and molinists had moved into a new phase – it was now *nationaux* versus *sacerdotaux*, the nation led by the parlement against the clerical establishment.[65]

The mid-century crisis has been studied as the prelude to the revolution, with d'Argenson as the interpreter of the signs of the times and the prophet of doom. It also needs to be studied as the decisive reactive moment in the formation of the anticlerical temper which was to characterise french history in future. The uncharitable conduct of churchmen was universally decried.[66] The necessity of the sacraments for salvation was brought into question.[67] Jansenist fortitude under persecution discredited the standard apologetical 'proofs' from the martyrs, just as convulsionist marvels had discredited the proof from miracles.[68] From the divisions of catholics men drew the conclusions Bossuet had drawn from the divisions of protestants.[69] The inner conflicts of the french church, exacerbated by

---

pp 223–45; Arles 1734—an attempt by the archbishop to deprive the aged visiting bishop of Castres of the last sacraments, L. Remacle, *Ultramontains et Gallicans au XVIIIe siècle. Honoré de Quiqueran de Beaujeu et Jacques de Forbin-Janson* (Marseille 1872) p 168; Rennes 1738, L.-M. Raison, 'Le Jansénisme à Rennes', *Annales de Bretagne* 48 (Rennes 1941) pp 245–77; Saumur 1739, *ibid* p 243; Paris 1738, Barbier 3 p 129; Amiens 1741, Levé pp 100–1); Douai 1741, Parguez p 110; Dax 1741, A. Degert, *Histoire des évêques de Dax* (Dax 1903) pp 391–7; Bayonne 1743—bishop Christophe de Beaumont in earlier days (Régnault 1 pp 93–4).

[64] Régnault 1 pp 159–60; A. Bernard, *Le Sermon au XVIIIe siècle* (Paris 1901) p 37; M. Vallery-Radot, *Un administrateur ecclésiastique à la fin de l'ancien régime: le cardinal de Luynes, archevêque de Sens* (Paris 1966) pp 56–8.

[65] *Journal et mémoires du marquis d'Argenson*, ed E. J. B. Rathery, 9 vols (Paris 1859–67) 8 p 313 (24 June, 1754).

[66] How did archbishop Christophe differ from St Christopher? 'Il ne veut ni porter Jésus-Christ ni souffrir qu'on le porte', *Lettres de Piron*, ed E. Lavaquary (Paris 1920) p 67.

[67] In enforcing respect for the bull, he accustomed people to pay no respect to the sacrament, Voltaire, *Histoire du Parlement de Paris*, cap 65.

[68] On miracles Barbier 2 pp 44, 501, and Diderot, *Pensées philosophiques*, ed R. Niklaus (Paris 1950) pp 38–9, caps 53–4. For martyrs, cap 55.

[69] For the phrase, A. Monod, *De Pascal à Chateaubriand* (Paris 1916) p 211.

the refusal of sacraments scandal, created an atmosphere of suspicion and hypocrisy which swallowed up and distorted reforming enthusiasms. With sardonic insight, Loménie de Brienne, a reforming, though unbelieving prelate, described the effect on the monastic orders, where 'jansenists who pride themselves on the regularity of their lives to accredit their party' fought against 'constitutionals who affect submission to the bull to dispense themselves from the rules of their order.'[70] The victory of the parlement left the jesuits exposed to the vengeance of the magistrates; in 1764 they were proscribed in France and in 1773 their order was disbanded by the pope at the behest of the catholic sovereigns. The *philosophes* rejoiced to see the church divided and discredited. 'During the war of the parlements and the bishops', wrote Voltaire to d'Alembert, 'reasonable men had a good time, and you had the freedom to enliven the *Encyclopédie* with truths no one would have dared to publish twenty years ago.'[71]

Sainte-Beuve spoke of that 'entirely political jansenism which allowed many to be of the party without being of the dogma, or indeed, of religion at all'. But why should this be a criticism? Issues of principle fundamental to the enlightenment lay behind the eighteenth-century political battle. Religious dogma was no longer relevant to the dispute; indeed, for long in the seventeenth-century, it had been but marginal. The five propositions summed up an idea of God which was properly rejected: the *Augustinus* contained some theological affirmations which one is glad to see abandoned. But the five propositions are not in the *Augustinus*, and once it is officially laid down that they are, we enter the dark underworld of intellectual confusion out of which *Unigenitus* emerges. It was the exigencies of seventeenth-century politics, secular and ecclesiastical, which produced the formulary and *Unigenitus*, between them an affront to the whole spirit of the enlightenment, and jansenists were right in their instinct to seize upon 'truth' and 'liberty' as the keywords to sum up their case and their dilemma. Putting it the other way round, authority was at risk; papacy and crown were committed, and neither Rome nor the monarchy of Louis XIV made a virtue of the cromwellian adjuration – to think it possible they might be mistaken. At the end of the line comes Fleury, recommitting authority because he believed authority was already irretrievably committed anyway, but behind

---

[70] P. Chevallier, *Loménie de Brienne et l'ordre monastique, 1766–89*, 2 vols (Paris 1959–60) 2 p 29.
[71] *Correspondence*, ed T. Besterman, 30 (Geneva 1958) p 197, 13 November 1756.

his display of force using subtlety, bribery and compromise. And last of all, comes archbishop Christophe de Beaumont, who was generally regarded, in the circle of royal government as well as by magistrates and the general public, as a fool. His conscience, Bernis told him, was a dark lantern which illuminated his own path but no one else's. In his literal way, he tried to enforce the ecclesiastical penalties the acceptance of a formulary and a bull which had emerged from a century of worldly manoeuvring. After studying the evils caused by so much intelligent political finesse it is sad to end with the disaster caused by sincere and intolerant blundering.

University of Oxford
Christ Church

'CHRIST'S KINGDOM NOT OF THIS WORLD:' THE CASE OF BENJAMIN HOADLY VERSUS WILLIAM LAW RECONSIDERED

by HENRY D. RACK

THE traditional reputations of Hoadly and Law could hardly be more sharply contrasted. Hoadly's latitudinarianism, his promotion on the bench for political reasons, his neglect of diocesan duties have long made him a favourite example for castigating the hanoverian episcopate.[1] Law has been much more fortunate. Almost universally cited as a happy exception to the lax theology of his age; credited with a religious appeal to men of all parties; and praised for his literary style and powers of argument, Law has enjoyed a generally uncritical press, despite the difficulties of reconciling the early, orthodox controversial and devotional writings with his later and mystical works.[2] Of the confrontation between Hoadly and Law over the Bangorian sermon, the prevailing opinion has been that of dean Hook: 'Law's "Letters" have never been answered, – may indeed be regarded as unanswerable'.[3] Some, indeed, have suggested that Hoadly failed to reply directly to Law either through fear or inability to do so.[4] Overton, however, with his customary fairness, allowed that Hoadly 'was a very able controversialist and not afraid of any antagonist'.[5] Hoadly claimed that others had replied to Law (who had not attempted to answer them), and that all of Law's most important points had been answered in Hoadly's *Answer to the Representation*. He also thought that 'considerable a writer as Mr. Law is; I hope the Committee [of

---

[1] The view taken of him, however, has always been strongly conditioned by political and ecclesiastical bias, and I hope to show elsewhere that it has not been uniformly unfavourable.

[2] A. K. Walker's recent *William Law: his Life and Work* (London 1973) is more critical of Law.

[3] W. F. Hook, 'The Bangorian Controversy' in *The Church Dictionary* (London 1842) quoted by [J. H.] Overton, [*The Life and Opinions of William Law*] (London 1881) p 20.

[4] Thomas Sherlock, *The Condition and Example of our Saviour Vindicated* (London 1718) p 62 thought Law 'a writer so considerable that I know but ONE good reason why his Lordship DOES NOT answer him'.

[5] Overton, p 19 n.

Convocation], as a body, are much more considerable, in the Dean's [Sherlock's] eyes . . . and him himself [the Dean] a much more considerable writer than Mr. Law'.[6] It is fair to say that Law may well have appeared a less important antagonist to contemporaries than he has to later historians: a non-juror producing his first writing was a less obviously significant figure to answer than established controversialists like Snape and Sherlock. In his account of the affair the dissenter Calamy singled them out but did not mention Law.[7]

It may be added that Law's much-praised controversial skill is not above criticism. One of his major techniques, for example, is the dangerous and not always convincing *reductio ad absurdum*, of which he made excessive use.[8]

In a short paper, however, it is only possible to study one small part, though a central one, of the Bangorian controversy: that is, the arguments about the nature of the church and its relationship to the state, with particular reference to the context in which they occurred.

Of the controversy generally[9] it is sufficient to recall that Hoadly, then bishop of Bangor, followed his *Preservative against the Principles and Practices of the Non-jurors* in 1716 with a sermon in 1717 on *The Nature of the Kingdom or Church of Christ* which provoked a vast pamphlet warfare. In the sermon he appeared to deny that there was any power on earth entitled to exercise the authority of Christ in his church, since any such power would in effect supersede the kingship of Christ. To his critics, then and later, Hoadly seemed to deny any authority or bond of unity and discipline in the church on earth; to go beyond erastianism to the point of destroying the very being of the church if not the very foundations of christianity itself – a suspicion strengthened later by his treatise on the Lord's Supper and hints of heterodoxy elsewhere in his writings.

It may be argued, however, that Hoadly's position has not been

---

[6] *An Answer to a late Book written by the Rev Dr Sherlock* (London 1718) in [B.] Hoadly, [*Works*], ed J. Hoadly, 3 vols (London 1773) 2, pp 694–5. See also his *An Answer to the Rev Dr Snape's Letter* (London 1717). For Law's ironical comment see his [*Three Letters to the Bishop of Bangor, 1717–19*] in [*Works*] ed G. Moreton, 9 vols (Setley 1892) 1, pp 88–9.

[7] [E.] Calamy, [*An Historical Account of My Own Life*] ed J. T. Rutt, 2 vols (London 1829–30) 2, pp 371–9.

[8] See the admirable account by Leslie Stephen, 'William Law' in *Hours in a Library* (London 1876) second series, pp 129–32 (omitted in 1892 ed).

[9] The best account is by P. B. Hessert, 'The Bangorian Controversy' (Edinburgh PhD thesis 1951). As Hessert's sympathetic account of Hoadly at important points resembles my own, I should make it clear that the argument of this paper was worked out before I saw his work.

properly understood. It is true that the context of the controversy has often been described. It was, in general, 'the blended fear of sacerdotal tyranny and Stuart autocracy',[10] heightened by the alliance of highflying ecclesiastics and extreme tory politicians in the period of ferocious party politics following the revolution of 1688. Hoadly had a long history of defending the revolution, but the writings we are concerned with appear to have been provoked by the posthumous publication of the non-juror George Hickes's *Constitution of the Catholick Church* (1716)[11] which denied the right of secular rulers to depose bishops and asserted independent ecclesiastical jurisdiction in matters spiritual, based on apostolic succession.[12]

Hoadly's more than erastian response embarrassed even his whig sympathisers, at least among the ecclesiastics, and a case could be made for saying that in the heat of controversy he used unguarded language implying more than he intended. Yet even when this is allowed for, it seems likely that the sharp contrasts between Hoadly's and Law's views of the church arise in large measure from two aspects of the profound crisis of conscience which anglicanism was undergoing from the late seventeenth century onwards. One problem was how to adjust thinking about the nature of the church and its authority in relation to politics and society in face of the destruction of divine-right monarchy and the grant of religious toleration. The other problem was how to define christianity itself, particularly in its anglican form, in face of roman catholic, protestant and deist forms of it. If Hoadly's answers to these problems appear confused and unsatisfactory they nevertheless seem to represent an attempt to grapple with a confused and changing social reality, while Law seems to be holding on to a disappearing past. If Hoadly's protestantism seemed a semi-rationalised form of christianity, Law's brand of high-churchmanship could easily be represented as a corruption of the protestant tradition, opening an avenue for a return to Rome, particularly when its political sympathies – especially among non-jurors – seemed to lie with the exiled Stuarts who had so recently attempted to subvert the established order both in church and state.

[10] *Religious Thought in the Eighteenth Century*, ed J. M. Creed and J. S. Boys Smith (Cambridge 1934) p xxxviii.
[11] So Hoadly's editor in Hoadly, 1 p xx note N.
[12] G. Hickes, *The Constitution of the Catholick Church* (London 1716) pp 64, 69, 89–93. But he allowed that the clergy could not infringe a king's rights or depose him. For a hostile description of highflying claims see [M.] Tindal, [*The*] *Rights [of the Christian Church Asserted*] (4 ed London 1709) pp 32–3.

Hoadly's view of the church, like his view of civil government, closely resembles that of Locke, and in important respects was conceived with the same ends in mind. In his *Letter on Toleration* Locke had defined the church as 'a free society of men, joining together of their own accord for the public worship of God in such manner as they believe will be acceptable to the Deity for the salvation of their souls'.[13] As to the powers of this church, Locke acknowledges a need for rules agreed by the members for the being of any society; and as the church is a free and voluntary society, only the society or its agreed officers can make them. The only sanctions possible for ecclesiastical laws are those suitable to the nature of matters in which external profession is useless without inner persuasion; and this is the case with religion. Hence only exhortation, admonition, advice and (as a last resort) expulsion can be used, physical coercion being ruled out. Locke's main concern was to establish the totally different ends, and therefore the independent and different modes of persuasion appropriate to church and state respectively, as a basis for proving the need for and validity of religious toleration. He added that 'sincere' religious belief cannot be forced by external penalties; hence persecution is self-defeating as a means to conversion. In the course of his argument he observed that the notion of a divinely-ordained episcopal succession had no scriptural foundation.[14]

Locke's sometimes rather embarrassing disciple, the deistic Matthew Tindal, spelled out the implications of his master's position. In religious matters men are in a 'natural' state 'subject to God and their own consciences only; since no man's religion, like his lands, descends from father to son, but everyone, when capable, is to chuse [*sic*] his own church. . . . And tho' no church, more than any other voluntary society, can hold together, except the members agree on some place, on the persons to officiate . . . yet none has a right to prescribe to another, but everyone has for himself a negative . . . not only before he joins himself to it, but afterwards', and this applies to doctrines as well as worship and ceremonies. Quoting the familiar 'where two or three are gathered together' Tindal concluded that 'when people meet together upon any other motive, than worshipping God according to that method they judge most agreeable to his will, they cannot deserve the name of a Church'. Moreover, while scripture

[13] [John] Locke, [*Epistola de Tolerantia. A Letter on Toleration*,] ed R. Klibansky and tr J. W. Gough (Oxford 1968) p 71.
[14] Locke pp 73–5.

sees the church as 'the Christian people' with or without their ministers, and the articles define it as 'a congregation of the faithful', divines have often made it 'the clergy, exclusively of the people', to the detriment of liberty. This is 'as ridiculous as if the drummers and trumpeters shou'd call themselves the army exclusive of all others'.[15]

Only a few months before the Bangor sermon, A. A. Sykes had preached on *The Difference between the Kingdom of Christ and the Kingdoms of this World* saying that Christ's kingdom is for the salvation of all who have faith in Christ and live according to the laws of the gospel; it is within the souls of men, internal and spiritual. The 'Church of Christ' comprehends the visible professors of christianity and so the kingdom of Christ is 'a society of men joined together by the alone laws of Christ' to confirm each other in their religion. Sykes then proceeded to elaborate the differences between the kingdom or church of Christ and that of the world in matters of government, sanctions and so on with a special view to demolishing priestly domination.[16]

Hoadly's views and aims in defining the church are on the same lines. The church or kingdom of Christ is 'the number of men, whether small or great, whether dispersed or united, who truly and sincerely are subject to Jesus Christ alone, as their lawgiver and Judge, in matters relating to the power of God, and their eternal salvation'.[17] Like Locke he was opposed to high views of episcopal succession. 'I think there may be regularity preserved, without the supposition of a succession, absolutely uninterrupted from the beginning'.[18] With the views of men like Hickes in mind, who upheld the independent powers of the ministry with the political dangers these seemed to imply, Hoadly maintained: 'As the Church of Christ is the Kingdom of Christ, He himself is King: and in this it is implied that He is himself the sole lawgiver to His subjects and himself the sole Judge *in the affairs of conscience and eternal salvation. And in this sense, therefore, His Kingdom is not of this world*; that he hath, *in these points*, left behind him no visible, humane [*sic*] authority; no vicegerent who can be said

---

[15] Tindal, *Rights*, pp 23–4, lxxxvii.

[16] A. A. Sykes, sermon preached in December 1716, published in 1717, quoted in [J.] Disney, [*Memoires of the Life and Writings of Arthur Ashley Sykes*] (London 1785) pp 43–5.

[17] [*A*] *Sermon* [*on the Nature of the Kingdom or Church of Christ*] (London 1717) in Hoadly, 2 p 406.

[18] [*An*] *Answer to the Representation* [*drawn up by the Committee of the Lower House of Convocation*] (London 1717) in Hoadly, 2 p 485. Even in his strong defence of episcopacy against Calamy in 1703–5, Hoadly did not see it as essential to make a church or to convey salvation: Hoadly, 2 pp 477, 479.

properly to supply His place; no interpreters, upon whom His subjects are absolutely to depend; no judges over the consciences or religion of His people'.[19]

All these writers had two aims in mind in their descriptions of the church, though the details of their descriptions varied according to which aim was uppermost. One was a concern to restrict the power of rulers, whether civil or ecclesiastical (though in this case particularly the latter); and the other was to serve the interests of religious toleration.[20] Locke, and still more evidently Tindal, saw the church, like the state, as a voluntary corporation in which the natural rights of the individual had within severe limits been given up to rulers for self-protection. Hoadly did not commit himself so far, as will become apparent in a moment; yet it was understandable that he should have been seen as advocating a position which more obviously fitted the voluntary assemblies of dissent than an established church.[21] This church, as elaborated by Locke and Tindal, seems admirably fitted to Macpherson's 'possessive individualism'.[22] Put more ecclesiologically, it seems like a secularised version of the old separatist ideal of the 'gathered church' – 'secularised' in so far as it seems to be ordered less by the divine initiative than by the human will, and pragmatically. The 'divine' element lies in the individual's subjection to conscience or, as Hoadly put it, to Christ as 'Law-giver and judge'.

It was Hoadly's view of the church and ministry which especially provoked the attack of William Law in his *Three Letters to the Bishop of Bangor* of 1717–19. Hoadly's radical mode of refuting extreme views of church authority seemed to Law, as it has seemed to many later observers, to have destroyed not only 'absolute' but all authority in the church.[23] It was, indeed, claimed at the time by the bishop's enemies that the sermon as originally preached was even more obviously open to this interpretation, and that before publication he had hastily covered himself by inserting qualifying words like 'absolute', 'properly' and so forth. This led to unedifying charges of

[19] *Sermon*, in Hoadly, 2 p 408 (my italics).
[20] He opposed the use of the sacrament as a test for political office and was willing to extend civil as well as religious rights to dissenters in writings of 1718 and 1736: Hoadly, 2 pp 697, 971.
[21] *Literary Anecdotes of the Eighteenth Century*, ed J. Nichols, 9 vols (London 1812–16) 9, p 85; compare Calamy, 2 p 371.
[22] C. B. Macpherson, *The Political Theory of Possessive Individualism* (Oxford 1962).
[23] Even Norman Sykes as an apologist for latitudinarianism balked at Hoadly's theory of the church in several of his writings, for example in *Church and State [in England in the Eighteenth Century]* (Cambridge 1934) pp 293–4.

280

lying from both sides, and the truth is probably beyond recovery.[24] William Law claimed, however, that even with the qualifying words Hoadly's position still destroyed the church and much else besides.

Law concentrated on three points in particular. First, that to make 'sincerity' the sole criterion of religion not only destroys the anglican church but all organised society and indeed christianity itself. It implies that 'if a man be not a hypocrite, it matters not what religion he is of': persecutors, martyrs, muggletonians, turks, unbelievers are all equally acceptable to God.[25] Secondly, Law argues that to deny an 'absolute' authority in the church is to deny what the church has never claimed, for example in its power of absolution,[26] and that 'all your Lordship's arguments against Church authority conclude with the same force against all degrees of authority' and 'falls as heavy upon the State, and makes all civil government unlawful'.[27] In reality, 'though Church authority be not absolute in a certain sense, yet if our Saviour and His apostles had any authority, the Church may have a real authority: for neither He nor His Apostles had such an absolute authority, as excludes all consideration and examination, which is your notion of absolute authority' and this can be established by Hoadly's own favourite appeal to the evidence of scripture alone.[28] Thirdly, Law took up Hoadly's claim that he was not subverting church government because the description of the church in his sermon referred only to 'the universal invisible Church, made up of those, who do truly and sincerely in their hearts, which are not open to mortal eyes, believe in Jesus Christ' and not to the visible church or any particular part of it and its discipline.[29] This, said Law, is against scripture and the articles and is irrelevant to the main question at issue, which is 'whether external communion with fanatics be lawful? Whether it be as safe to be in one external visible communion as another?' Hoadly's 'invisible Church' is 'a mere speculative conjecture, a creature of the imagination', though Law had already conceded that 'There is, no doubt of it, an invisible church – i.e., the number of beings that are in covenant with God, who are not seen by mortal eyes; and we may be

[24] For Hoadly's version see Hoadly, 2 pp 429–47. G. V. Bennett, *White Kennett* (London 1957) pp 139–45 makes a tangled tale as clear as the material allows.

[25] *Ibid* p 50. Compare [F.] Hare, [*Church Authority Vindicated*] (London 1719) p 26.

[26] Law, 1 pp 5–7.

[27] Law, 1 pp 16–17, compare p 115 where Law sees Hoadly's doctrine as equally destructive of all social relationships.

[28] Law, 1 p 16; and for his interpretation of 'My kingdom is not of this world', pp 106–13.

[29] *Answer to the Representation* in Hoadly, 2 pp 452, 477, 478, 481.

said to be members of this invisible church, as we are entitled to the same hopes and expectations. But to call the number of men and women who believe in Christ and observe His institutions, whether dispersed or united in this visible world, to call these the invisible Church, is as false and groundless as to call them the order of angels, or the Church of the Seraphims'.[30]

In similar vein Francis Hare wrote that the 'invisibility' of the church is a 'mere fiction': 'the Church as spoken of in Scripture, is either a particular visible society, or the collection of them.' The church 'is invisible only by abstraction, and as such has no existence but in the mind of him who so thinks of it. Nor are the members of the church otherwise invisible, than as God alone, who only knows the hearts of men, can certainly distinguish between the serious professor and the hypocrite'.[31] John Rogers, in one of the soberest contributions to the controversy, acknowledged that there is an invisible church subject to Christ alone as ruler, and a visible society with powers of discipline. Both views can be held together if understood with 'proper restrictions', but represent 'one Catholic Church, one society, of which Christ is head: but the mind considering this society in different respects, distinguishes it under these two ideas of visible and invisible'. Elsewhere, replying to A. A. Sykes, he thought they agreed on the restricted effects of ecclesiastical penalties in relation to salvation, but argued more strongly than Sykes (or Tindal) for church discipline since 'this visible society must . . . agree with all other visible societies, in those general properties which are essential to a visible society as such' – in terms of a 'mutual compact'.[32]

Were Law's criticisms fair and valid? Despite Law's formidable wit and his ruthless use of the *reductio ad absurdum*, it can be argued that he was far from completely demolishing the points which Hoadly was trying to make, and that part of the trouble was that they were talking about different ideas while using the same terms (such as 'Church'). There is the additional difficulty, already mentioned, that Hoadly never wrote a direct reply to Law, but the substance of such a reply may be gathered from his replies to the convocation

---

[30] Law, 1 pp 103, 106, 90.

[31] Hare, p 32. The last point is similar to Law's admission and was taken up by Hoadly in *An Answer to the Rev Dr Hare's Sermon* (London 1720) in Hoadly, 2 pp 856-7.

[32] John Rogers, *A Discourse of the Visible and Invisible Church* (4 ed London 1720) preface and p 1; *A Review of a Discourse of the Visible and Invisible Church* (2 ed London 1722) pp 335, 425. The appeal to pragmatic rather than scriptural and traditional arguments is noteworthy.

committee, to Snape and to Hare who between them made all Law's main criticisms in their own fashion.

First, on the question of 'sincerity' as the basis of salvation. Misleading though the term may be, the intention of it is reasonably plain. Hoadly spoke in terms of christianity, not of any truth there might be in other religions or atheism. Within christianity, he was attempting to ensure toleration in the same way as Locke, by arguing that true religion cannot be created by external sanctions or persecution. 'To please God' wrote Locke, 'he needs faith and inward sincerity'.[33] Salvation, for Hoadly, does not depend on adherence to a particular communion or on the peculiar powers attributed to its priests, but on sincere faith in Christ; and true worship can only come from inward understanding and sincerity, not from 'flattery' or 'force'.[34]

Secondly, on the question of whether Hoadly had denied all authority in the church. He claimed that he had not done so, partly because he had constantly qualified all his statements with such words as 'properly' and 'absolutely',[35] but more importantly because his description of the church was only concerned with matters of 'conscience' and 'eternal salvation', and such a church (as we have seen) he described as 'invisible'. But (said Hoadly) this does not affect the existence and powers of 'visible' churches including the church of England. At this point Hoadly is undeniably vague: he says he does not deny any powers proper to a christian church and ministry, but he says little positive on what they are. The most important positive duty of bishops and clergy is to be 'guides' to Christ as the true ruler; they are not to make supernaturalist claims to hold the keys of salvation; and men are to be free to judge and respond to guidance as they will.[36] Leslie Stephen remarked that the conflict between Hoadly and his opponents was based partly on a misunderstanding: they thought he was distinguishing between ecclesiastical and civil legislation, whereas in fact he was distinguishing between the spheres of morality and legislation; even more to the point, that his arguments would have been more cogent had he attacked the 'supernatural' rather than the

[33] Locke pp 99–100.
[34] *A Preservative against the Principles and Practices of the Nonjurors* (London 1716) in Hoadly, 1 pp 592–3; *Answer to the Representation* in Hoadly, 2 pp 508–9.
[35] So did A. A. Sykes in *Some Remarks on Mr Marshall's Defence* (London 1717), quoted in Disney, pp 52–5.
[36] Hoadly, 2 pp 420–7, 465, 472–7, 485, 463. Compare Tindal, *Rights*, pp 23–4; and Locke, pp 73, 77, who saw the 'arms' of the church as 'exhortation, admonition and advice'.

'absolute' power of the priesthood both in matters of discipline and of doctrine.[37] For in fact Hoadly and Law differed fundamentally in their views of the function of the visible church in the economy of salvation. For Hoadly, in the last resort, it is not primary; salvation does not depend on the visible church, though it may be aided by it. 'As to external visible order . . . this was not the great end of Christ's descending from heaven . . . every thing of this sort, is but of a secondary nature; and of a very low account, in comparison with those great points, upon which our Lord declares that the eternal salvation of all shall equally depend'.[38] For Law a true church, divinely-based on apostolic succession to guarantee the sacraments, is essential for salvation. 'If there be no uninterrupted succession, then there are no authorised ministers from Christ; if no such ministers, then no Christian sacraments; if no Christian sacraments, then no Christian covenant, whereof the sacraments are the stated and visible seals'.[39] It will be seen that Law had replaced one extreme view of the link between the visible church and salvation with another.

Law's third criticism, about Hoadly's use of 'invisible' to describe the church, is less easy to assess than appears at first sight. It certainly looks as if Hoadly introduced it in his defences of the sermon to safeguard himself against the charge that he was destroying church government; but it is fair to say that the description of the church in the sermon was most adequate if taken to be referring to the inner reality of religion which alone guarantees salvation, and is equally applicable to 'sincere' christians of all denominations or none. We have seen that this is in line with the Locke type of argument for toleration; but while Hoadly clearly agreed with this, in the sermon he was using it mainly to justify an attack on highflying demands for independent clerical power in the church. Law conceded that one could speak of an 'invisible' church as a term for the truly saved, known only to God; so did Hare and Rogers, even if they thought this simply a way of viewing the one church from the speculative angle of ultimate salvation. What they, and above all Law, wished to assert, was that the church on earth is a visible community, with a stronger degree of discipline than Hoadly allowed; and that not all churches had those true ministries, discipline and sacraments which alone could ensure

---

[37] L. Stephen, *History of English Thought in the Eighteenth Century*, 2 vols (New York 1962) 2 pp 139, 145.
[38] *Answer to the Representation*, in Hoadly, 2 p 562.
[39] Law, 1 p 9.

salvation. Hoadly could fairly claim that he was not ruling out church government; and his answer to what Law claimed was the point at issue – 'whether it be as safe to be in one external visible communion as another?' – had to be that in the last resort it *was* as safe, at least if the communion was a christian one. Law obviously rejected this, but it is not self-evident that Hoadly's was an impossible belief for an anglican, however much Law might wish to think so. Law, indeed, professed to find it impossible to see how Hoadly could claim to be loyal to anglicanism[39a] – to which Hoadly might have retorted that this was a dangerous criticism for a non-juror to make; and it is noticeable that Law carefully avoids any discussion of independent ecclesiastical jurisdiction as related to the powers of the state.

Nevertheless, there are problems in Hoadly's position. If the 'invisible' church is simply a description of sincere, saving religion, the question still arises of the appropriate visible form of the church; and so far as anglicanism is concerned, the relationship of both invisible and visible churches to the idea of establishment. It is remarkable, in view of the struggles going on at the time between highfliers and the government, and all the theorising about independent church power, and the very nature of the church itself, how little is said about the justification of establishment as such. Hoadly avoided the most awkward questions by firmly keeping his church of true believers 'invisible'. Locke and Tindal made matters far more difficult for themselves on the question of establishment by describing what appeared to be the visible church in terms of a voluntary, gathered community; and by drawing a sharp distinction between the nature, ends and methods of church and state; so also did A. A. Sykes.[40]

Law and other high church opponents of Hoadly and his supporters were trying to defend, indeed to recall, an older, less individualistic, more hierarchical view of society, which for them was embodied in ecclesiastical as well as in secular institutions. Modified ideals of divine right monarchy and a paternalistic society still had force after the revolution[40a]; and they were closely paralleled in highflying views of episcopal authority and discipline, though Law argued for

---

[39a] *Ibid* p 7.

[40] Locke pp 85–7; Tindal, *Rights*, pp lxxxv, 16–17; A. A. Sykes quoted by Disney, p 45; compare J. Toland, *Nazarenus* (London 1718) letter 2, p 34. See discussion in [G. R.] Cragg, [*Reason and Authority in the Eighteenth Century*] (Cambridge 1964) cap 7.

[40a] G. Straka, 'The Final Phase of Divine Right Theory in England, 1688–1702', *EHR*, 77 (1962) pp 638–58.

episcopal authority in theological terms as the necessary authority behind the sacraments to guarantee salvation. Such a church was not voluntary and it was liable to oppose or at best only reluctantly and inconsistently to allow for religious toleration. But the highfliers' claims to independent ecclesiastical jurisdiction co-existed only uneasily with divine right, or with post-revolution kingship; or indeed with the course of much anglican history since the reformation, and Law noticeably glossed over this issue. On the other hand, an established church supported by a sympathetic magistrate, remained the conventional wisdom of the time, not only for social reasons, but also because it seemed to fit an exclusive, disciplined church better than a church seen as a voluntary society. The latitudinarian and deistic writers had in mind two main interests: those of toleration (inside and outside the establishment); and those of the state and individual christians against clerical government. To establish these interests they utilised a view of religion held in any case for other reasons; a view which put a premium on inwardness, sincerity, individualism and voluntary effort. This view of religion was closely parallel to their political theory of 'possessive individualism' and both for religion and civil society drove them to artificial views of the making of community in terms of voluntary contract. For the purposes of their main concerns in religion, they made a sharp division between the role of the individual privately making his religious choice; and the role of the magistrate who is mainly concerned with public order and the defence of 'property'. This left two vital middle terms unclear: the form and sanctions of the church as a visible collection of believers; and the state's establishment of a particular religion. Hoadly, as we have seen, blurred the issue by confining the church of true believers to the invisible realm; for the visible church he tacitly accepted the traditional disciplines and the establishment while reducing the church's sanctions to persuasion voluntarily accepted by the individual in a manner in fact more appropriate to a visible counterpart of his invisible company of believers. Locke and Tindal seemed to go further. They made little play with the 'invisible' concept and described the church and its sanctions in terms which seemed inexorably to lead to a voluntary church, hardly compatible with an establishment.

One way to make sense of all this would be to say that these writers had three things in mind. First: true, sincere, inward religion; an individual adherence to Christ which some of them denoted by the symbol of the 'invisible' church. Secondly: the 'visible' church (or rather churches), which is a symbol for voluntary fellowships of otherwise 'invisible' christians who find they wish for various purposes to set up such communities. These societies allow for discipline but only on the general lines of Locke's 'contract' (with all the problems of historical reality and the way in which society actually functions, which this entails). But here it must be added that the coherence of this church and the powers of ecclesiastical rulers are very much less than those of the lockeian state which only allows rebellion and secession as a rare, last resort. Thirdly, the established church poses peculiar problems. Hoadly allows that it may be 'lawful and prudent for a legislature to establish a Church' yet it must only use 'penalties agreeable to the Christian religion' or 'to the ends of that civil government, which thinks fit to establish this Christian Church'.[41] Locke does not discuss the question directly, but his sharp distinction between the concerns of the magistrate and those of religion, so as to maintain toleration, allows for the fact that 'no doctrines, incompatible with human society, and contrary to the good morals which are necessary for the preservation of civil society are to be tolerated by the magistrate'.[42] Hence his denial of toleration to atheists and roman catholics, which he claims is not on grounds of religion but of social order. It might be argued, then, that establishment of a church is less for religious than for social purposes. Tindal uses the same argument. While he can bluntly write that 'the Church of England, which being established by Act of Parliament, is a perfect creature of the civil power; I mean the polity and discipline of it', he modifies this by saying that while 'the magistrate has all in religious matters which man is capable of, I do not design to carry this power so far as to make void the principle on which the Reformation is built, viz. the right everyone has of judging for himself, and of acting according to his judgment in all those things which relate only to God and his own conscience.' The magistrate's power is simply to punish good and evil for the sake of society, hence he can punish atheism and blasphemy which undermine good order; he can punish offences against God when they affect the duties to God 'which have an influence on human life, and conduce to the welfare and support of societies'. And he actually criticises magistrates for 'establishing their religion and Church by law' if this means 'annexing properties and privileges to the teachers of his own religion' and taking away men's natural rights of judging

[41] Hoadly, 2 pp 990, 508–9; compare 775–80.
[42] Locke pp 131–5.

for themselves in religion.[43] Established churches, then, seem to be largely for social purposes. Within them the members of the visible and invisible churches subsist as far as they voluntarily choose to be members. Such an establishment must be broad and undemanding in its dogmatic demands, and allow for the existence of other invisible true christians organised in visible voluntary churches outside it. Even some of the social functions of the church may be performed by these christians; and all are subject, but only for social ends, to the magistrate.

Such a picture is doubtless confusing, inconsistent, and awkward to reconcile with the reality of the eighteenth century establishment. Yet Law's picture of the church could also be criticised on these grounds. The explanation lies in the political but also the social confusion which afflicted the anglican church after the revolution.

From the point of view of political theory, Vereker has described this attempt to combine a 'voluntaryist' view of the church together with establishment as a 'divorce' theory: that is, an acceptance of traditional christian themes but not as part of a total christianised conception of the world. In this situation one conceives of a secular state and society with a theory to match; and, separately from this, the idea of membership of an invisible church concerned with a kingdom 'not of this world'. 'Church and State' he says 'become parallel disconnected institutions, the one held mystically together by faith and sincerity, the other depending on contract and compulsion'. The earlier, medieval view followed from the incarnation – the church is incarnate in society; there is a real union but separate identity of the partners. In the eighteenth century with a changing theology the corporate effort of the church in redemption was in effect transferred to a secular body as appropriate to a secular conception of a 'redeeming' society for which the church's means were not appropriate.[44] There are obvious attractions in this view, though it does not adequately bring out either the inconsistencies and blindness to some of the consequences of their views in the writers concerned, or the complicated compromises which marked the life of the eighteenth century church.

The anglican church between 1688 and 1714 (and indeed later) was undergoing what might fairly be termed a crisis of identity, certainly

[43] Tindal, *Rights*, pp v, lxxxv, 11–12, 16–17; *Of the Power of the Magistrate and the Rights of Mankind* (London 1697), reprinted in *Four Discourses* (London 1709) pp 132–3; *Rights*, p 25.
[44] C. H. Vereker, *Eighteenth Century Optimism* (Liverpool 1967) pp 18–22, 91–6.

a crisis of authority at several levels of theory and practice.[45] If the revolution did not immediately end divine right theory it certainly plunged it, with its corollaries of passive obedience and non-resistance, into almost hopeless confusion. The agony of conscience which churchmen of all schools of thought had to undergo as a result, helps to explain the peculiar, often hysterical ferocity of ecclesiastical conflict in the period. The problems of anglicans were worsened by the recognition, however incomplete, of the legality of dissent; and by the open advocacy of socinianism and deism, especially after the lapse of the licensing act in 1695. Nor were their problems simply ideological. The dissenting threat had important political and social dimensions; the clergy's status, self-esteem and ability to perform their social role were weakened by taxation, anti-clericalism and gibes at their low social standing. Rightly or wrongly, they felt the nation was passing through a moral crisis in which the church's traditional sanctions for religious and social discipline were becoming ineffective. In some cases the parochial system seemed to be breaking down in face of local population growth and the rivalry of dissent, in a way which almost foreshadows the much graver crisis of the early nineteenth century. As Holmes has pointed out, the toleration act by itself meant that the established church lost some of the major benefits of establishment without the corresponding gains which would have (or might have) accrued from total disestablishment.[46]

The party warfare of these years in the church reflected, amongst much else, two incompatible solutions to the church's problems.[47] What may be termed, roughly, the high church solution was based on a yearning after the closest possible return to the pre-1688 situation when church and state worked in harmony within a regime of uniformity and unquestioning obedience to authority; and on a reliance on the traditional expedient of political means to restore the status quo; for example, by politically-backed enforcement of the canons and discipline of the church. In opposition to this, a 'low church' minority saw the best hope for the church in acceptance of two unpleasant truths: that the church had only survived in 1688 by turning its back on its old political principles; and that in 1689 it had, in effect, been partially disestablished. Hence, instead of looking to the

---

[45] For what follows it will be obvious that I am indebted to *Britain after the Glorious Revolution* [1689–1714], ed G. Holmes (London 1969); and to his [*The Trial of*] *Doctor Sacheverell* (London 1973) cap 1.

[46] G. Holmes in *Britain after the Glorious Revolution*, p 26.

[47] G. Holmes, *Doctor Sacheverell*, p 32.

state it should 'accept the place in English society of a basically voluntary body working within the legal conditions of the Establishment'.[48] It should allow some latitude within its own pale; welcome toleration; and seek to re-establish the church's declining influence not by political activity nor the revival of ancient claims, but by furthering its social mission, practical and congregational work, and charity. This would entail more reliance on voluntary organisations and on the laity. In this sense, at least, the revolution had an indirect effect on social change, even if one hesitates to accept the notion of a 'moral revolution' in 1688 as applied to societies for the reformation of manners.[49]

The distinction between the two policies and their identification with high and low churchmen must not be pressed too hard; and certainly the eighteenth century church as a whole did not unambiguously follow either course. The establishment survived; the 'alliance' of church and state continued, though on partially altered terms; the establishment continued to be important for social welfare and control in view of the sparseness of state intervention, though voluntary lay agencies became increasingly important and multiplied when, at the end of the century, a more fundamental crisis began to afflict the church.

To return, finally, to Hoadly. Obviously he does not fit very neatly into either of the two policies offered to the church. He was hardly the type of low churchman to be held up as an exemplar or even advocate of parochial care, voluntaryist effort, moral reform. He fits all too easily into the category of 'political bishop' pure and simple. Yet in the Bangorian controversy can be seen, at least at the theoretical level, a stark clash between some aspects of the two opposed ways of viewing the church after 1688. Hesitantly and inconsistently in Hoadly, more radically in Locke and Tindal, we can see emerging the elements of a rationale for a 'voluntaryist' church as against the more traditionalist view of Law. Of Hoadly's sermon Norman Sykes remarked, with some justice, that it related less directly than some of his earlier writings to the immediate political and religious issues of the revolution, notably to the relationship between the non-jurors and the state. 'The practical choice lay' (wrote Sykes) 'not between a society

---

[48] G. V. Bennett in *Britain after the Glorious Revolution*, p 165.

[49] D. W. R. Bahlman, *The Moral Revolution of 1688* (Yale 1957). Although he sees the societies as filling a gap left by church and state (p 107) it is significant that on their failure the lay magistrates took over prosecutions.

divested of all authority in accordance with the Bangor Sermon, and a *societas perfecta* demanding entire freedom of action in spiritual matters from the State, but between the establishment as menaced by the actual policy of James II and as safeguarded by the provisions of the revolution settlement that the ruling monarch must always be in communion with it'.[50] The fact remains that if neither Law's nor Hoadly's views were acceptable as a justification for the new situation in the church, other apologists, including the redoubtable Warburton of the 'Alliance' could not make complete sense of the situation either.[51] Hoadly's influence, indeed, lived on – or at least views closely resembling his on the nature of the church, 'sincerity', and of course dislike of priestly pretensions, seem to be recurring features of lay religion.[52] Here long-standing erastian prejudices in the laity combined with a persistent suspicion that real religion is inward and individual to the point of creating a new theology of the church.

University of Manchester

[50] N. Sykes, *Church and State*, p 294. He thought Hoadly's doctrine of the church a 'veritable kingdom of fairies', presumably echoing Thomas Hobbes.
[51] W. Warburton, *The Alliance between Church and State* (London 1736). See R. W. Greaves, 'The Working of the Alliance' in *Essays in Modern English Church History* ed G. V. Bennett and J. D. Walsh (London 1966) pp 163–80 for an admirable analysis of how imperfectly Warburton's theory fitted the actual working of the church.
[52] Thomas Chubb the deist on the church in *Miscellaneous Tracts* (London 1730) pp 185, 201 practically quotes Hoadly. Similar language about the 'Kingdom of Christ' is frequently found (examples in Cragg, pp 194, 210–12). Lord Carteret shocked lord Egmont by saying that parliament 'might as well appoint priests to the office of bishop': *Egmont Diary*, HMC, 3 vols (London 1920–3) I, pp 106–7. Henry Venn the evangelical severely criticised contemporary 'sincerity' ideas in relation to salvation: *The Complete Duty of Man* (new ed London no date) p xxix (preface written in 1763).

A COLONIAL CONCORDAT:
TWO VIEWS OF CHRISTIANITY
AND CIVILISATION

by A. F. WALLS

SIERRA LEONE began as an explicitly christian colony, and as an overwhelmingly african one. The 1100 immigrants of african descent who effectively took over Granville Sharp's 'Province of Freedom' were as much children of the evangelical revival as the Clapham philanthropists who planned and financed the settlement. They brought other transatlantic imports to Africa besides evangelical religion; a material culture based on that of the plantation states where most of them had once lived (so they built their houses in the 'colonial' style, wore european clothes and spoke english) and radical political reflexes which came to be hardened and sharpened by the settled sense of grievance, first in Nova Scotia and then in Sierra Leone.[1]

The original colony, however, was transformed at the point of what seemed its unrelieved failure, by the success of one of the better known schemes of the men of Clapham. The act abolishing british participation in the slave trade in 1807, and the obligations gradually acknowledged for enforcing and policing these and similar measures, led to the crown relieving the private Clapham-sponsored company of the responsibility for the settlement. It also meant that such slave ships as were intercepted by the Navy were brought into Freetown's magnificent harbour and their unfortunate cargoes of slaves – uprooted, demoralised people, disorientated and often in poor physical shape from the conditions of their passage – put ashore to begin a new life in Sierra Leone.

Sierra Leone was now a crown colony; but the arrival of the new

---

[1] On the whole period covered by this article see [C.] Fyfe, [A History of Sierra Leone] (London 1962); and for an interpretation of the forces at work in Sierra Leone in the period of the settlement of the recaptives, [J.] Peterson, [Province of Freedom: a History of Sierra Leone 1787–1870] (London 1969). On the religious significance of the Nova Scotia settlers, see [A. F.] Walls, ['A Christian Experiment: the early Sierra Leone colony'], in The Mission of the Church and the Propagation of the Faith, SCH 6 (1970) pp 107–29.

population reinforced, rather than replaced, the former raison d'être of the settlement as a province of freedom for former slaves and a beacon light of christian civilisation in Africa.[2] Nor did it break at once the connexion with 'the saints': Clapham continued for many years to take an interest, sometimes a crucial one, in matters affecting the colony. The first expedient adopted for settling the newcomers, 'apprenticeship' to existing settlers, was clearly inadequate, once it began to dawn that the new population would soon vastly outnumber the old; but it was symbolic of the assumption that underlay the whole venture: that the only viable future for the recaptives lay in assimilation to certain european norms which the nova scotian african settlers already represented. If one word could sum up this assimilation, it was 'civilisation'.[3]

'Civilisation' was also the watchword of colonel, later Sir, Charles MacCarthy, one of the most remarkable colonial servants of the nineteenth century, and probably the most remarkable never to have had a full biography. He became governor in 1814, when the administration of the colony had become the topic of unpleasant public controversy in Britain. He was to remain for ten years, in which it was his peculiar talent to persuade a government bent on cutting expenditure to spend vastly more than most people ever believed an african colony was worth. For our purpose it is noteworthy that he was one of the authors of a concordat which underlay the first major success of the modern missionary movement.

His personal story is a curious one.[4] He was from a french emigré family: MacCarthy was the name of his irish mother. By origin and upbringing he was a roman catholic; and as his will indicates, the church of his origin retained his deepest convictions. But when he entered the king's service, he accepted the king's religion and all the consequences. This tells us something about his attitudes; he is an establishment man, and a soldier, with a very clear idea of where his duty lies, and an acceptance of the alliance of religion and duty. But he is not greatly concerned about doctrinal questions, and apt to be impatient, if not suspicious, when they are urged in the way of what he takes to be the job in hand. It accords with his sense of the fitness of things if the job in hand is carried out by members of the national

[2] See Peterson p 13.
[3] See CMS Archives CA 1 E5, Kenneth Macaulay to Zachary Macaulay 25 September 1815: 'The captured negroes and other natives do no doubt get polished by their constant intercourse with the former settlers.'
[4] See Fyfe p 124.

church, but he has no idea of any theological necessity in this. If he cannot get them, he will have methodists or anyone else who will do the job; accordingly his regular, and most potent, method of bullying the Church Missionary Society was to threaten that if they did not supply the men he wanted, he would ask someone else. For the rest, he is, as he put it to a missionary whom he esteemed highly, 'a worldly man'[5] by which he probably meant that he made no claim to more than perfunctory piety, that he allowed his temper and language to reflect the privilege of his rank,[6] and that he kept a mistress whom his position would not allow him to marry;[7] a worldly man who is neither sceptical nor cynical about religion; who respects higher piety and virtue than he has himself attained wherever he meets them, and who sees the acid test of piety to be its practical effects.

MacCarthy devoted his considerable energies to the task which he describes as the 'civilisation' of the recaptives. We should remember that their actual position was deplorable: they had lost their homeland, their society, their cohesion; effectively, they had lost their past. The arrivals of the earlier years, before sheer numbers gave the Yoruba a certain cultural dominance, reflected a wide variety of peoples all the way from Senegal to the Congo, a profusion of languages, backgrounds and cultures, none of them native to the area where they now were settled. The only identity possible for the recaptives was a new identity: MacCarthy gave them that, and in doing so, gave a decisive shape not only to west african, but to christian, history.

MacCarthy sought to have the ungainly human dumping grounds around the outskirts of Freetown[8] transformed into genuine village communities. Edward Ferrars of *Sense and Sensibility* – published three years before MacCarthy became governor – was, it may be remembered, better pleased by a troop of tidy, happy villagers than by the finest banditti in the world,[9] and it was MacCarthy's aim to make the

---

[5] MacCarthy to William Davies, Paris, 28 February 1821, printed in appendix to [*Extracts from the Journal of William*] *Davies,* [*1st, when a missionary at Sierra Leone*] (Llanidloes, preface dated 1835).

[6] See [Major] Ricketts, *Narrative of the Ashantee War* (London 1831) p 58: 'if [the superintendent of ordnance] had not suddenly disappeared . . . it is probable that if Sir Charles had had the means at the moment, he would have put his threat into execution of suspending him to a tree.'

[7] See Fyfe p 147.

[8] Three settlements outside Freetown – Leicester, Wilberforce and Hogbrook (renamed Regent's Town by MacCarthy) antedated MacCarthy's arrival. MacCarthy reorganised them and created ten more.

[9] Jane Austen, *Sense and Sensibility* cap 17.

broken humanity of the slave-ships into tidy, happy villagers of a sort miss Austen herself would recognise. And the means is miss Austen's means: the village clergyman, teaching men their duty, a duty which embraces all the relations of life, and produces happiness and every beneficent influence. Habits of industry, temperance, decent homes and better tended gardens would result.[10]

I have explained . . . my views as to the means most likely to forward the Civilization of Africa, more particularly of the Colony and of the numerous classes of captured Negroes who under the Blessing of Providence are indebted for their emancipation from a cruel slavery to Great Britain only.

I conceive that the first effectual step towards the establishment of Christianity will be found in the Division of this peninsula into Parishes, appointing to each a Clergyman to instruct their flock in Christianity, enlightening their minds to the various duties and advantages inherent to [sic] civilization – thus making Sierra Leone the base from whence future exertions may be extended, step by step to the very interior of Africa.[11]

It will be observed that MacCarthy here uses the words civilisation and christianity interchangeably. It is also characteristic that this letter concludes 'I am thoroughly convinced that in doing all I can to promote [this] I shall not only follow the line of my duty, but adhere most strongly to the benevolent wishes of His Royal Highness towards Africa'.

Whatever wishes the first gentleman of Europe may have had for Sierra Leone, the letter here quoted was to the CMS, and is intended as an explicit request that the society find and set aside the clergyman for each of these parishes. The idea was not new in his mind: MacCarthy's greatest disability was ever the chronic shortage of competent and dedicated people to oversee the settlements, and early he seems to have concluded that the most suitable people for the task would be clergymen;[12] despite the fact that, as no one knew better than he, the task required a variety of gifts, and, above all, administrative

---

[10] I have often heard him observing, after coming into my house, 'Davies, such and such a man, that lives in such a house, is one of your members, is he not?' 'How does your Excellency know?' 'Why, he has white-washed his house, his fence around the premises is good, his garden is clean and productive.' 'Your Excellency is right – he is a member, and Christianity alone can civilize: for godliness is profitable for all things, and when they get religion they will be industrious'. Davies, p 53.

[11] CMS Archives CA 1 E5, MacCarthy to Pratt, 15 June 1816.

[12] See CMS Archives CA 1 E5/71, MacCarthy to Pratt.

competence. But MacCarthy firmly links the material culture and pattern of civic order of his idea of civilisation, with its doctrinal and religious undergirding: and is happiest if the two are in the same hands. When the wesleyan missionary, William Davies, whom he had already made an alderman of Freetown, was ejected from his pastoral charge by the nova scotian methodists, MacCarthy at once snapped him up and put him in charge of the village of Leopold.[13]

Though west Africa had been the scene of the first operations of the CMS,[14] the Sierra Leone colony was little more than a supply base for the mission in Susu country, far beyond its borders. MacCarthy was always scathing about the Susu mission, holding it an unmitigated waste of time and manpower: what was the use of a school in the bush where nobody wanted the product on offer and where any converts among the children could never hope to withstand the pressures of tradition when they returned home? When the mission church is burned down, he can hardly conceal the glee in his condolences to the CMS as he dilates on the desirability of their transferring their operations to the colony, where no-one would be allowed to burn down their property and where they would have crowds of people eager to be taught.[15] The need of clergymen in the colony was also being urged by Kenneth Macaulay, Zachary's nephew, who traded in Freetown in a big way and who feared a methodist takeover with consequent incitement to civil disobedience.[16] At least one of the CMS missionaries – albeit one in whom the committee were for ever detecting 'a proud and independent spirit', so much so that Josiah Pratt once burst out, 'Is this man a Christian?'[17] – had argued for CMS to enter co-operation with government in the matter of 'the instruction' as it was called, of the recaptives.[18] In 1816 the CMS sent its first official deputation to west Africa, in the person of Edward Bickersteth, whose dispatches from Sierra Leone stress the need for effort to be concentrated on the colony, where he held they could use

[13] On Davies' ejection, see Walls. His period as superintendent at Leopold is only minimally reflected in the methodist missionary society archives, which hold his letters from Freetown, but is documented in the 1835 *memoir*.

[14] At the beginning of those operations known as 'The Society for Missions to Africa and the East.'

[15] CMS Archives CA 1 5E/71, MacCarthy to Pratt.

[16] *Ibid* Kenneth to Zachary Macaulay, 25 September 1815. Zachary Macaulay sent the letter on to CMS.

[17] *Ibid* Pratt to Garnon, 9 April 1817. The missionary in question was Leopold Butscher, 'a good man', as Garnon replied.

[18] See Peterson pp 67 *et seq.*

fifty missionaries and schoolmasters.[19] MacCarthy was delighted that
the visitor was seeing sense. Still better was it when CMS had a letter
from him printed in the *Missionary Register* with an indication that they
intended to act on it.[20]

When it came to the point CMS did accept the principle of what
MacCarthy wanted: they would appoint a clergyman and a schoolmaster for each village: Bickersteth had talked about a dozen men.[21]
And the colonial government would pay salaries[22] and MacCarthy had
already demonstrated his readiness to build churches. But for a long
time, CMS would not accept that this implied the closure of the
Susu mission. Too much had already been spent on the Susu mission;
so they proceeded to spend more. And the twelve men spoken of did
not immediately come: until the Susu mission was closed, there was
little hope of their doing so, and MacCarthy was not assuaged by talk
of three men being in training.[23] He blasted the hapless colonial
chaplain, who had evidently offered him the latest issue of the
Missionary Register, saying that there was no point in reading
the religious lies of people who had no intention of performing
what they promised, that Bickersteth got his facts wrong, and
that this was typical of people who never listened to informed
advice.[24]

In the end, the CMS were forced to close – temporarily, they hoped –
the Susu mission. Even so, the shortage of candidates, especially such
as were, or could be, ordained, and the high mortality among them,
meant that the ideal of the parson and the schoolmaster for each
parish was never realised: it was cause for rejoicing when one of
those functionaries could be supplied.[25] Meanwhile, CMS officials,

[19] CMS Archives CA 1 E5, Bickersteth to Pratt, 20 April 1816.
[20] *Missionary Register* July 1816.
[21] William Garnon, while deprecating MacCarthy's complaints about CMS
dilatoriness, urged the sending out of Bickersteth's twelve instead of a reply to his
letter. CMS Archives CA 1 E5A, Garnon to Pratt, 28 October 1816.
[22] In the private notes for Bickersteth, made prior to his visit, (CMS Archives
CA 1 E5/141) Pratt indicated 'The Society will undertake to supply all the required
teachers if it can retain reasonable control over them,' and outlined a scheme
whereby teachers appointed to the government would be regarded as connected
with the society, and their salaries paid through the society. A much smaller scale
affair than the parish system, was, of course, envisaged.
[23] CMS Archives CA 1 E5, Pratt to MacCarthy, 11 November 1816.
[24] CMS Archives CA 1 E5A, Garnon to Pratt, 28 October 1816.
[25] See A. F. Walls, 'Missionary Vocation and the Ministry: the first generation' in
New Testament Christianity for Africa and the World: Essays in honour of Harry Sawyerr,
ed M. E. Glasswell and E. W. Fashole-Luke (London 1974).

Two views of christianity and civilisation

facing a combination of increased commitments and economic recession, took MacCarthy's reactions very ill. Had it not been for their good offices in London, Pratt grumbled, the MacCarthy plan would never have got official approval, and for that matter, the british public would have been unlikely ever to hear much to the praise of Sir Charles MacCarthy were it not for the favourable notices he received in 'our numerous publications.'[26]

But there were strains of another sort in the concordat when it came to its practical outworking: and these arose from the way in which missionaries saw their vocation.

MacCarthy's ideal for his villages differed from the english prototype at one vital point: there was no squire, no resident landowner. The superintendent was judge and magistrate, town planner and master-builder, storekeeper and book keeper; he had to see to the making of bricks and the erection of woodwork, whether anyone had taught him such things or no: and then he had to keep school and evangelise the flock. When one adds the shadow of death, the fact that super-intendents were often sick and hardly ever well, it is hardly surprising that many felt the strain too great. There are plenty of complaints from missionaries that the pressures of 'secular' business left them no time or strength to attend to their missionary calling, or that their magisterial duties were incompatible with that of commending the gospel.[27] Not surprisingly the complaints are loudest from those who were not very good at secular business; but CMS undoubtedly began to fear for some whose pastoral and evangelistic concern flagged,[28] and one or two who were all too clearly finding their escape according to the most ancient convention.[29]

But some missionaries saw no more dichotomy between the tasks of the superintendency and their missionary vocation than did MacCarthy himself; and indeed, it is easy to see how one aspect of the work could support the other.[30] W. A. B. Johnson, though not a man

[26] CMS Archives CA I E5A, Pratt to Garnon, 9 April 1817.
[27] CA I E5, Wenzel to Pratt, 21 June 1816, and Pratt's reply *ibid* 2 November 1816. See CA I E7A Nylander to Bickersteth, 3 March 1819, and Peterson pp 132–5.
[28] CA I E5A, Pratt to Garnon, 9 April 1817.
[29] The sad decline of C. F. Wenzel is evident: see, for example, *ibid* Garnon to Pratt 28 October 1816.
[30] Near contemporaries and later writers have pointed to Johnson's magisterial powers as part of the secret of his missionary success (see Fyfe p 129, Peterson pp 116 *et seq.* and writers quoted) but it must be noticed that the experience of Wenzel and Nylander, quoted above, was that magisterial functions militated *against* missionary effectiveness.

of distinguished formal accomplishments[31] was clearly a most competent superintendent in MacCarthy's eyes as well as being a splendid missionary in the view of CMS. MacCarthy, though he often quarrelled with Johnson, gave him everything he needed for his church, and heaped upon him additional duties, often taken away from less capable missionaries, duties which Johnson invariably shouldered. And yet it is Johnson above all who shows that governor and missionary were not always at one in their understanding of the relation of christianity and civilisation.

It emerges most clearly over the question of baptism. In a civilised country as MacCarthy knows it, all are baptised, go to church (or at least *ought* to go to church) and learn their christian duty there. Johnson, a man who had known an agonising spiritual quest, a man in whom lutheran and moravian influences had been overlaid with Pell Street calvinism on the doctrine of grace, is looking for the evangelical progress of conviction of sin, mourning, personal trust, and assurance of forgiveness – for radical conversion, in fact, as a fruit of his preaching. And, despite his undoubted labours for the transformation of society, he regards little of what he is doing as of lasting value till he sees this; and indeed often doubted his missionary vocation in the months when he did not see it.

In the end he did see it – and indeed, with all the marks of a classical revival. But, with his packed church and overflowing prayer meetings, he still insists that a credible profession of belief must be given, credibility resting on demonstration of the marks of regeneration. MacCarthy resolved to have a quiet word with him:

His Excellency the Governor came here today. He led the conversation while we were in the garden to baptism. He wished I would baptize more people. I told him that I could not, unless God first baptised their hearts. He said that the reason so many were baptised on the Day of Pentecost was that the Apostles despised none. I replied that they were pricked in the heart, and that I was willing to baptise all that were thus pricked in the heart. He thought baptism an act of civilization, and that it was our duty to make them all Christians. He spoke in great warmth about these things, and I endeavoured to show him through Scripture

[31] He was a hanoverian, who had worked in a distillery and a sugar refinery in London. See [W. Jowett,] *Memoir [of the Rev. W. A. B.] Johnson* (London 1852). Nevertheless, though he says he did not understand english very well in 1812, he was writing it very effectively by 1816, and he was recognized as the best qualified of the three teachers sent out then, CA 1 E5/23.

passages the contrary. He gave it up at last; calling me and the society a set of fanatics . . .[32]

Some months later, MacCarthy tried again.

The Governor said a great deal about baptising all the people, which I refused. He said much about its necessity, but I kept to the word of God. He said that the Apostles, on Pentecost day, baptised 3000 at once. I replied that they were pricked in their hearts, and *as many as believed* were baptized . . . He could not answer this, but said that he would write to the Archbishop of Canterbury concerning the matter . . . and would send those refused to Mr Davies, for he thought Mr Davies' baptism as good as ours.[33]

MacCarthy probably recognised that indiscriminate baptism was impossible: but it worries him that *civilised* men, people who have accepted assimilation to european modes, should be turned away: it is a threat to his whole strategy of offering the advantages of civilisation. It is dividing the community, just where he wanted to unite it. So when this pigheaded missionary refuses to baptise without evidence of conversion, he concludes there must be bad theology somewhere. On getting the worst of a scriptural argument with the missionary, his professional instinct is to refer to higher authority. It would no doubt have puzzled the military man still further to realize that if the archbishop of Canterbury ever got his letter, he would be quite unable to do anything about it.

The church of Regent, by which these altercations took place, still stands, and largely as MacCarthy and Johnson left it. As if in witness to the concordat, it is now St Charles' Church; and its patron is not Charles Borromeo, nor Charles the Martyr, but Charles MacCarthy. The concordat, so perpetually under strain throughout its existence, barely outlasted MacCarthy's governorship. But it was enough to shape the future. The recaptives found their new identity, developed their own distinctive krio culture, and did so as a self-consciously christian community. Sierra Leone saw the first real success story of the modern missionary movement, the first sign of a mass movement towards the christian faith. The recaptives would be as

---

[32] Johnson, *Memoir* 94.

[33] *Ibid* p 125. Mr Davies was, of course, a wesleyan. Baptism was not the only matter where Johnson recognised an absolutism other than the governor's. He refused, for instance, to encourage the singing of 'God Save the King', on the ground that it was customarily sung over a beerpot, while fully agreeing with a perplexed MacCarthy that 'Honour the King' was an apostolic injunction, *ibid*.

incapable as their european contemporaries of distinguishing between the strictly 'religious' and the strictly 'secular' element in the package they were offered: but the nature of the part the 'Black Europeans' were to play, not only as the great acculturators of west Africa, but as its evangelists, suggests that the understandings of the relation of christianity and civilisation, and the imperatives behind them, among europeans had their analogue in african experience. The crucifixion of the catechist Moses Osoko is as much a witness to one, as his clerical umbrella is to the other.

University of Aberdeen

ALESSANDRO GAVAZZI: A BARNABITE FRIAR AND THE RISORGIMENTO (PRESIDENTIAL ADDRESS)

by BASIL HALL

Think now
History has many cunning passages, contrived corridors
And issues, deceives with whispering ambitions,
Guides us by vanities. Think now
She gives when our attention is distracted
And what she gives, gives with such supple confusions
That the giving famishes the craving. Gives too late
What's not believed in, or if still believed,
In memory only, reconsidered passion.[1]

ISTORIANS no doubt have problems enough without setting before themselves that 'memento mori' from Eliot, who, though he was describing an old man seeking to understand his own past, leaves nevertheless an echo in the mind disturbing to those who practise the historian's craft. We assume a confidence which in our heart of hearts we do not always, or should not always, possess. Eliot's words not only demonstrate the difficulty of one man understanding his own past, but also the historian's difficulty in understanding those whom they select for questioning from among the vast multitudes of the silent dead, whose deeds, artifacts, ideas, passions, hopes and memories have died with them. We dig into the past, obtain data from archives, brush off the objects found, collect statistics, annotate, arrange, describe, establish a chronology – but do we effectively understand the dead, especially since we are affected by our own beliefs, customs and ideologies? We are, of course, all aware of this: we silently scorn the lecturer who raises these diffident hesitations. For we know our duty: we examine all that we can, we describe our findings, we annotate them, we draw conclusions, or leave our demonstrations to speak for themselves. There are reasons, as I shall hope to show, that these considerations – Eliot's ominous words and our determination not to

[1] *The Complete Poems and Plays of T. S. Eliot*, (London 1969). *Gerontion*, p 38.

be disquieted by them – bear upon the subject of this paper, the almost forgotten Alessandro Gavazzi.

To collect materials for an account of the life and work of Alessandro Gavazzi is not difficult, though I had a major setback in a visit to Rome in not being able to find his manuscript autobiography;[2] and another in reading through a large collection made for Gavazzi of tiresomely repetitive close-printed newspaper cuttings from British newspapers of his rhetorical speeches, for many of them did not show their source or date.[3] Moreover, these cuttings could reduce him to the level of that anti-papal oratory popular in English-speaking victorian protestantism, and therefore to being not worth much more than a footnote in a volume of Dessain's full edition, still in progress, of Newman's letters and journals – and he may not even attain that

[2] A full description of this manuscript *Autobiografia* is given by Robert Sylvain, pp 517–18 of the second volume of his biography of Gavazzi (see n 23 below). [Armando] Lodolini had described the manuscript earlier in his [*Contributo alla biografia del Padre Alessandro Gavazzi*] *Rassegna storico del Risorgimento*, 43 (Rome 1956) pp 434–48. Extracts have been published by [Giorgio] Cencetti, [*Alcune pagine dell'autobiografia del P. Alessandro Gavazzi*], *Atti e Memorie della Deputazione di Storia patria per le Provincie di Romagna*, Nuova Serie 1 (Rome 1948), pp 153–73. I have used these extracts, the only original text available to me, as well as occasional and translated paragraphs in Sylvain's biography of Gavazzi, in this paper. I visited Rome in 1974 in order to see this manuscript autobiography and other materials concerning Gavazzi, which since 1950 had been in a permanent exhibition *Mostra didascalia* at the Archivio di Stato di Roma, Palazzo della Sapienza. I was told that it was unavailable since a process of centralising all archives was being undertaken by the city authorities. I inquired about a copy of the manuscript in the possession of G. Conti, a close relation of the Conti who had known and written the last and uncritical biography of Gavazzi, but I was told 'it was impossible to read the handwriting' and I could not gain admission to Sig. Conti. Judging by the extracts given by Cencetti, and Sylvain's translated citations, the autobiography should be a work of considerable importance for the history of the risorgimento, as well as the religious history of the nineteenth century in England and elsewhere as well as in Italy. Sylvain rightly describes it as strange that it remains unpublished, refers to it as 'ce précieux manuscrit', and states that 'les faits sont-ils indiqués avec suffisamment de précision et d'honnêteté: on n'y surprend jamais Gavazzi falsifiant une circonstance biografique ou historique. Nous avons vérifiée, toutes les fois que nous l'avons pu, l'exactitude de son récit par la comparaison avec des renseignements venant d'autres sources. Or ces recoupements ont toujours confirmé la véracité du mémorialiste'. This is the more significant since it is the judgment of a roman catholic historian, who is justifiably distressed by Gavazzi's 'excès de plume . . . par tirades d'injures à l'adresse de ses anciens confrères et de ces coreligionnaires de jadis . . .'

[3] These are in eight octavo volumes: there is also a quarto volume of cuttings called *Memorie* (as well as published works by Gavazzi in italian) in the library of the Facoltà Valdese di Teologia, Roma. These collections appear to have been made by Gavazzi himself, or those who acted from time to time as his secretaries. The closely printed cuttings are trying to read, and are accompanied often by not much more than a date.

Alessandro Gavazzi: a barnabite friar and the risorgimento

memorial. But those newspaper records do not show what Eliot called 'reconsidered passion', that passionate intensity with which Gavazzi was involved in the risorgimento in the period leading to the brief roman republic and its downfall. What they show is his talent for noisy and gesticulatory declamation. They do not demonstrate why he was adored by catholic crowds as the 'Savonarola of the piazzas' in the forties, and why he was still a useful supporter of Garibaldi's renewed attacks in Italy in the sixties when Gavazzi's vigorous speeches as a returned exile roused enthusiastic *vivas* from Naples to Venice.

If the historiography of the italian risorgimento is full of 'cunning passages' and 'contrived corridors' and 'supple confusions' not least because the literature is vast (autobiographies, diaries, letters, as well as materials in military, municipal and ecclesiastical archives) and discussion of it still arouses deep and bitter controversy in Italy.[4] Walter Maturi's book *Interpretazioni del Risorgimento* gives brief extracts and analyses from over fifty works from Denina's *Rivoluzioni d'Italia*, 1770 (and it is significant that the understanding of the risorgimento has to begin with eighteenth century roots) to those writings of the English historian Denis Mack Smith which were published by 1960. Even in the 692 pages of his book Maturi has not covered all historians but has selected certain writers to show varying interpretations and emphases. Given these varieties of interpretation listed by Maturi, against what clearly defined framework in the risorgimento can Gavazzi be placed? For some no doubt the politics of the left should suffice (whether anarchist-socialist, as shown recently in *Gesu Socialista* by Arnoldo Nesti, or earlier in the work of the marxist Antonio Gramsci who called the reunification of Italy 'a passive revolution') – but as Nesti notes at the beginning, Italy lacked an experience like the Paris commune.[5] There was too much utopian oratory, together with the powerful influence of the strongminded toughness of Garibaldi, so stubbornly concerned for 'liberty', in the risorgimento to make marxist analysis fruitful. In fact any purely political analysis of the risorgimento would leave out too much: there were so many non-political factors within the movement. In English terms the risorgimento was simply a struggle for liberal ideals and institutions as can

---

[4] The publicist, Indro Montanelli, in his *L'Italia del Risorgimento (1831–1861)* (Milan 1972) at p 685 under *Bibliografia* wrote: 'Una completa bibliografia di opere sul Risorgimento è impossibile da redigere perché richiederebbe un volume a parte.' This would be a conservative estimate.

[5] Arnaldo Nesti, *Gesu Socialista*, (Turin 1974) p 10.

be seen across the spectrum from Swinburne's lush poeticising *Songs before Sunrise* to Trevelyan's traditionally whig trilogy of praise for Garibaldi, of whom he wrote in his autobiography – 'Garibaldi attracted me because his life seemed to be the most poetic of all true stories'.[6] But Mack Smith, disillusioned after the war with Mussolini's Italy and Hitler's Germany, finds a fascist under many a risorgimento bed.[7] Perhaps Gavazzi was popular with the English in his exile here because, in spite of his oratorical gifts and anti-papalism, he showed no interest in political partisanship – his popularity, in certain areas, with working-class audiences does not imply that he raised political issues; rather it implies his diffused social concern for the italian poor and the probably latent 'orangeism' of those audiences.

Political analysis will not explain Gavazzi: for him religiously suffused patriotism was the essential matter. He had no use for Mazzini's republicanism, and no declared understanding of what might come of the piedmontese conservative state. Politically he was no more than a noise in the street – even though his oratory stirred like a trumpet. When he walked with an arm linked with Garibaldi in Rome in 1848 he was not demonstrating a political choice, he thought he was walking towards a nation and a church revived anew in Italy. Sociological analysis would not help. At the touch of a sociologist's finger Gavazzi would collapse like a pricked balloon, but the same could almost be said of Mazzini. If we turn to the history of the institutions created by the risorgimento, they seem to have been as bureaucratically ramshackle as those of modern Italy, before the new industrial technology began there in our time. The only institution created by Gavazzi faded away in a generation, though he could be an excellent organiser.[8] In the history of ideas Gavazzi would make little showing. He had a remarkable talent for oratory, and a ready pen: but

---

[6] George Macaulay Trevelyan, *An Autobiography and Other Essays*, (London 1949) p 13.

[7] Denis Mack Smith, *Cavour and Garibaldi: 1860* (Cambridge 1954); *Garibaldi, A Great Life in Brief* (London 1957); *Italy, A Modern History* (Michigan 1959). [W.] Maturi, [*Interpretazioni del Risorgimento*] (Turin 1962) p 688: 'Mack Smith è ossessionato dal problema del fascismo: nella storia d'Italia dal 1861 in poi tutto conduce al fascismo', and, 'garibaldinismo e fascismo', p 689. Maturi's judgment is not unique to himself, but is also noticed by recent historians. It is part of the purpose of this paper to suggest that Mack Smith's view is illiberal (and does not do justice to the idealism and religious convictions of many of those who took part in the risorgimento) though not calling in question the thoroughness of his scholarship nor, for example, his conception of the rôle of Cavour.

[8] That is, the *Chiesa Libera d'Italia*, eventually renamed *Chiesa Evangelica d'Italia*, see n 149 below.

he spoke too often and wrote too much amid an active daily life, for him to produce significant original ideas, or sustain a close analysis of themes requiring intellectual force and disciplined scholarship. His importance lay in his quickness in assimilating views current in his time and, through his own varied experience of life, providing these views with potency and an original exposition of them in speeches, pamphlets, journalism, and full-scale books. Gavazzi had a powerful personality sustained by great physical strength and energy, which assisted that flood of words which poured from him in speech and writing, and gave these their peculiar flavour and power. The style and the manner are now badly dated, but we can still see why he moved both Italians and English speakers on the platform and in print.

In view of these limitations few options are open in historical method apart from narrative. It will be by narration, especially of two re-markable periods of his life, combined with an attempt to discover what his views were in those two distinctive stages, that this study of Gavazzi will be attempted. For him the risorgimento was a religious passion more than a political programme. Unfortunately, we are not helped in understanding him because too little attention has been given by historians (although italian writers are aware of the need) to the religious passions within the risorgimento.[9] Amidst the multitude of books on the subject of Italian renewal a full-scale analysis of the religious energies behind the movement for italian unity has yet to be written. Pius IX spent half a life-time anathematising the risorgimento and his excommunications fell all over Italy like autumn leaves in Vallombrosa. Yet catholic historians, even if they are not dedicated to the attitudes of the jesuit journal famous in those years, *Civiltà Cattolica*, are hardly likely to be interested in compiling embarrassingly long lists of names of priests, secular and religious, who supported the piedmontese or Garibaldi, and even less likely perhaps to write with sympathetic understanding the history of the renegade priests, who found the strain of being at once loyal to Pius IX and to the aims of a united Italy too great to bear and left the church, while they still claimed to be christians.[10] Alessandro Gavazzi was one of these and they were no small company. Some came as exiles to England, the

---

[9] For example: [Georgio] Spini, [*Risorgimento e Protestanti*] (Naples 1956). [Arnaldo della] Torre, [*Cristianesimo in Italia dai filosofisti ai moderni*] (Milan no date). [Valdo] Vinay, [*Evangelici Italiani esuli a Londra durante il Risorgimento*] (Turin 1961).
[10] See n 103 for these priests.

home of liberalism and anti-papal protestantism. But he must not be confused with hypocritical confidence tricksters like Achilli, whose morals and intrigues seemed to English catholics to be typical of risorgimento renegade priests, and a public warning of the consequences of religious disobedience.[11] Nor may Gavazzi be associated with that group of anti-catholic polemicists from the inventive liar who wrote the *Awful Disclosures of Maria Monk*[12] in 1835, through the ex-priest Chiniquey who shocked and titillated victorian nerves in his book *The Woman, the priest and the confessional*, to well-intentioned evangelicals like Lancelot Holland who exposed to the protestant world the horrors of *Walled-up Nuns* in 1895.

Gavazzi's life-span from 1809 to 1889 had three crucial stages: 1847-9 which in his manuscript autobiography he called *Patria*, the years of exile 1849-59 entitled *Esiglio*, and the years of renewal in the attempt to reunite Italy 1859-68 which he called *Ritorno*. His life up to the age of thirty-eight he seems to have regarded as commonplace; its significance paled for him compared with the years of *Patria, Esiglio* and *Ritorno*.[13] He did not live to complete his autobiography, no doubt he felt he could leave to others who shared his final years with him an account of his life when in those last years 1868-89 he worked hard but

---

[11] Dr Giacinto Achilli, a former dominican friar described by [Wilfred] Ward in his [*Life of Cardinal Newman*] (London 1912) I, p 276, as 'an unfrocked priest, not only without a character of any kind, but one who might without exaggeration be described as a portent of immorality'. Ward, p 279, quotes cardinal Wiseman's detailed though florid indictment of Achilli's career as a seducer of women 'and worse'. However *Bell's Messenger* – an unusual place for the review of a religious work – wrote of Achilli's *Dealings with the Inquisition, or Papal Rome, her priests and her Jesuits with important disclosures* (London 1851): 'Dr Achilli's most valuable book which, independently of the most important information it contains, breathes a spirit of fervent piety and devotion which no one but a man thoroughly convinced of the truths of Christianity as set forth in the only infallible Word of Truth, could have used.' (I derive this citation from the second edition which contains extracts from reviews of the first edition.) It was this sort of acceptance by protestants of Achilli which helped him to bluff his way as an honest convert, and made Newman's task at the famous libel trial so difficult. Achilli's book has a thoroughly offensive self-righteous tone. His manuscript autobiography is in the British Museum.

[12] Eric Quayle, *The Collector's Book of Books* (London 1971) describes the first edition, and calls the book 'A one-time shocking tale of sex and murder in a nunnery in Montreal . . . invented by the revd. J. J. Slocum . . . who had a consuming hatred of the Roman Catholic Church'.

[13] See Cencetti, n 2 above. Sylvain, however, states that the first two parts are entitled: *La Famiglia* and *Il Chiostro*, p 517. This is not indicated by Cencetti in his introduction to the *Alcune pagine*, but Sylvain who knew the manuscript well must be correct. In the 'Introduzione' Gavazzi wrote . . . 'mi ritrarrò quale fui nella famiglia, nel chiostro, nella crociata, nell'esiglio e nel rimpatrio . . .'

Alessandro Gavazzi: a barnabite friar and the risorgimento

ineffectively to build up his free church of Italy.[14] A few brief extracts from his autobiography have been published and what is apparently the introduction appears under the ambiguous title 'The Beginning of the End' in which Gavazzi states that he will not concern himself with the philosophy of history, nor with 'theatrical situations', nor with the temptation to what he calls *romanzo* – but that he will follow the simple chronology of events as they happened beginning with his family, moving on to his claustral life, to the 'crusade' (1847–9), to the period of exile, and his return to see Italy at last united.[15] He adds with an old man's resignation and with some restrained pathos that he wrote not out of vanity or ambition, but to give the portrait of a man who had nothing other in his heart than to see his Italy crowned queen in the Campidoglio. This comes at the end of a long passage in which he begins by stating that he wishes to leave to posterity some memory of one who belonged to the elect company of those who during the period of the Italian revolutions sacrificed all for the motherland with no other compensation than insults and persecutions – and to claim to have attained in this company a modest niche.[16]

He added with some bitterness that he had an original sin which no baptism could cancel, namely that he belonged to no party. He had accepted only the liberalism of progress (this phrase has a mazzinian ring). He had followed one flag, that of Italy, but on it was the name of no sect or party. Gavazzi went on to deny that he was a legitimist monarchist believing in divine right for that would have been to restore medieval vassalage. He wrote that he had not remained as 'the priests *botteganti di sagrestia* [shopkeepers of the sacristy] those who dreamed only of prestige when their throne and dominion were lost'.[17] After he was 'no longer a priest and papist he had been first among those who fought . . . obscurantism, superstition, the syllabus and vaticanism'.[18] He was not a moderate other than in the sense of not going to extremes, but if moderate meant conservative then that

---

[14] The autobiography apparently ceases at 1870 ('*Ritorno, va de 1859 à 1870*': Sylvain p 517). Ludovico Conti, *In occasione del centenario della nascita di Alessandro Gavazzi: cenno biografico* (Rome 1909) – a pastor of Gavazzi's *Chiesa Libera d'Italia* who knew him well in his later years. Unfortunately, his account of these years has nothing of the force and interest of Gavazzi's own writing, and contains more of pious adulation than of useful analysis.

[15] Cencetti p 160.

[16] *Ibid* pp 157–60.

[17] *Ibid* p 158.

[18] *Ibid* . . . i traffici, l'oscurantismo, la superstizione, il sillabo, ed il vaticanismo . . . cordialemente mi odiano.

implied a 'camorra' of inept, ambitious, thieves and he was then no moderate.[19] (Conrad's garibaldino in *Nostromo* used to invoke Cavour's name as a curse, for he was 'the arch-intriguer sold to kings and tyrants'.)[20] Gavazzi added that he was not a republican: nor was he a *rosso* like so many garibaldini even if he had marched with them with the good will of their *gran Capitano*. He wrote that when he was challenged at Leghorn by those who said 'born Catholics should die Catholics', he replied that he was a catholic without catholicism, rather he had returned to the true religion of the italian fathers from whom these very catholics had apostatised.[21] Finally to those who said that 'his poor name would go down in dishonour to the grave', he would offer no defence but he would relate his actions which could speak for themselves.[22] The style of the autobiography is that of an ageing weakening mind, discursive with digressions, though it is not without flashes of the colourful pungent phrases which had made him the formidable orator who had thundered to vast receptive crowds in the great squares of Venice, Rome and Naples. Those generalisations of Gavazzi's introduction to his own account of his life need the framework of factual details to justify them. Since his autobiography is unpublished his other writings must be the basis for relating and understanding his life – this however would be a large undertaking. Robert Sylvain, who wrote a two-volume life of Gavazzi over fifteen years ago *(Alessandro Gavazzi Garibaldien, Clerc, Prédicant des Deux Mondes)*, provides a most useful bibliography of books, pamphlets and fly-sheets by Gavazzi numbering 138, and I could add more to that number.[23] Further, there are eight volumes of newspaper cuttings of Gavazzi's speeches in England, the United States, and Canada, a volume of cuttings from *L'Eco d'Italia*, and another volume of newspaper cuttings called *Memorie* which contains further materials and a collection of *Orations in England*.[24] Again there are four accounts of

---

[19] *Ibid* p 158: Non sono moderato. Se il nome in Italia non fosse stato, sconsacrato da una camorra d'inetti, d'ambiziosi, di egoisti, di broglioni, di ladri; vorrei anch'io essere dei moderati nel vero senso del liberalismo progressivo, conscio che gli estremi non durano.

[20] [Joseph] Conrad, [*Nostromo*] (London 1923) p 24.

[21] Cencetti p 158: . . . che chi è nato cattolico deve morire cattolico . . . perchè io tornai alla religione vera dei Padri Italiani, di cui essi cattolici non sono che antifrati di apostasia . . .

[22] *Ibid* p 159.

[23] Although Sylvain worked at the library of the Facoltà Valdese at Rome, he seems to have overlooked some of Gavazzi's pamphlets that are available there.

[24] *L'Eco d'Italia* was an italian newspaper for immigrants to New York, edited by Gavazzi's friend Secchi de Casali.

Alessandro Gavazzi: a barnabite friar and the risorgimento

Gavazzi's life, three published in the mid-nineteenth century, and the last in 1909, all written by men who knew him intimately and who used his personal anecdotes and letters.[25] Well, 'tis sufficient to say according to the proverb that here is God's plenty'. Moreover, Sylvain's full-scale work, and the shorter but excellent life by Luigi Santini nearly twenty years ago, seem to leave little room for me to write a paper.[26] But Sylvain pointed out in his preface that in his work he intended to fill an obvious gap in canadian and american historiography; further he apparently felt it necessary to analyse once again the myth that Pius IX could be seen as a potential head of the movement for italian unification and that the explanation must be made once again that Pius IX was the spiritual head of all catholics, whether they were italian or not. Sylvain rightly gave considerable space to the american and canadian visits of Gavazzi for this had not been done before. He set these visits against the background of the appearance of the american 'know-nothing' anti-catholic movement, and he described in detail the background of catholic history in Canada against which he set the meetings of Gavazzi in Quebec and Montreal which caused serious riots, and also showed how Gavazzi, on returning to the United States, helped to cause the ignominious flight of the pontifical delegate Msgr Gaetano Bedini.[27] He also gave in full the argument, traditional even to the extent of being well-worn, in defence of *Pio Nono* and his stand against the risorgimento. By comparison Sylvain

[25] Two are short admiring accounts – G. B. Nicolini (not to be confused with the neo-ghibelline writer G. B. Niccolini): *The Life of Father A. Gavazzi, Chief Chaplain to the Roman Army of Independence* (Edinburgh 1851). This was reissued at New York 'continued to the time of his visit to America', 1854. This bibliographical point is not noticed by Sylvain, in his admirable bibliography, p 526. G. M. Campanella, *Life of Father Gavazzi* (London 1851): Campanella was also a friar who had left catholicism for exile and protestantism and who also wrote and published an interesting autobiography cited below, n 60. The other two lives by men who knew Gavazzi are that of Conti in italian already mentioned above, and the [*Life of Alessandro Gavazzi*] by [J. W.] King (London 1857) which contains first-hand reports of Gavazzi's recollections of his life before he came to England as well as extracts from letters of Gavazzi and King used below.

[26] [Luigi] Santini, [*Alessandro Gavazzi*] (*Aspetti del problema religioso del Risorgimento*), Collezione storica del Risorgimento Italiano, 2, serie 3 (Modena 1955).

[27] Volume 2 of Sylvain's work, the pages of which are numbered consecutively from volume 1, contains from p 287 to p 442 (the remainder of the volume of text is completed by p 511) very detailed accounts of Gavazzi's visits to the USA and Canada, with much useful material on the history of roman catholicism in those countries. Sylvain, while objective and fair, writes in the manner of catholic historians before the second vatican council – the church is always right, this apologetic stance is occasionally wearing on the reader.

gave little space to Gavazzi's exile in Britain, and since he wrote more in sorrow than in anger about Gavazzi's apostasy, he still left open unanswered questions about the crisis of conscience created by the pope's opposition to yielding an inch of his temporal power. Santini's life is half the length of Sylvain's, since he wrote to a shorter perspective, and is generously sympathetic, but the period of the English exile of Gavazzi is written more factually than analytically, a statement which would also cover his account of Gavazzi's activities in the roman period 1847-9.

Both authors omit matters of importance. Why did Sylvain, who had studied at the British Museum and also examined the volumes of British newspaper cuttings in the library of the Facoltà Valdese at Rome, not inquire into the impact of Gavazzi's lectures in Britain? Why did he not ask who sponsored them, who supported him by their presence on his platforms, why did Gavazzi revisit certain towns more frequently than others, and were there riots there as in Ireland and in Canada? Why do both Sylvain and Santini almost ignore Gavazzi's attitude to Mazzini and his ideas and make hardly any reference to the possible influence on him of Rossini, Gioberti and others? On the question why Gavazzi became a barnabite friar the answer may not be known, but Sylvain concluded that he made his vows at sixteen without a true religious vocation because Gavazzi said in 1858 that 'claustral vows are a sacrilegious attack on individual liberty and amount to moral suicide'.[28] On this basis one could argue, and scholars both protestant and catholic have done so, that Luther, who also denounced monastic vows later in life, never had a true vocation for it. This unjustly poses a doubt on a man's integrity from the beginning. Giacomo Leopardi in one of his *Pensieri* wrote 'the years of childhood are in the memory of every man, the fabulous years of his life; as in a nation's memories the fabulous years are those of that nation's youth'.[29] I suggest that Gavazzi became a barnabite friar after education in one of the schools of the order in his native city of Bologna (which was in the papal states) because like his friend and fellow-barnabite Ugo Bassi who was to be a poet and martyr for italian unity, he had deep religious feeling 'in the fabulous years' of his

---

[28] Sylvain, 1, p 18, n 23, quoting Gavazzi's *My Recollections [of the Lives of the last Four Popes]* (London 1858) pp 8-9.

[29] Iris Origo and John Heath-Stubbs, *Giacomo Leopardi* - selected prose and poetry - (London 1966) p 195.

Alessandro Gavazzi: a barnabite friar and the risorgimento

youth.[30] This is still true even if we allow that the friars saw in the boy Alessandro, described later by a contemporary as being a precocious boy both in his physical and intellectual development, talents which would be useful to their order. Again the influence of his mother must not be overlooked: he was her second son, she had twenty children by his father and four more from a second marriage and she survived to a healthy and indomitable old age, proud of her sons – all this argues that she was a woman of powerful character. The family were devout catholics, and the fact that Gavazzi dedicated one book to his mother, using her name in the title, and also caused another book of his, in praise of a saint noted for almsgiving, to be beautifully bound in leather with a label on the front cover: *Se io viva ancor eccone O Madre il segno*, then there must have been a close link between mother and son.[31] Again, on the subject of his becoming a barnabite friar it is worth remembering that after he left the order and became what he called a catholic christian – he always refused to call himself a protestant which caused him some serious misunderstandings in exile – he maintained all his life two of his religious vows, namely, chastity (and though they tried hard enough no opponent could bring any calumny against him on this) and also poverty: in the first year of exile

[30] Ugo Bassi (1801–59), barnabite friar, poet, martyr in the struggle for Italian unity. In common with other men of the risorgimento his career is the subject of controversy between anti-clerical writers and catholics. He shared Gavazzi's religious background and training, and took part with him in the forties in impassioned oratory for the re-unification of Italy. He had a more sensitive and reserved character than Gavazzi. He was executed by the austrians and died a catholic, though expelled from his order shortly before his death. It was bitter reflection in exile on Bassi's treatment by the pope and the austrians, which led Gavazzi to deliver a funeral oration for his dead friend in London after which he began to turn from catholicism. Information on the career in the order of barnabites of both Bassi and Gavazzi can be found in [Giuseppe] Boffito, [*Scrittori barnabiti, o della Congregazione dei Chierici Regolari di San Paolo, 1533–1933, Biografia, Bibliografia, Iconografia,*] 4 vols (Florence 1933–37). An excellent catholic account of Bassi's life is: G. F. de Ruggiero, *Il Padre Ugo Bassi* (Rome 1936).

[31] *Il beato Giacomo Elemosinario Panegirico del P. Alessandro Gavazzi, Barnabita di Bologna* (Orvieto 1844). This book was well-printed on fine paper. The copy in the library of the Facoltà Valdese is bound in leather and the words cited are on the front cover printed on a leather label. Presumably after his mother's death Gavazzi placed it in his own library. For some time after the second world war, many books of Gavazzi's library were in the possession of the methodist church which took over Gavazzi's house and church (see below p 350). I have been informed by the reverend R. Kissack who for a period lived in Gavazzi's former house at Rome, that among books given to Gavazzi, was one from W. S. Landor. That Gavazzi attracted the attention of victorian English men of letters should not be overlooked in assessing his achievements, see n 111 below.

he came near to starvation, and all his life he gave to charities, and showed little worldly calculation in money matters.

When the congregation of clerks regular of St Paul named barnabites were founded in 1533 (a small order mostly confined to Italy), one of its declared aims was 'reform of the clergy and other social groups', though there is no evidence that Gavazzi obtained the basis of his later social conscience from his early barnabite training.[32] What he would have to undertake as part of his rule was study of the pauline epistles, education and mission work. In 1825 he travelled to the house of his order in Naples, a journey which impressed itself on his adolescent memory which revived again in 1858 when he described his horror on entering the beggar-ridden misery of the region outside of Rome.[33] On his early studies his later comment in 1864 was that the papacy required seminarists 'to be deep in the legends of the saints and in blaspheming liberty'.[34] How this word 'liberty' recurs among the men of the risorgimento! Conrad's garibaldino in far South America looked at the portrait of Garibaldi and muttered: 'this was your liberty: it gave you not only life but immortality as well.'[35] Obviously Gavazzi's phrase is an inadequate description of seminary training among the barnabites. For example, the barnabite friar Luigi Lambruschini at the age of twenty-three taught classical literature, philosophy, mathematics, dogmatic and moral theology, greek and hebrew. He was either another *doctor mirabilis* or the depth and originality of his courses were rather thin; nevertheless the subjects went beyond Gavazzi's minimising, and Lambruschini became distinguished as a cardinal and secretary of state at Rome.[36] The year after Gavazzi entered the barnabite house at Naples his father, who had been a professor of law at the university of Bologna, died. Gavazzi, perhaps to be near his widowed mother and her other children, was moved to the barnabite house at Marsa near Bologna, from which he frequently visited his family. He now began to study oratory in the frigid and florid style of the period. In 1829 on his way back to Naples he passed through Rome where Leo XII had just died and, as Gavazzi wrote

[32] Boffito 1 and 2.

[33] *My Recollections* p 10; again, on the squalor of the poorer districts of Rome, p 232.

[34] Gavazzi, *A mio padre Angelico, lettera* (Pistoia 1864) p 22, cited in Santini, p 17, who states that Gavazzi was not alone in this protest. Rosmini and others made similar though less pungent criticisms.

[35] Conrad p 21.

[36] He should not be confused with Raffaele Lambruschini one of the strongest supporters of the movement for reform in the catholic church. (See below p 336.) For Luigi Lambruschini's lecturing programme, see Santini p 17 n 6.

later, like a 'fanatical papist' (though at the time it was an act of a devout friar) he kissed the slippered foot of the corpse with veneration.[37]

At Naples where he taught in the barnabite college he published some poems in 1830, which show a young man's desire to burst into print rather than any taste or talent. He was ordained priest in 1832 and moved to various houses of the order, and in Alessandria in Piedmont in 1833 he founded the friendship with Ugo Bassi which lasted until Bassi was shot by austrian troops after the 'crusade'. In 1836 Gavazzi was becoming known as a preacher of talent, as was Bassi a little later. Both men were innovators as preachers; they imitated the new style of preaching that was introduced in France in Lamennais's time, popular in appeal in the attempt to restore catholicism after the revolutionary destruction of so much in french catholic life This new style involved using loud and soft changes of voice, and strenuous gestures, and here too possibly lay the origin of Gavazzi's later theatrical style of oratory though his temperament would draw him strongly to theatricality. Further, this change suggests that Bassi and Gavazzi may have known something of the views of Lamennais and his followers.

Gavazzi was invited to preach the lenten course of sermons in the great Frari church in Venice. However, the austrian police refused him permission to enter their territory. This is the first indication that Gavazzi might be something more than a devout barnabite whose sole concern was piety. Protestants are accused of seeing jesuit intrigues everywhere, but catholics have not been averse to this either: it must be stated, nevertheless, that jealousy existed between the jesuits and the barnabites and that the jesuits were particularly supporters of political legitimism, opponents of liberalism, and became increasingly powerful at Rome in the reign of Gregory XVI (1831–46) and in the reign of Pius IX, especially after his return to Rome in 1850. The strongest supporter of the jesuits in Piedmont was the foreign minister, count Solaro della Margarita, and he had caused the police to prevent Bassi from preaching a lenten course in Turin: perhaps the count had passed a hint about Gavazzi to the austrian police at Venice.[38] The king of

---

[37] *My Recollections* p 81.
[38] Count Solaro della Margarita wished to write a history of Italy to defend his position, which was that of leader of the piedmontese clericals opposed to all liberalism. See Maturi pp 228, 229. Against Gioberti's *gesuito moderno* he believed that opposition to the jesuits was 'war on governments, religion and God'. Sylvain p 42.

Piedmont grumbled incidentally that his life was poised between the daggers of the carbonari and the chocolate of the jesuits.

Of this period Gavazzi left no recollections later save to complain of the bad latinity of the order whose 'stupid systems' he said, 'absorbed the best years of our youth.'[39] In 1839 and 1840 he published a few small works of piety and some more tedious poetry – it is unfortunate that it is so easy to string verses together in italian. However, it was a poem which brought him his first real challenge from governmental authority. It was a sententious effort on the unpoetic subject of a steam-boat setting forth to steam from Turin to Venice; and it was issued during the second italian scientific congress which happened to be meeting in Turin.[40] Consciously or unconsciously the ebullient Gavazzi by issuing this poem at that time was in effect taking a nationalist attitude, for the members of the scientific congresses were hostile to the repressive governments in Italy. That Metternich of italian conservatives, count Solaro della Margarita, had stated that 'science and art were only the apparent pretext of the Congresses; their true aim was an Italian revolution'.[41] This hostile judgement was shared by Lambruschini and also the contemporary pope, Gregory XVI, who refused to allow railways and gas lighting into the papal states on the grounds that revolutionary views travelled by rail and, presumably, they could be more clearly illuminated by gas-light.[42] Moreover Gregory, wiser than the piedmontese, refused to allow the

[39] Gavazzi's comment appeared in *L'Eco d'Italia* (New York, 7 January 1854). Santini p 17, notes that Adolfo Omedeo in his *Le Missioni di riconquista cattolica nella Francia nella restaurazione, (Aspetti del cattolicesimo della restaurazione)* (Turin 1946) points to the poor training of the clergy at this period.

[40] *Cenni sul battello a vapore che per primo partirà da Torino per Venezia, coll'aggiunta di una poesia sullo stesso soggetto* (Turin 1840).

[41] Solaro della Margarita, *Memorandum storico-politico* (Turin 1930) p 138: Io avversai fin dall'alba queste congreghe tanto applaudite' because he knew that 'scienza e arte non essere che il pretesto apparente, il vero fine la rivoluzione italiana'.

[42] [Fredrik] Nielsen, [*The History of the Papacy in the nineteenth century*] (London 1906) 2, p 75: 'The moderate Liberalism which desired that the papacy should accommodate itself to modern times, was in his eyes [Cardinal Lambruschini] as dangerous as the revolutionary ideas of Mazzini; and the new Secretary of S ate [Lambruschini] regarded lighting by gas, railways and scientific congresses with as much suspicion as Liberalism.' However, it was Gregory XVI himself who opposed gas and railways. See *Gregorio XVI: [Miscellanea Commemorativa]*, part 2 (Roma 1948) p 343. Also G. Gioacchino Belli, in his *Sonnetti Romaneschi*, dialect verses which show the dislike of the romans for Gregory's administration (see below p 353 and n 140), has a poem on the subject of Gregory after death wanting to go to heaven; eventually he arrives there and meets saint Peter who asks him: 'How long was the journey?' 'A month' replied Gregory. 'Why so long?' asks St Peter. Gregory replies: 'Ben ti sta' gli soggiunse, poteri fare la strada ferrata e a quest'ora saresti già arrivato.'

italian scientific congresses to meet in any town of the papal states. Gavazzi made more trouble for himself in Piedmont by preaching powerfully in favour of orphanages for the lost children of the streets. This gave offence to the jesuits who disapproved of these orphanages because they had been invented by foreigners who were probably protestants. So Gavazzi was moved to Parma, somewhat under a cloud.

Since his preaching seemed too stirring he was appointed as chaplain to the male and female prisons in Parma (which would confine his oratory to the narrow limits of prison walls), where he found the conditions to be appalling. His attention was fully focused now on social questions and he published a booklet *Le Carceri* which showed compassionate sympathy for the harsh lives of the prisoners, their inability to find work after their sentences expired, and the tragic destitution of their families. Further, he published a book of devotions for prisoners, *L'Amico dei carceri* in 1844, which among other things stressed that prisoners could better endure their lot by living in the grace and fear of God, and that sanctification could be achieved by viewing the life of a prisoner as a life similar to that of a christian martyr of the first centuries of the church. There is no question that the barnabite Gavazzi was a fully committed priest of apostolic life and conviction. He crowned this period by writing a book on the recorded sayings of the founder of the barnabite order, Zaccaria, accompanied by a brief life of him. He even offered himself for missionary work in Burmah but this was not taken up, and a memoir on the necessity of foreign missions which he prepared for the chapter general of his order still survives in their archives.[43] At Orvieto in papal territory, he preached a panegyric on the local saint and almsgiver *Il Beato Giacomo Elemosinario* which he published in 1844. Perhaps Gavazzi intended to show the innocuousness of his preaching: it is certainly a dull exercise in that traditional italian rhetorical style which was carried over from the eighteenth century.[44] It was a copy of this

---

[43] *Sulle missioni straniere*, submitted for the consideration of the chapter general in 1844. It consists of twelve quarto sheets, and is now in the archives of the barnabites at Rome. To the credit of Gregory XVI it should be stated that he 'dedico viva attenzione alle missioni', for example he increased the number of vicars apostolic in China – see [K.] Bihlmeyer [and H.] Tuechle, [*Storia della Chiesa*], italian translation by Igino Rogger (Brescia 1962) 4, p 149, and also section 206. – though 'viva attenzione' is overstated.

[44] This book has been described above, n 31. A characteristic passage is: E insiemente che ei possa ascoltato esaudito perorare in pro vostro, ve lo accertino le sue ferite sostenute per amor di giustizia, e che in lui sono come meriti messi d'altri

book which Gavazzi caused to be beautifully bound and provided
with the inscription to his mother, referred to above, which can now
be seen in the library of the Facoltà Valdese at Rome. In 1845 at
Perugia he showed a rapid change of style for he preached a lenten
course which aroused such admiration that a pamphlet was published
entitled cordially *Omaggio di publica ammirazione e gratitudine all'esimio
sacro oratore padre Alessandro Gavazzi.*[45] From this it appears that
Gavazzi had preached on christian matrimony, denounced the growth
of luxury and effeminacy of manners – and most admirable Gavazzi –
he even rebuked the use of tobacco. Police spies were everywhere in
Italy and the police chief, Nardoni, reported to the governor of Rome
that Gavazzi had said some imprudent things. Gavazzi knew nothing
of this report and, carried away by the popular enthusiasm he was
creating, he turned a sermon intended in praise of the miraculous
madonna at Ancona into an impassioned attack on the sorrows of
Italy and italians, divided and oppressed by foreigners. The fact that
the miracle of the madonna of Ancona had consisted in her moving
her eyes to warn the people of the approach of french troops in the
napoleonic period, while it gave the ground for Gavazzi's observations, did not prevent the anger of the consuls of Austria and
Naples.[46] Gavazzi was slipping ever nearer to speaking out for the
risorgimento. Before long he was called to Rome by the order of pope
Gregory XVI, *ad audiendum verbum.* He went to Rome to the house of
his order, and from there being forbidden to preach he was sent to the
novice house at San Severino Marche in Umbria, a region
malonconiche e sinistre.[47] So he took up his pen again and wrote a book
of religious exercises, 1846, and no doubt brooded over his dislike

---

maggiori privilegi; sicurando Agostino che esse sono nel martire altrettanto
valevoli bocche a chieder grazie, ad ottenere favori. E non vorrà proteggervi?
Troppo vorrà. Giacchè chi meglio di esso si può conoscere di voi? Al vostro
Giacomo è cognita l'aura di questo cielo, l'aspetto di questa natura, il suono di
questa favella: i consapevoli colli della sua infanzia, il dolce loco che lo raccolse
bambino, il focolare di sua paterna casa a lui sono noti: palpita in quel suo caldissimo
petto un cuore pievese: egli è il naturale patrono della sua patria. (pp 28-9).

[45] Perugia, 1845. Lodolini, gives illustrative materials from the *Archivio di Stato di Roma,*
Direzione Generale di Polizia, anno 1847, Padre Alessandro Gavazzi, Busta 266. The
chief of papal police, Nardoni, when reporting Gavazzi's attacks considered his sermon
nevertheless to be 'sublime preaching'. See Lodolini p 436.

[46] Lodolini p 437.

[47] See L. Gualtieri, *Memorie di Ugo Bassi, Apostolo del Vangelo, Martire dell'independenza
Italiana* (Bologna 1861) p 49 for a description of this grim remote monastery in
Umbria where in 'solitude and silence' both Bassi and Gavazzi at different periods were
confined as a penance for politically dangerous preaching.

Alessandro Gavazzi: a barnabite friar and the risorgimento

for Gregory XVI on whom he was to make a most embittered attack in England in 1858.[48] The death of Gregory and the election of cardinal Mastai-Ferretti as the new pope, came some months later; both events were met with enthusiasm by liberals – Gregory had at first refused to make Giovanni Mastai-Ferretti a cardinal, because he said 'in the house of Mastai even the cats were liberal'.[49] Gavazzi benefited from the new pope's amnesty, wrote an enthusiastic set of verses to Pius IX and published them at Parma.[50] Gavazzi began preaching again, this occasion was at the funeral of the gloomy and reactionary count Maldonado Leopardi, who had contemptuously dismissed the writings of his son, Giacomo, today regarded as one of the finest of italian poets. The family were scandalised as Gavazzi thundered forth on the bad education of the nobles of the count's generation. If Giacomo Leopardi had survived he would have been sardonically amused at the denunciation given to that political bigotry of his father which had darkened his youth.[51] Unstoppable now that he had found his stride, Gavazzi, in the cathedral of Senigaglia (the town where the new pope's family had long resided, and where Pius's father was a count and gonfaloniere) preached an impassioned address to commemorate the birthday of Pius IX which was published about the same time as a new edition of the poems to Pius he had written earlier.[52] The volume, luxuriously bound, was presented to Pius by his younger brother count Giuseppe Mastai who knew Gavazzi. Gavazzi had not finished with the praises of Pius yet; for in the church of the virgins at Macerata he preached with immense verve a sermon on the subject of 'Mary and Pius IX', but Gavazzi quickly dismissed the needs of the Virgin 'since

[48] *My Recollections* pp 273 *et seq.*
[49] Nielsen, 2, p 114.
[50] *Pio IX Pontifice Massimo. Tributo di affetti di A. Gavazzi, Bolognese* (Florence 1846). Two specially bound copies were presented in turn to count Mastai and later the Pope. Among other emotional declarations in these poems is the following: Io amo Pio l'amo dell'amore onde si ama Dio senza limiti, senza misure, senza ragioni, tutto virilità e caldezza . . . Santini p 39.
[51] 'Paternal power, in every law-abiding country, brings about a kind of children's slavery, more stringent, because it is more domestic, and more oppressive than any law, and which . . . can never fail to produce a most damaging effect . . .' *Giacomo Leopardi* p 11. Gavazzi's sermon at the Count's funeral was published, *Nel funere del Conte Monaldo Leopardi, parole del p. Alessandro Gavazzi, Barnabita bolognese* (Loreto 1847).
[52] *Il genetliaco di Pio IX Pontefice Massimo. Discorso del P. Alessandro Gavazzi, Barnabita bolognese, recitato nel Duomo di Senigaglia, il 13 maggio 1847* (Senigaglia 1847). *Il busto di Pio Nono donata dai Romani ai Bolognese, Epigrafia e sonnetti di Alessandro Gavazzi* (Rome 1847).

she was so well-beloved she needed no special sermon, whereas there was real need to praise unreservedly Pius IX who was bringing in a new life to the Church', a fact Gavazzi helped forward by denouncing once again Gregory, the new pope's predecessor. The crowd in the packed church verged on the sacrilegious by applauding with wild enthusiasm. The papal legate, overwhelmed as much by the obvious political appeal of the sermon as by the thunderous applause it occasioned, wrote to the barnabite cardinal who was bishop of Ancona, who in turn wrote to the general of the order at Rome, stating that Gavazzi's democratic eloquence passed all limits and even censured governments: he admitted it was true that Gavazzi was a man of talent, well-informed, and of ardent temperament, but in need of restraint – so it would be better if Gavazzi could be called back to Rome.

He arrived in Rome in May 1847 and now began what he wrote of later as the first great period of his life. He found the people in a state of intense excitement, and after seeking through count Giuseppe Mastai an audience with the pope, obtained it. His heart, bursting with joy, he was about to kneel and kiss the pope's slippered foot, but with gracious condescension Pius gestured him to leave this and offered Gavazzi the fisherman's ring to kiss. Both spoke to each other for about half an hour with great cordiality and probably complete mutual misunderstanding. Gavazzi was carried away by the well-known charm of Pius and saw before him the pope who would renew the church and set himself at the head of a league of italian states if not of a united Italy. Pius saw an over-enthusiastic friar who had a great popular following, and who, if his oratory could be tamed, would be a useful instrument of papal support. Pius, whose charm was remarkable, smiled and asked Gavazzi whether he had been applauded in a church. The reply was quick-minded, and parried an implicit reprimand: 'No, they did not applaud me most holy Father, they applauded what was said of you'. Pius laughed and the audience continued in which the Pope admired the talents of Gavazzi's fellow barnabite, Ugo Bassi, and ended apparently with the command that Gavazzi was not to preach again on nationalism or political subjects.[53]

Gavazzi had not, however, suffered a severe check for he was

---

[53] Gavazzi related this interview in his *Autobiografia*, p 091284, according to Sylvain who translated some sentences from this conversation. Gavazzi also related the interview in [*The*] *Lectures Complete* [*of Father Gavazzi as Delivered in New York*] ed G. B. Nicolini (New York 1854) pp 259–60.

Alessandro Gavazzi: a barnabite friar and the risorgimento

appointed as assistant priest in a barnabite church in Rome. When the first anniversary of Pius arrived, a crowd of fifty thousand with banners waving and bands playing marched to the Quirinal palace to receive the papal benediction. On that evening Gavazzi preached to a vast crowd in the baths of Diocletian, a panegyric on Pius which lasted for an hour and a half and was followed by the *Te Deum* and enthusiastic applause.

Events in Rome were moving fast towards political confrontation between the papal government and popular democratic groups. Gavazzi indiscreetly chose at this point to preach a politically based sermon denouncing once more the evils of Gregory's pontificate and calling for liberal leadership from Pius IX. Because of this, and the extreme political tension at this time his superiors once again forbade him to preach. Later, during his exile, Gavazzi claimed that it was Pius himself who had put him under this interdiction. In January 1848 soldiers of the austrian General, Radetsky, killed a number of citizens in Milan and elsewhere in Lombardy during the risings that year.[54] In spite of the interdiction, Gavazzi took the pulpit in the former Pantheon and with deep emotion urged the romans to avenge the lombards who had died for Italy under the accursed austrians, and he repeated a similar outburst to the students in the chapel of the university. For this he was confined to a monastery near Rome, but the students found out where he had been placed, came out in force, serenaded him, and drew him in a carriage back to Rome. Once again Gavazzi passionately exhorted the romans to go to the aid of the lombards, speaking from the carriage; and his fiery oratory continued to its peak at the Colosseum with an appeal for volunteers for a 'holy war', indeed a new crusade.[55] On that day large numbers of roman citizens began to take action in the drama of the regeneration of Italy. Pio Nono, reluctant but smiling, gave his blessing to the newly enrolled troops who gathered in the vatican gardens in March 1848. He made Gavazzi chaplain general and he even had to endure the sight of the tri-coloured badge on Gavazzi's barnabite habit, excused on the dubious ground that it represented the colours of an italian religious

[54] [G. F-H. and J.] Berkeley, [*Italy in the Making January 1st 1848 to November 16th 1848*] (Cambridge 1848) p 19. The troubles began on 3 January in Milan, known as 'I Lutti di Lombardia'.

[55] This was called afterwards the opening of *il dramma della regenerazione d'Italia*; Gavazzi addressed a huge crowd of 40,000 calling for a *guerra santa*. Cardinal Manning was present and described the impression this vast passionate crowd made on him. E. S. Purcell, *Life of Cardinal Manning*, 1, pp 374–5.

order. Once again the pope and Gavazzi were at cross-purposes: Gavazzi wanted to take part in a crusade to throw the austrians out of Italy, whereas the pope ordered Durando, the general of the papal troops, not to cross the Po but merely to defend papal territory if it were attacked.[56] The papal army marched northward and four of Gavazzi's brothers marched with its chaplain general. At each stage of the march Gavazzi preached encouragingly to the troops and was heard with special enthusiasm in his native Bologna. At Parma he addressed huge crowds and brought in numbers of new recruits. From now on he began to be known as 'the new Peter the Hermit'. One who heard him preach said 'He who did not hear Gavazzi that day failed to hear eloquence never heard before'.[57] Gavazzi's themes

[56] This was the agonising dilemma for Pius IX – he had not intended attack by his troops on the austrians, but he must have known that once the enflamed patriotic youth of his states had marched north, they could not sit down at the frontier and do nothing to help the piedmontese. In any event he had placed the command of his army ultimately under orders from the king of Piedmont. But Pius had not formally declared war, and there was the possibility of his troops, if an attack commenced, being captured and shot out of hand as *franc-tireurs* by the austrians. The piedmontese and their supporters elsewhere in Italy including those in the papal states were determined to draw Pius into supporting the war on Austria. Massimo d'Azeglio, the piedmontese writer and politician, who had been appointed adjutant general to Durando, had a clear eye for the position and issued an order of the day on 5 April in the name of Pius which showed papal and piedmontese troops as conducting a crusade against the barbarous Radetsky: Durando approved of this attitude and intended to carry out its implications. See cap 9 *The papal difficulties*, in Berkeley p 153 *et seq*. Nevertheless the difficulties which Pius IX felt did not turn him aside from the fundamental conviction that the papal states were inviolably his province as ruler. The belgian ambassador at Rome, Van de Weyer, wrote to Leopold I, on 6 February 1859, (though this is a decade later, other evidence would bear out that the views of Pius had always been consistent on this point) citing a remark made by Pius IX to Odo Russell the British representative in Rome, who corresponded regularly on roman affairs with the foreign office (see below n 58): 'Quoiqu'il arrive ajoute le S. Père, je serai toujours pape; mais plutôt que de séculariser le gouvernement, je suis prêt à descendre aux catacombes, nouveau martyr de l'Eglise.' Archives Generales Royaume Bruxelles, Van de Weyer Papers, no 124: cited in Aloïs Simon, *Palmerston et les Etats Pontificaux en 1849, Rassegna Storica [del Risorgimento]*, 43 (Rome 1956), p 542. Simon added: 'En maintenant les Etats Pontificaux le Saint Siège voulait certes conserver certains droits acquis par l'histoire et surtout sauvegarder l'indépendence spirituelle du souverain pontife. mais il avait aussi une nostalgie de la théocratie.' *Ibid* p 543.

[57] Luigi Gualtieri, *Memorie de Ugo Bassi, apostolo del Vangelo, martire della Indipendenza Italiana* (Bologna 1861) pp 68–9. Sylvain regards Gualtieri as too much biased in favour of Gavazzi and Bassi, and states that he was responsible for some accepting too readily exaggerations about the circumstances of the death of Bassi which embittered Gavazzi and Garibaldi when these were reported to them verbally, and adds that Gualtieri's book was accepted too uncritically by [G. M.] Trevelyan in his *[Garibaldi's] Defence [of the Roman Republic]* (London 1907) p 308. Nevertheless no effective help was given by catholic prelates and clerical diplomats on Bassi's behalf, who it should be remembered was still a priest and had not carried arms.

were not only nationalist but also were concerned with the indifference of the rich to the poor, and attacked those whom he regarded as reactionary nobles and the conservative-minded clergy.

The pope feared that he was losing control of the situation, that there might be revolt in the papal states, that his troops might be involved in war with Austria, and that the international character of the papacy would be lost if he could be seen as supporting a war to unite Italy. On the 29 April he delivered his cold allocution in which he declared that he abhorred war, had an equal affection for all peoples, that austrians and italians were fellow-catholics, and that he had no intention of presiding over an italian republic, rather, italians must remain loyal and faithful to their respective legitimate sovereigns in Italy.[58] This open challenge caused great popular resentment against his government, and the allocution was seen by those who until then had looked to Pius to lead the movement for the regeneration of the nation and of the church as turning his back on them and siding with anti-nationalist conservatism. It would be difficult to exaggerate the effect of what Pius had said. It conclusively showed that Pius was

[58] The bitterness aroused by this allocution among italian patriots is understandable because the papal declaration helped in the defeat of the italians in 1848. It was in any case, as the events showed, fatal to the intention of Pius to preserve the temporal power. Patriots now saw that unity could only be achieved by challenging and overcoming papal rule in the papal states. Whether the danger of schism was as immediate and probable as Pius claimed is an open question. That his dilemma, however, was extremely difficult is plain: that his resolution of it and the way he became increasingly obstinate later in trying to repress the risorgimento were wise is less plain. For the allocution see the italian translation in L. C. Farini, *Lo stato romano dal anno 1815 al 1850,* 4 vols (Florence 1853) 2, p 92. The pope in addressing german language catholics claimed that considerable measures of reform had been under way in the papal states, therefore, since he was carrying out the advice of european governments, how could he be regarded as a revolutionary? How far Pius was effecting reforms can be seen from Odo Russell's despatches from Rome, *The Roman Question,* ed N. Blakiston (London 1962) which show how often Russell repeated the advice of the British government for the pope to reform his administration, to the irritation of Pius, in the years 1858–70. Reform obviously meant different things to Palmerston, and his successors, and to Pius. Russell's report of the opinion of Pius on italians is interesting: 'The Italians are a dissatisfied, interfering, turbulent, and intriguing race, they can never learn to govern themselves. It is impossible. . . . A hotheaded people like the Italians require a firm and just government to guide and take care of them . . .' Russell's reply, exemplifying the lack of justice, led Pius only to smile and take snuff, p 37.

The second part of the allocution was addressed to italians stating that Pius could not prevent volunteers from among his subjects fighting for Italy, but he had not declared war since he represented on earth the author of peace, and that his duty as sovereign pontiff was to show equal paternal love to all peoples. In the third part of his allocution he vigorously rejected the idea that he could preside over an italian republic, rather italians should remain loyal to their legitimate sovereigns – these included the austrians: the point that embittered Gavazzi and Italian patriots generally.

opposed to the risorgimento.[59] Gavazzi was badly shaken by the allocution, and fell back on the view that the pope had been manipulated by the curia and the jesuits. The papal army pushed on to Venice and its chaplain-general Gavazzi made heroic speeches in the piazza San Marco, though his views on the needs of the poor alienated the venetian leader Daniele Manin. The papal troops marched back to Treviso and formed the right wing of the piedmontese army in an unavailing attack on the austrians. Gavazzi, using his great physical strength, was prominent in rescuing wounded soldiers while under heavy fire.[60] The neapolitan troops withdrew to Naples, and the joint italian army thus weakened was defeated at Vicenza.

The impact of these experiences turned Gavazzi into a passionate political orator. He felt a bitter sense of betrayal – the betrayal of the idea of 'the crusade', betrayal by the neapolitans, and betrayal by the pope. He became a man 'for the people' (here he meant the supporters of an orderly liberal progress to unite Italy, not revolutionaries), and for 'italians of faithful hearts': these could be trusted, but not

[59] 'Thus vanished the dream of Gioberti.' A. M. Ghisalberti published the letters of count de Liederkerke de Beaufort to the belgian government in two differently titled books: from the second, *Rapporti delli cose di Roma (1848–1849)* (Rome 1949) Sylvain cites this quotation 1 p 327. For Gioberti see below p 332. The count's letters, like those of other despatches from foreign ambassadors or government representatives at Rome, including those of Odo Russell, give more objective reports on the events and attitudes of the time than those of the participants. The violent emotional reaction of the patriots of the papal states helped to plunge Rome into revolution against the pope. Within a few days of the allocution the papal government was losing control: the political clubs (*Circoli*) and the civic guard began to take over, Berkeley 3, p 185.

[60] Santini reports, p 63 n 30, a letter sent from Venice to Gavazzi's mother by three of her sons, Giovanni (a colonel of volunteers), Paolo (a sergeant-major) and Alessandro, describing their safety after the battle of Treviso, to be found in the appendix to G. Zaccagnini, *Pistoia durante il Risorgimento nazionale* (Pistoia 1940). G. B. Nicolini in his *Lectures Completes*, who was present at the battle describes Carlo, another brother of Gavazzi, shouting to Alessandro not to expose himself to the storm of austrian bullets but to shelter with him behind a tree: but Gavazzi ignored him and carried wounded men under fire to the ambulances. In his *Autobiografia*, in the section on the battle of Treviso, printed by Cencetti, Gavazzi does not refer to himself but he describes with pride how a troop of *miei Voluntarii* charged up a steep valley against the austrian guns which was a *preludio gloriossimo di quella di Balaklava in Crimea sotto la guida di Lord Cardigan*, p 167. Another brother of Gavazzi, Pietro, a doctor served in this campaign as an army surgeon. [G. M.] Campanella, [*Life in the cloister in the Papal court and in Exile: an Autobiography*] (London 1877), see above p 311, n 25, wrote in the appendix (p 9) that he visited Gavazzi's mother in Bologna in 1848 – she 'was truly one of the strong women of ancient times . . . inflamed with the love of country. She told us how all her five sons had exposed themselves bravely against the foreigner . . . the mother was truly worthy of such sons'.

princes, not politicians, not the pope.[61] The police of the papal states were ordered to arrest him, but they feared to do so in his native Bologna to which he had now returned. He moved on to Tuscany and then to Milan. In July the general of the barnabite order sent out rescripts of secularisation for both Gavazzi and Bassi. Insubordination and immorality would have been grounds for this but the latter was untrue so presumably the charge essentially was that they had gone beyond their office as religious in taking part in political demonstrations. Gavazzi never received the rescript in person, and by now had come to believe that the barnabite general had been pushed into issuing it by Pius who wished to conciliate the austrians at any price. Cardinal Oppizoni, the archbishop of Bologna, was embarrassed when he interviewed Gavazzi, who had returned to Bologna to quieten the wilder citizens, and did not show him the rescript. Gavazzi wrote later: 'It was not that we had betrayed our vows [when Bassi and he were ejected from their Order] it was because of the apostasy of the pontiff to the cause of Italy.'[62] Increasingly now Gavazzi was concerned with the rights of the people, not as a demagogue of revolution, but as a man deeply offended by the neglect of the poor, and the failure to provide pensions for those disabled in the struggle to free Italy from foreign rule. Garibaldi had now landed at Nice and was poised ready with his gathering legion to recommence the struggle. He came to Bologna and Gavazzi and Garibaldi addressed in turn, from the hotel balcony of the most impressive hotel in the city, a great crowd which had gathered to welcome the guerrilla leader.[63] It has been assumed with some probability that Gavazzi persuaded Garibaldi not to march with his legion against the austrians who were gathered round Venice, but to remain in the papal states since significant changes might occur there.[64] The pope's response to Gavazzi's welcome to Garibaldi was to write to cardinal Amat, the papal legate at Bologna, that Gavazzi should be arrested forthwith and placed in a lunatic

[61] Sylvain, I, pp 174, 175, translates a passage from Gavazzi's, *L'Italia inerme e accattona*, p 45, demonstrating this.

[62] Sylvain I, p 175.

[63] Cencetti p 169. Also see *Un Esperimento*, number 8, *Garibaldi a Bologna*, an enthusiastic article by Gavazzi describing the scene at the hotel. This journal by Gavazzi ran for eight numbers, 17 October to 11 November 1848, Bologna. (Library of Facoltà Valdese, Rome.)

[64] Ermana Loevinson, *Garibaldi e la sua legione nello Statto Romano*, 3 vols (Rome 1902–7) I, p 11. Holding back Garibaldi and his legion near to Rome was of fundamental importance, and Gavazzi was the most probable influence in this. Also see T. Casini, *Garibaldi nell'Emilia*, *Archivio Emiliano* (Modena 1907) p 182.

asylum.[65] The problem was to find someone who could effectively fulfil this order. Not for the first or last time in his life, Gavazzi when presented by a hostile attack was prepared to defend himself by force. He snatched up a large knife from the refectory table of the barnabite house when the police came at night to take him, until the barnabite superior, his former teacher, persuaded the police to withdraw from their sacrilegious assault in a conventual building. 'Death before prison', Gavazzi had shouted when the police pursued him into the refectory.[66] It can easily be seen why Garibaldi, always suspicious of priests, made Gavazzi chaplain to his forces: he accepted and doubtless preferred not Gavazzi's too ready rhetoric on the piazzas, but the bold fortitude (which his legionaries would respect) of a priest who had shown that he really meant what for romantic revolutionaries was no more than a melodramatic slogan: 'Give me liberty or give me death'.[67] Now the pope authorised general Zucchi at Bologna to take Gavazzi by force even from a sacred conventual building in contravention of canon law. Zucchi arrested Gavazzi with a troop of soldiers and gave orders for him to be removed to the prison for immoral priests at Corneto. But the armed troop, while eating at an inn at Viterbo the following night, with Gavazzi under guard, were challenged by the civic guard there, some of whom had served in 'the crusade' and recognised not a shamefaced broken priest but their former chaplain general. The civic guard took him from Zucchi's men and Gavazzi celebrated his release at a public banquet in Viterbo – and, inevitably, made a lengthy after dinner speech.[68]

What he had apparently foreseen and warned Garibaldi to expect

[65] *Epistolario di Luigi Carlo Farini*, ed Luigi Rava, 4 vols (Bologna 1911–35) 2, p 668, for the pope's demand to cardinal Amat; also see M. Minghetti *Miei Ricordi* 3 vols (Turin 1889–90) 2, p 398. These references are cited by Sylvain, who is better on the literature favourable to the clerical interpretation of these events than with that of the men of the risorgimento.

[66] Cencetti p 171, '. . . che morte si, ma giammai mi avrebbero avuto prigione.'

[67] Garibaldi in his *Memorie Autobiografiche* (Florence 1888) does not write directly of Gavazzi – there are many omissions of persons in this collection of not over-articulate reflections – but various contemporary writers and journalists show that Garibaldi respected Gavazzi's courage and appointed him more than once as chaplain and organiser of ambulances. Moreover, he was glad of Gavazzi's aid in Naples and elsewhere as one who could enhearten his soldiers and obtain popular support by his irresistible oratory. The slogan originated with the american, Patrick Henry: it had a more literal meaning for many young italians who died believing it, than for Henry's more cautious hearers.

[68] The bishop of Montefiascone and Corneto was deeply alarmed at the prospect of Gavazzi being incarcerated in the 'Ergastulum' for immoral priests, since he was sure disturbances would occur, but the papal administration was now in disarray after the

had now taken place. Papal authority was challenged at Rome: the moderate Rossi, who was trying to introduce a form of representative government at Rome, was murdered. Faced by revolution Pius fled disguised to Gaeta in the neapolitan kingdom. Garibaldi came with his legion and Gavazzi also entered Rome, and his arm in Garibaldi's walked through cheering crowds who, like himself, expected a brave new world to be born.[69] Garibaldi, more down to earth, wary of Mazzini's dreams of a *Respublica Romana* restored, and aware of the dangers of foreign intervention especially that of a french army, prepared for the attack. Gavazzi was appointed chaplain and organizer of ambulances for the roman troops of the republic which had been proclaimed. He was now, while still a priest, fully committed as a revolutionary, a servant of the triumvirate ruling the republic, and rejoicing to be a comrade of Garibaldi's legionaries. An incident from this period was to form a colourful part of his later anti-papal oratory, the breaking open of the prison of the holy office; Gavazzi was among the first to explore its dark chambers and look horrified on heaps of human bones, and the concealed trap of an underground pit containing human hair and putrefying remains. The prison was ordered to be cleaned out and turned into a lodging house for the poor.[70]

---

murder of Rossi. A. Zappoli, *L'arresto di Padre Gavazzi*, an article in *La Constituente*, 25 November 1848. Sylvain cites here G. Natali, *Il padre Gavazzi e l'entrata di Garibaldi nello Stato Pontifico* in *Il Comune di Bologna*, 21 (1934).

[69] The prominence of Gavazzi at this stage is shown by the fact that it was he who after assisting at mass on easter Sunday in St Peter's, blessed the crowd with the blessed sacrament from the vatican loggia. He wrote: 'Io feci benedire il popolo dalla gran loggia Vaticana nel giorno di Pasqua col Santissimo Sacramento.' (*Eco d'Italia*, 1 October 1853.) The mass at St Peter's was sung by a piedmontese priest who had been inhibited for supporting the risorgimento. To usurp thus the privileged papal altar was a sacrilege which seems not to have worried Spola, the celebrant, nor Gavazzi, the assistant, nor the vast crowd who gathered there.

[70] Luigi Bianchi, *Incidents in the Life of an Italian* (London 1859). Bianchi describes himself as present, and saw a chamber high in the roof with heaps of bones. He added (p 146) that an aged bishop and two nuns were set free. This matter has long been a disputed difficulty. Gavazzi recounted these horrors later in Britain and North America when the inquisition was one of his most successful anti-papal subjects. Clerical writers affirm that the bones, furnace and instruments of torture were hastily set up in the prison of the holy office – there was a cemetery nearby – as an exhibition of papal cruelty. Anti-clerical writers deny this. Gavazzi claimed to have been the first to enter the prison and his horrified description points to visible evidence. I have found no instance of calculated lying on matters of fact by Gavazzi elsewhere, but this, of course, does not preclude his being the victim of a theatrical display by republican anti-clericals who had worked hard as scene-shifters in the hours before he entere1 the prison on 1 April 1849.

It was stated above that in writing on Gavazzi 'few options are open apart from narrative': however, it was added, that Gavazzi can be seen as exemplifying the religious crisis created by the risorgimento for many catholics. The narrative of what happened to him from his entry into the barnabite order at sixteen to his becoming a chaplain and organiser of ambulances under Garibaldi during the roman revolution at thirty-nine, has been given. The question must now be asked, what forces were at work in the italian church which transformed the innocent novice, the loyal catholic, the devout writer of works of piety, the admirer of Pius IX into the impassioned orator of the crusade against the austrians and, for him, a conservative revolution, chaplain to the troops of the anti-clerical Garibaldi, and soon after into a vigorous denouncer of the papacy and of roman catholicism? Leopardi had written: '. . . in a nation's memories the fabulous years are those of that nation's youth', and though he did not live to see them the fabulous years of Italy's youth were those of the risorgimento: but here we enter a confusing maze of interpretations, as was suggested above, when we seek to study that movement. To understand Gavazzi, and many other priests or laymen who were pulled between conflicting loyalties, we must consider the force of religious energies in the risorgimento. If we ignore this religious force then Gavazzi becomes at worst no more than a renegade, a ranting second-rate actor in a demagogic melodrama; at best, a self-willed friar who lost his vocation and betrayed his church.

The risorgimento is commonly understood to have begun in Italy in 1831, when Gavazzi was twenty-two. Five years before this Lamennais had written prophetically: 'Society awaits, in order to be reborn, a new activity in christianity, a great deed noble in itself: henceforth it will not be with diplomacy that the world will be saved.'[71] It was by diplomacy and war, with Cavour and Garibaldi as significant exemplars, that Italy was united; but diplomacy and war must have ideas and emotions behind them to rouse men to support or endure them. There had to be ideas and purpose to justify the italian dead at Treviso and many later battlegrounds. Lampedusa in *The Leopard* describes a sicilian, the prince of Salina, reflecting in 1860 on the corpse of a young soldier of the fifth regiment who had crawled into his gardens to die. 'Soldiers become soldiers in order . . . to die in defence of their king. . . . The image of that gutted corpse often

---

[71] Translated from Paul Dudon, *Lettres inédites de Lamennais à Ventura, Etudes*, I (March 1910) p 612. The date of this letter to Ventura was 14 May 1826.

reappeared as if crying to be given peace . . . for to die for someone or something is to do well and is in order, provided that he who does so knows or feels sure for whom or for what be is dying . . . "He died for the King [of Naples] it is clear, who represents order, continuity, decency, right, honour . . . who alone defends the Church" . . . but kings should not fall below a certain level for generations, for if they do the idea they represent suffers also.'[72] The kings referred to had been the product of Metternich's reaction, restored by the congress of Vienna, but incompetent in their absolutism; on the principle of throne and altar such men were supported by Gregory XVI for whom conservative repression was the truth of God and liberalism in any form the instrument of the devil. That conservative intention gave the austrian empire the chief control not only immediately in Lombardy and Venetia but mediately elsewhere in Italy – and in the south was that kingdom where Lampedusa's prince saw the idea of kingship and honour degraded by repression and corruption. Italians, however regional their traditional loyalty, felt that change must come, and that change could only come by new principles, by new aspirations and ideas. In searching for these ideas and emotions more attention should be given to religious writers and also clergy and devout laymen active in the risorgimento; and, in doing so, the later effort by members of the catholic church in Italy to minimise or distort the history of that movement should not be overlooked.[73] That catholics should be indignant at the vulgar and violent anti-clericalism of many partisans of italian unity is obviously acceptable, but that should not carry with it indifference to the agony of conscience of religious men who sought what they believed to be for their country's good. 'History has many cunning passages, contrived corridors . . . deceives with whispering ambitions . . .' Eliot's words echo in the memory when one remembers that the christian democratic party,

---

[72] Tomasi di Lampedusa, *Il Gattopardo* (Milan 1958). Translated here from the 1963 Feltrinelli edition, pp 13–14.

[73] [Anthony P.] Campanella, [*Giuseppe Garibaldi e la Tradizione Garibaldina una*] *bibliografia* [*dal 1807 al 1970*], Comitato dell'Instituto Internazionale di Studi Garibaldini, 2 vols (Geneva 1971). 'The roman catholic church, the perennial enemy of liberal garibaldian principles . . . has, through its vast network of churches, schools and propaganda media . . . precluded any dissemination of the true facts concerning him.' To this church 'Garibaldi represents the anti-Christ par excellence'. He adds that the christian democratic party of Italy sought consistently to undermine Garibaldi's prestige and neglected the publication of his correspondence. The phrase 'true facts' show Campanella as too emotionally committed, but the basis of his criticism is sound.

dominant in Italy since 1945, has sought consistently to undermine Garibaldi's prestige, neglected his house and documents, and blamed him for the fiasco of fascism.[74] But it was beyond irony when that party pushed Garibaldi into the background and supported the touring club of Italy in publishing a volume honouring Pius IX as the real hero of the occasion when the events of 1860 were celebrated in 1961.[75] This and other examples from recent times eliminate the crisis of conscience of Gavazzi and many others like him, and convey the impression that whatever was religiously valid in the risorgimento must be seen through a distorting hindsight.

What was 'religiously valid' goes back further than 1831. There were two strong influences, both originating in France, jansenism and the catholic renewal begun by Lamennais and his followers. The kingdom of Piedmont, the heartland for the reunification of Italy, was neighbour to France and therefore it had been open to jansenist influences. Italian jansenism showed its power at the synod of Pistoia, 1786, held in Tuscany under bishop Scipione Ricci.[76] Among the fifty-seven points for reform made at the synod were reform of the liturgy, including the encouragement of reading the bible in italian; the revision of disciplinary procedure including reform of the religious orders; the introduction of synodical government; the obligatory residence of parish priests; the closing of the holy office. The synod, which established a comprehensive statement of italian jansenism, showed through their decisions a decentralised anti-papal tendency. The memory of the work of bishop Ricci remained long after the synod had been condemned by a papal bull in 1798, including his hostility to 'scholastic inventions', and, particularly, the idea that ecclesiastical reform was necessary and possible. Jansenism's power lay in its moralistic drive, its strong appeal to the conscience, which impelled to action for religious renewal. If ecclesiastical reform was blocked by repressive conservative governments supporting the throne and altar principle backed by the papacy, then anxious consciences could ask, Was the church not of greater importance than the civil power? In northern Italy the university of Turin had been a jansenist powerhouse until the jesuits obtained control of it after 1821 –

---

[74] Campanella *bibliographia*. The citations are from his introduction.

[75] *Ibid.* He adds thus 'honouring the great enemy of italian independence'.

[76] Maturi, pp 602–3, refers to three historians who have discussed the influence of jansenism in northern Italy. For brief statements on Ricci and the synod of Pistoia, Bihlmeyer-Tuechle 4, pp 57, 103, with accompanying references to the literature of the subject.

a fact, though comparatively small in itself, which had, no doubt, some bearing on Charles Albert's reference to the jesuits' chocolate and to Cavour's attitude to religious orders later. The conflict concerning the synod of Pistoia, pursued through books and pamphlets, lasted for years. Here were ideas catholic, moral, reforming and practical which lingered on in northern Italy. Mazzini had in his youth known the moral purposiveness of jansenism.

Again, the proximity of France led to the influence of Lamennais whose work increasingly emphasised loyalty to the papal principle against that of the union of throne and altar, the absolutist anachronism which he found so exasperating either under the restored Bourbon or the 'citizen king' in France.[77] For him a renewed catholicism in which the essence of christianity was freedom, and in which the rights of the poor must be claimed, turned for support not to kings but to the papacy. When Lamennais countered the condemnation of his views by Gregory XVI in *Mirari vos*, 1832, with his *Paroles d'un croyant* in 1834, he showed that it was possible for catholics to be loyal to the faith of the church while rejecting the church's contemporary rôle in politics including the important stumbling-block of the temporal power of the pope in the papal states. This had considerable influence on catholic intellectuals which the encyclical *Singulari nos*, 1834, failed to overcome. Manzoni – the devout author of that historical novel *I Promessi Sposi* which presented the ideal of catholicism at its best – who accepted the reformist and liberalising views of the neo-guelfs, wrote of Lamennais that he was the sole voice in France for justice, truth and liberty. The neo-guelfs, whatever they owed to catholic writers elsewhere in Europe, were inspired by italian problems and italian ideas to resolve them. The catholic intellectual and religious elements in the risorgimento were born among the neo-guelfs, those liberal catholics who questioned the traditional assumptions of the rôle of the church in society and in relation to the state.

Liberal catholic views would owe something to the cultural renewal in the eighteenth century in Italy shown in the work of the historians Giannone and Muratori, and the philosophy of Vico which is still

---

[77] For a brief view of the later views of Lamennais see *Catholicisme*, publ Centre Interdisciplinaire des Facultés catholiques de Lille, 6 (Paris 1967) cols 1721, 1722. A. R. Vidler, *Prophecy and Papacy* (London 1954) unfortunately ends before examining the later years of Lamennais in which his social and political views were so widely influential.

seminal today.[78] But the tracing of the genealogical descent of ideas is difficult and it is dangerous to be too positive about lines of descent and influence. Republicanism and the 'principles of eighty nine' were brought into Italy following on the french revolution and the napoleonic invasion: the carbonari were part of the consequence. Mazzini took the republicanism of the revolution as a weapon against the nexus of throne and altar, and used the nationalism which was part of the reaction to the revolution to urge an association of free european nations inspired by the vague theistic overtones of 'God and the People' in which Italy would be free, united, and helping to renew humanity.[79] But the neo-guelfs opposed to these vaguely defined aspirations, a catholicism renewed, politically liberal, and looking to guidance from the papacy disentangled from the net of the temporal power and giving leadership to an Italy freed and reborn. The intellectual force of this liberal catholic movement, which opposed the views of Mazzini's party of 'young italy' and the methods of their network of secret societies, was provided by two priests and philosophers, Vincenzo Gioberti and Antonio Rosmini.[80] They started from the same basis as the christian romanticism shown by Manzoni – a romanticism which, however fruitful in ideas, had lacked political realism. Gioberti was a piedmontese who became a priest and was attracted to the movement for a united Italy, and was banished at the same time as Mazzini in 1833 because of his vigorous liberal political views. From his exile in Brussels in the following years he wrote various works which gripped a younger generation of laymen and priests, not so

[78] Maturi also cites a chain of those who demonstrated ideas of national independence for Italy: Machiavelli – Vico – Cuoco – Mazzini – Gioberti, p 526. P. Giannone (d 1748) was a historian who wrote on his native Naples with a strong anti-papal bias and who believed in minimising hierarchical control of the church. A. Muratori (d 1750) is a name famous among ecclesiastical historians for his integrity, diligence and objectivity as a scholar, whose ecclesiastical position can be seen reflected in the dislike shown to him and his works by the jesuits. G. B. Vico (d 1744) wrote the remarkable *Scienza Nuova* (Naples 1725) showing the history of civilisation as a spiral, though Vico's view of history as guided by God's providence has little interest to historians in our time. His interest in language influenced James Joyce, 'a lord of language'.

[79] Luigi Salvatorelli, *Il problema religioso nel Risorgimento*, [*Rassegna Storica*], anno 43, fasc 1 (1956) p 213: '. . . il Mazzini fece del Risorgimento italiano, e anzi della sistemazione europea in associazione di nazioni libere, una esigenza della religione "Dio e Popolo".' – this excluded the papacy. Also see Mazzini, *Opere* 4, p 1; 5, pp 42, 43 (Salvatorelli's reference) – (see n 89 below).

[80] Torre. Torre claims that Gioberti affirmed that Italy contained in itself, above all through its religion, all the conditions required for its material and political renewal. For a list of Gioberti's major writings see Maturi, p 721, and for the historiography on Gioberti see Maturi's index.

much by his philosophical works, anti-scholastic in form and grounded on the assertion of the intuitive vision of God, as by his writings on the recovery of national independence combined with religious renewal which were so influential. His *Il Primato morale e civile degli Italiani* affirmed the idealised vision of the papacy as guiding an italian confederation of states and as the moral arbiter of the nations. He took a view wholly opposed to that of Mazzini on the papacy, since Gioberti showed that the papacy was necessary for Italy, because through it national unity could be blessed by unity of faith. What Lamennais found helpful in France in Chateaubriand's *Génie du Christianisme*, Gioberti's italian disciples found in Manzoni's idealised view of italian catholicism in the seventeenth century, and in Gioberti's own eloquent prose. Manzoni's remarkable novel *I Promessi Sposi* first began to appear in 1825 and achieved its final form in 1840–2, emphasised tolerance, freedom, human brotherhood purified by a religion of peace and love in a catholicism that ignored 'curialism' and jesuit triumphalism.[81] Here was the rallying point for new ideas on combining political liberalism, catholic belief, social improvement, church renewal under a pope with the vision to guide the nation forward, while avoiding the anti-clericalism and violence of the republican groups. Gioberti's *Prolegomini del Primato morale e civile degli Italiani*, 1845, turned against Austria, the oppressor nation carefully unnamed in his previous book, and also attacked the jesuits whom he had come to dislike in his Turin years for he regarded them as pro-austrian and the fuglemen of reaction and oppression in the name of curial necessity – moreover they had vigorously attacked his earlier work. He crowned his anti-jesuit polemic with a study in five volumes published in 1846 *Il Gesuito moderno*. Powerful propaganda for the neo-guelfs can also be found in count Cesare Balbo's *Delle Speranze d'Italia* of 1844 exhorting patriots to defy the austrians, and the book by the moderate but determined statesman Massimo d'Azeglio, the son-in-law of Manzoni, *Degli ultimi casi di Romagna*, 1846, making clear to Europe at large the miserable condition of the people immediately under papal government.[82]

[81] Manzoni's novel still attracts numbers of readers, and has had a renewal of life in a new English version. The viewpoint of Manzoni has been described in Maturi (p 40) as *una formula felice*, namely 'nel considerare come ideale dello storico la fusione del Vico e del Muratori, della filosofia e della filologia, dal gusto di vedere le cose dall'alto con genialità di pensiero e del gusto del particolare preciso appurato dopo pazienti indagini archivistiche'. Nevertheless it is a moving story, and owes something to the powerful influence of Walter Scott on the continent.

[82] Massimo d'Azeglio was a potent figure, his *I miei ricordi* – best edition edited by

But Gioberti and others, it is now increasingly clear, were equalled and surpassed by another priest Antonio Rosmini who in 1830 had published an invigorating study of the origin of ideas, and in 1842 issued his *Filosofia di diritto della politica*. The following year, together with count Balbo, he produced a pamphlet on a new constitution, especially concerned with the papal states – this was the feverish period of constitution-making in the various italian states.[83] Pope Pius IX, whose attempts at change led the elderly Metternich to his ironical comment, 'I had foreseen everything but a liberal pope', was interested in Rosmini's views, including the publication, which had been in manuscript since 1832, of his *Delle cinque piaghe della Santa Chiesa* which set down ways of reform and renewal in the church in which Rosmini took for starting point the principles of the men of the sixteenth-century oratory of divine love, Sadoleto, Contarini, Caraffa and Pole. He emphasized better education for ordinary laity, and also for the priests, pointing out the poor quality of seminary training. His constitutional programme, which interested Pius IX, proposed that the states of Italy should be free of foreign rule, united and meeting together in a governing body at Rome under papal protection.

Reform or liberal catholicism in Italy, with or without political concerns, from jansenism through Lamennais to Rosmini and Manzoni, is known ground to historians of the period to whom the previous paragraphs should be a familiar summary. But this summary is the necessary setting for discussing the change of Gavazzi from a pious young friar with a talent for preaching, to the orator ejected from his order who shared in the roman revolution which led to the flight of the pope and Garibaldi's first major conflict for italian unity. Unfortunately, citations by Sylvain, and the extracts in an italian journal, from Gavazzi's autobiography show an old man reviewing distant memories of action: he apparently was uninterested in explaining his development by recalling his intellectual progress in describing what books he read in his youth and young manhood, or what men he

---

Ghisalberti (Milan 1963) – is one of the better autobiographies of the first half of the nineteenth century – he was an artist, a professional soldier and politician, and author. His observations and judgments are shrewd, and forceful.

[83] Rosmini is attracting attention among catholic writers today because his views are more acceptable to their contemporary theological needs than those of the ultimately antagonistic Gioberti and Lamennais. But it is significant that references to him are few in Maturi's index.

talked to who were familiar with the ideas of reformed catholicism and of the neo-guelfs. Gavazzi remembers the fires of old passions, of heroic adventures, and of courageous oratory – intellectual analysis, the origin and significance of particular ideas, did not interest him. This was to be a major weakness of his platform oratory in England and North America, and it also accounts for the ephemeral quality of many of his writings in which, in those I have been able to find and read, he makes no effective mention of the thought of the makers of the liberal catholic tradition. Nor, when he had ceased to be a catholic, do his writings and speeches show the intellectual's concern with depth, and the scholar's concern with precision, in the use of history and theology.

Gavazzi was a man who did not originate ideas or put together with original intellectual labour a continuous analysis of social, political or religious matters. His mind was quick to assimilate by hearing others talk, and to skim through an article or a book, grasping here and there a telling phrase or an idea which could be given an emotional colouring: from this assimilation he derived the content of his oratory, his books and pamphlets. What emerges from his sermons and books before 1845 are, first, that he had accepted in his early years as a barnabite the excellent if somewhat routine religious emphases of his order, which enabled him to express traditional piety dressed in the conventional rhetoric of the period; secondly, we can see that these traditional and worthy pieties were increasingly energised with ideas on social matters (the needs of the poor, the prisoners, the dispossessed, the indifference and selfishness of the rich and the nobles), and on religious reform (the concern for improvements in the training of priests, the questioning of the superficial quality in the lives of many monks and nuns, the search for something fresh and quickening, the increase of piety, and irritation with the creaking bureaucratic machinery of the church). However, the phrases and themes he began to use increasingly in the years 1838–45, so far as they can be obtained from his comparatively few publications of this period, are difficult to identify as showing the influence of specific authors or movements. He may well not have known, or attached importance to, the names of liberal or reform catholics, and in any event if he knew the names or was aware of the sources and aims of a movement, since his knowledge probably came not so much from careful and systematic reading as from listening to others, he would not have been able to give a considered and cogent presentation of, or judgment on, the work of particular authors. Since the Gavazzi family were bolognese (though of venetian origin) they would share in Bologna's concern as the lay-capital of the papal states to be forward-looking and resentful of ecclesiastical conservatism in politics, although his father appears to have been conservative in outlook.[84] Giuseppe Patuzzi, a maternal uncle of Gavazzi, took part in the revolution at Bologna in 1831 and emigrated to France in 1836; he was to be praised for his patriotism later by his nephew.[85] Gavazzi felt other influences showing zeal for liberty besides that of his mother's family (and his mother, especially dear to Gavazzi, showed pride in the patriotism of her sons), his father's successor in the chair of civil law at the university of Bologna, Antonio Silvani, who had been briefly exiled after 1831 because of his liberal views, became a close friend of the young barnabite. Silvani was much concerned with constitutional changes and his conversation must have affected Gavazzi.[86] In preaching in San Petronio at Bologna on the immaculate conception Gavazzi contrived to exalt the historical greatness of Bologna and its future political rôle. It was about this period that he had become a close friend of Ugo Bassi, who had become an advocate of 'liberty' and social reform. Again, Gavazzi's various travels included Turin more than once, where liberal views were discussed. These visits together with the friendship of Silvani who was concerned with political reform, and of Bassi an older man than Gavazzi and burning with zeal for Italy – all these are influences on an impressionable young preacher of strong character. From these may come some elements of remembered jansenism and its moral earnestness, which could reinforce ideas on the church as aiding social justice derived from Lamennais and his followers, for example Raffaele Lambruschini in Italy. Beyond this it would be speculation: but by the late thirties it is certain that Gavazzi, while ignoring the methods and propaganda of the secret societies, had available for his sermons themes which showed concern for political and social reform, and patriotic zeal for Italy, and which echo those of the contemporary writers on reformed catholicism.[87]

---

[84] Sylvain cites the manuscript of Gavazzi's *Autobiografia*, p 091024 for Gavazzi's view of his father as a conservative if not a reactionary.

[85] *My Recollections* pp 196–7: '. . . my only uncle, the general of the civic guard [at Bologna] who afterwards merited the honour of being exiled for the cause of Italy, and died in exile. The reader will, I trust, pardon my honest family pride.'

[86] Santini p 31. Silvani again renewed relationship with Gavazzi in 1847.

[87] King, p 96 quotes Gavazzi: 'During my seven years' exile I have never seen Mazzini nor have I corresponded with him. . . . I am the last to approve him as a political

Alessandro Gavazzi: a barnabite friar and the risorgimento

Whether he owed anything to Mazzini, and the movement of 'young italy', is worth investigation but difficult to determine: Mazzini's phrase 'God and the people' could find an echo in Gavazzi's sermons and writings, but this would not tie him to Mazzini's views. Gavazzi always opposed republicanism as a valid political future for Italy, although in his patriotic zeal to help Garibaldi to defend Rome against the french army in 1849 he could not help working under the roman republic's brief triumvirate. The idea of an analogy between the experiences and aspirations of italians and those of the jews of scripture was not uncommon at that time: both were a martyr people overwhelmed by domestic and foreign tyranny, and as the jews hoped that after Babylon there would come a restoration of land and people, so italians yearned for unity and freedom from foreign domination.[88] Mazzini believed that Italy could only be freed from foreign rule and united with the aid of religion. Gavazzi could readily accept this. When Mazzini said: 'We need a new religion, a religion of duty', Gavazzi might well agree about duty but he could not have accepted Mazzini's vague theism as an adequate religion.[89] Gavazzi's reform principles were closer to those of the neo-guelfs than to Mazzini and his republicanism. Gioberti's *Il Primato morale e civile degli Italiani* which appeared in 1833 stole Mazzini's thunder. It is reasonable to believe that the books of Balbo and Gioberti's book influenced the eager young barnabites Bassi and Gavazzi, who at the same period were aware of the views associated with the disciples of Lamennais. Again, Pius VII, for Gavazzi's generation, had been the pope who had endured insults and oppression by the french and could be idealised (and was idealised with purpose by Rosmini in a panegyric on the death of Pius VII) as a heroic figure opposing foreign oppression of italians, and a symbol of neo-guelf aspirations for a 'liberal' pope.[90] Perhaps here lies the enthusiasm of Gavazzi when Pius IX was enthroned. But whether Rosmini's later works were studied and assimilated by Gavazzi is an open question, and is probably doubtful. He had found sufficient fuel

---

leader.' Mazzini instituted secret societies. There is no evidence to connect Gavazzi with freemasonry, in Italy a politically oriented and anti-clerical body – moreover his brusque common sense would have no taste for its rituals.

[88] Spini p 76.

[89] Torre quotes Mazzini as demanding a new religion, a religion of duty in which there would be three dogmas, the existence of God, the law of progress, and the general co-operation of men (cited from Mazzini's *Fide e Avenire*).

[90] Santini p 5 'Pio VII che, spogliato dal regno e condotto prigioniero a Savona, assorgeva a simbolo della nazionalità oppressa'.

after 1845 to feed the furnace of his oratory, without needing Rosmini's patient study of philosophical constitution-making which envisaged a new Italy of federal states under the guidance of Pius IX.

A stronger possibility of influence on Gavazzi is that which could be called neo-ghibellinism whose basic principle differed from that of the neo-guelfs (who saw the papacy as taking the lead in purifying society and the church) in declaring that the papacy was incapable of such leadership since it had become too corrupt to reform itself much less Italy. The neo-ghibelline group less easy to describe because it was less homogeneous than the neo-guelfs, held to the same view as the latter that religion must be maintained as the necessary source of moral energy and as the formative principle by which the reunification of Italy should be attained. But unlike the neo-guelfs, the neo-ghibellines had differing views on how this religion should be expressed. Mazzini believed that 'religious thought purifies the individual and to try to act without religion is false'.[91] Gabriele Rossetti stated a central theme of this group: *il cristianismo in se stesso e virtu morale che si trasforme in forza politica è vigor privato da cui deriva il pubblico; è nobilita individuale da cui proviene la nazionale.*[92] The heroic figures of the christian past in Italy for the neo-ghibellines were Dante, Petrarch, Tasso, Machiavelli and Sarpi, and they viewed the papacy, in the light of the writings of these men of a former age, as still the source of corruption in contemporary Italy. Niccolo Tommaseo who was to become one of the heroes of the 'five days of Milan' which caused the austrian reprisals leading to 'the crusade' of 1847-9, wrote that Italy would not be made a nation again until it first reacquired the purity of the religion of its ancestors before there had been brought in the dogma of purgatory and the practice of the confessional which was 'the school of corruption'. Tommaseo knew Gavazzi and attacking the confessional as a source of moral corruption was to become one of Gavazzi's standard lecture subjects. Further, Gavazzi later published a little book in England called *The Priest in Absolution* attacking the revival of confession in the church of England by father Knox Little at St Albans, Cheetwood, Manchester, and father A. H.

[91] Torre p 96, citing Mazzini *Opere* 4, 1.
[92] Torre p 118, citing Rossetti's *Roma verso la meta del secolo XIX* (London 1840). Gabriele Rossetti was to make a famous name for himself in exile in England not so much by his writings or by his becoming professor of italian at the newly founded King's College, London, but by becoming the father of a remarkable literary family – Christina, Dante Gabriel, and William Michael. He adopted strong anti-catholic polemical views and, in later life, some degree of protestant evangelicalism. Vinay p 123.

Mackonochie in Holborn, London.[93] When Mazzini wrote to Lamennais in 1834, the year in which Lamennais was condemned by the pope: 'The papacy has killed faith under a materialism more dangerous and abject than that of the eighteenth century . . . papal materialism proceeds from the mantle of jesuitism . . . the papacy has suffocated love in a sea of blood . . .'[94] Gavazzi would find an echo for his own later thinking – not that he derived such judgments necessarily from Mazzini but from those who held such views among the people he knew in the forties. The tragedy, *Arnoldo da Brescia*, by G. B. Niccolini is a significant document of the ideals of this group of which he was a leading member.[95] Gavazzi was to lecture later in exile on Dante as a heroic symbol of purer religion and defiance of papal political activity. From various echoes in his later speeches and writings Gavazzi showed he was more influenced by the neo-ghibelline attitude after his exile in 1849. But one other source of influence on Gavazzi at a later stage was that of the political leadership of Piedmont, especially that of Cavour.

Gavazzi's career up to the fall of the brief roman republic has been outlined, the period of his exile in Britain will be considered later; in his autobiography he called the years 1859–68 *Ritorno*, and at this point his relationship as an opponent of the catholic church, as well as the papacy, to Cavour's political views will conclude this examination of the interconnection of his religious convictions and the political environment of this second and different experience of the stages taken towards italian unity.

By now Gavazzi was wholly opposed to the roman catholic church, as well as anti-papal, and had adopted most of the principles of evangelical protestantism, though with strong reservations on the doctrine of grace, and moulded this protestantism to his own pattern. (He was obnoxious to the Plymouth brethren, who had made some powerful italian converts, and to the strongly evangelical presbyterian

[93] *The Priest in Absolution: an Exposure*, 'by Alessandro Gavazzi, Minister of the Free Christian Church in Italy' (London 1877). The following sentence (p 31) has a period flavour: 'And yet, after the experience of centuries, Dr Pusey dares to assert, in one of his letters to the *Daily Express* that a great injustice has been committed towards "a large body of well-educated English clergymen, in thinking that any clergy of ours would ask anything, or English wives and daughters listen to, what it would be unfit for father or husband to hear".'

[94] Torre cites Mazzini writing these words to Lamennais, and gives *Opere* 5, pp 42, 44, as the reference.

[95] 'Niccolini non era democratico, ma liberale laico.' Maturi, p 403.

congregations in Italy, because of his modifications to traditional protestant evangelical orthodoxy.)[96] Not long after his return to Italy he prepared a pamphlet *Sulla necessitá d'una religione per gl'Italiani* which shows he was not only negatively anti-papal but he was also searching for a way of relating the patriotic desire for unity and reform to a new way of religion. His problem was that he was unattracted by the forms of protestantism already developed in Italy, waldensians, Plymouth brethren, presbyterians or other evangelical groups. In 1860 he also challenged the view, propagated by Napoleon III, that Italy needed a french alliance and also now took a positive stand against Mazzini's republicanism in favour of an Italy strong under the piedmontese monarchy. It would be most useful to know what was Gavazzi's attitude to Cavour, and especially to Cavour's initiative to break the deadlock between the piedmontese creation of italian unity and that papal intransigence seen in Pio Nono's *non possumus* to the suggestion that he should give up the papal states. In October 1860 Cavour spoke for all italians seeking reunification when he said in Parliament: *La nostra stella e di fare che la città eterna . . . diventi la splendida capitale del regno italico.*[97] 8176 secular priests and 767 religious, especially men from the south, signed a petition to the pope in favour of Cavour's utterance: 'two voices cry aloud *Viva il Papa e Viva Roma Metropoli del Nuovo Regno* – it will be your blessed destiny to harmonise them.'[98] Pius replied with his by now usual and immediate threat to excommunicate all the signatories unless they immediately withdrew. This shows both the feeling among catholic clergy, and the obstinate difficulty in solving the problem. Cavour's other and even better-known way to break the deadlock was his declaration: *Libera chiesa in libero stato*[99] – 'moral forces overcome moral

---

[96] Gavazzi wrote *Che sia il plimuttismo: Studio storico-polemico* (Florence 1876) in order to counteract their infiltration of his free churches. His sources were: *The Errors of Darby and the Plymouth Sect, The Record* (1862); *Plymouth Brethrenism: its ecclesiastical and doctrinal teachings, British Quarterly Review* (October 1873); *The Heresies of the Plymouth Brethren,* J. L. Carson (Coleraine 1862); *Brethrenism or the special teachings ecclesiastical and doctrinal of the Brethren, or Plymouth Brethren,* Duncan Macintosh (London 1872); *A Catechism of the doctrine of the Plymouth Brethren* (London 1866). There were several scottish presbyterian ministers working in Italy – R. Stewart of Leghorn who worked with the valdesi, and J. MacDougall whose work was among English-speaking presbyterians in Italy, were among these. The latter showed sympathy to Gavazzi, but Stewart strongly opposed him in Italy and in Scotland. Gavazzi found Stewart a constant thorn in the flesh.

[97] Torre p 167.

[98] *Ibid* p 167.

[99] There has long been discussion on the origin of this famous phrase. E. Passerin

obstacles.' He was attempting to persuade Pius that by giving up the temporal power the pope would acquire greater not less freedom.

Gavazzi's concern for a new religion for italians could fit this pattern; he was later to institute a free church in Italy, claiming to be uncommitted to traditional protestantism, expressing the religion of the early church at Rome, and dissociated from the curialism and triumphalism of the catholic church.[100] Unfortunately so many of Gavazzi's writings are expressed in terms of personal experiences and recollections that once again one cannot be sure how much he knew of Cavour's views on religious matters. He begins frequently from personal griefs, observations and hopes and expresses these in rhetorical terms which can in certain phrases resemble Cavour's statements at this period, but this is not sufficient proof. Moreover, his concern not to be identified with one political party or party leader may have led to his generalising his assertions, and also he may have been aware of the protestant origins of Cavour's famous phrase and was wary of using it. In any case the piedmontese government regarded Gavazzi as a trouble maker.

A more powerful and sympathetic figure for Gavazzi was Garibaldi, to whom he wrote offering his services in 1860, and whom he followed to Sicily and shared in his successes there, once again acting as organiser of ambulances, and encouraging the 'thousand' with his inspiring oratory – while Pio Nono wrote desperately in a private letter of the *pirati e predoni* who formed that 'pernicious band of desperate men'.[101]

It was stated above that Gavazzi was far from being alone in being a priest who helped the cause of italian unity, even though his own character and experiences and eventual protestantism were very different from that of the others. Many of the lower clergy, especially in the south, were devoted to Garibaldi's campaign: a large number of

---

d'Entrèves, *Rassegna Storica* 41 (1954) pp 494–506 argued that Cavour adopted it from Montalembert the french liberal catholic associated with the famous journal *L'Avenir* and the historian of the monks of the West. Montalembert claimed this himself. But Cavour wished Rome to be the capital of Italy and Montalembert did not; moreover he was an ardent ultramontanist which Cavour was certainly not. It is more likely that Cavour, who knew french-speaking Switzerland well, derived it from Alexandre Vinet the distinguished theologian of Lausanne, who broke away from the cantonal state church to found *une église libre*. What is not in doubt is that Cavour opposed any authority being given to the catholic church in temporal affairs.
[100] See p 355 below.
[101] A. Monti, *Pio IX e il Risorgimento italiano* (Bari 1928) cites this from a letter of Pius to monsignor Papardo, 9 June 1860.

them even formed a *legione ecclesiastica* which was attached to the XVI Cosenz division, commanded by a sicilian priest, Paolo Sardo.[102] A number of articles and monographs have been written about priests who took part in the risorgimento. There were three distinguished priests in Salerno, for example, who left their posts to follow the 'thousand', an abbot Sacchi, Vincenzo Padula, and Ovidio Filippo Patella, who were men of learning detesting the social evils and religious corruption deriving from bourbon absolutism in the kingdom of Naples – they found prison, exile and the horrors of battlefields. Two of these men eventually took up again their priestly functions after the reunification of Italy.[103] Men like these, including Gavazzi, could no longer accept Cavour's utterance in the chamber of deputies: 'The Roman Question cannot be solved by the sword: only moral forces overcome moral obstacles.' Better known was one of the remarkable priests of the risorgimento, Gregorio Ugdulena, erudite, devout, patriotic and a lover of liberty; his contribution was political, from being a former university teacher he became a strong influence in the parliament of united Italy.[104] These men differed from Gavazzi in believing that *il gran rifiuto* of Pius IX did not cancel out the principles of the neo-guelfs: they showed that many catholics, including priests, believed that the movement for Italian unity, freedom from foreign occupation and constitutional liberty could be reconciled with catholicism. But between these priests, who remained in Italy and sought that reconciliation between church and nation, and Gavazzi lay his bitter years of exile in which he had become a protestant, though a peculiarly gavazzian protestant. To understand the cause of that separation his activities in exile must be examined.

Since Gavazzi had taken part in the defence of Rome against the french and supported therefore the revolution, he was declared a rebel and sought by the police. He was fortunate to get a passport from the american consul, and with better chance than Bassi, who was caught and shot by the austrians in the north, he escaped with Garibaldi, and, after separating from him, reached Leghorn and sailed for London.[105] He reached unknown England, penniless, heart-broken, ignorant of the

[102] Santini p 143.
[103] Beniamino Palumbo, *Preti del Risorgimento, Rassegna Storica* 43 (1956) pp 511 *et seq.*
[104] *Ibid* pp 513, 514.
[105] King p 40 – Freeman, the american consul, had attended the celebrations after the flight of Pius from Rome, and american opinion supported the republican ideal, and opposed the temporal power of the pope.

language, and drifted into that mixed, sometimes raffish, group of italian exiles already gathered in Soho. He survived on ten shillings a week he earned by giving italian lessons: once he was saved from extreme hunger by meeting another exile, a former colonel of the pontifical volunteers.[106] He still felt strongly his priestly vocation and, shocked by the irreligion of many of the exiles, he tried to minister to them. He interrupted an anti-catholic meeting of italians and others by shouting aloud his allegiance to the catholic faith and his priest-hood.[107] When he received news of the execution near Bologna, by orders of the austrian general Gorzkowski, of his friend Ugo Bassi, whom monsignor Bedini (appointed as the papal representative in the legations) had done nothing to aid, Gavazzi, mourning his friend – and bitterly remembering Bedini whom he was to attack in the United States later – delivered a funeral address which he published at his own expense.

Cardinal Wiseman inhibited him from continuing his activities as a priest, even though Gavazzi claimed in an interview with Wiseman that he had a special commission from the pope.[108] Gavazzi might have drifted downwards into obscure semi-starvation if he had not been taken up at this stage by another inhibited priest, the irishman Francis Mahony, who had trained for the jesuit order, but had not continued in it, became a priest in Italy, returned to his native Cork but 'instead of observing the modesty which adorns and the deference which promotes a young chaplain, he indulged his talent for caricature at the expense of personages whom prudence at least might have counselled him to let alone' . . . 'He became a half-pay soldier of the church minus the half-pay'.[109] Mahony used his brilliant gift for languages, especially latin and greek, and his equally remarkable gift of English prose style, to become one of the circle of writers for *Fraser's Magazine* in 1834, and sit with Thackeray, Southey, Carlyle and other supporters of the 'Queen of the Monthlies' in 'their tavern-in-the-town-conviviality', singing their favourite *All Round my Hat I wear a Green*

---

[106] Campanella p 137.

[107] Santini p 103: 'era frate e frate sarebbe rimasto per sempre.'

[108] King p 47. Wiseman inhibited him as soon as Gavazzi's sermons in italian were announced at a small chapel near Soho Square: Gavazzi refused to recognise the inhibition after an interview with Wiseman who said Gavazzi needed a licence from the pope.

[109] [Ethel] Mannin, [*Two Studies in Integrity: Gerald Griffin and the Rev. Francis Mahony*] (London 1954) p 147. The first quotation is from the reverend George O'Neill, SJ, who wrote a centenary study of Mahony for the National Literary Society in 1905. The second quotation is from a writer in the *North British Review* (December 1866).

Willow, which Mahony could turn into greek or latin, french or italian verse with remarkable speed. Mahony wrote under the pen-name of 'Father Prout', famous once though now forgotten.[110]

He heard Gavazzi deliver his oration for Bassi, found it impressive, and, himself fervently opposed to ultramontanism, offered Gavazzi help. Mahony obtained the Princess Theatre lecture room, off Oxford Street, for him where Gavazzi gave twelve lectures on the character of Pius IX, the influence of the jesuits, and related subjects, beginning 5 January 1851, one of which was attended by Palmerston who wrote: 'I went one day to hear Gavazzi's harangue against the abuses of the Catholic Church. He spoke for an hour and a half to several hundred hearers with much eloquence and effect.'[111] Mahony translated these lectures for the *Daily News*, and they were collected as a booklet, *Orations by Father Gavazzi*, later in 1851. Gavazzi's attacks, since they were based on first-hand experience and that useful addiction to auto-biographical illustration so frequent in his speeches and writings, were bound to be popular when given soon after the establishment of the catholic hierarchy in July 1850 by Pius IX. Palmerston's support and that of other distinguished men, together with Mahony's brilliant and precise English rendering of Gavazzi's oratory, brought Gavazzi out into the foreground where various groups of protestants could provide him with audiences. But they were puzzled and since they were all too familiar with heresy-hunting they frequently wanted to know whether Gavazzi was an orthodox protestant. His biographer, J. W. King, in his book published in 1857, put their questions thus:

> What is your friend Gavazzi? Yes, yes, the uttering of great truths, the aspirations of a nobly patriotic and truly Christian heart are all very well. But there is no profession. Of what peculiar creed is he now? To what section of the Protestant faith does he belong? When did light first break in upon him? Was there no terrible wrestling with the Man of Sin? . . . Evangelical Christianity is not a straw's worth if he does not cast aside that suspicious toga

[110] Mannin pp 152, 153.

[111] Campanella p 135: 'A numerous attendance of persons of every social position filled the large rooms in which these lectures were given. I remember to have seen Earl Russell, and Lord Palmerston several times at the lectures given by the generous patriot'. The quotation from Palmerston is in E. Ashley, *The Life of H. J. Temple, Viscount Palmerston* (London 1876) 1, p 257. In 1850 Ruskin broke an engagement to hear Gavazzi lecture, and Carlyle told his wife Gavazzi was a blockhead – but somebody had enthusiastically claimed that Gavazzi reminded him of Carlyle. W. H. Rudman, *Italian Nationalism and English Letters* (London 1940) p 229.

[Gavazzi's barnabite habit], preach from the pulpit and yield himself up to the Faith as it is in the Church.[112]

King's rendering of these doubts shows the narrow mind and raucous voice of victorian protestantism. Newspaper reporters, more worldly, wrote: 'He is the Shakespeare of actors and has no living rival . . . magnificent voice and physical strength . . . He speaks English with wonderful accuracy but with a foreign accent . . . He pours denunciation [upon the Church of Rome], not from the Protestant but from the Catholic point of view.'[113] It is true that Gavazzi had set himself earnestly to learn English and in time gained a sound grip of the language and fluency in it; but exact reporting of his addresses and his few surviving letters in English show some oddities and italianate phrasing – his accent, moreover, was stronger than the report quoted suggests.

Gavazzi's reply to British protestant doubts about his protestant views is given by King, who quotes a letter from Gavazzi to himself:

When and how and why I came out of Rome I need not discuss here, for I detest all public exhibitions of conversion, as smelling of business and hypocrisy . . . As a lecturer and expounder of my principles, as you well know, I never forget to declare solemnly that I am no Protestant for I have nothing to Protest against. My aim . . . is not to protest against Rome, but to destroy the whole system, root and branch. There is nothing to reform in the Church of Rome, which is nothing but an abuse from beginning to end . . . As an Italian, however, there are still further and grave reasons for declining to embrace any Protestant denomination. It could entirely destroy my hopes of the future evangelisation of Italy. It may be wrong but so strong are the prejudices of Italians against Protestantism at large that, to go to them in a Protestant name would be like driving from my platforms the very people I look for . . . I take the opportunity to exclaim against those societies that spend their money, in sending and maintaining missionaries in Italy. I say publicly that this is the way to strengthen Romanism . . . Let the work be left to the Italians themselves aided by Protestant advice and prayers only. . . . There was a Christianity in Rome before there was any catholicity . . . It is to that primitive, apostolic, evangelical Christian church that

[112] King p 49.
[113] King p 53.

345

I anxiously look for a return . . . let everyone know that I am an unsectarian, independent, evangelical Christian.[114]

This shows why so many British protestants were uneasy about him: he would not conform to their pattern. Either because of his seminary training, or from simple conviction, he detested what was thought of as essential to evangelical protestantism in English dissent, and emphasised in the non-established presbyterianism of Scotland, the doctrine of grace focusing on original sin and predestination, denying free-will and emphasising personal assurance and final perseverance. In his last years in Italy when he formed his free church he was harassed by strongly evangelical groups supported by British funds especially the *plimuttisi*, and he turned aside from the waldensians because he regarded them not as italians but as half-french, and infected with calvinistic predestinarian doctrines.[115] This extract also shows Gavazzi's concern to prevent another kind of foreign intervention in Italy than that which had made him proclaim 'the crusade' against Austria, the religious divisions of foreign protestantism – the problems of italian unification were bad enough without adding to them. Further, Gavazzi's conception of what a true church should be is briefly mentioned: essentially he wanted to pass by all the problems posed by catholicism and protestantism, and take as his model a simplified view of the christian community shown in the new testament. His hostility to historical forces, and his emphasis on Paul as the apostle of the romans show the influences he derived from his italian nationalism. This refusal to face historical facts was a characteristic of the *littérateurs* of the risorgimento – and who now would consult Chateaubriand's *Génie du Christianisme* for its historical analysis however great its value as a document of romanticism?

Soon after getting established in London, Gavazzi like many another political exile before and after him obtained a reader's ticket for the British Museum, and read widely in questions concerning the protestant controversy with Rome, early church history, and the authority of the bible. He would hardly be concerned with the painstaking analyses of the scholar, but he would be reading omnivorously, pursuing questions he had not asked himself before. Somewhere in these first two years in England but, for the reason he himself gave to King we do not know when, he decided against the catholic church.

[114] King p 63.
[115] Spini pp 192 *et seq*, and also Paolo Sanfilippo, *Il Protestantismo Italiano nel Risorgimento* (Rome no date) pp 31 *et seq*.

Alessandro Gavazzi: a barnabite friar and the risorgimento

G. M. Campanella a fellow exile who published in 1877 his *Life in the Cloister, in the Papal Court and in Exile – An Autobiography*, and dedicated it to Gavazzi, wrote of the poorest of the italian refugees being on the slippery slope to crime from despair: 'In this unfortunate position Gavazzi was as if both materially and morally sent by Providence to the rescue, for he not only gave succour in money [derived from collections at his lectures] to those most near falling on the slippery way, but he also gave them persuasive and useful advice and counsel of morality and patriotism.'[116] Gavazzi never forgot the patriotism – but in justice to him we should remember Massimo d'Azeglio's words, and he had an astute and cool judgment and wide experience as a politician and diplomatist: 'We must create italians if we would have an Italy.'[117]

Gavazzi was now established as a public lecturer on the 'evils of the papacy' and travelled to the major towns of the British Isles to thunder forth his denunciations. It would be a useful study to establish who were the various sponsors of these occasions, why he returned several times to certain towns, who were the clergy or prominent laymen appearing on his platforms since something more could be learned in closer detail about victorian protestantism in the fifties and in the return visits he made in later years. From the volumes of newspaper cuttings which survive on these addresses (unfortunately cut so close that names and dates and sometimes places are not given) his standard subjects were: the bible and the papal system; the pope and his double-headed supremacy; monks and nuns; transubstantiation; popedom, and the temporal power of the pope; worship of the virgin Mary and the saints; auricular confession; the inquisition; the present state and future hope of Italy; the jesuits.[118] His oratory even reverberated as far as holy Russia since N. A. Dobroliubov published some of them in his *Sobranie Socineniy* at Petersburg, 1862, now housed in the Lenin state library at Moscow – the translator was something of a political demagogue, and Russia would welcome, in any case, an attack on roman catholicism.[119]

116 Campanella.
117 Massimo d'Azeglio, *Things I Remember*, trans E. R. Vincent (London 1966) p 311.
118 All of these topics recur frequently in newspaper reports of his meetings in the volume of newspaper cuttings and printed ephemera, *Memorie*, and also in the volumes of newspaper cuttings *Orations*, in the Facoltà Valdese at Rome. These topics are also to be found in *Lectures of Gavazzi at New York* (New York 1854).
119 Campanella *Bibliografia*, no 7819. Nikolai Aleksandrovic Dobrolinbov, *Otez Aleksandr Gavazzi, i ego propovedi*, in *Sobranie Socineniy* (Petersburg 1862 and 1911).

Dr Spence Watson of Newcastle-upon-Tyne, wrote to G. M. Trevelyan who had asked for information about Gavazzi that in his youth nearly half a century before he had been present at some of his meetings:

He was far too eloquent not to be verbose, and he certainly was violent. I remember little of what he said in his lectures. His description of the prisons of the Inquisition and of the immorality of the priesthood were exceedingly vivid; but he struck me, after all, as being a genuine man with the faults which one would expect to find in a clergyman who had certainly a strong love of his country and had gone through much for it, but who had become so used to stirring great audiences that that which was a means to excite interest in the matters in which he absolutely believed, in the first instance, had become in itself an end. He lectured in a long black gown, and the great action that he used, and the way in which he threw his gown about him and off again was very theatrical, but it had a certain effectiveness.[120]

Other witnesses, unnamed reporters for provincial newspapers give a similar description though lacking in Spence Watson's insight on 'the means' and 'the end'. In his first two years in England Gavazzi used an interpreter; but before long he dispensed with this aid and from the Woolwich Athenaeum to the Carlisle Athenaeum (with 'the very Rev. the Dean and his lady present') and the Free Trade Hall in Manchester he exposed the errors of Rome. Questions were asked about him in the house of commons, for example by Mr Moore attacking Peel, who said in the prose style Dickens had had to endure in his youth as a press reporter: 'The low Jacobins of the continent were said to see the Gamaliels at whose feet the honourable baronet loved to sit, and the expressions he had used were worthy of his tutelage, for he recognised in them the philosophy of Mazzini and the apostasy of Gavazzi.' (Peel had been one of Gavazzi's audience at the Princess Theatre lecture room: and Moore was pro-austrian). Gavazzi challenged him with the vigour if not the language of a garibaldino in *The Globe*: '. . . I need not suggest to you that your own name ω'μωρε signifies in that language, especially as one Erasmus (an apostate of the same extent as myself) has written a *Moriae Encomium*. If you know as much Italian as Greek, I invite you to hear me tomorrow at Wallis Rooms on the whole subject' – did Mahony suggest that gambit?[121]

[120] Trevelyan, *Defence* p 76, n 2.
[121] *Orations [of Fr. Gavazzi (Decade the Second)]* (London 1851) p 69. (Mahony had

Alessandro Gavazzi: a barnabite friar and the risorgimento

In the *Memorie* a quarto volume of newspaper cuttings in the Facoltà Valdese library at Rome, Gavazzi's public addresses are reported, those which he made in the later sixties and early seventies when returning to seek funds for his new free church of Italy. There is a typical handbill: 'Workmen's Hall, Birkenhead, Father [sic] Gavazzi will deliver his farewell lecture previous to his departure for Rome, on the New Dogma of Papal Infallibility and its startling consequences. Rev. Dr. Blakeney in the chair. Tickets – Body 1s, Gallery 6d.'[122] These prices suggest that by comparatively expensive tickets irish labourers might be kept out. The question of where, and with what consequences and how often, Gavazzi was attacked in towns where a large irish population existed also needs investigation. The cuttings in the *Memorie*, like those volumes of newspaper cuttings dealing with his visits to Quebec and Montreal in the late fifties detailed at length by Sylvain, barely mention trouble – Gavazzi or his secretary preferred to collect for posterity his own words to additional news reports of rioting before or after meetings.

A small attendance at Glasgow in 1865 for a lecture on the french in Rome was blamed by Gavazzi on one of the self-appointed watchdogs against his heresies, Stewart, an ardent predestinarian – but perhaps a cold November night to hear about the french had no compelling power for Glaswegians. [123] At the Music Hall, Newcastle-upon-Tyne, the reverend Wildon Carr who presided presumably led the applause after Gavazzi's comparison of cloister life to 'a little lady in a large crinoline – a very small quantity of substance in a very large envelope'.[124] *The Scotsman* for 1865, shows him denouncing the Davenport brothers for hearing voices from the dead; elsewhere we learn the young men's improvement society at the Liverpool institute under the chairmanship of the reverend M. Clegg was edified by him. In 1854 the *Manchester Guardian* reported a lecture by Gavazzi when the chairman for the occasion, an energetic 'no popery' man, was the evangelical churchman canon Hugh Stowell of Christ Church, Salford, who informed the audience that Gavazzi wanted a real king in Italy and 'not a wretched drivelling old woman'.[125] In 1856 Gavazzi

---

helped with the translations of Gavazzi's first lectures.) Gavazzi replied in *The Globe*, 18 March, with this reference to ω'μωρε.

[122] *Memorie* pp 3, 4.

[123] *Memorie*, cutting from *Daily Review* of Glasgow for 7 November 1865.

[124] *Memorie* p 43.

[125] *Orations* p 82.

toured South Wales, and he appeared there again in 1863. But a
correspondent to *Y Faner ac Amserau y Cymru* who reported hearing
him in Siloh calvinist methodist chapel, Aberystwyth, described the
sermon as 'containing more philosophical ingenuity than practical
substance' – a guarded way of saying that though Gavazzi was an
impressive anti-papal orator yet he did not satisfy calvinist methodist
standards for the content of a sermon.[126] These brief allusions to his
tours on the anti-papal circuits may be brought to the following
climax given in an address at St George's presbyterian church,
Southport, where he refers to a new house and church built for his free
church 'on the bank of the Tiber at the feet [*sic*] of the castle of S.
Angelo. Turning to his left on his balcony he could see the Vatican a
few hundred yards away, and some beautiful morning he and the
Pope would open their respective windows and if they caught each
other's eyes he would bid his holiness good morning because he could
preach the Gospel freely and the Pope less cheerful would be looking
impotently over Rome'.[127] By this period in the late seventies Gavazzi
had apparently mellowed – but one essential goal of his life had been
achieved, a united Italy and the abolition of papal civil government
over italians.

Something should be said about a few at least of his writings: many
were ephemeral, consisting of journalism, as well as sermons and
lectures, but some were set pieces. His early attempt at the traditional
rhetorical style of pulpit oratory is tedious, and its interest lies in
showing how greatly he changed later in theme, style and manner.
His nearest approach to a full-scale work of scholarship was his book
on saint Peter, *La Favola del Viaggio di S. Pietro a Roma*, 1868, where
in three parts forming 320 pages he sought to prove that Peter had never
been to Rome nor was he martyred there, nor, therefore, was he the
first bishop of Rome, nor were the papal claims for special authority
justified. In all this his aim would be to challenge in advance the
rumours of the coming vatican council I and the probability of a
declaration of papal infallibility. In the preface Gavazzi contemptuously
wrote of the *vanità puerile* and *religione da teatro* of Pius, and the famous
non possumus was dismissed as mere 'feminine obstinacy'. The book is
built up on negations derived from wide but superficial reading, and

[126] I owe this information to a member of the staff of the national library of Wales,
Aberystwyth; another member provided the translation of the reporter's welsh phrase
in *Y Faner*.
[127] *Memorie* p 210, *Southport Daily News* (the newspaper cutting is cut too close to give
the date, but it must have been on a visit to England by Gavazzi after 1870).

in the light of modern scholarship displays some eccentricities; but at the time most convinced protestant controversialists in England as elsewhere would have agreed with his main themes. Gavazzi asserts that it is clear from the bible that Peter's commission was not to be in Rome but in Babylon – and he adds that 'Hebrews were numerous in Assyria'.[128] He continues that historical tradition is against it: Eusebius was simply wrong and there is no proven episcopal descent from Peter; Ignatius was rhetorical; Papias was credulous; Hegesippus was spurious as were also the *Apostolic Constitutions* and the *Clementine Recognitions*; and he cuts down the erroneous assumptions in Tertullian, Origen and Cyprian. He concludes by showing that archaeology is no help; the cathedral of saint Peter is in no sense his.[129] For a good knock-down method of argument Humpty Dumpty could not have done better, but he would have been less verbose.

Among his writings in English two are worth mention and quotation: *My Recollections of the Last Four Popes, and of Rome in their Times*, 1858, and *No Union with Rome: an Anti-Eirenicon*, 1866. Cardinal Wiseman, for Gavazzi a fanatic on three counts – he had an irish father, he was born in Spain, he was educated at Rome – had addressed a large gathering at Myddleton Hall, Islington, on Pius VII, Leo XII, Pius VIII, Gregory XVI and Pius IX praising their virtues and achievements.[130] A few days later Gavazzi furiously rebutted Wiseman's eulogies in the same auditorium. He then produced, extended into a book, the substance of his attack on Cardinal Wiseman's bland and graceful periods. In the preface he warms up with this judgment of Wiseman: 'The author, to spare his readers all intellectual fatigue has, with a charity which deserves to be transmitted to posterity, taken care to say nothing.'[131] Later in the book a memory of his youth when he first visited Rome and crossed the frontier at Radicofani into the papal states came back to him: 'What is the sign by which the traveller perceives that he has entered the dominions of the priests? The appearance of squalor, poverty and wretchedness, which surrounds him on every hand . . . a heap of dirty cottages ironically called the town of Radicofani . . . The Roman States . . . the desert of Italy, and

---

[128] These arguments are from the first section.
[129] These arguments are from sections 2 and 3.
[130] [Cardinal N. P.] Wiseman, *Recollections [of the Last Four Popes and of Rome in their times]* (London 1858). Gavazzi, *My Recollections* in the preface, p v, wrote: 'In answer to his lecture on the Four Popes I delivered one after in the same place. How did they resemble each other? As much as Italy and Ireland.'
[131] *Ibid* p vi.

more than the desert, the opprobrium of the peninsula.'[132] The
jesuits received a dismissive sentence: '. . . the fatal order . . . its own
confession, which I have many times heard boldy repeated by Jesuits,
[is] that its sole aim is to push back our age to feudalism, to ignorance,
and the state of Catholic servility anterior to the French Revolution.'[133]
Wiseman incautiously had said of Gregory XVI: 'I am not aware
that there was a single political execution in his pontificate.' Gavazzi's
response was blunt: 'May God pardon all liars! . . . in 1843 alone . . . in
Bologna . . . six were condemned to death for political crimes, and the
sentence was executed . . .'[134] Gavazzi's intense patriotism overcame
what little tact he possessed when he even attacked one of England's
heroes by exploding into these words: '. . . history, so long as the world
shall last, will bear witness to the ineffaceable infamy of Nelson.'[135]
Gavazzi must have startled even hardened protestants, when referring
to his 'imprisonment' under Gregory XVI at San Severino monastery,
by stating that friends at Rome, including a roman colonel in the
pontifical army, sent him a list of concubines of the prelates, cardinals
and even of Gregory himself, 'with the exception of Lambruschini',
so that by seeking this feminine aid he could obtain release – 'I scorned
[this] method and preferred to remain in captivity rather than obtain
my freedom by such vile instrumentality'.[136] However, Gavazzi's
height of scorn for Gregory XVI, his *bête noire*, is found in this
astonishing sentence: 'Meanwhile, let the admirers of the succession
of St. Peter delight themselves in their holy Pope, "the virtuous
Gregory", who, on his part, stretched upon the couches of the
beauteous Gaetanina, and surrounded by a coronet of youthful satellites,
exclaims from his apostolic heart, *Deus nobis haec otia fecit*.'[137] Sylvain
understandably loses his calm control, in describing Gavazzi's career,
at this point: '. . . la masse d'anecdotes dont ces pages regorgent,
suffisent, pensons-nous, à demontrer *ab absurdo* que l'on ne peut ajouter
foi aux assertions d'un pamphlétaire qui n'hésite pas à confier au
papier les ragots les plus infects avec une absence désarmante d'esprit

[132] *Ibid* p 10. [133] *Ibid* p 38. [134] *Ibid* p 200.
[135] *Ibid* p 255. *The Encyclopaedia Britannica*, (11 ed, New York 1911) 19, p 355, pompously
stated: 'The story of Nelson's visit to Naples in the June of 1799 will probably remain
a subject for perpetual discussion' – this means he acted in a discreditable manner.
Emma Hamilton persuaded Nelson to support the queen of Naples and the feeble
bourbon king, and he acted entirely arbitrarily in quelling republicans and hanging
their leaders. Gavazzi was one of those italians who evidently neither forgot nor
forgave this.
[136] *Ibid* p 274.
[137] *Ibid* p 277, see also n 140 below.

critique.'[138] Two points are worth making about Gavazzi's violent polemic: first, he believed the truth of what he was saying, he was no sly inventive Achilli, nor was it his intention to be merely scurrilous; the second point is that his anecdotes about Gregory were based on well-known popular assumptions in Rome which were wittily put in dialect verses by Giuseppi Belli and passed about as flysheets. Mazzini quoted one when in exile in England; the italian political exiles would have known these and the romans among them would know how popular opinion supported these wry judgments.[139] Members of Gregory's own order published two commemorative volumes in honour of him in 1948, and one of the contributors dealt fully with Belli's verses on that pope which are freely quoted without the indignation of Sylvain, rather they are used as helping to build up a portrait of that period.[140] The real thrust of Gavazzi's argument is to discredit the popes praised in cardinal Wiseman's book and to draw the attention of English-speaking readers to the evils of papal government in Italy: 'The evil government of the priests went to such lengths, that it became a proverb in the Roman States, "Better be under the Turks than under the priests". Can Wiseman deny these

---

[138] Sylvain, 2 p 459.

[139] Mazzini copied a sonnet of Belli's in his London exile in a letter to a friend, see A. M. Ghisalberti, at *Gregorio XVI* 2 p 350 (see n 140 below).

[140] 'Il carabiniere A. Bianchi Giovini', wrote *Il Papa e la sua Corte* (Rome 1860) according to A. M. Ghisalberti, 'Gregorio XVI [e il Risorgimento'], in *Gregorio XVI*, 2, and described the 'fig-like' nose of Gregory and of his *abuso del vino*. Ghisalberti also refers to Gaetano Moroni's beautiful wife, and quotes Belli's poem of 1835, *Er Papa Omo*, in his *Sonnetti Romaneschi* no 1533 (see n 42 above):

> A Palazzo der Papa c'è un giardino
> Co un boschetto e in ner bosco un padijone
> Pien de sofà a la turca e de potrone
> E de bottije de rosojo e vino,
> C'eppoi ne le su' stanzie un cammerino
> Co 'una porta de dietro a un credenzone
> Che mette a una scaletta, e in concrusione
> Corisponne ar quartier di Ghitanino
> Ghitanino è ammojato: la su' moje
> É una donna de garbo, assai divota
> Der vicario de Dio che lega e scioje
> Oh, nun vojo dì antro: e ho-ffatto male
> Anzi a pparla cusì, dove se nota
> Oggni pelo e se pensa ar criminale.

See *Tuttii Sonnetti Romaneschi*, ed Bruno Cagli, 5 vols (Rome 1964–5) 4, p 361. These pieces of Belli's were not immediately printed but passed around in manuscript. Gavazzi's use of this material shows that touch of vulgarity referred to (below p 356). In any event Wiseman had already gracefully dealt with Gregory's large nose in his *Recollections*.

facts?'[141] Gavazzi also shows his neo-ghibelline allegiance: '—if the substitution of the Orleans for the Bourbon branch was legitimate in France [this is aimed at the legitimist principle of Metternich supported by the Jesuits and Pius IX], it can but be legitimate in the Roman States to substitute a popular and Italian government for the cruel anomaly of the Papacy'.[142] If nothing else the passion of the writer, and the autobiographical basis of his attack, give interest to this forgotten book. The style has energy and pungent phrasing. Gavazzi can hardly have achieved this without some help, even if this was limited to proof-reading. 'Father Prout' was in Paris during this period, and perhaps had no hand in the preparation of the text but the sentence quoted above about Gregory XVI has a twist and a latin tag which echo his style. King and others of Gavazzi's English friends lacked this sarcastic stylistic force.

Gavazzi's *No union with Rome* is an indignant onslaught on tractarian respect for roman catholicism; it is an odd chance that his preface is dated from 88 Newman Street. Gavazzi was indignant at Pusey's reunion scheme, and had been profoundly suspicious of the Oxford movement since his first visit to England.[143] 'You, Doctor [Pusey], with utter want of charity and logic, assert that rationalism was given us by Lutheranism, as Socinianism was given us by Calvinism . . . where is the English Church? In the homeopathic fraction of Oxford, a Tom Thumb of Anglicanism . . . I shall advise him [Pusey] to go to Rome to study Romanism better than he has done from his books or in the company of Newman, who strives to retain in his new faith a portion of the liberty he enjoyed in the English Church.'[144] When Gavazzi explained to readers his own religious views – this book is an interesting *apologia* for them, since it contains an exposition of his unusual religious position – Pusey, if he had troubled to read it would have been shocked by Gavazzi's dismissal of the athanasian creed as 'the apocryphal composition of a half-crazy monk, [which] reduces itself to the riddle of a sphynx, while, in its condemnatory clauses, it belongs to the religion of Belial or Juggernaut.'[145] But for Pusey there

[141] *My Recollections* p 51.
[142] *Ibid* pp 185, 186.
[143] H. P. Liddon, *Life of E. B. Pusey* (London 1898) 4, p 107. Pusey wrote to Keble a letter which he called his 'First Eirenicon' – this was a defence of the catholicity of the church of England against an attack on it by archbishop Manning in 1864. But it also contains suggestions on how re-union could be achieved between Rome and Canterbury.
[144] *No Union with Rome: an Anti-Eirenicon* (London 1866) pp 50, 51.
[145] *Ibid* p 277.

would be nothing to choose between a Gavazzi and an Achilli – false and renegade priests both. Gavazzi's religious position is seen in these sentences: 'As I belong neither to the English Church nor to any other Protestant denomination, my sole aim in Italy being the revival of the Church of Rome as it was in the glorious days of the Apostle Paul, so I feel myself called upon only to defend the great principles of Christianity common to all . . . in all the confessions of the reformed Churches there is what I call human and theological doctrine in open questions and in the mode of explaining dogma . . . I have in my favour . . . the patristic axiom of the great Augustine, *in dubiis libertas* . . . I am an Evangelical Christian of the Italian Church, as established in Rome by the Apostle St. Paul, without Pope and without Popery.'[146] He had a valid and prophetic criticism of protestant proselytising in Italy: '. . . sad experience has taught me that the sects which send agents and missionaries to evangelize Italy have nothing in view but the glorification of their own denomination, by the transplanting of which to Italy we shall end miserably with religious strife and divisions . . .'[147] The archons of ecumenism in our day since they appear to regard the study of church history as unfruitful, or indeed as 'irrelevant', may not know that Gavazzi wrote in 1866: '. . . the reader may see how logical I am in that while I strive to promote the unity and brotherhood of the Churches of Italy . . . it is but natural that I should desire to see the reunion of the different denominations of England', nor may they know of the failure of his great efforts in setting up a free church of Italy uncommitted to dogmatic niceties, and free of the mortmain of past history which he had hoped, therefore, could be the basis for uniting protestants.[148] In his last aim – a church which would draw to it the diverse and divided protestant bodies – he achieved no success. His indefatigable tours abroad to raise funds made possible the establishing of a number of congregations, a theological college and central church 'at the foot of S. Angelo', but after 1896 there was no future. The *plimuttisi* he had feared found places in his congregation and divided them; his pastors wanted more 'order'; and the *Chiesa Evangelica d'Italia* disappeared largely into the wesleyan and episcopal methodist churches in Italy after 1905.[149]

[146] *Ibid* p 96.   [147] *Ibid* p 299.

[148] *Ibid* p 299. See Santini p 185 *et seq*, chapter unnumbered, entitled 'Problemi delle giovani Chiese protestanti italiane (1877–1883)'.

[149] *Sixteenth Evangelization Report of the Free Christian Church in Italy* (Glasgow 1887); J. R. McDougall prepared this report, and after 1896 he stated that this church had no independent future.

Eliot's words that history 'gives too late what's not believed in' echo again in the mind: the religious passion of the risorgimento (for it began, in spite of the secret societies, or Mazzini's well-intentioned intrigues, as a religious crisis) had faltered by 1870. Gavazzi had found a new birth of religious conviction and aims through 'the crusade', and then had had to readjust painfully, and ultimately unsuccessfully, to a new religious position. History has left him as a shadow 'in memory only reconsidered passion'. Is reconsideration of Gavazzi worth the trouble? Neither Pusey nor Eliot in their respective generations would have thought so. My own implied judgments that politically he was a noise in the street, and religiously not much more than rhetoric on public platforms, are perhaps too harsh. We may remember Jowett's no doubt justified criticism of an essay by Cosmo Gordon Lang when the future archbishop was an undergraduate at Balliol: 'Words are not always ideas, nor are ideas always realities' – this dictum could apply to Gavazzi.[150] For all his theatricality, and the vulgar streak that irritated the young poet Mameli[151] to aversion when dying, Gavazzi deserves to be remembered as a brave, patriotic and religious man, who took far-ranging decisions on principle, and not for self-advancement, who shows us that great movements in the past are misunderstood by historians if they ignore or reject the significance of the religious convictions of those who participated in them. An epigraph for Gavazzi could be the words he placed on his book which he had dedicated to his mother: *Se io viva ancor eccone O Madre il segno* – he still lives when we see *il segno* of religious aspirations in the risorgimento.

[150] J. G. Lockhart, *The Life of Cosmo Gordon Lang* (London 1949) p 27.
[151] Trevelyan, *Defence* p 308.

CHURCH AND STATE IN BORNEO:
THE ANGLICAN BISHOPRIC

by BRIAN TAYLOR

W HEN James Brooke became rajah of Sarawak in 1841, his enterprise – the acquiring of territorial sovereign rule by a private British citizen – was regarded with doubt and hesitation in official circles in London, and all three white rajahs were always very sensitive about their status. But when James Brooke visited England in 1847–8 there was no doubt about his personal standing as a romantic figure. Moreover, he added to the strength of the British presence in south-east Asia, which was needed to discourage Dutch assertiveness, and so he was lionised, and knighted, and among other things given an honorary doctorate by the university of Oxford. While he was there, about £500 was collected by members of the university, who considered that a mission to Borneo 'ought to go forth under the superintendence of a Bishop from the very first'.[1] This was sound doctrinal theory, but unlikely to be put into practice then or indeed since. But the idea was there, and the money was funded, and the church in Borneo did not have to wait as long as many places for episcopal ministrations, or for an episcopate of its own. Plans for a mission to Sarawak had already been made, and the first two missionaries sailed with their families at the end of 1847, and landed in Sarawak on 29 June 1848.

As Borneo was not included in any diocese, the missionaries were within the ecclesiastical jurisdiction claimed by the bishop of London,[2] and the leader of the mission, Francis Thomas McDougall, was licensed by bishop Blomfield on 22 November 1850 'to perform the Office of Principal Chaplain to the British Residents in the Island of Borneo in the East Indies, and also to Act as Senior Missionary there'. His original companion, William Bodham Wright, was licensed the same day,[3]

---

[1] USPG archives, Borneo box 2, E. C. Woollcombe, fellow of Balliol, to T. F. Stooks, secretary of the Borneo church mission, 17 June 1851.

[2] For a discussion of the origin of this jurisdiction in the disciplinary policy of Laud, and made more formal by Compton, see A. L. Cross, *The Anglican Episcopate and the American Colonies* (London 1902) caps 1, 2.

[3] Guildhall library MS 9532A4, London diocesan act book 1842–53, p 150.

but by then he had already left for Singapore, which was within the diocese of Calcutta. When Reginald Heber was consecrated bishop of Calcutta in 1823, his patent (issued 27 May 1823) enlarged his diocese, which already included the whole of India and Ceylon, by adding New South Wales and Tasmania, and all territories within the area of the East India Company's charter, which included Penang. Singapore and Malacca were brought under company rule (and therefore within the jurisdiction of the bishop of Calcutta) in 1824, and the three straits settlements were given a unified administration in 1826.[4]

In September 1850, Daniel Wilson, the fifth bishop of Calcutta, received a letter from the bishop of London asking him to go to Borneo and 'consecrate the new church recently erected by Sir James Brooke, the Rajah of Sarawak. A voyage of fourteen weeks and a journey of four thousand miles, was thus suggested, by the stroke of a pen, to a Bishop in his seventy-third year!'[5] In fact, Wilson intended to go to Singapore during his fifth visitation, and McDougall had written to suggest that he might cross to Sarawak without much added trouble.[6] St Thomas's church and cemetery Sarawak (as the town of Kuching was still called) were consecrated on 22 January 1851, and confirmation was administered to two candidates. The consecration was entered in Blomfield's register.[7]

A few days later, James Brooke wrote to McDougall.

> The Government of course is the ultimate judge of what concerns the safety of the country, or is likely to disturb the public peace but there ought to be some power in the Church itself, to give unity of design and execution . . . How is this done? Have you the ecclesiastical authority to control and direct other clergymen? If you have not, and I do not perceive that you can have, what objection would there be, to making you the Bishop of Sarawak? There would be no objection on my part; and I consider, certainly, that some authority within the church it-self is necessary to control the clergy; and to offer to the Government a responsible person, with whom it could treat,

---

[4] For the growth and then reduction of the diocese of Calcutta, see C. J. Grimes, *Towards an Indian Church* (London 1946) pp 53–83.

[5] J. Bateman, *The Life of the Right Rev. Daniel Wilson, D.D.* (London 1860) 2, p 328.

[6] USPG archives, Borneo box 1, Wilson to McDougall, 21 June 1850; McDougall to Stooks, 12 August 1850.

[7] Guildhall library MS 9531/31, Blomfield's register 1848–56.

and in whom it could confide. The details I must leave with you . . .[8]

In January 1852 Brooke was again in Oxford, and revived interest in the university in the proposals for a bishopric in Sarawak – and his own state was as far as his concern went. McDougall had a broader concern. Towards the end of 1852 he wrote of the need of more clergymen, including asians, who would need proper supervision – 'that unity & discipline which apostolic rule and order can alone import to the Mission of the Church'. Although most of his work might lie in Sarawak, there was always the possibility of expansion further north in Borneo, and also the needs of the clergy and congregations of the mainland, still in the diocese of Calcutta, would become more pressing. But McDougall knew that the whole thing depended on the goodwill of the autocratic rajah of Sarawak, whether his motives were really the good of the church (as the Oxford dons hoped) or the prestige of his own establishment; and so he wrote rather sententiously, 'Nothing but planting the Church in its complete organization & with the power of local reproduction & increase can effectually aid Sir James Brooke in his noble efforts for the benefit of the aborigines of Borneo, or consolidate the good already done'.[9]

The details of the foundation and endowment of the bishopric can be left aside, but the way that the constitutional problem was dealt with must be noticed. The archbishop of Canterbury could not consecrate without licence from the crown, and the crown would not issue a licence, or set up a diocese where it had no jurisdiction; and certainly the rajah would not accept any infringement of his sovereign authority. The answer was found in the small and thinly populated island of Labuan, off the cost of Borneo, which had become a British colony in 1846. On 6 August 1855, letters patent were issued, erecting the 'Island of Labuan and its Dependencies into a Bishops See or Diocese to be styled the Bishoprick of Labuan'. McDougall was to be the first bishop, by royal nomination and appointment. He and his successors 'shall be subject and subordinate to the Archiepiscopal See of Canterbury . . . in the same manner as any Bishop of any See within the Province of Canterbury . . .' Archbishop Sumner was to issue a commission to the bishops of Calcutta, Madras, Colombo, Victoria

---

[8] USPG archives, Borneo box 1, J. Brooke, who was in Singapore on his way to England, to McDougall, 28 January 1851.

[9] USPG archives, E/Pre H Borneo and Calcutta, undated and unaddressed paper by McDougall.

[Hong Kong] and Mauritius, or any three of them, to consecrate as soon as possible.[10] McDougall was consecrated in Calcutta cathedral on 18 October 1855 by bishop Wilson, with bishop Dealtry of Madras and bishop Smith of Victoria – the first consecration to a colonial bishopric to take place outside of England. On 1 January 1856, the bishop of Labuan was made also the bishop of Sarawak, by the rajah's ordinance.

> Whereas for the maintenance of religion and for the promotion of Piety within the State of Sarawak, it is desired by the native and foreign inhabitants professing the doctrines of the Church of England in the said State, that there be a Bishop, and that the Right Reverend Francis Thomas McDougall, Bishop of Labuan, should be received and acknowledged as the Bishop of Sarawak, It is ordained that the Right Reverend Francis Thomas McDougall be appointed Bishop of Sarawak with powers to exercise all the ecclesiastical functions pertaining to the episcopal office, as recognized by the Order of the Church of England.
>
> And the Right Reverend Francis Thomas McDougall is accordingly Bishop of Sarawak.
>
> Given under our hand and seal this first day of January in the year of our Lord 1856.[11]

This arrangement lasted for nearly a hundred years. Bishops were appointed to the colonial see of Labuan, but care had to be taken that each new bishop was acceptable to the rajah for appointment as bishop of Sarawak.

The circumstances of the joint bishopric changed considerably. In 1856, the state of Sarawak was very small, but it became very much bigger in 1861, and further additions were made up to 1905, and the area of the bishop's jurisdiction increased with the size of the state. But it was in the diocese of Labuan that there were most changes, and it very soon ceased to be little more than a legal fiction. Wilson would have happily parted with the straits settlements, but while they were ruled by the East India Company that was not easily done. McDougall performed episcopal acts for him, including the ordination to the priesthood of his own original assistant, W. B. Wright,[12] and he consecrated a cemetery in Singapore for Wilson's successor, bishop Cotton.[13]

---

[10] PRO, copy of patent roll (chancery) 19 Victoria, pt 2 no 4.
[11] Printed in *The Borneo Chronicle*, centenary number (Uxbridge 1955) p 11.
[12] On 9 August 1857. Singapore diocesan records, record book 3 (1838–63).
[13] On 15 November 1864. Calcutta diocesan register.

Church and state in Borneo: the anglican bishopric

During the 1860s, relations between McDougall and rajah James Brooke grew steadily worse, and the bishop was looking for ways of moving the centre of his work away from Sarawak. In 1861 he wrote to the secretary of the Society for the Propagation of the Gospel saying that he had heard that the colonial office had decided that Labuan and the straits settlements should become one colony. He assumed that this would lead to the separation of the straits settlements from the diocese of Calcutta and their addition to his diocese of Labuan. This would make it possible for the main centre of the mission to be moved to Singapore. 'In the present political position of Sarawak it is most desirable that our missions should not appear to be connected with the local government in any way but should really appear to the natives purely what they are, Missions of the English Church; connected with the chief English station in Singapore and wholly independent of Sir J. Brooke and his officials.'[14] Labuan did not become part of the straits settlements until 1907, but by the straits transfer bill of 1866, the settlements were separated from India, where the East India Company's rule had ended in 1858, and became a colony, by order in council, at the end of the year. An act of parliament was needed to transfer the new colony to the diocese of Labuan. In the meanwhile, McDougall resigned from his double bishopric. His letter of resignation was received by the colonial office on 1 July 1868.[15] James Brooke had died on 11 June, but before his death he agreed with McDougall that the new bishop of Sarawak should be Walter Chambers, who had worked in the state since 1851. Charles Brooke, who succeeded as rajah, had already approved of the nomination.[16] Chambers sailed to England and was called to discuss the whole question with archbishop Tait, who had received a petition in 1866 from the English residents in Singapore, asking that the straits settlements should be transferred to the diocese of Labuan. There was an alternative suggestion that they should, with Labuan, be added to the diocese of Victoria, Hong Kong, but Tait made up his mind that the former course was preferable, and recommended that Chambers should be appointed to the enlarged diocese. He was able to assure the secretary of state for the colonies that the bishop of Calcutta approved of the change.[17] Approval was given, and Chambers was

[14] USPG archives, Borneo – letters received 2, McDougall to E. Hawkins, 23 May 1861.
[15] PRO, CO 144/28.
[16] USPG archives, Borneo – letters received 2, C. Brooke to McDougall, 24 May 1868.
[17] PRO, CO 144/30, Tait to secretary of state for the colonies, 22 February and 30 April and 5 June 1869.

consecrated on 29 June 1869 in Westminster abbey, while correspondence continued about the legal details. The act of parliament for the
separation from the diocese of Calcutta of the straits settlements, now
to 'be and be taken a part of the said See or Diocese of Labuan to all
intents and purposes whatsoever', and to be removed from the
metropolitan authority of the bishop of Calcutta to that of the
archbishop of Canterbury was passed on 8 October 1869, and letters
patent were issued naming Chambers as bishop.[18] He was authorised
by the Crown 'to select any suitable Church within the Diocese to be
his Cathedral Church',[19] and St Andrew's Singapore became the
cathedral of the diocese of Labuan on 20 December 1870,[20] and
Chambers was enthroned there. He had already been installed on 5 June
1870 in St Thomas's Kuching, which was to be called the 'diocesan
church', to safeguard the dignity of the church in Sarawak. No record
of a rajah's patent formally appointing Chambers as bishop of Sarawak
has been found. Rajah Charles Brooke had only just arrived in
Sarawak with his bride, and perhaps the matter was overlooked.

When Chambers announced his resignation in 1879, there was no
obvious successor. Rajah Brooke had no preference.[21] McDougall,
who was consulted, also had no-one to suggest, but he warned
archbishop Tait's chaplain, Randall Davidson, that whoever was
chosen must be acceptable to the rajah.[22] In October 1880, H. W.
Tucker, the new secretary of the SPG, recommended the venerable
George Frederick Hose, archdeacon of Singapore. Tait offered him the
appointment, and received a telegram of acceptance from Hose on
9 December 1880.[23] Chambers resigned officially early in 1881, and
Hose was consecrated on 26 May in Lambeth palace chapel. When
the archbishop applied for a licence to consecrate, he was told that
letters patent were no longer issued, because they so frequently led to
legal disputes. The licence was for 'one of Our Possessions abroad',
with no mention of Labuan, but Tait gave Hose a commission to
exercise episcopal authority.[24] The new bishop was installed in the
cathedral in Singapore on 27 November 1881, and went on to

[18] PRO, copy of patent roll (chancery) 33 Victoria, pt 1 no 12.
[19] PRO, CO 404/5.
[20] Lok Keng Ann, *Fifty Years of the Anglican Church in Singapore Island 1909–1959*
(Singapore 1963) p 2. There is an undated copy in the Kuching diocesan register 1.
[21] L[ambeth] P[alace] L[ibrary], Tait 1880 L 28 Bp of Labuan, C. Brooke to Tait, 26
December 1879.
[22] *Ibid*, Tait 1880 L 28 Bp of Labuan, McDougall to Davidson, 8 January 1880.
[23] *Ibid*, Tait 1880 L 28 Bp of Labuan.
[24] Singapore diocesan records, record book 5; royal licence, notarial act, and commission.

Sarawak in January. The rajah's patent for Hose as 'Bishop of the Church of England over the Territory of Sarawak' was issued the day he landed, 17 January 1882.[25] Just before his consecration, Hose asked the archbishop for permission to alter the name of the diocese of Labuan to Singapore, as Labuan was insignificant, and it would be inconvenient when his letters went there by mistake. Tait gave his unofficial approval for Hose to use the title 'bishop of Singapore, Labuan and Sarawak,' to indicate that Singapore was the main centre of his work.[26] Hose was usually known as the bishop of Singapore, or Singapore and Sarawak, but legally all of his bishopric outside Sarawak was still the diocese of Labuan, and this became apparent again towards the end of his long episcopate, when there was a move to divide the diocese, and erect a new see for Singapore and Malaya.

Hose notified archbishop Davidson in October 1907 that he would resign in the following year, but the questions of the future of his bishopric, and who should succeed him were being discussed before then. Arrangements were made for the new diocese of Singapore, and its first bishop was consecrated on 24 August 1909. The diocese of Labuan now was limited to Borneo, but was of growing significance, because for over twenty years there had been anglican work in the state of British North Borneo. The secretary of the SPG at this time was bishop H. H. Montgomery, and he summed up the situation regarding Sarawak exactly: 'the position of the Bishop in Sarawak is a most delicate one, for the Rajah is an absolute autocrat'.[27] No doubt because of the long interval since the appointment of Hose, Montgomery thought it wise to go to the colonial office to enquire if they wished to claim the right to appoint a bishop for Labuan. He was told that the appointment lay with the archbishop.[28] The obvious person for selection was the archdeacon of Sarawak, Arthur Frederick Sharp, but he was not acceptable to rajah Brooke, who was in England at the time, and saw the archbishop on 6 December 1907 about the matter. He agreed that the archbishop should appoint, and the archbishop said that he wanted to act in co-operation with the rajah. Before the interview ended, Brooke expressed his opinion that Sharp was unsuitable, and followed this up with letters, culminating in an ultimatum, 'I can confidently assure your Grace that the Archdeacon

[25] Kuching diocesan register 1. LPL, Davidson box 1 Labuan 1916.
[26] LPL, Tait 1881 Singapore and Labuan, Hose to Tait, 17 May 1881. USPG archives, Borneo – letters received 2, Tait to Hose, 18 May 1881.
[27] *Ibid*, Davidson 1909 S8 Sarawak, Montgomery to Davidson, undated memorandum.
[28] *Ibid*, Davidson 1909 S8 Sarawak, Montgomery to Davidson, 5 December 1907.

is not a suitable man for the post – and I shall never give him authority to act, and hold diocesan jurisdiction in Sarawak'.[29] Davidson did not like being defied, especially as he wished to appoint Sharp, whom he had already interviewed, but Montgomery urged him not to provoke a confrontation. 'The Rajah could make life unendurable to a man – stop rights of way, withdraw grants, shut schools etc: and there is no redress';[30] and he might have added that Brooke could refuse to allow an unwelcome bishop to land in the state. There was then a long pause for thought, until the end of 1908, when Davidson decided to offer the appointment to William Robert Mounsey, the secretary of the New Guinea mission.[31] After Mounsey had accepted the bishopric, Davidson wrote to inform the rajah, asking him to do for Mounsey as he had for Hose, and give him a 'document accrediting him and commending him'.[32] Mounsey was consecrated in Lambeth palace chapel on 25 March 1909, and enthroned in St Thomas's Kuching, now called the pro-cathedral, on 4 July. The rajah's patent contained no significant alteration from that issued to Hose. The government of North Borneo made itself heard, as this was the first new bishop in its history. The government secretary wrote to Mounsey asking for official notification that the state was in the diocese of Labuan, as the information was necessary for correspondence about land titles. Mounsey replied rather crisply.

> The jurisdiction of the Bishop of Labuan and Sarawak in matters spiritual extends over Borneo. I send you this information merely as information, as I imagine that the Government of British North Borneo is concerned with temporal matters only, and I can admit no question as to my jurisdiction in spiritual affairs. I am anxious that everything should be put on a proper footing, but I must point out that for twenty years or more no question seems to have been raised as to the Bishop's jurisdiction.

He passed on the request to the archbishop. Much earlier he had written, 'When a new bishop is sent out a highly formal document would please our Governments'.[33]

[29] *Ibid*, Davidson 1909 S8 Sarawak, C. Brooke to Davidson, 20 February 1908.
[30] *Ibid*, Davidson 1909 S8 Sarawak, Montgomery to Davidson, 24 February 1908.
[31] *Ibid*, Davidson 1909 S8 Sarawak, Davidson to Mounsey, 8 January 1909; Mounsey to Davidson, 10 January 1909.
[32] *Ibid*, Davidson 1909 S8 Sarawak, Davidson to C. Brooke, 25 January 1909.
[33] Kuching diocesan register 1, A. C. Pearson to Mounsey, 8 August 1910; Mounsey to Pearson, 28 August 1910. LPL, Davidson 1910 L1 Labuan, Mounsey to Davidson, 29 February 1910.

Mounsey's episcopate was short; his resignation on 31 October 1916 was announced in the previous June. Montgomery made a note that Charles Brooke, now in his eighty-eighth year, and the forty-ninth year of his reign, would be even more suspicious and difficult to please.[34] In August the archbishop received a letter from the rajah.

> The Right Revd. W. R. Mounsey having resigned his appointment, as Bishop in the Borneo diocese I am desirous of filling up the vacancy as soon as possible – and after close inquiry and ascertaining the feeling of the Sarawak Lay European inhabitants I find that the Revd. C. Beamish will be the right man for the appointment and I would ask Your Grace to consecrate this gentleman as soon as convenient – in order that I may grant him a License to act in his sacerdotal duties in the State of Sarawak.
>
> I would mention that the three previous Bishops MacDougal, Chambers and Hose all three were chosen by the Rajahs of Sarawak – the last two by myself – & a private unofficial letter from the late Archbishop Tait – to me mentioned that if I would nominate a man for that post he would appoint him to be Bishop of the Borneo Diocese and I chose Archdeacon Hose of Singapore.[35]

The rajah's letter, inaccurate in many details, and ignoring the wishes and interests of the church people in North Borneo and Labuan, and of the asians in his own state, and not mentioning that very few of the Sarawak europeans, not including himself, took any regular part in the worship and life of the church, caused anxious discussion between archbishop Davidson and bishop Montgomery, who took advice from everyone available on the rights and precedents concerning the appointment to the double bishopric. The details need not concern us.[36] Throughout the long correspondence, the fact of the rajah's undisputed veto was always in mind, but the archbishop was determined that he would not be forced into appointing anyone who was not suited to be bishop of all the territories in Borneo. The reverend C. N. B. Beamish, mentioned in the rajah's letter, did not seem to be entirely suitable, and in fact became a roman catholic soon afterwards. Finally, Davidson chose the reverend Ernest Denny Logie Danson, who was working in Malaya. He had been recommended by the

[34] LPL, Davidson box 1 Labuan 1916, memorandum by Montgomery, 23 June 1916.
[35] *Ibid*, Davidson box 1 Labuan 1916, C. Brooke to Davidson, 6 July 1916.
[36] The papers are in LPL, Davidson box 1 Labuan 1916.

bishop of Singapore to Mounsey, who also had a favourable opinion of him from the bishop of Glasgow. Charles Brooke arrived in England early in 1917, but as a dying man. The archbishop was obliged to negotiate with the rajah's adviser, H. F. Deshon, and with the Sarawak state advisory council in London. They asked for time to consult the rajah's heir, who was travelling to the east, but Davidson sensed that he could now act resolutely without fear of being countered by a veto, and offered the bishopric to Danson. The state advisory council notified the rajah's son, but before he could reply, Charles Brooke had died, on 17 May 1917, and so his approval was one of his first acts as rajah Vyner Brooke.

Danson was consecrated in Lambeth palace chapel on 21 September 1917. On the same day the archbishop issued letters notifying the rajah of Sarawak, and the governors of the Straits Settlements (for Labuan) and of North Borneo of the consecration. On 13 December he gave Danson letters of introduction to the three governments. At the bishop's enthronement in Kuching on 19 May 1918, before the reading of the rajah's patent, a mandate from the archbishop was read, which stated that Danson was consecrated to 'exercise his Office of Bishop in Labuan, Sarawak, North Borneo, Brunei and the rest of the Island of Borneo and in the Islands belonging and adjacent thereto'.[37] This emphasised the spiritual supremacy of the archbishop in appointing a bishop for the whole of the Borneo states, and also pointed towards the extension of the work of the church to the state of Brunei, which had been hoped for by Mounsey.

During the reign of Vyner Brooke, there were two appointments to the bishopric, Noel Baring Hudson, who was consecrated on 28 October 1931, and Francis Septimus Hollis, consecrated on 7 June 1938. Archbishop Lang was able to choose these bishops, after taking advice, without any fear that the third white rajah would act as his father had done. When each bishop was enthroned (14 February 1932 and 28 August 1938) the archbishop's mandate was read before the rajah's patent. Copies of the papers relating to the consecrations, and letters introducing the new bishops were sent to the governments of the states. In North Borneo the consecration papers were seen and acknowledged in 1931, and marked with the note, 'I take it no action is required'. In 1938 reference was made to the procedure followed in 1931, and the same was done.[38] The church's affairs were no longer of

---

[37] Kuching diocesan register 1.
[38] Sabah central archives, file 64 church and state.

such great interest to the state authorities. In the muslim state of Brunei, the growing work of the church was permitted by the government, without any suggestion that the sultan might intervene in the appointment of a bishop.

By the time of bishop Hollis's resignation in 1948, the political situation had completely changed. Brunei was and is still a British protectorate, but Sarawak and North Borneo, which now embraced Labuan, had become British colonies in 1946. The double bishopric was unified into one diocese when Nigel Edmund Cornwall was chosen by archbishop Fisher, and consecrated bishop of Borneo on 1 November 1949. He was enthroned in Kuching on 20 December. The diocese of Borneo was divided in 1962. The state of North Borneo became the diocese of Jesselton, which was inaugurated on 24 July, when James Wong Chang Ling was enthroned as bishop. He had been assistant bishop in the diocese of Borneo since 1960, and was appointed diocesan bishop by archbishop Ramsey. Sarawak and Brunei became the diocese of Kuching on 13 August, with bishop Cornwall as its diocesan until his resignation at the end of October.

The bishops in Borneo are still appointed by the archbishop of Canterbury, after proper consultation, as there is no province of south-east Asia. Bishop Cornwall's successor in Kuching was Nicholas Allenby SSM (consecrated on 30 November 1962 and enthroned on 13 January 1963). Later in 1963, on 16 September, further political changes came, when the two colonies, Sarawak and North Borneo, became states of the new nation of Malaysia, and North Borneo's name was altered to Sabah. Bishop Wong resigned on 30 September 1964, and was succeeded as bishop of Jesselton by Roland Koh Peck Chiang, who was born in Sabah. He had been consecrated assistant bishop of Singapore in 1958, and had been bishop suffragan of Kuala Lumpur since 1961. Bishop Allenby resigned on 31 October 1968, and was succeeded by the Sarawak-born Basil Temengong (consecrated in Kuching on 6 December, and enthroned on 8 December 1968). None of these appointments met with difficulties, but that was not the case after the translation of bishop Koh from Sabah (as the diocese of Jesselton had been called since 1968) to the new diocese of West Malaysia, where he was enthroned on 7 April 1970. The state of Sabah's policy of indigenisation is operated through a system of permits for residence and work, which severely restricted the choice that the archbishop was able to make. In 1971, government approval was obtained for Luke Chhoa Heng Sze, the archdeacon of North

Malaya. He was consecrated in Lambeth palace chapel on 30
November, and enthroned on 25 January 1972. Even greater difficulty
has been experienced by the roman catholic church in Sabah. Bishop
Peter Chung, a malaysian citizen, was consecrated on 15 November
1970, but has never been permitted to reside in Sabah. His episcopal
duties have to be carried out in short visits to the state.[39] To record
these problems is in no way to criticise the state government's policy.
It is a reminder that church institutions and personnel are subject to
civil authority. In many periods of history the main way in which
the state influenced or controlled the church has been at the appointment of bishops. This paper has sought to shew that this has been true
for most of Borneo's anglican history.

Leicester

[39] Bishop Chung to the present writer, 6 April 1974.

GLADSTONE AND THE NONCONFORMISTS:
A RELIGIOUS AFFINITY IN POLITICS

by D. W. BEBBINGTON

NONCONFORMISTS had an attitude of veneration for Gladstone. They admired his political skills; they were grateful for the legislative benefits he had brought them like the abolition of compulsory church rates and the opening of higher degrees at the ancient universities; and they were roused by his displays of oratorical power. Yet their respect for Gladstone went far beyond what was due to the able leader of a political party. There was amongst nonconformists by 1890 what a correspondent of *The Times* called a 'fascination, amounting to fetishism, of the great name and personality of Mr Gladstone.'[1] This was not primarily a result of sympathy in political policy, despite a general concurrence of nonconformists with Gladstone in the principles of peace, retrenchment and reform. In many other areas of policy there was disagreement. The overriding aim of political dissent, the aim of religious equality, was not shared by Gladstone; he was usually absent from parliamentary debates on the contagious diseases acts against which nonconformist feeling was high;[2] and as temperance political pressure gathered momentum among nonconformists in the later years of his life, Gladstone stood aside.[3] Nonconformists were always more whole-heartedly behind Gladstone in opposition, when he was denouncing the wrongs of conservative administrations, than behind Gladstone in office, when he was ignoring the wishes of nonconformist electors. Yet, despite policy differences, from at least 1868 until Gladstone's death thirty years later nonconformists as a whole were enthusiastic Gladstonians, supporters of the man. The explanation lies in the fact that undergirding the political relationship was a religious affinity. At a meeting of ten leading nonconformist ministers in 1889,

---

[1] 'A Congregational Minister' to the editor, [*The*] *Times*, 29 December 1890 p 4.

[2] F. B. Smith, 'Ethics and Disease in the Later Nineteenth Century: the Contagious Diseases Acts', *H St* 15 (1971) p 134. *The Methodist Times* (London), 28 April 1892 p 397.

[3] Gladstone told a methodist MP that he himself was baffled by the drink question. W. E. Gladstone to Thomas Snape, [*The*] *C[hristian*] *W[orld]* (London) 10 October 1895 p 758.

according to the diary of the baptist John Clifford, when the prospects of the liberal party were under discussion, 'the conversation turned chiefly on the religious fibre of the prospective leaders. Suppose Gladstone gone, what have we to look to? The outlook was thought to be very unpromising.'[4] It was the 'religious fibre' of Gladstone that brought him esteem. It was primarily religion that bound the nonconformists in personal loyalty to Gladstone.

However, there was a great gulf fixed between evangelical nonconformists and Gladstone, the dedicated high churchman. 'Perhaps,' reflected the editor of *The Freeman*, a baptist weekly, on Gladstone's death, 'many a student a hundred years hence will be puzzled by the enthusiastic allegiance of Nonconformists to the greatest Churchman of the nineteenth century.'[5] Gladstone saw the church of England as the national branch of the catholic church founded by Christ and preserved down the ages by the apostolic succession. He believed that a man entered the church through baptismal regeneration, that the church of England should enjoy at least sisterly relations with other branches of the historic church including the roman catholic and that the state should recognise and aid the teaching of the church of England. Nonconformists, by contrast, thought little of the doctrine of the church. They held that conversion was the entry to christian discipleship, that the roman church obscured the way of salvation and increasingly from the 1830s (apart from the wesleyans) that the church of England should be disestablished. Gladstone originally entered politics as a defender of precisely what dissenters were beginning to attack, the church of England as established.

Gladstone modified his churchmanship hardly at all in the years when nonconformists were his loyal supporters. A whole series of minor incidents occurred to disappoint his nonconformist friends at what they saw as his illiberality. Once when staying as the guest of J. J. Colman, the congregational 'mustard king' of Norwich, Gladstone insisted, despite his host's attempts at persuasion, on attending church rather than chapel.[6] Dr Parker of the congregational City Temple asked Gladstone in 1891 for his opinion of the practice of clergymen taking nonconformist services. 'With all respect for those clergymen who are willing to preach in Nonconformist pulpits,' Gladstone

---

[4] Sir James Marchant, *Dr John Clifford, C.H.: life, letters and reminiscences* (London 1924) p 82.

[5] [*The*] *Freeman* (London) 27 May 1898 p 290.

[6] [J. G.] Rogers, [*An*] *Autobiography* (London 1903) pp 238 *et seq.*

replied, 'I must say they do not form a proper conception of their own Church.'[7] And when editing the works of bishop Butler for publication in 1896, Gladstone went out of his way to guard the bishop from any appearance of commending interdenominational cooperation.[8] A wesleyan review called attention to this point as curious, but it was simply a part of what Gladstone conceived to be consistent churchmanship.[9] He tried to sway the vatican in favour of recognising anglican orders; and, as Vidler has argued, he never abandoned his establishment principles as the ideal for any nation.[10] Gladstone was what nonconformists in the 1890s usually called a sacerdotalist, and, what was worse, he was a pro-popish, establishmentarian sacerdotalist. Nonconformists were far from agreeing with Gladstone in matters of religion.

Yet one of the reasons for nonconformist disagreement with Gladstone had a corollary that helped to bridge the gulf. Many nonconformists argued for disestablishment on what they called the voluntary principle, the principle that 'religion ought to be indebted to the *voluntary* offering of its friends.'[11] The state should not help or hinder, or in any way interfere with, the progress of religion. Hence the state church should be disestablished; but hence, too, the state should not take note of men's religious opinions. If a voluntary practised what he preached, this meant that he, like the state, should respect the right to their own convictions of all public men – including Gladstone. This was what leading disestablishers like Edward Miall, editor of *The Nonconformist*, believed: they might disagree sharply with Gladstone over spiritual truth, but in assessing him as a statesman they felt bound 'to set aside the religious predilections, tastes, and convictions by which he is governed as a private individual.'[12] Many nonconformists were far less prepared to disregard, for example, Gladstone's apparent leanings to catholicism; but doctrinaire voluntaries, men who had been glad to cooperate with catholics in support of Irish disestablishment, were ready to ignore them. It was a

[7] Joseph Parker, 'Mr Gladstone close at hand: a personal sketch,' *The New Review*, 4 (London March 1891) p 209.
[8] *The Works of Joseph Butler, D.C.L.,* ed W. E. Gladstone (Oxford 1896) 2, p 291 n.
[9] 'Mr Gladstone's "Butler" ', [*The*] L[*ondon*] Q[*uarterly*] R[*eview*], 87 (London January 1897) p 249.
[10] Compare A. R. Vidler, *The Orb and the Cross: a normative study in the relations of Church and state with reference to Gladstone's early writings* (London 1945).
[11] [Joseph] Angus, [*The*] *Voluntary System, a prize essay, in reply to the lectures of Dr Chalmers on Church establishments* (London 1839) p 22.
[12] [*The*] *Noncon[formist]* (London) 12 August 1874 p 761.

matter of principle to a substantial number of nonconformists, especially those most active in public life, to overlook those aspects of Gladstone's religion that they disliked.

What demands attention are those aspects of Gladstone's religion that formed a bond with the nonconformists. Foremost among them was the way in which his religion, dominating the man, moulded his political style. It was primarily christianity put into practice that drew them. Gladstone was admired as what John Clifford called 'the typical Christian statesman.'[13] Long before he first stood out, in 1864, as champion of a policy generally embraced by nonconformists, parliamentary reform, Gladstone had been respected by their leaders. Mrs Beecher Stowe, author of *Uncle Tom's Cabin*, was impressed with Gladstone on a visit to London in 1853. 'It is a commentary on his character', she wrote, 'that, although one of the highest of the High Church, we have never heard him spoken of among the Dissenters otherwise than as an excellent and highly-conscientious man.'[14] The euphoria of nonconformists over irish disestablishment owed not a little to a sense that a noble christian politician was deigning to take up what they thought of as a dissenting issue. Again and again from then on nonconformists singled out for praise Gladstone's 'conscientiousness' and 'earnestness.'[15] These two qualities reflected the religious attitude that nonconformists thought they themselves should adopt in political life. Gladstone realised their highest ideal of political behaviour.

There was also in practice a close similarity between the two religiously-charged outlooks of Gladstone and of his dissenting followers, perhaps most strikingly illustrated at the time of the bulgarian agitation. Gladstone had been in the cabinet at the time of the crimean war which had confirmed Turkey in her charge of christian peoples. In 1876 she was abusing her trust by atrocities in Bulgaria. 'Gladstone,' noted John Bright in his diary, 'burdened with a sense of responsibility in connection with his share in the Crimean War, and anxious to urge that sense of responsibility on the conscience of the nation.'[16] Already *The Nonconformist* had commented: 'Turkey owes the integrity of her empire to our policy [in the Crimean War],

---

[13] G. W. Byrt, *John Clifford: a fighting Free Churchman* (London 1947) p 127.

[14] [J. E.] Ritchie, [*The Real*] *Gladstone* [*: an anecdotal biography*] (London 1898) p 251.

[15] For example J. G. Rogers, 'Mr Gladstone', *BQR* 79 (January 1884) p 32. [*The*]*B*[*aptist*] *Mag*[*azine*], 60 (London February 1869) p 99.

[16] 26 April 1877. *The Diaries of John Bright*, ed R. A. J. Walling (London 1930) p 390.

Gladstone and the nonconformists

and this is the use she makes of it . . . But that war was certainly
supported by an enormous preponderance of public opinion at the
time. And the only profitable use which can, at the present moment,
be made of that fact is to realise the responsibility which it has entailed
upon us now.'[17] Here was a common conscientiousness, an identical
moral awareness of past action entailing present responsibility. During
the Bulgarian agitation Gladstone became aware of this identity, and
never afterwards forgot it.[18] Nonconformists were most delighted with
Gladstone whenever he again dramatically demonstrated what were
seen as christian principles in politics, perhaps especially in the
midlothian campaign and at Parnell's fall. Gladstone, to nonconformists, was 'the incarnation . . . of the highest ideal of political
morality', 'a man who regarded politics as a part of Christian duty'
or (according to an opponent) 'a kind of superfine blend of the
Statesman and the Saint'.[19] Here was a religious bond that found
expression in politics.

Outside the sphere of politics the religious bond was perhaps less
obtrusive to observers but it was substantial to the parties concerned.
There was the legacy of Gladstone's early environment. His training,
he recalled in 1892, taught him to regard evangelicalism as 'another
name for Christianity.'[20] He had been brought up in a family that
visited Charles Simeon and Hannah More, in which the evangelical
Christian Observer was read and which founded churches for
evangelical clergymen. The spirit was of evangelical inclusiveness, not
of church exclusiveness. His mother commonly sat under dissenting
divines, and even consulted one about the choice of a clergyman.[21]
Gladstone's earliest religious convictions were those of an evangelicalism
that sat comparatively loose to churchmanship. 'I hope,' he later wrote
of this position, 'that my mind has dropped nothing affirmative.'[22]
He dropped what he conceived as negative in his opinions, the
damnatory part about roman catholics, heretics and heathens; and he
added his steady loyalty to the church of England. But the evangelical

---

[17] *Noncon*, 6 September 1876 p 894.
[18] For example *Times*, 19 April 1878 p 6. [W. E.] Gladstone, ['The Place of] Heresy and
Schism [in the Modern Christian Church', *Later Gleanings*] (London 1898) p 288.
[19] Samuel Smith, *My Life-Work* (London 1902) p 138. *The Congregationalist* (London
February 1875) p 66. Cited by John Morley, *The Life of William Ewart Gladstone*
(London 1903) 2, p 506. *The Liberal Unionist* (London) 1 October 1889 p 56.
[20] [*The Prime Ministers' Papers: W. E. Gladstone: 1:*] *Autobiographica*, ed John Brooke
and Mary Sorensen (London 1971) p 36.
[21] [*The*] *B[ritish] W[eekly]* (London) 29 October 1891 p 5.
[22] *Autobiographica*, p 152.

373

D. W. BEBBINGTON

affirmations, common ground with most nonconformists, remained. He was at one with them in christian orthodoxy. In an article on 'The Courses of Religious Thought' of 1876, Gladstone characterised five schools of thought: the ultramontane, accepting the papal monarchy; the historical, accepting the visibility of the church; the protestant evangelical, accepting the Trinity and the incarnation; the theistic, rejecting dogma; and the 'negative', rejecting providence.[23] His own anglican position fell within the historical school; evangelical nonconformists within the protestant evangelical school. They were linked in what he once called 'the undenominational religion of heaven' that united the first three schools in the doctrines of the Trinity and the incarnation.[24] From unitarians, falling within the theistic school, he felt divorced by their denials, and his feelings found public expression: at a dinner during the year of office of the first lord mayor of Liverpool, for instance, the unitarian chaplain was conscious of Gladstone's contempt for him and for the grace he had offered.[25] Other nonconformists, though, enjoyed his sympathy. 'Myself', he wrote in 1864 to Newman Hall, a moderate congregationalist, 'in profession at least, a somewhat stiff Churchman, I value beyond all price the concurrence of the great mass of Christians in those doctrines and propositions of religion which lie nearest the seat of life.'[26] There was an awareness of unity in beliefs that Gladstone had held from his youth up.

The shared evangelical heritage of Gladstone and the nonconformists was not simply a matter of orthodoxy. It was also about 'the seat of life' itself, about the conscience as well as the mind, about the heart as well as the head. Gladstone's known views on preaching well illustrate the point. He advocated what he once called 'searching preaching', sermons by preachers that should 'lay upon the souls and the consciences of their hearers their moral obligations, and probe their hearts.'[27] Preaching, he said on another occasion, must be of Christ, 'not merely of facts about Him and notions about Him, but of His person, His work, His character, His simple, yet unfathomable sayings . . .'

---

[23] W. E. Gladstone, 'The Courses of Religious Thought', Gleanings [of Past Years] (London 1879) 3, p 101.
[24] Gladstone, 'Heresy and Schism' p 300.
[25] L. P. Jacks, The Confession of an Octogenarian (London 1942) p 144.
[26] W. E. Gladstone to Newman Hall, 14 May 1868. Newman Hall, An Autobiography (London 1898) p 265.
[27] [W. T.] Stead, [Character Sketch:] Mr Gladstone, [The Review of Reviews], 5 (London April 1892) p 362.

374

Gladstone and the nonconformists

This declaration was made when Gladstone was attending a conference on 'Pew and Pulpit', organised in 1877 by Dr Parker at the City Temple: he spoke of being on 'common ground' with nonconformists, of being able to talk 'as Christians' about preaching.[28] Searching preaching was to be preaching of Christ: moral obligations were to be connected with the person of Christ – a connection which, in Gladstone's view, was the great achievement of the evangelical revival.[29] Gladstone felt himself as firmly wedded to that achievement as did the nonconformists. As well as moral obligations themselves, in Gladstone's opinion, the failure of men to fulfil their moral obligations in the sight of Christ, their sin, needed stress. In 1869 he congratulated Joseph Angus, president of the baptist Stepney College, on proposing to include human sinfulness in an unidentified literary project since it appeared to him that 'weak notions on that subject lay very near the root of the main religious difficulties of the day.'[30] One nonconformist preacher in particular did not neglect such themes: C. H. Spurgeon. Gladstone admired Spurgeon for what he called his testimony 'of sin, of righteousness and of judgment.'[31] Spurgeon, according to Gladstone, was an upholder of searching preaching; and he paid tribute to the 'great earnestness and power' of the baptist preacher.[32] In order to hear Spurgeon, Gladstone broke his normal custom and attended a dissenting service. On 8 January 1882 he visited the metropolitan tabernacle, to the delight of nonconformists.[33] A common satisfaction in preaching on the themes of duty, sin and Christ was a bond between Gladstone and the nonconformists as sons of the evangelical revival.

If Gladstone was sympathetic to nonconformists as evangelicals, he was less critical of nonconformists as dissenters than many men of high church conviction. His first book *The State in its Relations with the Church*, published in 1838, gained a reputation among dissenters for intolerance, not least because of Macaulay's review. His premises, as dissenting critics noticed, suggested that his conclusions should include

[28] *Times*, 23 March 1877 p 10.
[29] W. E. Gladstone, 'The Evangelical Movement: its parentage, progress, and issue,' *Gleanings* (1879) 7, pp 222 *et seq.*
[30] W. E. Gladstone to Joseph Angus, 9 December 1869. MS in possession of the reverend Dr E. A. Payne, to whom I am grateful for this reference.
[31] W. E. Gladstone to C. H. Spurgeon, 18 June 1884. *Correspondence on Church and Religion of William Ewart Gladstone*, ed D. C. Lathbury (London 1910) 2, p 325.
[32] Stead, 'Mr Gladstone', p 362. W. E. Gladstone to J. W. Harrald *CW*, 10 March 1892 p 198.
[33] *Freeman*, 13 January 1882 p 21.

the coercion of all subjects into observance of the faith of the state.[34] Some of Gladstone's dissenting constituents at Newark grew uneasy, and expressed fears at the 1841 election that he wished 'to exercise the civil power' for the purpose of 'compelling conformity.' However, Gladstone was able to disclaim all desire even to limit the civil privileges of dissenters, and to rebut the charge by sending a copy of the third edition of his book which he was confident would dispel apprehensions.[35] He was far less intolerant, even in theory, than his reputation suggested. In his *Church Principles considered in their Results,* of 1840, Gladstone argued that independency as a church polity was indefensible since it evacuated the term 'the Catholic Church' of all meaning; and yet he went on to contend that dissenters who exhibited holy lives gave evidence of being within the bounds of Christ's church.[36] The advocate of catholic principles, he soon afterwards put forward, can admit all that sectarian bodies claim for themselves – that their sacraments are but edifying signs, that their churches are human and voluntary associations and yet that their members who have faith are in the church invisible.[37] The wesleyans, often still attenders at the parish church, he would have been delighted to see reincorporated into the church on the pattern of a roman catholic order.[38] Gladstone certainly believed in these early years that dissent, since it rejected the authority of a teaching church, exalted too highly the right of private judgement of scripture and so could readily slide into heresy.[39] Yet his church principles were from the beginning adjusted to take account of the existence of dissent, and even to make a favourable estimate of dissenting brands of churchmanship. In later years he was able to build on this foundation a fuller appreciation of nonconformity as a religious body.

The religious resemblance in later years extended beyond matters of the spiritual life, of orthodoxy and of preaching, to matters of churchmanship. First there was a common anti-erastianism. On Gladstone's side, this was the result of a long-standing conviction that the church must have freedom for its spiritual work. In *Church Principles* he denounced erastianism as a sin, arguing that the church

[34] Angus, *Voluntary System* p 183.
[35] Ritchie, *Gladstone* p 19.
[36] [W. E.] Gladstone, *Church Principles [considered in their Results]* (London 1840) pp 96, 417.
[37] W. E. Gladstone, 'Present Aspect of the Church', *Gleanings* (1879) 5, p 78.
[38] Gladstone, *Church Principles* p 423.
[39] *Autobiographica* p 50.

could not properly be a creature of the state since the church was
there before any existing state.[40] In the 1890s he wrote of erastianism
as a base doctrine that confounded the church with the world.[41] On
the side of nonconformists, hostility to state manipulation of the
church could be a direct deduction from the voluntary principle. Dr
Guinness Rogers, congregational preacher and a leader of the disestablishers, recalled that 'Erastianism was distasteful to both Mr
Gladstone and ourselves, and the intensity of his own convictions made
him the more capable of understanding and respecting ours.'[42]
Wesleyans could approach Gladstone's position even more closely
than Guinness Rogers, since they generally did not reject the principle
of a state church until the last years of the century yet valued highly
freedom from state interference. Orthodox nonconformists other
than wesleyans were widely divided from Gladstone over whether
ideally a church should be recognised by the state; yet anti-
erastianism was common ground with Gladstone even in the area of
church-state relations.

Agreement that state control of religion was wrong proved specially
influential at one point in the relations of Gladstone with the nonconformists. In 1874, at a time when nonconformists were lukewarm
in their allegiance to the liberal party on account of Forster's education
policy, Disraeli's new conservative ministry introduced ecclesiastical
bills that flew in the face of voluntaries' wishes: the church of Scotland
patronage bill to end patronage in scottish parishes and the public
worship regulation bill to restrict the growth of ritualism in the church
of England. Gladstone emerged from a post-election period of withdrawal from politics to oppose both. He urged that the measures
constituted unjust interference in church affairs. English nonconformists, as well as scottish non-members of the established church, were
rallied to renewed enthusiasm for his policies and for the party of which
he was leader. It could hardly be otherwise when he declared himself
in one debate no 'idolator of Establishments' and in the other a defender
of 'the liberties of the congregation.'[43] Nonconformists concurred in
Gladstone's recoil 'from the coarseness of Erastianism.'[44] Hopes then

---

[40] Gladstone, *Church Principles* pp 96 *et seq.*
[41] Gladstone, 'Heresy and Schism' p 302.
[42] Rogers, *Autobiography* p 221. Compare G. I. T. Machin, 'Gladstone and
Nonconformity in the 1860s: the formation of an alliance, *HJ*, 17, 2 (1974)
p 354.
[43] *Noncon*, 8 July 1874, p 641; 15 July 1874 pp 666 *et seq.*
[44] *Ibid* 12 August 1874 p 761.

kindled that Gladstone was making progress towards the voluntary principle never entirely disappeared.[45]

A second affinity of churchmanship was grounded in hostility to ultramontanism. The popular anti-catholicism that affected most nineteenth-century Englishmen was strongly ingrained in nonconformists. Their wariness of the designs of the vatican embraced not only a repudiation of roman catholic teachings and a revulsion for romish religious practices like the confessional, but also a vigilance against attempts to extend papal political influence. Gladstone respected both the teachings and the practices of the roman church, but deplored the temporal power of the pope. His respect for roman catholicism was sometimes more obvious than his reservations about papal power. During Gladstone's first administration, his sympathy for Rome was a matter of deep suspicion to many nonconformists, especially to those most evangelical and least voluntary in outlook.[46] Popular protestant propaganda put out by defenders of the irish established church in 1868 and 1869 had the effect of raising questions in many nonconformist minds: Gladstone had, after all, visited the pope in 1866, and his high churchmanship was well known. Then the irish university bill of 1873, which at first appeared a satisfactory measure to nonconformists, on closer inspection proved to have been drafted with jesuit-like ingenuity to ensure a catholic dominance in the proposed irish university within a few years. Finally Gladstone's opposition to the public worship regulation bill, however welcome to disestablishers, was interpreted as anti-protestant by those sections of nonconformity most jealous of the nation's protestant heritage.[47] By 1874 rumours of Gladstone's crypto-popery were widely spread.

However, in the autumn of that year he published an article on 'Ritualism and Ritual' criticising, in an aside, the effect of the promulgation of papal infallibility in 1870 in allegedly subverting the civil allegiance of catholics. Controversy burst around him, and he felt constrained to defend his position in a series of further articles. Gladstone's best-selling pamphlet *The Vatican Decrees*, thought the editor of *The Baptist Magazine*, had 'opened the eyes of the public to

[45] *Ibid* 7 June 1876 p 565. Rogers, *Autobiography* pp 223 *et seq.*
[46] [J. H.] Rigg, ['Mr Gladstone's Ecclesiastical] Opinions', *LQR*, 43 (January 1875) p 405. *B Mag*, 66 (November 1874) pp 690 *et seq. Noncon*, 11 November 1874 p 1078. The author of the first article is identified by John Telford, *The Life of James Harrison Rigg, D.D., 1821–1909* (London 1909) p 179.
[47] *B Mag*, 65 (March 1873) pp 127 *et seq*; 65 (April 1873) p 173.

the true character and aims of Ultramontanism, now the supreme power in the Roman Catholic Church.'[48] After 1874 Gladstone was clearly no papist – unless one chose to believe, with an anonymous dyed-in-the-wool no-popery nonconformist pamphleteer, that Gladstone issued the pamphlet at the very time when his romish tendencies were about to be revealed and so proved his jesuitical skill.[49] A leading wesleyan, Dr J. H. Rigg, pointed out that Gladstone still entertained 'Oxford sacramental superstitions';[50] and Edward Miall in *The Nonconformist* regretted that Gladstone did not see universal disestablishment as the panacea that should destroy, among other evils, the pretensions of the pope.[51] Yet both Rigg representing the most evangelical section and Miall representing the most voluntary section of nonconformity were pleased to find that Gladstone repudiated the temporal claims of the papacy.

A third ecclesiastical similarity between Gladstone and the non-conformists was their denominational allegiance. In the late nineteenth century nonconformists were elaborating central and regional committees, funds and agencies, all reflecting denominational self-awareness. This was no novelty for the wesleyans, but for con-gregationalists and baptists it was more recent, the fruit in part of the union meetings begun earlier in the century, in part of celebrations of the bicentenary of the great ejection of 1662. By the 1870s, nearly all prominent nonconformists would think of themselves as loyal members of a denomination, even though they would normally desire to avoid exclusiveness. 'I profess to be a denominationalist,' said the baptist Charles Williams of Accrington in 1878, though adding, 'I hope to God I may never be a sectarian.'[52] Gladstone's loyalty to the church of England was analogous. Although denominational allegiance separated the nonconformists from Gladstone, it also bound them to him: allegiance to *a* denomination was something they had in common. '. . . I am one of those', declared Gladstone, sure of an enthusiastic response, at the Nottingham congregational institute in 1887, 'who think that none of us ought to be ashamed of what may be termed our denominational connexions (cheers), because they all belong to those conscientious convictions which we regard as the proper foundation

[48] *Ibid* 67 (January 1875) p 5.

[49] *Mr Gladstone exposed! by a Nonconformist* (London [1891]) p 9.

[50] Rigg, 'Opinions' p 398.

[51] *Noncon*, 3 March 1875 p 214.

[52] *Freeman*, 1 November 1878 p 551. Cited by J. H. Lea, 'Charles Williams of Accrington, 1827–1907', *The Baptist Quarterly*, 23, 4 (London 1969) p 184.

of religious belief and action.'[53] Gladstone could sympathise with
loyalty to a churchmanship other than his own. Nonconformists, for
their part, could honour a man for loyalty to his own church. It is
no wonder that, as a liberal high churchman wrote of Gladstone,
nonconformists 'felt that even ecclesiastically he had much in
common with them, and they with him, though they might not all
find it easy to put their impressions into words.'[54]

The affinities between the religious attitudes of Gladstone and the
nonconformists could draw them together the more effectively
because in his later years Gladstone refrained from writing of his
church principles. It was not until his final retirement from the
premiership in 1894 that he set out his views systematically, as he had
last done over half a century before. Up to 1894 nonconformists could
but guess the nature of his views and hope they were more liberal
than they feared. In the article Gladstone argued that, according to
Christ, schismatics were to be treated as heathen, yet that the passage
of time meant that nonconformists, receiving their faith by tradition,
had none of the culpability of the creators of heresy and schism.[55]
Despite the goodwill that undoubtedly prompted the article, it strained
the goodwill of those for whose benefit it was written. John Clifford,
one of the most eminent nonconformist preachers, took issue with the
article in a sermon. He refused to be freed of the stigma of heresy at
the expense of his forefathers' reputation. Further, not all nonconformists had received their faith by tradition. 'Some, many,'
continued Clifford, 'have accepted the doctrines they hold after mature
study, and have deliberately chosen to enter this or that body of
Christians. According to Mr Gladstone's dictum, then, how bad must
they be.'[56] And Clifford located Gladstone's error in his doctrine of the
church. As soon as they were expressed, Gladstone's church principles,
however charitably set out, remained a stumbling block.

Yet on the same Sunday evening that Clifford criticised Gladstone's
article, another baptist minister expressed his gratitude for a second
article by Gladstone that defended the doctrine of the atonement.[57]
From his first resignation as prime minister in 1874 until two years
before his death Gladstone occupied much of his leisure in composing

[53] *Times*, 20 October 1887 p 6.
[54] Malcolm MacColl, 'Mr Gladstone as a Theologian', *The Life of William Ewart Gladstone*,
ed Sir Wemyss Reid (London 1899) p 253.
[55] Gladstone, 'Heresy and Schism' pp 280 *et seq*, 292 *et seq*.
[56] *CW*, 6 September 1894 p 655.
[57] *BW*, 6 September 1894 p 309.

similar apologetic for the christian faith. Gladstone was seen during the 1880s and early 1890s as a defender of christianity against unbelief rather than as a protagonist of church principles. Some of these writings had, according to the wesleyan review, a ' "revivalistic" intensity . . . not far short of the intenser preachings of John Wesley or Charles Haddon Spurgeon.'[58] Such a quality commended the writer to nonconformists. Much of Gladstone's apologetic was based on Butler, and especially his argument from analogy for the acceptance of revelation. To a wesleyan reviewer, Gladstone's studies subsidiary to an edition of Butler seemed dated, and A. M. Fairbairn, principal of the nonconformist Mansfield College, Oxford, had written in 1887 that 'no man who knows what he is about now cites Butler as a final or adequate apologetic . . .'[59] Again, there was dissatisfaction with Gladstone's work in defence of the authority of the bible, *The Impregnable Rock of Holy Scripture* (1890), on the ground that higher criticism was conceded too many points.[60] On the other hand, a later *Christian World* editorial suggested that Gladstone was far too conservative in his critical views of the old testament.[61] Yet the general response to Gladstone's writings, including *The Impregnable Rock*, was highly favourable. It was the fact that Gladstone wrote christian apologetic rather than its content that was important.[62] His intention more than his achievement helped to consolidate his reputation among nonconformists.

The special relationship between Gladstone and the nonconformists was the result of religious resemblance in more ways than might be supposed. Even in the areas where contrasts were sharpest – over the establishment, sympathy for Rome and denominational loyalty – there were affinities. The very distance between the premises of Gladstone and the nonconformists in these areas seems to have strengthened nonconformist admiration for the liberal leader: to discover a great deal in common beyond a vital christianity put into practice, despite basic differences, was a welcome surprise. Nonconformists therefore trusted Gladstone as a politician, even – most of them – in the home rule crisis. And one of the chief nonconformists who felt compelled to withdraw his loyalty in 1886, Dr R. W. Dale, provides confirmation

---

[58] 'Mr Gladstone's "Butler" ', *LQR*, 87 (January 1897) p 248.
[59] *Ibid* p 254. A. M. Fairbairn, 'Christianity and the Service of Man', *The Congregational Review*, 1 (April 1887) p 304.
[60] ['Mr Gladstone as a] Religious Teacher', *LQR*, 90 (July 1898) p 322.
[61] *CW*, 30 May 1895 p 427.
[62] For example 'Religious Teacher', p 325.

that it was a religious bond that accounted for the fervour of non-conformist enthusiasm for Gladstone. 'This enthusiasm', he said in 1894, 'was mainly due to their faith in the reality and depth of his religious life, and thus he had the support of those who are the heirs and descendants of the Puritans.'[63]

University of Cambridge
Fitzwilliam College

[63] *CW*, 8 March 1894 p 165.

THE POLITICS OF THE ENABLING ACT (1919)

by DAVID M. THOMPSON

I doubt whether any event in the constitutional history of Church and State (wrote Randall Davidson in February 1921) has ever been wrought out with so little friction, and on so smooth a current as this great change . . . I think it is indisputable that if we had failed in December 1919 to get through Parliament what is popularly known as the Enabling Bill, we might have waited for it for many a long year with increasing and most harmful loss of enthusiasm, and growth of irritation among the progressive groups. Instead of this we have had a continuous stream of praise and thankful gratulation at the way in which the new system has begun to work.[1]

These words are a useful reminder that contemporaries were surprised at the easy passage of the enabling act, and that its success therefore requires explanation. The 'rightness of the cause' has tended to obscure the fact that right causes often fail. Moreover subsequent criticisms of the act, and particularly the disappointment of the life and liberty movement with what followed, have tended to minimise the significance of the changes it made.[2] Nevertheless the charisma of William Temple and Dick Sheppard seems to have led even the critics to attribute the act's success to the life and liberty movement;[3] viscount Wolmer's church self-government association has been relegated to the sidelines; and the verdict of bishop Bell (who in 1919 was Davidson's chaplain) that 'Its achievement was due to Randall Davidson more than to any other single person'[4] has been forgotten. In this paper I shall argue that the political success of the enabling act requires a political explanation, that parliamentary tactics in both the house of commons and the house of lords are therefore of prime importance, and that the significance of the success is enhanced by a

---

[1] [Lambeth Palace MS,] D[avidson] P[apers], 14, memo of 6 February 1921.
[2] For example [H. H.] Henson, [*Retrospect of an Unimportant Life*], 1, (London 1942) pp 301–2; F. A. Iremonger, *William Temple* (London 1948) p 281; [K. A.] Thompson, [*Bureaucracy and Church Reform*] (Oxford 1970) pp 156–78.
[3] For example, Thompson p 175.
[4] [G. K. A.] Bell, [*Randall Davidson*] (3 ed London 1952) p 980.

fact which has never been discussed before – the initial opposition of
the government of the day.

The background to the enabling act is well known. In 1913 lord
Halifax and viscount Wolmer used the opportunity of an anti-
disestablishment motion from Sir Alfred Cripps in the representative
church council to request the setting up of a committee to investigate
the possibility of a system of legislative devolution for the church of
England. The archbishops appointed a committee under the chairmanship of the earl of Selborne which reported in July 1916. It
recommended that the representative church council, suitably reformed, should be given legislative powers in church matters, subject
to a parliamentary veto. The report was officially welcomed by the
bishops in the spring of 1917, though Davidson remarked that it was
obviously impossible to do anything during the war. Those who felt a
greater sense of urgency set up the life and liberty movement in July
1917 to press for early action to secure freedom for the church 'in the
sense of full power to manage its own life'. Meanwhile the representative church council appointed a grand committee to consider the report.
That committee reported in November 1918, endorsing the 1916
proposals, except for the significant alteration of the franchise for
electors to parochial church councils from confirmation to baptism.
The report was accepted by the representative church council in
February 1919 and the next step was to approach parliament for the
necessary legislation.[5]

The proposals were, however, controversial both inside and outside
the church of England. Davidson expected 'ructions and wide
divisions' in the representative church council meeting in February
1919 and was 'agreeably surprised to find how well everyone be-
haved'.[6] Within the church there were those, best represented by
Hensley Henson, who saw self-government as reducing the church of
England to one denomination among many. Henson wrote a series of
letters to the Times in 1919 arguing that under the proposals the
church would cease to be 'the Church of the English nation, in which
every Englishman has rights, and for which every Englishman has
responsibility'. It would 'disallow for ever the hope of "compre-
hension"'. Henson also feared that the new church assembly would be
dominated by hard-line anglo-catholics – he had already described
the life and liberty movement as 'Gore's crowd'.[7] Evangelicals also

[5] Bell pp 956–70. [6] DP, 13, memo of 2 March 1919.
[7] Times, 19 May 1919, 15 December 1919; Henson pp 206–11, 301–6.

feared anglo-catholic influence, especially on the matter of prayer book revision, as Joynson-Hicks made clear in the house of commons.[8] All of these feared that this might be the first step towards disestablishment.

Outside the church there was a tendency to argue that disestablishment was the only condition on which self-government would be permissible. This was the view taken by those who sponsored the opposition in the commons, Thomas Broad and major Barnes. Some nonconformists, however, welcomed the bill as a step towards full liberty, i.e. disestablishment: W. B. Selbie of Mansfield College, Oxford, writing to the *Times* on 2 June 1919, was one of these. He was replying to P. T. Forsyth, who had also criticised the scant opportunity for parliament to discuss legislation under the new arrangements and claimed that this abrupt attempt to settle the church and state question was another setback to reunion conversations.[9]

But the weightiest opposition, as Davidson recognised, came on constitutional grounds and was represented by lord Haldane, a former lord chancellor. Haldane moved a negative amendment on the second reading of the enabling bill in the house of lords. Whilst making it clear that he had no objection to helping the church to regulate its own affairs, he held that the bill as drafted sought to narrow the basis of the national church and to remove the restraint on the power and authority of the episcopacy which parliament had for centuries imposed. In particular he objected to the omission of the constitution of the national assembly from the bill or a schedule of it (which he realised had been done on principle and not by accident); he drew attention to the novelty of the crown receiving advice on legislation directly from an ecclesiastical committee of the privy council rather than from the constitutionally appointed ministers; and he criticised the provision that measures submitted under the bill would become law without debate after forty days unless either house moved to reject them, on the grounds that this would blackmail the government into making time to debate measures of which they disapproved.[10]

More than any other person Haldane drew the government's attention to the significance of the bill. Tom Jones, assistant secretary to the cabinet, lunched with Haldane on 17 May 1919 and the bill was the first topic of conversation. Jones said he thought the cabinet had

---

[8] H[ouse of] C[ommons] Debates, 5 series, 120, col 1852.
[9] Times 28 May 1919, 16 June 1919. The first setback was the insistence on the historic episcopate.
[10] H[ouse of] L[ords] Debates, 5 series, 34, cols 993–1015.

probably never heard of the bill, but promised to draw Bonar Law's attention to it.[11] In response to a request from Herbert Fisher, chairman of the home affairs committee of the cabinet, Bell sent him details of the bill and the home affairs committee discussed it on 28 May. Fisher said that 'it was a very important measure, and very controversial, destroying as it did the Elizabethan and Caroline settlements. It would confer on the Church of England all the advantages of disestablishment without any of its disadvantages, and was certain to be hotly contested.' He felt drastic amendments were necessary. Munro, secretary of state for Scotland agreed that it was acutely controversial and added that the free churches in Scotland 'disliked the Bill intensely'. Sir Alfred Mond said that he thought the bill objectionable in principle. But it was agreed that the strong part of the church's case was the difficulties caused by the congestion of parliamentary business, though Fisher thought that the new system of standing committees in the commons would help this. It was decided that, subject to the prime minister's approval, the government should not accept the bill in its present form but should indicate its readiness to help the church to expedite internal reforms. On 2 June Fisher discussed the bill with Lloyd George when he saw him in Paris.[12]

The debate on the second reading of the bill began in the lords on 3 June, but as the next day was Derby day it was adjourned until 1 July. In the intervening month pressure against the bill intensified: this was the period of the correspondence in the *Times*. The executive committee of the national liberal federation, the executive of the national free church council and the general body of dissenting ministers in London all passed resolutions against the bill on the grounds that the special privileges retained by the church of England were inconsistent with self-government. The free church council added that it made parliamentary control void and exposed 'our Protestant liberties and rights to attack by default, rather than by free and open discussion'. The dissenting ministers said that it imperilled the movement towards christian unity.[13] These were significant pressures for liberals in the government. There were also manoeuvres of a different kind. On 21 June Sir Claud Schuster, permanent secretary at the lord

---

[11] T. Jones, *Whitehall Diary*, I, ed K. Middlemas (London 1969) p 86.
[12] [PRO MS] CAB 24/80, no GT 7349, Bell-Fisher 26 May 1919; CAB 26/1, H.A.C. 30 § 2, 28 May 1919; [Bodleian Library MSS], Fisher Diary, 2 June 1919.
[13] DP 'enabling bill' file: national liberal federation, 18 June 1919; national free church council, 24 June 1919; dissenting ministers, 4 July 1919.

chancellor's office, wrote to Fisher to ask for government help with the union of benefices bill, which had passed the house of lords in 1918 and 1919 but had made no progress in the house of commons. This was discussed in the home affairs committee on 26 June when Fisher explained the fear that it would again be shelved unless the government took charge of it and found time for it in the commons. He said that

> The Lord Chancellor advised that this should be done, firstly, because he was of the opinion that the Bill in itself was a good one, and secondly, because the Government had already decided to ask the House of Lords to reject the Enabling Bill on the ground that there was at present no evidence that the new procedure in the House of Commons would not enable the Church to pass such non-contentious legislation as was necessary for good administration. It would be a good thing, therefore, since the Government were going to reject the Enabling Bill, that they should afford facilities for the passage of the Benefices Bill.

It was decided to assist the bill through the commons with the home secretary in charge; and in the resumed lords' debate Birkenhead was able to repudiate Lang's claim that the union of benefices bill was meeting great difficulty in the commons.[14] The full cabinet considered the enabling bill on 30 June 1919. Birkenhead spoke strongly against it saying that after examining it 'he had now reached the conclusion that the Bill was a thoroughly bad one and something less than candid. It was engineered by a small body of men in the Church who had in view a purpose which was not represented in the Bill. It compromised the whole position of the National Church and the question of Disestablishment.' Curzon suggested that Birkenhead ought to modify his strong condemnation when he spoke in the house, lest it embarrass members on the government side who wished to support it. He expected it to obtain a second reading in the lords, but (like Munro in the home affairs committee) thought it was unlikely to pass the commons. Lloyd George saw no reason for the government to take sides and it was agreed that there should be a free vote.[15] It was clear, however, that the cabinet felt it could afford to be neutral because the bill would eventually fail.

How much of this was known to Davidson is not clear; but he had

[14] CAB 24/82, GT 7557, Schuster-Fisher 21 June 1919; CAB 26/1, H.A.C. 32 § 3, 26 June 1919; HL Debates, 5 series, 35, cols 94–5, compare col 30.
[15] CAB 23/10, War Cabinet 586 § 2, 30 June 1919.

always believed that the support of men 'of the important classes' was vital, which was why he had refused to act when pressed by life and liberty in 1917.[16] He also took care in presenting the measure to the representative church council to remove 'it largely out of the realm of fine-drawn theories and imperishable principles of right and wrong and the historic relation of Church and State . . . to the prosaic level of administrative efficiency and the difficulty of doing our work properly'.[17] The same tone is echoed in his description of his speech in the lords:

> My speech in introducing the Bill into the House of Lords was studiously different from what could be called a war cry. I brought the measure forward as a businesslike plan for enabling the Church of England to do its work better not as a constitutional change which was going to shatter the chains of an enslaved Church and emancipate us from a hampering bondage. The result was to take the wind out of the sails of the opponents who from the constitutional, or the Erastian, or the evangelical side (and all of these had potential champions) wanted to hold up our measure to obloquy in Parliament and secure its defeat.[18]

But that memorandum was written after the ultimate success of the bill. Davidson's success was not only due to his speech; it was due to his parliamentary tactics generally.

Haldane was an old friend of the archbishop, and he had been anxious to make it clear as early as 21 May that his grounds for opposing the measure were constitutional and not a lack of sympathy with its purpose.[19] Sir Lewis Dibdin, the leading ecclesiastical lawyer of his day, wrote to Davidson on 8 June saying that he felt a compromise would have to be reached, as the government could hardly support the bill after Haldane's speech. Davidson replied on 13 June that he was open to reasoned amendment and invited Dibdin to breakfast on 18 June for talks. Dibdin then consulted various opponents of the measure including Haldane, Wickham Steed (editor of the *Times*) and Henson. It seemed that Haldane was prepared to compromise in committee, but in view of his position as a leader of the extreme radical peers 'he would rather that the generosity seemed to come by compromise or compulsion, as it were, than on his own

---

[16] DP, 13, memo of 9 December 1917 (compare Bell, p 965).
[17] *Ibid* 13, memo of 2 March 1919.
[18] *Ibid* 14, memo of 6 February 1921.
[19] *Ibid* 13, memo of 6 July 1919; 'church and state' file, Haldane-Davidson 21 May 1919.

initiative'.[20] The committee stage was taken on 10 July, and Davidson conferred with Salisbury, Selborne, Grey (joint honorary secretary of the church enabling bill committee in the lords) and others about the amendments on the previous day. More than half the amendments were lost or withdrawn, with one significant exception. Davidson described the debate as follows:

> . . . we got through much better than I had anticipated – the division giving a majority of 41 (*sic*). I believe this to have been largely due to my determination not to let myself be forced into an attitude of opposition, still less of angry opposition, towards Haldane etc. They had no hostility to the principles of the measure as expanded by me i.e. that we need means of facilitating ecclesiastical legislation. They only objected to the procedure, and their objections were largely met by my conceding that Parliament must vote in favour of passing a measure when it has been passed through the Privy Council, not merely must abstain from a resolution against it.[21]

F. B. Meyer told the archbishop that these amendments would 'greatly meet Free Church objection'; and when the bill passed its report stage and third reading on 15 and 21 July, Wolmer wrote to Davidson thanking him for his 'brilliant and self-sacrificing leadership' and apologising for the impatience of himself and others in the past.[22] Wolmer was the man who had once accused Davidson of sitting on the fence like Balfour did over free trade and tariff reform.[23]

The bill was through the lords: but this was only half the battle because church bills had always fared better there, and as we have seen the government did not expect it to get through the commons. The work of rallying support in the commons fell to Wolmer. He already had 177 MPs on his church enabling bill committee, and since October 1918 he had been in touch with Scottish presbyterians and English nonconformists (through the good offices of Scott Lidgett and Shakespere).[24] The day after the third reading in the lords Wolmer

---

[20] *Ibid* 'church and state' file, Dibdin-Davidson, 8 June 1919, Davidson-Dibdin, 13 June 1919: (compare Bell, p 977, Thompson, pp 168-9. I do not share Thompson's sinister interpretation of this episode).

[21] *Ibid* 13, memo of 6/13 July 1919. Bell wrongly calls viscount Finlay the lord chancellor.

[22] *Ibid* 6, fol 41, Meyer-Davidson 11 July 1919; fol 42, Wolmer-Davidson, 26 July 1919.

[23] *Ibid* 14, memo of 6 February 1921.

[24] CAB 24/80, GT 7349 (printed list inside 'Explanation of the National Assembly of the Church of England (Powers) Bill: its cause and justification': issued by the joint parliamentary church enabling bill committee); DP, 'church and state' file, Wolmer-Davidson, 28 October 1918.

lunched with Fisher and he also wrote to Bonar Law, leader of the house of commons.[25] (Davidson had thought that contact with Bonar Law would be more useful than with Lloyd George.)[26] Eventually the cabinet was persuaded on 14 October to give time to the bill in the commons and this was announced on 29 October.[27] The debate on the second reading took place on 7 November, when it was introduced by Sir Edward Beauchamp who took exactly the same line as Davidson: Wolmer did not speak in the debate. An amendment declining a second reading on the ground that disestablishment and disendowment was the best method of achieving the aims was moved by Thomas Broad, a former congregational minister, and seconded by major Barnes. The latter compared the proposals to bolshevism, which he defined as 'a desire to combine a democratic form with autocratic effects'. Various criticisms were made but lord Robert Cecil, who also admired Davidson's tactics in the lords, was conciliatory about possible amendments in committee. The amendment was lost by 304 votes to 16. The majority included 126 MPs on the church enabling bill committee, and 233 unionists and coalition unionists (i.e. two thirds of the unionists in the house).[28] In committee Wolmer and his colleagues accepted two significant amendments from Sir Ryland Adkins, a congregationalist, who led the nonconformist members who had been in conference with Wolmer. One changed the ecclesiastical committee of the privy council into an ecclesiastical committee of both houses of parliament; the other provided that the enabling act itself could not be amended by its own procedure. The third reading was approved without a division on 5 December; the lords accepted the commons amendments on 15 December and the royal assent was given on 23 December.[29]

There is no doubt that the speed of the commons surprised even the promoters. Davidson attributed it to the method adopted:

[25] Fisher Diary, 7 July 1919, 22 July 1919; DP, 6, fol 42, Wolmer-Davidson 26 July 1919.
[26] DP, 'enabling act' file, Davidson-Wolmer, 3 March 1919.
[27] Fisher Diary, 14 October 1919 (CAB 23/12, War Cabinet 630 § 9, 14 October 1919 says that consideration was adjourned until the leader of the house of lords and the lord chancellor were present, but there is no further reference to the matter in the cabinet minutes): HC Debates, 5 series, 120 col 661.
[28] HC Debates, 5 series, 120, cols 1817–95; analysis of the division list based on Dod's Parliamentary Companion, 1920, and the list of the church enabling bill committee referred to earlier.
[29] HC Debates, 5 series, 121, col 1801; 122, cols 838–66; HL Debates, 5 series, 38, cols 15–22, 537.

The politics of the enabling act (1919)

Our success in the House of Lords, where the critics like Haldane and others were forced to admit the reasonableness of my plea, encouraged the promoters of the Bill to take the same line in the House of Commons with the result that the measure, to everybody's amazement, got through just before Christmas. It is a pleasure to me to recognise that the frankest admission was made forthwith, and since, by such men as Wolmer, Temple, Sheppard and many others, that my leadership had been right after all. It was an example of the advantage of having old men as well as young men in a great movement. For my own mode of handling it was the outcome of what is now a very long experience of public affairs, and a pretty sound knowledge of what Parliament will and won't tolerate.[30]

Was he right? Despite his self-satisfaction I believe that in general he was: certainly he was right in saying that 'the vociferousness which they (Life and Liberty) wanted would have been the very thing to wreck . . . the Enabling Bill in its cradle'.[31] But the nature of parliamentary success in an enterprise of this kind is such that it can never be the achievement of one man. If Davidson's method was right, then he alone cannot claim success. His stress on administrative efficiency did not prevent the wider issues of principle being raised: they stand out in all the debates. But because he put administrative efficiency first, he was ready to concede enough to defuse the explosion over principle, even though he recognised that his concessions might not be popular outside parliament.[32] In each house major changes were made in the form of the bill, all of them restoring elements of parliamentary control originally lacking. Success in the lords was probably always likely, but the promoters converted initial government hostility into benevolent neutrality; and the disestablishment tone of the opposition in the commons probably helped the bill further.

Why did the government change its mind? Partly because Lloyd George did not see the need to take sides; partly because of the concessions made; partly because the government never expected the bill to succeed in the commons anyway. But the general political situation is also relevant. Two other matters involving the church were the concern of the government at this time. One was the revised financial settlement for the disestablished Welsh church which was reached in July 1919 and which Davidson supported in the lords

[30] DP, 14, memo of 6 February 1921. [31] *Ibid.*
[32] *HL Debates*, 5 series, 35, cols 471–2. Lord Phillimore expressed disapproval.

391

despite Salisbury's attempt to wreck it. The other was Fisher's negotiations with church leaders about the religious difficulty in education which also began in July 1919. In both these matters the government had every reason to want Davidson's support.[33] The transport bill, the rail strike in September, and the drafting of the Irish home rule bill in the autumn also drew the government's attention elsewhere, and even threatened its unity. Alongside these the enabling bill seemed a small matter. But it never did become a government measure: they simply provided parliamentary time.

The success of the enabling act, therefore, was not a foregone conclusion: it requires a political explanation. Davidson's concessions in the lords and Wolmer's in the commons are part of the explanation. Sympathy with the ideal of spiritual freedom and hopes for reunion may have swung some nonconformists in favour of the bill in the commons; the suspicions of anglican evangelicals were at least partly met. It is in fact plausible to argue that the church of England was lucky to get the bill through when it did, and it is possible that the commons' reaction to the prayer book measure in 1927 and 1928 is more typical of their attitude to ecclesiastical legislation as a whole. (I suspect that the real watershed here is not the enabling act but the 1944 education act.) It is worth remembering too that the original opponents still had reservations. In the final lords debate on the bill Haldane said,

> The assembly which is set up will be, unlike the present Church of England, not an assembly of the nation at large, not the Church of the nation at large, but the Church of a fragment of that nation ... A current has been set moving which, in the long run I think, will lead to the Disestablishment of the Church.[34]

By 1939 Henson was converted to disestablishment. If the recommendations of the Chadwick report on church and state are adopted, and certainly if Miss Pitt's memorandum of dissent to that report gains wide acceptance, then perhaps it will not be too fanciful to see Davidson as the initiator of a gradual move towards disestablishment and Haldane as the man who tried to save the church of England from itself: history has known such ironies before. One thing at least is clear: the church is entangled in secular politics, and never more so than at the moment of its apparent liberation.

University of Cambridge
Fitzwilliam College

[33] Bell, pp 982–5, 1126–30.   [34] *HL Debates*, 5 series, 38, cols 18, 20.

THE PRESBYTERIAN CHURCH IN IRELAND
AND
THE GOVERNMENT OF IRELAND ACT (1920)

by JOHN M. BARKLEY

THE government of Ireland act (1920)[1] did not fall, like Athene,[2] fully fledged from the head of Zeus, so its historical development has to be considered if the presbyterian attitude to it is to be understood.

Presbyterians in Ireland had been second-class citizens up to 1780, and from then until the act of disestablishment in 1870[3] a tolerated church.[4] This was a vital factor when they were called upon to face the issue of home rule in 1886. A second was that they were a minority, the majority of whose members lived in Ulster,[5] whose community interests with Britain had been accentuated by industrialisation.[6] They owed little or nothing to an irish parliament or Dublin so far as relief from legal disabilities and their standard of living were concerned.[7] A third factor was the 'vote tory manifesto' of 'catholic nationalism' in 1885 which ended liberalism as a party in Ulster politics leaving presbyterianism without a political party of its own liberal ethos.[8] Politically, presbyterians had now no option but to choose between the toryism of the former ascendancy and an aggressive catholic nationalism which at times resorted to force and violence against the union with Britain on which their standard of living and economic welfare depended.

---

[1] 10 & 11 Geo V cap 67.
[2] Hesiod, *Theogony* 886; Pindar, *Olympia* vii 35.
[3] 32 & 33 Vict cap 42.
[4] D and A Kennedy, *An Outline of Irish History* (Belfast nd) p 101; [J. M.] Barkley, [*St Enoch's Congregation, 1872–1972*] (Belfast 1972) pp 18–37; J. C. Beckett, *The Making of Modern Ireland, 1603–1923* (London 1961) pp 159–61.
[5] M[inutes of the] G[eneral] A[ssembly] (1886) statistics p 22.
[6] T. W. Moody, *The Ulster Question, 1603–1973* (Dublin 1974) p 15; [E. R. R.] Green, [*The Lagan Valley, 1800–1850*] (London 1949).
[7] J. C. Beckett, *Protestant Dissent in Ireland, 1687–1780* (London 1948); [W. T.] Latimer, [*History of the Irish Presbyterians*] (Belfast 1902); Green.
[8] [W. S.] Armour, [*Armour of Ballymoney*] (London 1934) pp 73–5; C. C. O'Brien, *Parnell and his Party* (Oxford 1957) p 105; L. P. Curtis, *Coercion and Conciliation in Ireland, 1880–1892* (London 1963) pp 62–8; Latimer p 521.

In these circumstances Gladstone's first home rule bill, 1886, which made no provision for irish representation at Westminster, was opposed by irish presbyterians because it tended 'to imperil the legislative union between Great Britain and Ireland'; would 'lead to the ascendancy of one class and creed in matters pertaining to religion, education and civil administration', and provided no 'guarantees, moral or material, which would safeguard the rights and privileges of minorities throughout Ireland against encroachment of a majority vested with legislative and executive functions'.[9]

So strong was this feeling that the distinguished home ruler, the reverend J. B. Armour (Ballymoney) for a time joined the liberal unionists in opposing it, because the bill 'seemed to him to lend itself to the agitation for separatism, and because there appeared insufficient protection for minority rights'.[10]

In other words, presbyterians having escaped from the yoke of an anglican ascendancy in 1870 were unanimous in their opposition to the establishment of a roman catholic ascendancy in 1886.

Gladstone's second bill in 1893, unlike the first, provided for continued irish representation in the imperial parliament. While some raised the same objections against it, a critical analysis of all the evidence shows that the general assembly was about equally divided on the issue.[11]

When we come to Asquith's bill we find the assembly in 1913 receiving a memorial, signed by 131,351 'members and adherents . . . against the Home Rule Bill now before Parliament', and the assembly itself expressing its opposition by 921 votes to 43.[12] This is a very different situation from that of twenty years earlier. What had brought about the change? While there were many influences, including increased orange-tory activity and economics, the really determining factor so far as presbyterians were concerned was the promulgation of the *Ne temere* decree by pope Pius X in 1908,[13] and its aftermath in the McCann case.[14]

[9] MGA (1886) p 104.
[10] Armour pp 75–95.
[11] MGA (1893) p 556; Armour pp 106–14; Barkley pp 78–81.
[12] MGA (1913) pp 635–6.
[13] H. Denzinger, *Enchiridion Symbolorum*, ed A. Schometzer (Freiburg im Breisgau 1965) paras 3468–74.
[14] MGA (1911) p 84; W. Corkey, *The M'Cann Case* (Edinburgh 1912). The M'Canns were members of Townsend Street presbyterian church, Belfast, in which Dr Corkey was the minister.

The presbyterian church and the government of Ireland act

Alexander McCann, a roman catholic, was married to Agnes Jane Barclay by the reverend R. M. McC. Gilmour (Ballymena) in High Street presbyterian church, Antrim, on 16 May, 1908.[15] Later, on the basis of the *Ne temere* decree, the McCanns were informed by father Hubert that they were not married at all, and efforts were made to induce Mrs McCann to consent to be 'married' by a roman catholic priest. This she refused to do.[16] In consequence she was 'deserted by her husband, and deprived of her children and her household effects and left homeless and penniless on the streets of Belfast'.[17] The impact of this upon a people the legality of whose marriages were open to dispute in the courts up to 1845, that is, within the living memory of some, was inflammatory, and understandably so.[18]

The extent of its influence on the presbyterian attitude to home rule may be seen in the resolution passed on 1 February, 1912, at what is generally referred to as the 'Presbyterian Convention' (although it had no church authority and was an ad hoc meeting called by a group of individuals and attended by several thousand people). Following an introductory sentence, it continues

> Under Home Rule as foreshadowed, the Parliament and executive alike are certain to be controlled by a majority subject to the dictation of the authors of *Ne temere* and *Motu proprio* decrees against whose domination all safeguards designed for the protection of the Protestant minority . . . would be valueless.[19]

In other words, presbyterians, who had so recently escaped from an anglican denial of the validity of their marriages and the legitimacy of their children, were not going to risk finding themselves in a situation where it was possible for the church of Rome to place them in the same position, if it could possibly be avoided.

Asquith's bill became an act in 1914, but it was accompanied by two conditions. Its implementation was suspended (i) until the war was over, and (ii) until parliament had had an opportunity by amending legislation to make special provision for Ulster.[20] The result of the

---

[15] High Street presbyterian church, Antrim, marriage register 16 May 1908.
[16] MGA (1911) p 84.
[17] *Ibid* p 84.
[18] 11 Geo II cap 10; 21 & 22 Geo III cap 25; 5 & 6 Vict cap 113; 6 & 7 Vict cap 39; 7 & 8 Vict cap 81; Tullylish presbyterian church marriage register 10 January 1828; *The Queen versus Millis* (*Writ of Error*), Opinion of Lord Campbell 10 August 1843; *Banner of Ulster* July 1842–April 1844.
[19] *Witness* 2 February 1912.
[20] Moody p 24.

latter was Lloyd George's bill for the better government of Ireland, which the reverend J. B. Armour described in the general assembly in 1920 as 'a measure wanted by few and hated by almost all' and expressed the hope that it 'will never reach the Statute Book'.[21]

However, the government of Ireland act did become law on 23 December, 1920. It provided for the setting up of two parliaments – one for the counties of Antrim, Armagh, Down, Fermanagh, Londonderry and Tyrone in the north and another for the remainder of the country.[22] Each government was to consist of a senate and a commons.[23] It provided for the setting up of a council of Ireland 'with a view to the eventual establishment of a Parliament for the whole of Ireland',[24] and provision for the establishing of such a parliament was included in the act.[25] It also provided for forty-six members returned by constituencies in Ireland 'to serve in the Parliament of the United Kingdom'.[26]

This act was accepted in the north, where king George V opened parliament on 22 June, 1921, and the following day the government appointed its representatives to the council of Ireland.[27] It was rejected in the south, where, after what is generally referred to as the war for independence, articles of agreement for a treaty between Great Britain and Ireland[28] (in Ireland commonly referred to as 'The Treaty') were signed on 6 December, 1921. This gave the south 'dominion status' outside the United Kingdom but within the British empire. The treaty was rejected by the more intransigent republicans and a bitter civil war followed in the south between the pro-treaty and anti-treaty forces, 1922–23.

The treaty gave the north power to decide whether it would remain under the government of Ireland act (1920), or place itself under the parliament of the Irish Free State;[29] and provided for the setting

[21] MGA (1920) p 1136.
[22] Sec 1.
[23] Secs 13–4; schs 2, 3, 5.
[24] Sec 2.
[25] Sec 3.
[26] Sec 19. Twelve from the north and thirty-four from the south.
[27] *Hansard* 23 June 1921 Commons cols 17–8; Senate col 15.
[28] Articles of Agreement for a Treaty between Great Britain and Ireland 1921 Cmd 1560; Saorstat Eireann, public general Acts 1922 pp 44–8. *Irish Times* 9 January 1922; some contend the treaty was signed 'under duress', for example, F. Pakenham, *Peace by Ordeal* (London 1935), but see Michael Collins in *Illustrated Sunday Herald* (5 February 1922) and bishop Cohalan of Cork in the *Belfast News-Letter* (12 February 1923) and the *Witness* (16 February 1923).
[29] Arts 11–12.

up of a boundary commission to 'determine in accordance with the wishes of the inhabitants, so far as may be compatible with economic and geographic conditions, the boundaries between Northern Ireland and the rest of Ireland'.[30]

The treaty was 'given the force of law' by Dail Eireann on 6 December, 1922, with the establishment of Saorstat Eireann,[31] and the following day the northern houses decided to remain under the government of Ireland act (1920).[32] To this decision it is probable that few northern presbyterians objected, because, if one omits the three Ulster counties of Donegal, Monaghan and Cavan because of murder and burning-down of homes, terrorism and insecurity, presbyterian numbers had been reduced between Easter, 1916, and 31 March, 1922, in the presbytery of Athlone by 30%, of Connaught by 36%, of Cork by 45%, of Dublin by 16% and of Munster by 44%.[33]

To the general assembly's state of the country committee fell the responsibility of dealing with and reporting on the situation, and it is significant that each year, 1921–4, its report was 'adopted unanimously', as was the government committee's report in 1925. Following the passing of the government of Ireland Act, the state of the country committee presented its first report to the general assembly in June, 1921.[34] Having referred to the constitution and aims of Sinn Fein, it lists a number of atrocities, states that 'in some districts the Protestant population is being entirely exterminated', deplores the fact that 'there seems no Christian public opinion to condemn them or help bring to justice the perpetrators', and calls upon the authorities to protect lives and property 'irrespective of creed or class'. Then turning to the act it says

> This change in the government of Ireland was not sought by the members of the Presbyterian Church. We have repeatedly declared that we were anxious to remain within the Imperial Parliament and immediately under its jurisdiction. But our people, for the sake of peace, accepted the Act, and they are prepared to loyally carry out its provisions, so as to bring about settled government and establish law and order in our land.

Presbyterians had never sought the partition of the country,[35] so on the fact of two parliaments it pointed out that 'in the United States

[30] Art 12.
[31] Constitution of the Irish Free State (Saorstat Eireann) Act 1922.
[32] *Hansard* Senate cols 277–8; Commons cols 1146a–50, 7 December 1922.
[33] MGA (1916) statistics p 12; MGA (1922) statistics p 144; Barkley pp 104–5.
[34] R[eports of the] G[eneral] A[ssembly] (1921) pp 78–80.
[35] RGA (1925) p 92.

each State has its separate legislature, but the people in the different States live in harmony and fellowship', stating that the same can be true in Ireland. On the effect of partition on the church it says, 'We know that while most of the Presbyterians are under the Northern Parliament, a large and important section of our Church will owe allegiance to the Southern legislature. But the unity of our Church will not be impaired by being under separate legislatures . . .' The report concludes by setting out the principles of Presbyterianism and applying them to the situation.

> One of the fundamental principles of the reformed faith is the right of every man to think for himself according to the light which God has given him. True to that principle our Presbyterian people wish to live at peace with their Roman Catholic fellow-countrymen in the new order of things in Ireland.

In its resolutions[36] the general assembly recorded 'its deepest abhorrence of the unspeakable crimes against humanity which are being perpetrated throughout our land and which have brought reproach on the name of Ireland in every part of the civilised world'; expressed its sympathy with all 'who are exposed to terror and outrage . . . and with the friends and relations of those who have suffered'; and advised 'all the members of our Church to exercise self-restraint in the present crisis, and to seek to allay bitterness and bring about a better feeling, so that peace and harmony may be speedily restored in our land'.

The government of Ireland act (1920) provided 'for four bishops of the Roman Catholic Church and also for two bishops of the Church of Ireland to represent these Churches in the Southern Senate'.[37] As no provision was made for any presbyterian representation though they numbered about 53,000 members in the south, the assembly instructed the moderator to approach lord French, lord lieutenant, on the subject. He admitted that 'the proposal to give representation to the Presbyterian Church was perfectly reasonable'.[38] With the south's rejection of the act the matter ended there. The assembly's debate and decision, however, reveal (i) that no exception was taken to the roman catholic or anglican hierarchies being represented in the southern senate, and (ii) that it believed in the right of a minority to representation in the legislature and that this should be constitutionally guaranteed.

[36] MGA (1921) pp 46–7.
[37] Sch 2 pt 3.
[38] RGA (1921) p 80; MGA (1921) pp 46–7.

The presbyterian church and the government of Ireland act

Not only did the assembly accept the act 'for the sake of peace', it adopted a positive and constructive approach. It drew up 'A Programme of Social Reform' dealing with educational, industrial, social, moral and benevolent reform.[39] The aim was 'to set out proposals' which are 'manifestly just' and 'in harmony with the spirit of Christ'. The preamble concludes, 'We believe the programme contains those reforms which, in the interests of the kingdom of God, ought to be attempted and may be achieved within the next ten years'.

The attitude of presbyterians as revealed in the 1921 general assembly may be summarised as follows:—(i) they wished to remain one country but inside the United Kingdom; (ii) they were prepared to accept a solution they did not want 'for the sake of peace'; (iii) they accepted constitutional procedures and were as opposed to the use of force and terrorism as they had been in 1793[40] and 1914;[41] (iv) they sought the brotherhood of north and south and were not opposed to a council of Ireland;[42] (v) they maintained the unity of the church in spite of territorial division; (vi) their concept of unity permitted diversity and was not narrowly territorially limited; (vii) they acknowledged the authority of conscience; (viii) they had respect to the views and rights of roman catholics; (ix) they believed in a constitutionally guaranteed place for minorities in government; (x) they recognised the necessity for social reform and approached it on the basis of the common good; and (xi) they cared deeply about the the good name of Ireland.

The report of the general assembly in 1922,[43] after references to the activities 'of numerous gunmen', continues 'By their [IRA] operations during the three months beginning the 1st of February and ending 1st May, 1922, no fewer than 51 Protestants were slain in Belfast, and upwards of 150 Protestants wounded, while thousands of pounds worth of valuable property belonging to Protestants was burnt.' About two-thirds of those shot and wounded were presbyterians. This is the background to the assembly in June, 1922. On the re-action to this situation, the report says, 'These crimes have led to violent reactions and cruel reprisals, which are justly condemned by all right thinking

[39] RGA (1921) pp 70–2.

[40] Records of the General Synod of Ulster 3, pp 156–7.

[41] MGA (1914) p 908.

[42] Incidentally when the northern government appointed its representatives to the council of Ireland several of them were presbyterians see *Hansard* 23 June 1921. Senate col 15, Commons cols 17–8.

[43] RGA pp 102–3.

people', and expresses 'warm admiration for the self-restraint . . . that has been shown by the overwhelming majority in this city in the face of the strongest provocation'. Following a brief reference to the uncertainties and atrocities arising from the boundary question, the section on the north concludes, 'We believe that there are large numbers of Roman Catholics in Northern Ireland who are law-abiding citizens, and we hope the day is not far distant when the lawless elements shall be overcome and well-disposed citizens shall be found working together for the common good'.

Then the report turns to a consideration of the situation in the south. It opens

> With the acceptance of the Treaty and the formation of a Provisional Government, it was hoped that peace would be brought about in the Southern Area of Ireland, where upwards of 50,000 members of our Church reside. These hopes were doomed to failure.

Having referred to the activities of 'gangs of irresponsible gunmen', it says, 'The withdrawal of all Imperial Forces from Southern Ireland and the desertion of law-abiding citizens, both Roman Catholic and Protestant, who have now no protection for life or property, is one of the darkest stains in the annals of British administration'.

On the other hand, the report speaks of instances of 'kindness received from Roman Catholics who are . . . immediate neighbours'; and then proceeds to discuss the decline in presbyterian numbers, saying, 'We have reliable information regarding many members of our Church who have been shot, or maltreated, or deprived of their property and compelled to leave the country on various pretexts'. Indeed, the state of the country committee dealt with over four hundred cases of the murder or the burning-out of presbyterians, apart from other atrocities, during the years 1919–24.[44] The southern section ends,

> We know that the members of our Presbyterian Church in Southern Ireland are prepared to co-operate whole-heartedly with their Roman Catholic fellow-countrymen for the establishment of a settled government and for the best interests of their beloved land. We hope and pray that men in Ireland of every creed and class may soon be found working together for the highest good of that community in which their lot may be cast.

[44] This information was supplied by the late Dr William McDowell, who was a member of the state of the country committee.

The resolutions[45] condemn 'all acts of violence and destruction of property, as contrary to the law of God and a crime against society'; urge 'upon all members of this Church the duty of . . . seeking to establish law and order and promote peace and goodwill throughout Ireland'; express sympathy to all 'who . . . have been driven from their homes or whose loved ones have been cruelly done to death'; and remind 'ministers of the necessity of inculcating in their pulpit ministrations the duties and obligations of good citizenship as part of the Christian life'.

The 1922 assembly supplements our knowledge of presbyterian attitudes on several issues – (i) reprisals are condemned without equivocation; (ii) they are prepared to give honour where honour is due; and (iii) they emphasise 'good citizenship as a Christian obligation'.

The report to the general assembly in 1923,[46] states that 'there is now a sense of security for life and property' in the north, but in the south

> The condition of our Presbyterian people in many districts in the Free State is still deplorable . . . Respectable homes are raided by irresponsible bands of young men who loot and destroy at their pleasure . . . carrying off the very stock from the farms . . . In many cases land has been seized from the rightful owner, and up to the present there is no redress . . . Many have been compelled to leave under threat of death. If the present rate of migration continues it can only be a short time until all our Presbyterian Churches in the South of Ireland have disappeared except those in the large centres of population, and even there we find already a marked decrease in numbers.

The assembly then called on the British exchequer to compensate the 'hundreds of Protestant families' who 'have been driven from their homes and from their country' and 'are in destitution . . . because of their loyalty to the British Government, and because they believed the British people would never betray them'.

The report in 1923 is noteworthy for two new features. It contains (i) the first reference to the condemnation by a member of the roman catholic hierarchy of the 'cruel and coarse manner' in which protestants were being 'persecuted', and (ii) an analysis of why presbyterians 'suffer a great deal worse than their Roman Catholic brethren'. While it is

[45] MGA (1922) p 40.
[46] RGA (1923) pp 103–5.

401

clear from both Dr Michael Fogarty's (bishop of Killaloe) lenten pastoral[47] and the assembly's report that presbyterians did not 'suffer specifically because they were Presbyterians', it is evident that there was a sectarian element in events. Finally, the assembly declared itself 'fully assured that all the members of the Church within the Free State fulfil the duty of co-operating with the Government as by law established'.

With the restoration of law and order in the north and the success of the government forces in the south, the assembly in 1924 was so certain that a peaceful settlement was possible that it 'discharged' the committee on the state of the country, any outstanding questions to be dealt with by the government committee.[48] The one question still to be settled was the boundary between north and south. On this the government committee reported in 1925.[49]

> Opposed as our Church has always been to the partition of the United Kingdom, the other partition – between one part of Ireland and another – was never desired by it. It was only reluctantly accepted as the lesser of two evils between which it was necessary to choose . . . We greatly regret that the Boundary Question has been raised at the present time, and in the form it has assumed. If local adjustments of the Boundary are thought necessary for the convenience of those who live near the border, there could be no objection to their being carried out in a just and friendly way; but we strongly protest against a large section of the Six Counties, given to the Northern Government in the Act of 1920, being wrested from it.[50]

The assembly's attitude was conciliatory and left room for negotiation. On 3 December, 1925, the three governments – of Britain, Northern Ireland and the Free State–signed an agreement on the issue.[51] This is notable for four things – (i) It confirmed the boundaries of Northern Ireland and the Free State as defined in the government of Ireland act (1920);[52] (ii) It relieved the Free State of certain financial

[47] 11 February 1923.
[48] MGA (1924) p 59; RGA (1925) p 92.
[49] RGA (1925) p 92.
[50] The 'two evils' between which the church had to choose were 'civil war' and 'partition'. To avoid the former, if possible, it accepted 'for the sake of peace' the government of Ireland act (1920).
[51] Ireland (Confirmation of Agreement) Act 1925, 15 & 16 Geo V cap 27; Statutes of Oireachtas, Saorstat Eiarenn no 40.
[52] Sec I.

The presbyterian church and the government of Ireland act

obligations;[53] (iii) The powers of the council of Ireland in relation to Northern Ireland were transferred to the parliament and government of Northern Ireland;[54] and (iv) The agreement had an international status in that it was duly lodged with the league of nations.[55]

The settlement was welcomed in the church's weekly newspaper, *The Witness*.[56] This may be why it was not referred to at the 1926 meeting of assembly, which appointed the Sunday before saint Patrick's day (13 March 1927) as a day of prayer 'for the peace and prosperity of our land'.[57]

To sum up, presbyterians, having accepted a political solution they did not want 'for the sake of peace', the legal issues of which had now been finalised 'in amity'[58] by the governments of Britain, Northern Ireland and the Free State with the resolve 'mutually to aid one another in a spirit of neighbourly comradeship',[59] and conditions having become relatively peaceful even though some nationalists in the north were carrying out 'a campaign of what amounted almost to civil disobedience',[60] as christmas day 1925 approached, hoped that 'the spirit of brotherhood and goodwill would soon obtain over the whole country'.

Presbyterian College, Belfast

[53] Sec 2.
[54] Sec 5.
[55] *League of Nations Treaties Series* 44.
[56] *Witness* 11 December 1925.
[57] MGA (1926) p 23.
[58] Ireland (Confirmation of Agreement) Act 1925, preamble.
[59] *Ibid.*
[60] F. S. L. Lyons, *Ireland since the Famine* (London 1971) p 685.

THE BARMEN DECLARATION (MAY 1934)

by OWEN GEOFFREY REES

THE exposition delivered at the synod of Barmen on Wednesday, 30 May 1934, by *Pfarrer* Hans Asmussen gives us the exact purpose and intention of the committee which had drawn up the six articles of the theological declaration.[1] It is made quite clear that the fundamental concern of the declaration is divine revelation. In the several articles of the declaration the uniqueness of the revelation in Christ is asserted and the uniqueness of the church as the body which is entrusted with the proclamation of that revelation is equally carefully emphasised. The church is alone in her responsibility and any attempt by the world to usurp that responsibility must be rejected. These great claims for the church are made because the church is more than a sociological entity, and the church must ever remain that which she truly is. Positions of responsibility within the church should be exercised with humility, for thus only can church order correspond to the inner essence of the church. The limits which separate the church and the state must be strictly observed and neither the church nor the state should presume to exercise authority in that which does not belong to it. And finally, the freedom of the Holy Spirit must be known, and the guidance of the Holy Spirit must be felt in the church. These statements are the culmination of a series of events in which the German evangelical church had been seriously disturbed by the national socialist policy of *Gleichschaltung*. Together with this there had been an attempt in various parts of the church to modify its doctrinal position and in that way to admit elements of racial nationalism. Finally, there had been since the collapse of Germany at the end of the great war a formidable amount of political theology which discovered manifestations of God's will and purpose otherwise than in the revelation of Jesus Christ. It is these three aspects of the life of the church which created a crisis which brought about the first confessing synod of the German evangelical church at Barmen on 29 to 31 May 1934.

[1] G. Niemöller, *Die erste Bekenntnissynode der Deutschen Evangelischen Kirche zu Barmen*, 2, *Text-Dokumente-Berichte*, A[rbeiten zur] G[eschichte des] K[irchenkampfes] 6 (Göttingen 1959) pp 49–66.

When Hitler had become chancellor on 30 January 1933, the danger for the church was not immediately visible. Indeed, the solemn inauguration of the new era in the garrison church at Potsdam on 21 March 1933 and the declaration by Hitler in his first *Reichstag* speech concerning the relationship of the 'National Government' to the two confessions and his expectation that both would take part in the 'national and moral restoration of our people', gave room for optimism. National enthusiasm for the unity of the German people found expression in the life of the church and was accompanied by a revival of plans for reform and of the desire for the creation of an evangelical *Reichskirche*. On 11 July 1933, the various *Landeskirchen* accepted a new constitution which bound them together in a federal *Reichskirche*. At the same time however, the pressure of the policy of *Gleichschaltung*, that is, the close integrating of all public activities under the control of the state had been felt when the election of von Bodelschwingh as *Reichsbischof* on 27 May had been vehemently opposed by the state authorities and Hitler's nominee, the former army chaplain, Ludwig Müller, through the endeavours of the German christians was imposed upon the German evangelical church and elected *Reichsbischof* on 27 September. Within six months of the original enthusiasm for national regeneration, the church had felt the harsh pressure of the new government. It had also discovered that the aryan paragraph of 6 September 1933 was to be enforced not only in the state but also in the church and that pastors and church officials of non-aryan blood were to be deprived of their office. It was very few of the clergy who were affected by this law but nevertheless it was a sinister indication of the danger in which the church stood. A small group of pastors who were seriously alarmed by the turn of events met under the guidance of Martin Niemöller and formed the pastors' emergency league on 21 September 1933, and the situation was made alarmingly more serious by the demonstration of the German christians at the *Sportpalast* in Berlin on 13 November of that same year. Already the German christians had secured control of the synods of several of the *Landeskirchen* and at the *Sportpalast* wild assertions had been made which seriously endangered the integrity of the confessional position of the evangelical church. It was as a direct outcome of the challenge of 1933 that the synod of Barmen was called.

It is important to realise that the synod was primarily concerned with the crisis of faith and of identity within the church, rather than with the threat of state control. Furthermore it is significant that the involvement of the national socialist party in the affairs of the German evangelical church, and in particular its deliberate attempt to incorporate the church in the unified state system, was not in accordance with traditional attitude of the party towards matters of religion.[2] The party programme in point 24 had expressed its support of a 'positive christianity' but in practice the party had been consistently reserved on matters of religious allegiance of any kind, at least until 1930. This involved not only an attitude of reserve towards christianity but also towards any other religious group and this attitude is illustrated in the dismissal of one of the *Altkämpfer*, Artur Dinter from the post of *Gauleiter* of Thuringia in 1927, and soon afterwards he was expelled from the party. The reason for this was that Dinter was the founder of the *völkish* movement *Deutsche Volkskirche* and it was the wish of the party clearly to dissociate itself from this movement. However, in 1930 a tactical change of attitude took place and the new policy was that of a co-ordination of the church with the state. The German christians were the means by which such a policy was possible. However, it is important to remember that the involvement of the party was the result of tactical considerations and the return of the party to an attitude of indifference and indeed hostility, towards church was soon brought about by the difficulties which attended the policy of co-ordinating the church into the state system. While the German christians continued with their purpose of co-ordinating the church as closely as possible with the state, the party gradually retreated from its involvement in this matter. Accordingly, from 1933 onwards, both the government and the party gradually resumed the position of neutrality. Those elements in the party which wished to make a clear distinction between the national socialist ideology and the christian faith secured an increasing preponderance and they were able to press forward with their desire to eliminate the influence of the church from public life. In October 1933 Rudolf Hess brought to an end the general requirement that every non-catholic national socialist should subscribe to a German christian church when he declared that no party member should be placed under any disadvantage should he acknowledge no confessional adherence. On the other hand, the German christians did not accept this change of front as an indication that the party had abandoned the plan for a *Reichkirche* closely bound to national socialism, and it is with the persistent efforts of the German

---

[2] K. Meier, 'Kirche und Nationalsozialismus' in Zur Geschichte des Kirchenkampfes, Gesammelte Aufsätze, AGK 15 (1965).

christians to manipulate the life and work of the church that the synod of Barmen was immediately concerned.

The German christian movement consisted of two separate groups, the *Kirchenbewegung Deutsche Christen* and the *Glaubensbewegung Deutsche Christen*.[3] The *Kirchenbewegung Deutsche Christen* began with the work of two young *Vikare* in the lutheran church in Bavaria, Siegfried Leffler and Julius Leutheuser. Serving together in Augsburg, they were clearly committed to national socialism and averse to confessional theology. They withdrew from the bavarian *Landeskirche* in 1927 and found parishes next to each other in the district of Wierstal near Altenburg in Thuringia, and here no impediment was placed in the way of their ardent propaganda for national socialism. The name *Deutsche Christen* was probably used for the first time in 1929 to refer to the followers of the two pastors. Leffler and Leutheuser established a local group of national socialists in February 1930 and in that year the German christian group was vigorously involved in political work for the party. Most probably it was the same people who in large measure supported both the party and the German christian movement. The German christians were able in due course to gain influence in church affairs by putting forward their own lists in church elections and in the election for the *Landeskirchentag* in Thuringia in January 1933, the German christians gained thirty per cent of the votes and sixteen out of the total of fifty-one seats. In the following weeks they were able to secure the expulsion of the six representatives of the *Religiösen Sozialisten* and following this they were able to secure the support of the other members of the assembly and, in consequence, a party which closely combined religious and political enthusiasm had secured control of the Thuringian *Landeskirche*. The two leaders believed that from the great movement under Hitler's leadership there must come an upsurge both of national and religious renewal. They saw the history of the German people in terms of *Heilsgeschichte*, a history through which God was fulfilling his purpose both for them and for the world. For that reason, the christian church in Germany would derive new vitality from these great events and, because these were great national events, it followed that the territorial churches of the reformation should now be united in a national evangelical church and further, that even the difference between the catholic and evangelical traditions should be overcome in a supra-confessional national church.

[3] K. Meier, *Die Deutschen Christen* (Göttingen 1964).

The Barmen declaration, May 1934

The second division of German christians, the *Glaubensbewegung Deutsche Christen* took its rise from far more practical and political reasons. The leader of the national socialist party in the prussian *Landtag*, Wilhelm Kube, saw the possibility of increasing the political influence of the party by securing successes in the church elections. He called for a league of evangelical national socialists and in February 1932 a meeting of 'ecclesiastically minded' national socialists from various parts of Germany took place in Berlin. The name evangelical national socialists was considered to be unsuitable for the winning of influence in the church and accordingly the term 'German christians' which was suggested by Hitler, was accepted with the approval of the thuringian German christians. In May 1932, pastor Hossenfelder was officially entrusted by Gregor Strasser, on behalf of the national socialist party, with the task of fighting the old prussian church elections. The new party was accordingly seen to enjoy the clear approval of the national socialist leadership, and it now began to serve not only the purposes of the prussian national socialist group but also began to be seen as the church party which was clearly in accord with the national socialist party in its work in every part of Germany.

The *Glaubensbewegung Deutsche Christen* was officially inaugurated at a meeting in Berlin in June 1932, and the guide-lines of its work were proclaimed. It was declared that its purpose was a summoning of men of faith to a new-ordering of the church. It was not a confessional front but a national movement which sought to discover new life for the church. A part of its aim was to overcome the fragmentation into *Landeskirchen* through the formation of an evangelical *Reichskirche*. The movement pledged itself to the service of 'positive christianity' and recognised in 'race, *Volkstum* and nation', 'orders of life ordained by God'. It bound itself to a new ordering of the church in which extensive recognition was given to national socialism. The ideological basis of the *Glaubensbewegung Deutsche Christen* was seen as the religious counterpart of national socialism and in return it was hoped that from national socialism new life might flow for the renewal of the church. The presence of Frick and Göring as guests of honour at the first national assembly of the movement in April 1933 appeared to give substance to these aspirations. The assembly provided a great impetus to the *Glaubensbewegung Deutsche Christen* because it made clear that the movement was fully committed to the reshaping of the *Landeskirchen* into a *Reichskirche*. Many of those who now joined were drawn by this hope of achieving a *Reichskirche*, rather than by the

409

radical racial ideas of the movement. The aspirations and motives of those who joined the movement were only vaguely defined and they were held together by the sense of participation in a national renewal which included the church and of which the party was seen as the supreme instrument. However, there had appeared a change in the attitude of the national socialists towards the *Glaubensbewegung Deutsche Christen*. From the late summer of 1933, the party leadership sought to give the impression that the time of revolution had come to an end and that it was now the time of the harmonious evolution of the nation. The previous positive support which it had given to the *Glaubensbewegung Deutsche Christen* changed to an attitude of neutrality and this change seriously affected the future prospects of the movement. The *Sportpalast* demonstration of November 1933 was intended as the first step in an effort to revive enthusiasm for the *Glaubensbewegung*. Over twenty thousand were present at the meeting and sixty flags belonging to various regional sections of the movement were dedicated. The speech of Gauobmann Dr Krause was significant of the increasingly radical trend of the movement. He spoke of the great numbers of Germans who had returned to the church, and he declared that in order that they might feel truly at home there, its worship and its confessions should be freed from everything which was un-German, and especially that it should be rid of the old testament with its morality of reward. He declared further that it would be necessary to remove from the new testament those parts which were distorted and heretical; that it would have to be purged of the theology of the rabbi Paul, which was a falsification of the original good tidings 'love thy neighbour as thyself'. The truth of the matter was that 'the whole course of development of dialectical theology from Paul to Barth has made our heavenly Father into an intellectual pawn'. The aims of the movement were summed up in a series of resolutions demanding the removal of recalcitrant pastors, the energetic implementation of the aryan paragraph and the removal of jewish elements from the worship and the confession of the church. Further, it called for a German *Volkskirche*, cleansed from all oriental misrepresentation, to proclaim a heroic Jesus as the basis of a genuine christianity which would produce men who knew themselves to be children of God and who were bound to that which is divine in themselves and in their people. Finally it was declared that the true service of God is fulfilled in the service of one's own people and that the movement was bound together in the struggle to fulfil the task given to it by God, of working together for a strong and valiant *Volkskirche*, in which would be seen the fulfilment of the German reformation, and which alone would do justice to the total claim of the national socialist state.

The protest at Barmen therefore began with the sounding of an alarm against the usurpation of power and authority in the church by the German christian movement, together with a clear statement of the supreme and unique authority of Jesus Christ as the Word of God. This had been clearly indicated by the two verses which stood at the head of the first article; John 14: 6; 'I am the way, and the truth, and the life: no one cometh unto the Father, but by me'. John 10: 1, 9: 'Verily, verily, I say unto you, He that entereth not by the door into the fold of the sheep, but climbeth up some other way, the same is a thief and a robber. I am the door: by me if any man enter in, he shall be saved'. In the first article it is declared 'We reject the false teaching that the Church should, apart from the Word of God alone, accept other events and powers, conceptions and truths as God's revelation'. In his theological exposition Asmussen declared that the church had no other loyalty but to the Word become flesh in Christ and to the Word preached through Him, and that this was now being challenged. The church and her members were being asked to recognise the great events of 1933 as ordained by God, to be taken into account in the proclamation and the interpretation of scripture, and as rightly demanding obedience side by side with the scriptures. Asmussen declared that their protest was in truth against that development which for more than two hundred years had gradually devastated the church. To accept historical events side by side with the scriptures was akin to the similar acceptance of reason, culture, aesthetic experience, progress or any other power. All these belong to the world which in Christ alone can find redemption. The further rejection of the German christian position is made clear in the second article where it is said 'We reject as false the teaching that there are parts of our life where we must acknowledge other Lords than Jesus Christ, that there are parts of our life where we have no need of the justification and sanctification in Him'. Asmussen declares that these words speak to a world which claims to be the church and also, that it speaks to those christians who have bound themselves to this world. The fifth article deals with the responsibilities and duties of the christian towards the state. 1 Peter 2: 17, 'Fear God. Honour the king' is the scriptural key to the relationship between the church and the state. Asmussen in the theological exposition declares without reserve that members of the confessing front are held by divine command in obedience and in loyalty to the *Volk* and to the state. State and church each works in its own realm. The one is that of the law the other is that of the gospel. Each overstepping of the bounds by one or the other leads to a bondage which is foreign to its nature. If the state proclaims an eternal kingdom, an eternal law and an eternal righteousness then it corrupts both itself and the people. On the other hand if the church sets out to proclaim an earthly kingdom and the righteousness of a human society, then it oversteps its bounds and it drags the state with it into its own slough. The article states, 'We reject the false teaching that the state could, over and above its own particular task, become the single and total order of human life and accordingly itself fulfil the vocation of the Church. We reject the false teaching that the Church should and could, beyond its own task, accept the form of the state, with its particular tasks and values, and thus become an organ of the state'. Asmussen then declared that it was impossible to accept the view that the basic idea of the contemporary form of state, on which otherwise no judgement was passed, could be identified with the wisdom of God. Neither could it be accepted that the standard of righteousness which prevailed in the state was the standard of divine righteousness.

The exaltation of the idea of *Volk* and state into a divine ordinance possessing an absolute quality which gave to it the nature of revelation, and the claim that in the events of the recent revolution was to be seen a manifestation of God's saving purpose which was on a par with the saving events of the biblical history, was unequivocally rejected at Barmen. However, it might well be thought that these were no more than rash statements of the German christians which, because of their manifest extravagance, could easily be recognised as possessing very little serious significance. In truth however, there lay behind them a considerable body of serious theological writing which sought to derive from the doctrine of creation a body of teaching concerning God's purpose for the political life of the nation.[4] The most radical of such theological writings was that of Emanuel Hirsch who sought, in the confusion of the period immediately after 1918 to discover a new inspiration for national feeling.[5] He maintained that the wishes and the interests of the individual should be subordinate to those of the nation

---

[4] W. Tilgner, *Volksnomostheologie und Schöpfungsglaube*, AGK 16 (1966).

[5] G. Schneider-Flume, *Die politische Theologie Emanuel Hirschs 1918–33*, *Europäische Hochschulschriften*, Reihe 23, Bd 5 (Bern-Frankfurt/M 1971).

and it was to this task of a theological exposition of the claim upon the individual of the *Volk* and of the nation that he gave a great deal of his attention during the next twenty years. In his book *Deutschlands Schicksal, Staat, Volk und Menschheit im Lichte einer ethischen Geschichtsansicht*[6] Emanuel Hirsch sets out the objective of a social-ethical revolution in which the orders of *Volk* and nation are acknowledged as parts of God's will in creation and, in face of the liberal tendencies towards disintegration, he defends these orders as God-given responsibilities. He emphasises the truth of a national *Volks*-state as a 'boundary' established by God, and the conception of conscience which had been emphasised in the Luther renaissance plays an important part in his thought concerning the state. The individual conscience is identified with the *Volk* conscience and the duty of the individual is identified with the duty of the whole people. In his book *Die Liebe zum Vaterland*[7] he propounds the concept of *Volkheit* as a principle of creation which is given concrete expression in the moral demand of a nation-state. Because *Volkheit* is a principle of creation, obedience to it is not obedience to an earthly law but obedience to the eternal. In it is discovered a metaphysical law which leads to the position that the created order of the people is seen as the law of God, and the history of the people is to be seen as a second spring of revelation. The revelation given in Christ is 'God's eternal act of reconciliation', but it does not impose a moral demand upon life. Morality and its claim to obedience are much more to be discovered in *Volkheit* which, as an ordinance of creation, declares the will of God concerning both the people and the individual. He derives from Fichte the conception of the various peoples of the world charged with the task of bringing to pass God's purposes in history. Every nation must fulfil its own task as it is discovered in its collective conscience and in the conscience of its individual members. Hirsch perceives the address of the divine 'Thou', the 'Lord of history', in the orders of life and in this objectifying of the divine demand he finds the way to overcome the introspection of idealism. Because morally bound existence is manifested in the orders of *Volk* and nation, it follows that the service of these orders now acquires a quality of divinity and by this metaphysical exaltation of the earthly and historical order of creation, Hirsch contributed profoundly to the development of a German christian *Schöpfungstheologie*. In 1934, when he published his lectures which had

[6] Göttingen 1921.
[7] Langensalza 1924.

been delivered in the previous year,[8] he acknowledged the identity of his own thought with the theology of the German christians and furthermore he recognised in Hitler's national socialism the new power of leadership, which in its bond with the German spirit, would set right the mistakes of past German history.

A further important contribution to nationalist theology was made by two theologians at the university of Erlangen, Paul Althaus and Werner Elert. Althaus was one of the main representatives of the Luther renaissance, and from his Luther studies he developed his theology of orders. He revived Luther's two-kingdom theology and therein he discerns a double lordship of God. On the one hand there are the moral responsibilities imposed upon the individual in his personal relationships and on the other, the orders and institutions of creation impose upon him a further responsibility of obedience. National existence is one of these orders of creation and the claims of the nation are made known in its history. The christian fulfils his duty towards God by his active participation in the orders of life and by such participation he fulfils Jesus's law of love. Althaus first gave systematic expression to his theology of orders in his book *Staatsgedanke und Reich Gottes*.[9] He declared that only an authoritarian state firmly established in the people could bring about the national renewal of the German people. Love and faith must be substantiated in the orders of state and of people, because these orders are necessary presuppositions of the kingdom of God. Althaus understood *Volkheit* not as the biological identity of the people, but rather as 'God's gift and creation'. This gift and creation is given to men as men and is not a part of Christ's work. It was in the wars of independence that the German people had first discovered their unity as a *Volk* and it was then that the state and the people became one. Because of this the state was enabled to transcend its basic function of exercising justice and restraining evil, and to advance to become the creative will of God for his people. In the political events of 1933 Althaus saw another creative expression of the national state. The new state was an 'order' to which both the conscience of the people and the Word of God testified. Althaus saw his theology of orders as the natural expression of the old protestant teaching of the *Vocatio generalis* and he gave his own expression to this in the doctrine of general revelation, the *Ur-*

[8] *Die gegenwärtige geistige Lage im Spiegel philosophischer und theologischer Besinnung, Akademische Vorlesungen zum Verständnis des Deutschen Jahres 1933* (Göttingen 1934).
[9] Langensalza 1923.

Offenbarung. Such a doctrine, while it gives divine sanction to the nation and the people, does not however ascribe to the history of particular peoples and nations a revelatory quality. Althaus reserved for the history of the old and the new testament alone the attribute of revelation. Thus no nation can claim for its own history the character of finality and the church on the other hand, can never be released from bearing witness to the uniqueness of the history contained in the old and new testament. Althaus makes it manifestly clear that he completely rejected the teachings of the German christians and that he could not accept the teaching that the history of the German nation possessed any quality of salvation. Yet his theology appears to approach very closely to a double revelation, in spite of the fact that Althaus declares that the *Ur-Offenbarung* is that wider conception of revelation which is the presupposition of all christian revelation.

Werner Elert became professor at Erlangen in 1923 and from that time onwards he associated himself very closely with the nationalist aspect of German lutheranism. His *Die Lehre des Luthertums im Abrisz*[10] and his article 'Das Luthertum und die Nationen'[11] gave clear expression to his new point of view. A fundamental presupposition of his political theological thought is the claim that a lutheran national theology has its deepest roots in the reformation. He took his stand with Luther when he taught that the revelation of Christ began in the incarnation and from this he argues that reformation theology cannot be reconciled with the rejection of the significance of historical existence. On the contrary particular national existences are 'willed by the creator himself'. Further, he declared that while the redemption frees us from the guilt which is involved in all our earthly ties, it does not abolish those ties, especially the ties of blood, which are willed by the Creator himself. Elert developed his *Schöpfungstheologie* in a comprehensive form in his classical work *Morphologie des Luthertums.*[12] Here he declares that the orders of creation are ordained by God and that they impose upon us a direct ethical and moral duty. He safeguards the revelation in Christ by saying that the orders of creation speak only of the hidden God and that they must be fulfilled and purified by the God who is made known in Jesus Christ. However, as in the case of Althaus, it is also true of Elert that he finds it difficult to subordinate the pressure of *völkish* and national thought-categories.

[10] Munich 1924.
[11] *Allgemeine Evangelisch-lutherische Kirchenzeitung* 1925.
[12] 2 vols (Munich 1931–2).

The deep contrast between the *Schöpfungstheologie* of the Erlangen school and the theology of the Barmen declaration is seen in the *Ansbacher Ratschlag*[13] which was issued in June 1934 as an explicit rejection of the Barmen declaration. The *Ratschlag* owes its basic form to Elert and it was only after several changes had been made that Althaus was able to associate himself with it. It declared that the Word of God speaks to us both as law and gospel. The law meets us in the total reality of our life, and it is brought to light through God's revelation. By it each one of us is bound both to that situation to which he is called by God and to the natural orders to which we are subjected, such as family, *Volk* and race. Furthermore, we are bound to a particular family, a particular *Volk* and a particular race and, because God's will meets us in our here and now, it binds us to the particular historical moment in which we find ourselves. The natural orders are not only the manifestations of God's will, but they are also the means through which God creates and sustains our earthly life. In relation to these basic ideas, the *Ratschlag* then sets out the task which awaits the church. The church is to proclaim the law of God by making clear the orders in their sublimity, its members are to accept the demands of the orders as they are manifested in the present historical situation, and the church must in its own structure, reflect the existing orders. As the demands of the particular orders vary with the historical situation, so must the church in its constitution and cultus be related to these changes. In relation to the ever changing demands of the historical situation there must be a continuing reformation of the church and the fulfilling of this reformation in the church of our own time must be brought about both by our theological work and by our church activity.

By its own deliberate assertion of the *Schöpfungstheologie* the *Ansbacher Ratschlag* serves to bring out the intensity of the Barmen theological declaration as a statement about the total sufficiency of divine revelation in Christ and as a decisive rejection of all natural theology and in particular of *Schöpfungstheologie*. It was only by this emphasis on theological principle that the confessional church was able to maintain the long and hard struggle for its own integrity and survival. Karl Barth assesses the importance of the theological declaration and of the first article in particular when he declares,

---

[13] G. Niemöller, *Die erste Bekenntnissynode der Deutschen Evangelischen Kirche zu Barmen, I, Geschichte, Kritik und Bedeutung der Synode und ihrer Theologischen Erklärung, AGK 5* (1959) pp 143–6.

The Barmen declaration, May 1934

The fact that in 1934 the basic opposition could be made which is laid down in this article, and that, in spite of all uncertainty and reverses, this opposition could since prove and maintain itself as the nerve of the whole attitude of the confessional church in a position of the severest tribulation, is something which, however things may develop, we can already describe as one of the most notable events in modern church history.[14]

St Michael's College, Llandaff

[14] K. Barth, *Church Dogmatics*, 2, 1. (English trans Edinburgh 1957) p 176.

CHURCH AND POLITICS:
DOROTHY BUXTON
AND THE GERMAN CHURCH STRUGGLE

by KEITH ROBBINS

THE German church struggle in the nineteen thirties inevitably involved christians in Germany in a reconsideration of their attitudes towards politics, but its significance was not confined to Germany. The fate of Martin Niemöller, in particular, was a matter of lively concern in Britain.[1] Conway contends that 'the English-speaking public was all the more disposed to give every credit to the "Bekennende Kirche" because all the books published in English before the war were wholeheartedly on their side.' English-speaking authors, he adds, unanimously, if one-sidedly, saw the struggle as one of church versus state, good versus evil, and confessing church versus nazi storm-troopers. A brief study of the activities of one of the writers mentioned by Conway, Mrs Dorothy Buxton, reveals that the 'English-speaking public' was not quite as unanimous in its interpretation of church and politics in Germany as the contemporary literary works might suggest.[2]

Mrs Buxton was no stranger to the techniques of political campaigning. Her husband, Charles Roden Buxton, was an active liberal and then labour politician all his life, though only for short periods was he a member of parliament. During the first world war he had been associated with the union of democratic control and had campaigned for peace by negotiation. He believed that the treaty of Versailles was a disgrace which would have evil consequences. His wife, a niece of Sir Richard Jebb, the Cambridge classical scholar, largely shared his views on these matters. During the war, she had compiled for the *Cambridge Magazine* items from the foreign press and was able to demonstrate to her own satisfaction that not all Germans shared a desire for extravagant war-aims. After the war, they

---

[1] See my article 'Martin Niemöller, the German Church Struggle and English Opinion' *JEH* 21, 2 (April 1970).

[2] [J. S.] Conway, [*The Nazi Persecution of the Churches, 1933–45*] (London 1968) pp xvii–iii.

both continued to maintain their interest in international affairs. Buxton was active as chairman of the labour party advisory committee on foreign affairs. Mrs Buxton gained a considerable knowledge of social conditions in Europe – her sister pioneered the save the children fund.[3]

The rise of the nazis in Germany worried the Buxtons, though it did not greatly surprise them. They did not sympathise with the methods and ideals of the nazis, but for years they had argued that the allied treatment of Germany would lead to such a reaction. After 1933, therefore, they were torn in different directions believing that British guilt required some expiation but also realising that the nazis might well destroy those liberal christian values to which they were committed. As the years passed, their reactions differed. Charles, with his eyes on the disaster of another war, grew more and more determined to fight a lonely struggle to avoid it, at almost any cost.[4] Dorothy, as she learnt more of the nazi treatment of christians in Germany, felt that if war did come British intervention could be justified.

Dorothy Buxton's knowledge of Germany was not superficial, nor was her interest merely passing. She devoted a great deal of time and money to gaining information from Germany and drawing the attention of British people to the situation. There were, however, considerable problems because some of the information was confidential and might cause harm to people in Germany if it were made generally available. There was also the constant danger that protests from Britain would make it easy for the nazis to brand christians in Germany as traitors. Initially, she was herself prepared to admit that, however disturbing, events in Germany admitted of more than one explanation. It might be reasonable to wait and see. It was possible that extravagant things were being said and done in the first flush of the revolution and they would later be regretted and abandoned. In 1935, she determined to go to Germany herself and investigate the position of the churches. Dr Bell, bishop of Chichester, whom she consulted, warned her that people would be unwilling to give information – 'the externals and the internals are so often different, and people are very, very reserved.'[5] She also wanted to find out about

[3] F. Wilson, *Rebel Daughter of a Country House* (London 1967).

[4] V. de Bunsen, *Charles Roden Buxton* (London 1948).

[5] [R. C. D.] Jasper, [*George*] Bell, [*Bishop of Chichester*] (London 1967). G. Bell to D. Buxton, 4 February 1935. A letter in the possession of Miss Eglantyne Buxton. Any letters in her possession are hereafter referred to as Buxton Papers (A).

concentration camps. J. H. Oldham, whom she asked, shared her anxiety on this score but doubted whether the problems of the confessing church 'should be complicated by the introduction of the other question, in spite of the fact that it is one in regard to which the Christian Church ought in normal times to take vigorous action.'[6] Not for the last time, Oldham's reservation raised the problem of 'politics'. In the event, Dorothy did go to Germany, reporting on her return that everyone she had talked to 'seemed oppressed and bound with the apparent necessity of extreme caution.'[7]

By 1936, the following year, however, she did not believe that judgment could any longer be suspended. From this point on, she tried in a variety of ways to make the English christian public aware of what was happening in Germany. She was not a theologian and made no attempt to write a theological guide to the complexities of the conflict. Nevertheless, although like her husband she had joined the society of friends, she was in general sympathy with the confessing standpoint. Inevitably, therefore, she came into conflict with the bishop of Gloucester. Arthur Headlam was the leading English exponent of the view that christianity in Germany could not be identified simply with the confessing church. He urged sympathy and understanding rather than condemnation, though he was himself critical of certain aspects of the new Germany.[8] In February 1935, for example, he wrote to Rosenberg that he was much disturbed by accounts of the existence of concentration camps and of restrictions on pastors. The secular power was interfering in matters which were strictly religious. The anti-semitism of Streicher and his paper was deplorable and only alienated British public opinion.[9] In October 1935, he was hopeful that the German government would make a new start and allow the German church to work out its own salvation.[10] Throughout 1936, while deploring particular episodes, he remained optimistic. Mrs Buxton, however, by the end of the year, became more dispirited. Dr Micklem, principal of Mansfield College, Oxford, who was also

---

[6] J. H. Oldham to D. Buxton, 1 February 1935, Buxton Papers (A). Oldham was a leading figure in the developing ecumenical movement. See his *Church, Community and State* (London 1935).

[7] Jasper, *Bell*, p 205.

[8] [R. C. D.] Jasper, [*A. C.*] *Headlam: [Life and Letters of a Bishop]* (London 1960) pp 292–3.

[9] Headlam to Rosenberg, 25 February 1935 quoted in Jasper, *Headlam*, p 295. See also *Das politische Tagebuch Alfred Rosenbergs 1934/35 und 1939/40*, ed H.-G. Seraphim (Munich 1964) p 65.

[10] Headlam to Miss P. L. Wingfield, 28 October 1935, Jasper, *Headlam*, p 296.

deeply interested in the German question, agreed that from a worldly point of view, the prospects of the confessing church were gloomy, but he doubted whether the church in Germany had been as alive and as christian as it now was at any time since the Reformation. It was a difficult task to keep public opinion informed of German developments, but he hoped that she would continue her 'quite invaluable work'.[11]

The bishop of Chichester visited Germany from 28 January to 1 February 1937 and had a long round of talks with various church leaders, including Lilje, Niemöller and Dibelius. Bell learnt of the increasing tension between Zoellner and Kerrl, and the German conviction that 'the future of the Evangelical Church must depend on public opinion in England.' Public opinion in England, however, did not speak with one voice. Just before Bell's visit, the reverend Dr A. J. Macdonald, at the bishop of Gloucester's request, also met church leaders and produced a different interpretation of the situation. In acknowledging Bell's report and covering letter, the archbishop of Canterbury related that Macdonald was critical of 'the more decisive attitudes of people like Niemöller' and was even prepared to recognise some merit in many 'German Christians'. Macdonald thought that the attitude of some of the leaders of the confessing church towards the 'Church Committees' had hindered a reasonable reconciliation between church and state.[12] The disagreement was acute because at this juncture Zoellner resigned. In a letter to *The Times* on 24 February 1937, Headlam also lamented what he regarded as the failure of the confessing church leaders to give Zoellner adequate support. Hitler had offered new church elections and he believed it was unwise to assume that this was only a clever device to injure the church further. 'We have no reason' he concluded 'for thinking that the Chancellor's action is not a wise and honest attempt at a settlement'.[13] Mrs Buxton refused to accept this interpretation. She wrote to Headlam that she did not believe his claim that police interference had diminished after Zoellner's appointment. Indeed, his resignation had been basically because he had been refused permission to go to Lübeck where some confessing pastors had been

[11] N. Micklem to D. Buxton, 3 January 1937. A letter in the possession of the author. Letters in his possession are hereafter referred to as Buxton Papers (B). N. Micklem, *The Box and the Puppets* (London 1957).

[12] Jasper, *Bell*, pp 217–20. See also the article by Macdonald in *The Nineteenth Century*, March 1937.

[13] *The Times*, 24 February 1937.

dismissed by a local German christian bishop.[14] In other words, no great opportunity had been lost.

Mrs Buxton's scepticism about the regime's intentions was increased in these months because she was horrified by the fate of Dr Weissler, former head of the secretariat of the confessing church. After the 1936 olympic games were safely over, he was arrested, presumably for his part in drawing up a protest memorandum submitted to Hitler by the confessing church in May 1936.[15] A few months after his arrest it was announced that he had committed suicide. Mrs Buxton tried to obtain signatures for a letter to *The Times* implying scepticism about the suicide and deploring the fact that he should have been imprisoned simply because he had allegedly given a copy of the memorandum to the foreign press. She told those she approached that she had come to the conclusion that letters of this kind were an important means of expressing solidarity with the confessing church. The replies she received reveal that not all her correspondents were so certain.

The moderator of the free church federal council, the reverend M. E. Aubrey, a baptist, replied that Dr Hans Bohm of Berlin had urged that the British free churches refrain from any public action unless they received some indication from Berlin. Aubrey feared that signing the letter 'might simply be an irritant to the persecuting party in Germany'.[16] Hensley Henson, bishop of Durham, shared the consternation of 'all who care for the future of religion in Germany and the possibility of any honest & lasting co-operation with her.' Yet he feared that any comment he made would be discounted 'as coming from a known opponent of the Hitler regime'.[17] The bishop of Croydon agreed to sign the proposed letter, though he feared that it might do more harm than good.[18] Lord Hugh Cecil declined, believing that an imputation of murder needed more than suspicion to justify it. Furthermore, he believed that there was always a danger that tyrants would finish off those captives whose sufferings excited foreign sympathy. In his view, there were signs that Hitler did not possess that absolute control exercised by Mussolini and, quite possibly, 'was told

[14] D. Buxton to A. C. Headlam, 17 June 1937. In an unsorted collection of Buxton Papers in Lambeth Palace library, London, hereafter referred to as Buxton Papers (C) 5a.
[15] Conway p 164.
[16] M. E. Aubrey to D. F. Buxton, 2 March 1937, Buxton Papers (B). Aubrey was general secretary of the baptist union.
[17] H. H. Henson to D. F. Buxton, 2 March 1937, Buxton Papers (B). For Henson see H. H. Henson, *Retrospect of an unimportant life*, 2 (London 1943) and E. F. Braley, *Letters of Herbert Hensley Henson* (London 1950).
[18] Bishop of Croydon to D. F. Buxton, 3 March 1937, Buxton Papers (B).

nothing about the crimes'. Except for callous indifference, therefore, he had no responsibility.[19] The bishop of Fulham (the anglican bishop for north and central Europe) also declined, explaining that if he took a public stand he would probably be refused entry into Germany. He had seen Niemöller and all the leaders of the different sides in December and feared that a letter would not bring peace, but more persecution.[20] In reply, Mrs Buxton acknowledged Fulham's misgivings, but argued that 'on the whole it must surely be harmful that the authorities in Germany should be able to count on the ignorance of the British public. If they feel they are being watched, and that some of the terrible happenings are realised over here, it must surely exercise some restraining influence.'[21] The bishop of Gloucester replied that he would write to bishop Heckel in Berlin telling him what a very bad impression these 'strange events' created in England. He added his thanks for some translations of German neo-paganistic literature Mrs Buxton had enclosed, but felt that she exaggerated 'the extent to which the Germans are prepared to listen to Rosenberg, and so on.'[22] The bishop of Birmingham, Dr Barnes, added another twist in his reply. He wished to go on record as an admirer of the 'Christianity and heroism' of the confessional leaders rather than of their theology. The murder of Weissler was a grave scandal. It was almost incredible that 'the Nazi tyranny in Germany should be a development of the twentieth century.'[23]

When the letter did appear in *The Times* on 11 March 1937, Aubrey wrote approving of it. He also sought some political advice. Should he go over to Germany in his capacity as moderator? Would not those who were unfriendly towards the confessional church consider such a step foreign interference in the concerns of the German people? He felt that it was 'rather difficult to persuade Germans that as individuals we cherish friendly sentiments towards their nation while at the same time we are critical of the actions of rulers for whom they have a regard that is almost akin to adoration.'[24] Mrs Buxton advised him to go. She believed that there were many among the persecuted christians of Germany who longed for any sign of sympathy from English

---

[19] Lord Hugh Cecil to D. F. Buxton, 10 March 1937, *ibid.*
[20] Bishop of Fulham to D. F. Buxton, 2 March 1937, *ibid.*
[21] D. F. Buxton to bishop of Fulham, 9 March 1937, *ibid.*
[22] A. C. Headlam to D. Buxton, 4 March 1937 and 10 March 1937, *ibid.*
[23] Bishop of Birmingham to D. F. Buxton, 8 March 1937, *ibid.*
[24] *The Times*, 11 March 1937; M. E. Aubrey to D. F. Buxton, 24 March 1937, Buxton Papers (B).

christians.[25] In the event, the moderator decided not to go but to seek an interview with the German ambassador in order to express his disquiet. Karl Barth, however, questioned the value of demands in the liberal tradition for 'freedom of expression' for the confessing church. Aubrey, who described himself as 'by no means a Barthian' felt there was some value in the reminder that real freedom would be gained by men who wished to 'declare the Gospel rather than by those who simply want freedom.'[26] Mrs Buxton was not sure that Barth was right. If he was, why had confessional church leaders recently pressed for a visit to Germany? Was he right to be so certain that representations to Germany never had any effect, particularly since the German government was apparently anxious to be on good terms with Britain? Finally, she wondered whether Barth represented the views of the confessional church as a whole.[27]

In this month, April 1937, Micklem was in Germany, first in the Rhineland and then in Berlin. One of the problems discussed was the question of German participation in the Oxford conference on church, community and state, scheduled for later in the year. Mrs Buxton was most anxious for a fully representative delegation from Germany to appear so that full publicity could be given to the German situation. On his return, Micklem reported to Mrs Buxton that the confessing church delegation would be prevented from attending.[28] He agreed that the whole situation was extremely confusing. What was really needed was an 'oecumenical bureau of information'.[29] British efforts to help in Germany were hindered by 'lamentable disorganization'. Of course, disorganization was not the only problem, for there was continuing disagreement about the 'facts'. At the spring meeting of the church of England council on foreign relations, for example, Bell and the dean of Chichester, Duncan-Jones, had successfully opposed the incorporation of MacDonald's report into the council's official *Survey*. Nevertheless, Headlam insisted on a preface emphasising the difficulties of forming a judgment on the realities of the situation. Much of the difficulty, he held, sprang from the inability of the German mind to compromise. Tension was increased because each group held to its opinion without any willingness to see the other point of view.

[25] D. F. Buxton to M. E. Aubrey, 29 March 1937, *ibid.*
[26] M. E. Aubrey to D. F. Buxton, 23 April 1937, *ibid.*
[27] D. F. Buxton to M. E. Aubrey, 27 April 1937, *ibid.*
[28] N. Micklem to D. F. Buxton, 7 May 1937, *ibid.*
[29] N. Micklem to D. F. Buxton, 13 May 1937, *ibid.*

In the second place, he distrusted the tendency of English opinion to become 'furiously partisan' about events in foreign countries when it could not possibly comprehend the full context. The confessing church did not have the monopoly of true religion. Citing figures, he held that by the end of 1936 'the great majority of the German pastors were living peacefully in their own parishes and were doing very good work.' He criticised anti-semitic propaganda and crude neo-paganism, but thought it wrong to judge national socialism by the foolish utterances of the more extreme members of the party. It was better to ascribe to Hitler good intentions rather than treat him as if he were a criminal. Finally, he urged all christians in Germany to recognise the need for unity to help the nation in a crisis of its history. It was wiser for the confessional churchmen to join with all the other 'Orthodox Lutherans' rather than to stand in isolation.[30]

When the *Survey* was presented to the church assembly on 22 June 1937, Bell vigorously contested these views and the archbishop of Canterbury insisted that they were in no way official but simply Headlam's own. Mrs Buxton also challenged Headlam.[31] The bishop replied that persecution was too emotive a term to describe the situation in Germany, 'though there may be very stupid interference'. A recent set of arrests, he contended, arose because certain German pastors deliberately banded themselves together to disobey an edict of the government which forbade the reading out during a service of the names of those who had left the Church. 'If the Government feel it wise to forbid it,' he wrote 'I do not think we can complain very much, but, at any rate, there can be no demand of conscience that the Pastors should disobey it. They are deliberately irritating the Government, and they cannot complain if as a result of that they are arrested; and it seems to me very foolish on our part to encourage them in these principles. They are exactly what a good Christian clergyman ought not to indulge in.'[32] Mrs Buxton was not convinced, agreeing with Aubrey that it was an 'appalling utterance'.[33]

At this time, the summer of 1937, she was deeply immersed in the final stages of her pamphlet, *The Church Struggle in Germany* which was

---

[30] *Fourth Survey on the Affairs of the Continental Churches (German Evangelical Church), April 1936 to April 1937* (London June 1937). Preface by the bishop of Gloucester.
[31] D. F. Buxton to A. C. Headlam, 17 June 1937, Buxton Papers (C) 5a.
[32] A. C. Headlam to D. Buxton, 29 June 1937, *ibid*.
[33] M. E. Aubrey to D. F. Buxton, 2 July 1937, *ibid*.

published early in July by the *kulturkampf* association.[34] This association is somewhat shrouded in mystery. A report on church matters in the third reich, *Kulturkampf*, had appeared in French and German from 1936, and then in English from early in 1937. It had a circulation of some 2,500 copies and Mrs Buxton ardently sent it to editors of various journals in the hope that information it contained would appear in their own columns.[35] In her own pamphlet, Mrs Buxton gave a brief survey of the outstanding events in the church struggle from March 1933. She accepted that the full story might seem incredible to some readers, but believed her facts were correct. She had no doubt, however, that 'Hitler and his regime are the supreme creation of the Treaty of Versailles'. The peace treaty, 'a terrific denial of Christianity', prepared the way for the religion of race. Hitler wanted to see a fusion of politics and religion, but his religion was one of hate, not love. Therefore, christians in England, who shared responsibility for his rise to power, could not turn a deaf ear to cries from Germany. 'If many Germans to-day deny Christ' she concluded 'and His supreme law of universal love, let us not forget that we of the Allies denied Him first.'[36]

The booklet was well-received. Hensley Henson felt that it was a powerful statement and the facts it contained should not be swept away by the 'intense desire to get into friendly relations with Hitlerite Germany'. We are confronted, he added, 'by a frantic nation, obsessed by a false idea.' He thought the condemnation of Versailles was somewhat severe, wondering what would have happened if the the boot had been on the other foot.[37] William Temple, however, found her conclusion most impressive, and Bell found nothing to take exception to in her judgment.[38] Other reviewers tended to ignore the section on Versailles, though the editor of the anglican paper, *The Guardian* agreed that the church struggle and the consequences of the treaty could not be separated.[39] The booklet quickly went into a

---

[34] In order to protect her informants she simply described herself as 'An English Protestant'. [*The*] *Church Struggle* [*in Germany. A Survey of Four Years, March 1933–July 1937*] (London 1937).

[35] See A. Wiener's article 'Untersuchungen zum Widerhall des deutschen Kirchenkampfes in England, 1933–38; in *On the track of tyranny; Essays presented by the Wiener Library to Leonard G. Montefiore*, ed M. Beloff (London 1961).

[36] *Church Struggle* pp 23–4.

[37] H. H. Henson to D. F. Buxton, 14 July 1937.

[38] W. Temple to D. F. Buxton, 14 July 1937; G. Bell to D. F. Buxton, 13 August 1937, Buxton Papers (B).

[39] G. Mayfield to D. F. Buxton, 20 August 1937, Buxton Papers (B).

second edition, but Mrs Buxton was rather at a loss to know what to do next. With the arrest of Niemöller the situation seemed to be deteriorating in Germany. As Micklem had forecast, there were endless difficulties concerning the German delegation to the Oxford conference. The bishop of Chichester was also depressed at this time, worried by what he believed to be the decreasing attention given to the German church struggle in Britain.[40] The Anglo-German political situation was very delicate. Lord Halifax was about to visit Germany and prominent people approached by Bell were unwilling to write letters to *The Times* about the German church lest they be accused, one way or the other, of trying to influence the politicians.

Nevertheless, to counteract this apparent malaise, Mrs Buxton drafted another letter which she hoped to see published with an impressive list of signatories. The letter mentioned that it was difficult to see how a christian church in Germany could survive as an outward organisation. It outlined recent speeches by Herr Kerrl and concluded that the culminating blows could be expected shortly. Niemöller and his fellow-pastors in prison had sacrificed themselves, not only to the cause of religious freedom, but also to the cause of christianity. However, it did indeed prove difficult to obtain signatures. A number of bishops, understandably, were unwilling to commit their names to collective letters when they could not check some of the statements that were made. Many others felt that a letter would not do any good, and might even lead to harm. Hensley Henson was prepared to write simply on his own behalf. It was paradoxical to him that at the very juncture that serious politicians were casting about for some reconciliation with Germany, Germany was embarking on an antichristian policy which made it difficult to regard any approaches to her 'without something like moral repugnance.'[41] The bishop of London, on the other hand, although sympathetic, felt that he was working to the same end by personal influence through the ambassador. 'My policy' he wrote 'is to make friends with Germany, and thus acquire an influence over her, which we have not got at present.'[42] The bishop of Ripon agreed with the proposed letter, but wrote that he had decided not to put his name in print 'with regard to affairs which are outside my proper diocesan job . . .'[43] The dean of St

[40] Jasper, *Bell*, p 235.
[41] H. Henson to D. F. Buxton, 7 December 1937, Buxton Papers (C).
[42] Bishop of London to D. F. Buxton, 14 December 1937, *ibid.*
[43] Bishop of Ripon to D. F. Buxton, 28 December 1937, *ibid.*

Paul's confessed that he was simply perplexed about the situation. He had been in Hesse during the summer and 'at the time I could find no evidence of religious persecution, and nobody complained to me about it.'[44]

Another large group of episcopal correspondents indicated that they would do whatever the bishop of Chichester recommended. Bell was not in fact very enthusiastic about Mrs Buxton's idea. People would rightly comment that all the bishops who might sign did not really know the facts of the situation. He did not want to sign himself because of several impending meetings, but suggested that Mrs Buxton might send the letter under her own name. 'Why should not' he added 'a Church survive as an outward organisation even if it is persecuted to the very depths?'[45] When the letter finally appeared in *The Times* on 20 December 1937 with a small number of episcopal signatures, Bell felt even more strongly that it was a wrong move. The notion of 'culminating blows' in the destruction of the church would be regarded by some of the most stalwart members of the German evangelical church 'as almost surrender'.[46] Micklem, on the other hand, felt that it was a 'most admirable' letter. He thought 'you are much more likely to be accurate on some of these points than is the Bishop.'[47]

Meanwhile, Mrs Buxton kept a vigilant eye on the press. Whenever correspondents to any newspaper wrote arguing that the third reich had taken a strictly impartial stand on religious question in return for ecclesiastical abstention from politics, she sent a letter denying the claim. In an article in *The Spectator* in February 1938, she traced the evolution of the new concepts of justice in Germany, concluding that in essence 'all crimes are reduced to an act of treason against the National Socialist State.'[48] She conceded that there were some 'undisturbed areas' in the German church, but this was 'In so far as the officials of the Church are willing to accept the persecution of Jews and refrain from befriending victims of the Secret Police, or fellow-Christians with some degree of Jewish blood.' Niemöller was being detained, despite being found not guilty on all points of substance,

---

[44] W. R. Matthews to D. F. Buxton, 8 December 1937, *ibid.*
[45] G. Bell to D. F. Buxton, 7 December 1937, 13 December 1937, 16 December 1937, Buxton Papers (B). See also Jasper, *Bell*, p 235.
[46] G. Bell to D. F. Buxton, 20 December 1937, Buxton Papers (B).
[47] N. Micklem to D. F. Buxton, 21 December 1937, 13 January 1938, 21 January 1938, *ibid.*
[48] A special correspondent, 'Justice in Germany', *The Spectator*, 18 February 1938.

because he was 'incapable of juggling, either with his conscience or with his mind.'[49] Impressed by Karl Barth's lecture, 'Trouble and Promise in the struggle of the Church in Germany' delivered in Oxford on 4 March 1938, she at once took steps to see whether it could be printed in a cheap edition for wide circulation.[50] She acted as hostess for Barth so that he could meet a group of some thirty leading church people. All the while, she continued her regular work of circulating translations of statements by nazi leaders and details concerning the plight of individual pastors. On receiving one such collection of testimonies by imprisoned pastors, Aubrey wrote that it was quite clear that a rebirth of christian faith and life was taking place in Germany. Prayer apart, however, what could be done to help? The international situation was perplexing, he wrote in May 1938, and concluded 'If only our country could get on better terms with Germany diplomatically . . . we should be able to bring real pressure to bear.'[51] Mrs Buxton had become more sceptical.

On the anniversary of Niemöller's arrest, she described his dilemma in an anonymous article in *The Spectator*. She dismissed the contention that Hitler was not deeply implicated in the church struggle. It would be an insult to his intelligence to suppose that the campaign had escaped his attention or did not represent his own wishes.[52] Besides this article, she gathered together a group of admirals to write to *The Times* about the former German naval officer. They recorded their respect for a former valiant foe now suffering for no less a cause than that of common christian faith.[53]

Mrs Buxton next found herself in a fresh public controversy with the bishop of Gloucester. Headlam had paid a further visit to Germany, but did not change his views as a result. He admitted that a section, but only a section, of those in authority in Germany was antagonistic to christianity but still believed that the best way of meeting this antagonism was that adopted by 'five-sixths' of German pastors rather than that advocated by the confessional church. The paramount need was for a united church, but the confessing leaders prevented this and in doing so irritated the authorities against the church.[54] Mrs

---

[49] Q.R.S. (D. F. Buxton), 'Dr Niemoller and the Confessional Church', *Time and Tide*, 5 March 1938.
[50] K. Barth to D. F. Buxton, 28 May 1938, Buxton Papers (B).
[51] M. E. Aubrey to D. F. Buxton, 13 May 1938, *ibid*.
[52] A special correspondent, 'Dr Niemöller's ordeal', *The Spectator*, 1 July 1938.
[53] *The Times*, 28 July 1938.
[54] *Ibid*, 20 July 1938.

Buxton felt that the bishop had been misled by 'official' Germany. There was another Germany where to speak the truth might land the speaker in a concentration camp.[55] Headlam reiterated that all sections of the German church were anxious to be friendly with the church of England and resented the way in which British interest was lavished on the confessing church. 'The theology of the German Christians' he wrote 'is much more in accordance with our ideas than those of the Confessional Church.' The confessing church was largely under reformed influence and the theology of Karl Barth, and there was a considerable opposition to episcopacy.[56] Mrs Buxton, however, had now completed arrangements for the publication of Barth's Oxford lecture and now asked the Swiss theologian for an introduction, telling him that the majority of her fellow-countrymen were in 'deplorable ignorance' on the subject.[57] Barth obliged with a fierce introduction declaring that British christians would be forced to see in the cause of the confessional church their own cause as well.'[58]

Besides the Barth lecture, Mrs Buxton was also responsible for the English edition of letters from imprisoned German pastors.[59] It was well received and sold well. Nevertheless, in the late summer of 1938 events, both ecclesiastically and politically, seemed to be moving to a crisis. The Munich crisis produced strains on all sides. Charles Roden Buxton and his brother lord Noel-Buxton were both keen advocates of appeasement but Dorothy was acutely conscious of the consequences for christians of an international settlement which avoided war but perpetuated nazi rule.[60] In Germany, a service of intercession drawn up by a small group of confessing leaders at the height of the sudeten crisis was denounced by the nazi hierarchy as high treason and the lutheran provincial bishops dissociated themselves from it.[61] To complicate matters further, Barth wrote to the Czech theologian Hromadka declaring that every Czech soldier who fought nazism did so in the cause of Christ. In the end, Mrs Buxton was reasonably

---

[55] *Ibid*, 10 August 1938.
[56] The bishop of Gloucester, 'The German Church', *The Guardian*, 2 September 1938.
[57] D. F. Buxton to K. Barth, 20 September 1938, Buxton Papers (B).
[58] K. Barth, *The German Church Struggle; Tribulation and Promise* (London 1938). Foreword.
[59] *I was in Prison*, ed D. F. Buxton (London 1938).
[60] K. G. Robbins, *Munich 1938* (London 1968). D. C. Watt, 'Christian Essay in Appeasement; Lord Lothian and his Quaker Friends', *Wiener Library Bulletin*, 14, 2 (London 1960).
[61] Mrs Buxton was responsible for the fact that the service was reproduced in *The British Weekly*, 1 December 1938.

satisfied with the settlement, yet did not have much confidence that it would be permanent.

In any case, it did not result in any improvement in the situation of the confessing church. She therefore continued her watch on the press.[62] Early in February 1939, for example, the *Church of England Newspaper* published an article from an Englishwoman who had long been resident in Germany. She claimed that if one defined christianity as the acceptance of the spiritual meaning of Christ's teaching, with a sincere effort to apply it to everyday life, 'one may discern Christianity as the "Leitmotiv" of the National Socialist philosophy in Germany'.[63] In a long letter to the editor Mrs Buxton pointed to nazi racial theory and treatment of jews, but he declined to publish it arguing that it would only inflame passions still further at a time when so many were trying to get a better understanding and closer co-operation with Germany. He added that he had heard that after Hitler came to power some of the church began to act politically.[64] Naturally, if the church was paid by the state a dictator would say that it ought not to carry on propaganda against the state. In a further letter, Mrs Buxton expressed surprise and shock, stating that she had tried in vain to get information from the bishop of Gloucester and others about the precise 'political propaganda' in which the confessing church had indulged.[65] In the end, after a further contribution from the bishop of Gloucester, the editor finally allowed Mrs Buxton space to express her own views.[66]

While challenging the editor about the 'political' confessing church, Mrs Buxton added that, personally, she would not mind if such information was discovered, being convinced that 'until Christians do "interfere" more in politics our world will go from bad to worse.' She never claimed that her own role was a major one. She never possessed political power nor aspired directly to possess it. Her work was rather in the field of propaganda and personal relations, creating a network of contacts and information. Her own position, however, revealed how double-edged was her injunction to christians to 'inter-

---

[62] See, for example, an exchange of letters in *The Scotsman*, 6–26 January 1939.

[63] *The Church of England Newspaper*, 10 February 1939.

[64] D. F. Buxton to the editor, *Church of England Newspaper*, 13 February 1939; editor, *Church of England Newspaper*, 21 February 1939, Buxton Papers (B).

[65] D. F. Buxton to the editor, *Church of England Newspaper*, 23 February 1939, *ibid.*

[66] Articles in the *Church of England Newspaper*, 17 March 1939 and 31 March 1939; editor, *Church of England Newspaper* to D. F. Buxton, 3 April 1939; D. F. Buxton in the *Church of England Newspaper* 6 April 1939.

Dorothy Buxton and the German church struggle

fere' more in politics. It is at least arguable that the two causes most dear to the heart of the Buxtons, international appeasement of Germany and support for the oppressed christians of Germany, were incompatible. In the end, in 1939, a choice had to be made between the horrors of war and the horrors of nazism. Dorothy tended to go one way and Charles the other. Interference in politics was, after all, a choice of evils.

University College of North Wales,
Bangor

433

ABBREVIATIONS

AASRP	*Associated Archaeological Societies Reports and Papers*
AAWG	*Abhandlungen der Akademie der Wissenschaften zu Göttingen*, [*Gesellschaft* to 1942] (Göttingen 1843–)
AAWL	*Abhandlungen der Akademie der Wissenschaften und der Literatur* (Mainz 1950–)
ABAW	*Abhandlungen der Bayerischen Akademie der Wissenchaften* (Munich 1835–)
Abt	Abteilung
ACO	*Acta Conciliorum Oecumenicorum*, ed E. Schwartz (Berlin/Leipzig 1914–40)
ACW	*Ancient Christian Writers*, ed J. Quasten and J. C. Plumpe (Westminster, Maryland/London 1946–)
ADAW	*Abhandlungen der Deutschen* [till 1944 *Preussischen*] *Akademie der Wissenschaften zu Berlin* (Berlin 1815–)
AHP	*Archivum historiae pontificiae* (Rome 1963–)
AHR	*American Historical Review* (New York 1895–)
An Bol	*Analecta Bollandiana* (Brussels 1882–)
Annales	*Annales: Economies, Sociétés, Civilisations* (Paris 1946–)
AR	*Archivum Romanicum* (Geneva/Florence 1917–41)
ARG	*Archiv für Reformationsgeschichte* (Berlin/Leipzig/Gütersloh 1903–)
ASAW	*Abhandlungen der Sächsischen Akademie der Wissenschaften in Leipzig*, [*Gesellschaft* to 1920] (Leipzig 1850–)
ASB	*Acta Sanctorum Bollandiana* (Brussels etc. 1643–)
ASC	*Anglo Saxon Chronicle*
ASL	*Archivio storico Lombardo*, 1–62 (Milan 1874–1935); ns 1–10 (Milan 1936–47)
ASOC	*Analecta Sacri Ordinis Cisterciensis* [*Analecta Cisterciensia* since 1965] (Rome 1945–)
ASOSB	*Acta Sanctorum Ordinis Sancti Benedicti*, ed L. D'Achery and J. Mabillon (Paris 1668–1701)
ASP	*Archivio della Società* [*Deputazione* from 1935] *Romana di Storia Patria* (Rome 1878–1934, 1935–)
AV	*Archivio Veneto* (Venice 1871–): [1891–1921, *Nuovo Archivio Veneto*; 1922–6, *Archivio Veneto-Tridentino*]
B	*Byzantion* (Paris/Brussels 1924–)
Bale, *Catalogus*	John Bale, *Scriptorum Illustrium Maioris Brytanniae Catalogus*, 2 parts (Basel 1557, 1559)
Bale, *Index*	John Bale, *Index Britanniae Scriptorum*, ed R. L. Poole and M. Bateson (Oxford 1902) *Anecdota Oxoniensia*, medieval and modern series 9
Bale, *Summarium*	John Bale, *Illustrium Maioris Britanniae Scriptorum Summarium* (Ipswich 1548, reissued Wesel 1549)
BEC	*Bibliothèque de l'école des chartes* (Paris 1839–)
Beck	H-G. Beck, *Kirche und theologische Literatur im byzantinischen Reich* (Munich 1959)
Bernard	E. Bernard, *Catalogi Librorum Manuscriptorum Angliae et Hiberniae* (Oxford 1697)
BHG	*Bibliotheca hagiographica graeca* (2 ed Brussels 1909)

ABBREVIATIONS

BHI	*Bibliotheca historica Italica*, ed A. Ceruti, 4 vols (Milan 1876–85), 2 series, 3 vols (Milan 1901–33)
BHR	*Bibliothèque d'Humanisme et Renaissance* (Paris/Geneva 1941–)
BIHR	*Bulletin of the Institute of Historical Research* (London 1923–)
BJRL	*Bulletin of the John Rylands Library* (Manchester 1903–)
BL	British Library, London
BM	British Museum, London
Bouquet	M. Bouquet, *Recueil des historiens des Gaules et de la France. Rerum gallicarum et francicarum scriptores,* 24 vols (Paris 1738–1904); new ed L. Delisle, 1–19 (Paris 1868–80)
BQR	*British Quarterly Review* (London 1845–86)
Broadmead Records	*The Records of a Church of Christ, meeting in Broadmead, Bristol 1640–87,* HKS (London 1848)
BS	*Byzantinoslavica* (Prague 1929–)
Bucer, *Deutsche Schriften*	*Martin Bucers Deutsche Schriften,* ed R. Stupperich et al (Gütersloh/Paris 1960–)
Bucer, *Opera Latina*	*Martini Buceri Opera Latina,* ed F. Wendel et al (Paris/Gütersloh 1955–)
BZ	*Byzantinische Zeitschrift* (Leipzig 1892–)
CA	*Cahiers Archéologiques. Fin de L'Antiquité et Moyen-âge* (Paris 1945–)
CAH	*Cambridge Ancient History* (Cambridge 1923–39)
CalRev	*Calamy Revised,* ed A. G. Mathews (Oxford 1934)
Calvin, *Opera*	*Ioannis Calvini Opera Quae Supersunt Omnia,* ed G. Baum et al, *Corpus Reformatorum* 59 vols (Brunswick/Berlin 1863–1900)
Cardwell, *Documentary Annals*	*Documentary Annals of the Reformed Church of England,* ed E. Cardwell, 2 vols (Oxford 1839)
Cardwell, *Synodalia*	*Synodalia,* ed. E. Cardwell, 2 vols. (Oxford 1842)
CC	*Corpus Christianorum* (Turnholt 1952–)
CH	*Church History* (New York/Chicago 1932–)
CHB	*Cambridge History of the Bible*
CHistS	*Church History Society* (London 1886–92)
CHJ	*Cambridge Historical Journal* (Cambridge 1925–57)
CIG	*Corpus Inscriptionum Graecarum,* ed A. Boeckh, J. Franz, E. Curtius, A. Kirchhoff, 4 vols (Berlin 1825–77)
CMH	*Cambridge Medieval History*
CModH	*Cambridge Modern History*
COCR	*Collectanea Ordinis Cisterciensium Reformatorum* (Rome/Westmalle 1934–)
COD	*Conciliorum oecumenicorum decreta* (3 ed Bologna 1973)
CR	*Corpus Reformatorum,* ed C. G. Bretschneider et al (Halle etc. 1834–)
CS	*Cartularium Saxonicum,* ed W. de G. Birch, 3 vols (London 1885–93)
CSCO	*Corpus Scriptorum Christianorum Orientalium* (Paris 1903–)
CSEL	*Corpus Scriptorum Ecclesiasticorum Latinorum* (Vienna 1866–)
CSer	*Camden Series* (London 1838–)
CSHByz	*Corpus Scriptorum Historiae Byzantinae* (Bonn 1828–97)
CYS	*Canterbury and York Society* (London 1907–)
DA	*Deutsches Archiv für [Geschichte, –Weimar 1937–43] die Erforschung des Mittelalters* (Cologne/Graz 1950–)

ABBREVIATIONS

DACL | *Dictionnaire d'Archéologie chrétienne et de Liturgie*, ed F. Cabrol and H. Leclercq (Paris 1924–)
DDC | *Dictionnaire de Droit Canonique*, ed R. Naz (Paris 1935–)
DHGE | *Dictionnaire d'Histoire et de Géographie ecclésiastiques*, ed A. Baudrillart *et al* (Paris 1912–)
DNB | *Dictionary of National Biography* (London 1885–)
DOP | *Dumbarton Oaks Papers* (Cambridge, Mass., 1941–)
DR | F. Dölger, *Regesten der Kaiserurkunden des oströmischen Reiches (Corpus der griechischen Urkunden des Mittelalters und der neueren Zeit*, Reihe A, Abt. I), 5 vols: 1 (565–1025); 2 (1025–1204); 3 (1204–1282); 4 (1282–1341); 5 (1341–1453) (Munich-Berlin 1924–65)
DSAM | *Dictionnaire de Spiritualité, Ascetique et Mystique*, ed M. Viller (Paris 1932–)
DTC | *Dictionnaire de Théologie Catholique*, ed A. Vacant, E. Mangenot, E. Amann, 15 vols (Paris 1903–50)
Ec.HR | *Economic History Review* (London 1927–)
EEBS | Ἐπετηρὶς Ἑταιρείας Βυζαντινῶν Σπουδῶν (Athens 1924–)
EETS | *Early English Text Society*
EHD | *English Historical Documents* (London 1953–)
EHR | *English Historical Review* (London 1886–)
EO | *Echos d'Orient* (Constantinople/Paris 1897–1942)
EYC | *Early Yorkshire Charters*, ed W. Farrer and C. T. Clay, 12 vols (Edinburgh/Wakefield 1914–65)
FGH | *Die Fragmente der griechischen Historiker*, ed F. Jacoby (Berlin 1926–30)
FM | *Histoire de l'église depuis les origines jusqu'à nos jours*, ed A. Fliche and V. Martin (Paris 1935–)
Gangraena | T. Edwards, *Gangraena*, 3 parts (London 1646)
GCS | *Die griechischen christlichen Schriftsteller der erste drei Jahrhunderte* (Leipzig 1897–)
Gee and Hardy | *Documents Illustrative of English Church History* ed H. Gee and W. J. Hardy (London 1896)
Grumel, Regestes | V. Grumel, *Les Regestes des Actes du Patriarcat de Constantinople*, 1: *Les Actes des Patriarches*, I: 381–715; II: 715–1043; III: 1043–1206 (Socii Assumptionistae Chalcedonenses, 1931, 1936, 1947)
Grundmann | H. Grundmann, *Religiöse Bewegungen im Mittelalter* (Berlin 1935, 2 ed Darmstadt 1970)
HBS | *Henry Bradshaw Society* (London/Canterbury 1891–)
HE | *Historia Ecclesiastica*
HistSt | *Historical Studies* (Melbourne 1940–)
HJ | *Historical Journal* (Cambridge 1958–)
HJch | *Historisches Jahrbuch der Görres Gesellschaft* (Cologne 1880 ff, Munich 1950–)
HKS | Hanserd Knollys Society (London 1847–)
HL | C. J. Hefele and H. Leclercq, *Histore des Conciles*, 10 vols (Paris 1907–35)
HMC | Historical Manuscripts Commission
Hooker, *Works* | *The Works of . . . Mr. Richard Hooker*, ed J. Keble, 7 ed rev R. W. Church and F. Paget, 3 vols (Oxford 1888)
Houedene | *Chronica Magistri Rogeri de Houedene*, ed W. Stubbs, 4 vols, *RS* 51 (London 1868–71)

ABBREVIATIONS

HRH	*The Heads of Religious Houses, England and Wales, 940–1216,* ed D. Knowles, C. N. L. Brooke, V. C. M. London (Cambridge 1972)
HS	*Hispania sacra* (Madrid 1948–)
HTR	*Harvard Theological Review* (New York/Cambridge, Mass., 1908–)
HZ	*Historische Zeitschrift* (Munich 1859–)
IER	*Irish Ecclesiastical Record* (Dublin 1864–)
Jaffé	*Regesta Pontificum Romanorum ab condita ecclesia ad a. 1198,* 2 ed S. Loewenfeld, F. Kaltenbrunner, P. Ewald, 2 vols (Berlin 1885–8, repr Graz 1958)
JBS	*Journal of British Studies* (Hartford, Conn., 1961–)
JEH	*Journal of Ecclesiastical History* (London 1950–)
JFHS	*Journal of the Friends Historical Society* (London/Philadelphia 1903–)
JHI	*Journal of the History of Ideas* (London 1940–)
JHSChW	*Journal of the Historical Society of the Church in Wales* (Cardiff 1947–)
JMH	*Journal of Modern History* (Chicago 1929–)
JRH	*Journal of Religious History* (Sydney 1960–)
JRS	*Journal of Roman Studies* (London 1910–)
JRSAI	*Journal of the Royal Society of Antiquaries of Ireland* (Dublin 1871–)
JSArch	*Journal of the Society of Archivists* (London 1955–)
JTS	*Journal of Theological Studies* (London 1899–)
Knox, *Works*	*The Works of John Knox,* ed D. Laing, Bannatyne Club/Wodrow Society, 6 vols (Edinburgh 1846–64)
Laurent, *Regestes*	V. Laurent, *Les Regestes des Actes du Patriarcat de Constantinople,* I : *Les Actes des Patriarches,* IV : *Les Regestes de 1208 à 1309* (Paris 1971)
Lloyd, *Formularies of Faith*	*Formularies of Faith Put Forth by Authority during the Reign of Henry VIII,* ed C. Lloyd (Oxford 1825)
LRS	*Lincoln Record Society*
LQR	*Law Quarterly Review* (London 1885–)
LThK	*Lexikon für Theologie und Kirche,* ed J. Höfer and K. Rahnes (2 ed Freiburg-im-Breisgau 1957–)
LW	*Luther's Works,* ed. J. Pelikan and H. T. Lehman, american edition (St. Louis/Philadelphia, 1955–)
MA	*Monasticon Anglicanum,* ed R. Dodsworth and W. Dugdale, 3 vols (London 1655–73); new ed J. Caley, H. Ellis, B. Bandinel, 6 vols in 8 (London 1817–30)
Mansi	J. D. Mansi, *Sacrorum conciliorum nova et amplissima collectio,* 31 vols (Florence/Venice 1757–98); new impression and continuation, ed L. Petit and J. B. Martin, 60 vols (Paris 1899–1927)
Med A	*Medium Aevum* (Oxford 1932–)
MGH	*Monumenta Germaniae Historica inde ab a. c. 500 usque ad a. 1500,* ed G. H. Pertz etc (Berlin, Hanover 1826–)
AA	*Auctores Antiquissimi*
Cap	*Capitularia*
Conc	*Concilia*
Const	*Constitutiones*
Dip	*Diplomata*

Epp	*Epistolae*
Form	*Formularia*
Leg	*Leges*
Lib	*Libelli de Lite*
SS	*Scriptores*
SRG	*Scriptores rerum Germanicarum in usum scholarum*
SRL	*Scriptores rerum langobardicarum et italicarum*
SRM	*Scriptores rerum merovingicarum*
MM	F. Miklosich and J. Müller, *Acta et Diplomata Graeca medii aevi sacra et profana*, 6 vols (Vienna 1860–90)
More, *Works*	*The Complete Works of St. Thomas More*, ed R. S. Sylvester et al, Yale edition (New Haven/London 1963–)
Moyen Age	*Le moyen âge. Revue d'histoire et de philologie* (Paris 1888–)
MS	Manuscript
Muratori	L. A. Muratori, *Rerum italicarum scriptores*, 25 vols (Milan 1723–51); new ed G. Carducci and V. Fiorini, 34 vols in 109 fasc (Città di Castello/Bologna 1900–)
NCE	*New Catholic Encyclopedia*, 15 vols (New York 1967)
NCModH	*New Cambridge Modern History*, 14 vols (Cambridge 1957–70)
NF	*Neue Folge*
NH	*Northern History* (Leeds 1966–)
ns	new series
OCP	*Orientalia Christiana Periodica* (Rome 1935–)
ODCC	*Oxford Dictionary of the Christian Church*, ed F. L. Cross (Oxford 1957)
PBA	*Proceedings of the British Academy*
PG	*Patrologia Graeca*, ed J. P. Migne, 161 vols (Paris 1857–66)
PhK	Philosophisch-historische Klasse
PL	*Patrologia Latina*, ed J. P. Migne, 217+4 index vols (Paris 1841–64)
PO	*Patrologia Orientalis*, ed J. Graffin and F. Nau (Paris 1903–)
Potthast	*Regesta Pontificum Romanorum inde ab a. post Christum natum 1198 ad a. 1304*, ed A. Potthast, 2 vols (1874–5 repr Graz 1957)
PP	*Past and Present* (London 1952–)
PRIA	*Proceedings of the Royal Irish Academy* (Dublin 1836–)
PRO	Public Record Office
PS	Parker Society (Cambridge 1841–55)
PW	*Paulys Realencyklopädie der klassischen Altertumwissenschaft*, new ed G. Wissowa and W. Kroll (Stuttgart 1893–)
QFIAB	*Quellen & Forschungen aus italienischen Archiven und Bibliotheken* (Rome 1897–)
RB	*Revue Bénédictine* (Maredsous 1884–)
RE	*Realencyclopädie für protestantische Theologie*, ed A. Hauck, 24 vols (3 ed Leipzig 1896–1913)
REB	*Revue des Etudes Byzantines* (Bucharest/Paris 1946–)
RecS	Record Series
RH	*Revue historique* (Paris 1876–)
RHD	*Revue d'histoire du droit* (Haarlem, Gronigen 1923–)
RHDFE	*Revue historique du droit francais et étranger* (Paris 1922–)
RHE	*Revue d'Histoire Ecclesiastique* (Louvain 1900–)
RHEF	*Revue d'Histoire de l'Eglise de France* (Paris 1910–)
RR	*Regesta Regum Anglo-Normannorum*, ed H. W. C. Davis, H. A. Cronne, Charles Johnson, R. H. C. Davis, 4 vols (Oxford 1913–69)

ABBREVIATIONS

RS	*Rerum Brittanicarum Medii Aevi Scriptores,* 99 vols (London 1858–1911). *Rolls Series*
RSR	*Revue des sciences religieuses* (Strasbourg 1921–)
RTAM	*Recherches de théologie ancienne et mediévale* (Louvain 1929–)
RSI	*Rivista di storia della chiesa in Italia* (Rome 1947–)
RStI	*Rivista storica italiana* (Naples 1884–)
S	*Sitzungsberichte*
SA	*Studia Anselmiana* (Rome 1933–)
SBAW	*Sitzungsberichte der bayerischen Akademie der Wissenschaften,* PhK (Munich 1871–)
SCH	*Studies in Church History* (London 1964–)
SCR	*Sources chrétiennes,* ed H. de Lubac and J. Daniélou (Paris 1941–)
SGre	*Studi Gregoriani,* ed G. Borino, 7 vols (Rome 1947–61)
SGra	*Studia Gratiana,* ed J. Forchielli and A. M. Stickler (Bologna 1953–)
SMon	*Studia Monastica* (Montserrat, Barcelona 1959–)
Speculum	*Speculum, A Journal of Medieval Studies* (Cambridge, Mass 1926–)
SpicFr	*Spicilegium Friburgense* (Freiburg 1957–)
SS	*Surtees Society* (Durham 1835–)
STC	*A Short-Title Catalogue of Books Printed in England, Scotland and Ireland and of English Books Printed Abroad 1475–1640,* ed A. W. Pollard and G. R. Redgrave (London 1926)
Strype, *Annals*	John Strype, *Annals of the Reformation and Establishment of Religion . . . during Queen Elizabeth's Happy Reign,* 4 vols in 7 (Oxford 1824)
Strype, *Cranmer*	John Strype, *Memorials of . . . Thomas Cranmer,* 2 vols (Oxford 1840)
Strype, *Grindal*	John Strype, *The History of the Life and Acts of . . . Edmund Grindal* (Oxford 1821)
Strype, *Memorials*	John Strype, *Ecclesiastical Memorials, Relating Chiefly to Religion, and the Reformation of it . . . under King Henry VIII, King Edward VI, and Queen Mary I,* 3 vols in 6 (Oxford 1822)
Strype, *Parker*	John Strype, *The Life and Acts of Matthew Parker,* 3 vols (Oxford 1821)
Strype, *Whitgift*	John Strype, *The Life and Acts of John Whitgift,* 3 vols (Oxford 1822)
SVRG	*Schriften des Vereins für Reformationsgeschichte* (Halle/Leipzig/Gütersloh 1883–)
TCBiblS	*Transactions of the Cambridge Bibliographical Society* (Cambridge 1949–)
THSCym	*Transactions of the Historical Society of Cymmrodorion* (London 1822–)
TRHS	*Transactions of the Royal Historical Society* (London 1871–)
TU	*Texte und Untersuchungen zur Geschichte der altchristlichen Literatur. Archiv für die griechisch-christlichen Schriftstellen der ersten drei Jahrhumderte* (Leipzig/Berlin 1882–)
VCH	*Victoria County History* (London 1900–)
VHM	G. Tiraboschi, *Vetera Humiliatorum Monumenta,* 3 vols (Milan 1766–8)
VV	*Vizantijskij Vremennik* 1–25 (St Petersburg 1894–1927), ns 1 (26) (Leningrad 1947–)

WA	D. *Martin Luthers Werke*, ed J. C. F. Knaake (Weimar 1883–) [*Weimarer Ausgabe*]
WA Br	*Briefwechsel*
WA DB	*Deutsche Bibel*
WA TR	*Tischreden*
WelHR	*Welsh History Review* (Cardiff 1960–)
Wharton	H. Wharton, *Anglia Sacra*, 2 parts (London 1691)
Wilkins	*Concilia Magnae Britanniae et Hiberniae A.D. 446–1717*, 4 vols, ed D. Wilkins (London 1737)
YAJ	*Yorkshire Archaeological Journal* (London/Leeds 1870–)
Zanoni	L. Zanoni, *Gli Umiliati nei loro rapporti con l'eresia, l'industria della lana ed i communi nei secoli xii e xiii, Biblioteca Historica Italica*, 2 series, 2 (Milan 1911)
ZKG	*Zeitschrift für Kirchengeschichte* (Gotha/Stuttgart 1878–)
ZRG	*Zeitschrift der Savigny-Stiftung für Rechtsgeschichte* (Weimar)
–GA	*Germanistische Abteilung* (1863–)
–KA	*Kanonistische Abteilung* (1911–)
–RA	*Romanistische Abteilung* (1880–)
ZRGG	*Zeitschrift für Religions- und Geistesgeschichte* (Marburg 1948–)
Zwingli, *Werke*	*Huldreich Zwinglis Sämmtliche Werke*, ed E. Egli et al, *CR* (Berlin/Leipzig/Zurich 1905–)